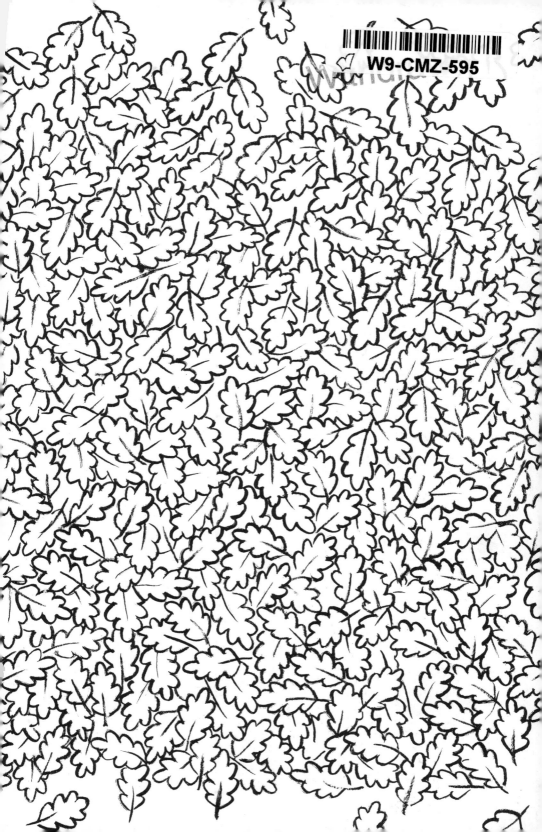

HUMMINGBIRD HEART

TRAVIS DANDRO

DRAWN AND QUARTERLY

THANKS TO ALL
OF MY FAMILY AND FRIENDS

AND EVERYONE AT D+Q

drawnandQuarterly.com
travisdandro.com

ISBN 978-1-77046-562-6
First edition: June 2022
Printed in Turkey
10 9 8 7 6 5 4 3 2 1

Published in The USA by Drawn & Quarterly,
a client publisher of Farrar, Straus, and Giroux
Published in Canada by Drawn & Quarterly,
a client publisher of Raincoast Books.
Published in The United Kingdom by
Drawn & Quarterly, a client publisher
of Publishers Group UK.

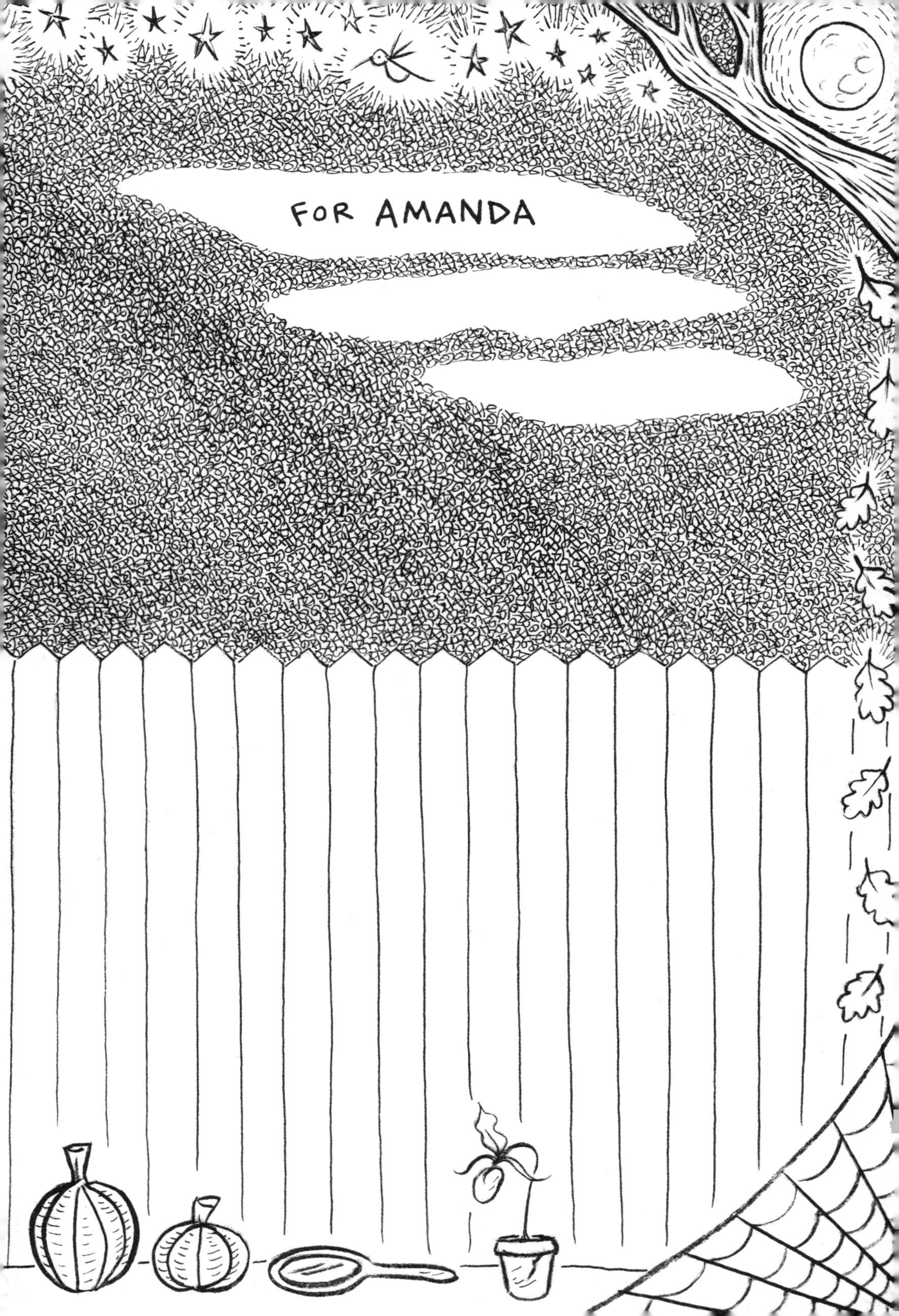
FOR AMANDA

LEICESTER,
MASSACHUSETTS

AUGUST
1991

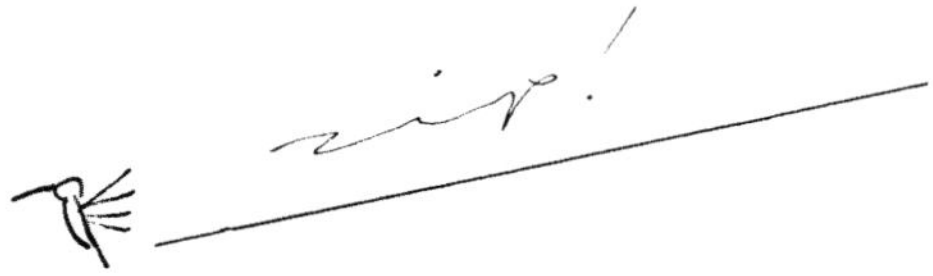
zip!

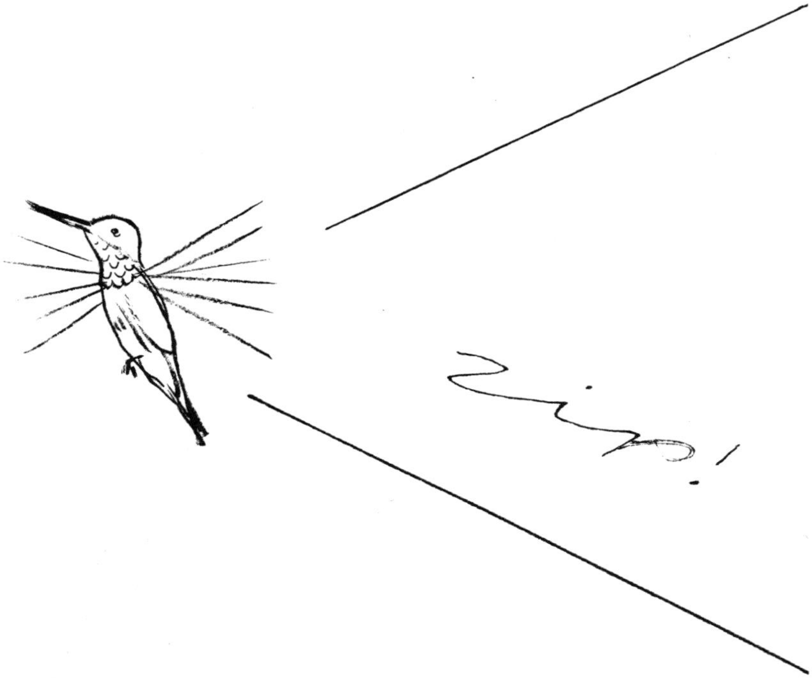
Zip!

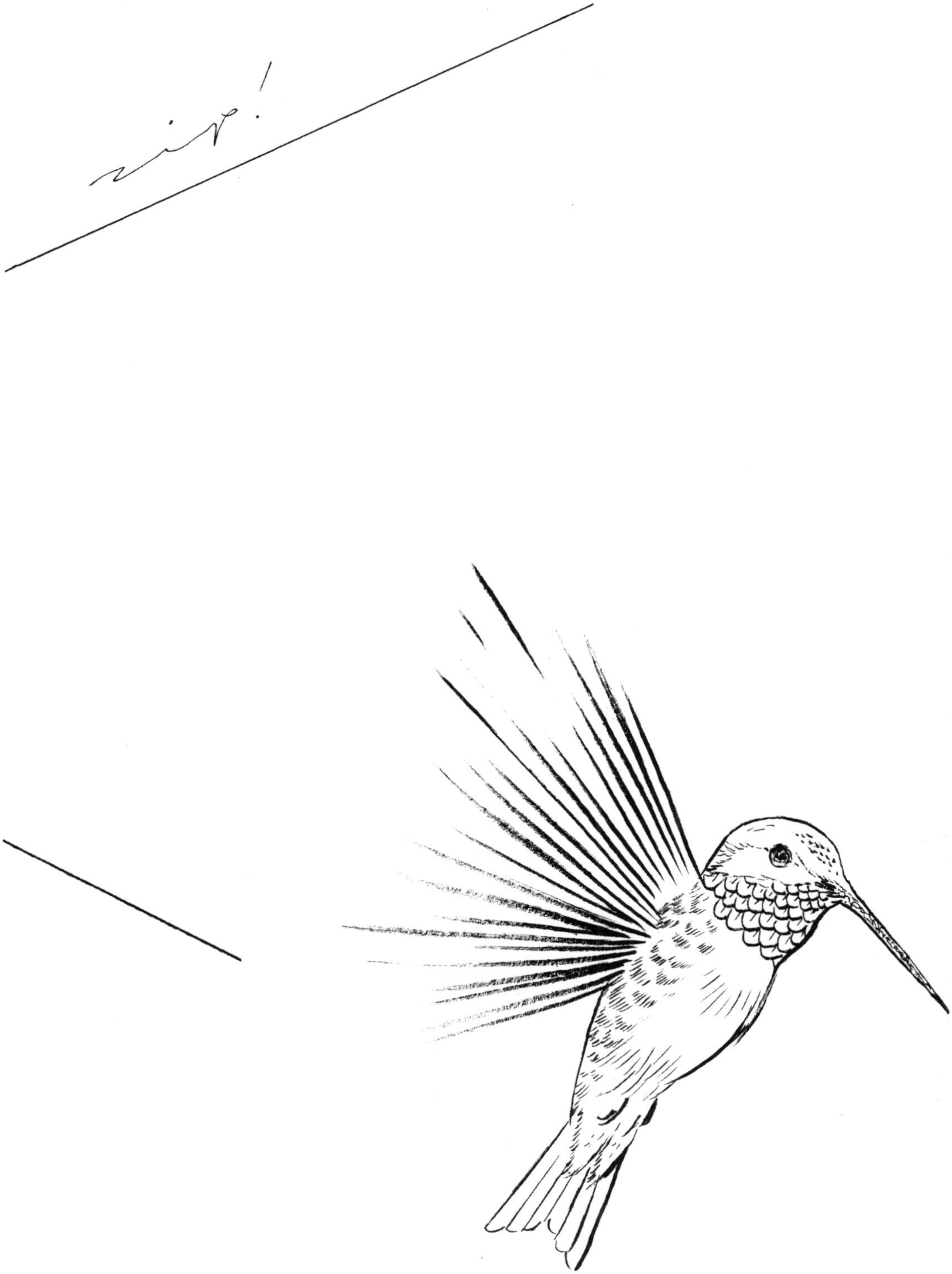
zip!

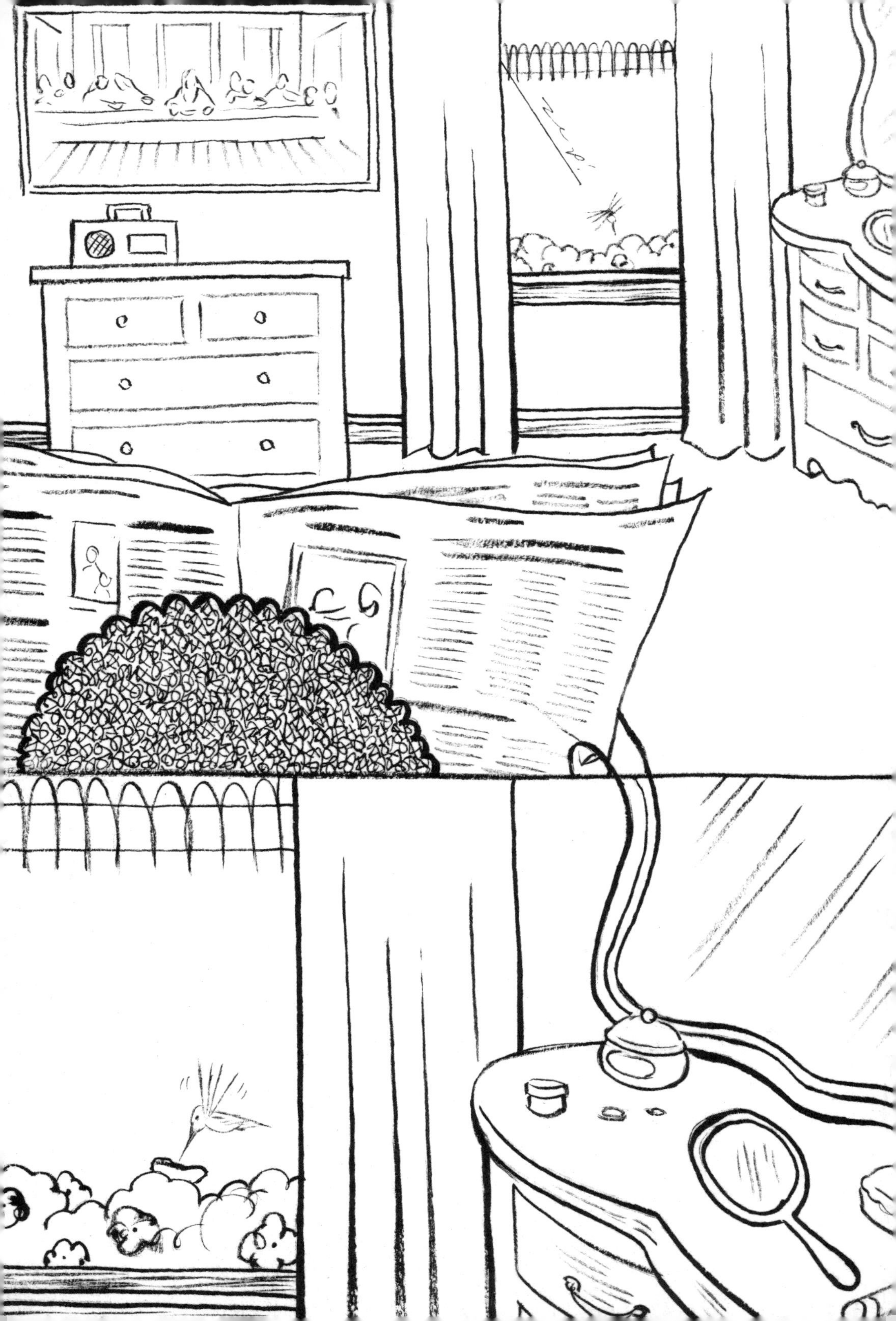

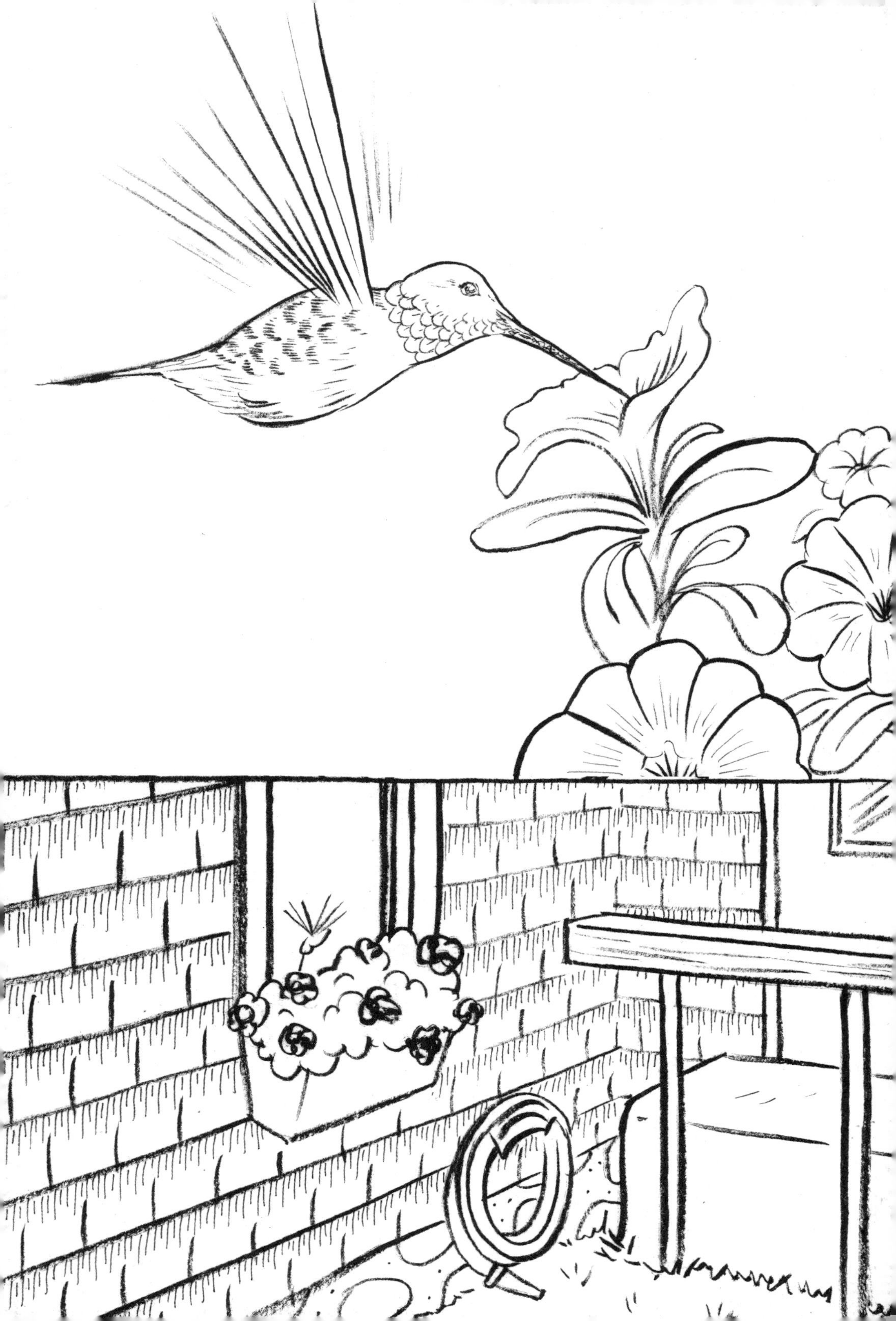

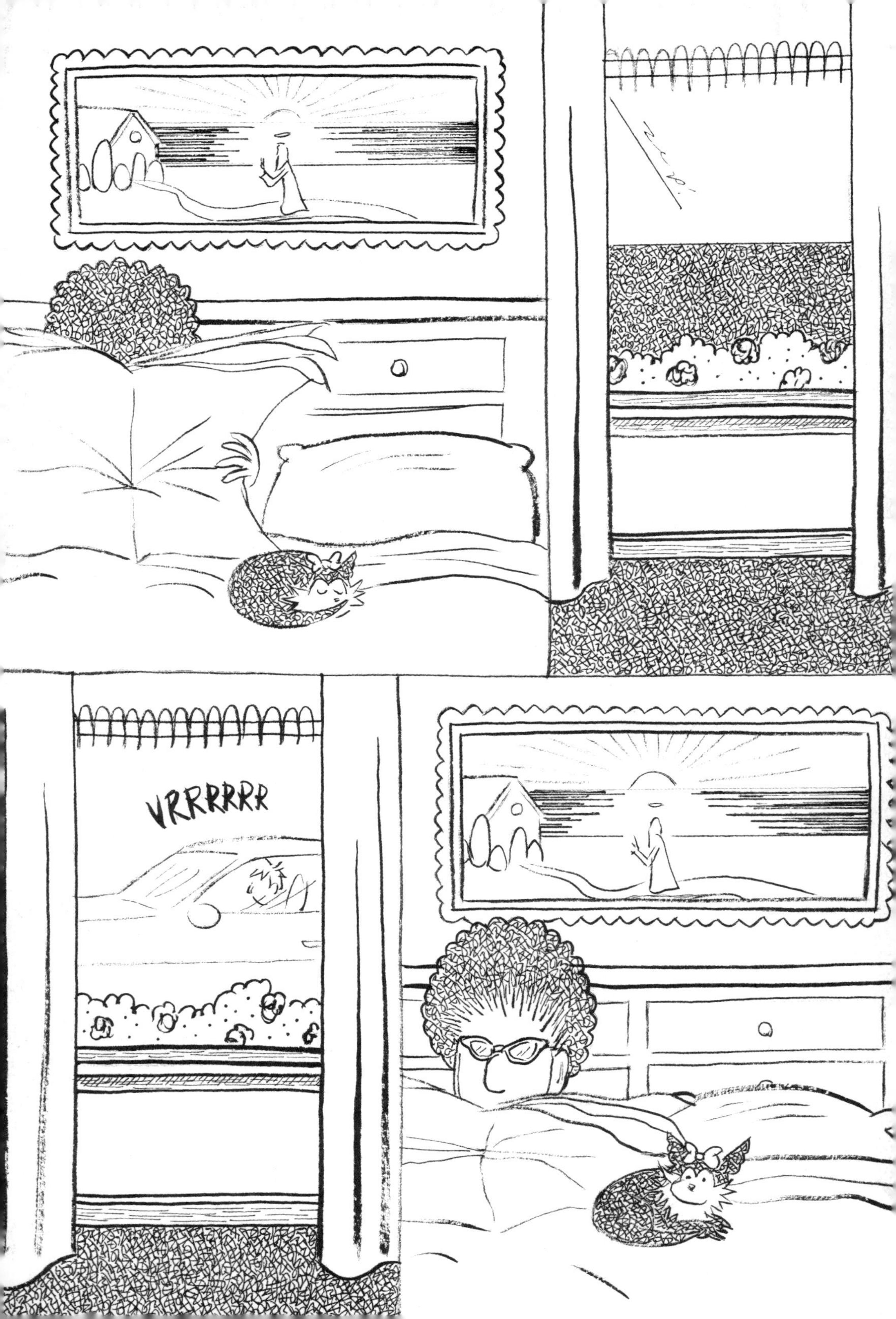
VRRRRRR

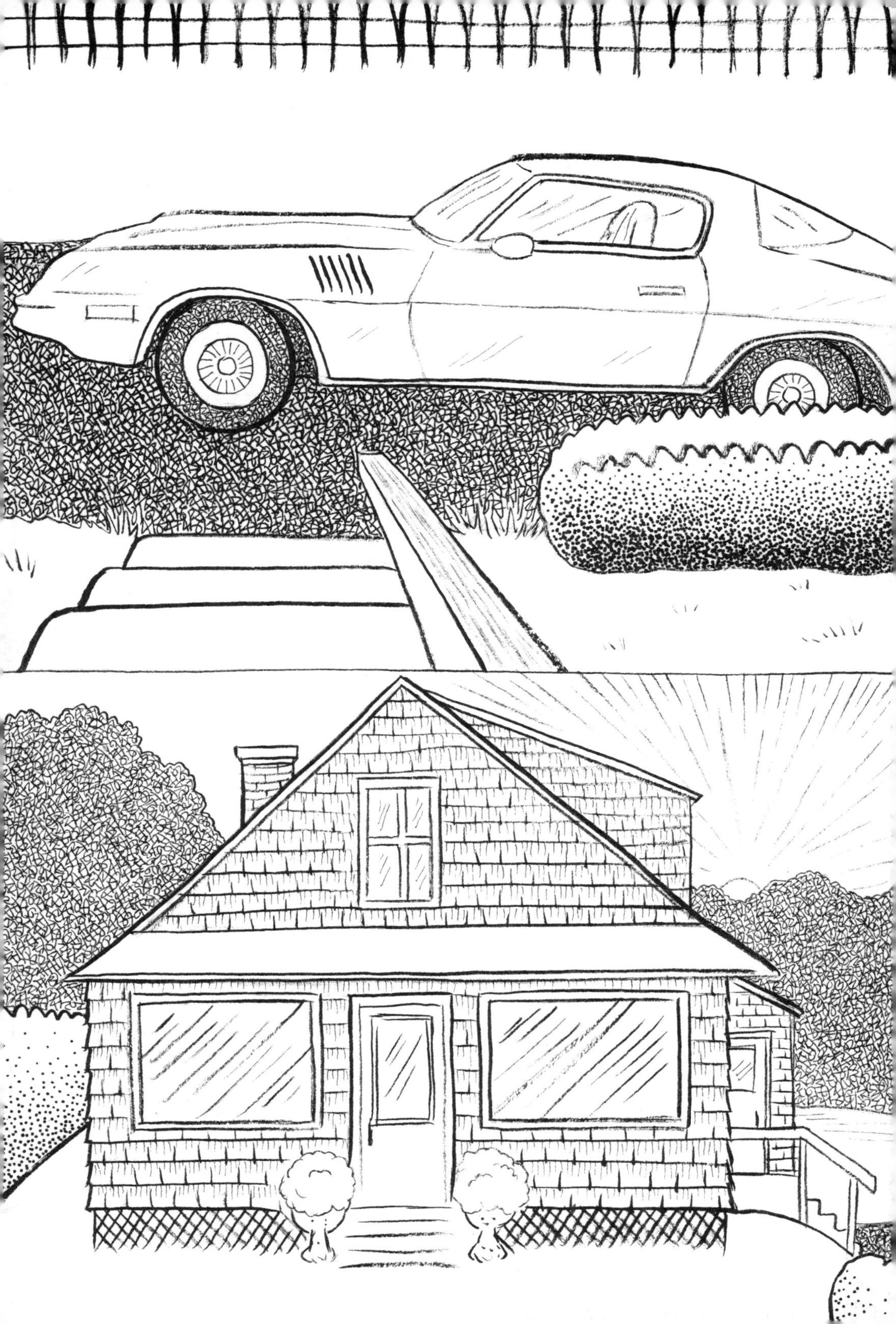

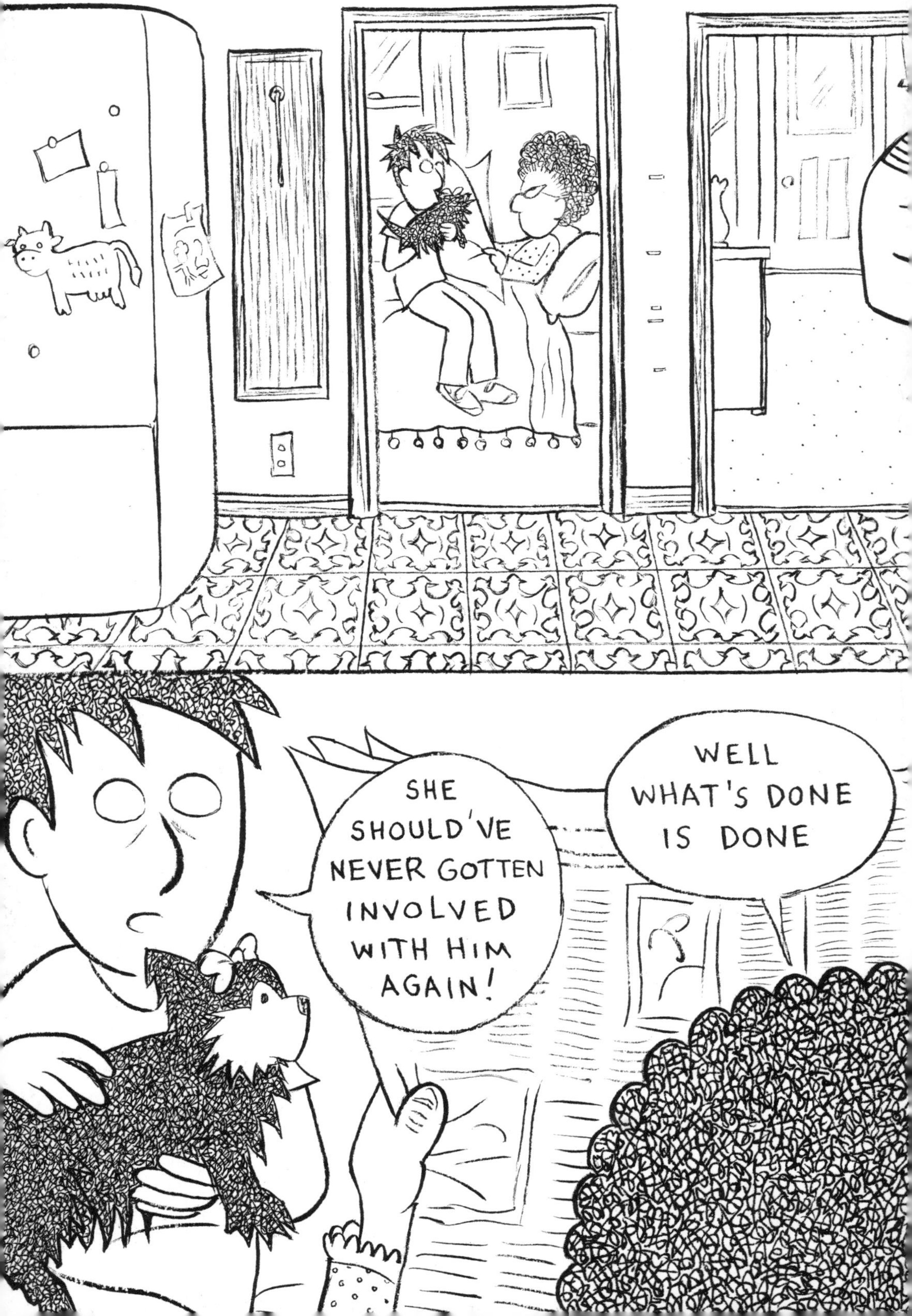
SHE SHOULD'VE NEVER GOTTEN INVOLVED WITH HIM AGAIN!
WELL WHAT'S DONE IS DONE

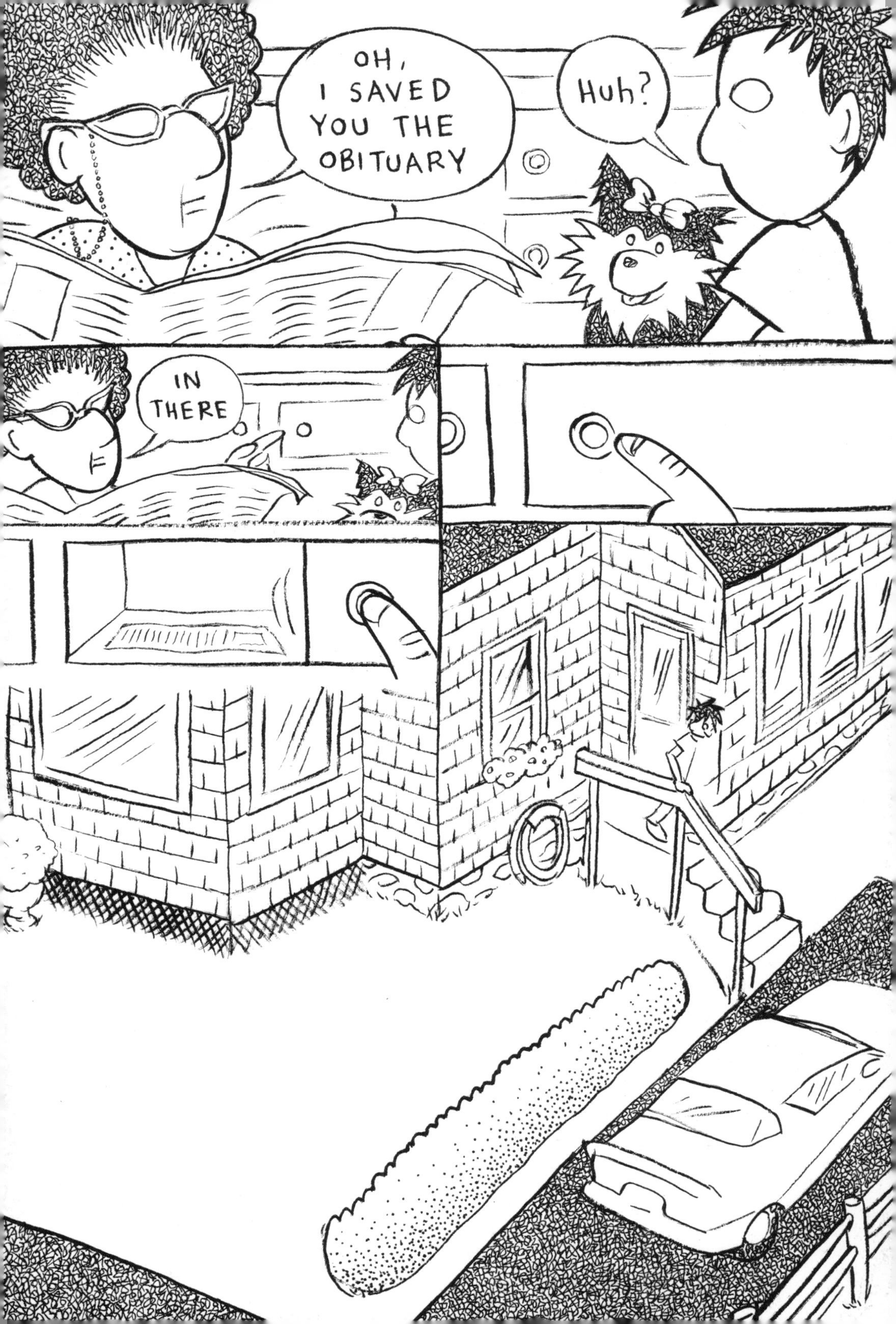
OH, I SAVED YOU THE OBITUARY
Huh?
IN THERE

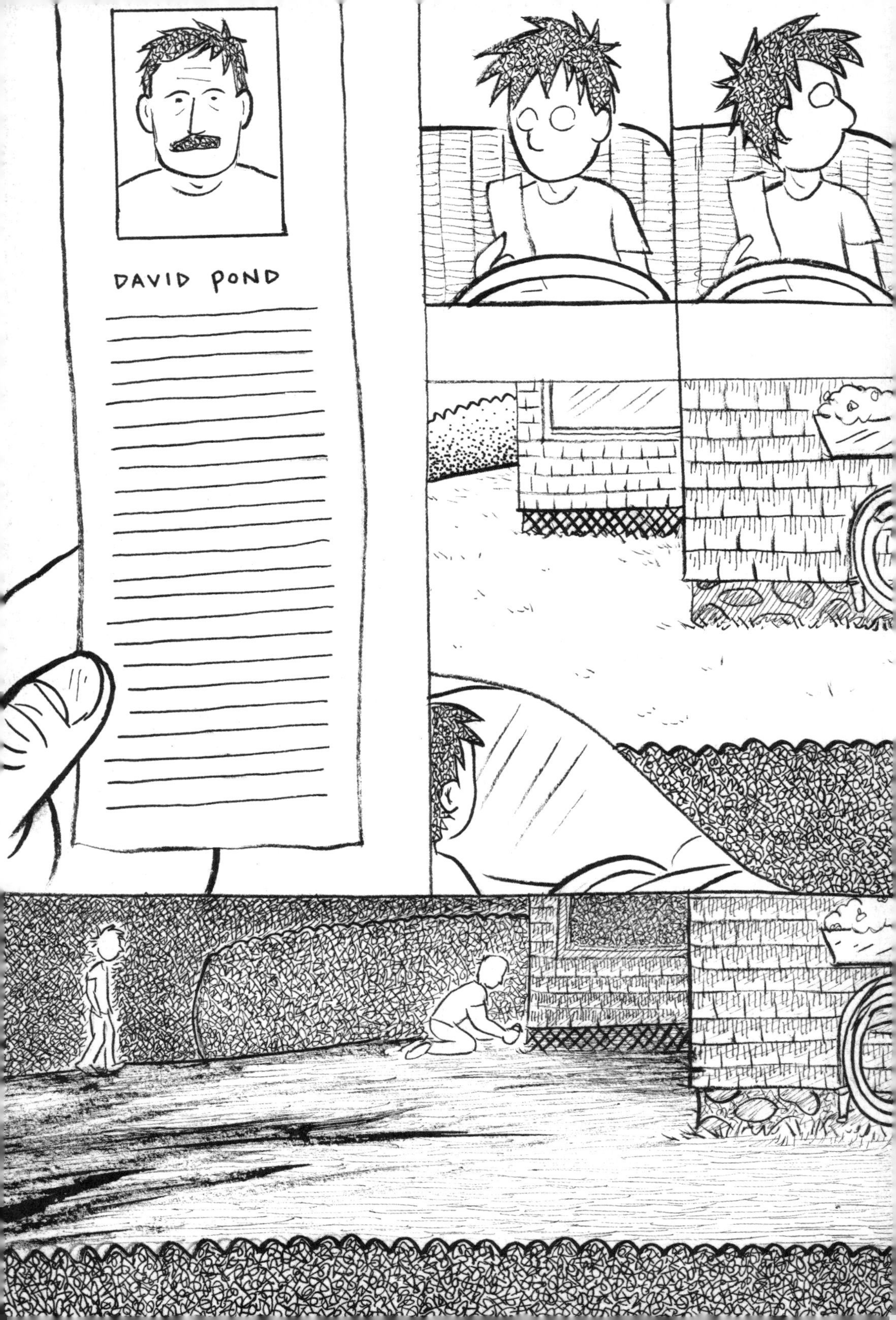
DAVID POND

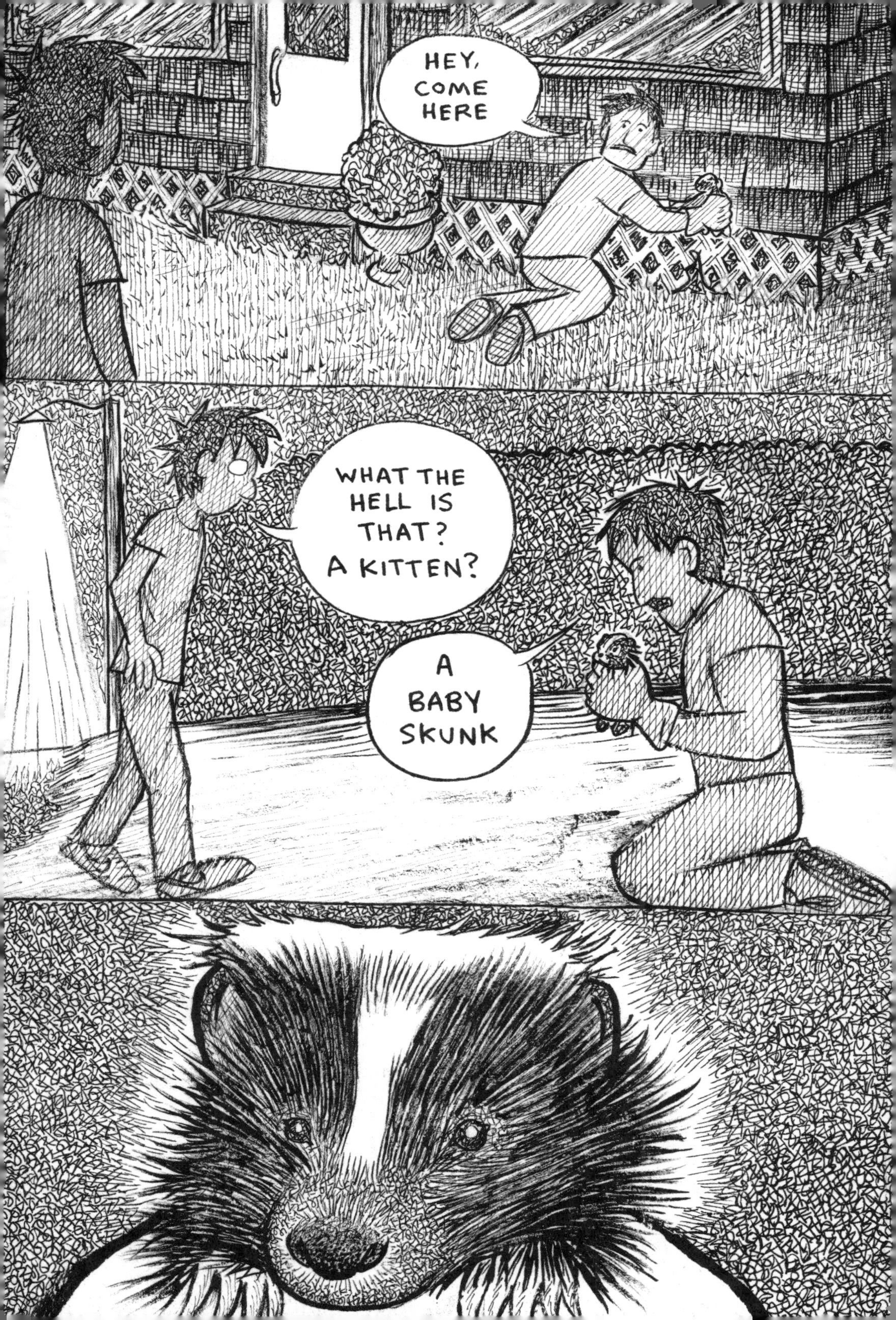
HEY, COME HERE
WHAT THE HELL IS THAT? A KITTEN?
A BABY SKUNK

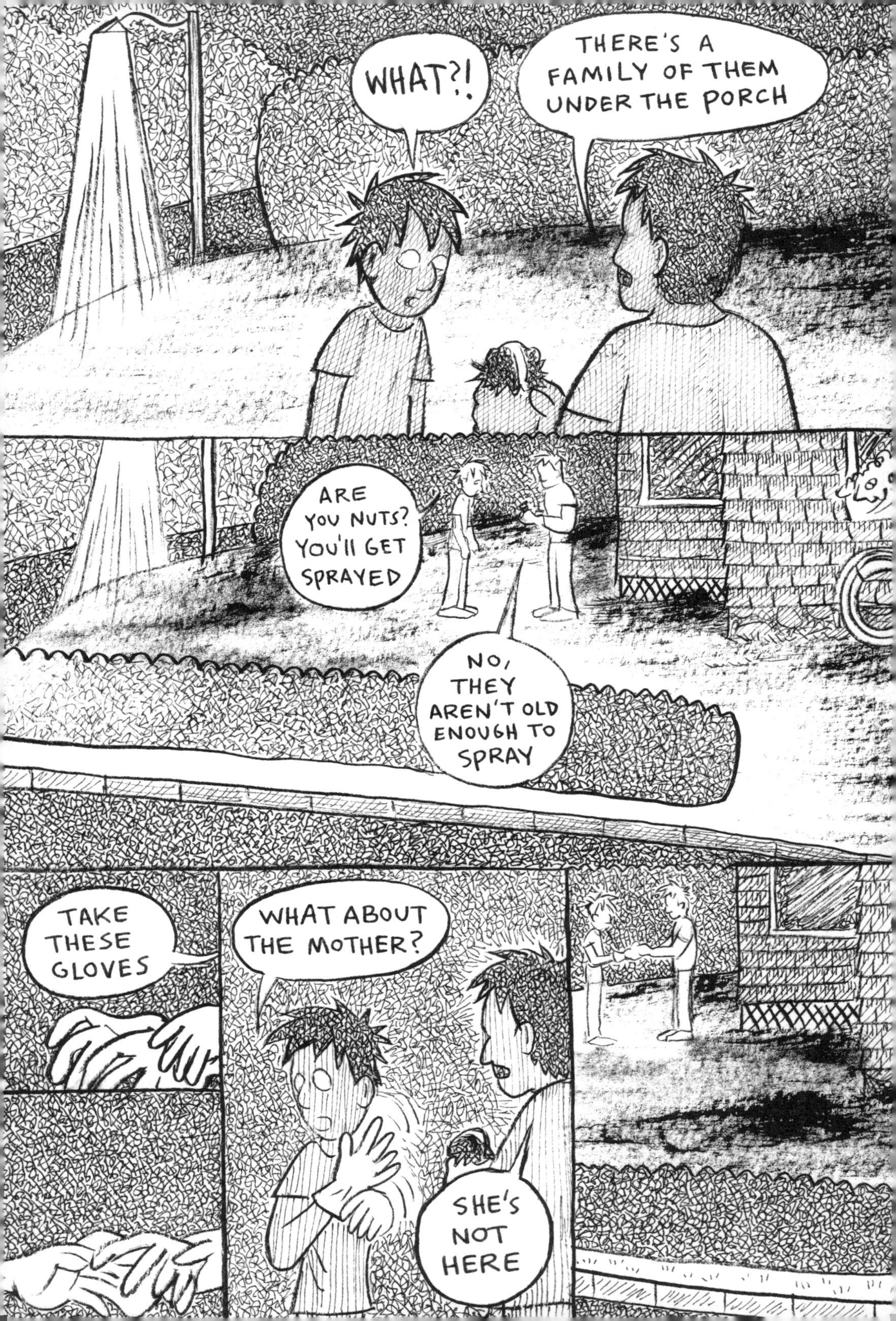
WHAT?!
THERE'S A FAMILY OF THEM UNDER THE PORCH
ARE YOU NUTS? YOU'll GET SPRAYED
NO, THEY AREN'T OLD ENOUGH TO SPRAY
TAKE THESE GLOVES
WHAT ABOUT THE MOTHER?
SHE'S NOT HERE

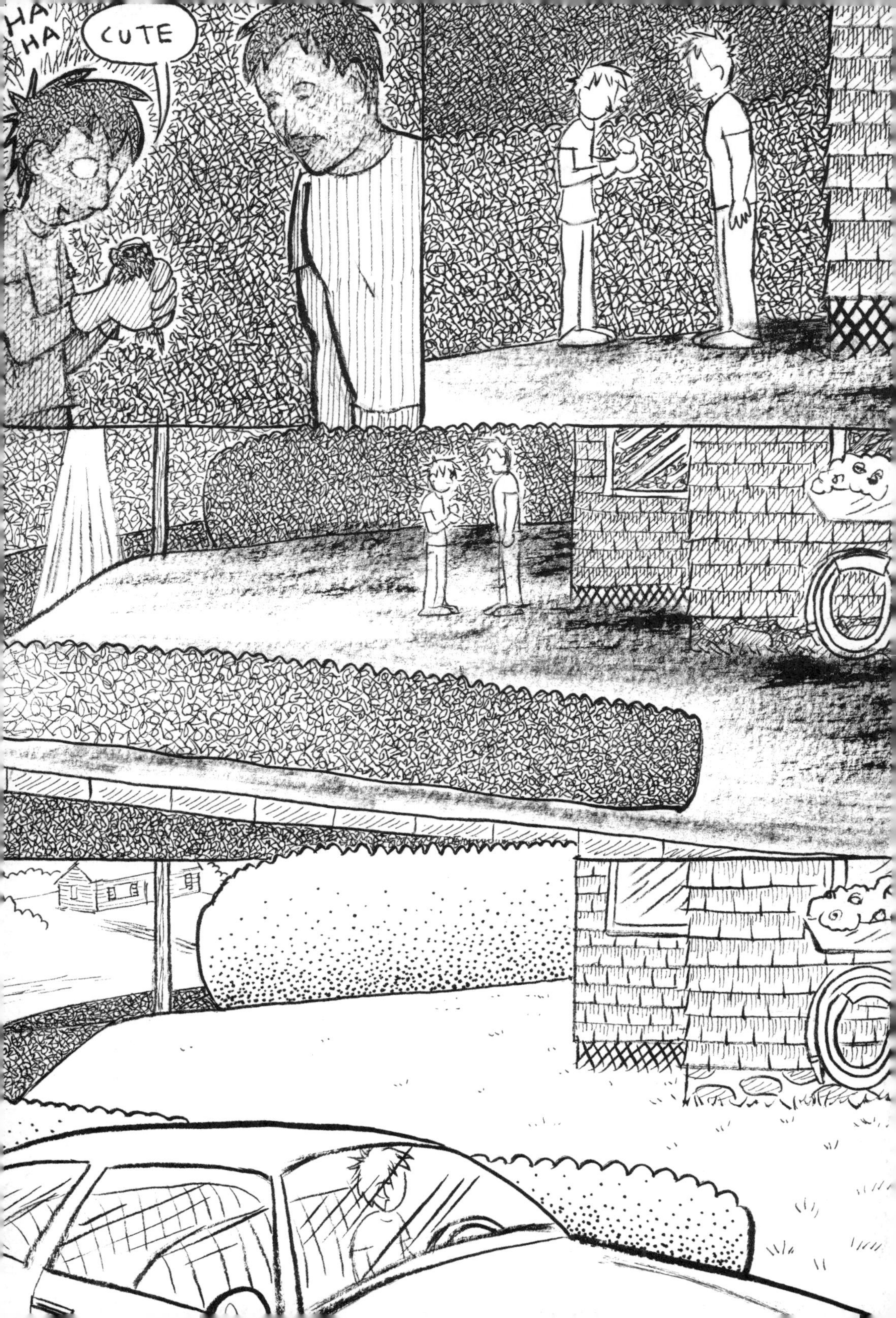
HA HA
CUTE

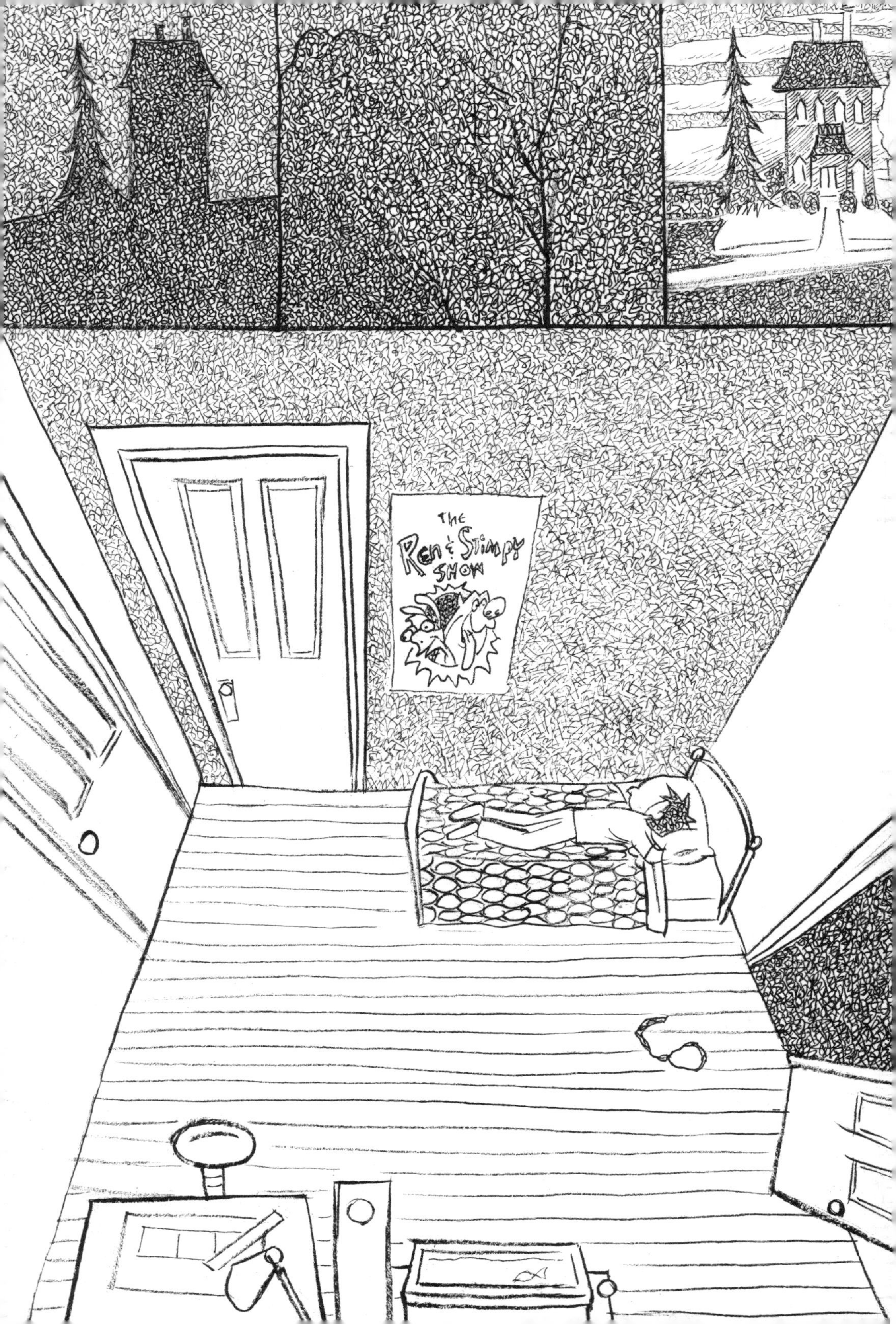
THE
Ren & Stimpy
SHOW

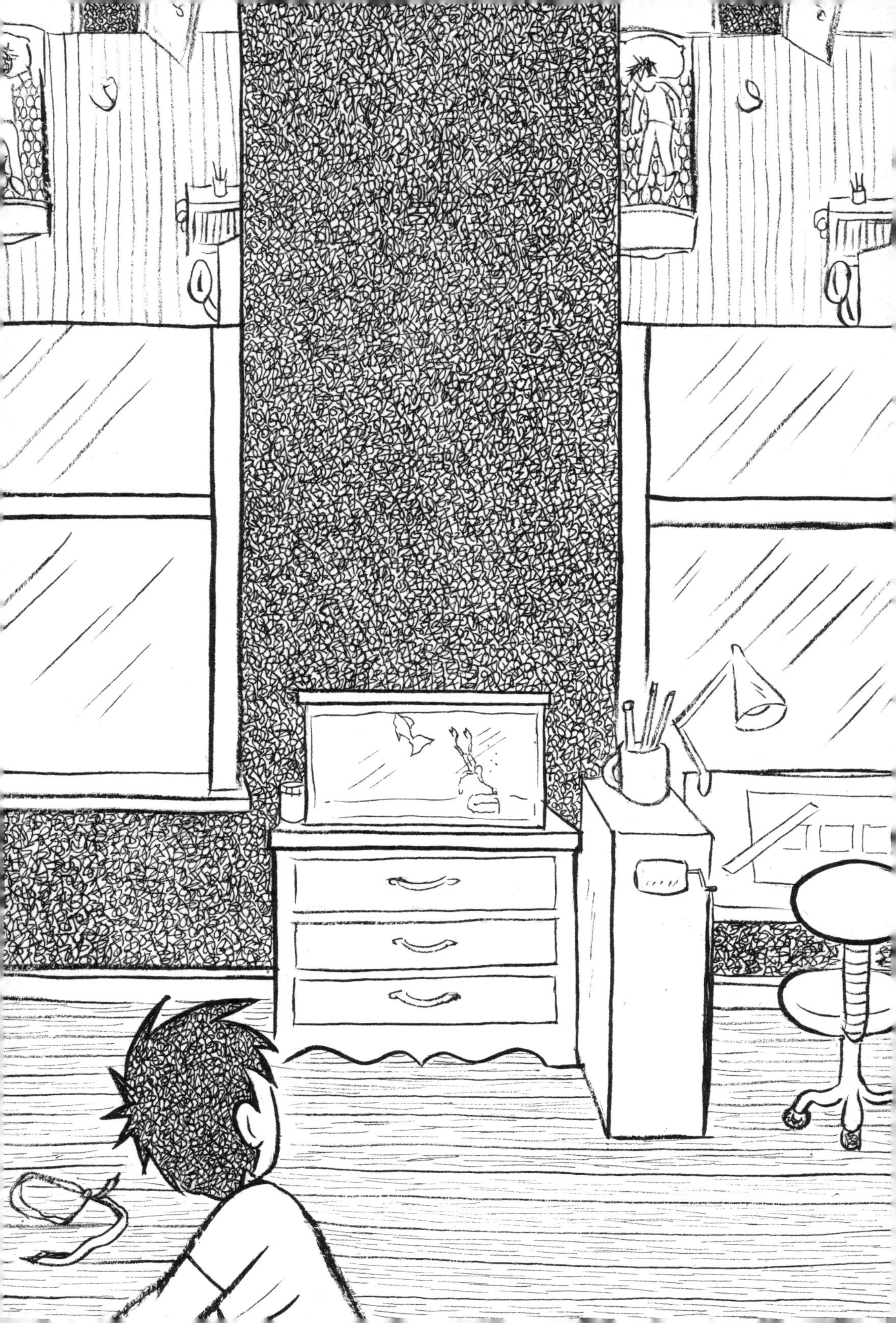

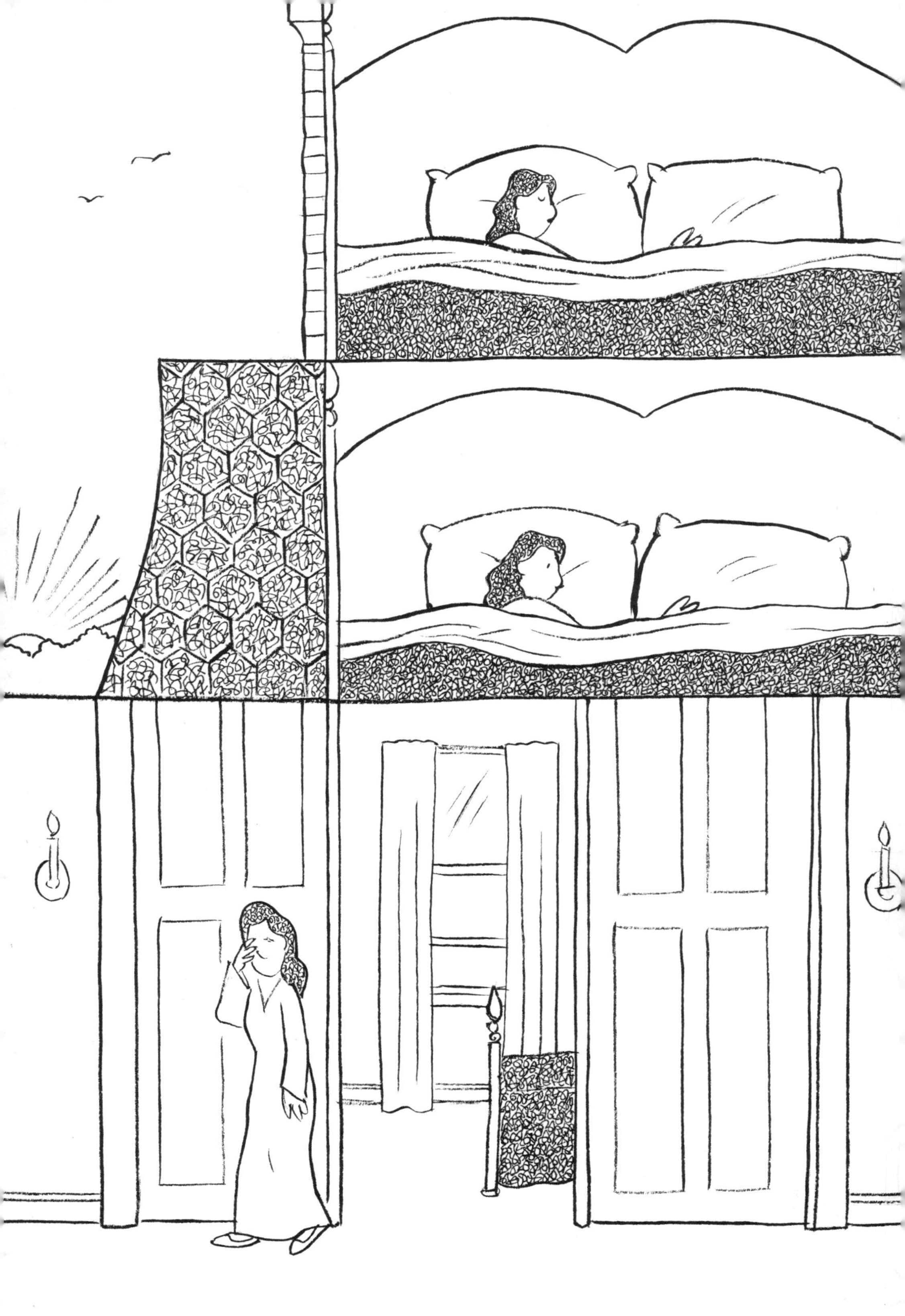

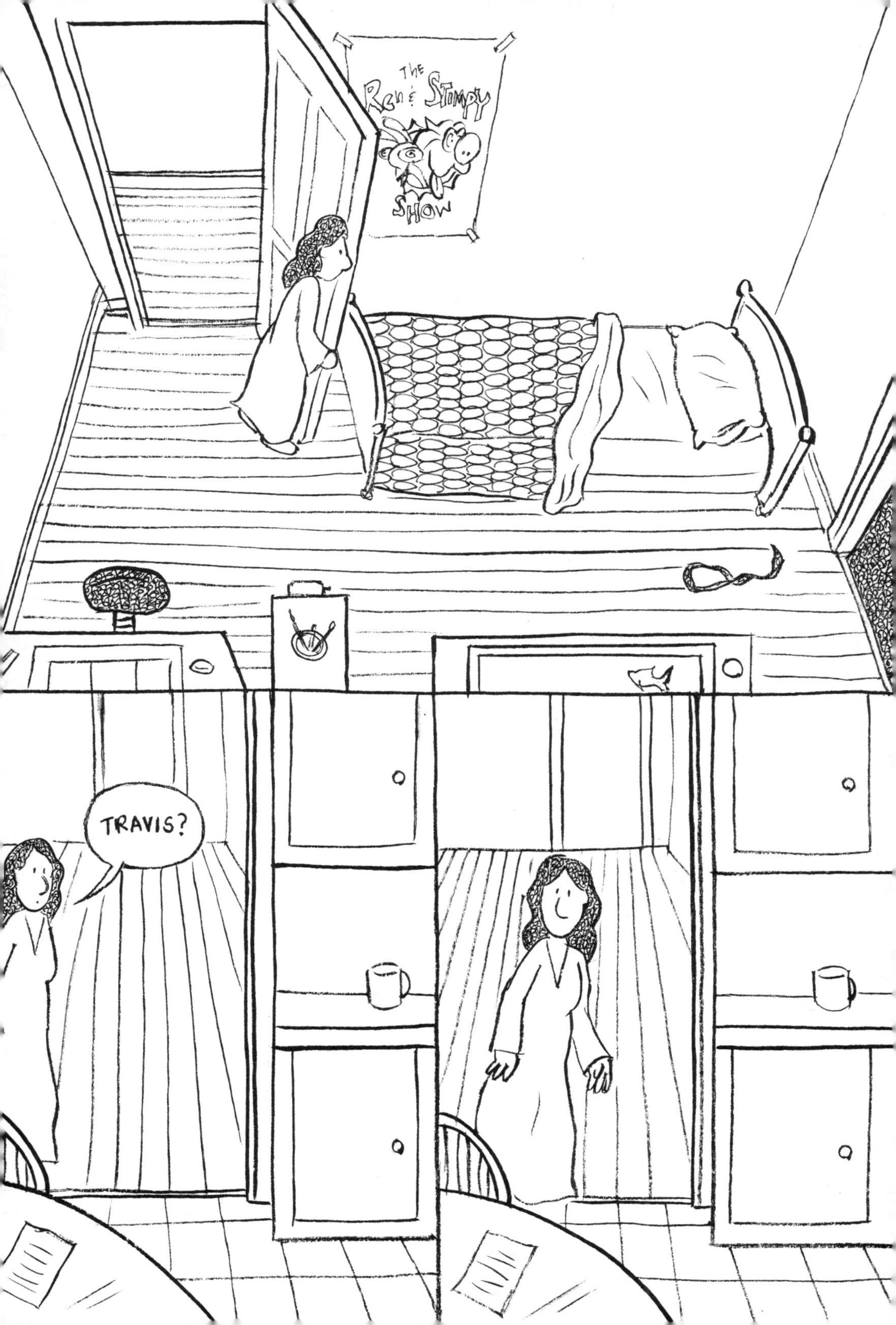
THE REN & STIMPY SHOW
TRAVIS?

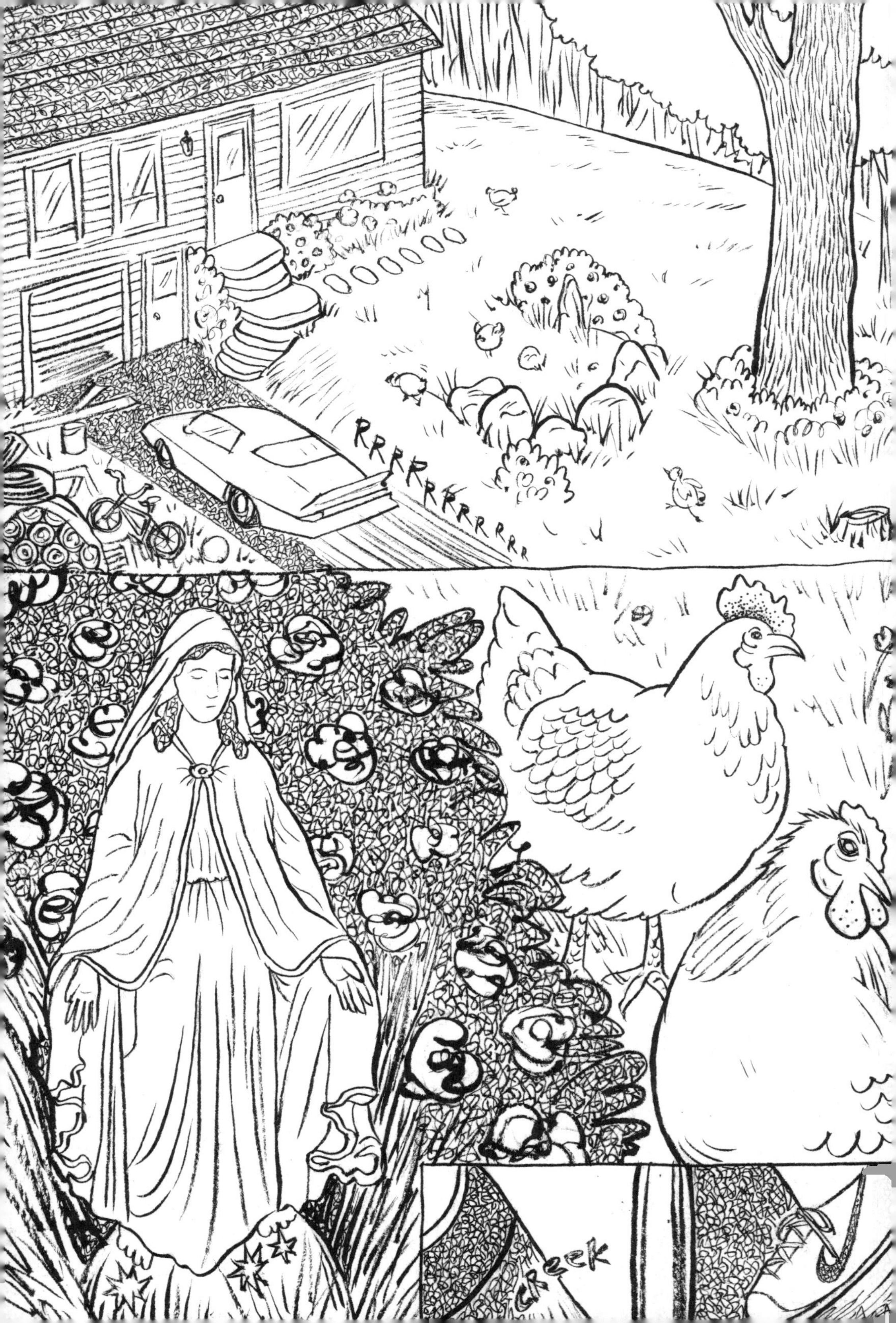
RRRRRRRRRRR
CReeK

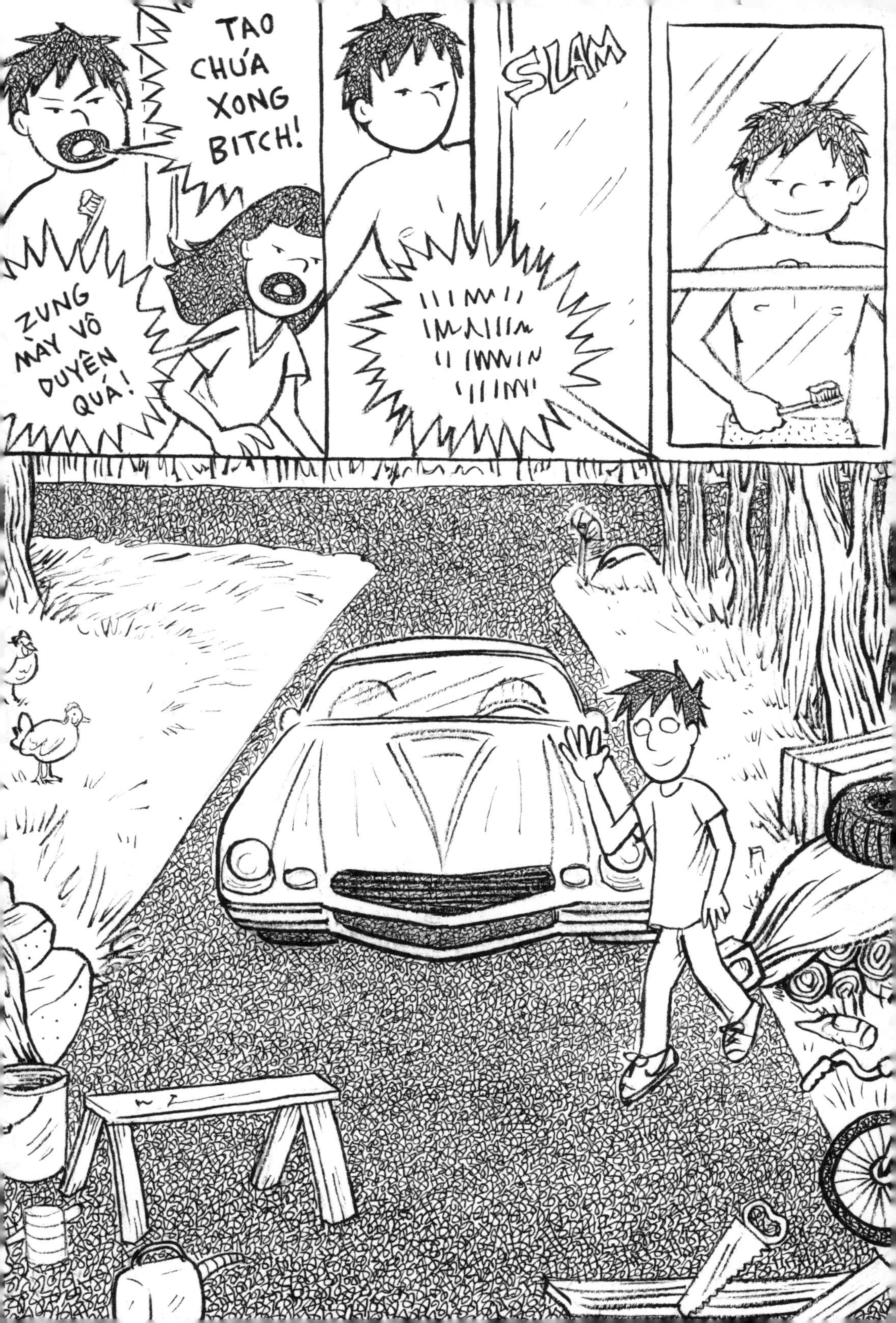
TAO CHƯA XONG BITCH!
ZUNG MÀY VÔ DUYÊN QUÁ!
SLAM

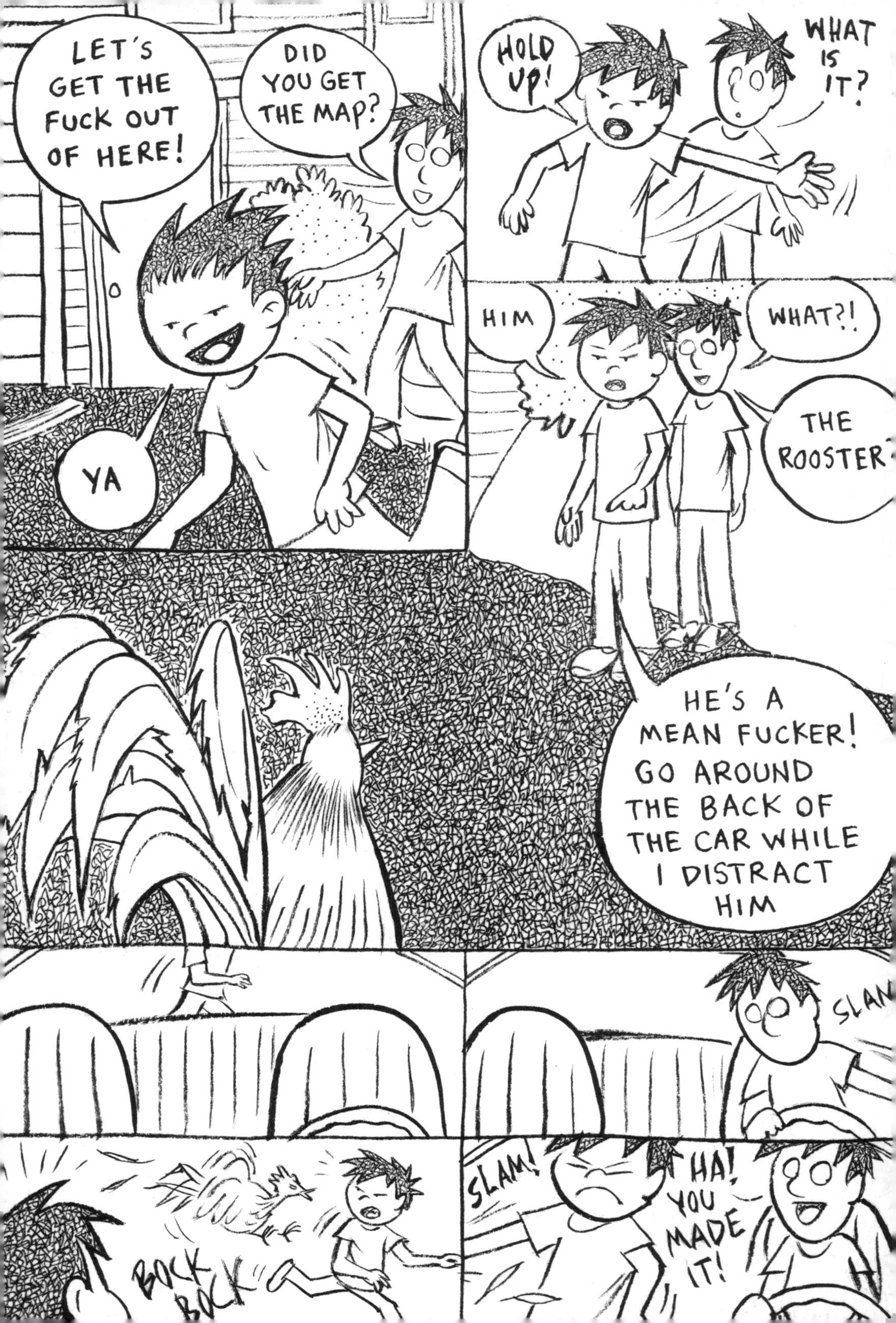

LET'S GET THE FUCK OUT OF HERE!
DID YOU GET THE MAP?
YA
HOLD UP!
WHAT IS IT?
HIM
WHAT?!
THE ROOSTER?
HE'S A MEAN FUCKER! GO AROUND THE BACK OF THE CAR WHILE I DISTRACT HIM
SLAM
BOCK BOCK
SLAM!
HA! YOU MADE IT!

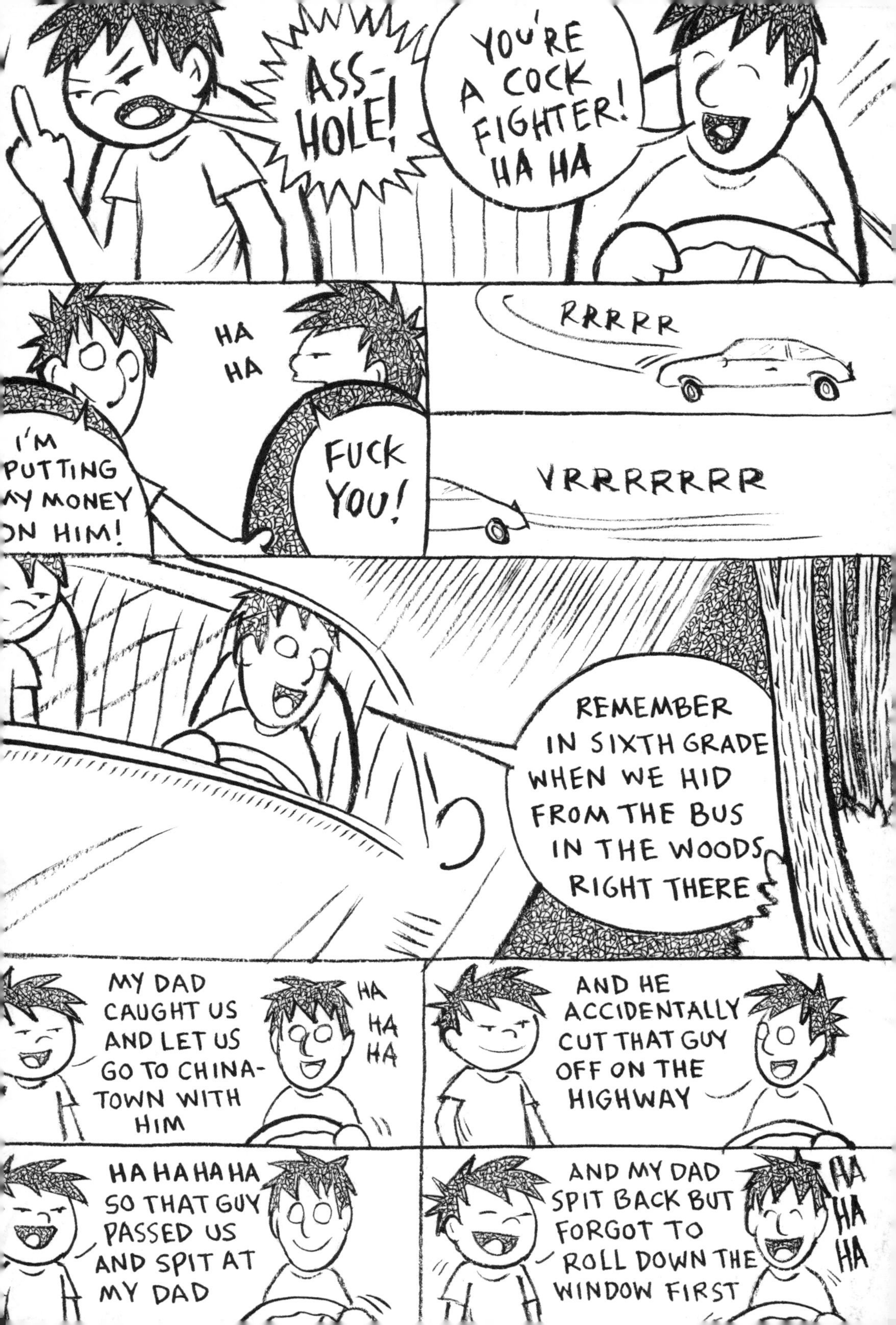
ASS-HOLE!
YOU'RE A COCK FIGHTER! HA HA
HA HA
I'M PUTTING MY MONEY ON HIM!
FUCK YOU!
RRRRR
VRRRRRRR
REMEMBER IN SIXTH GRADE WHEN WE HID FROM THE BUS IN THE WOODS RIGHT THERE
MY DAD CAUGHT US AND LET US GO TO CHINA-TOWN WITH HIM
HA HA HA
AND HE ACCIDENTALLY CUT THAT GUY OFF ON THE HIGHWAY
HA HA HA HA SO THAT GUY PASSED US AND SPIT AT MY DAD
AND MY DAD SPIT BACK BUT FORGOT TO ROLL DOWN THE WINDOW FIRST
HA HA HA

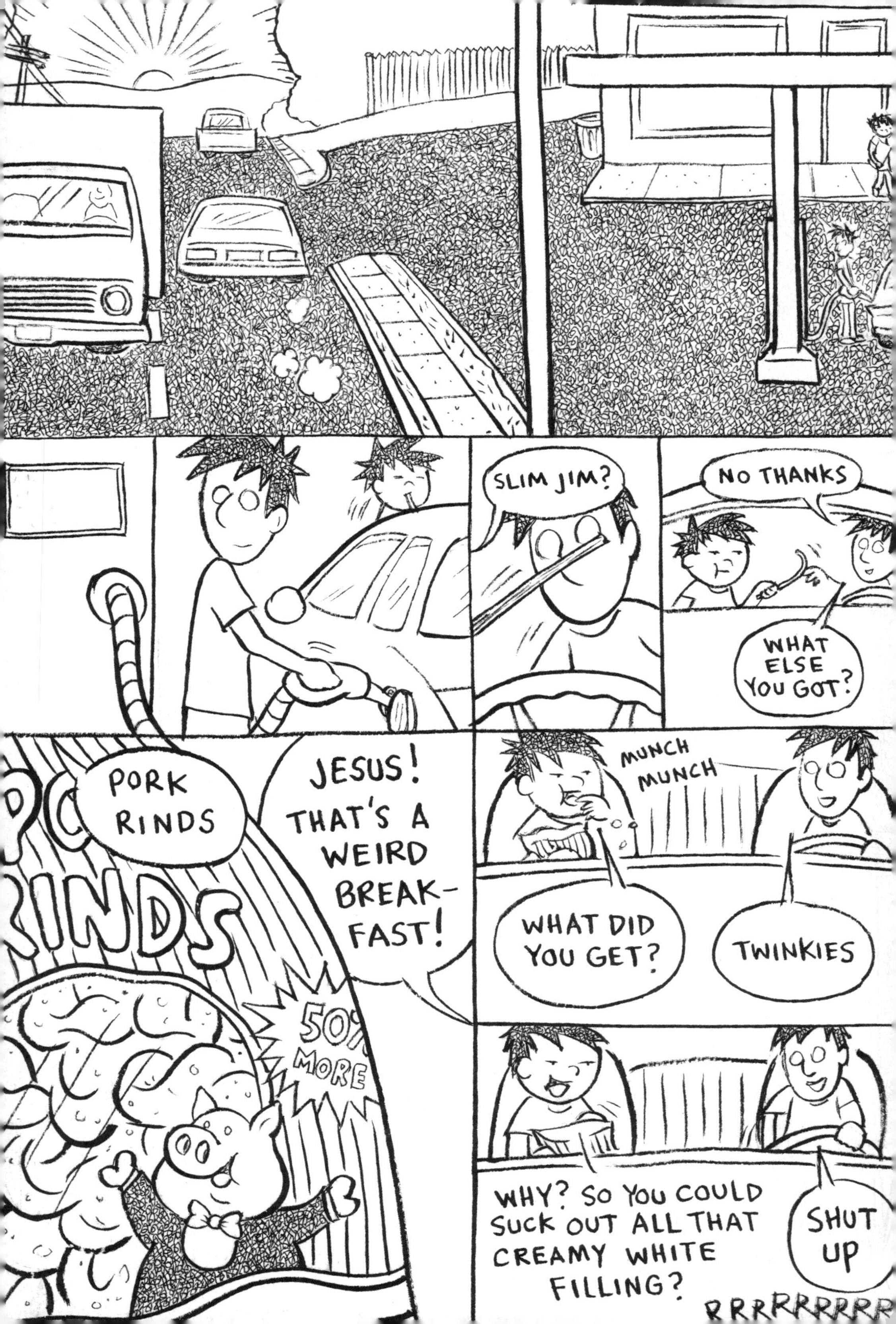
SLIM JIM?
NO THANKS
WHAT ELSE YOU GOT?
PORK RINDS
JESUS! THAT'S A WEIRD BREAK-FAST!
50% MORE
MUNCH MUNCH
WHAT DID YOU GET?
TWINKIES
WHY? SO YOU COULD SUCK OUT ALL THAT CREAMY WHITE FILLING?
SHUT UP
RRRRRRRRR

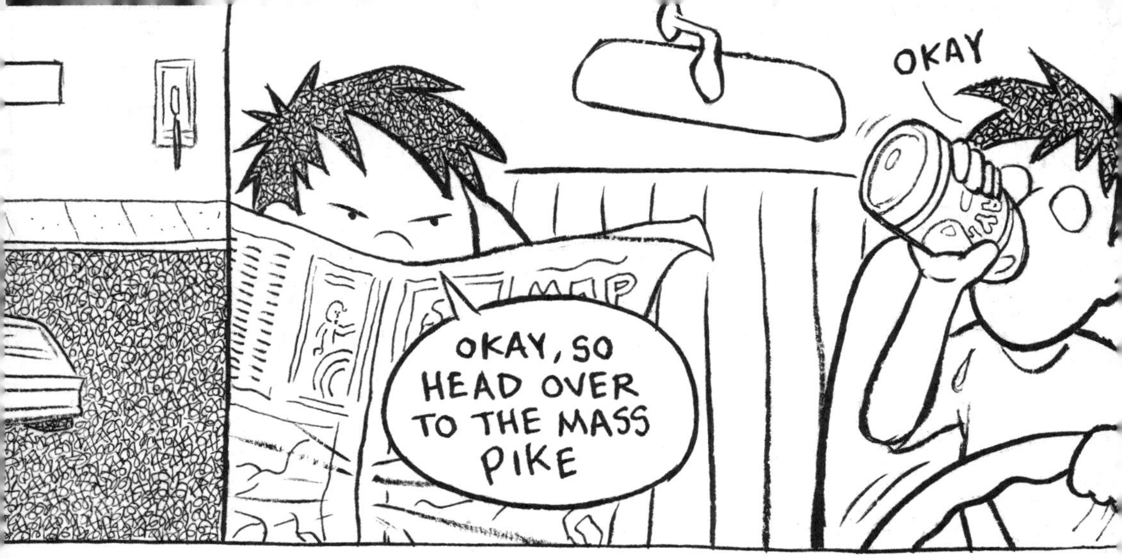
OKAY, SO HEAD OVER TO THE MASS PIKE
OKAY

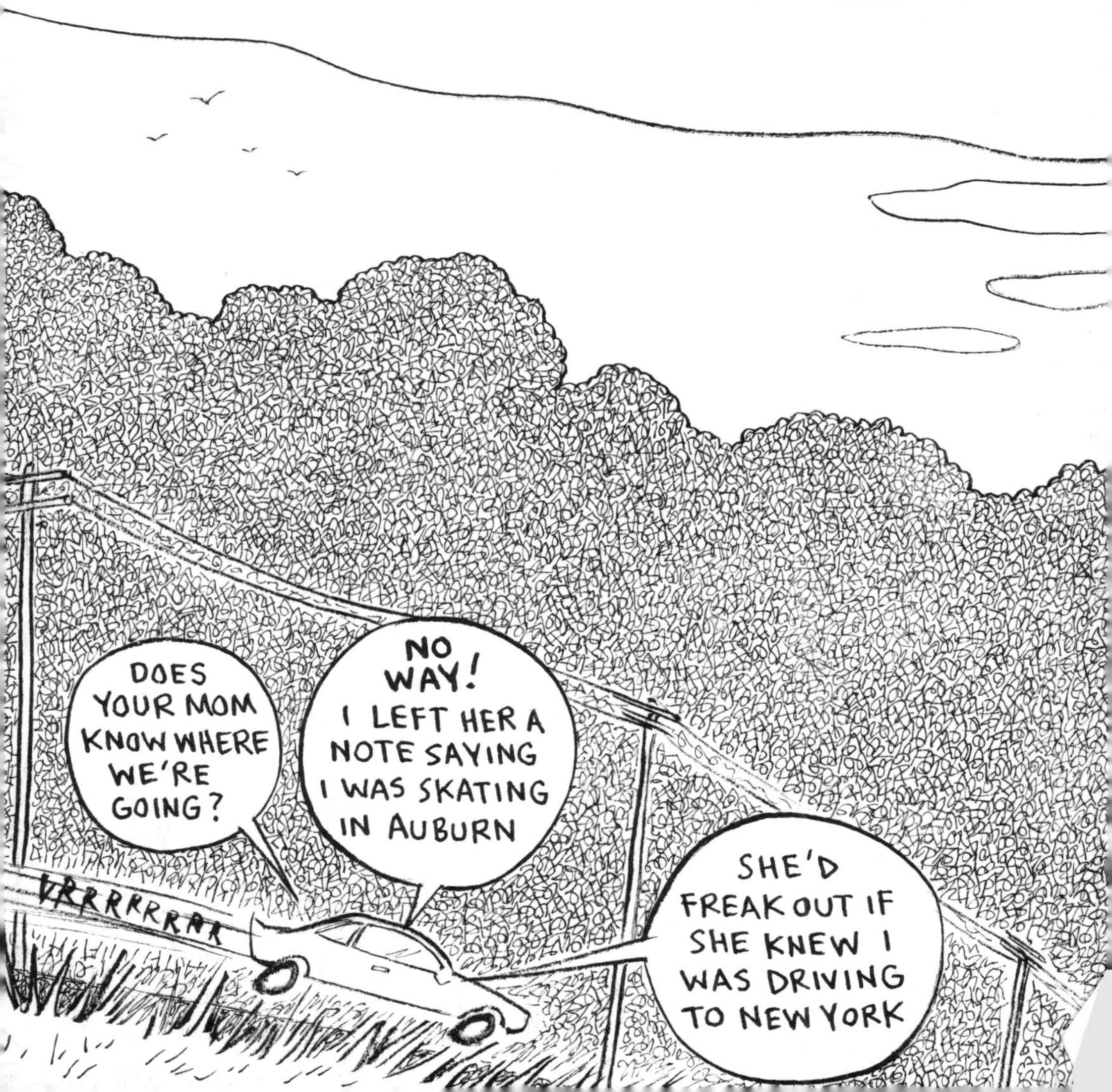
VRRRRRRRR
DOES YOUR MOM KNOW WHERE WE'RE GOING?
NO WAY! I LEFT HER A NOTE SAYING I WAS SKATING IN AUBURN
SHE'D FREAK OUT IF SHE KNEW I WAS DRIVING TO NEW YORK

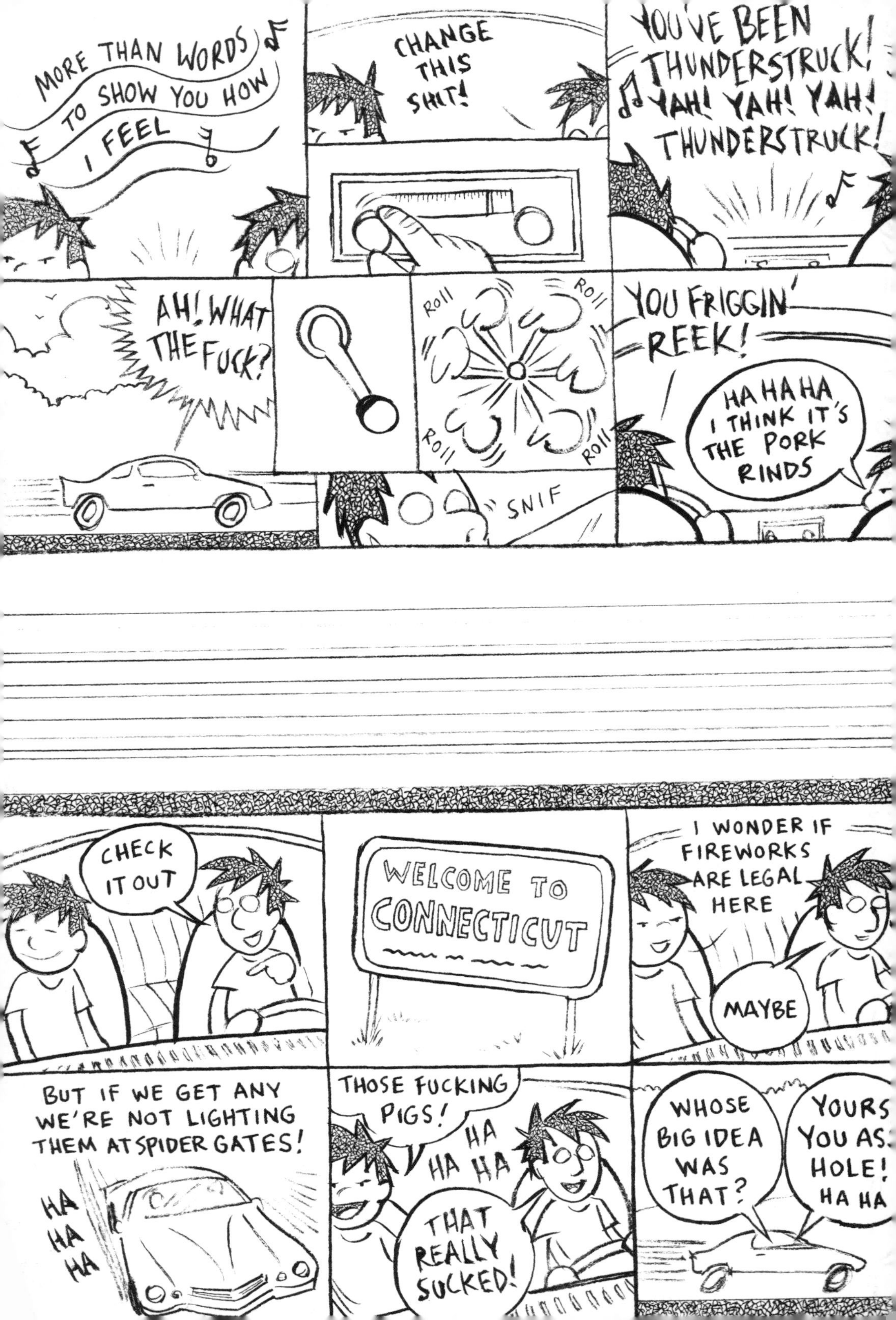

MORE THAN WORDS TO SHOW YOU HOW I FEEL
CHANGE THIS SHIT!
YOU'VE BEEN THUNDERSTRUCK! YAH! YAH! YAH! THUNDERSTRUCK!
AH! WHAT THE FUCK?
ROLL
ROLL
ROLL
ROLL
SNIF
YOU FRIGGIN' REEK!
HA HA HA, I THINK IT'S THE PORK RINDS
CHECK IT OUT
WELCOME TO CONNECTICUT
I WONDER IF FIREWORKS ARE LEGAL HERE
MAYBE
BUT IF WE GET ANY WE'RE NOT LIGHTING THEM AT SPIDER GATES!
HA HA HA
THOSE FUCKING PIGS!
HA HA HA
THAT REALLY SUCKED!
WHOSE BIG IDEA WAS THAT?
YOURS YOU AS HOLE! HA HA

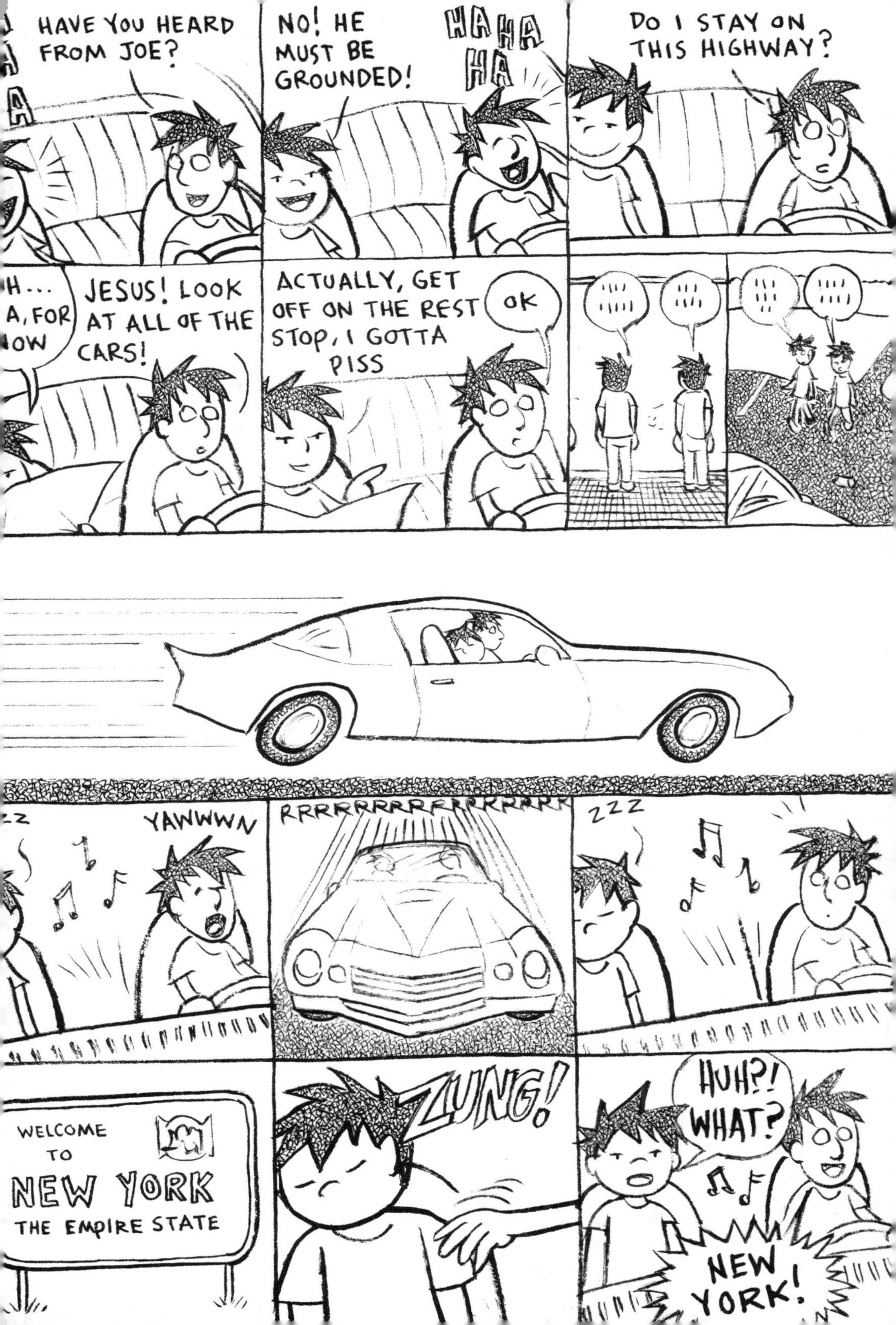
HAVE YOU HEARD FROM JOE?
NO! HE MUST BE GROUNDED!
HAHA HA
DO I STAY ON THIS HIGHWAY?
JESUS! LOOK AT ALL OF THE CARS!
ACTUALLY, GET OFF ON THE REST STOP, I GOTTA PISS
OK
YAWWWN
RRRRRRRRRRRRRRRR
ZZZ
WELCOME TO NEW YORK THE EMPIRE STATE
ZUNG!
HUH?! WHAT?
NEW YORK!

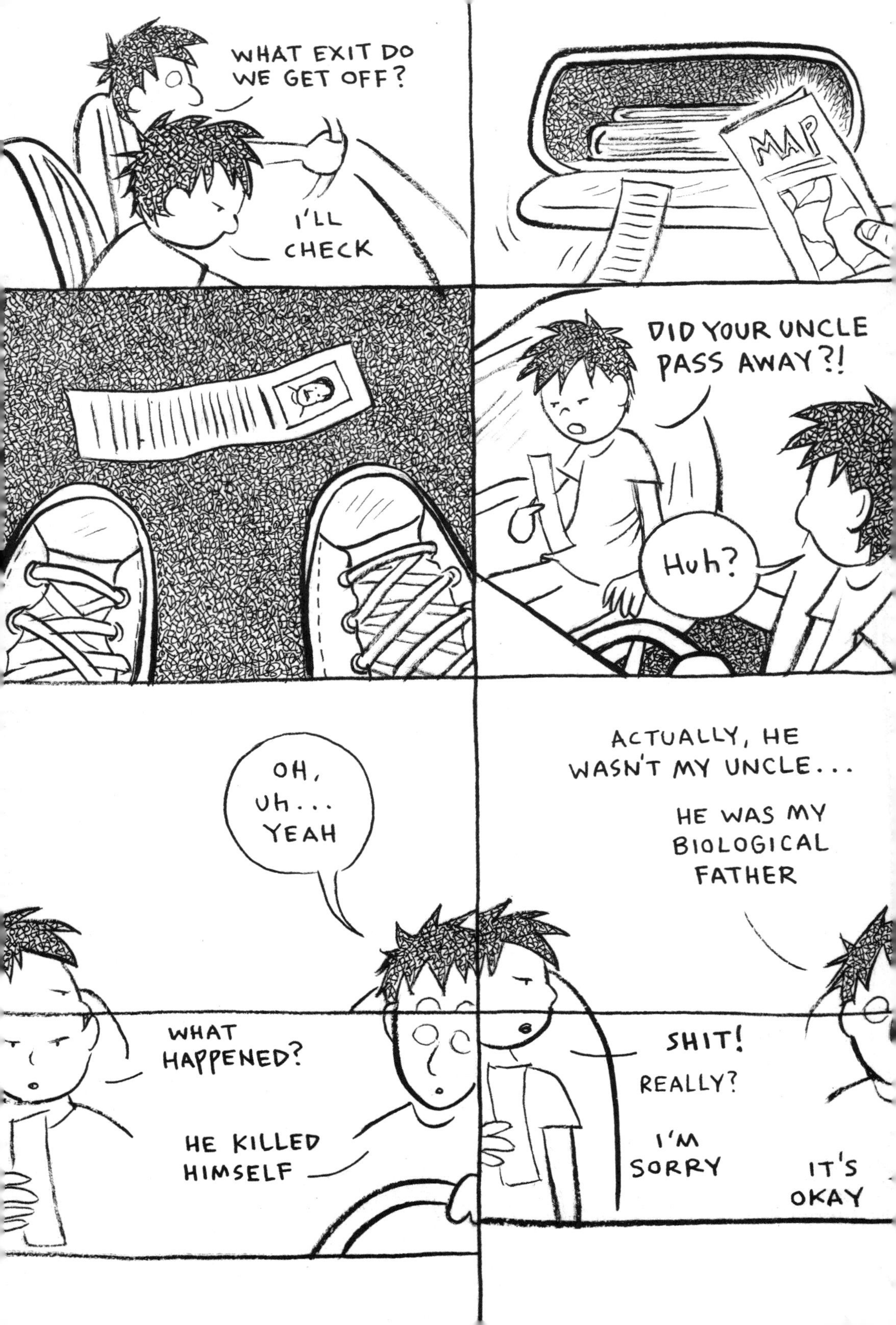
WHAT EXIT DO WE GET OFF?
I'LL CHECK
MAP
DID YOUR UNCLE PASS AWAY?!
Huh?
OH, UH... YEAH
ACTUALLY, HE WASN'T MY UNCLE...
HE WAS MY BIOLOGICAL FATHER
WHAT HAPPENED?
HE KILLED HIMSELF
SHIT!
REALLY?
I'M SORRY
IT'S OKAY

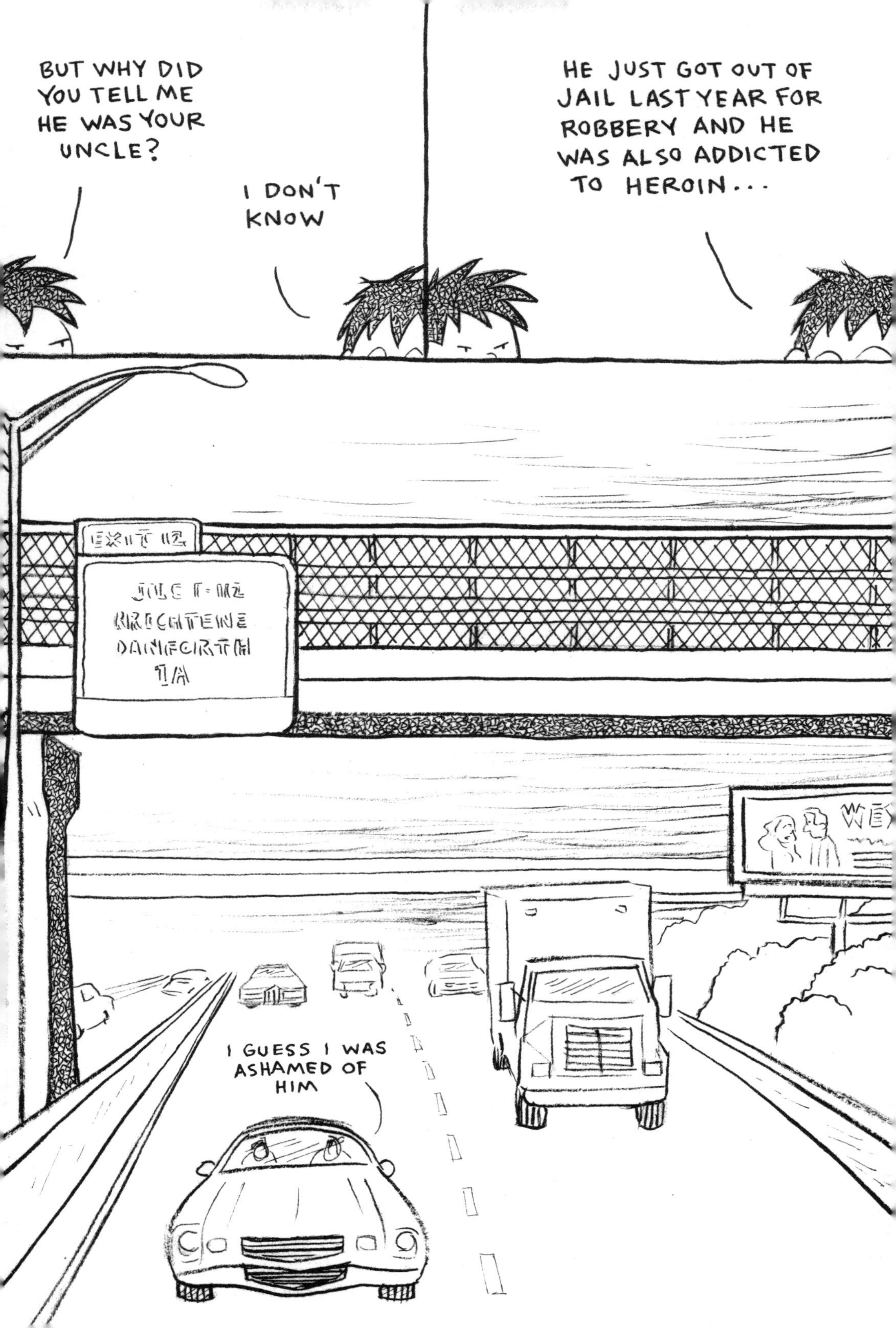
BUT WHY DID YOU TELL ME HE WAS YOUR UNCLE?
I DON'T KNOW
HE JUST GOT OUT OF JAIL LAST YEAR FOR ROBBERY AND HE WAS ALSO ADDICTED TO HEROIN...
I GUESS I WAS ASHAMED OF HIM

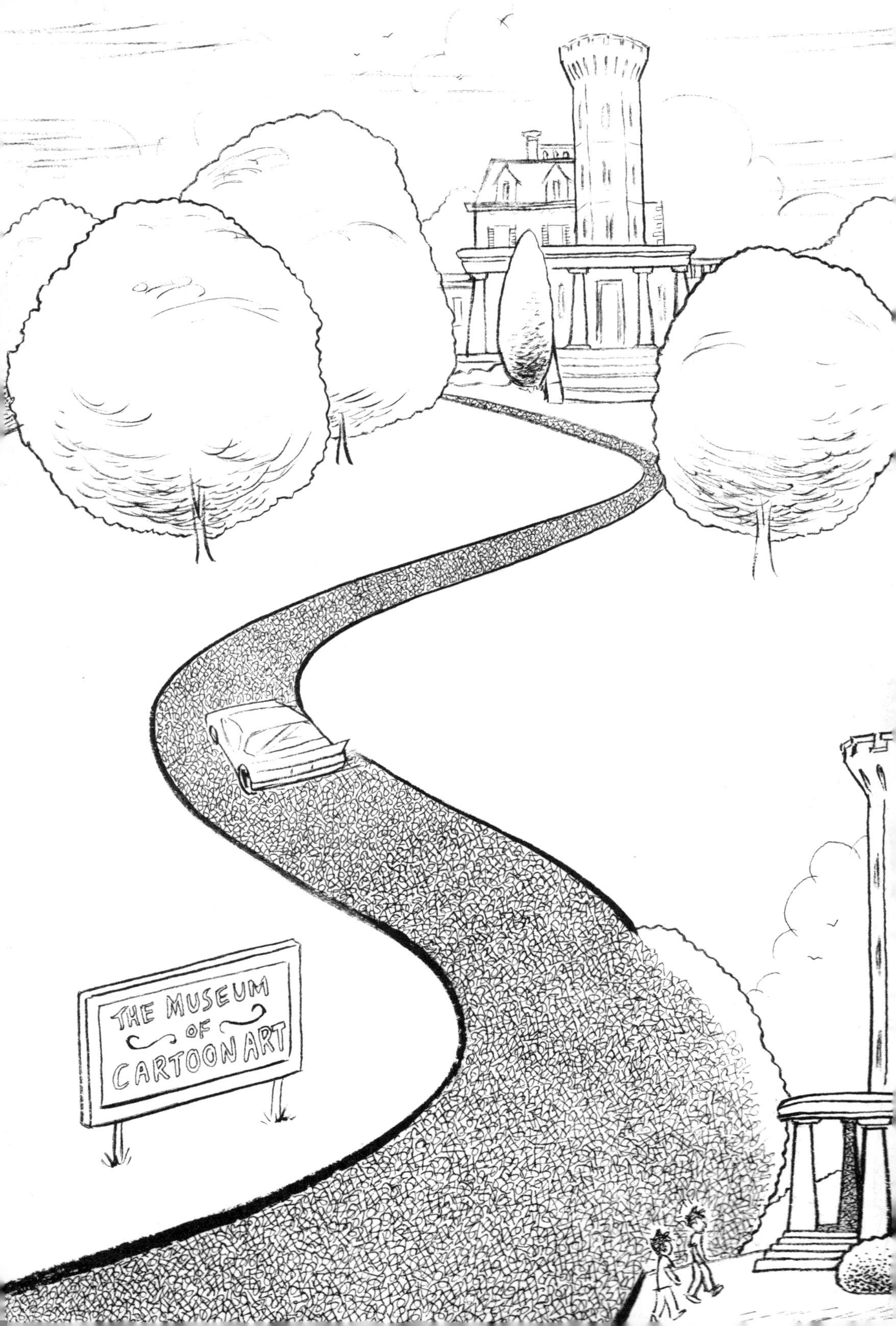
THE MUSEUM OF CARTOON ART

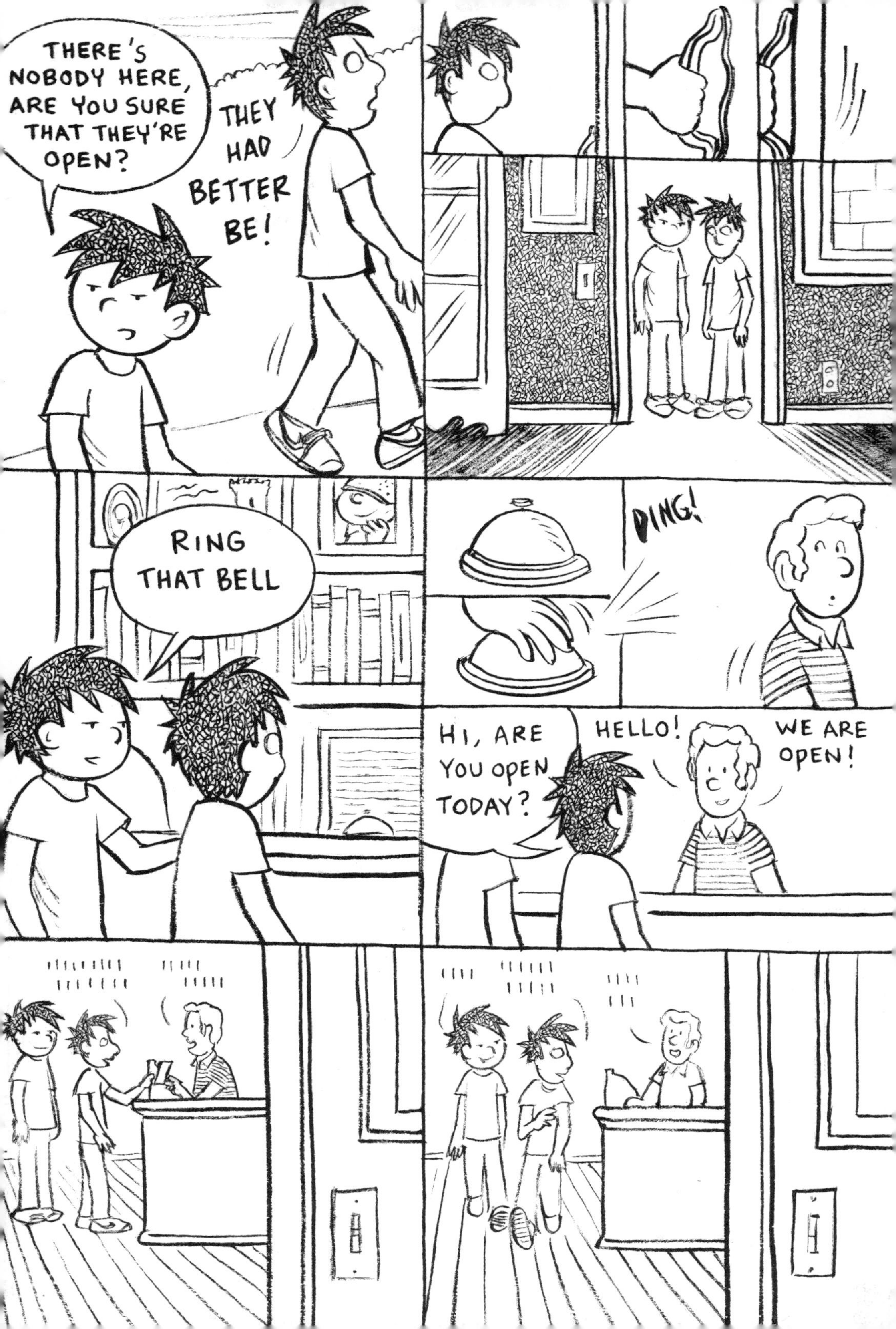
THERE'S NOBODY HERE, ARE YOU SURE THAT THEY'RE OPEN?
THEY HAD BETTER BE!
RING THAT BELL
DING!
HI, ARE YOU OPEN TODAY?
HELLO!
WE ARE OPEN!

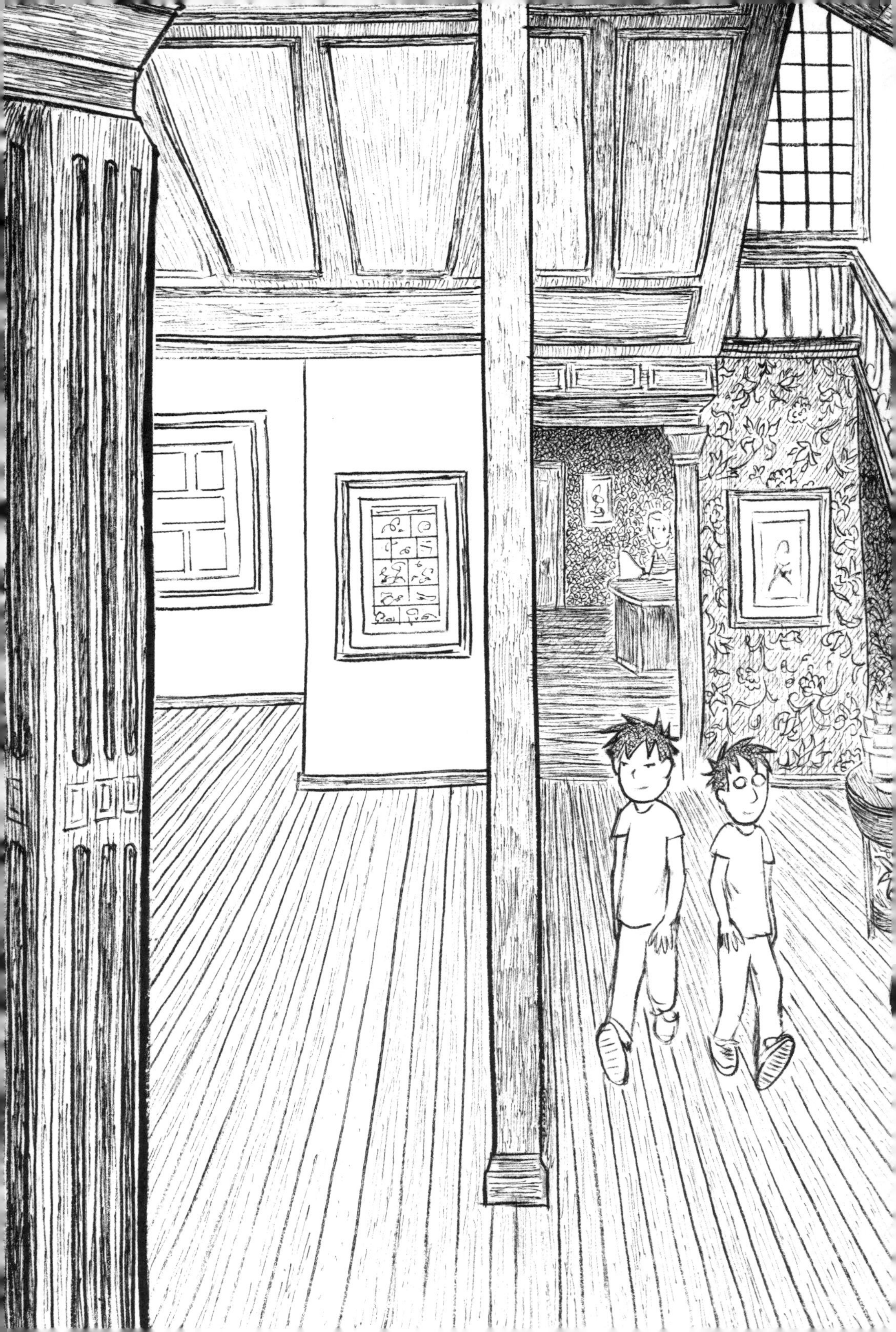

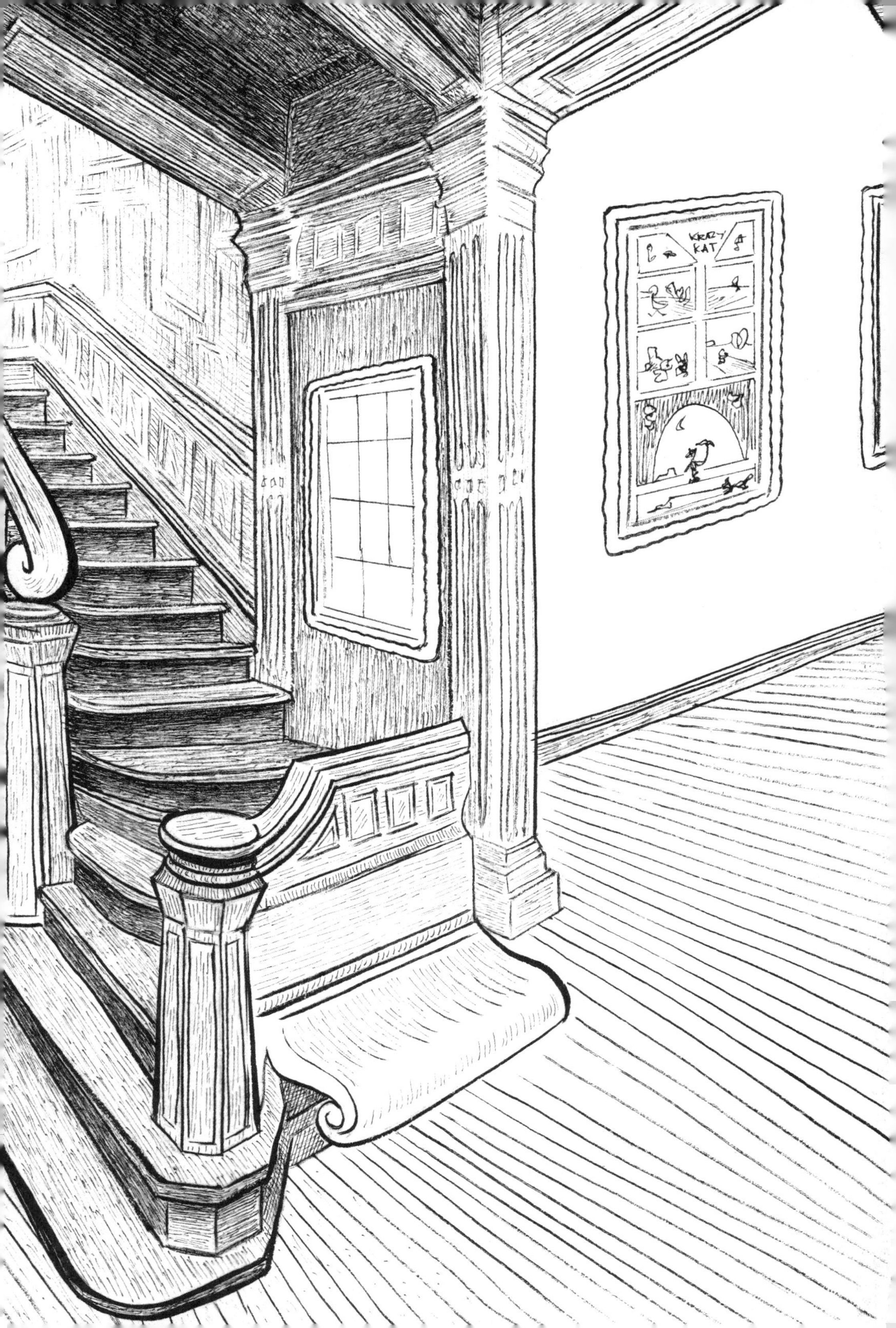
KRAZY
KAT

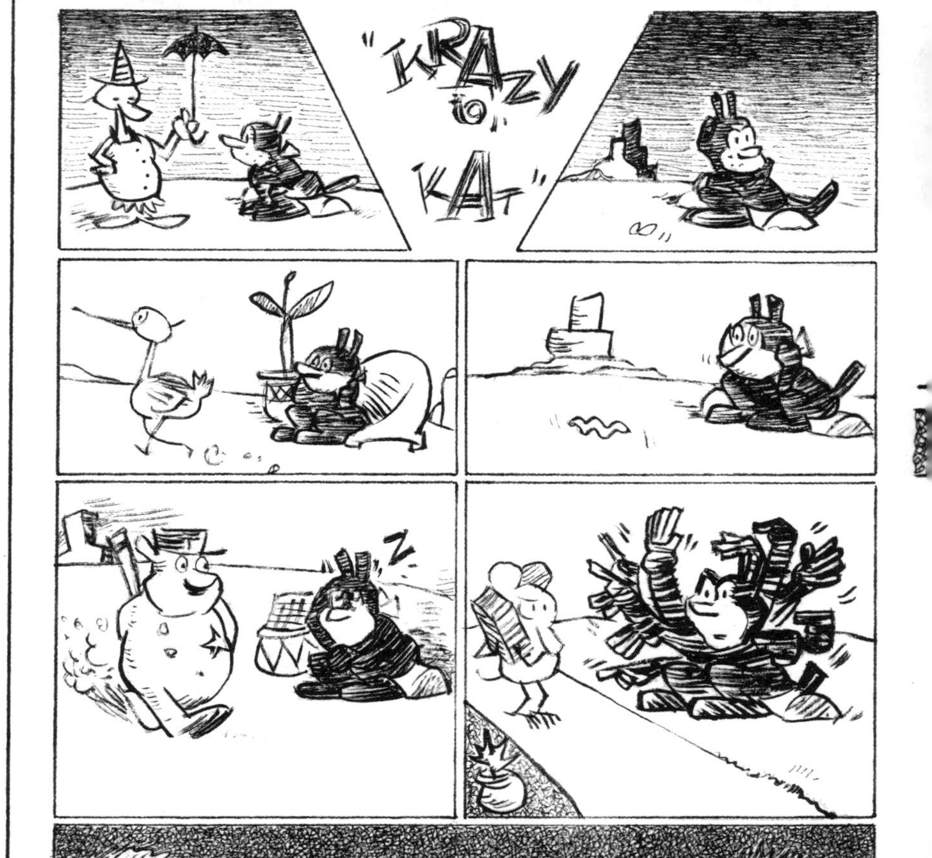
"KRAZY
KAT"

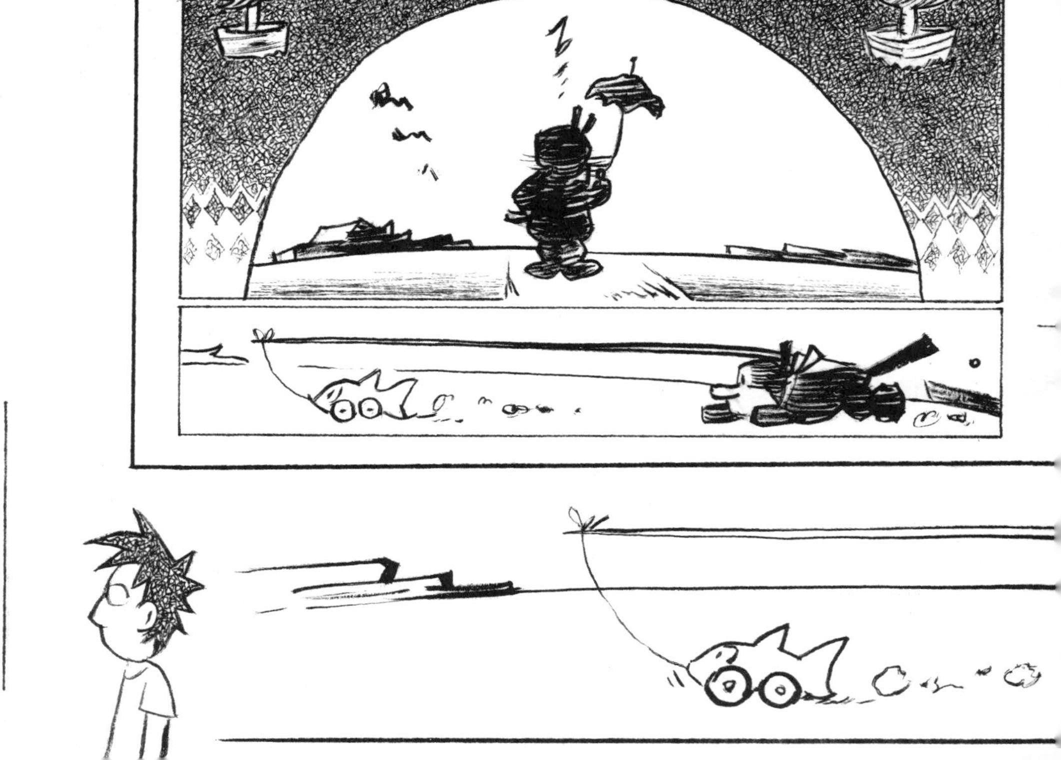

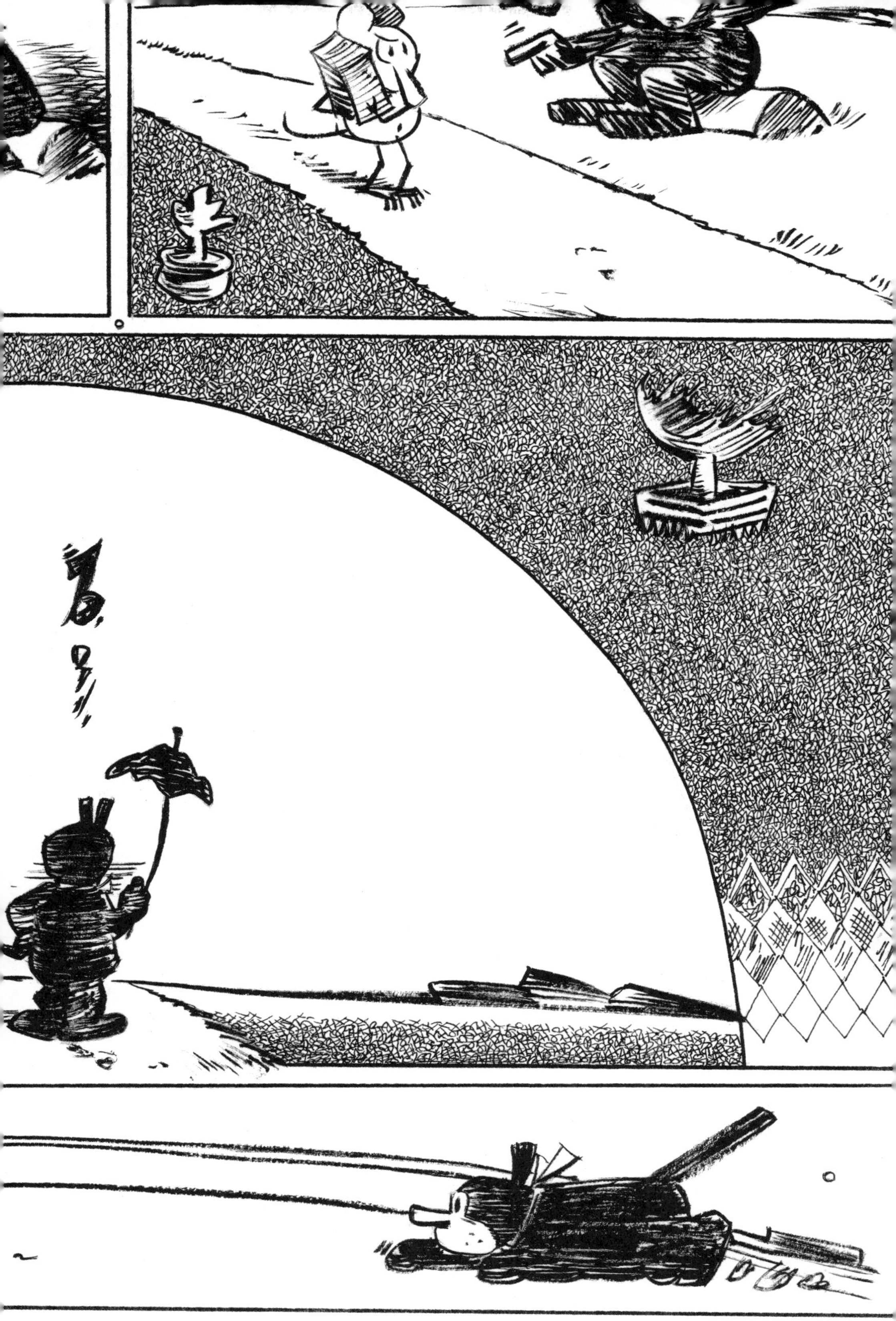

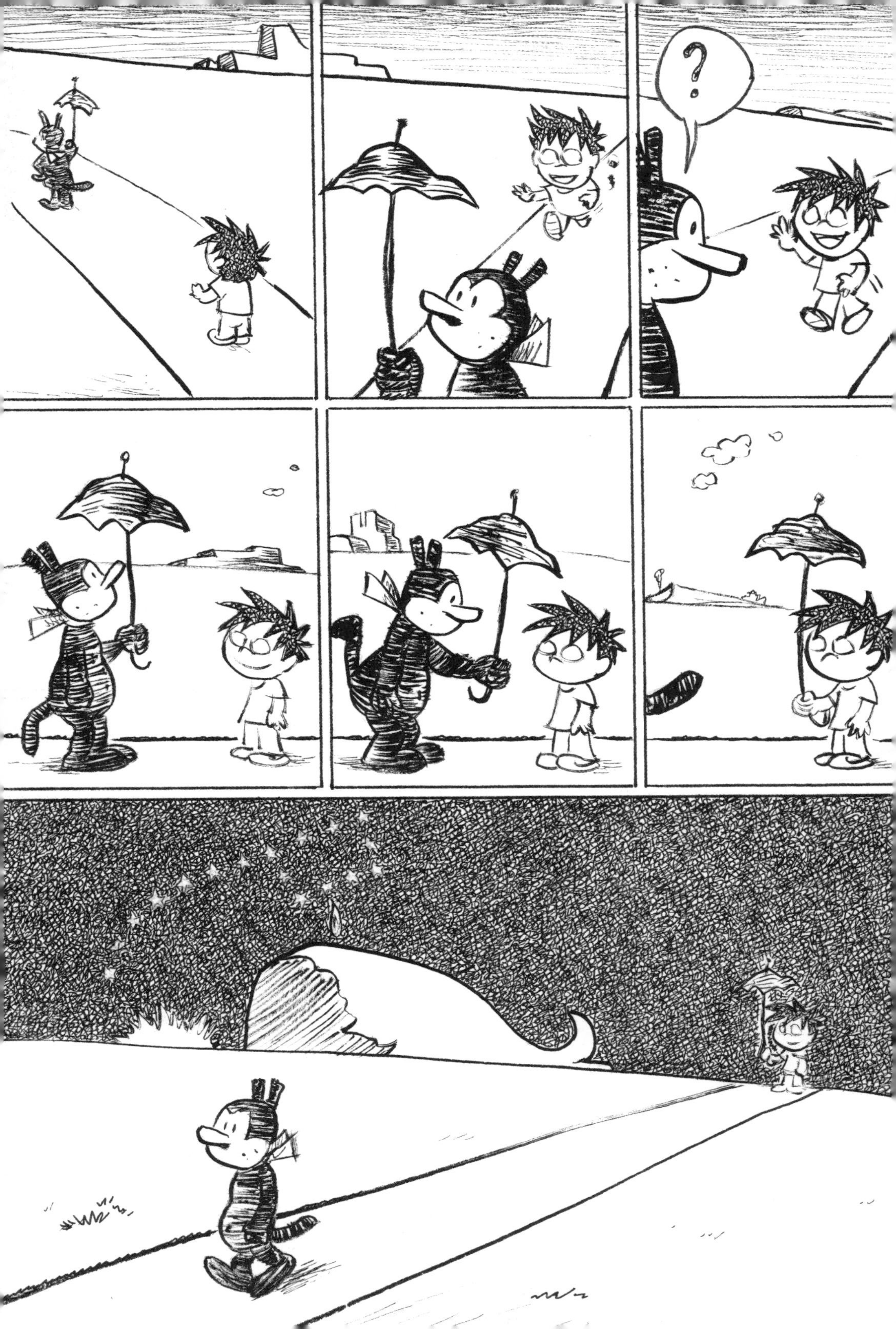
?

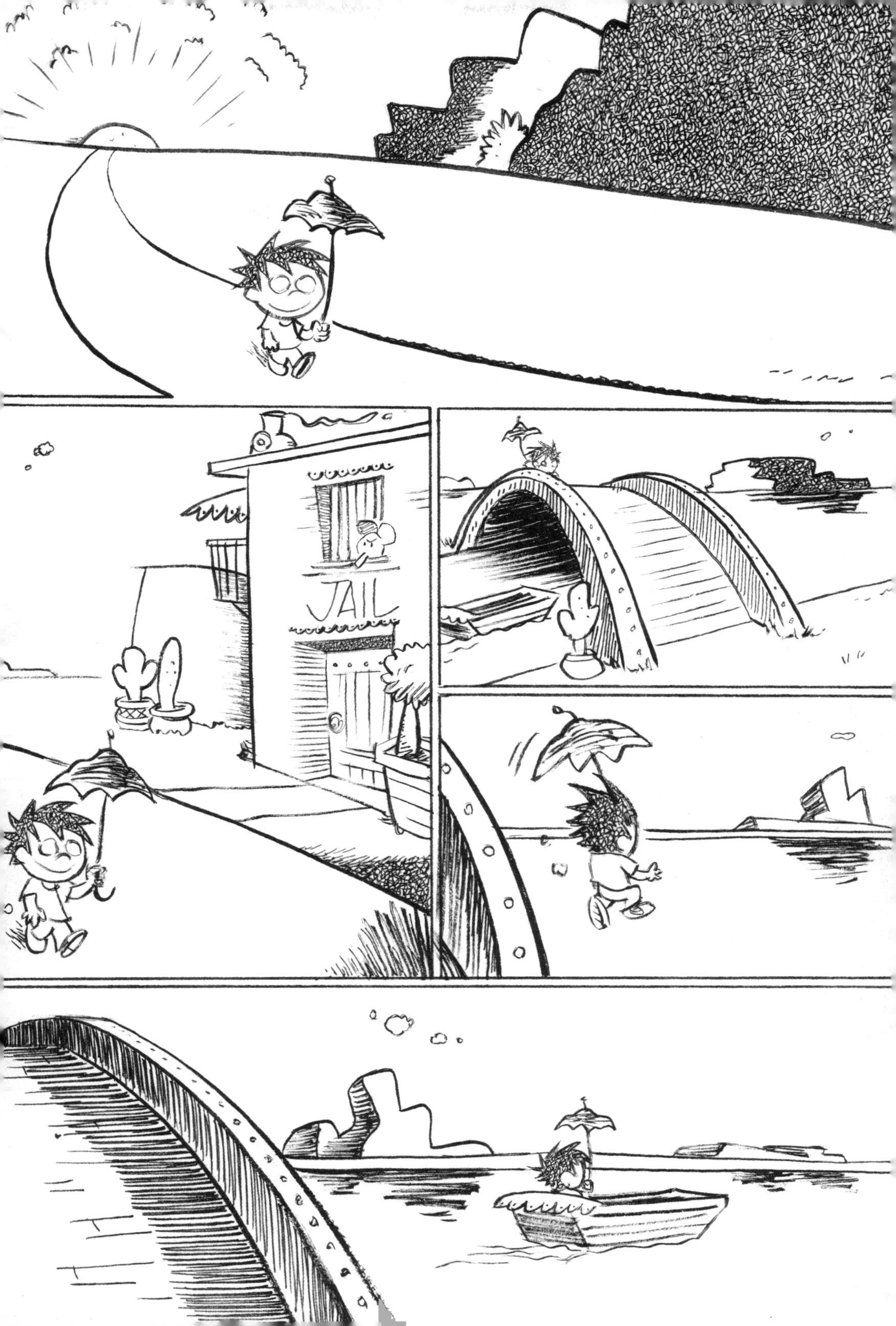
JAIL

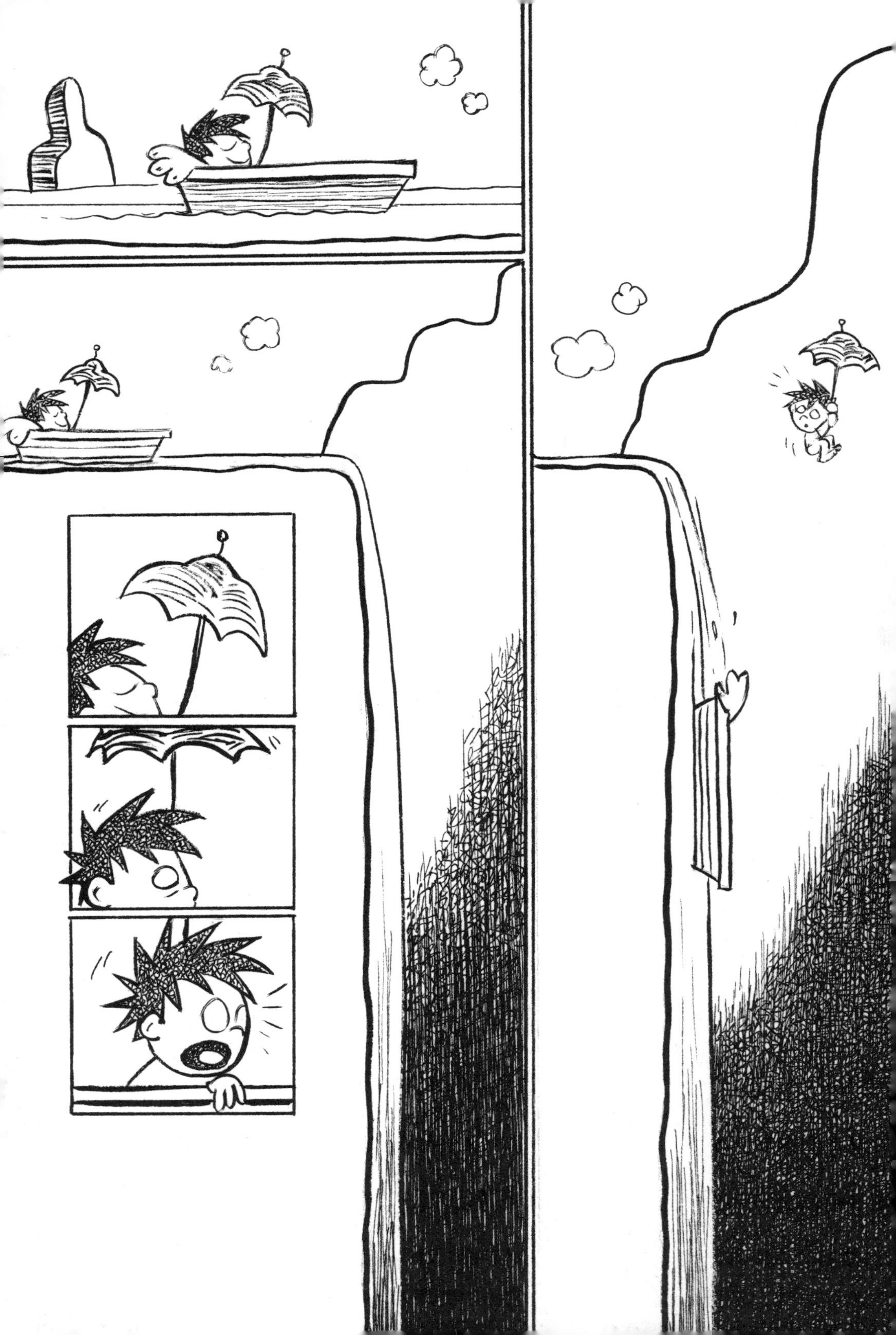

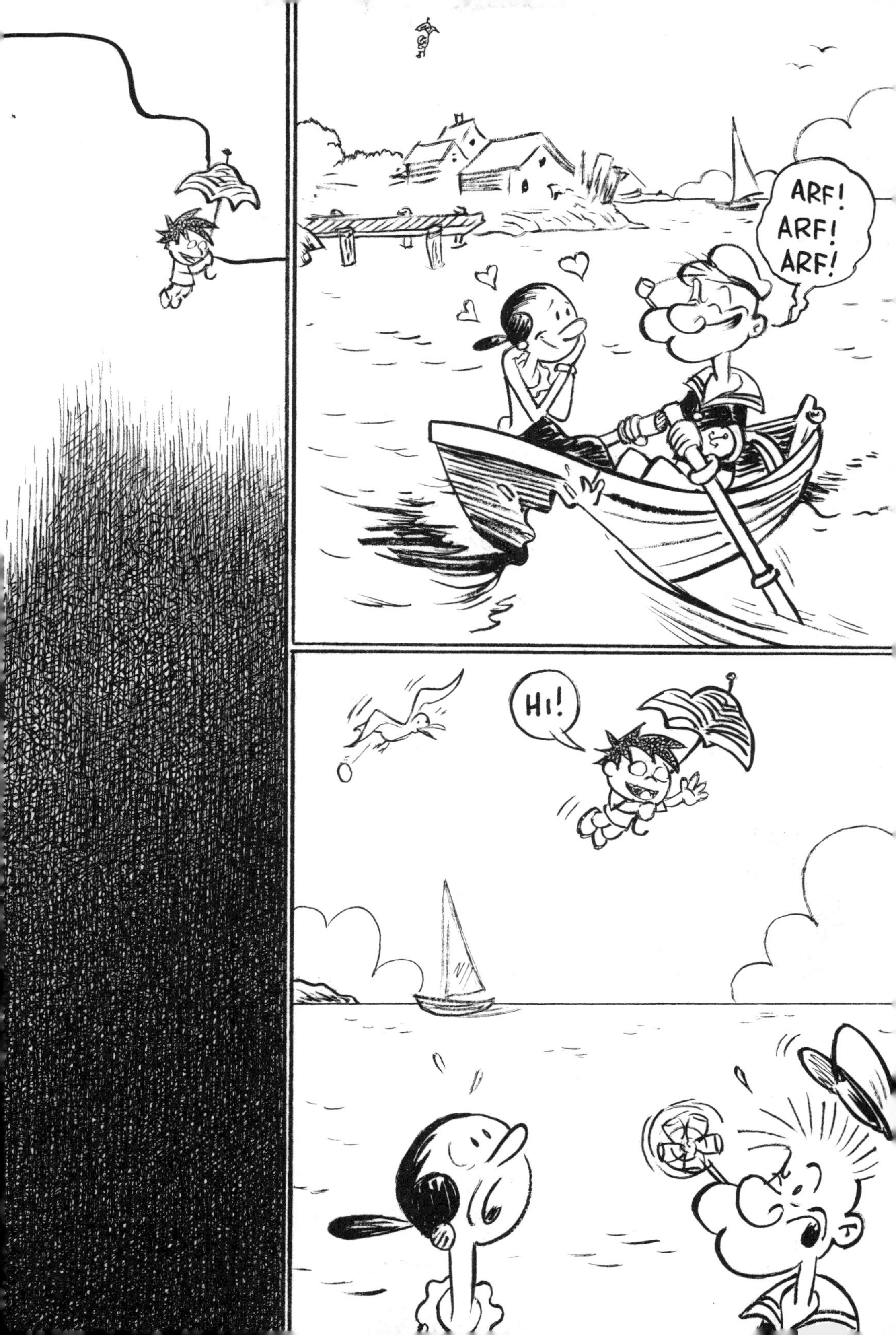
ARF! ARF! ARF!
HI!

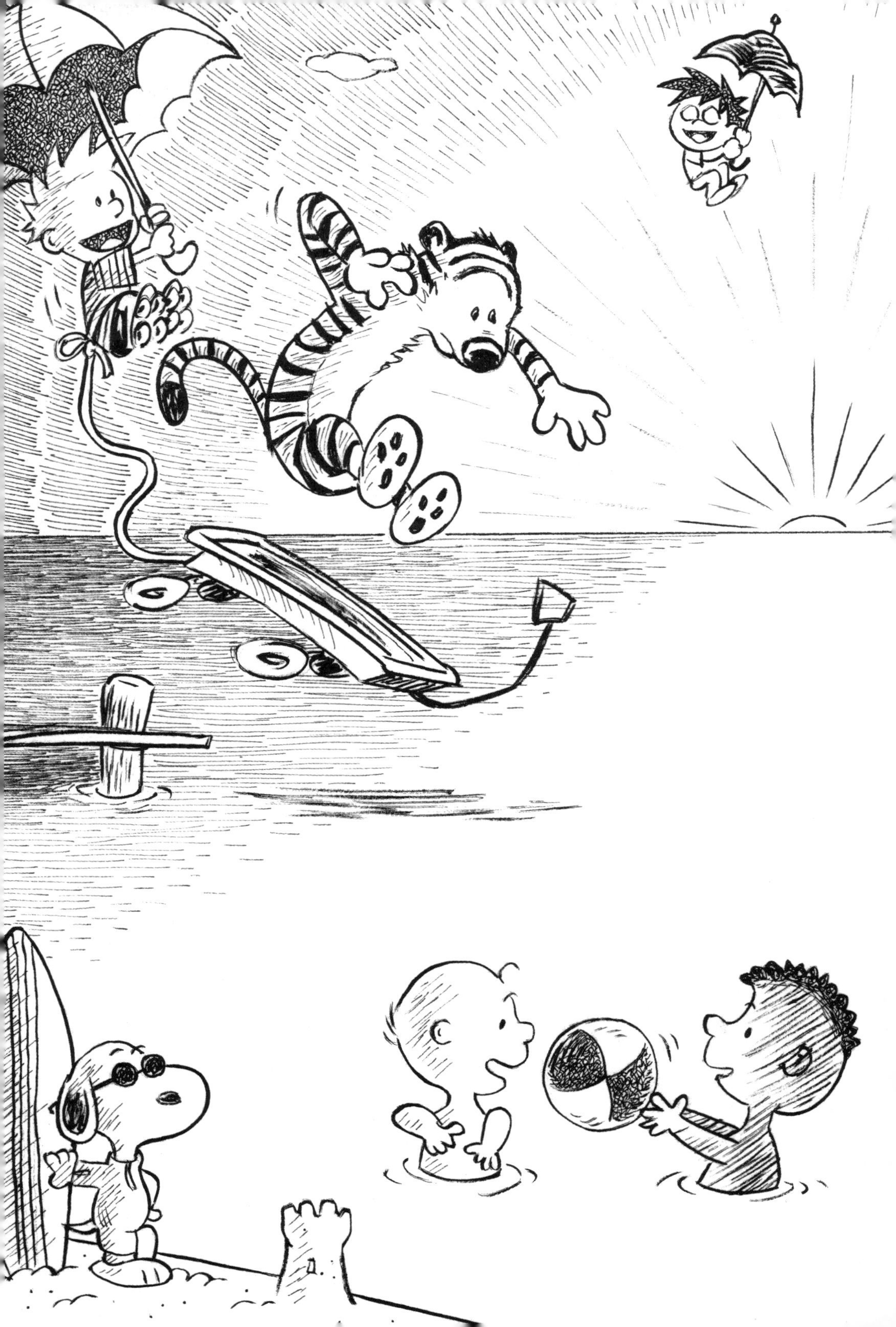

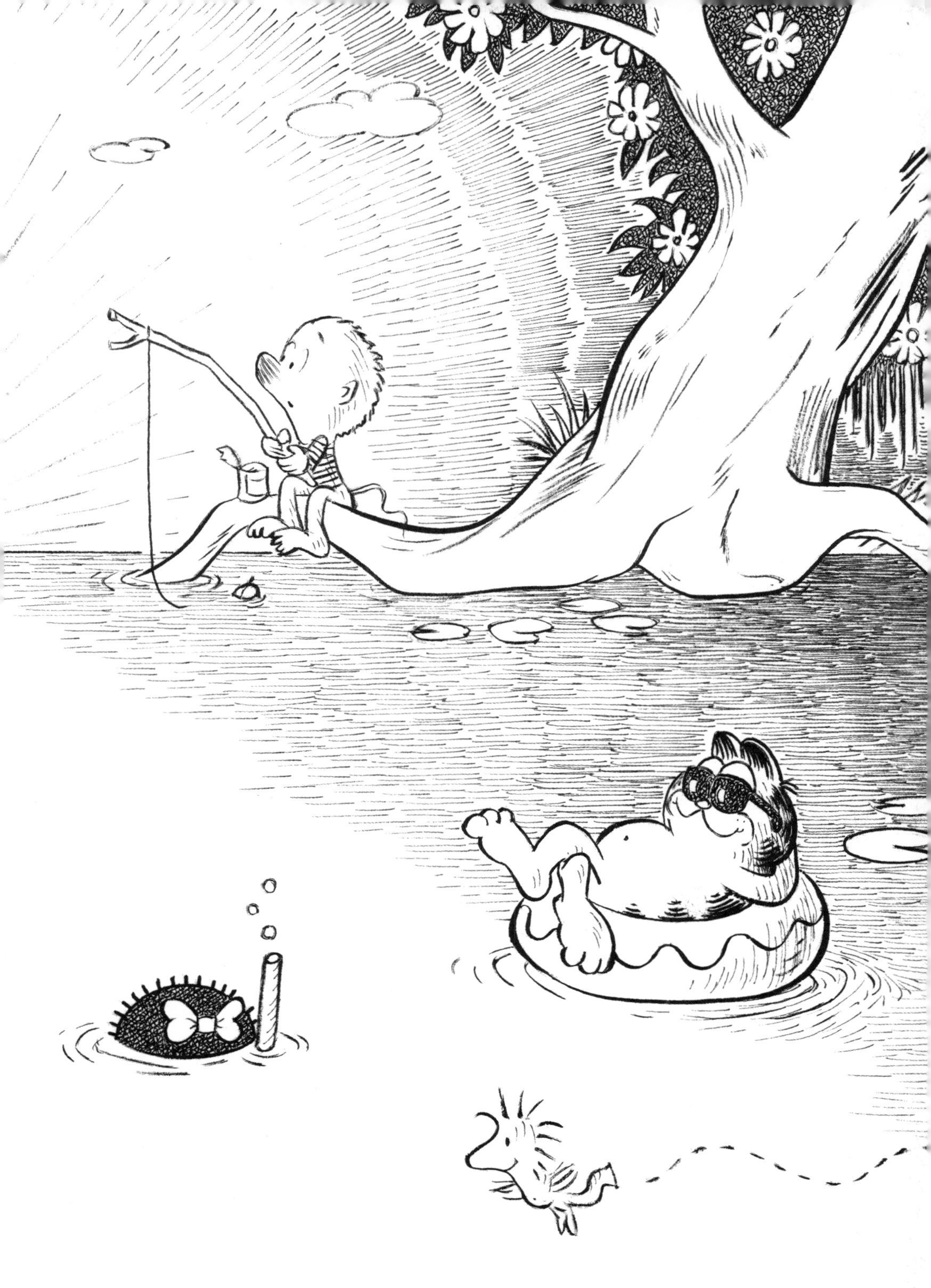

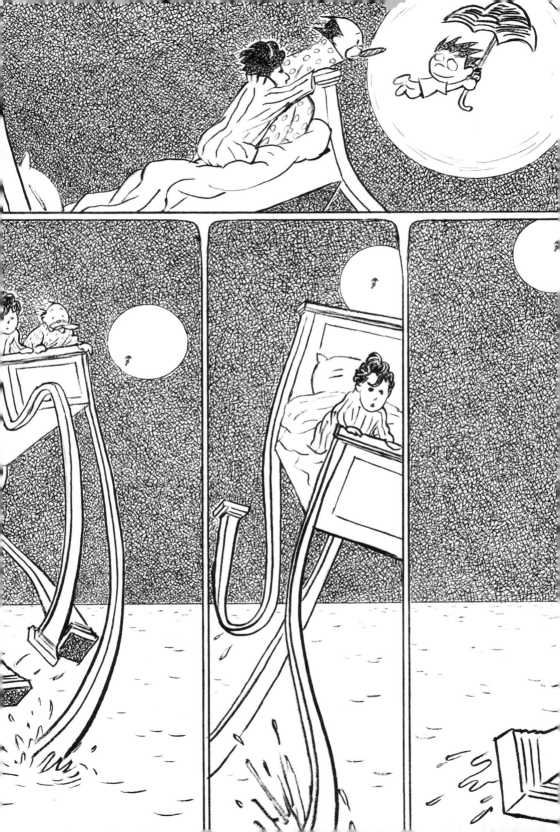

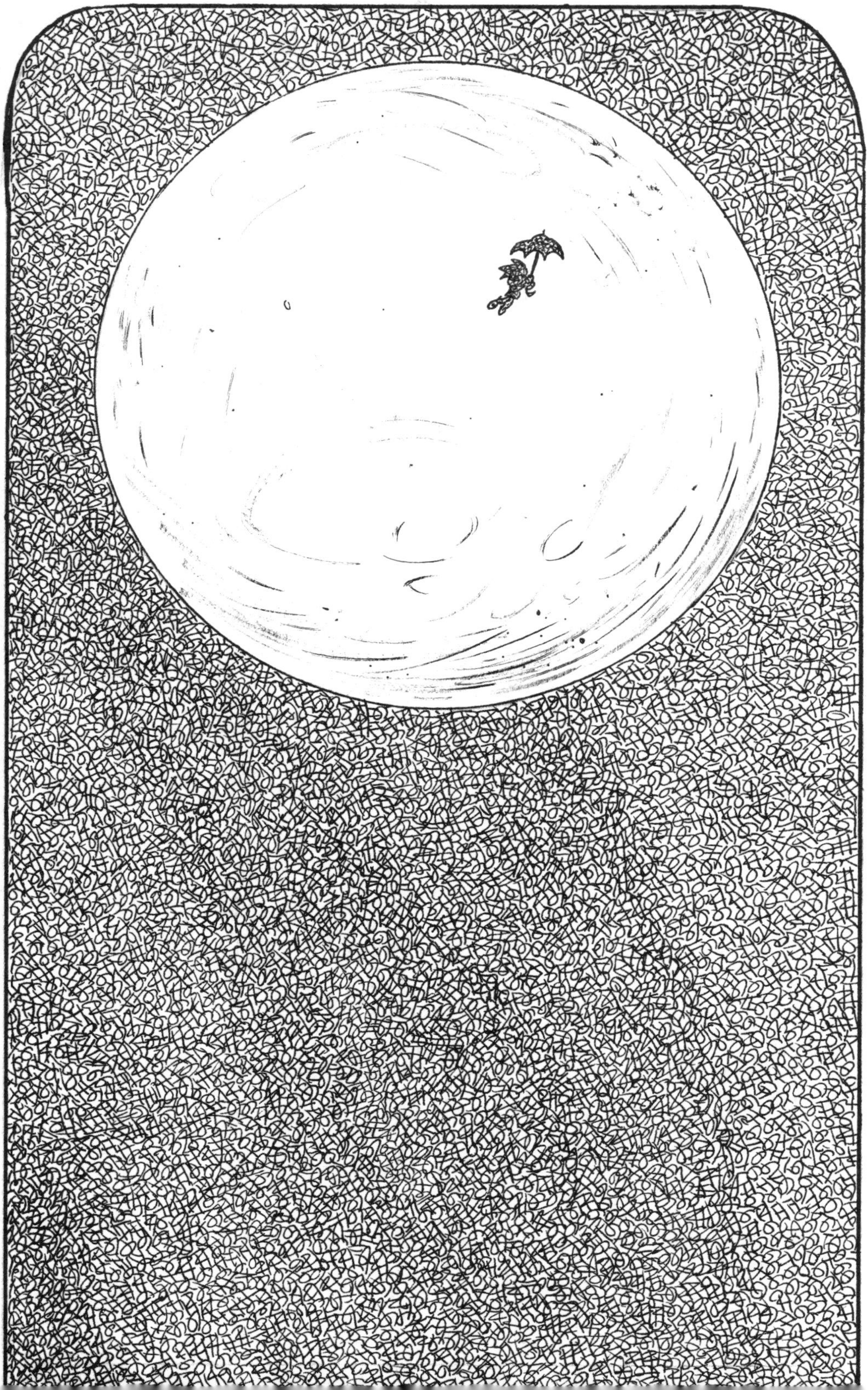

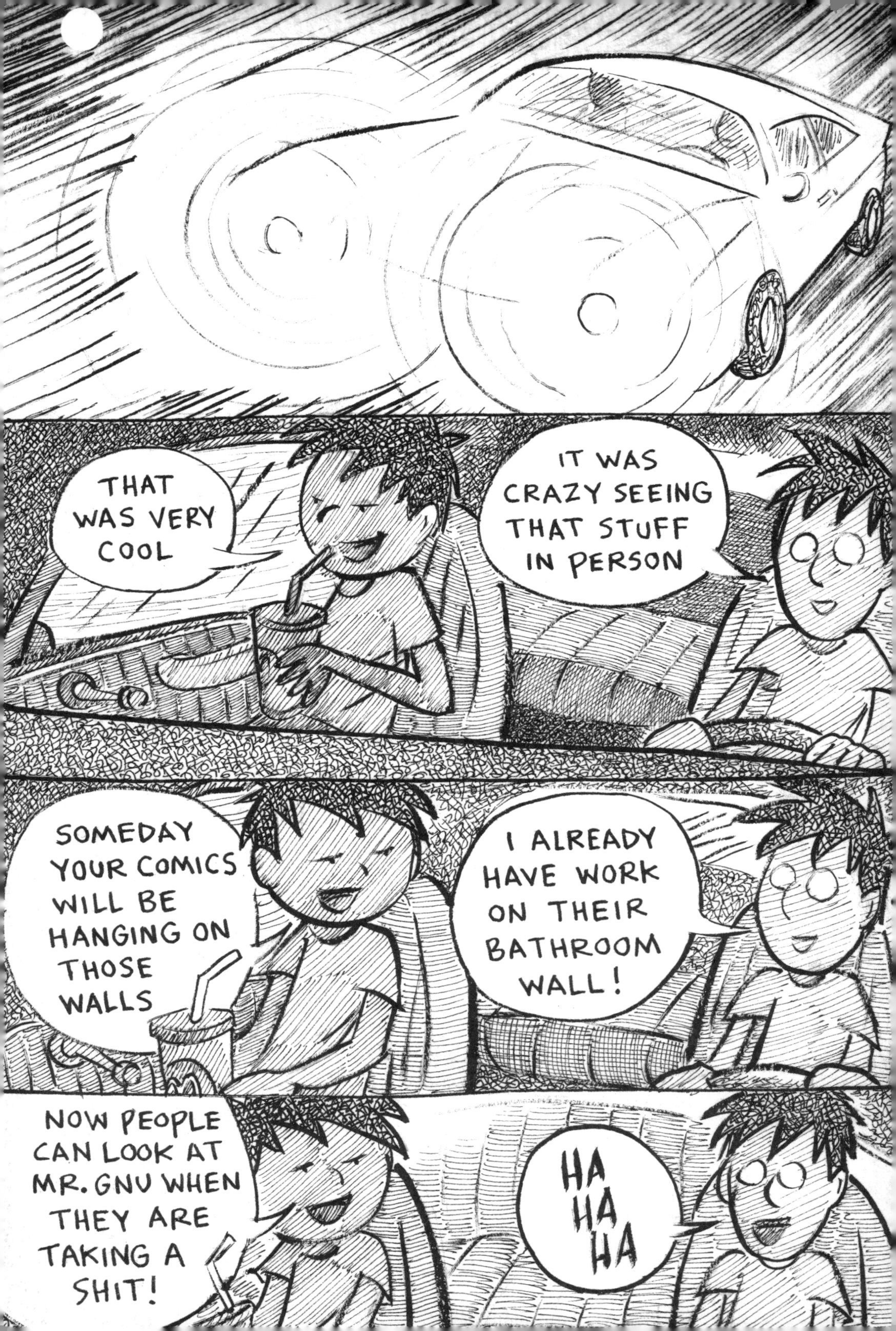
THAT WAS VERY COOL
IT WAS CRAZY SEEING THAT STUFF IN PERSON
SOMEDAY YOUR COMICS WILL BE HANGING ON THOSE WALLS
I ALREADY HAVE WORK ON THEIR BATHROOM WALL!
NOW PEOPLE CAN LOOK AT MR. GNU WHEN THEY ARE TAKING A SHIT!
HA HA HA

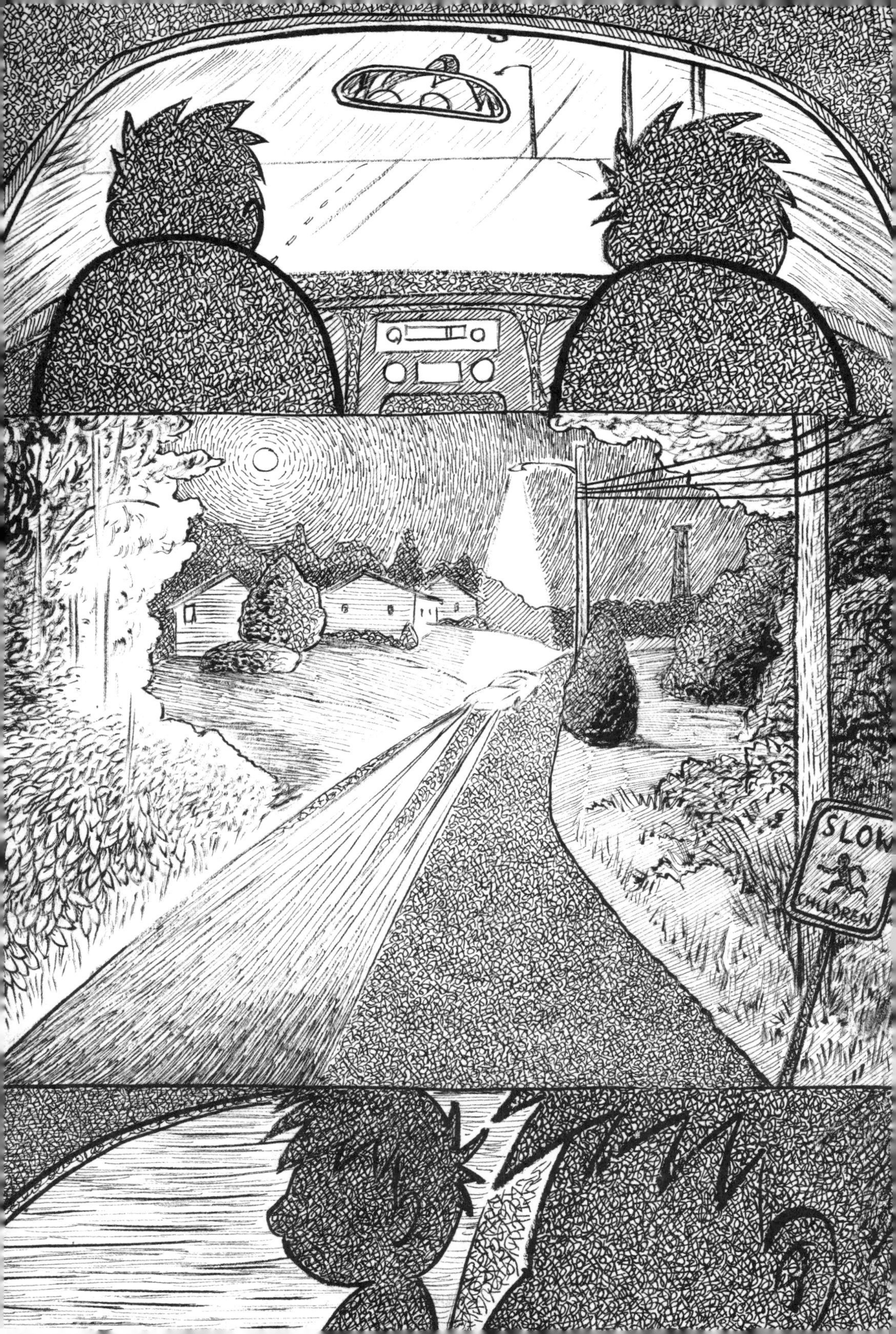
SLOW
CHILDREN

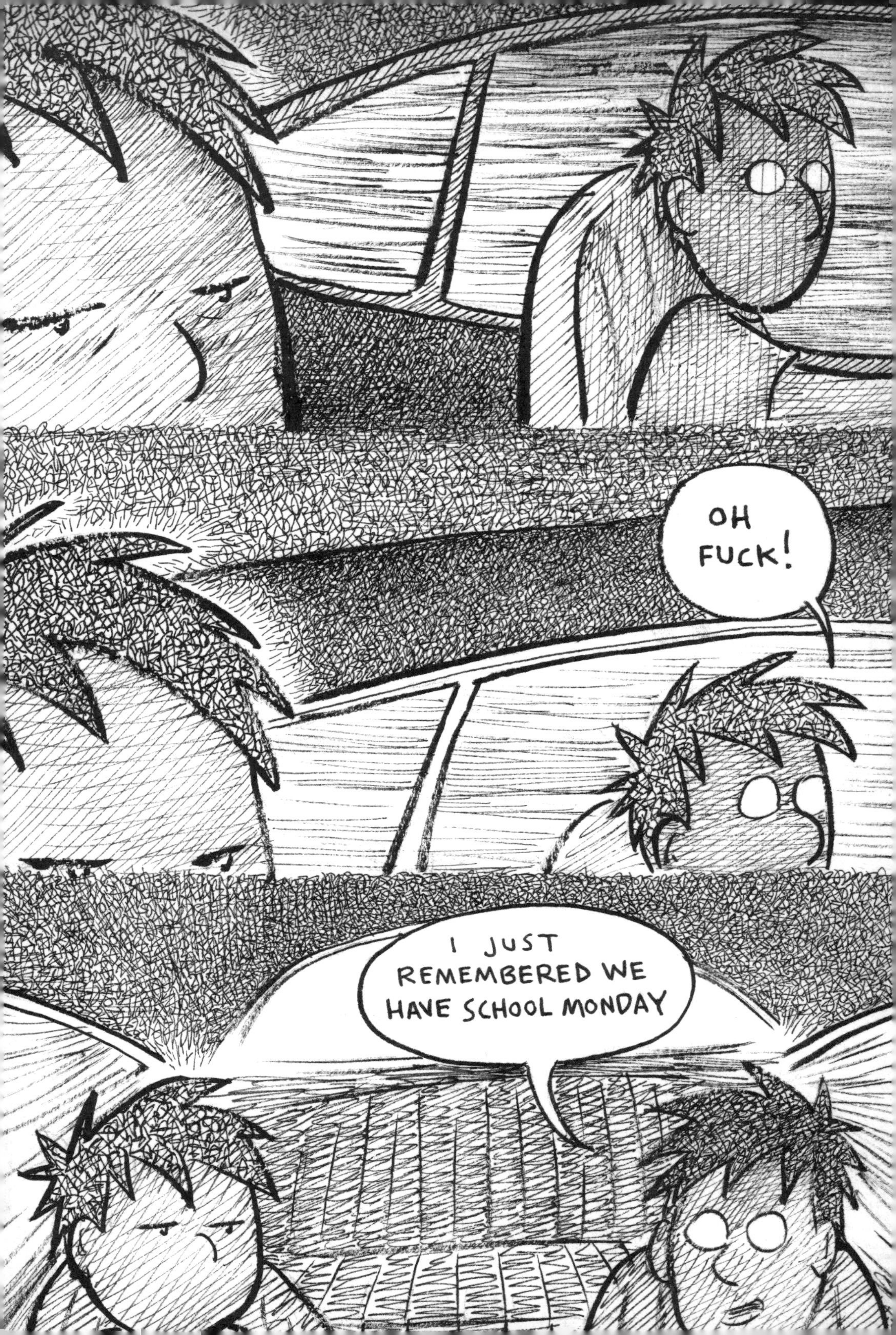
OH FUCK!
I JUST REMEMBERED WE HAVE SCHOOL MONDAY

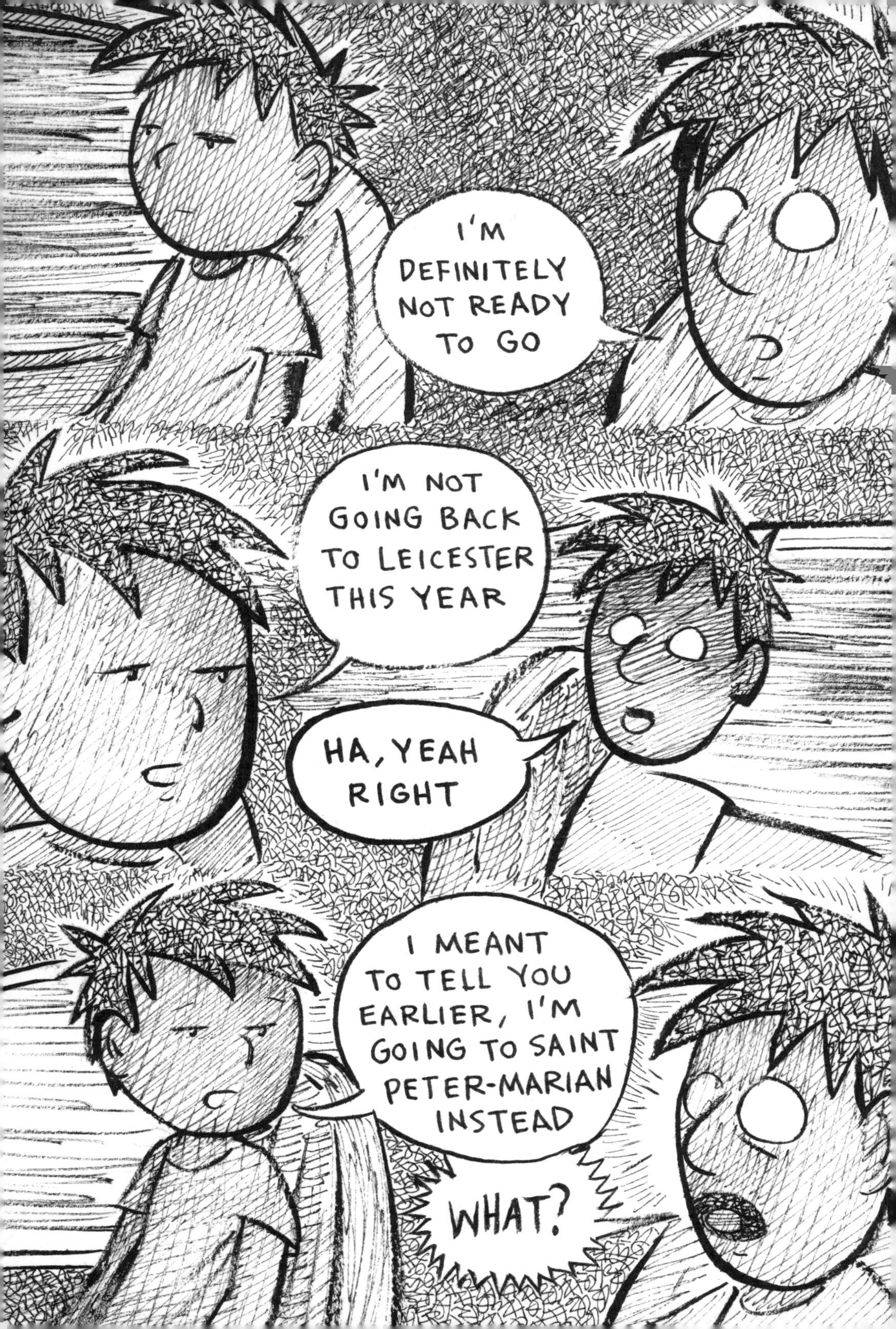
I'M DEFINITELY NOT READY TO GO
I'M NOT GOING BACK TO LEICESTER THIS YEAR
HA, YEAH RIGHT
I MEANT TO TELL YOU EARLIER, I'M GOING TO SAINT PETER-MARIAN INSTEAD
WHAT?

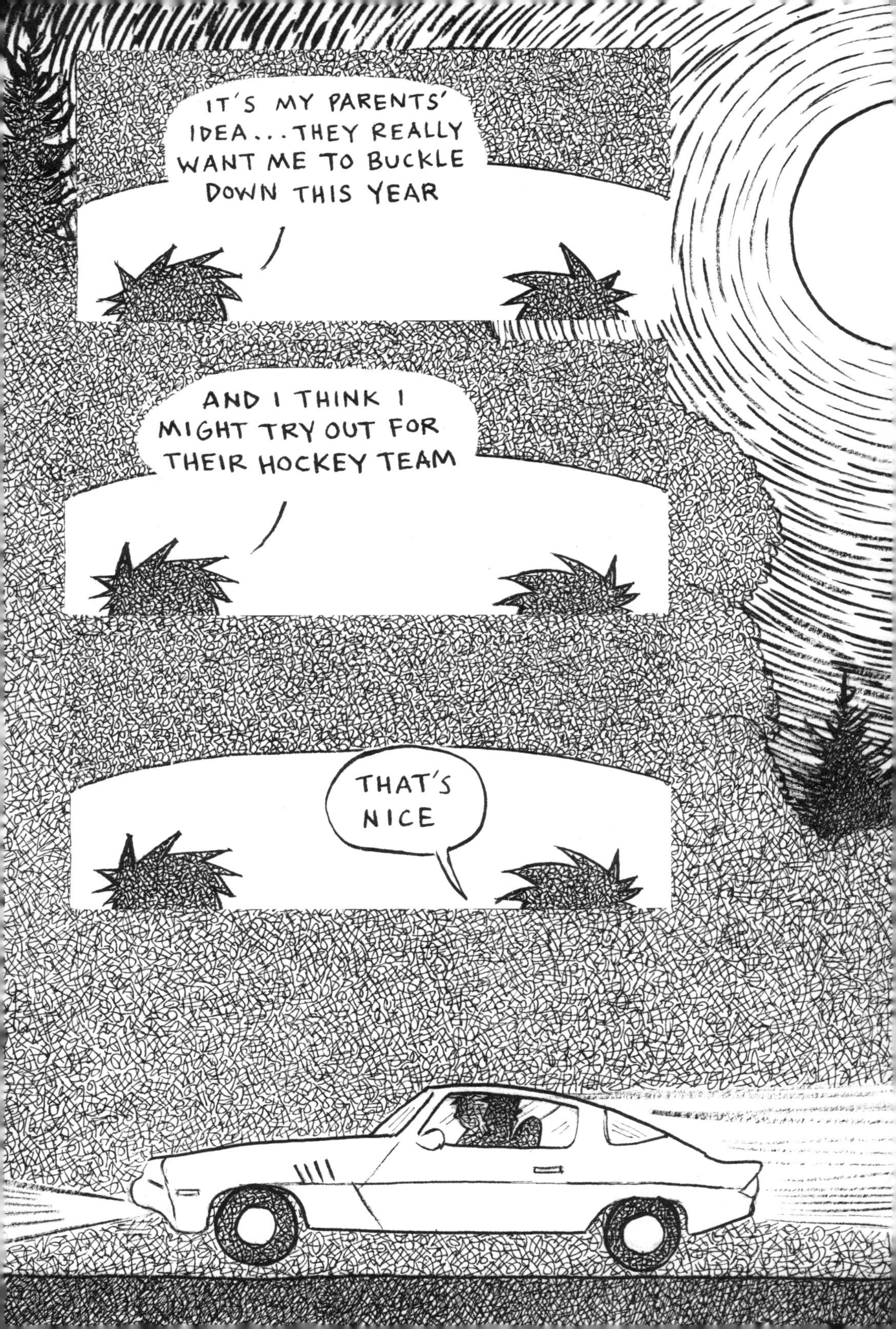
IT'S MY PARENTS' IDEA... THEY REALLY WANT ME TO BUCKLE DOWN THIS YEAR
AND I THINK I MIGHT TRY OUT FOR THEIR HOCKEY TEAM
THAT'S NICE

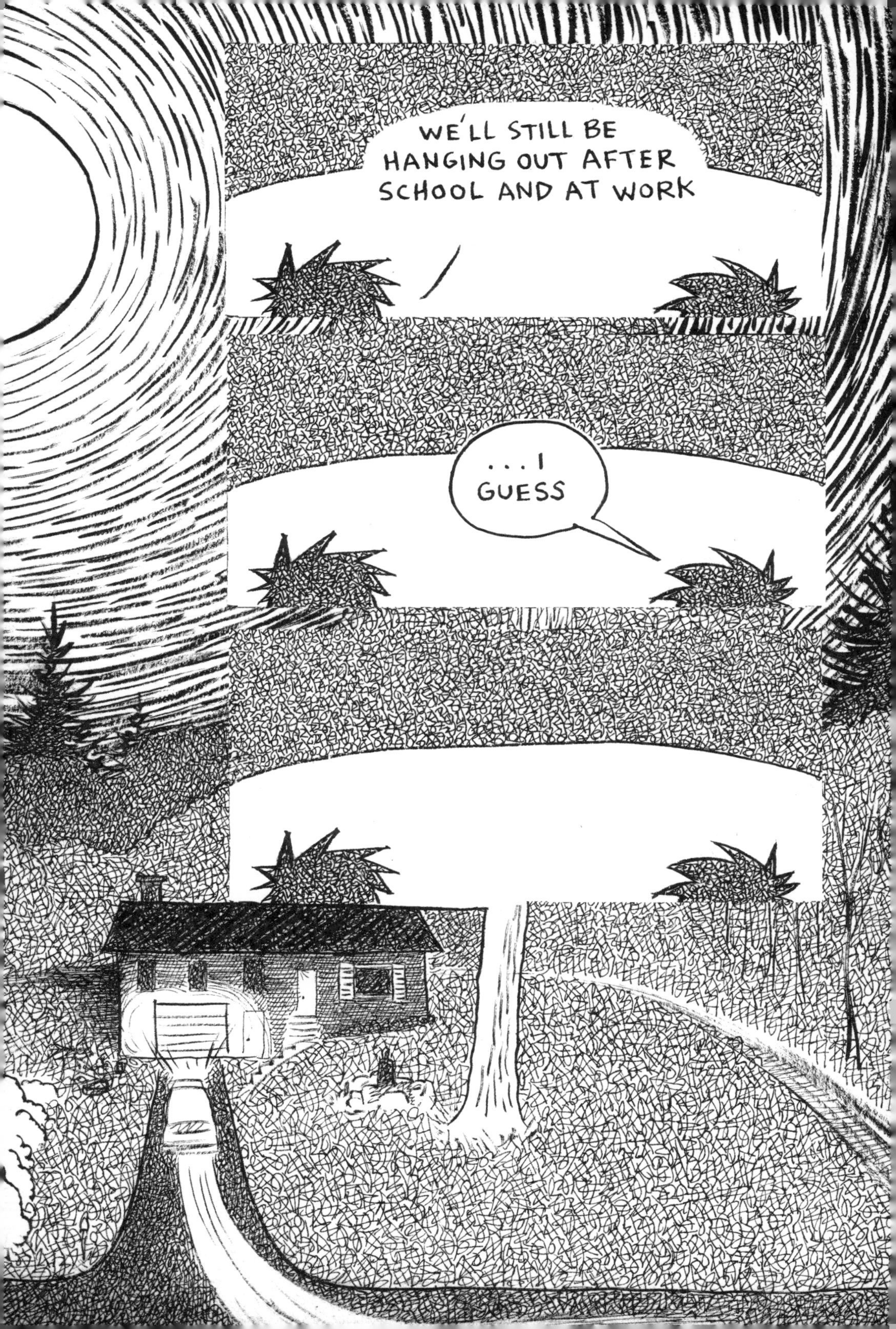
WE'LL STILL BE HANGING OUT AFTER SCHOOL AND AT WORK
...I GUESS

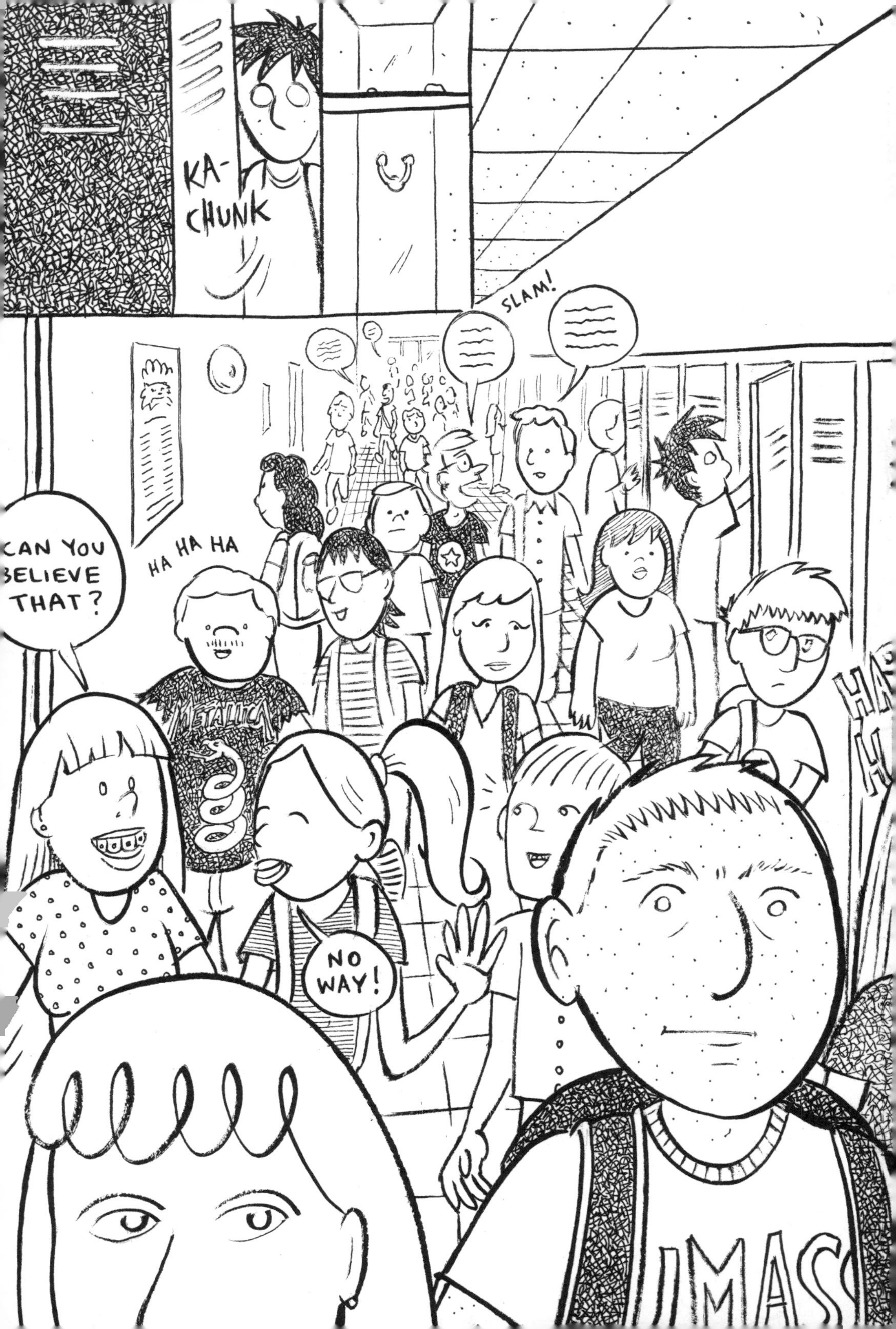
KA-CHUNK
SLAM!
CAN YOU BELIEVE THAT?
HA HA HA
METALLICA
NO WAY!

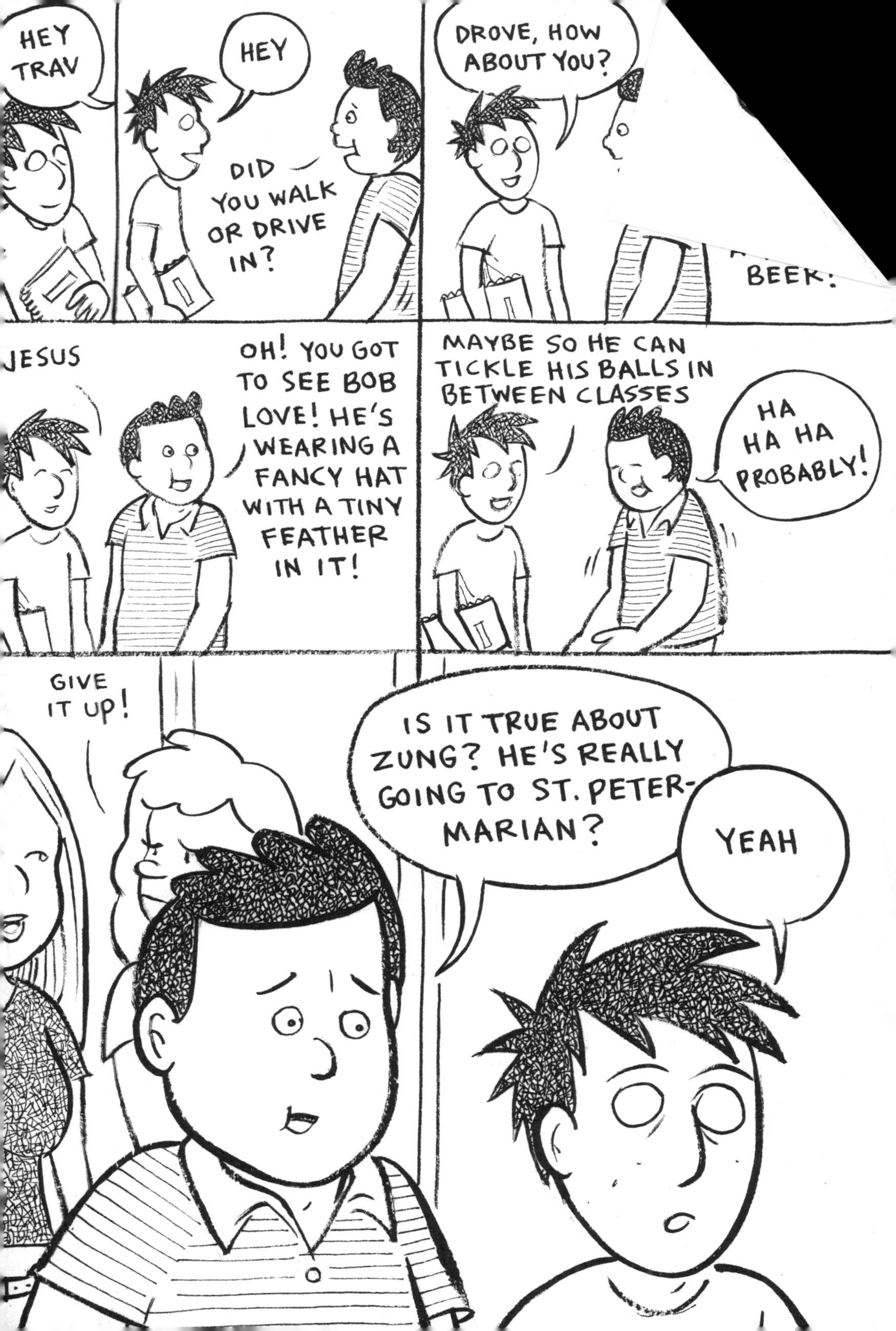
HEY TRAV
HEY
DID YOU WALK OR DRIVE IN?
DROVE, HOW ABOUT YOU?
JESUS
OH! YOU GOT TO SEE BOB LOVE! HE'S WEARING A FANCY HAT WITH A TINY FEATHER IN IT!
MAYBE SO HE CAN TICKLE HIS BALLS IN BETWEEN CLASSES
HA HA HA PROBABLY!
GIVE IT UP!
IS IT TRUE ABOUT ZUNG? HE'S REALLY GOING TO ST. PETER-MARIAN?
YEAH

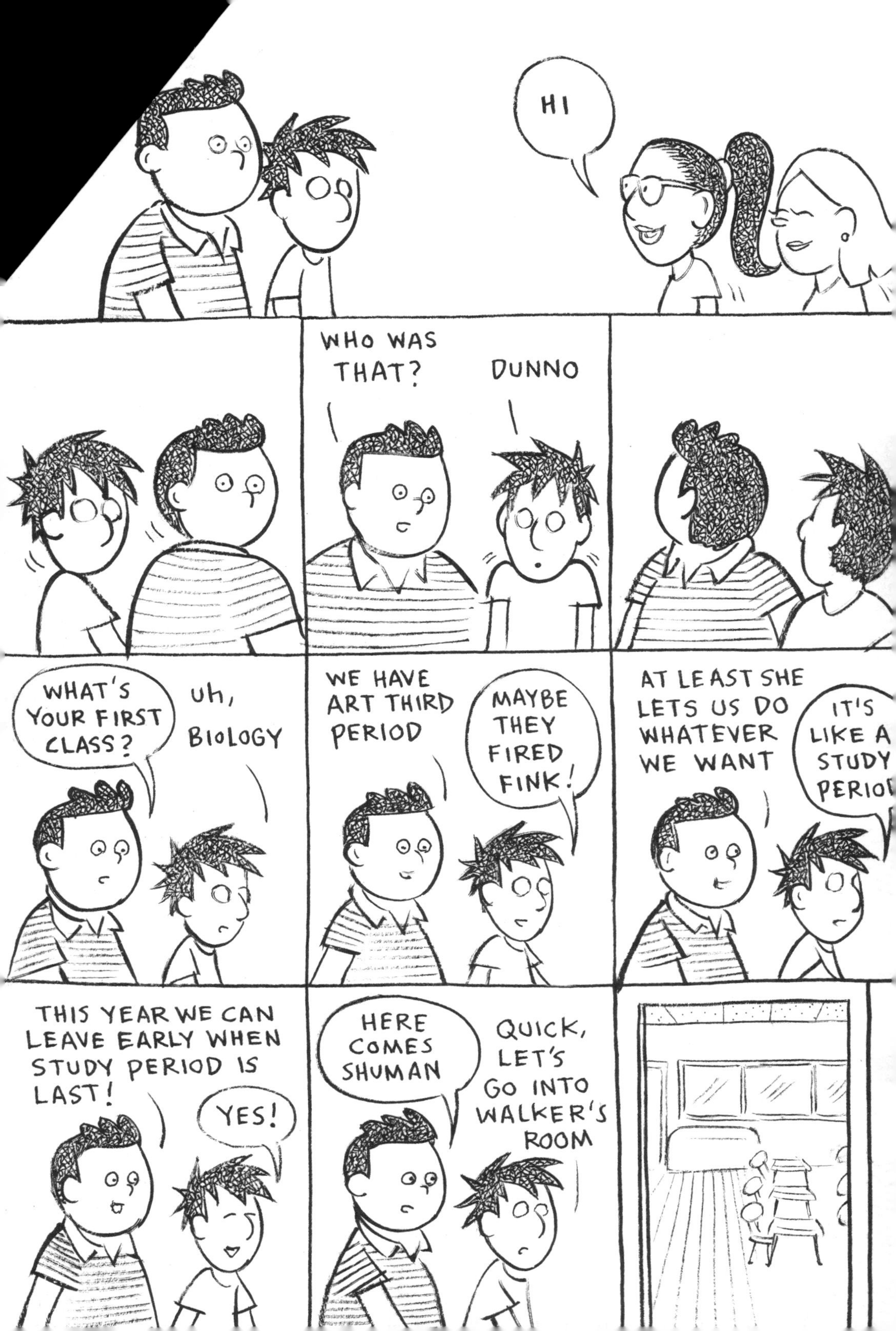
HI
WHO WAS THAT?
DUNNO
WHAT'S YOUR FIRST CLASS?
uh, BIOLOGY
WE HAVE ART THIRD PERIOD
MAYBE THEY FIRED FINK!
AT LEAST SHE LETS US DO WHATEVER WE WANT
IT'S LIKE A STUDY PERIOD
THIS YEAR WE CAN LEAVE EARLY WHEN STUDY PERIOD IS LAST!
YES!
HERE COMES SHUMAN
QUICK, LET'S GO INTO WALKER'S ROOM

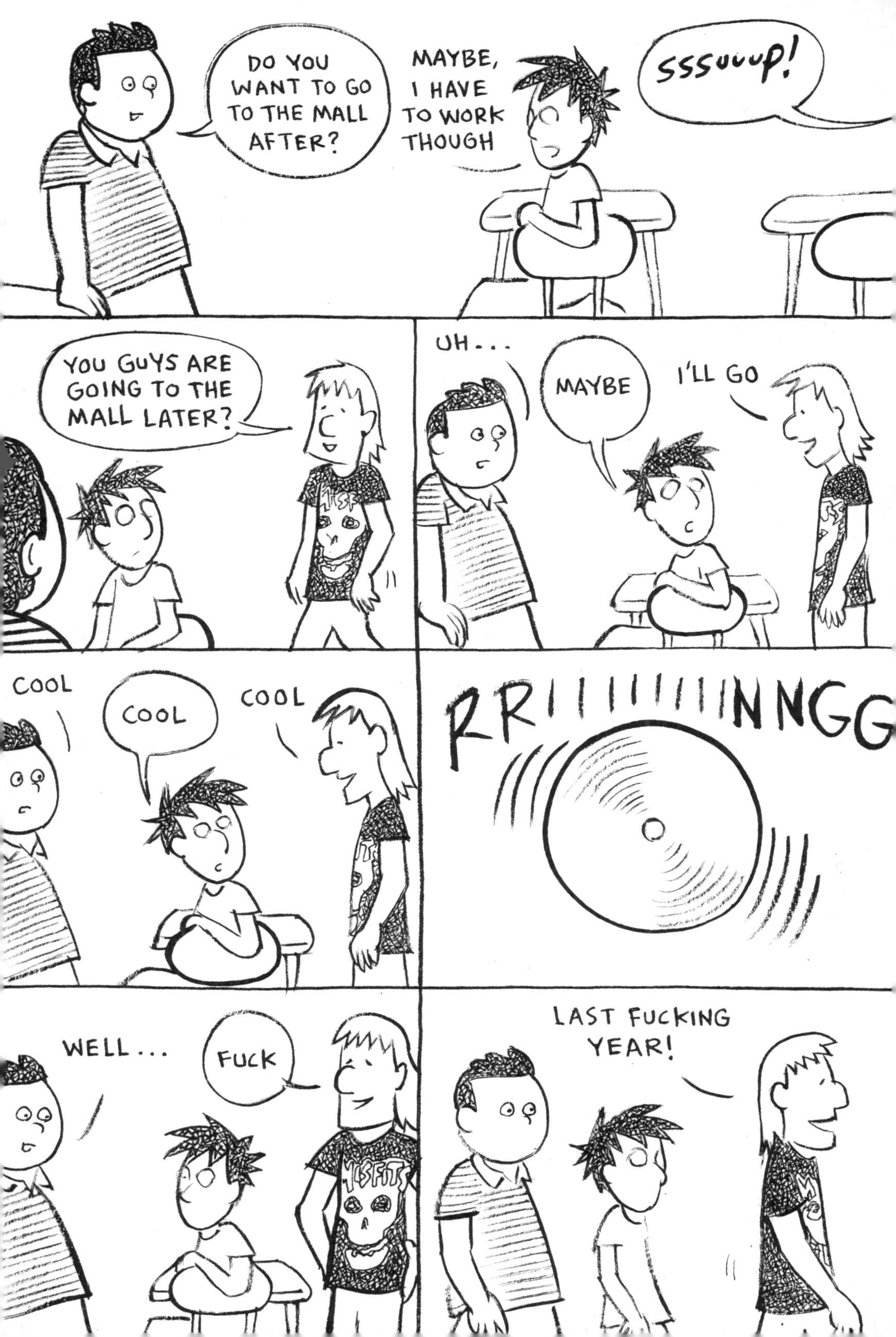
DO YOU WANT TO GO TO THE MALL AFTER?
MAYBE, I HAVE TO WORK THOUGH
SSSUUUP!
YOU GUYS ARE GOING TO THE MALL LATER?
UH...
MAYBE
I'LL GO
COOL
COOL
COOL
RRIIIIIIIINNGG
WELL...
FUCK
LAST FUCKING YEAR!

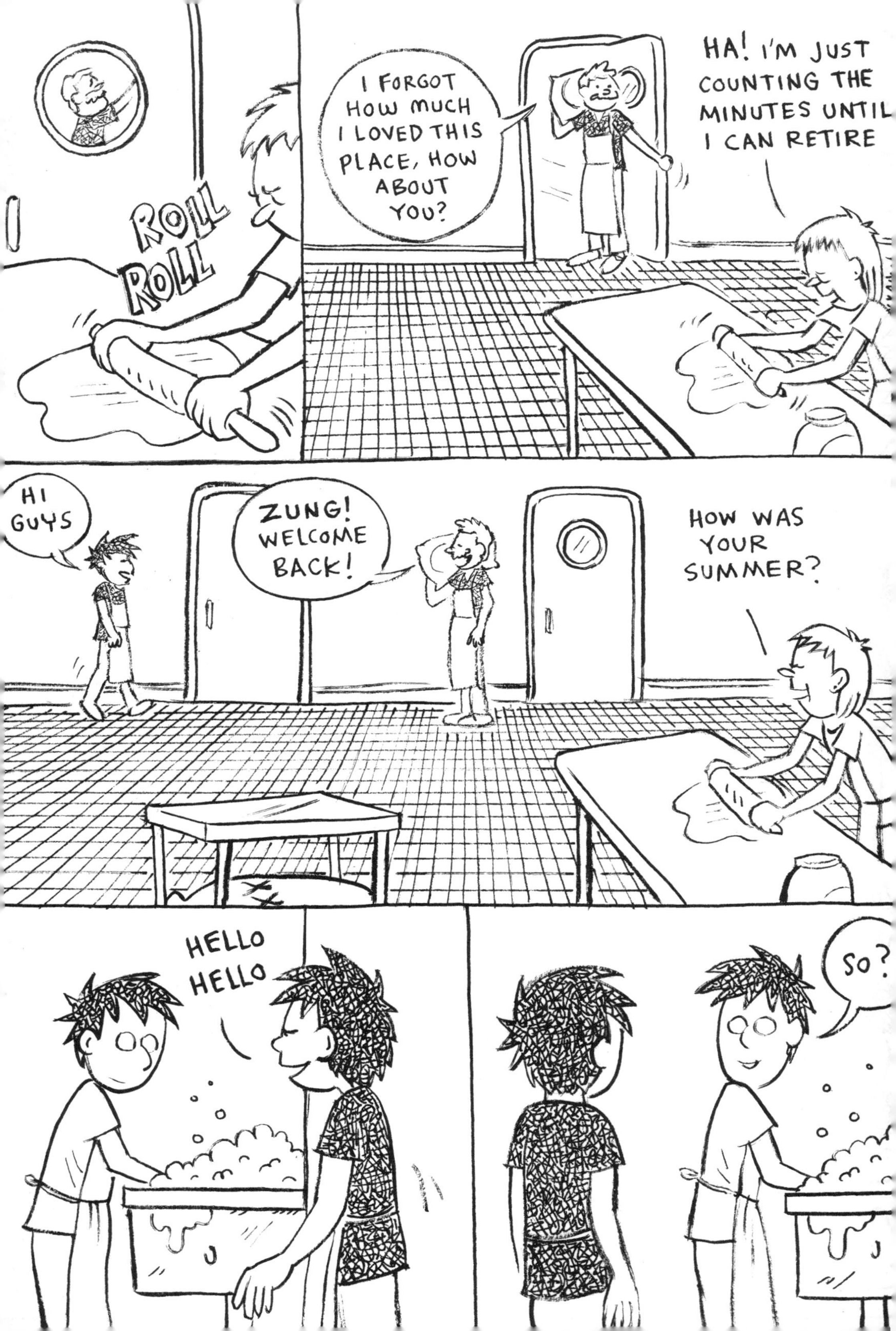
ROLL
ROLL
I FORGOT HOW MUCH I LOVED THIS PLACE, HOW ABOUT YOU?
HA! I'M JUST COUNTING THE MINUTES UNTIL I CAN RETIRE
HI GUYS
ZUNG! WELCOME BACK!
HOW WAS YOUR SUMMER?
HELLO HELLO
SO?

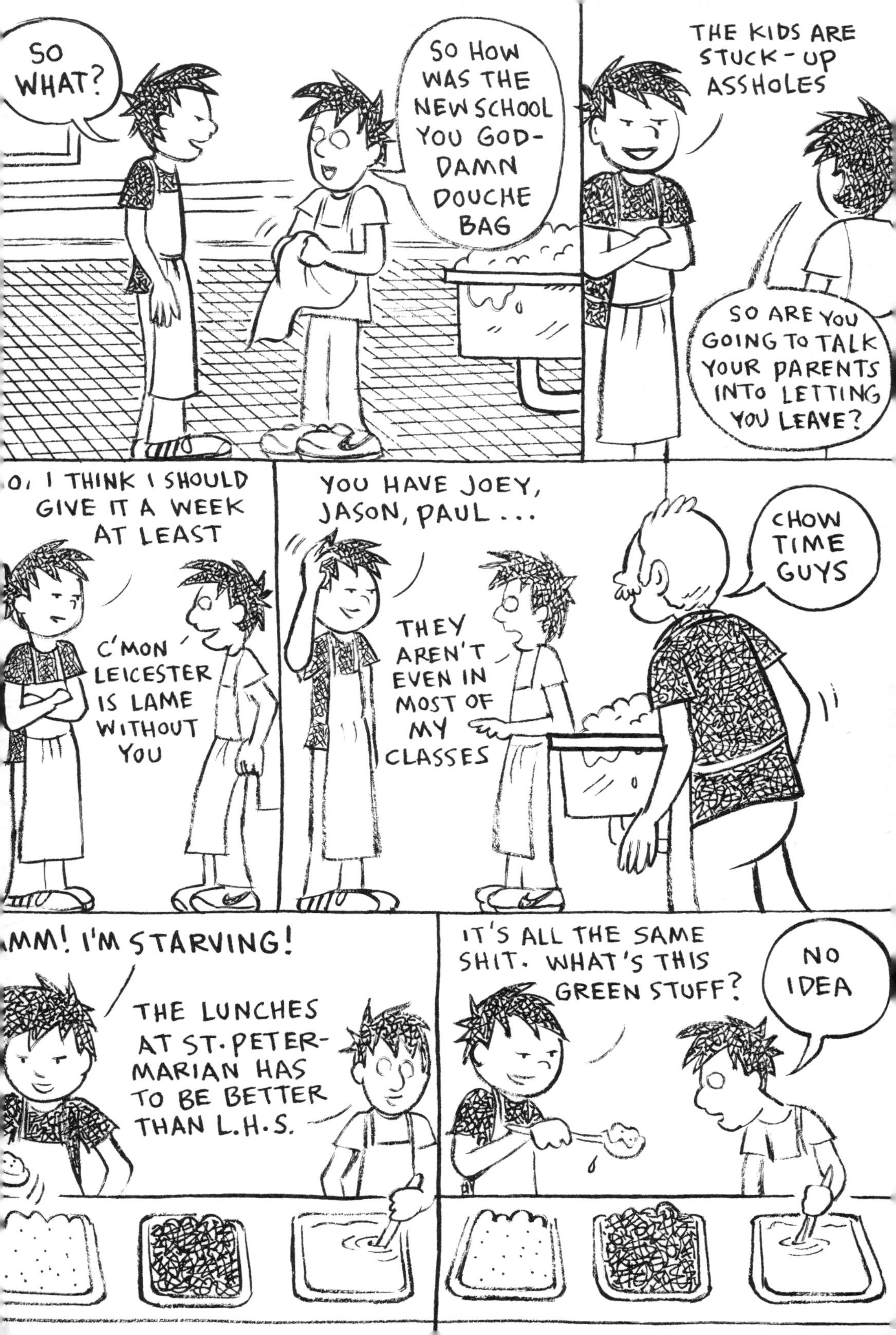
SO WHAT?
SO HOW WAS THE NEW SCHOOL YOU GOD-DAMN DOUCHE BAG
THE KIDS ARE STUCK-UP ASSHOLES
SO ARE YOU GOING TO TALK YOUR PARENTS INTO LETTING YOU LEAVE?
O, I THINK I SHOULD GIVE IT A WEEK AT LEAST
C'MON LEICESTER IS LAME WITHOUT YOU
YOU HAVE JOEY, JASON, PAUL...
THEY AREN'T EVEN IN MOST OF MY CLASSES
CHOW TIME GUYS
MM! I'M STARVING!
THE LUNCHES AT ST. PETER-MARIAN HAS TO BE BETTER THAN L.H.S.
IT'S ALL THE SAME SHIT. WHAT'S THIS GREEN STUFF?
NO IDEA

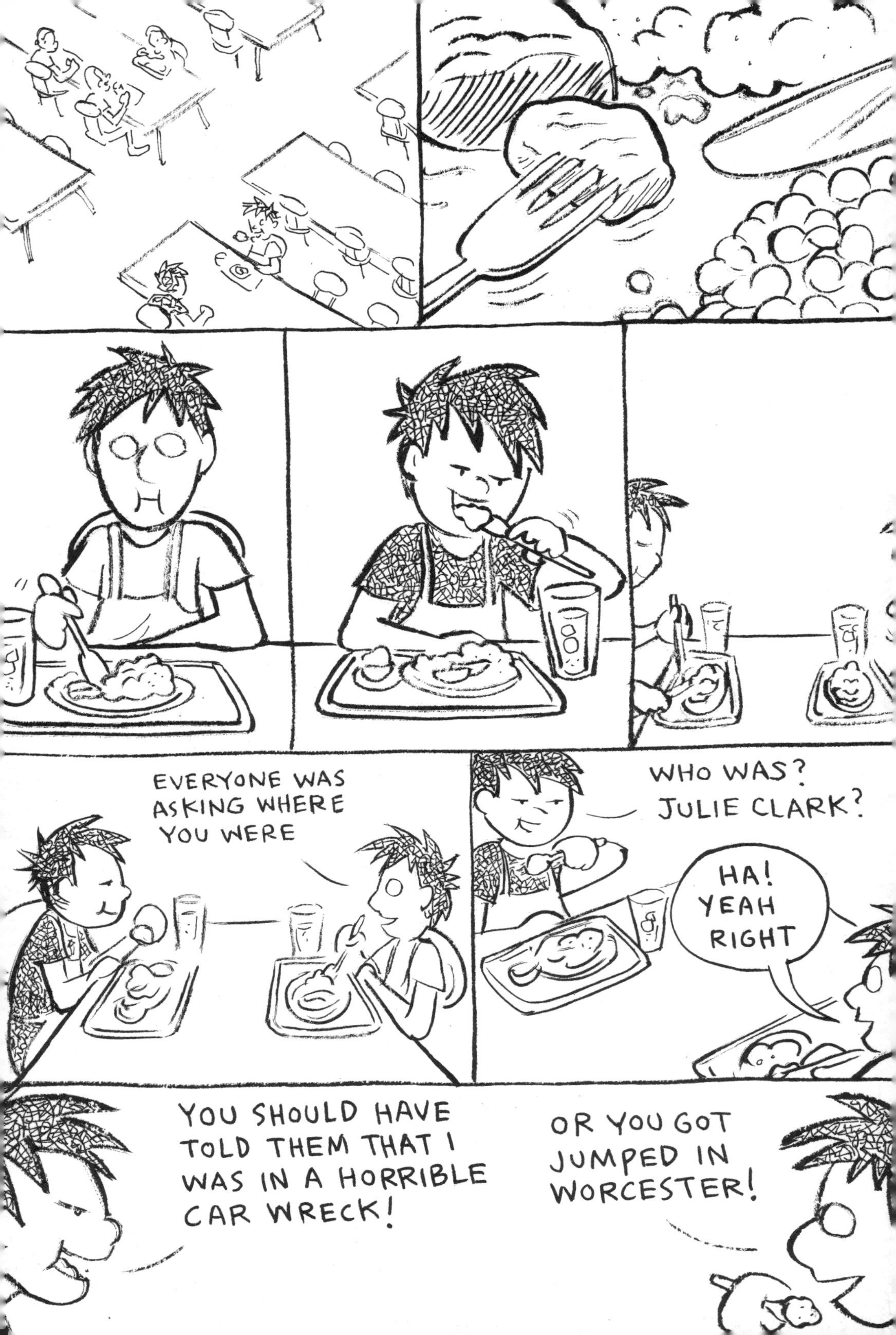
EVERYONE WAS ASKING WHERE YOU WERE
WHO WAS? JULIE CLARK?
HA! YEAH RIGHT
YOU SHOULD HAVE TOLD THEM THAT I WAS IN A HORRIBLE CAR WRECK!
OR YOU GOT JUMPED IN WORCESTER!

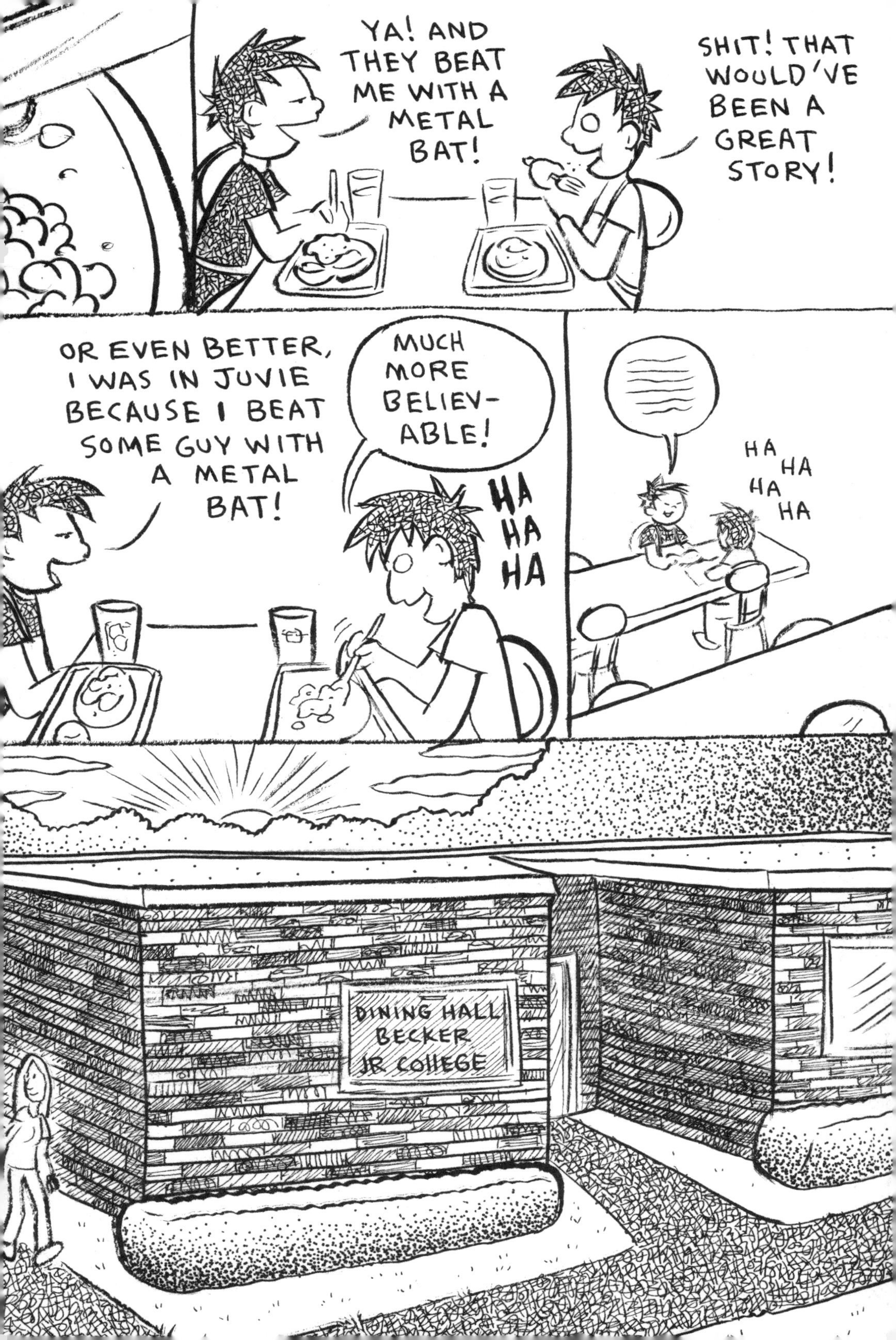
YA! AND THEY BEAT ME WITH A METAL BAT!
SHIT! THAT WOULD'VE BEEN A GREAT STORY!
OR EVEN BETTER, I WAS IN JUVIE BECAUSE I BEAT SOME GUY WITH A METAL BAT!
MUCH MORE BELIEV-ABLE!
HA HA HA
HA HA HA HA
DINING HALL BECKER JR COLLEGE

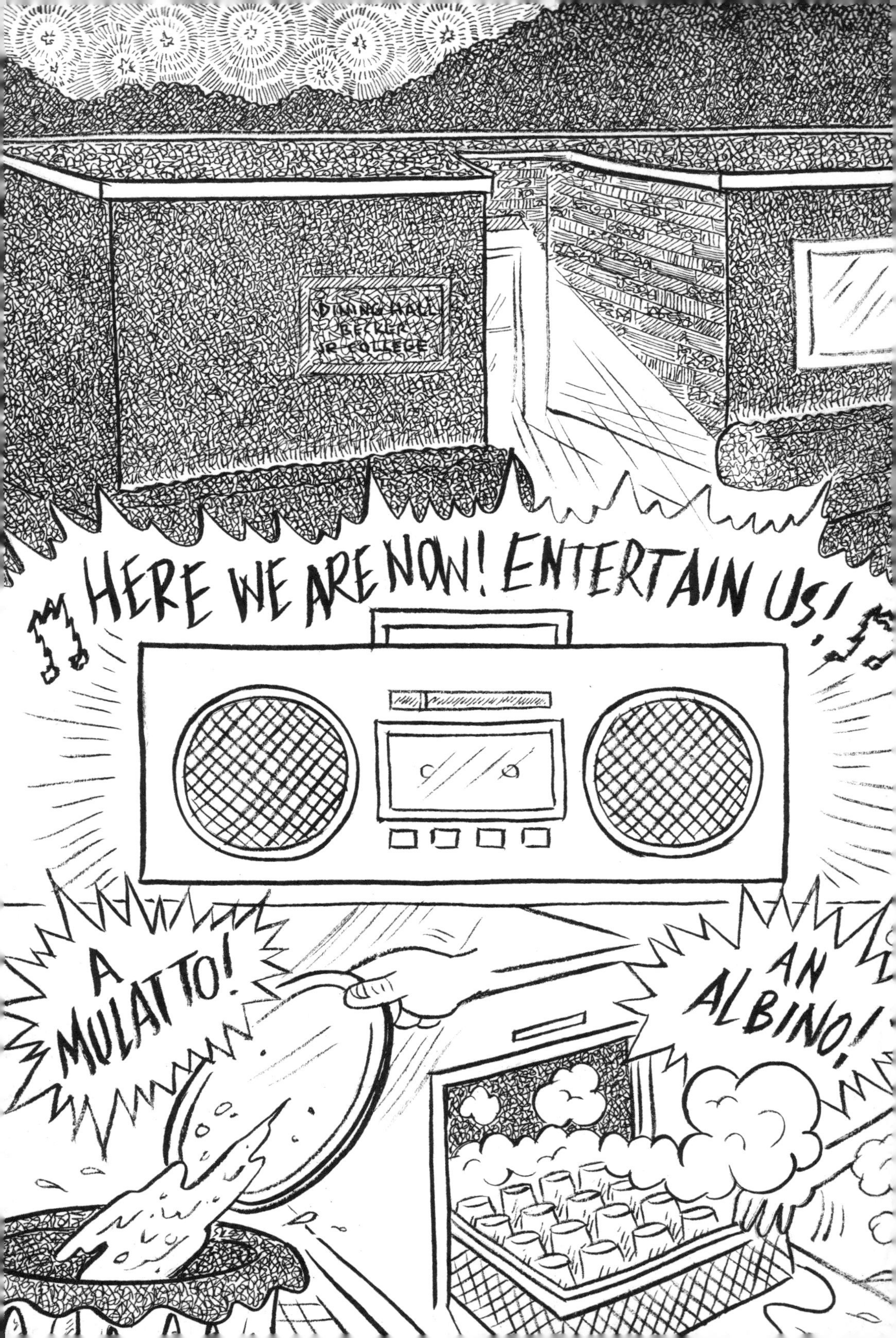
DINING HALL
BECKER
JR COLLEGE
HERE WE ARE NOW! ENTERTAIN US!
A MULATTO!
AN ALBINO!

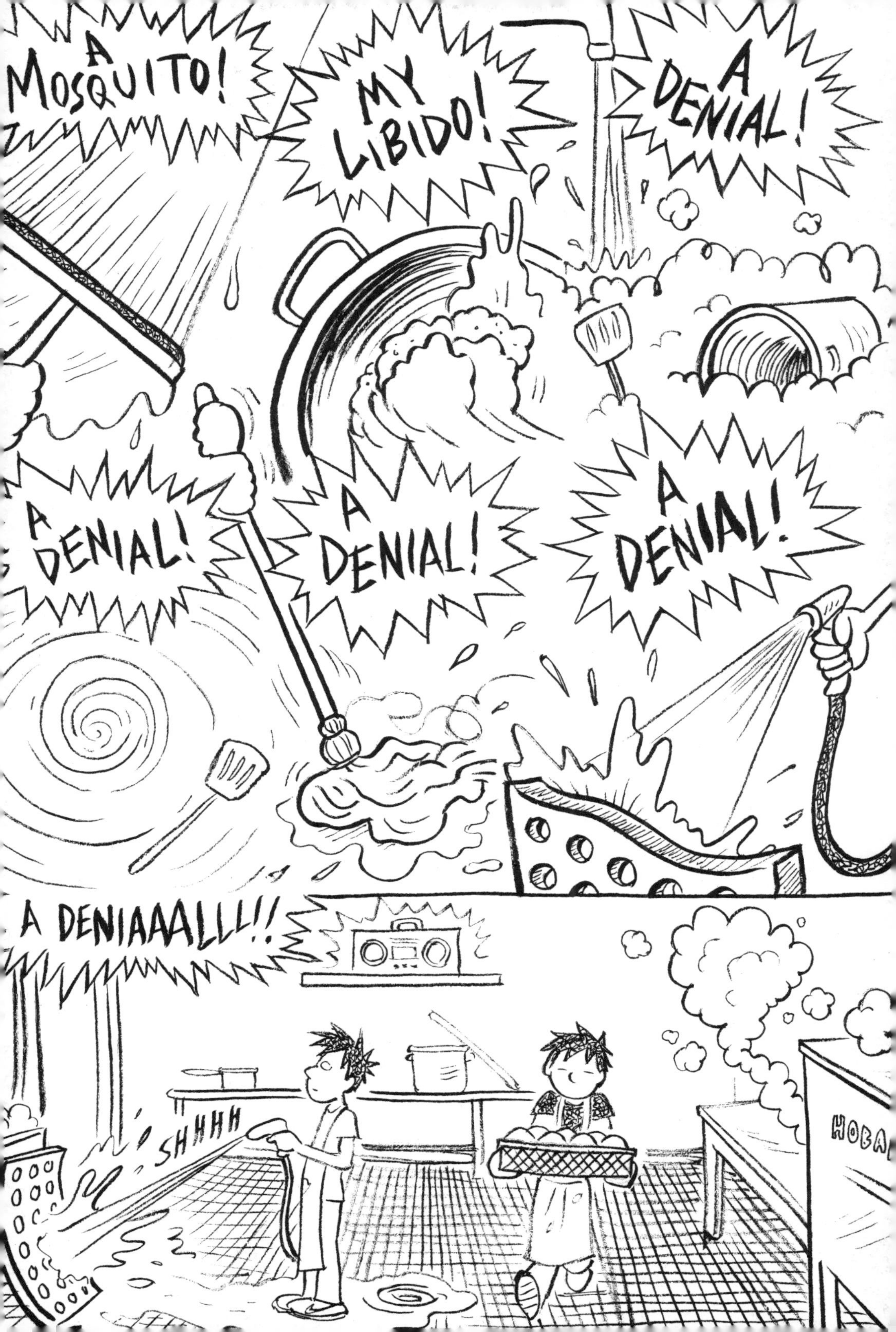
A MOSQUITO!
MY LIBIDO!
A DENIAL!
A DENIAL!
A DENIAL!
A DENIAL!
A DENIAAALLL!!
SHHHH
HOBA

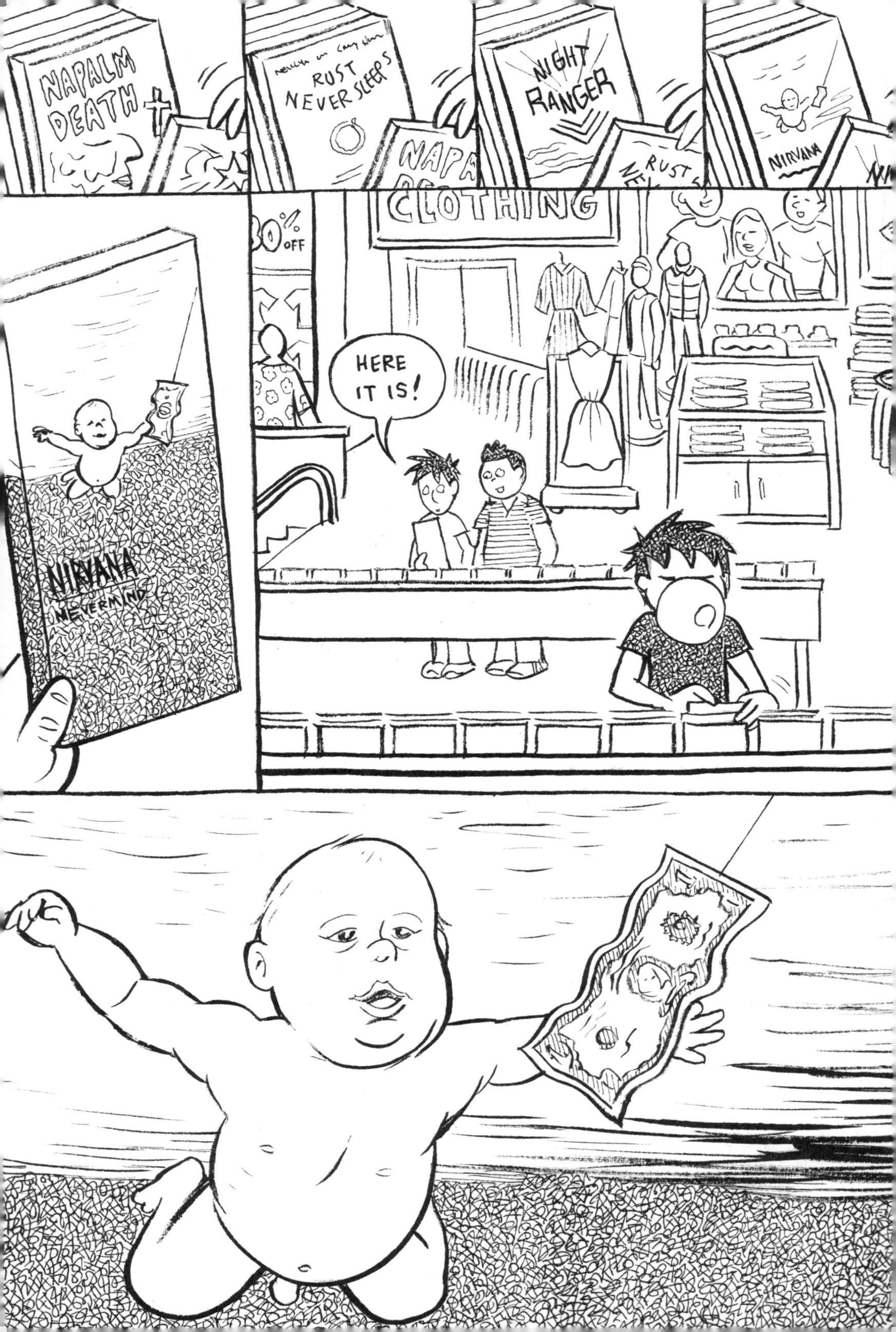
NAPALM DEATH
RUST NEVER SLEEPS
NIGHT RANGER
NIRVANA
CLOTHING
30% OFF
HERE IT IS!
NIRVANA
NEVERMIND

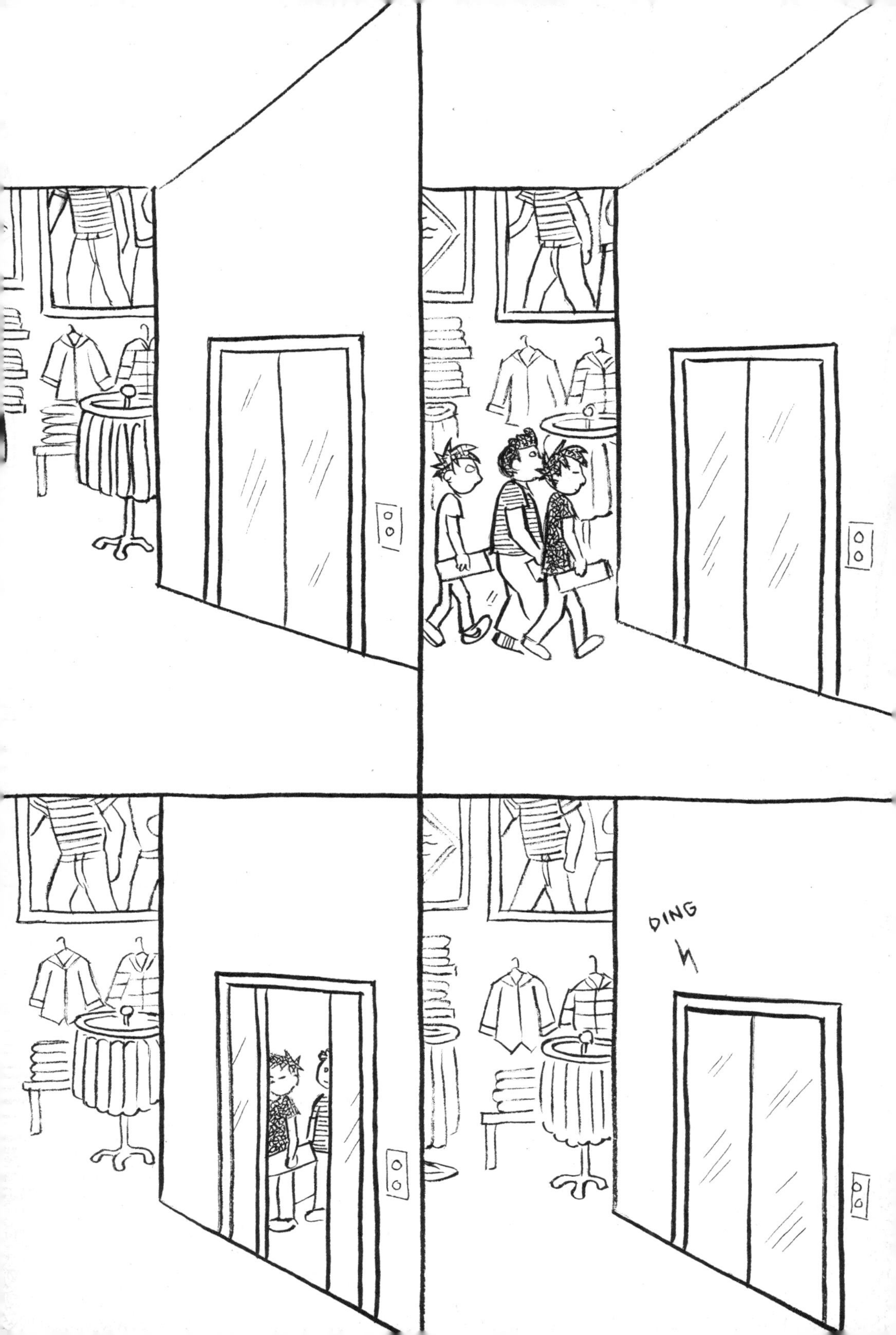
DING

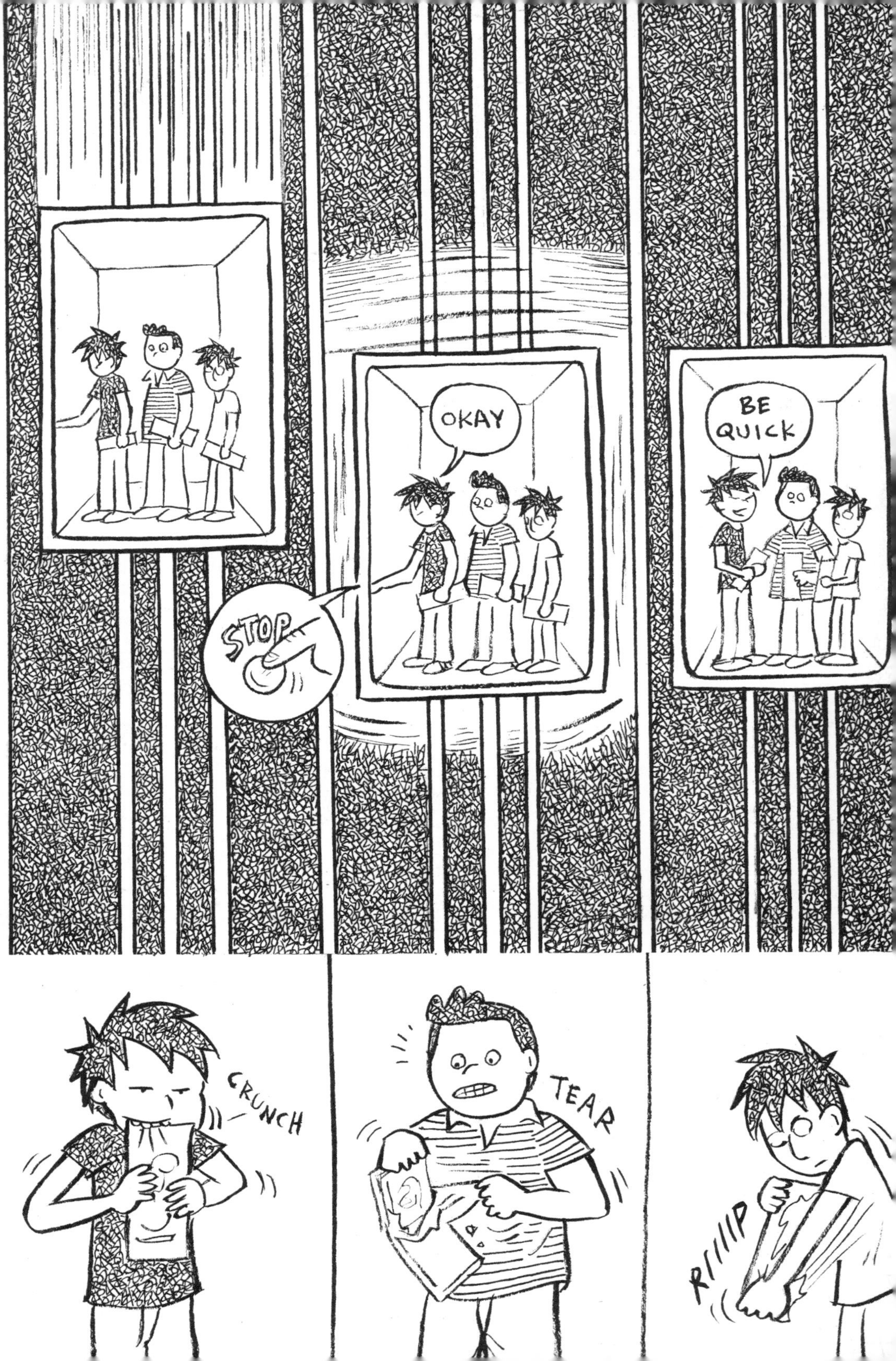
STOP
OKAY
BE QUICK
CRUNCH
TEAR
RIIIIP

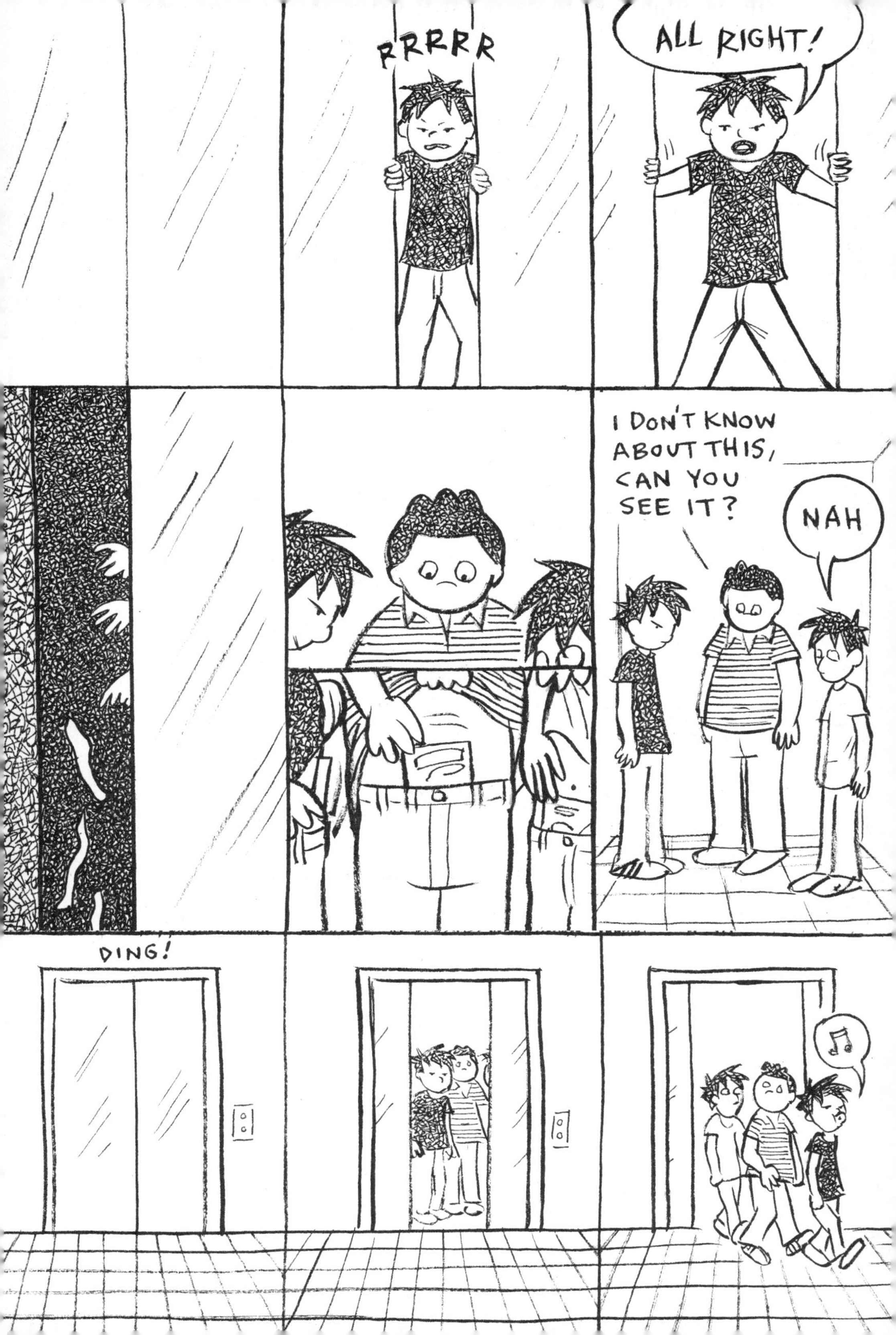
RRRRR
ALL RIGHT!
I DON'T KNOW ABOUT THIS, CAN YOU SEE IT?
NAH
DING!

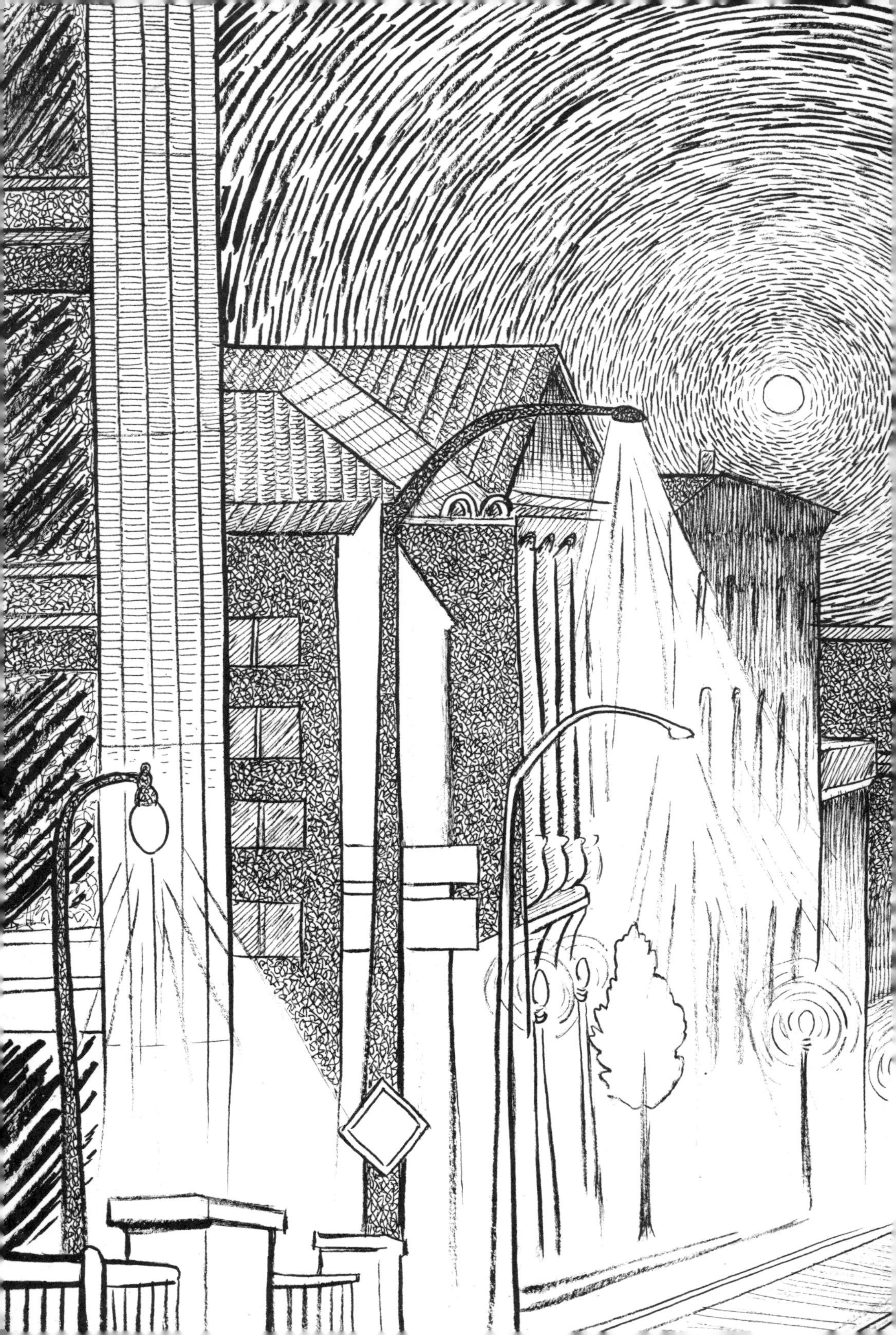

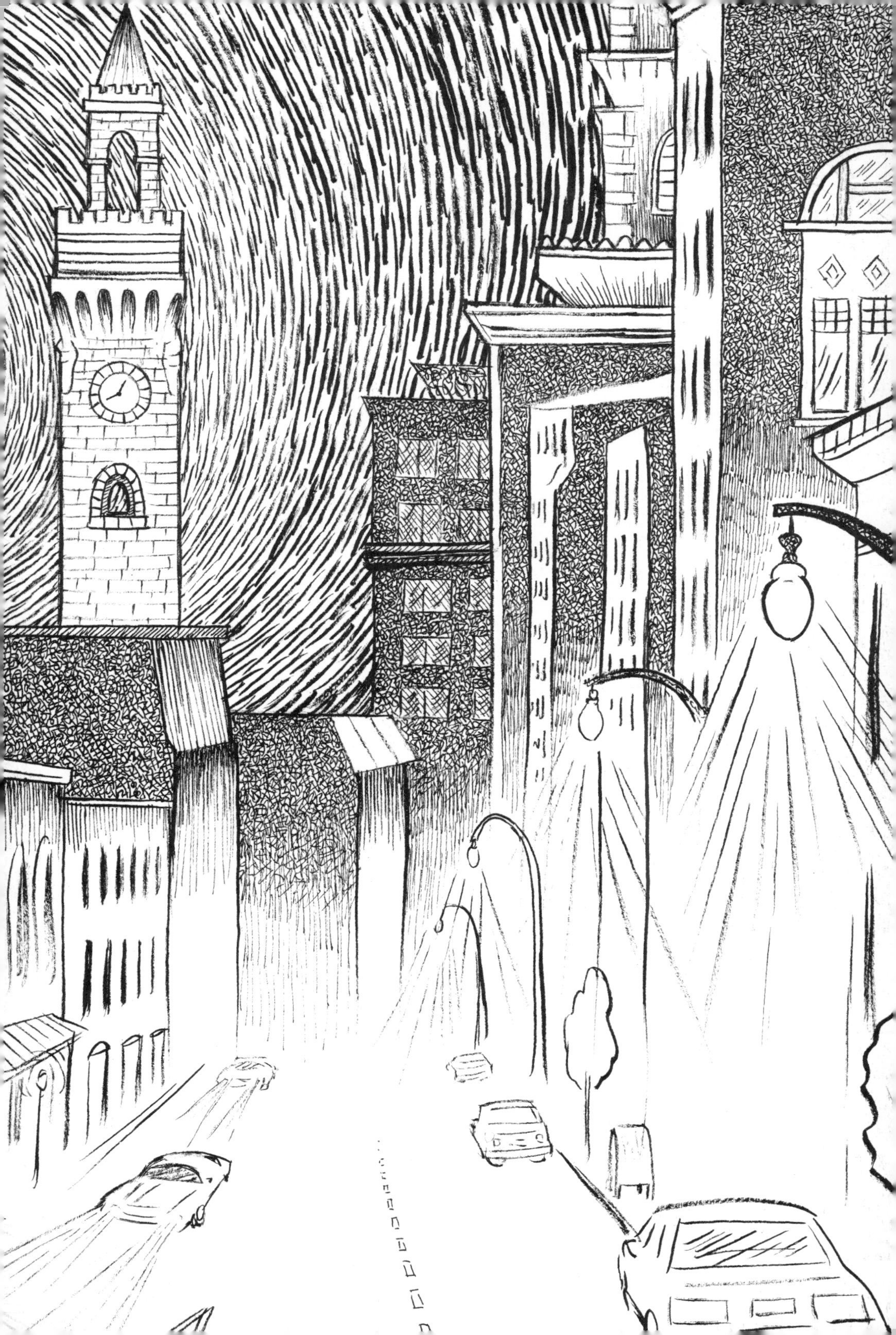

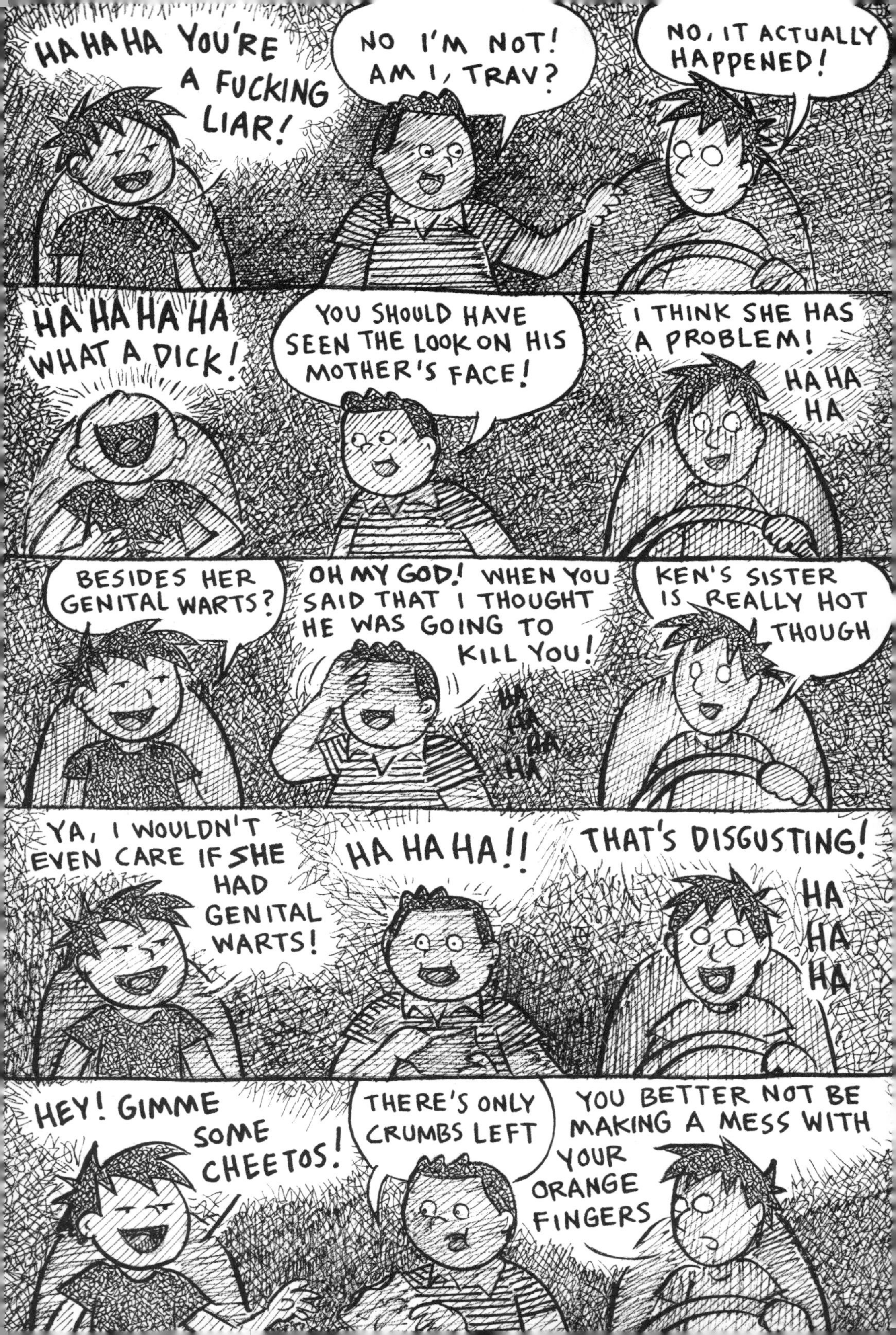
HA HA HA YOU'RE A FUCKING LIAR!
NO I'M NOT! AM I, TRAV?
NO, IT ACTUALLY HAPPENED!
HA HA HA HA WHAT A DICK!
YOU SHOULD HAVE SEEN THE LOOK ON HIS MOTHER'S FACE!
I THINK SHE HAS A PROBLEM!
HA HA HA
BESIDES HER GENITAL WARTS?
OH MY GOD! WHEN YOU SAID THAT I THOUGHT HE WAS GOING TO KILL YOU!
HA HA HA HA
KEN'S SISTER IS REALLY HOT THOUGH
YA, I WOULDN'T EVEN CARE IF SHE HAD GENITAL WARTS!
HA HA HA!!
THAT'S DISGUSTING!
HA HA HA
HEY! GIMME SOME CHEETOS!
THERE'S ONLY CRUMBS LEFT
YOU BETTER NOT BE MAKING A MESS WITH YOUR ORANGE FINGERS

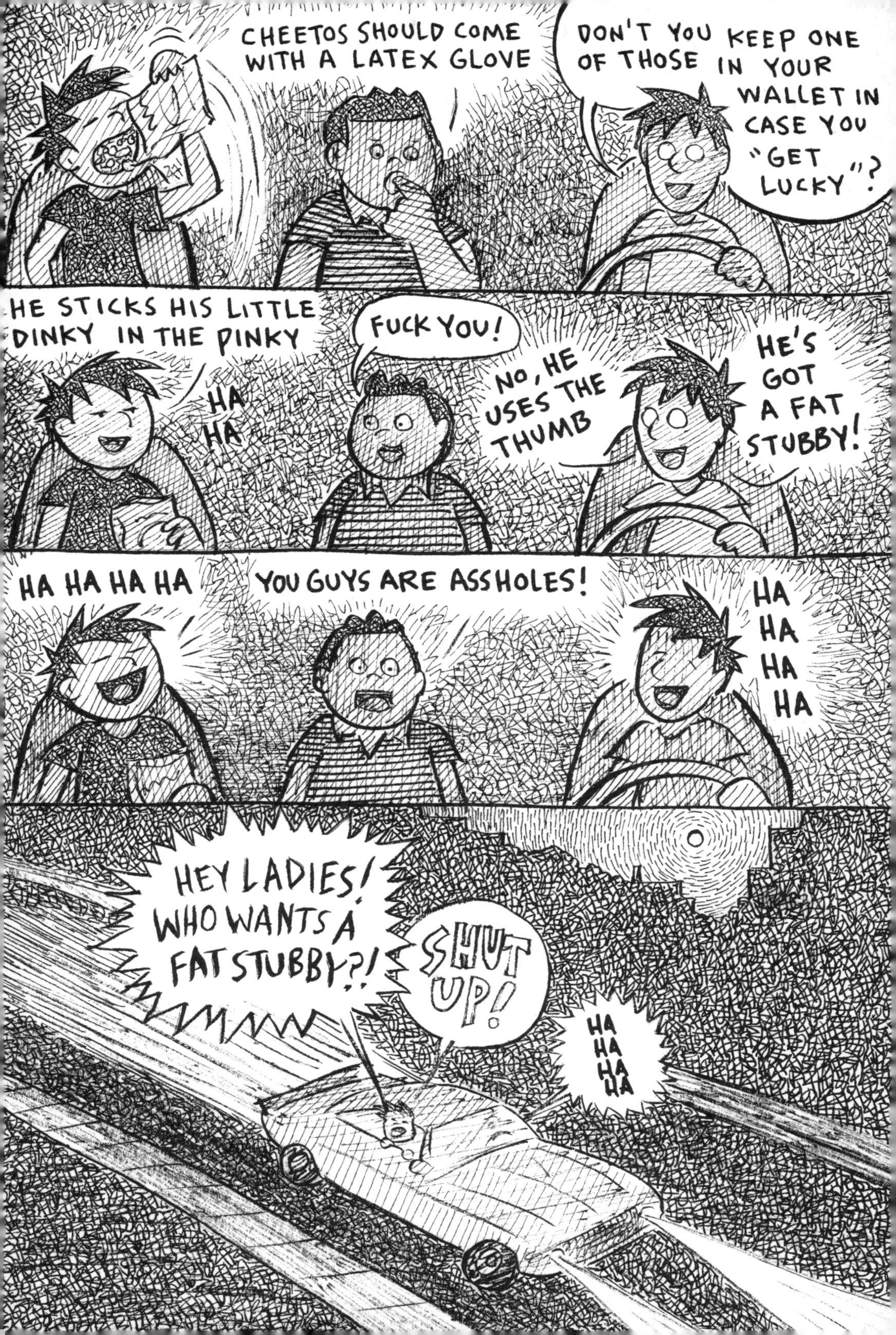
CHEETOS SHOULD COME WITH A LATEX GLOVE
DON'T YOU KEEP ONE OF THOSE IN YOUR WALLET IN CASE YOU "GET LUCKY"?
HE STICKS HIS LITTLE DINKY IN THE PINKY
HA HA
FUCK YOU!
NO, HE USES THE THUMB
HE'S GOT A FAT STUBBY!
HA HA HA HA
YOU GUYS ARE ASSHOLES!
HA HA HA HA
HEY LADIES! WHO WANTS A FAT STUBBY?!
SHUT UP!
HA HA HA HA

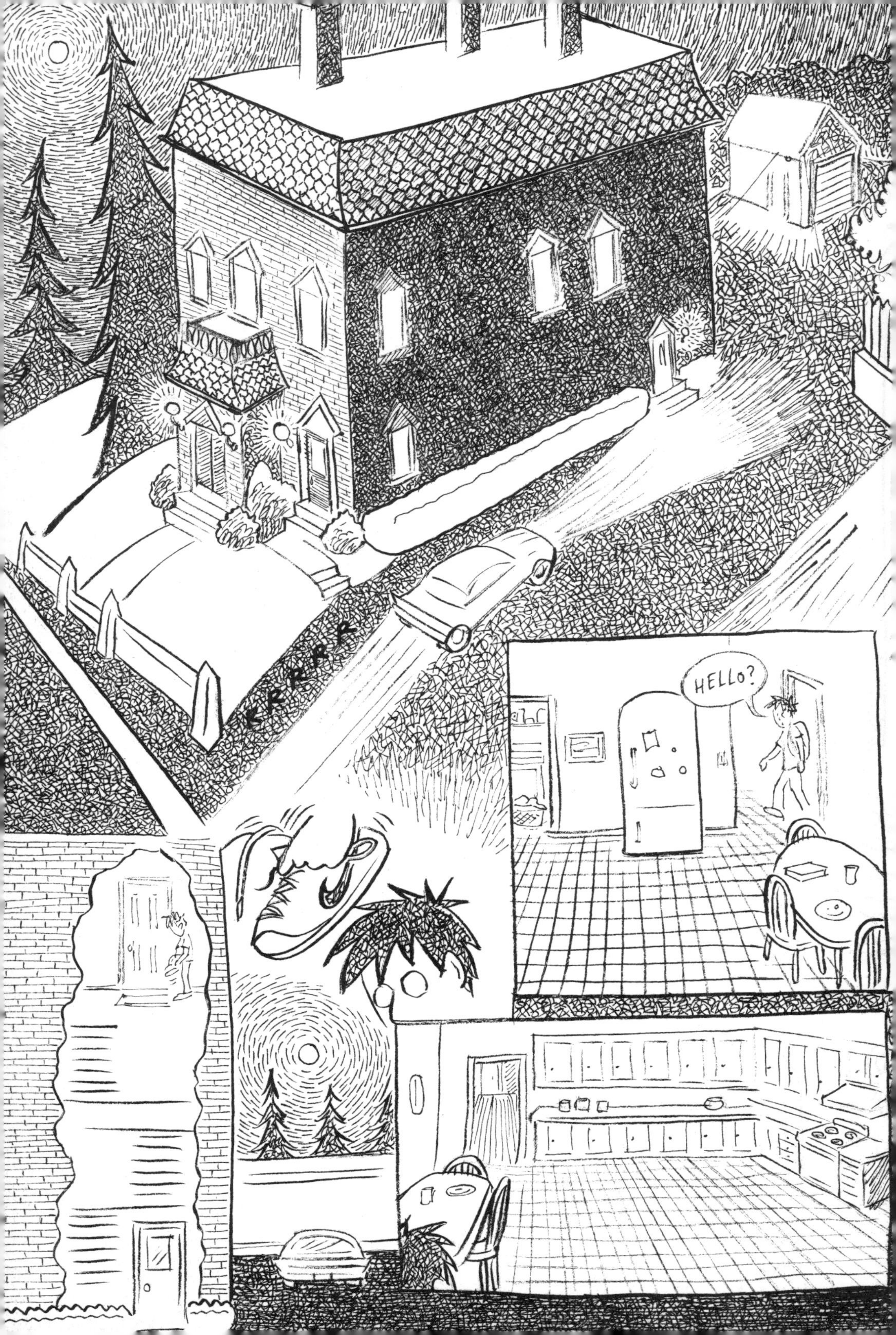
KRRRR
HELLO?

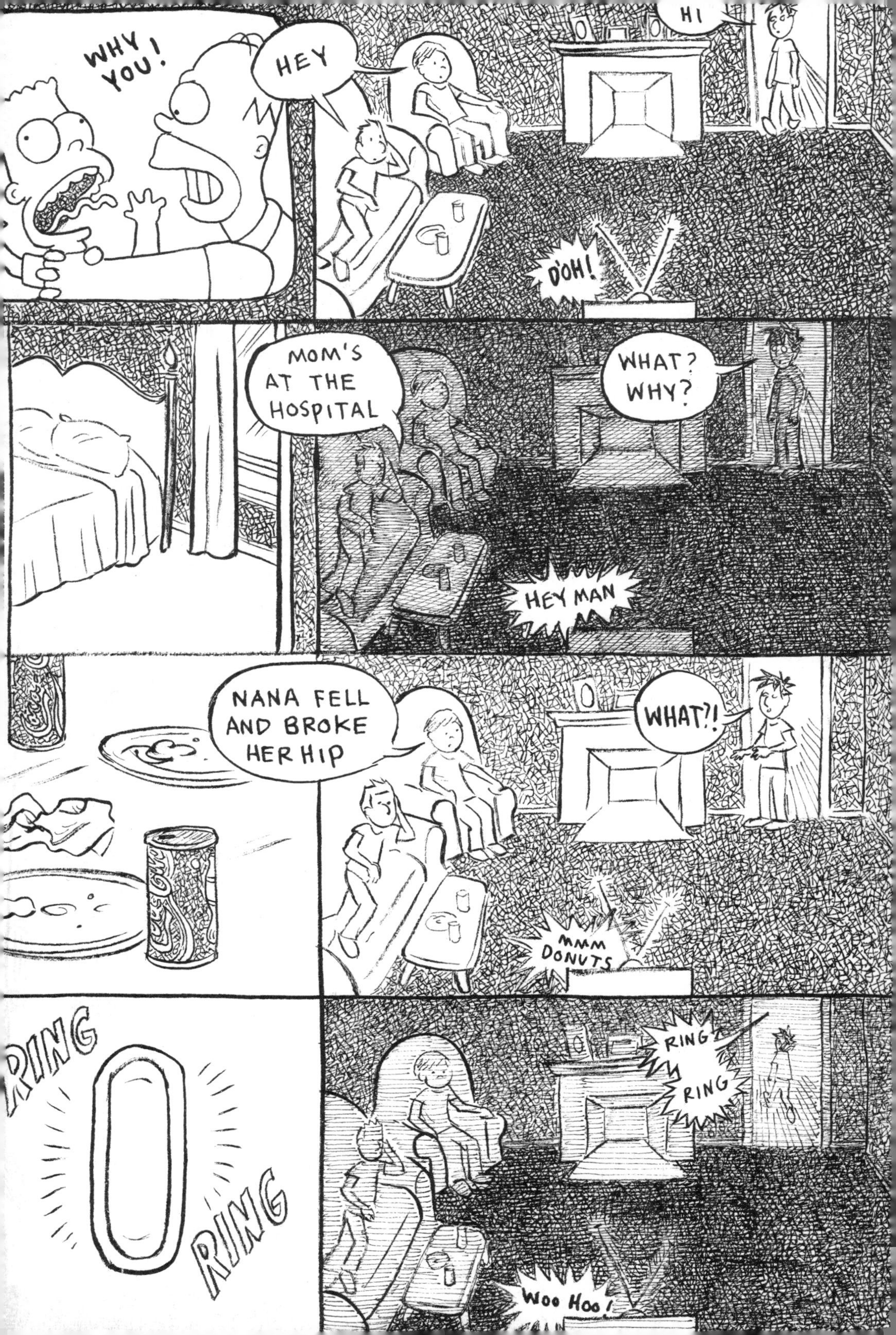
WHY YOU!
HEY
HI
D'OH!
MOM'S AT THE HOSPITAL
WHAT? WHY?
HEY MAN
NANA FELL AND BROKE HER HIP
WHAT?!
MMM DONUTS
RING
RING
RING
RING
WOO HOO!

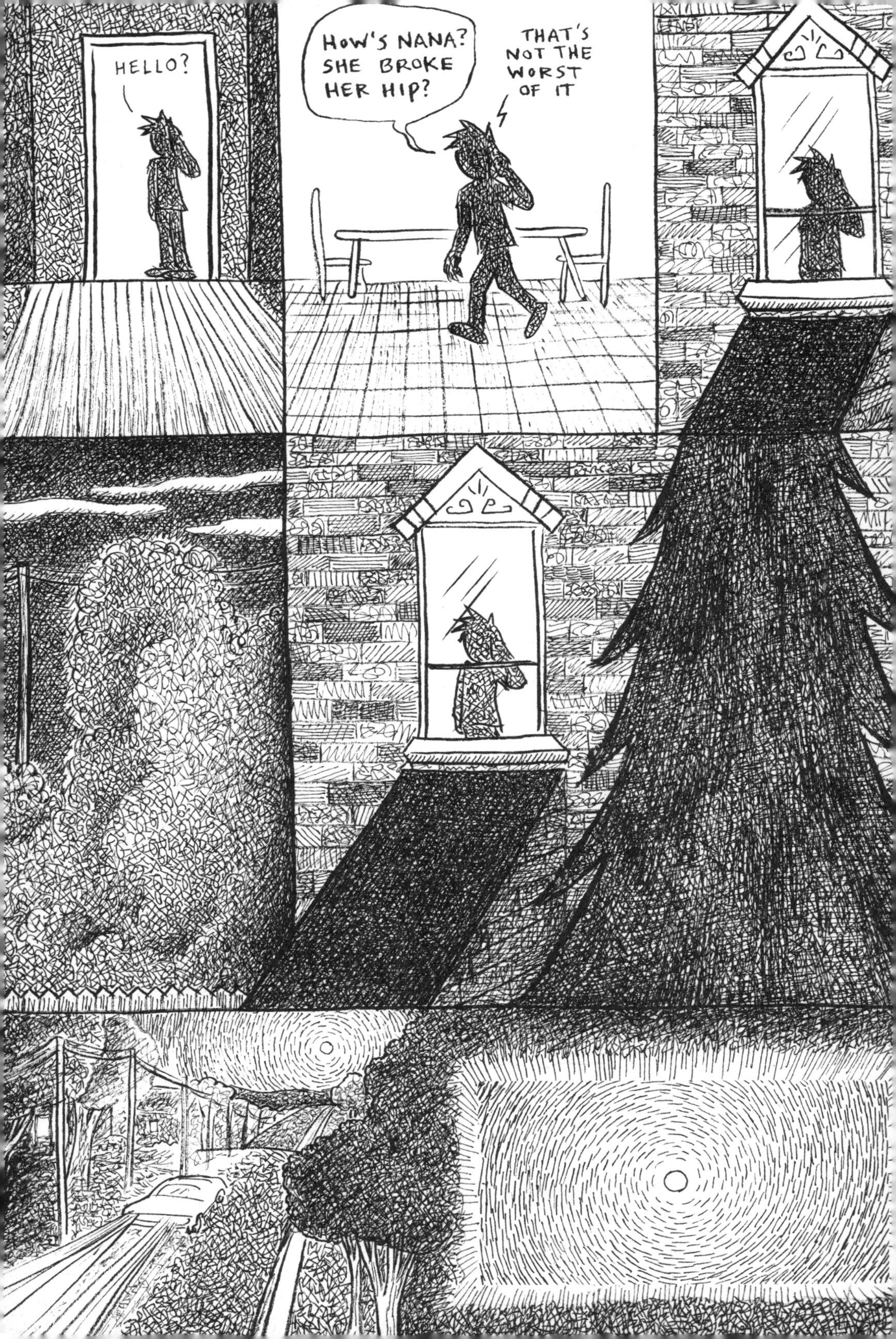
HELLO?
HOW'S NANA? SHE BROKE HER HIP?
THAT'S NOT THE WORST OF IT

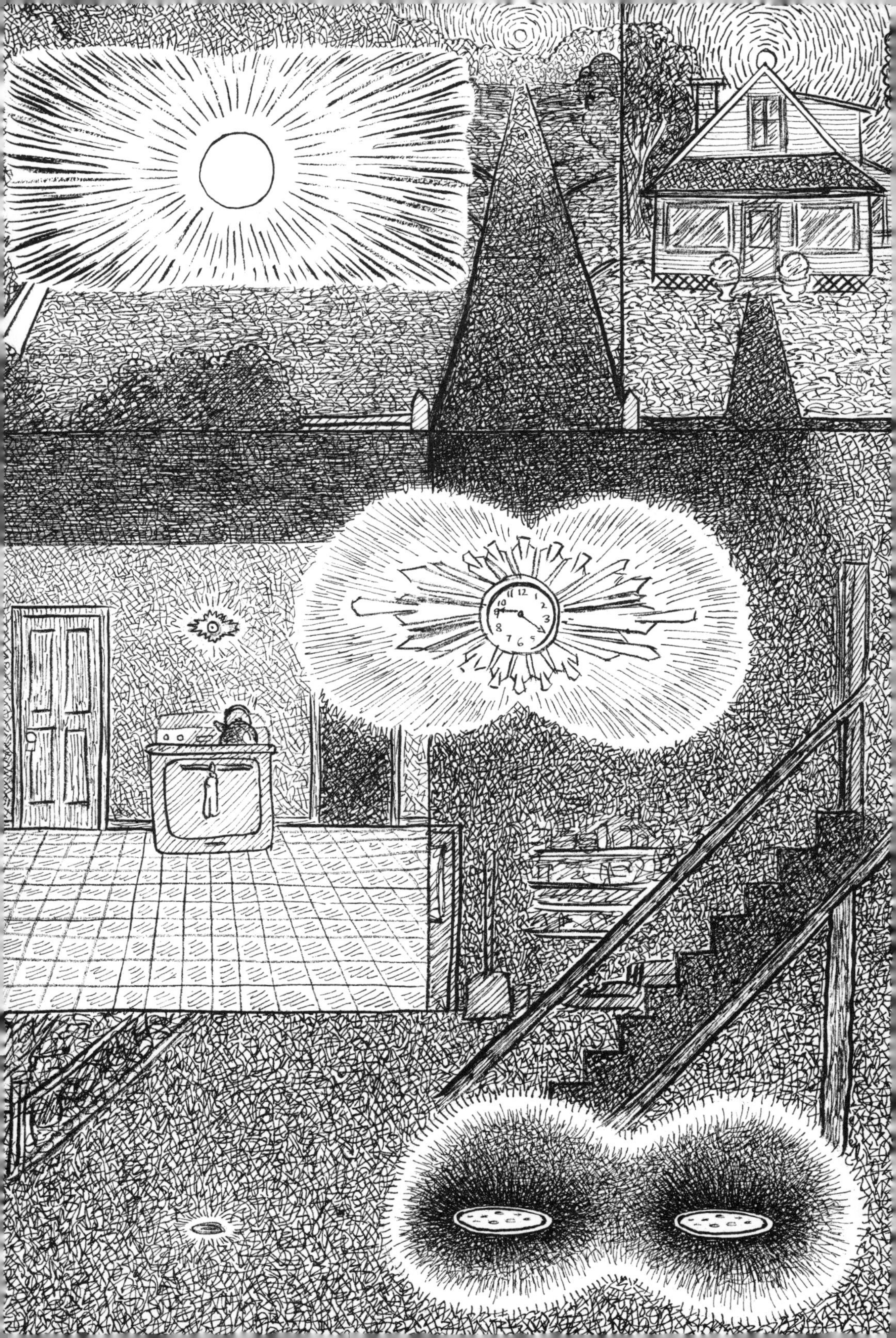

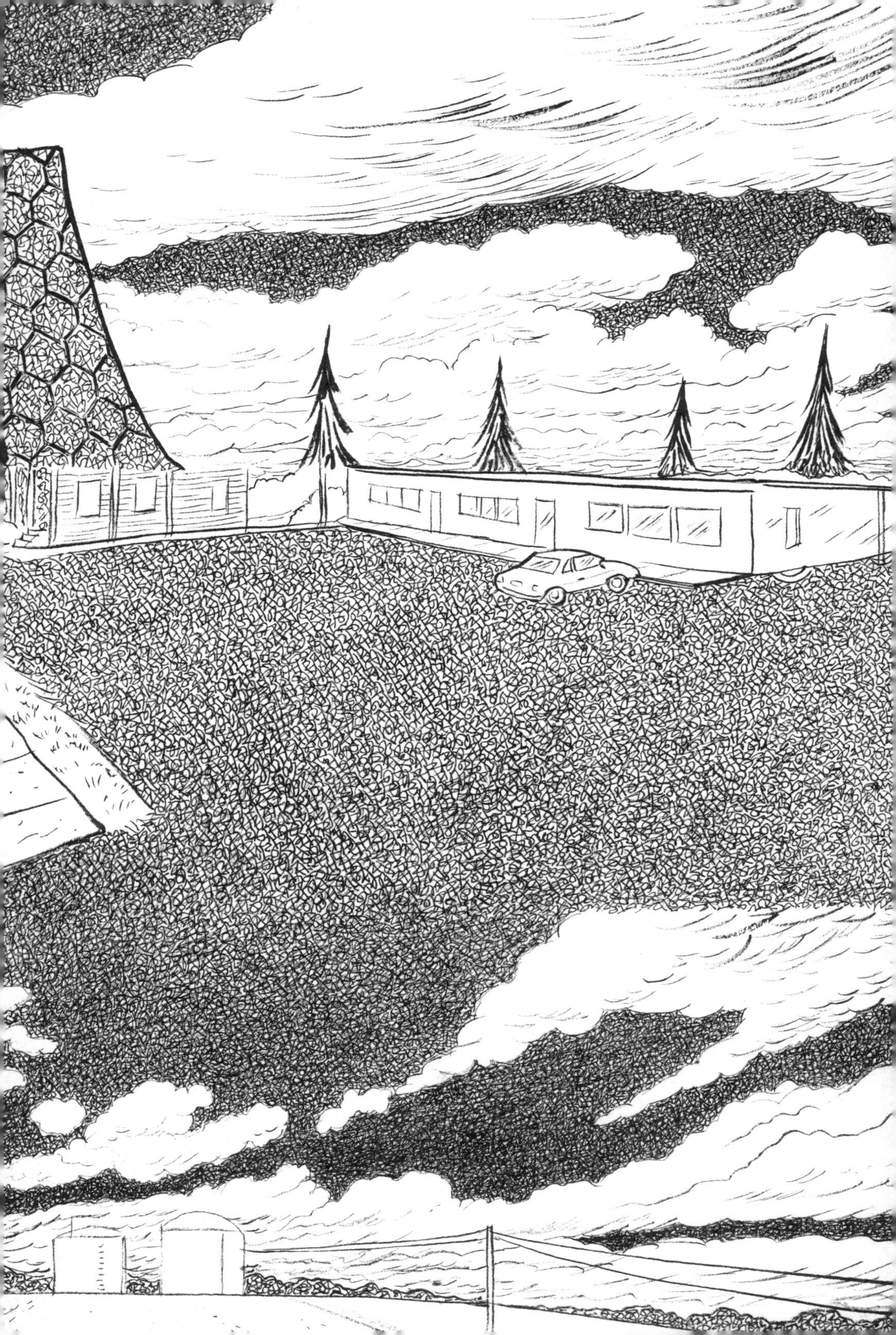

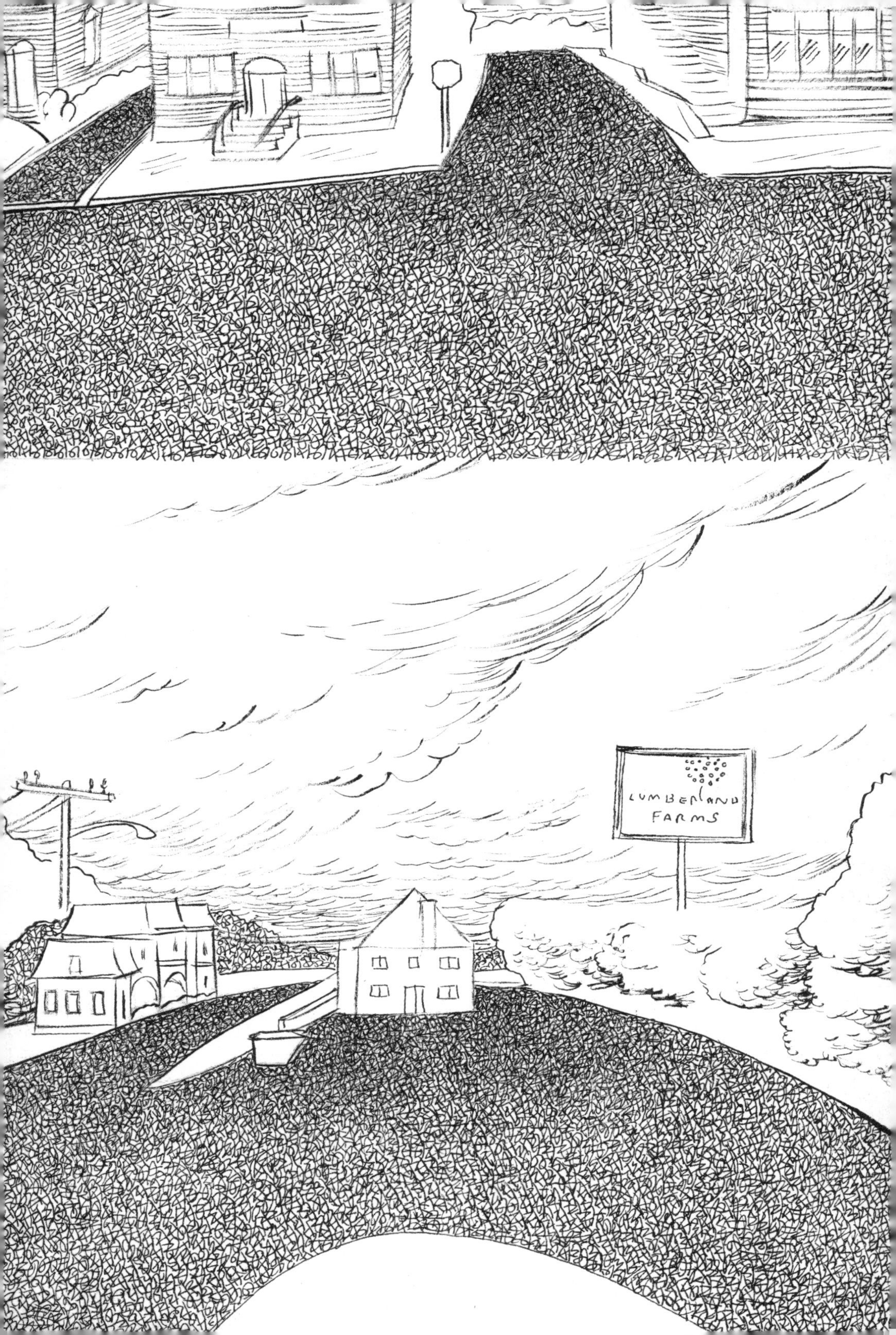
LUMBERLAND
FARMS

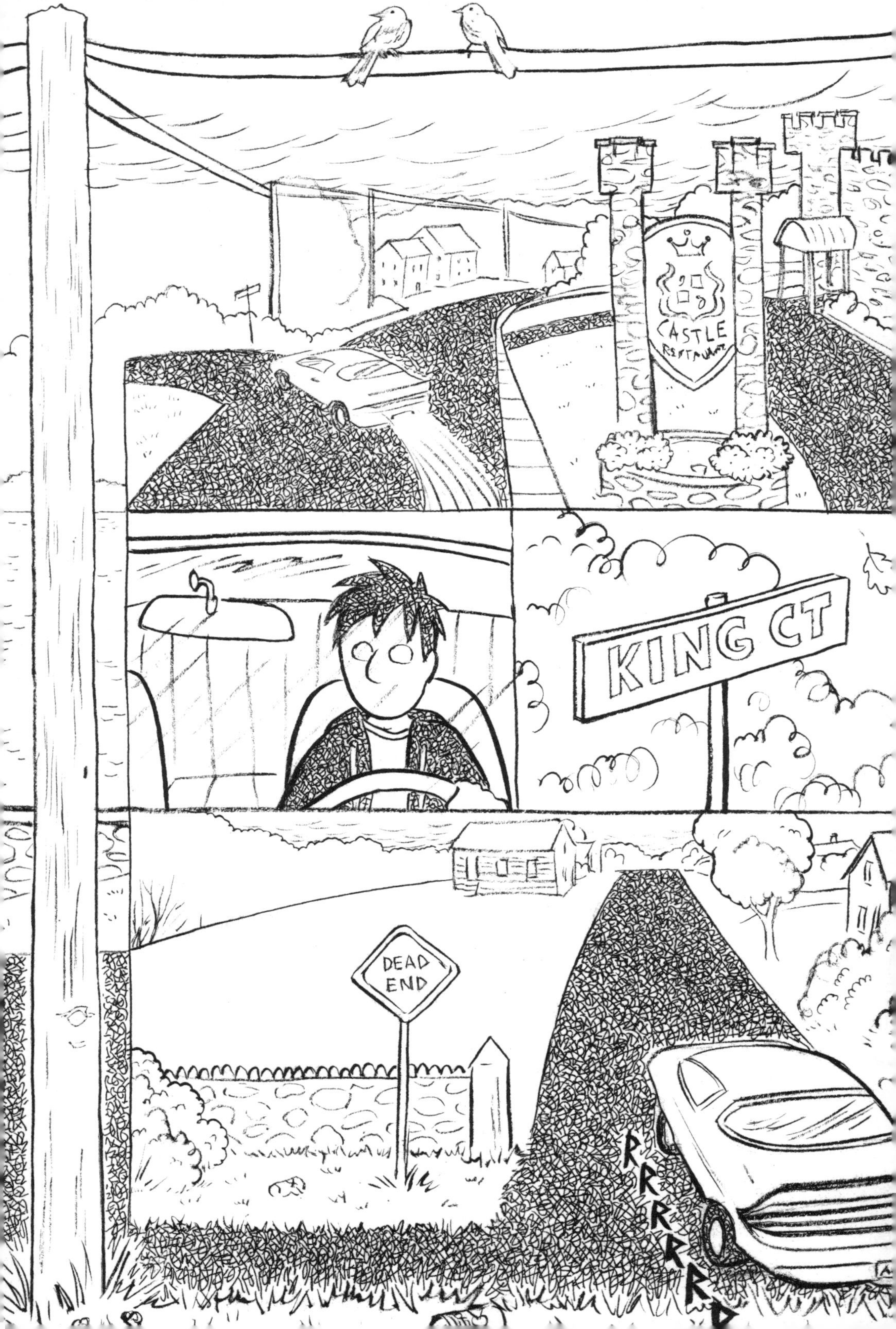
CASTLE
KING CT
DEAD END
RRRRRRD

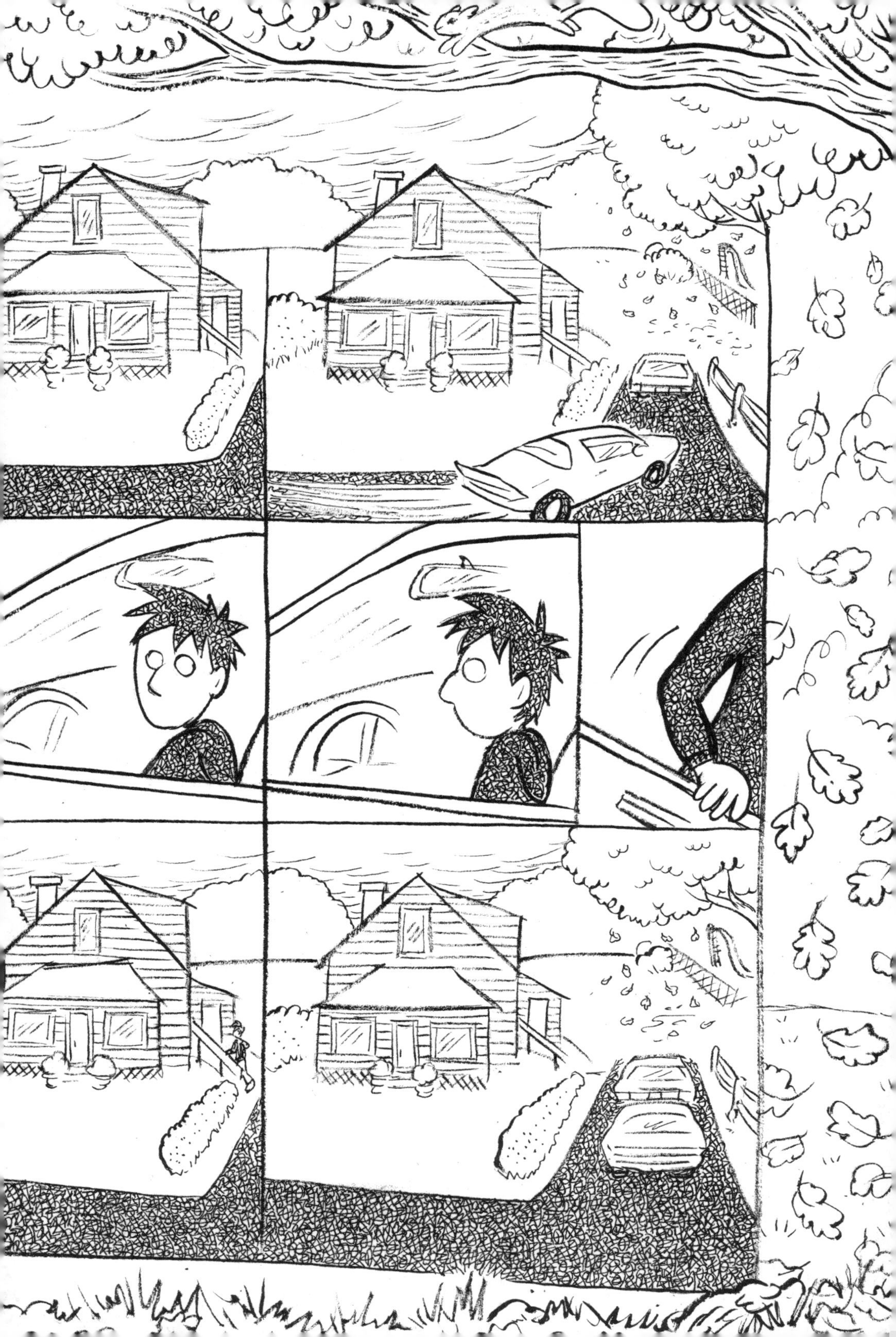

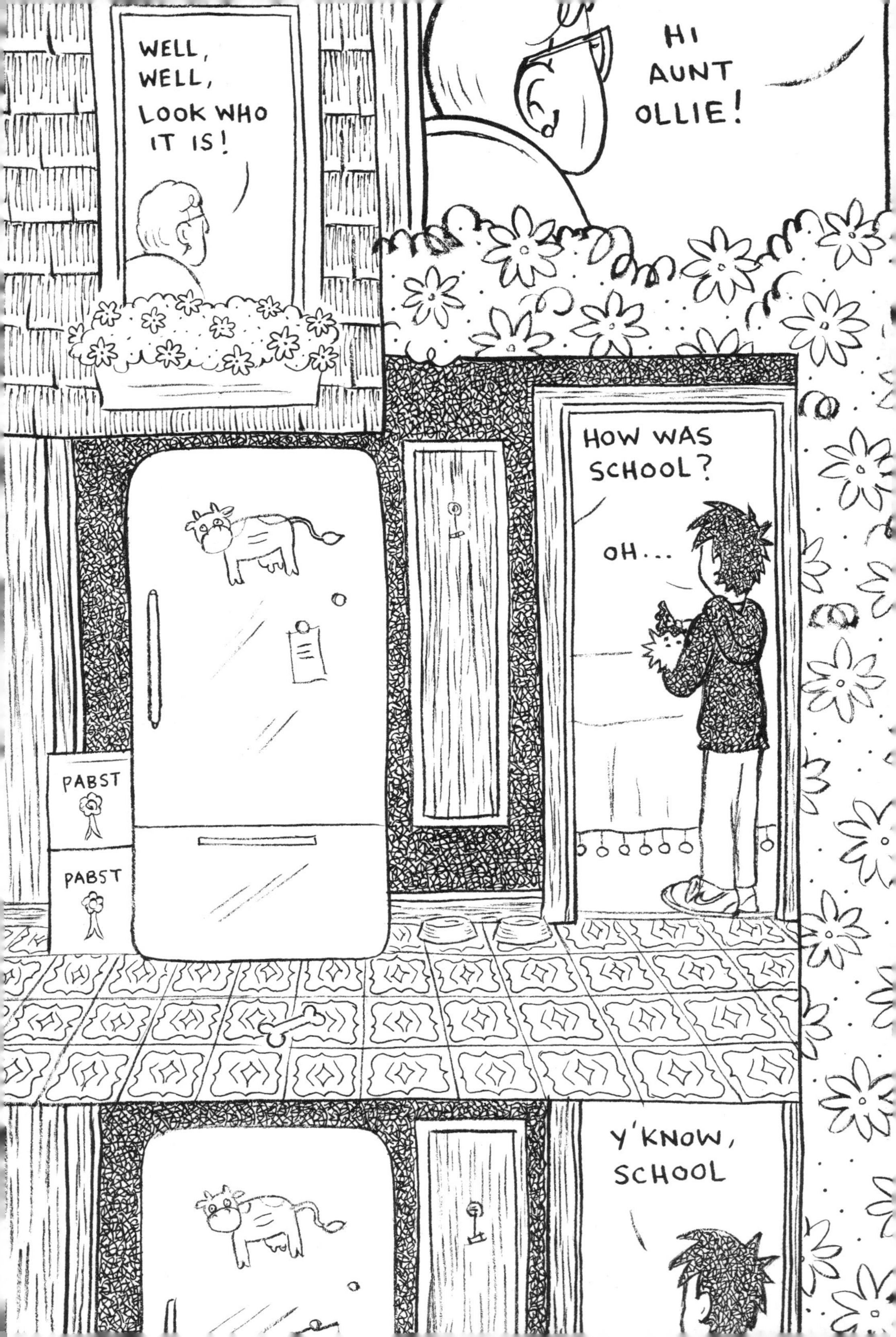
WELL, WELL, LOOK WHO IT IS!
HI AUNT OLLIE!
HOW WAS SCHOOL?
OH...
PABST
PABST
Y'KNOW, SCHOOL

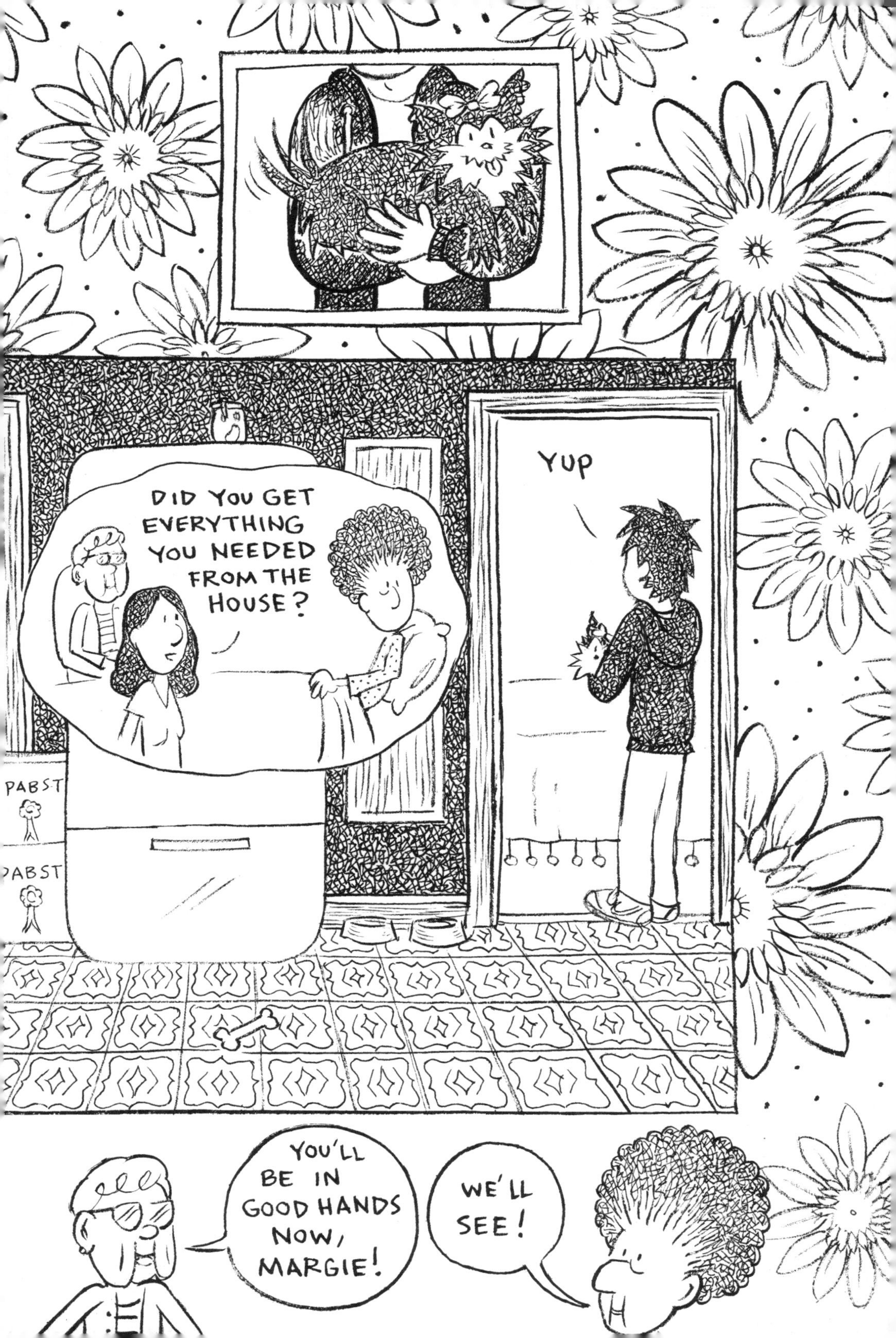
PABST
PABST
DID YOU GET EVERYTHING YOU NEEDED FROM THE HOUSE?
YUP
YOU'LL BE IN GOOD HANDS NOW, MARGIE!
WE'LL SEE!

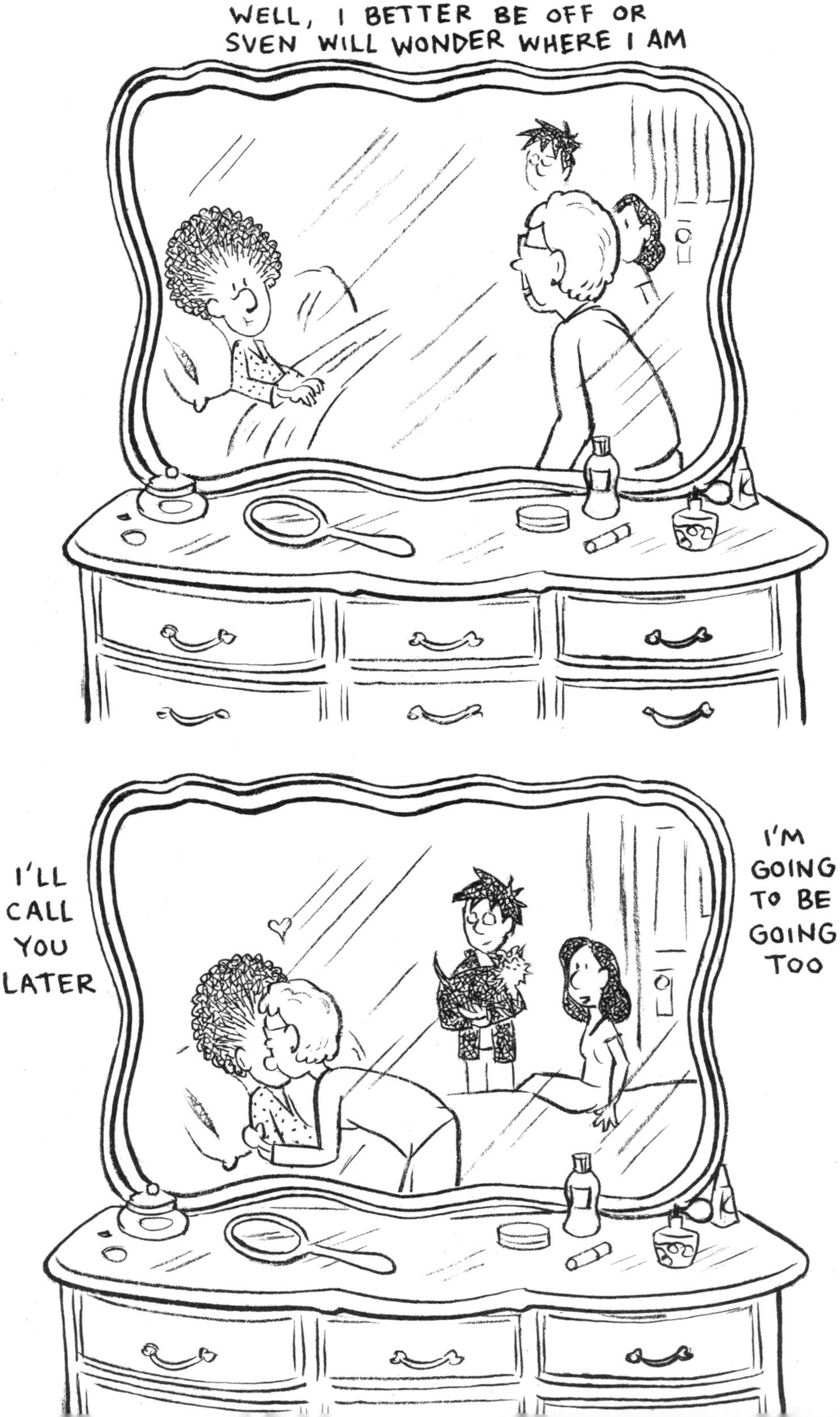
WELL, I BETTER BE OFF OR SVEN WILL WONDER WHERE I AM
I'LL CALL YOU LATER
I'M GOING TO BE GOING TOO

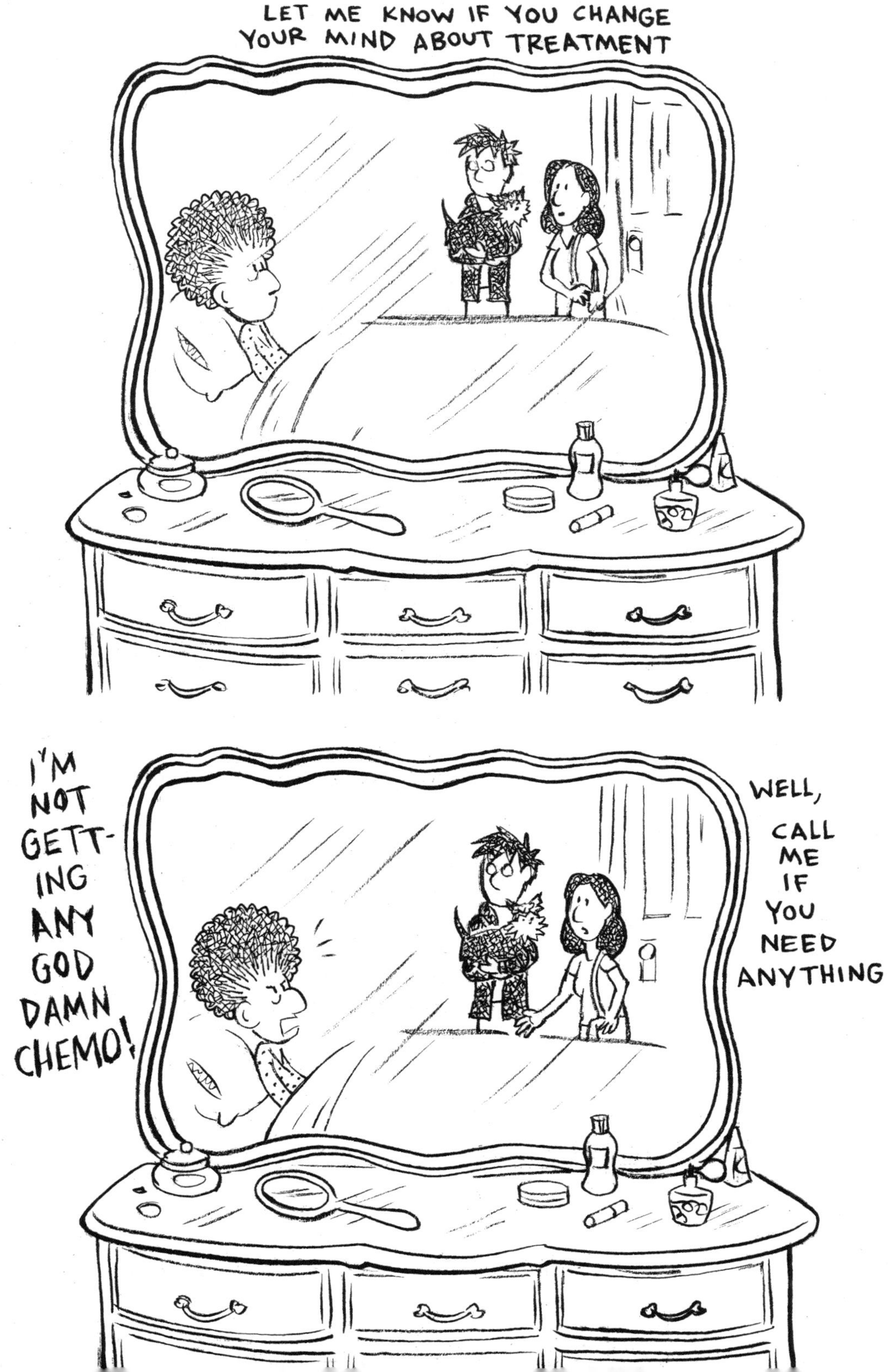
LET ME KNOW IF YOU CHANGE YOUR MIND ABOUT TREATMENT
I'M NOT GETT-ING ANY GOD DAMN CHEMO!
WELL, CALL ME IF YOU NEED ANYTHING

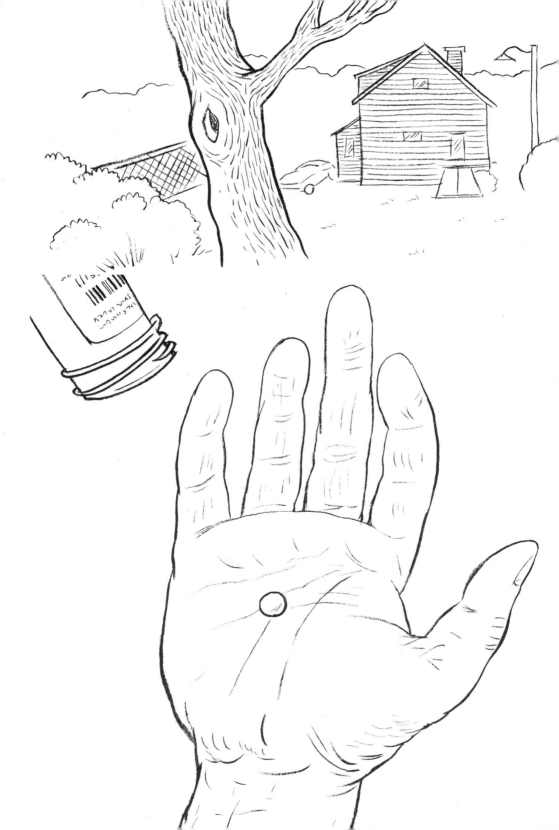

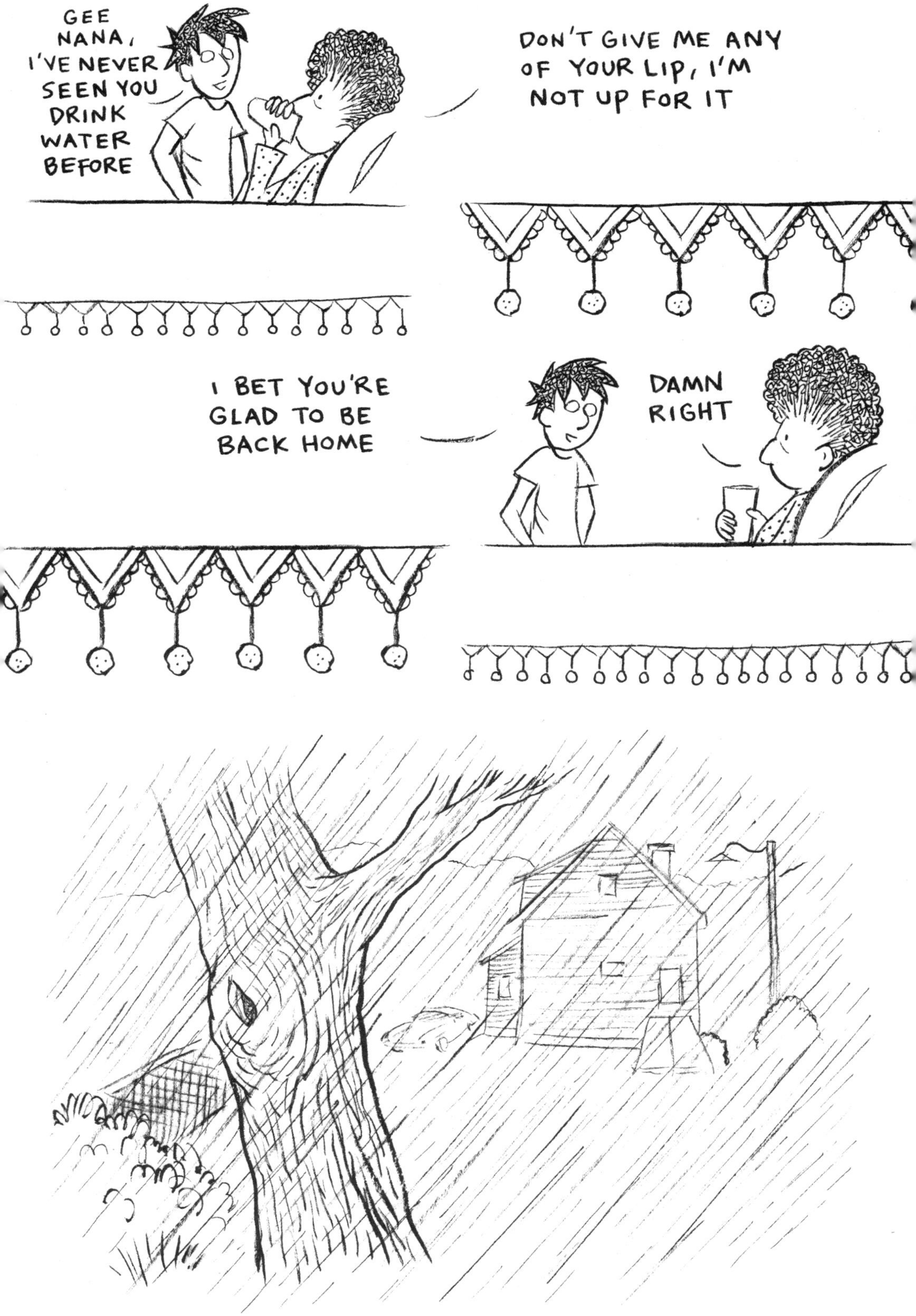
GEE NANA, I'VE NEVER SEEN YOU DRINK WATER BEFORE
DON'T GIVE ME ANY OF YOUR LIP, I'M NOT UP FOR IT
I BET YOU'RE GLAD TO BE BACK HOME
DAMN RIGHT

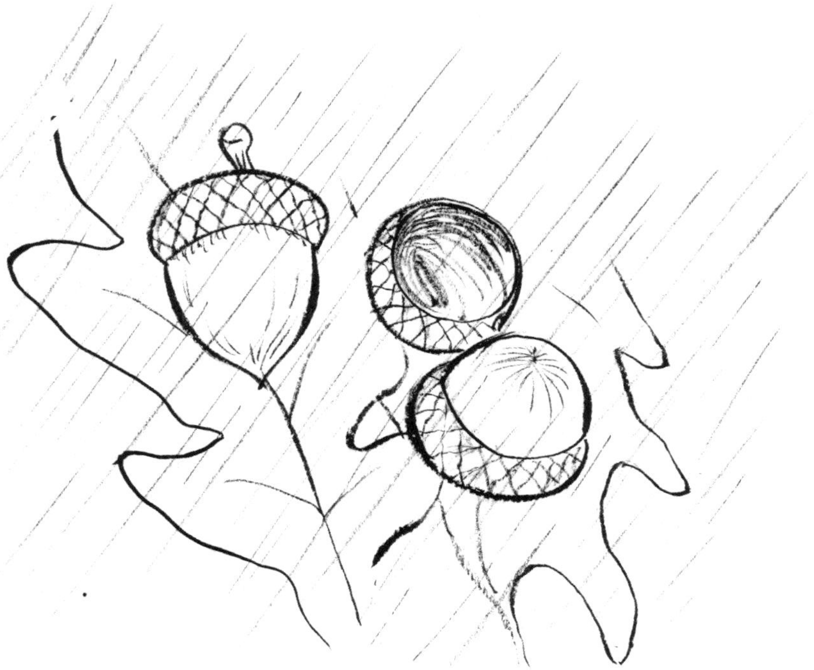

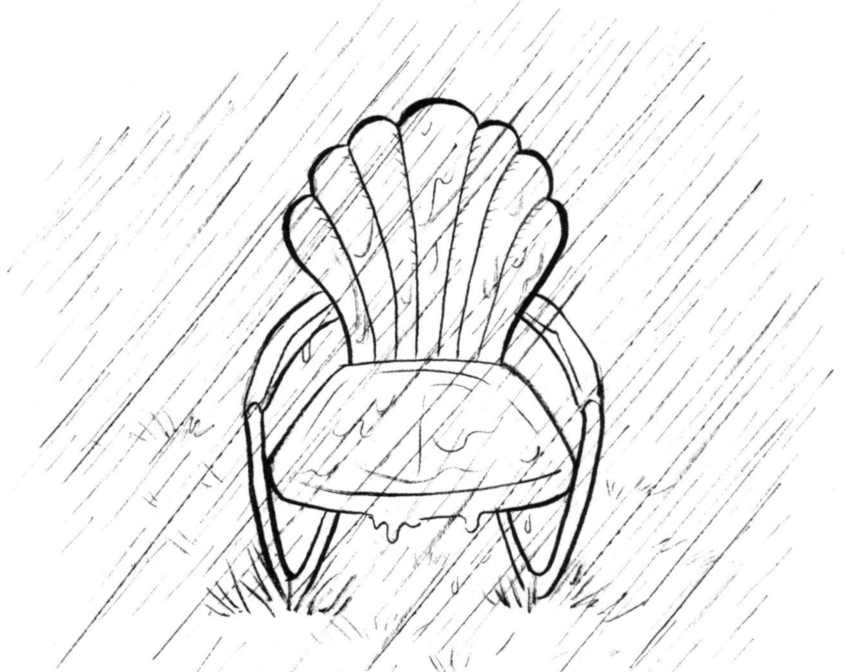

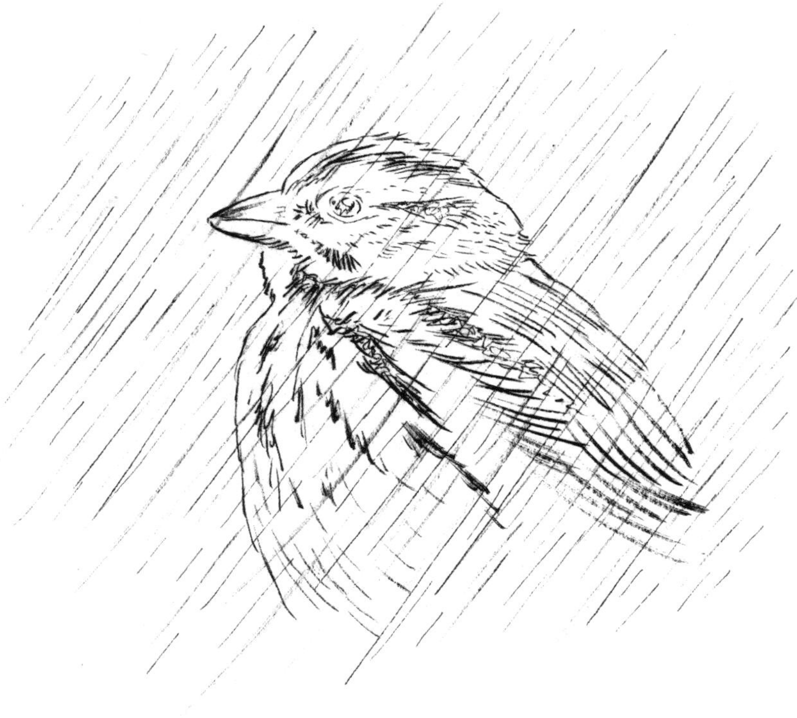

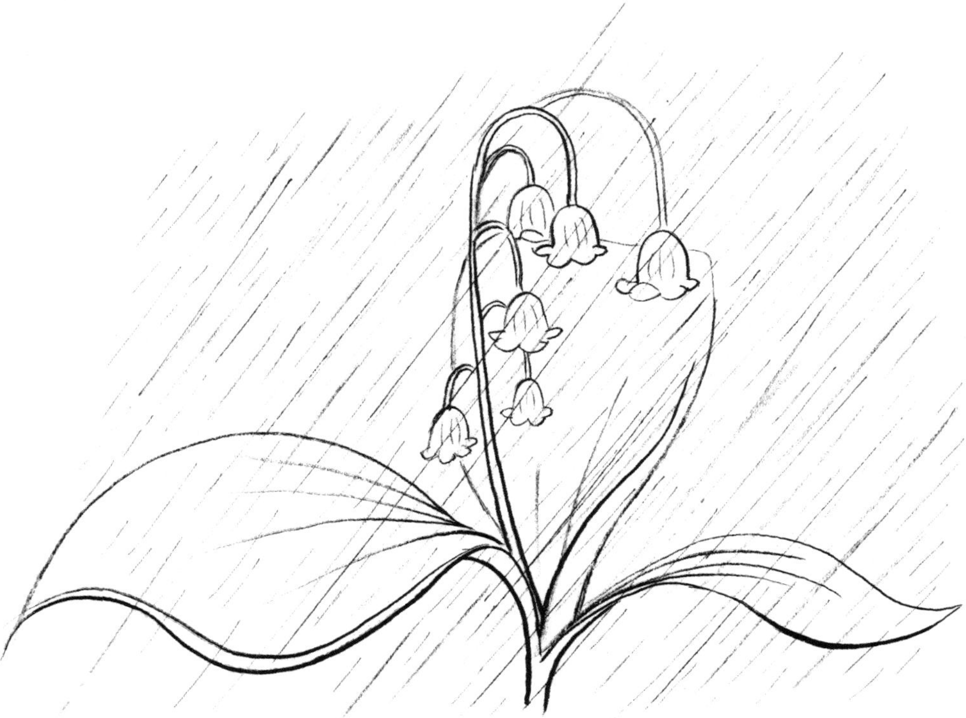

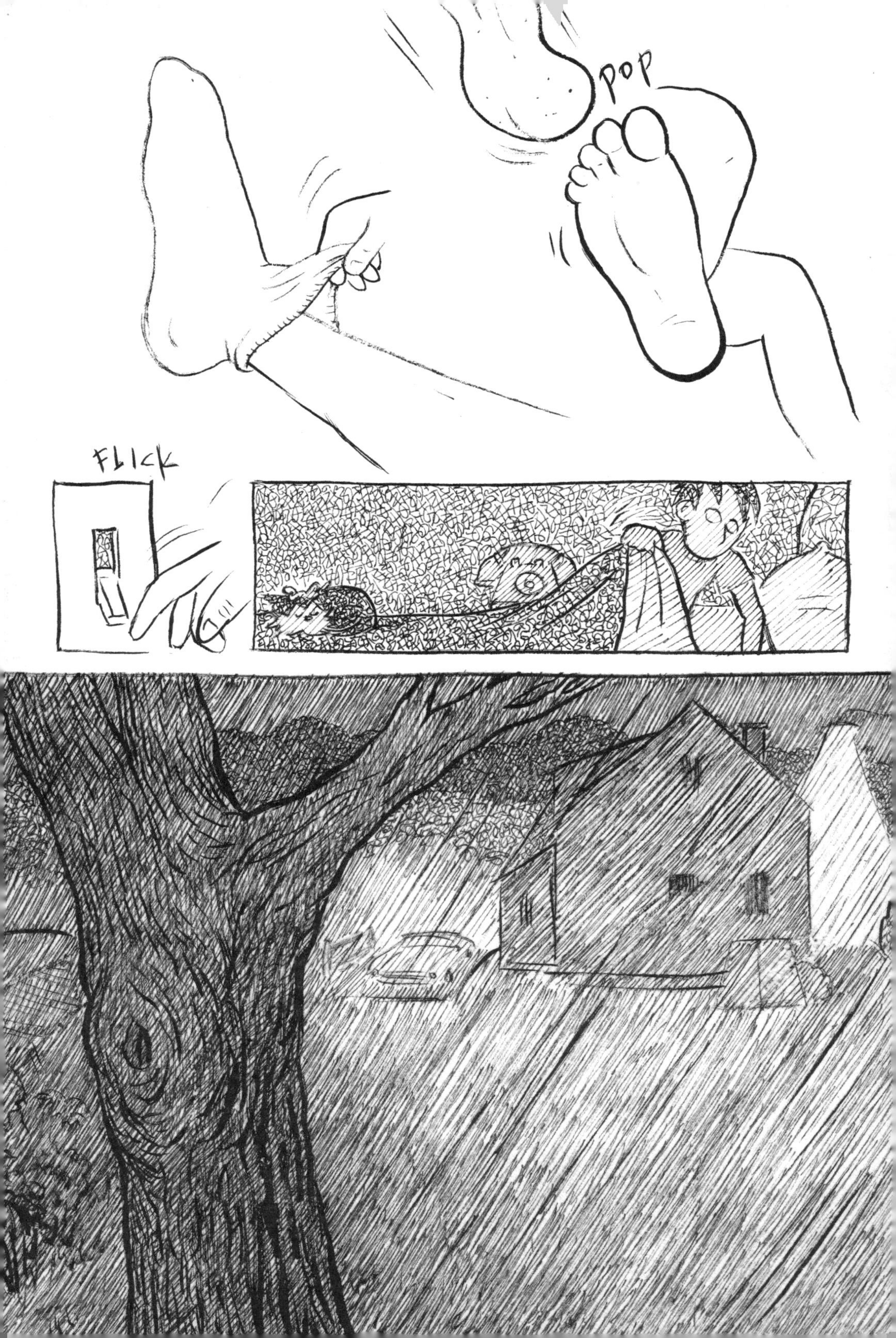
POP
FLICK

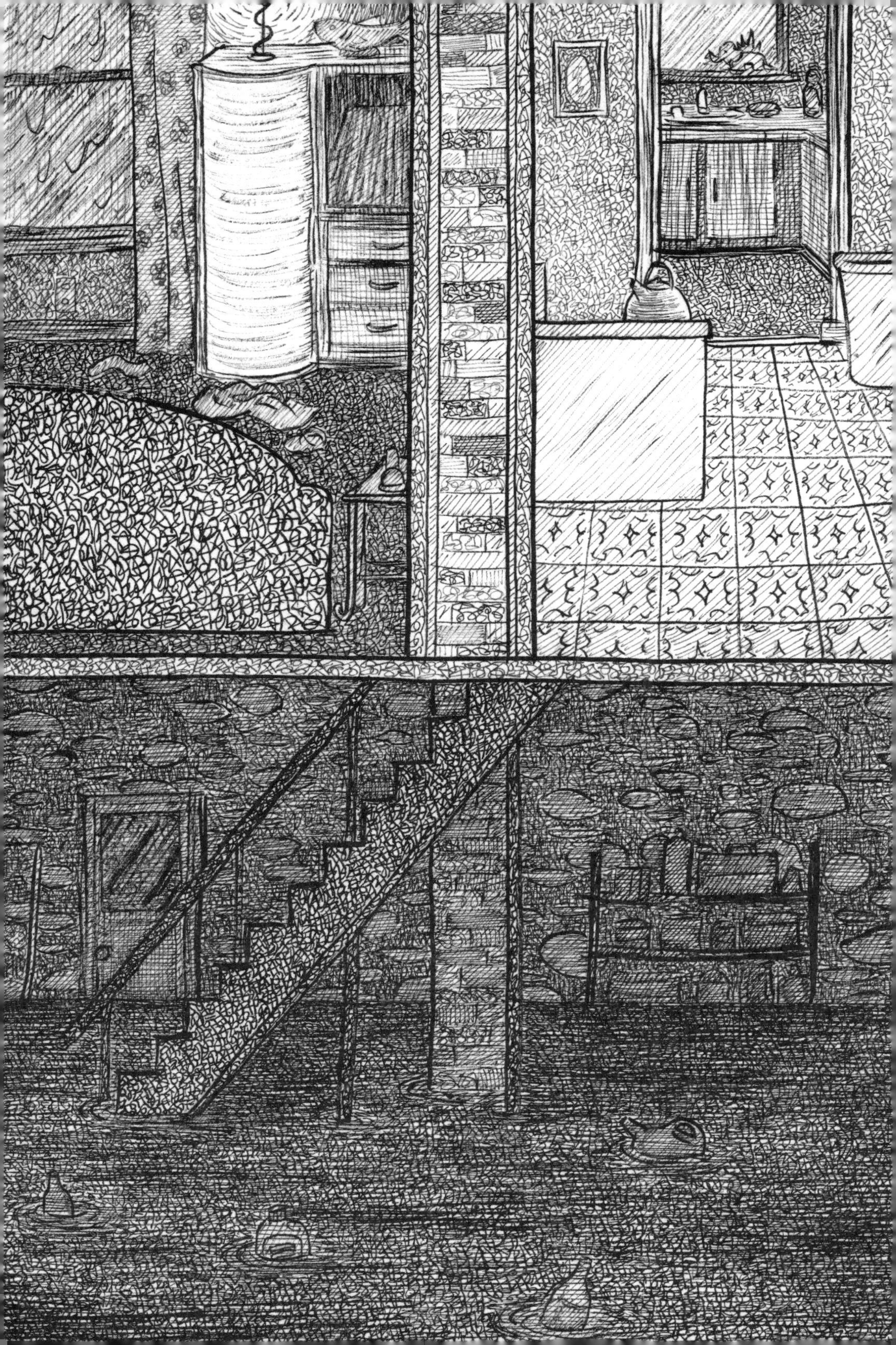

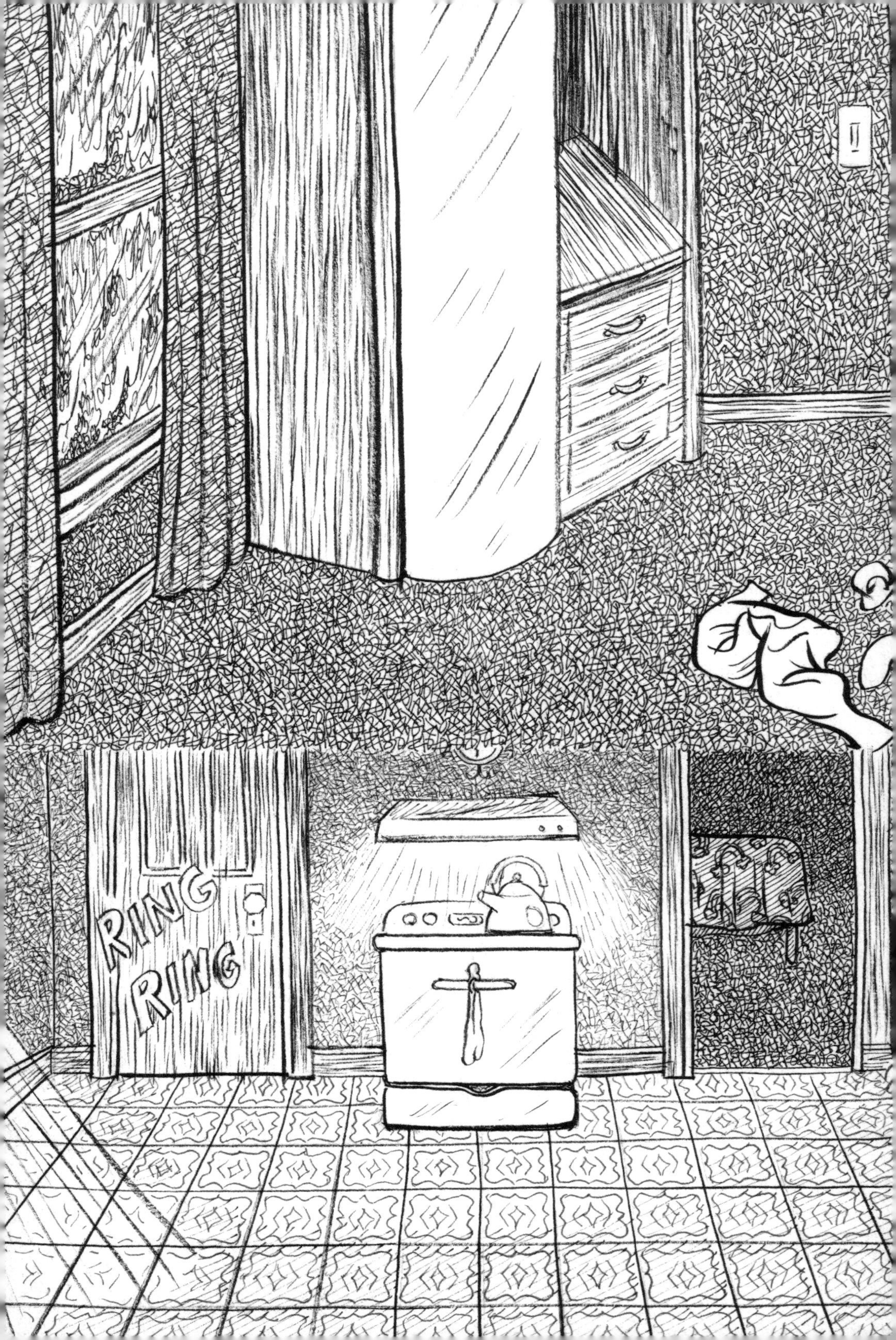
RING
RING

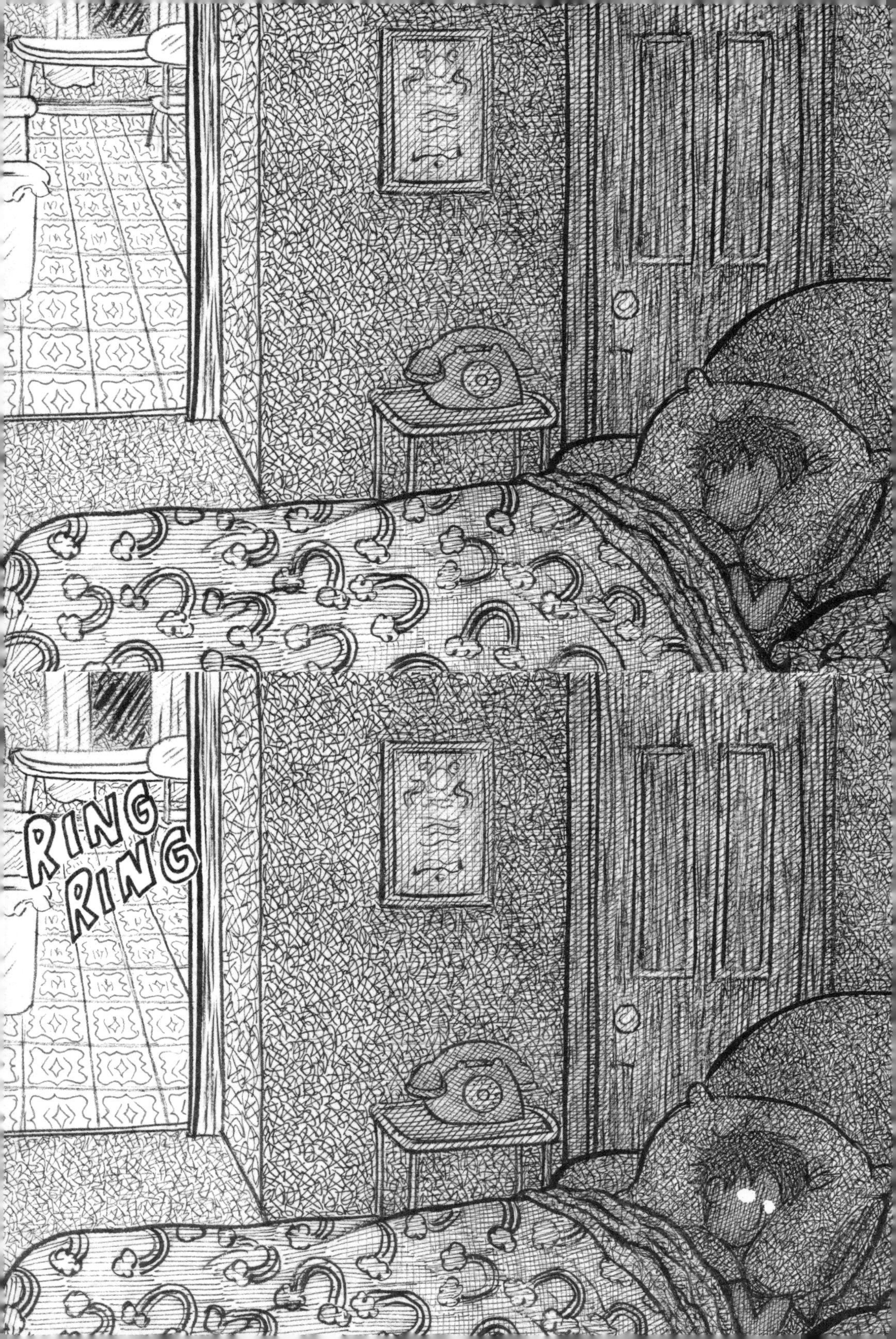
RING RING

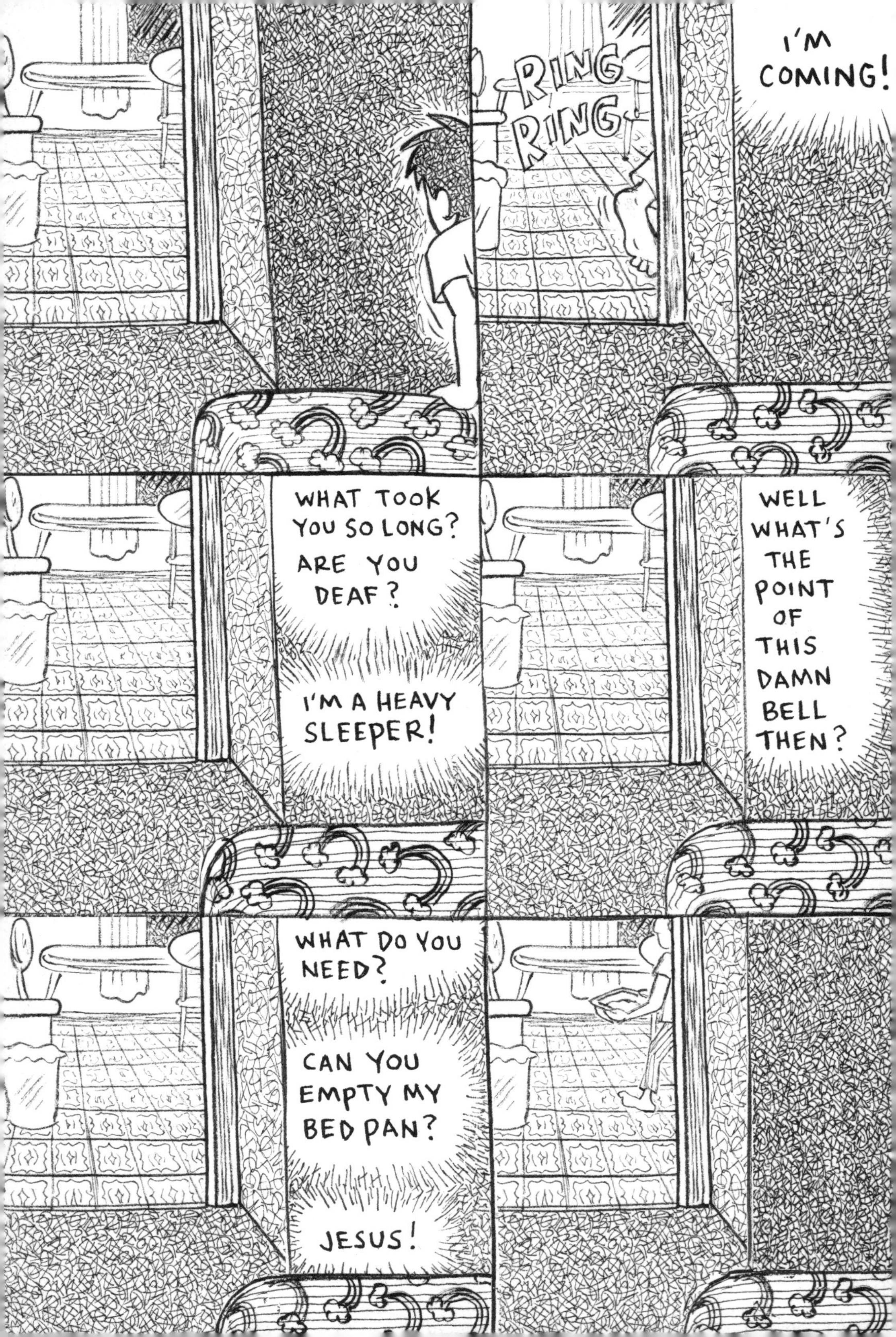
RING RING
I'M COMING!
WHAT TOOK YOU SO LONG? ARE YOU DEAF?
I'M A HEAVY SLEEPER!
WELL WHAT'S THE POINT OF THIS DAMN BELL THEN?
WHAT DO YOU NEED?
CAN YOU EMPTY MY BED PAN?
JESUS!

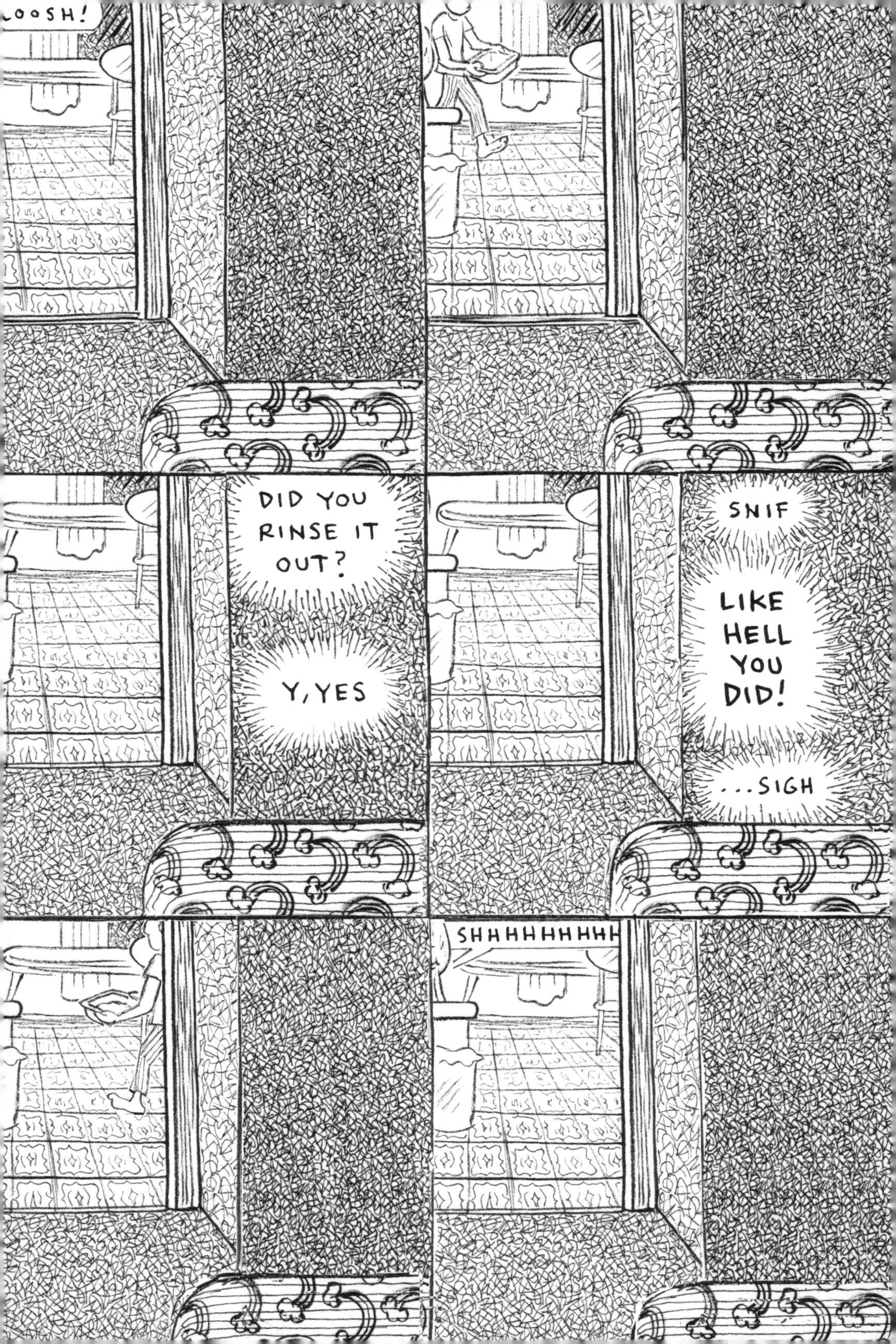
OOSH!
DID YOU RINSE IT OUT?
Y, YES
SNIF
LIKE HELL YOU DID!
...SIGH
SHHHHHHHHH

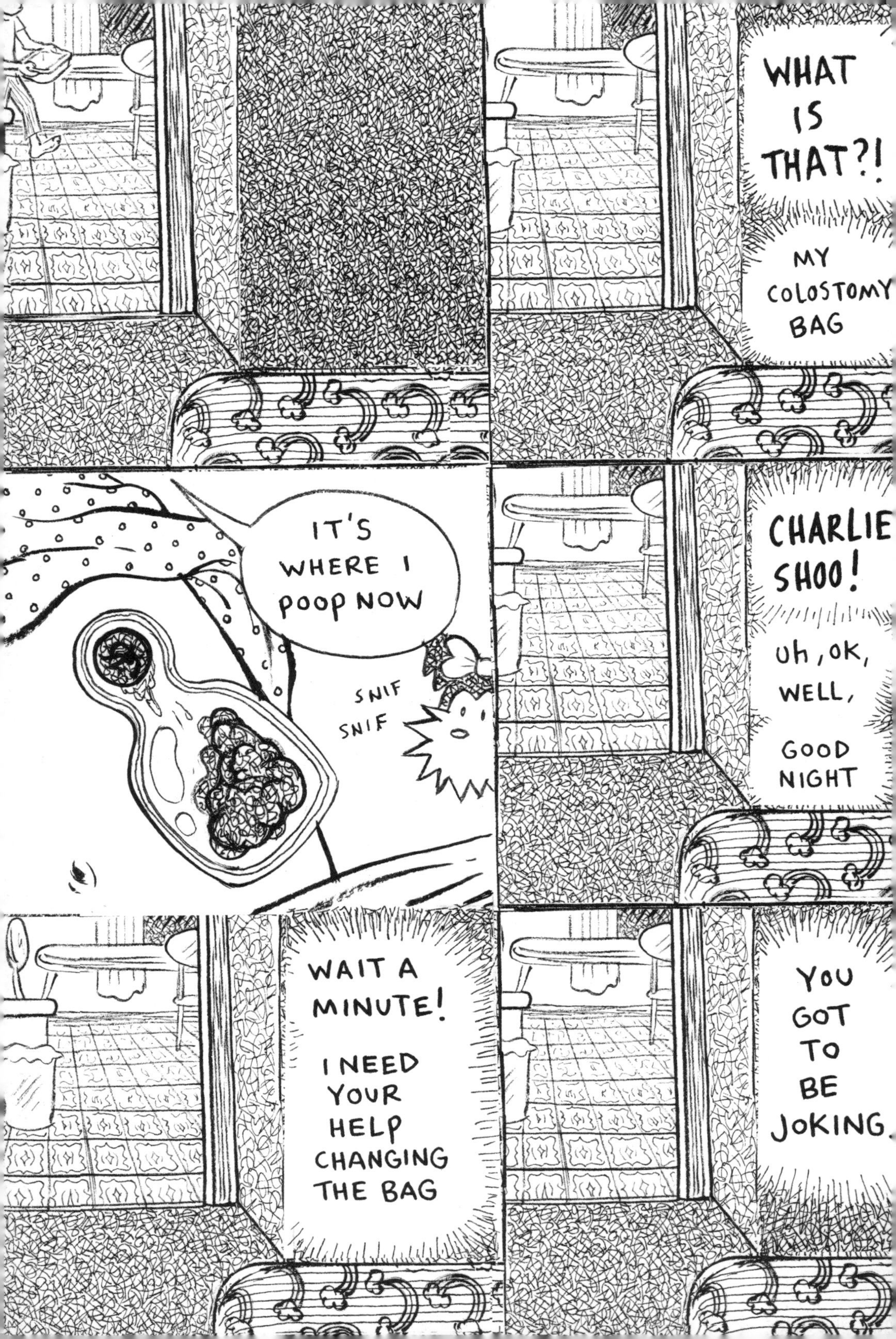
WHAT IS THAT?!
MY COLOSTOMY BAG
IT'S WHERE I POOP NOW
SNIF SNIF
CHARLIE SHOO!
Uh, OK, WELL,
GOOD NIGHT
WAIT A MINUTE!
I NEED YOUR HELP CHANGING THE BAG
YOU GOT TO BE JOKING.

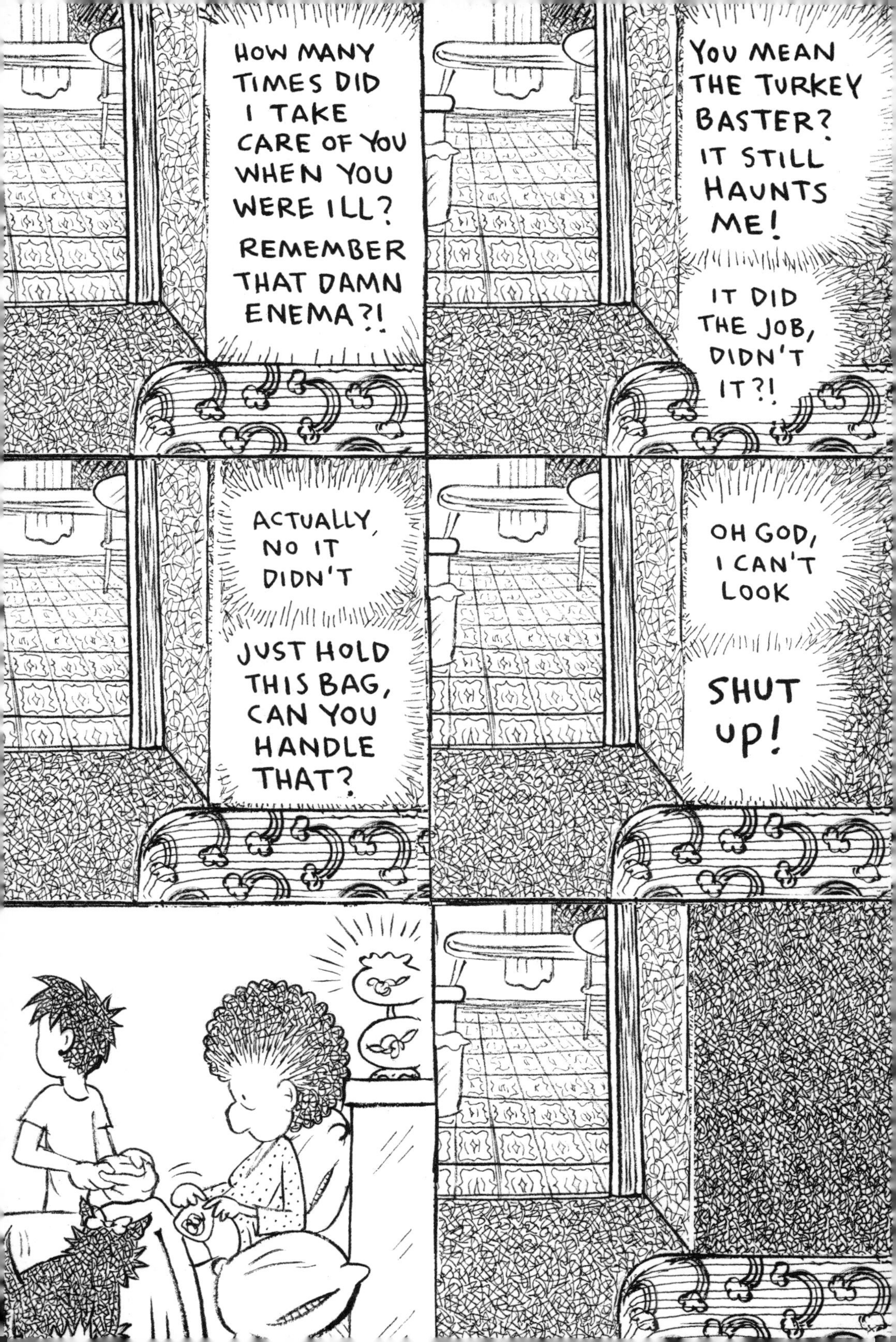
HOW MANY TIMES DID I TAKE CARE OF YOU WHEN YOU WERE ILL? REMEMBER THAT DAMN ENEMA?!
YOU MEAN THE TURKEY BASTER? IT STILL HAUNTS ME!
IT DID THE JOB, DIDN'T IT?!
ACTUALLY, NO IT DIDN'T
JUST HOLD THIS BAG, CAN YOU HANDLE THAT?
OH GOD, I CAN'T LOOK
SHUT UP!

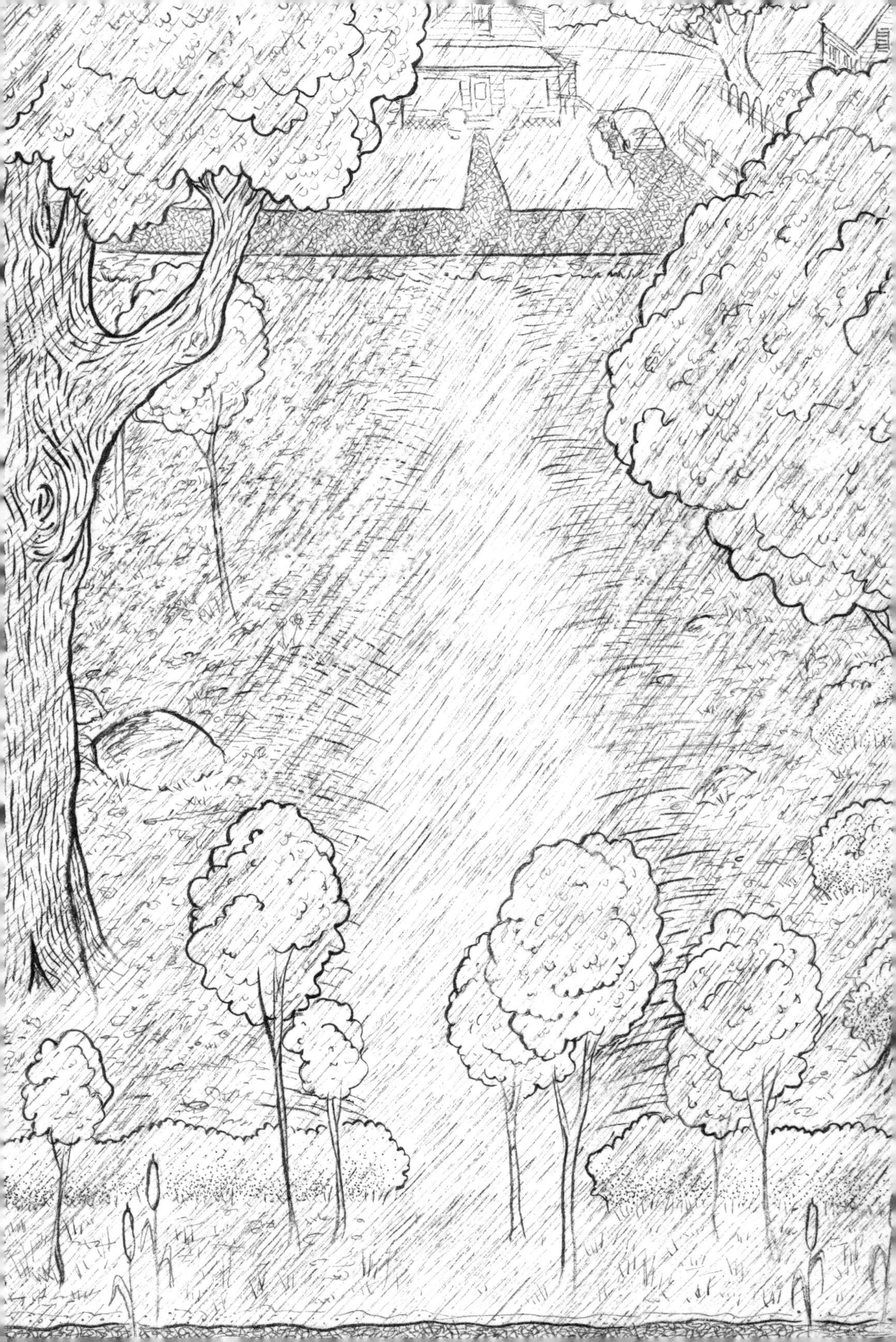

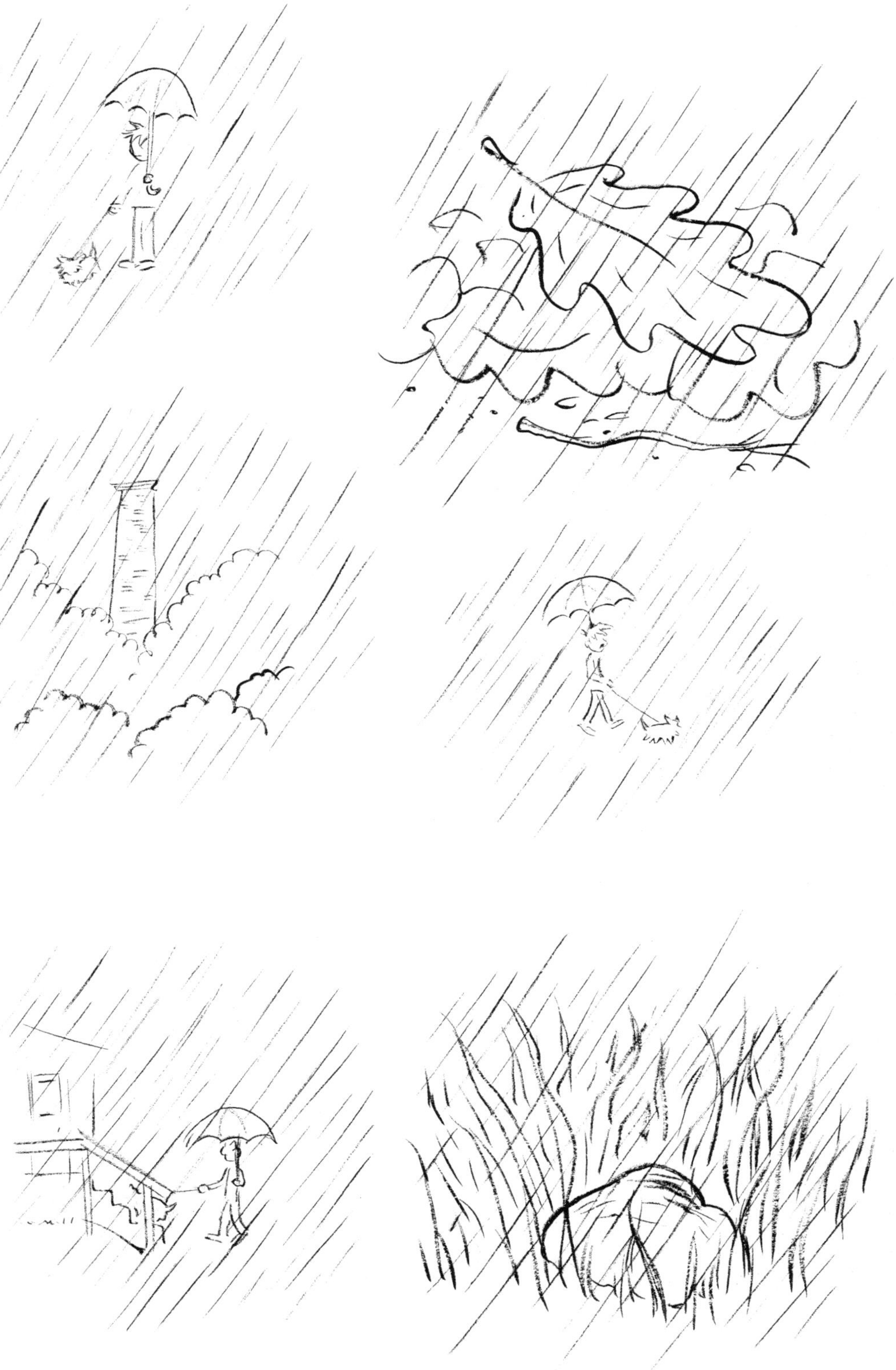

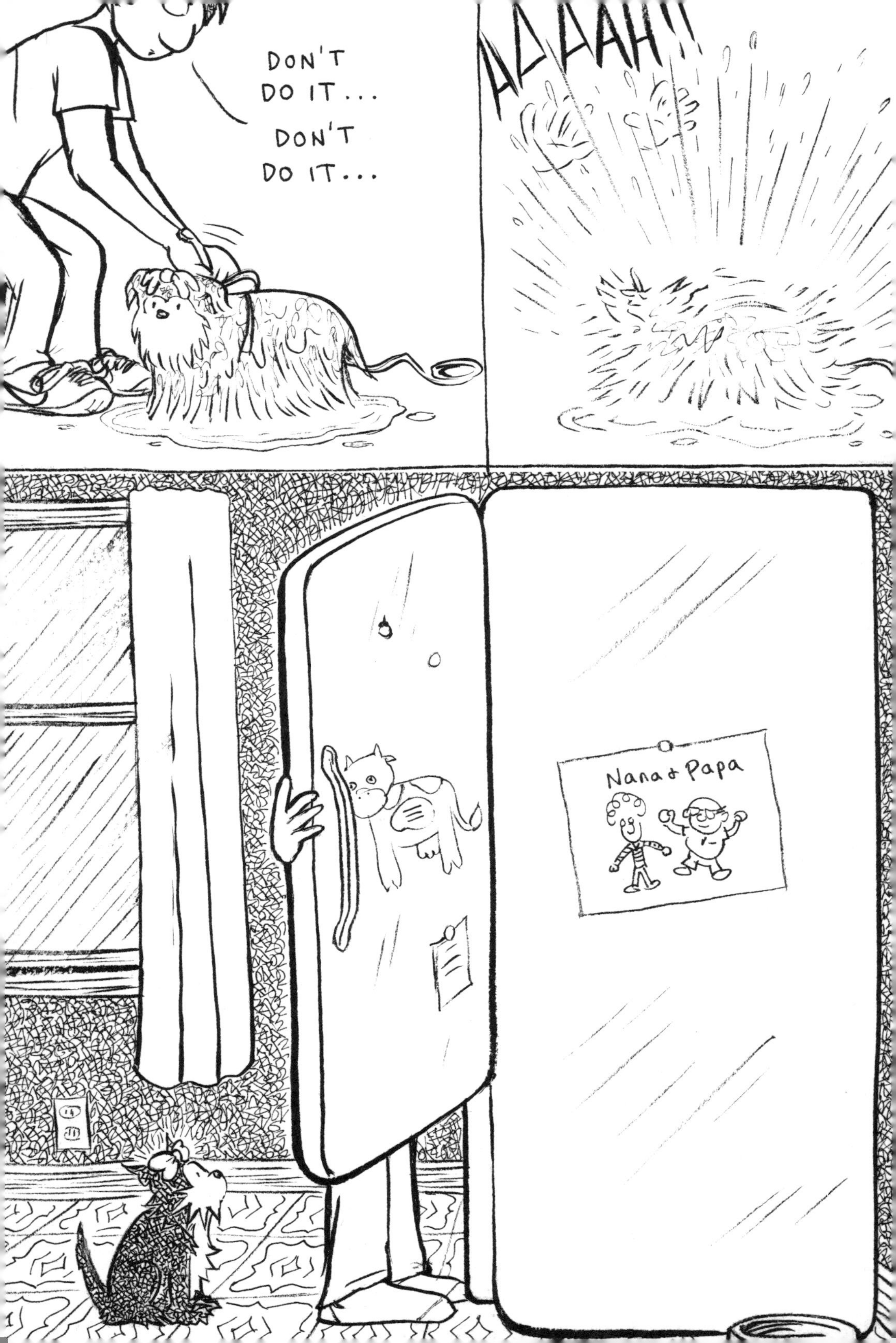
DON'T DO IT...
DON'T DO IT...
AAAAH!!
Nana + Papa

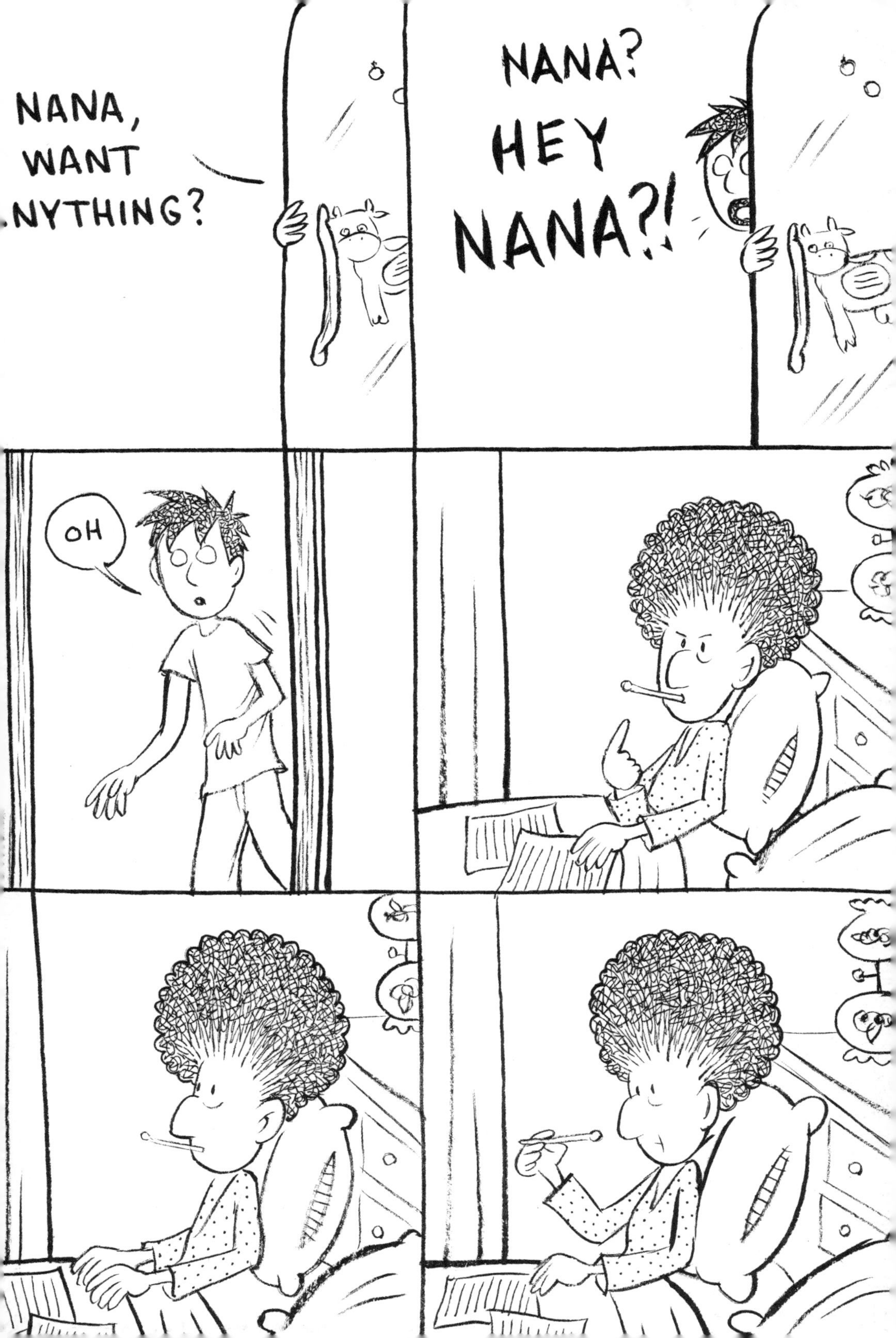
NANA, WANT NYTHING?
NANA?
HEY NANA?!
OH

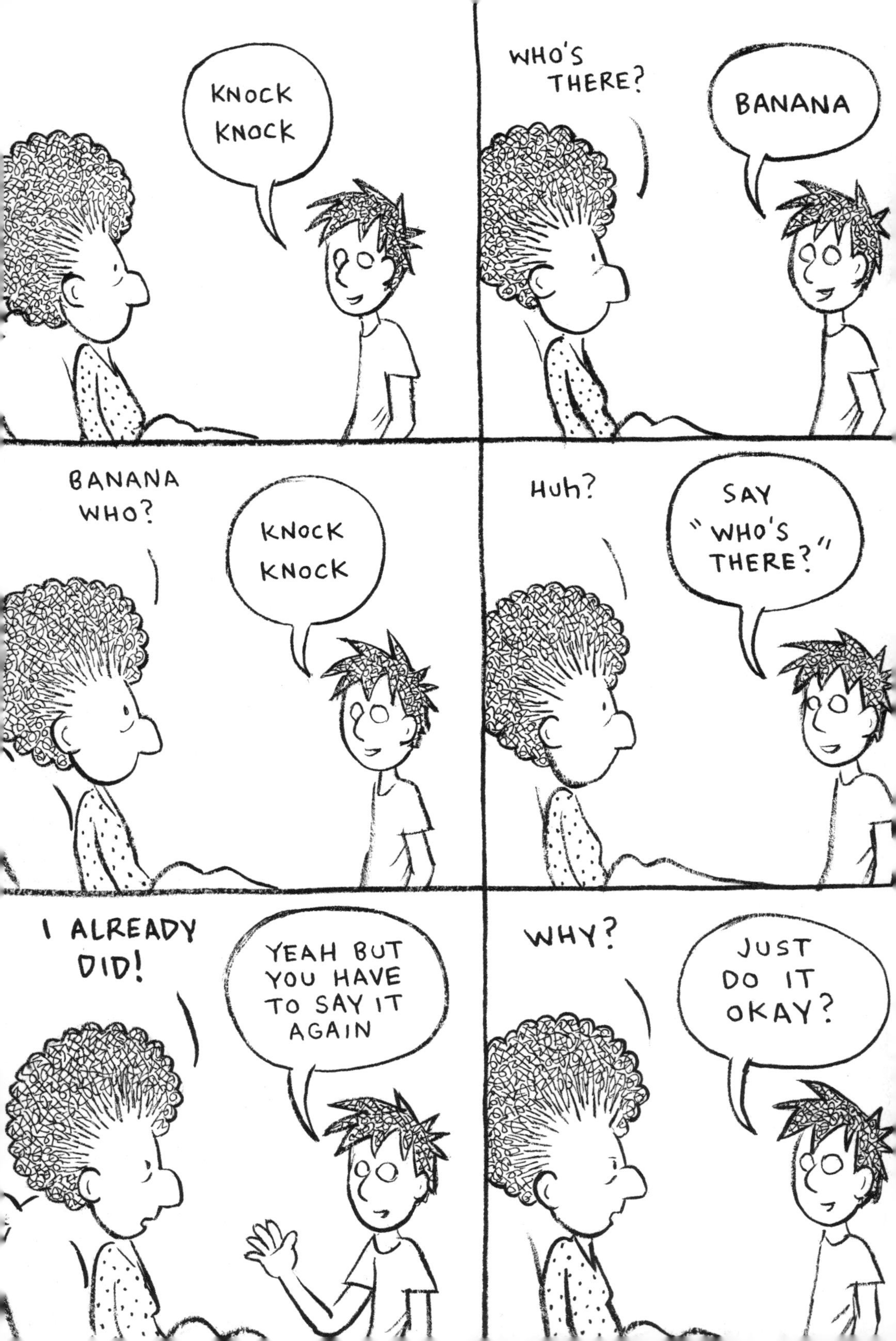
KNOCK KNOCK
WHO'S THERE?
BANANA
BANANA WHO?
KNOCK KNOCK
Huh?
SAY "WHO'S THERE?"
I ALREADY DID!
YEAH BUT YOU HAVE TO SAY IT AGAIN
WHY?
JUST DO IT OKAY?

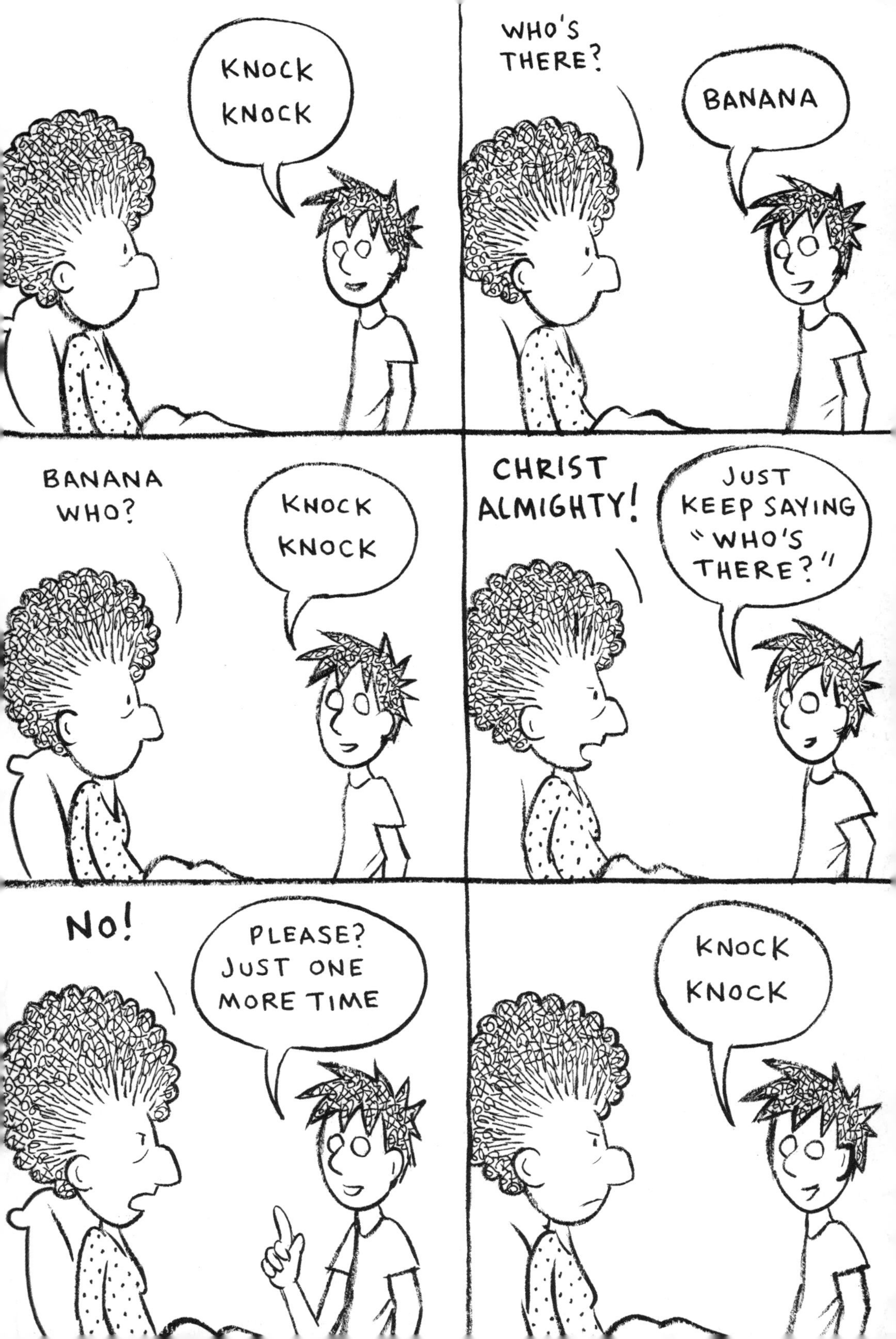
KNOCK KNOCK
WHO'S THERE?
BANANA
BANANA WHO?
KNOCK KNOCK
CHRIST ALMIGHTY!
JUST KEEP SAYING "WHO'S THERE?"
NO!
PLEASE? JUST ONE MORE TIME
KNOCK KNOCK

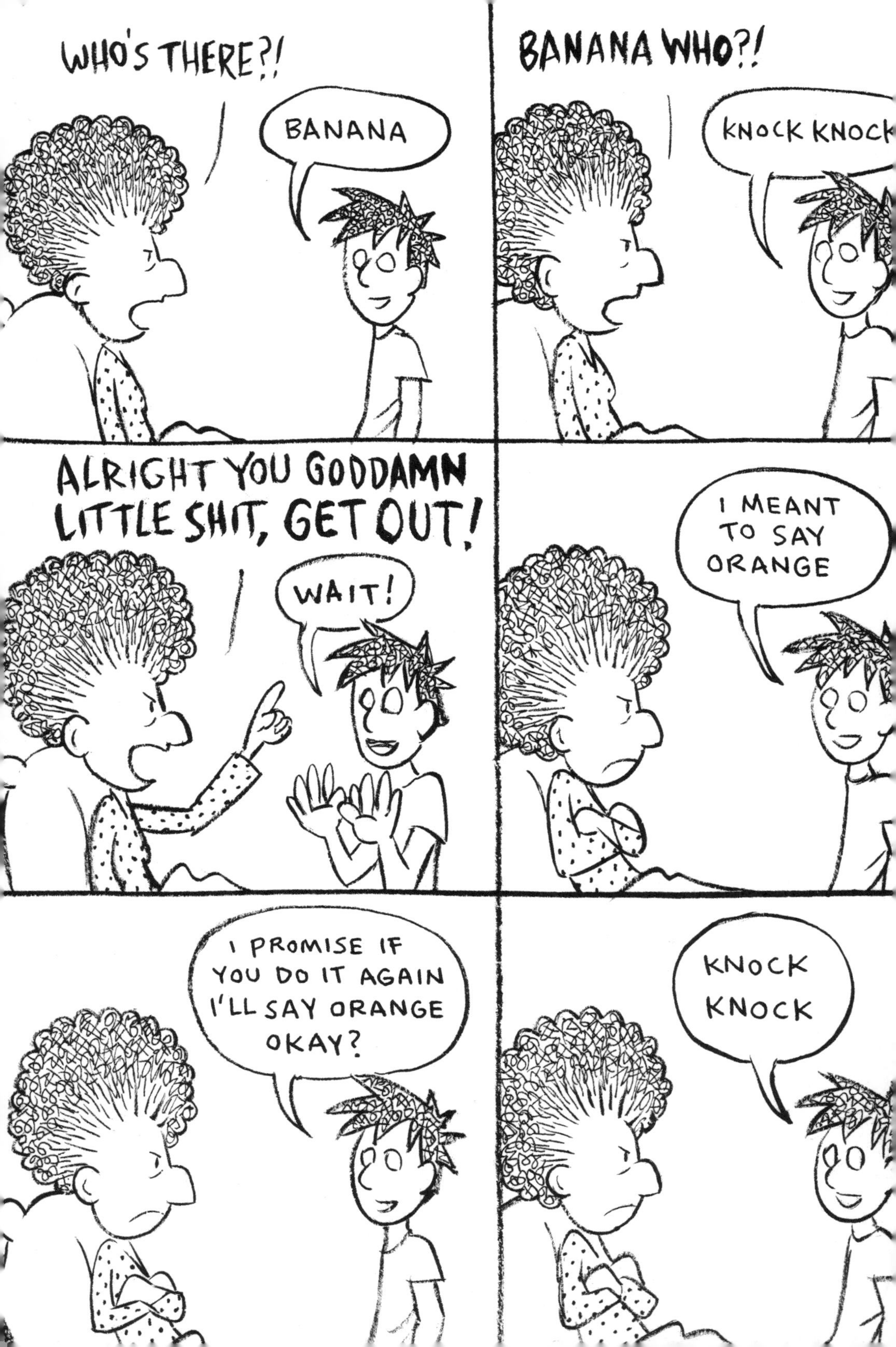
WHO'S THERE?!
BANANA
BANANA WHO?!
KNOCK KNOCK
ALRIGHT YOU GODDAMN LITTLE SHIT, GET OUT!
WAIT!
I MEANT TO SAY ORANGE
I PROMISE IF YOU DO IT AGAIN I'LL SAY ORANGE OKAY?
KNOCK KNOCK

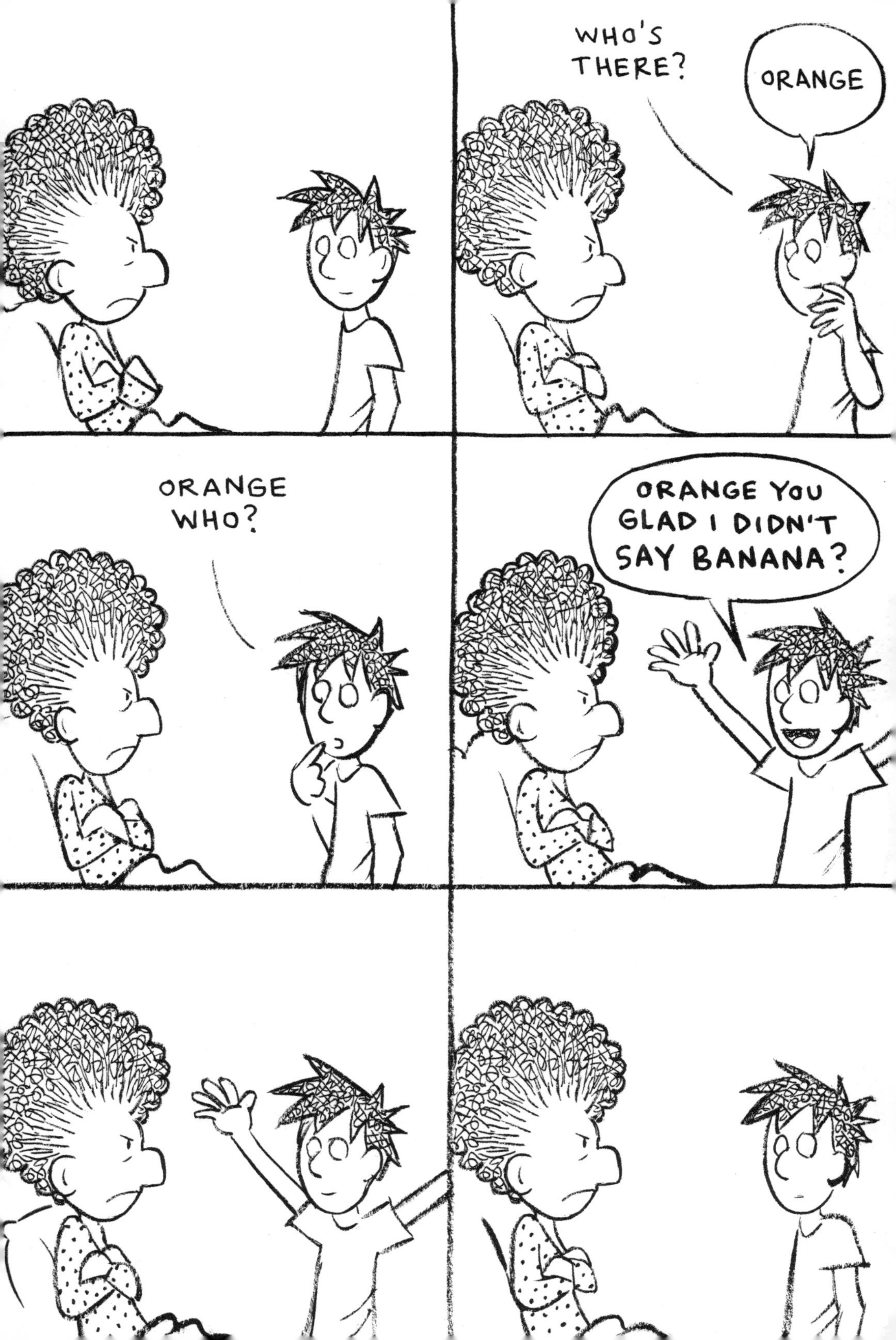
WHO'S THERE?
ORANGE
ORANGE WHO?
ORANGE YOU GLAD I DIDN'T SAY BANANA?

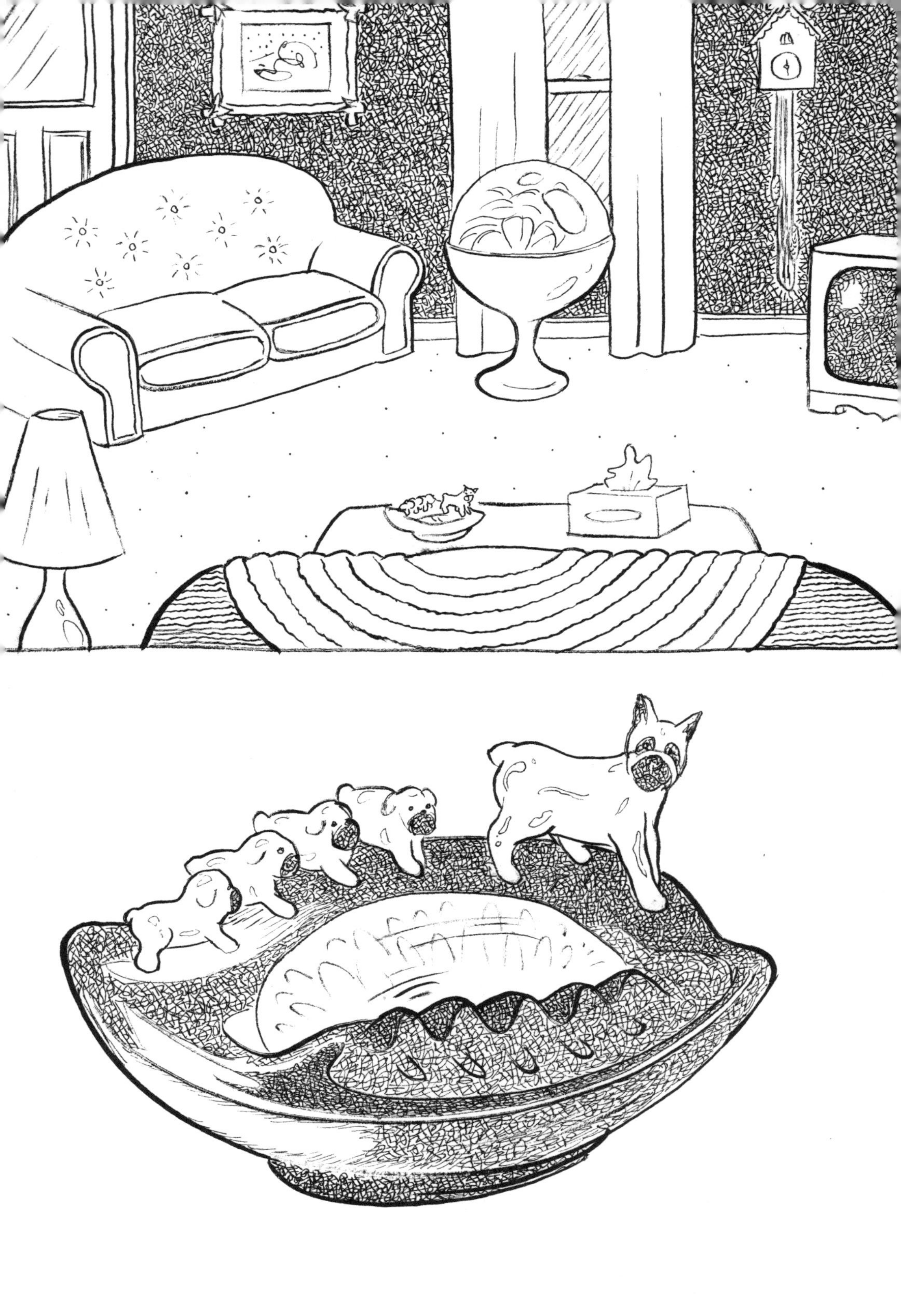

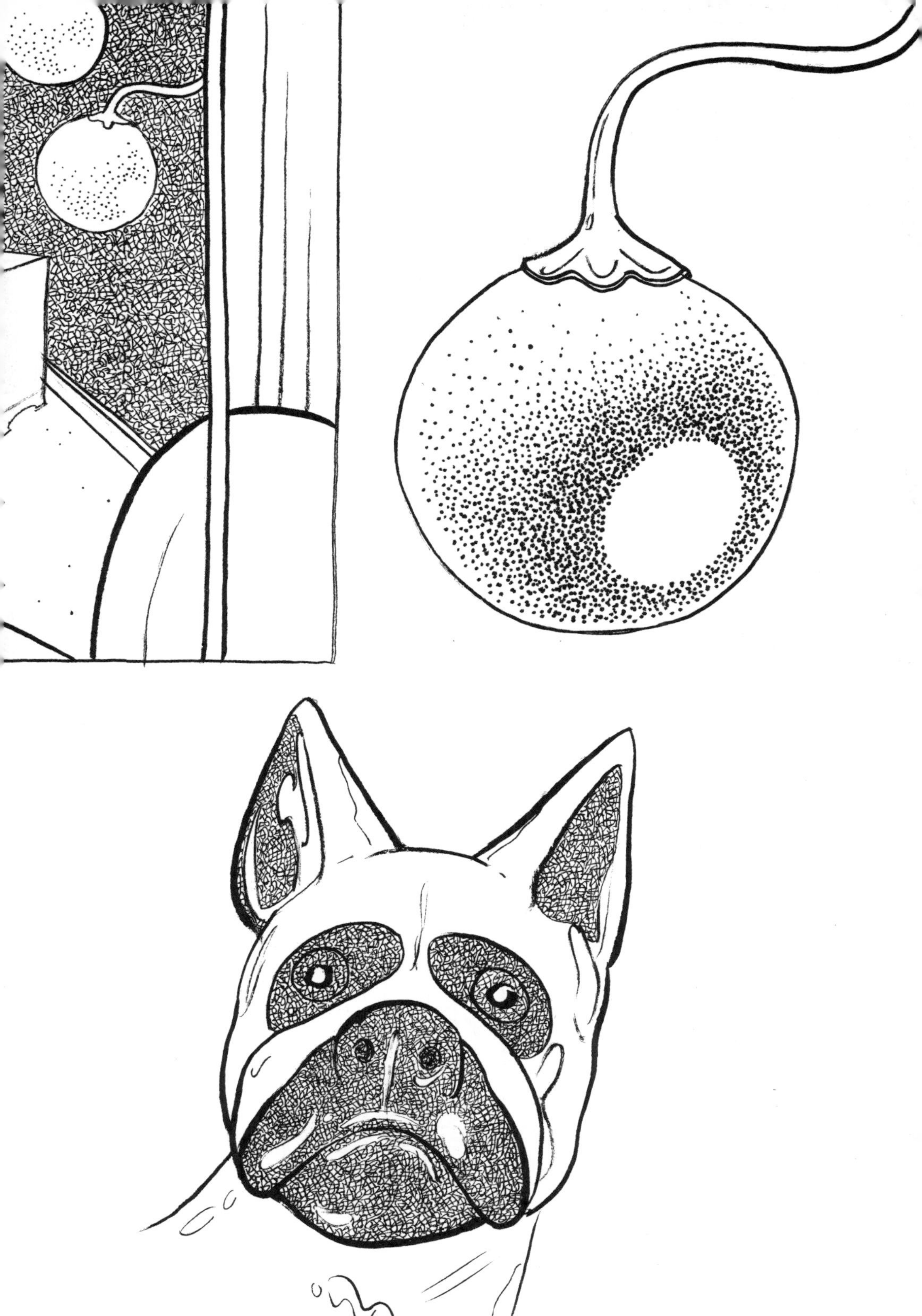

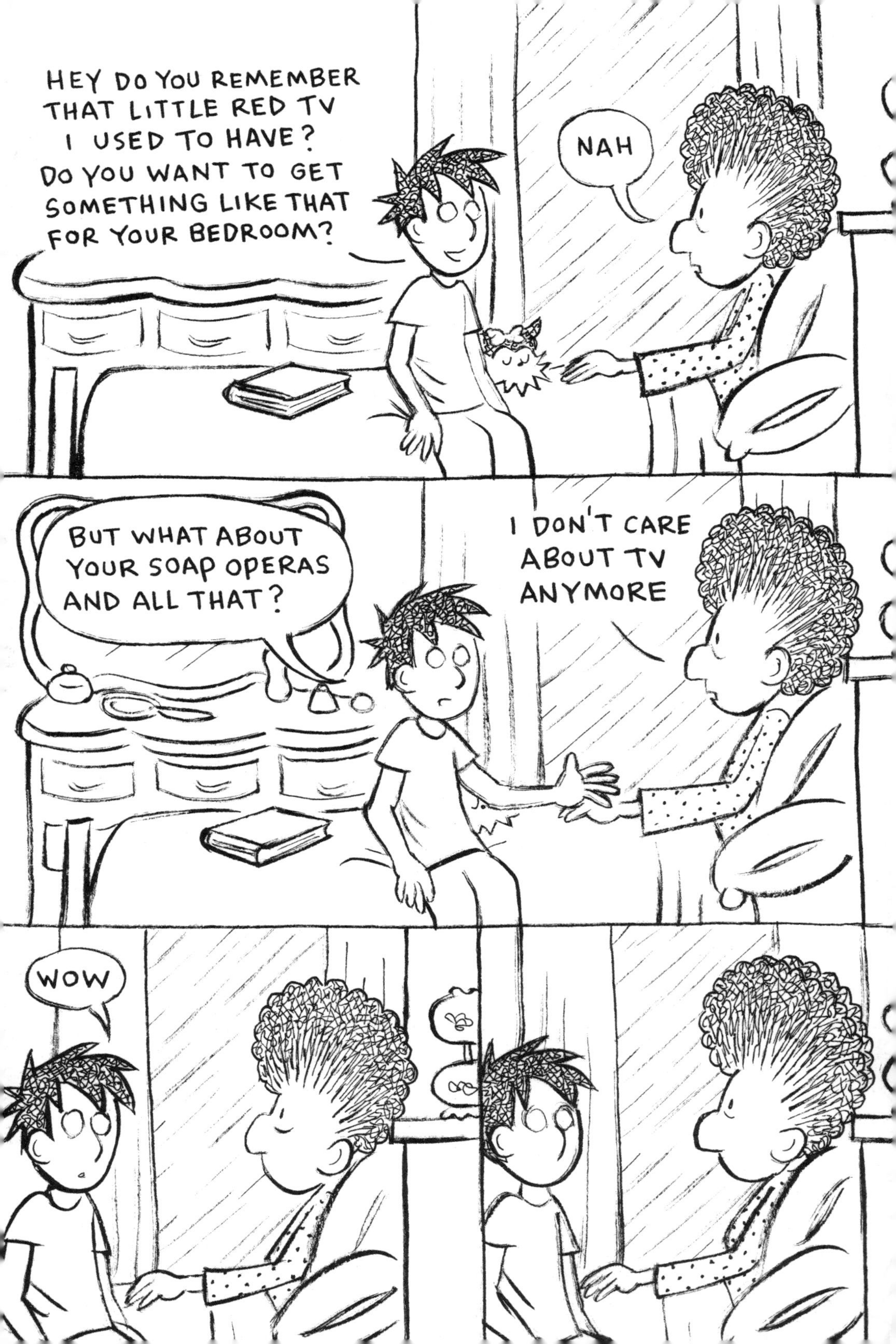
HEY DO YOU REMEMBER THAT LITTLE RED TV I USED TO HAVE? DO YOU WANT TO GET SOMETHING LIKE THAT FOR YOUR BEDROOM?
NAH
BUT WHAT ABOUT YOUR SOAP OPERAS AND ALL THAT?
I DON'T CARE ABOUT TV ANYMORE
WOW

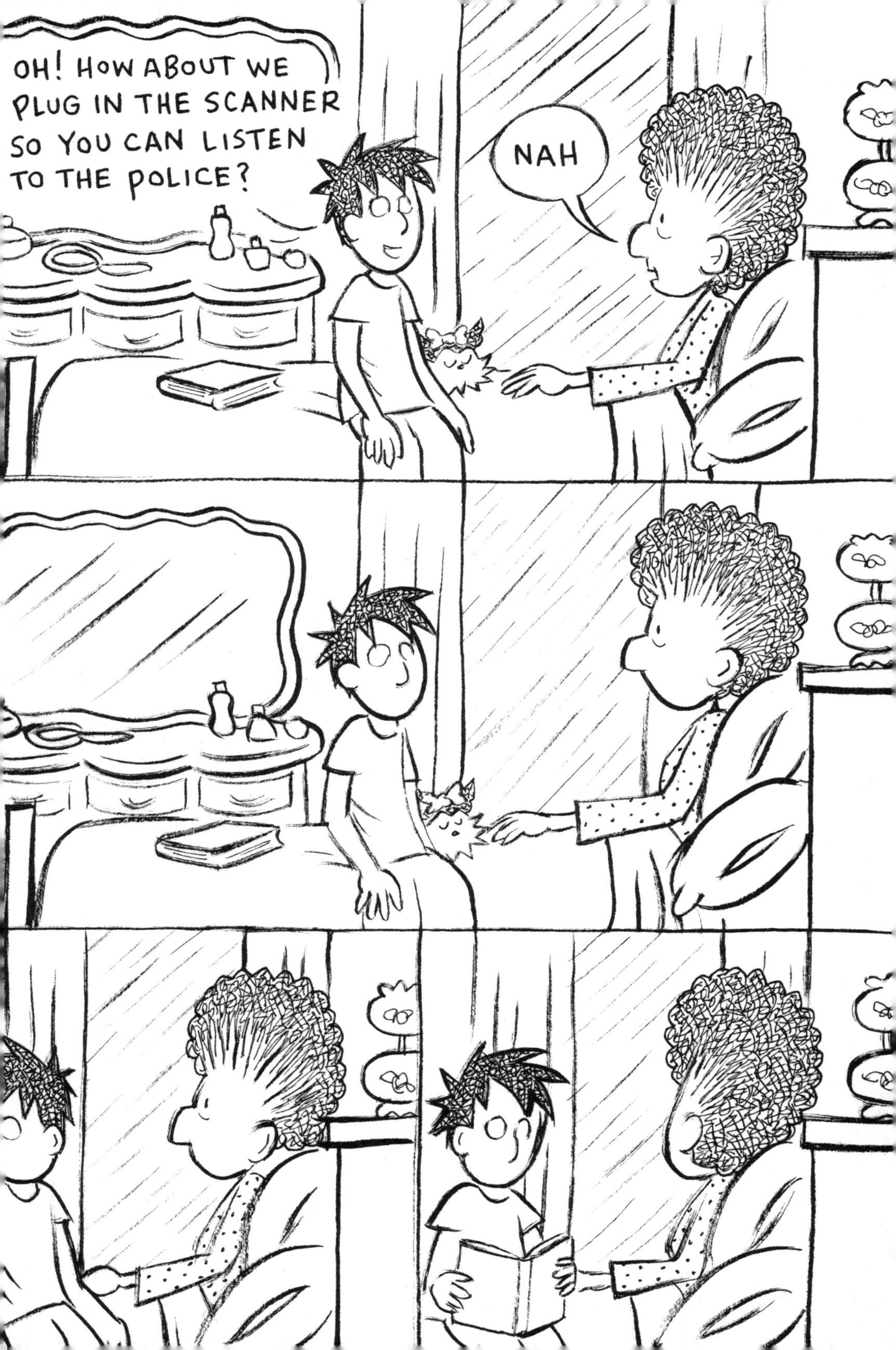
OH! HOW ABOUT WE PLUG IN THE SCANNER SO YOU CAN LISTEN TO THE POLICE?
NAH

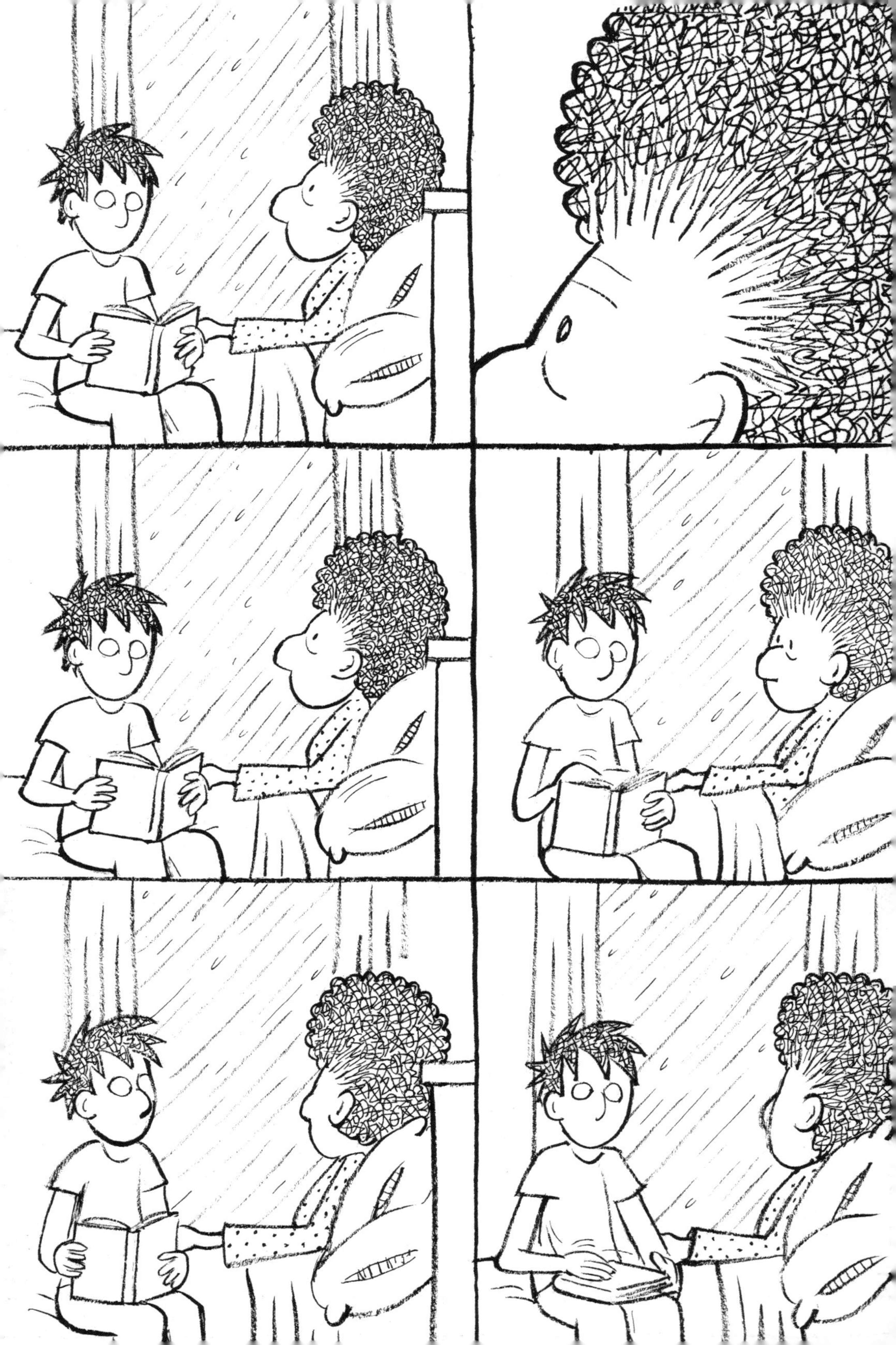

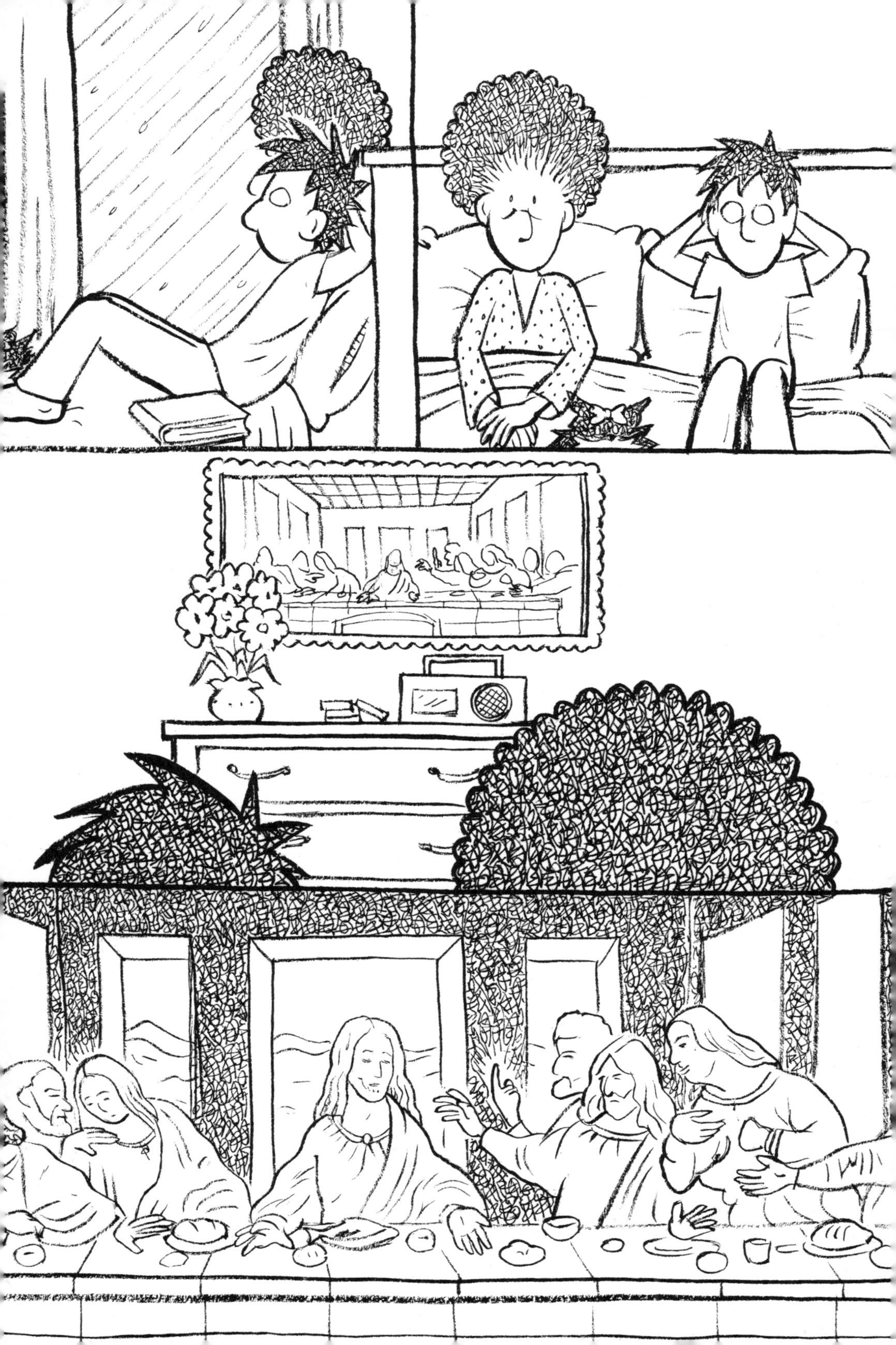

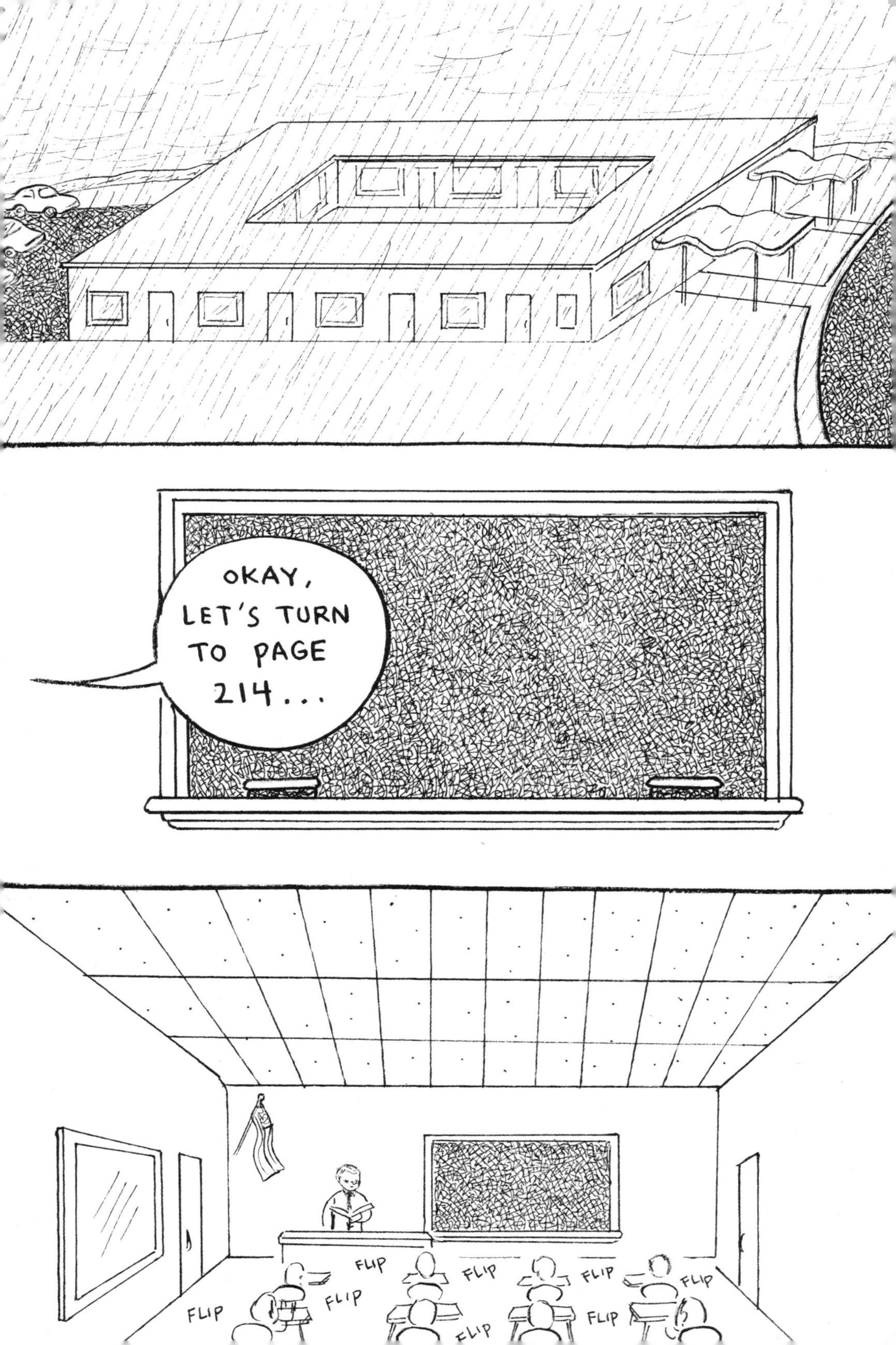

OKAY, LET'S TURN TO PAGE 214...
FLIP
FLIP
FLIP
FLIP
FLIP
FLIP
FLIP
FLIP

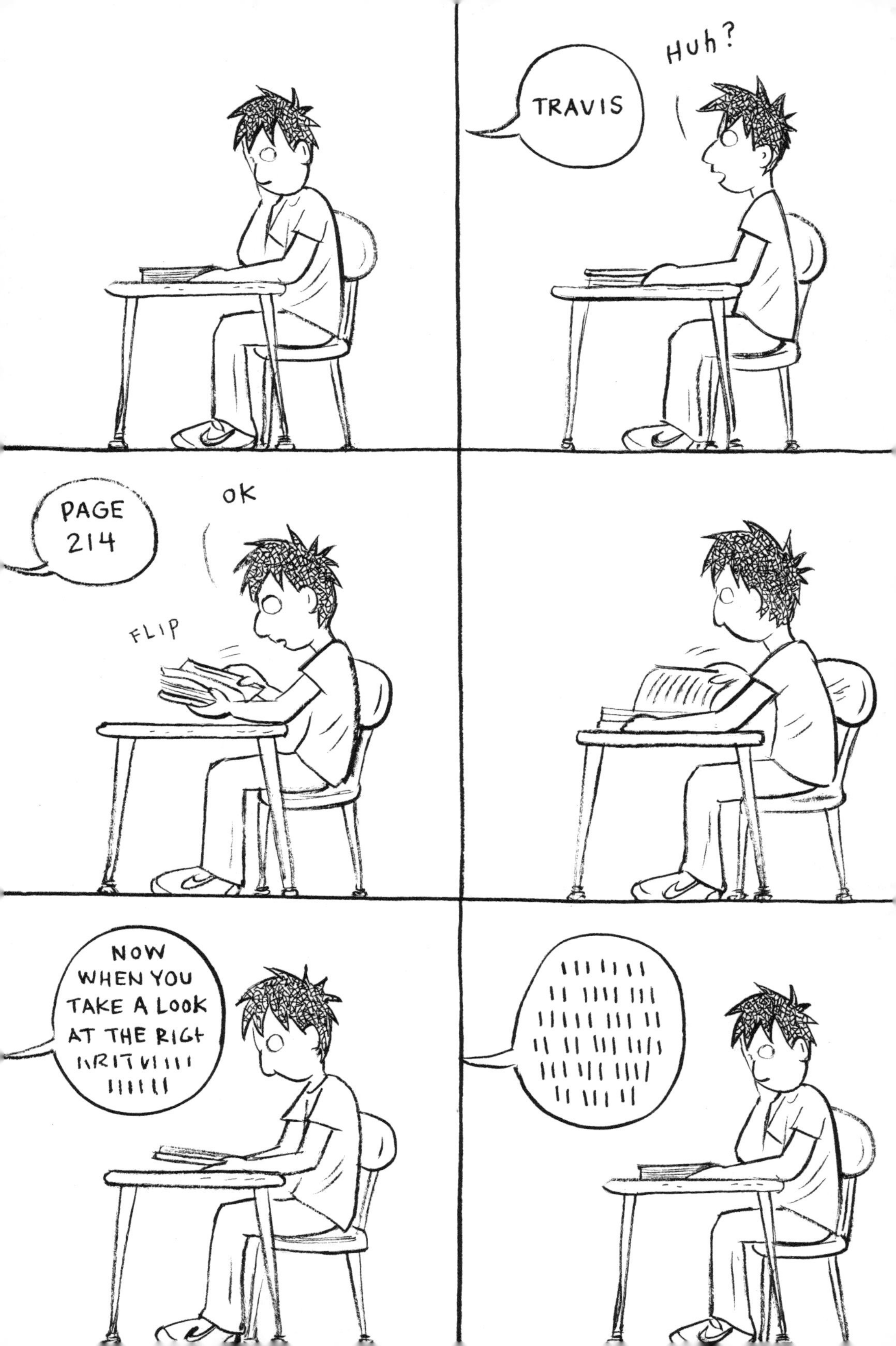
TRAVIS
Huh?
PAGE 214
OK
FLIP
NOW WHEN YOU TAKE A LOOK AT THE RIG

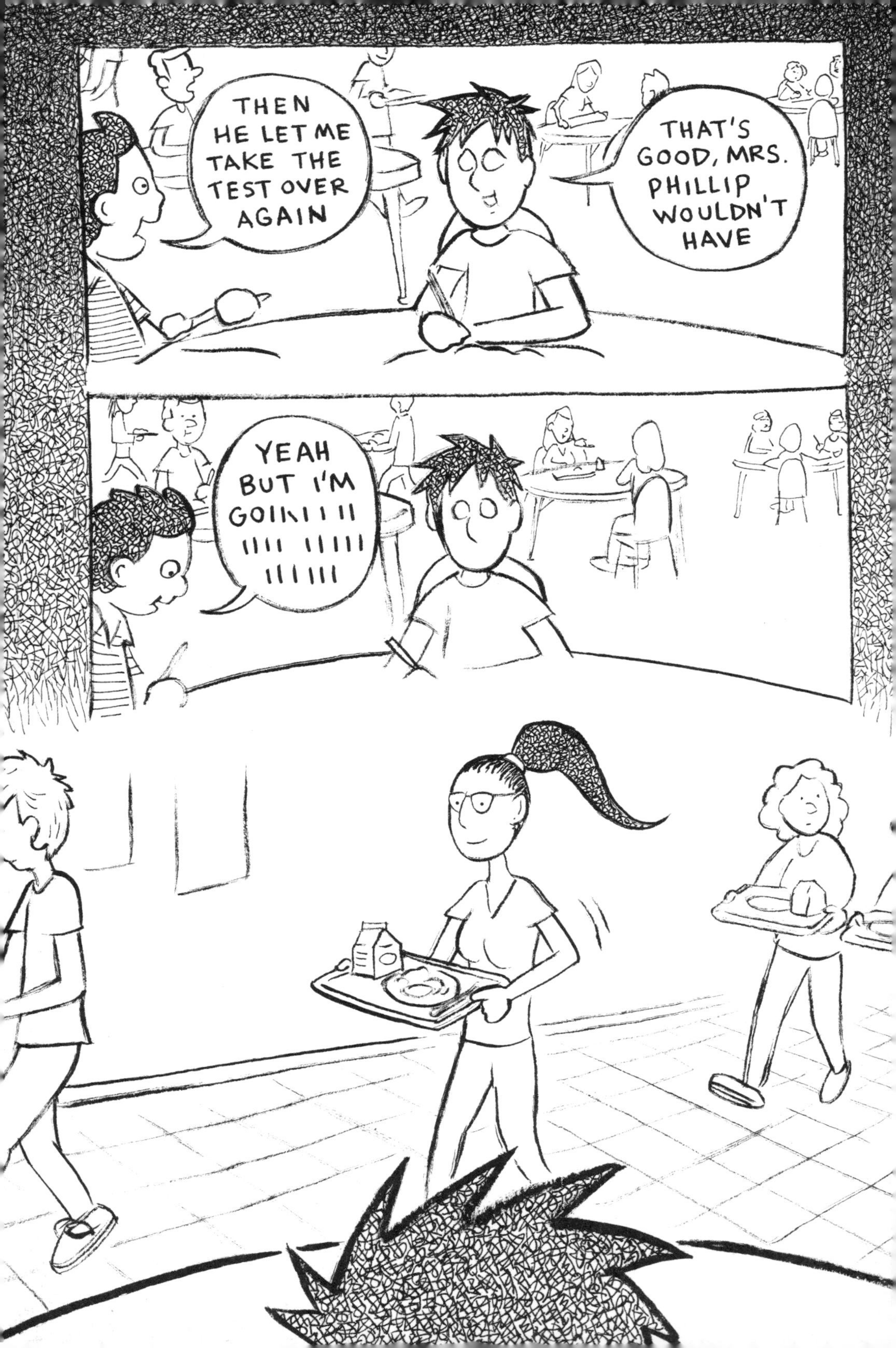
THEN HE LET ME TAKE THE TEST OVER AGAIN
THAT'S GOOD, MRS. PHILLIP WOULDN'T HAVE
YEAH BUT I'M GOI

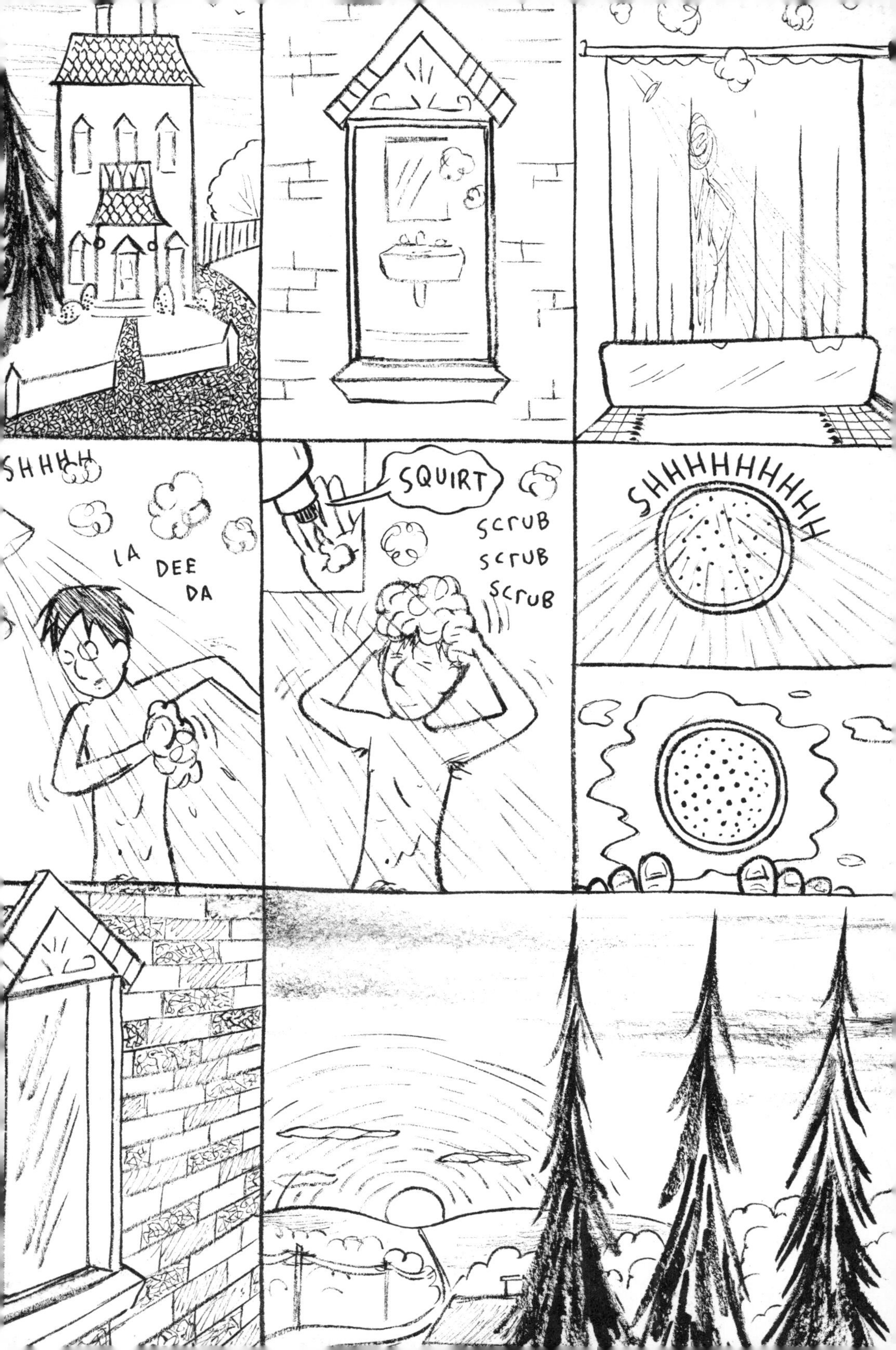
SHHHH
LA
DEE
DA
SQUIRT
SCRUB
SCRUB
SCRUB
SHHHHHHHHH

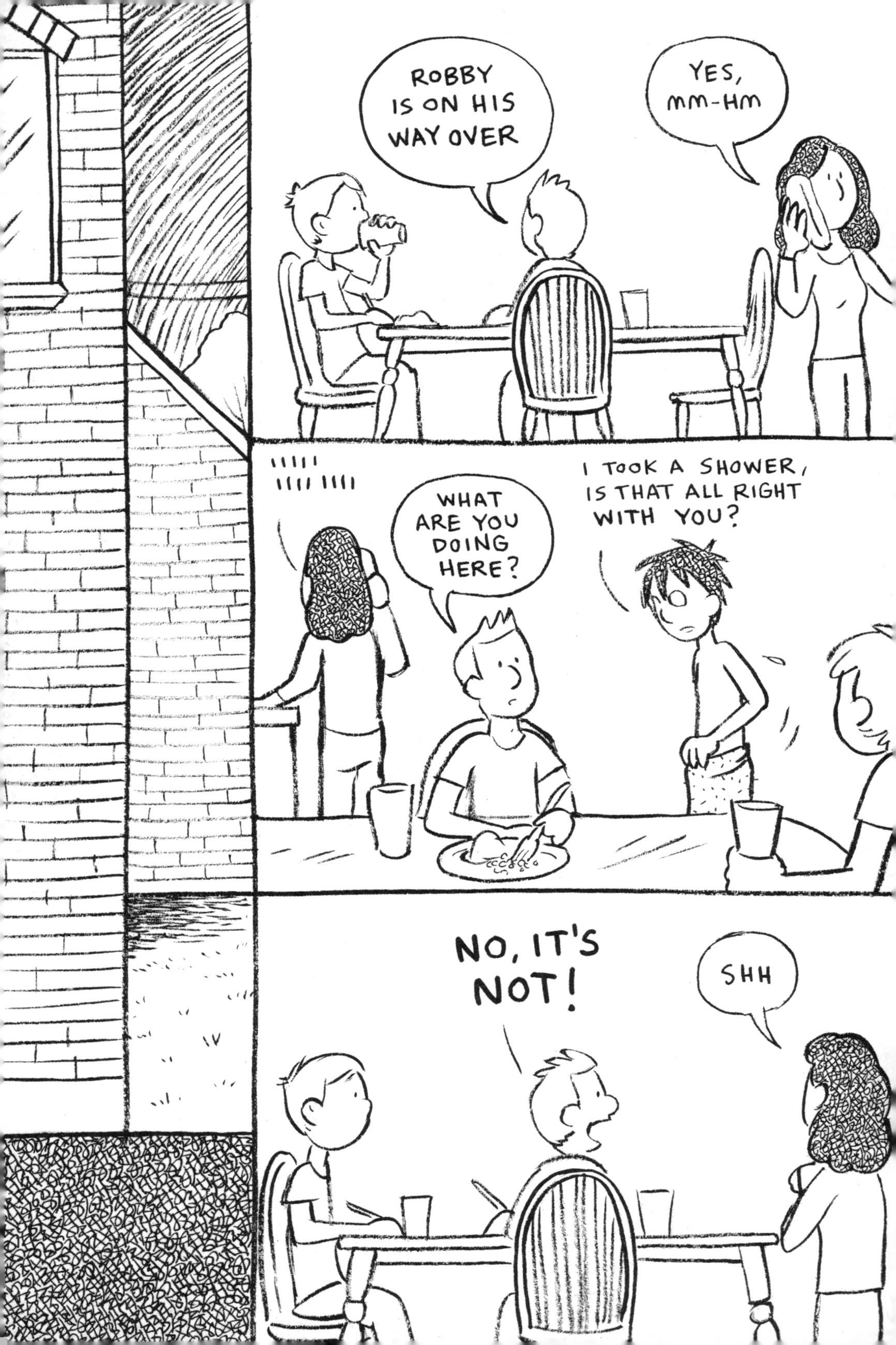
ROBBY IS ON HIS WAY OVER
YES, MM-HM
WHAT ARE YOU DOING HERE?
I TOOK A SHOWER, IS THAT ALL RIGHT WITH YOU?
NO, IT'S NOT!
SHH

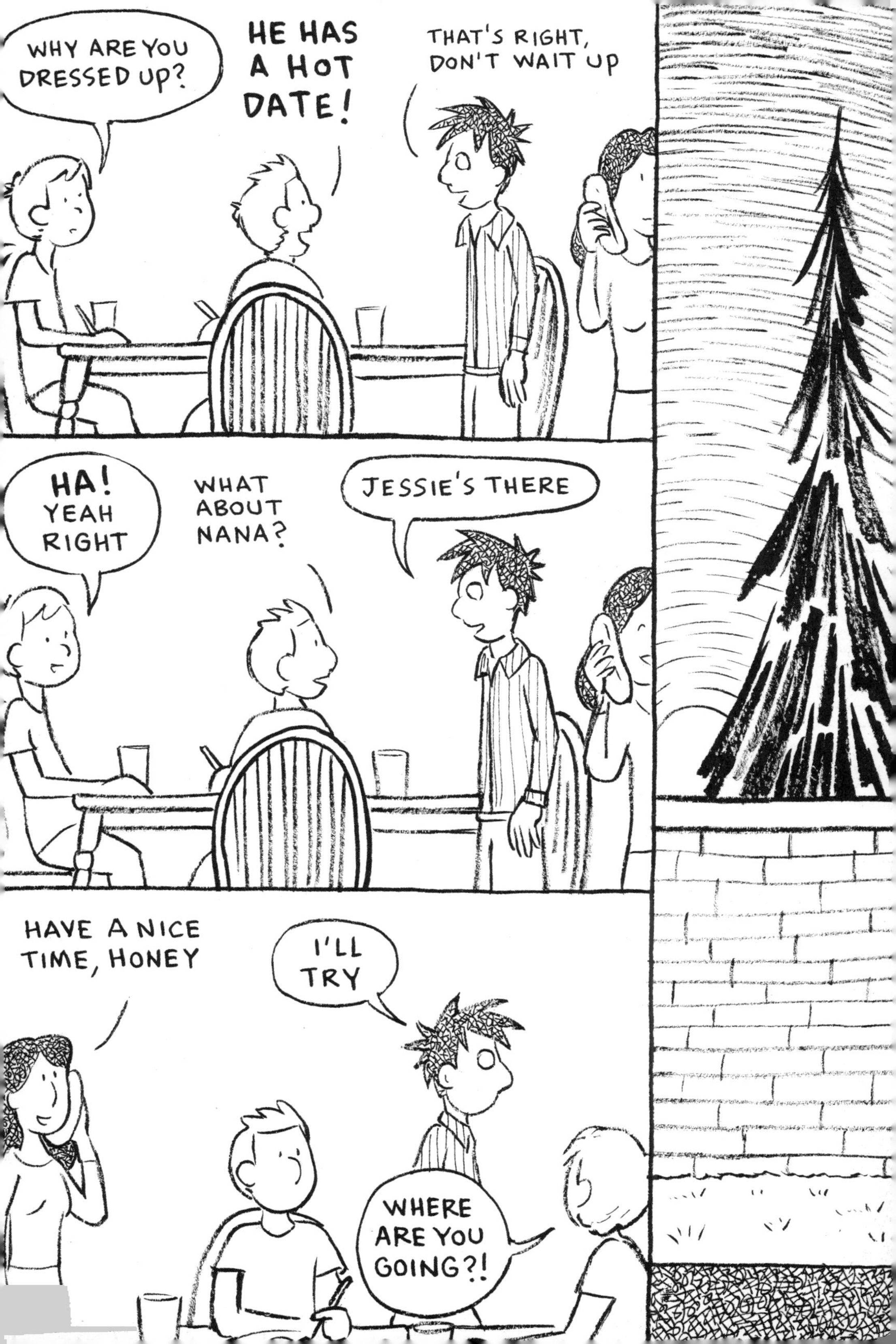
WHY ARE YOU DRESSED UP?
HE HAS A HOT DATE!
THAT'S RIGHT, DON'T WAIT UP
HA! YEAH RIGHT
WHAT ABOUT NANA?
JESSIE'S THERE
HAVE A NICE TIME, HONEY
I'LL TRY
WHERE ARE YOU GOING?!

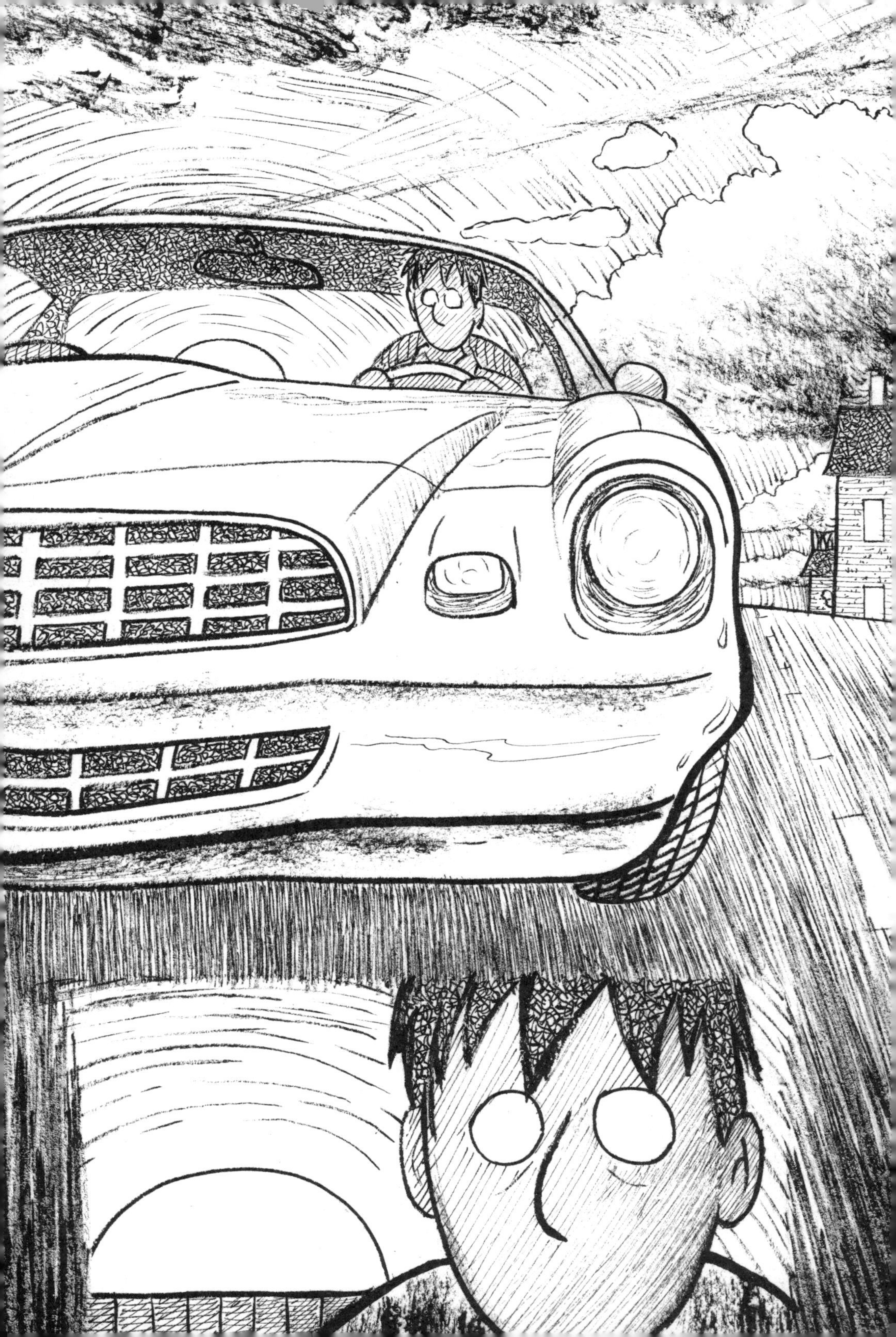

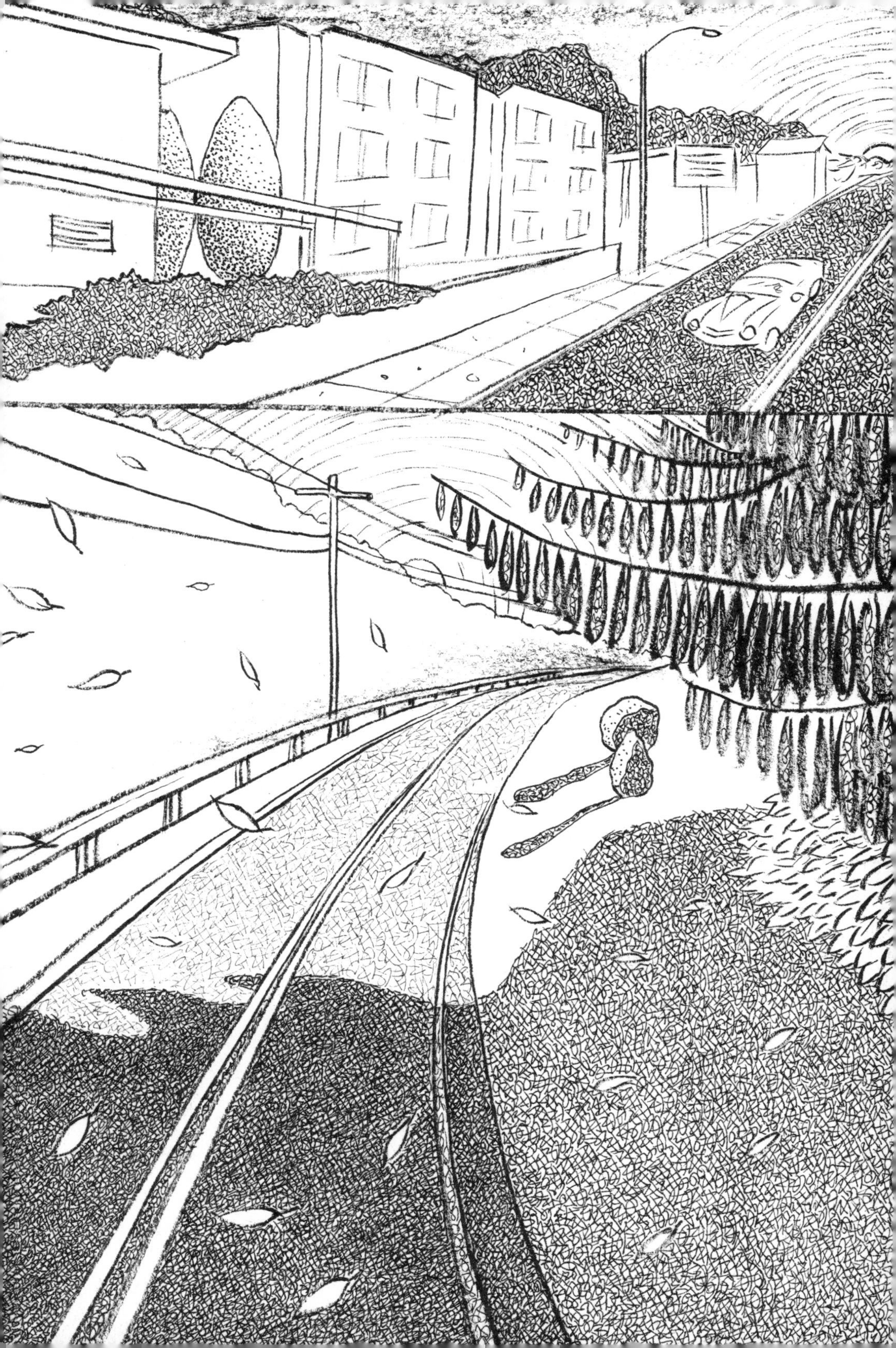

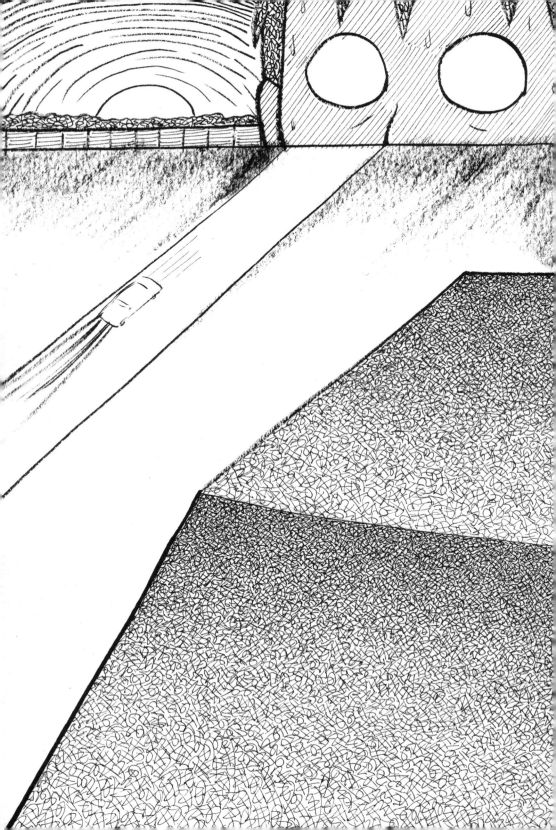

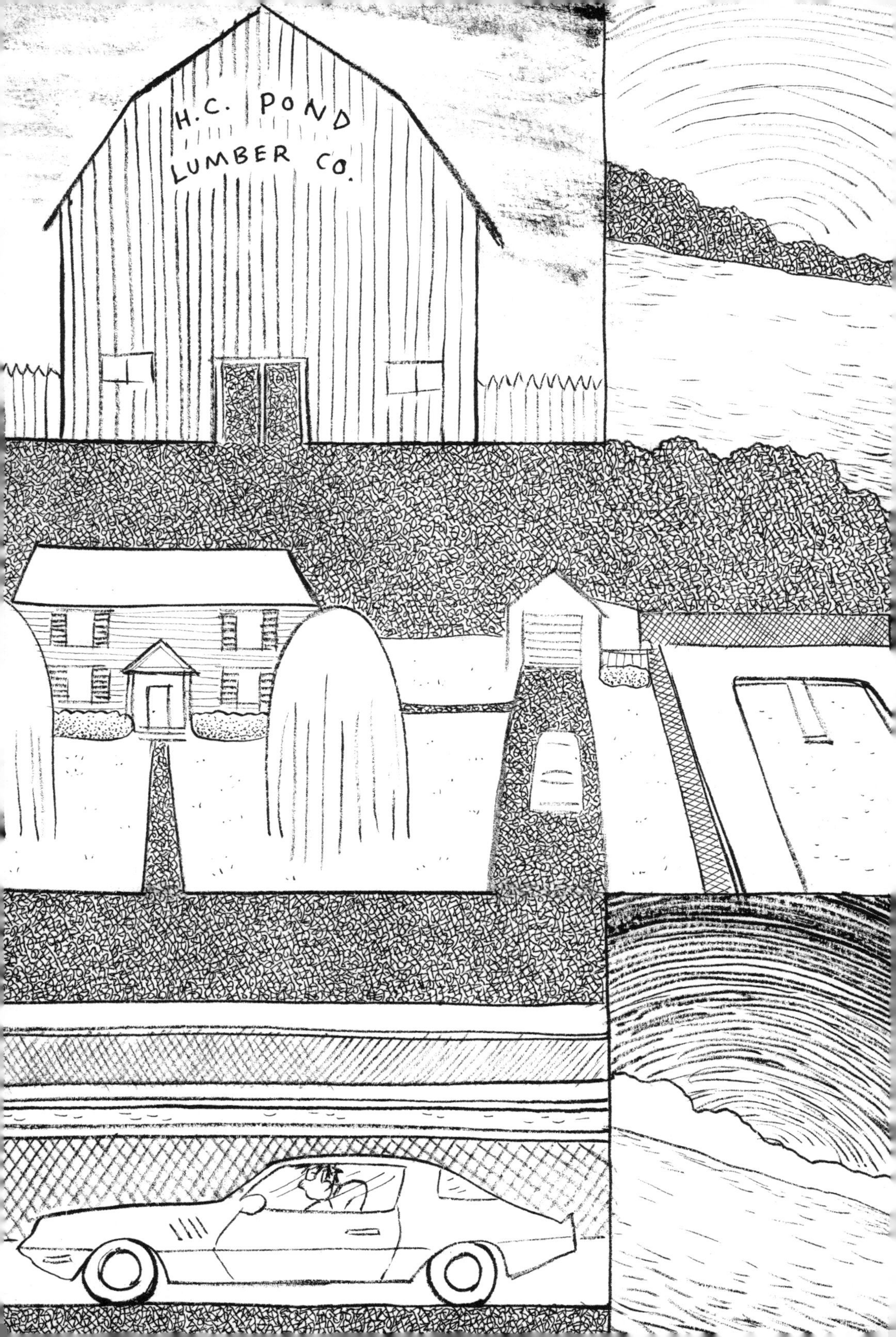
H.C. POND
LUMBER CO.

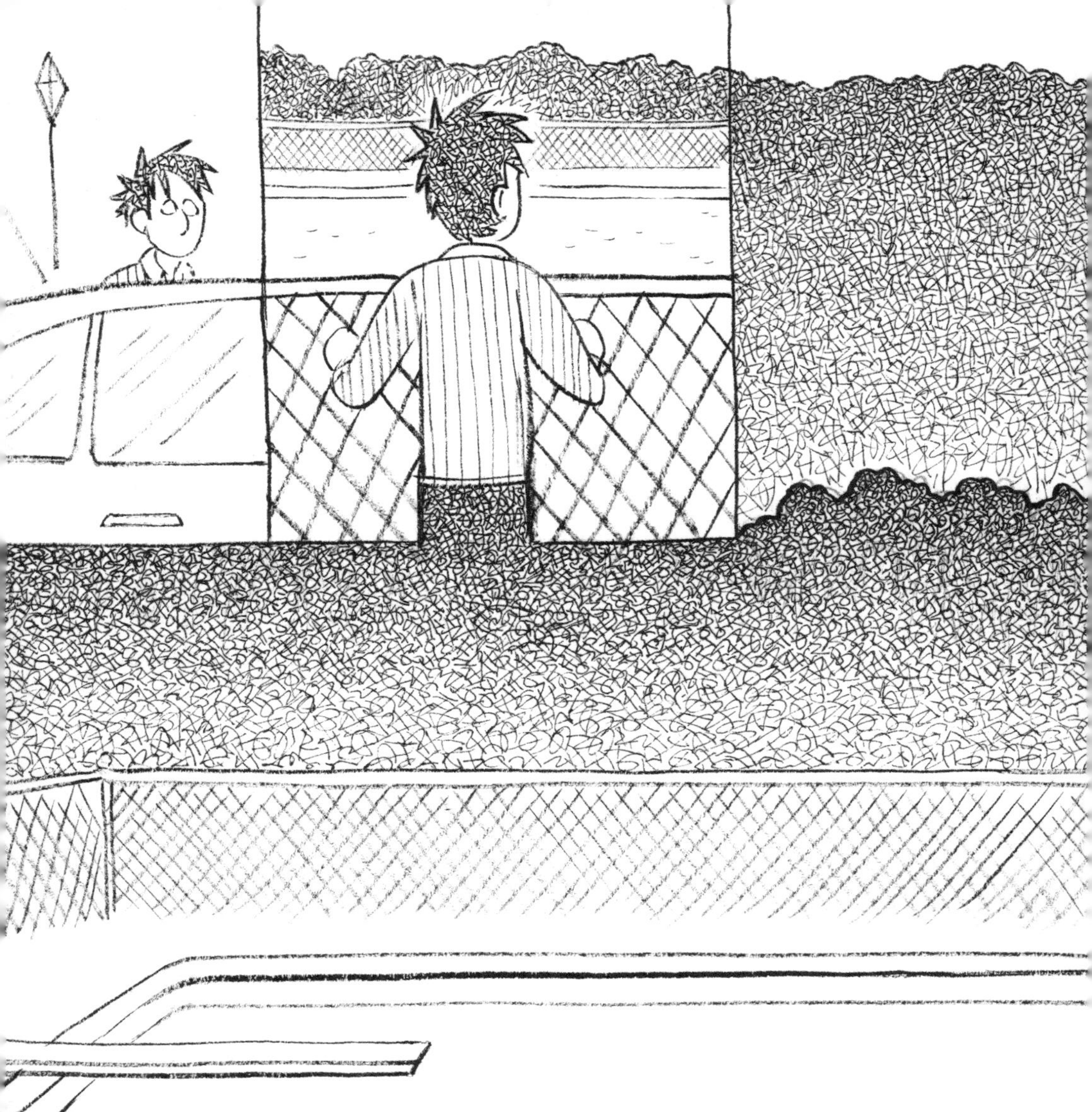

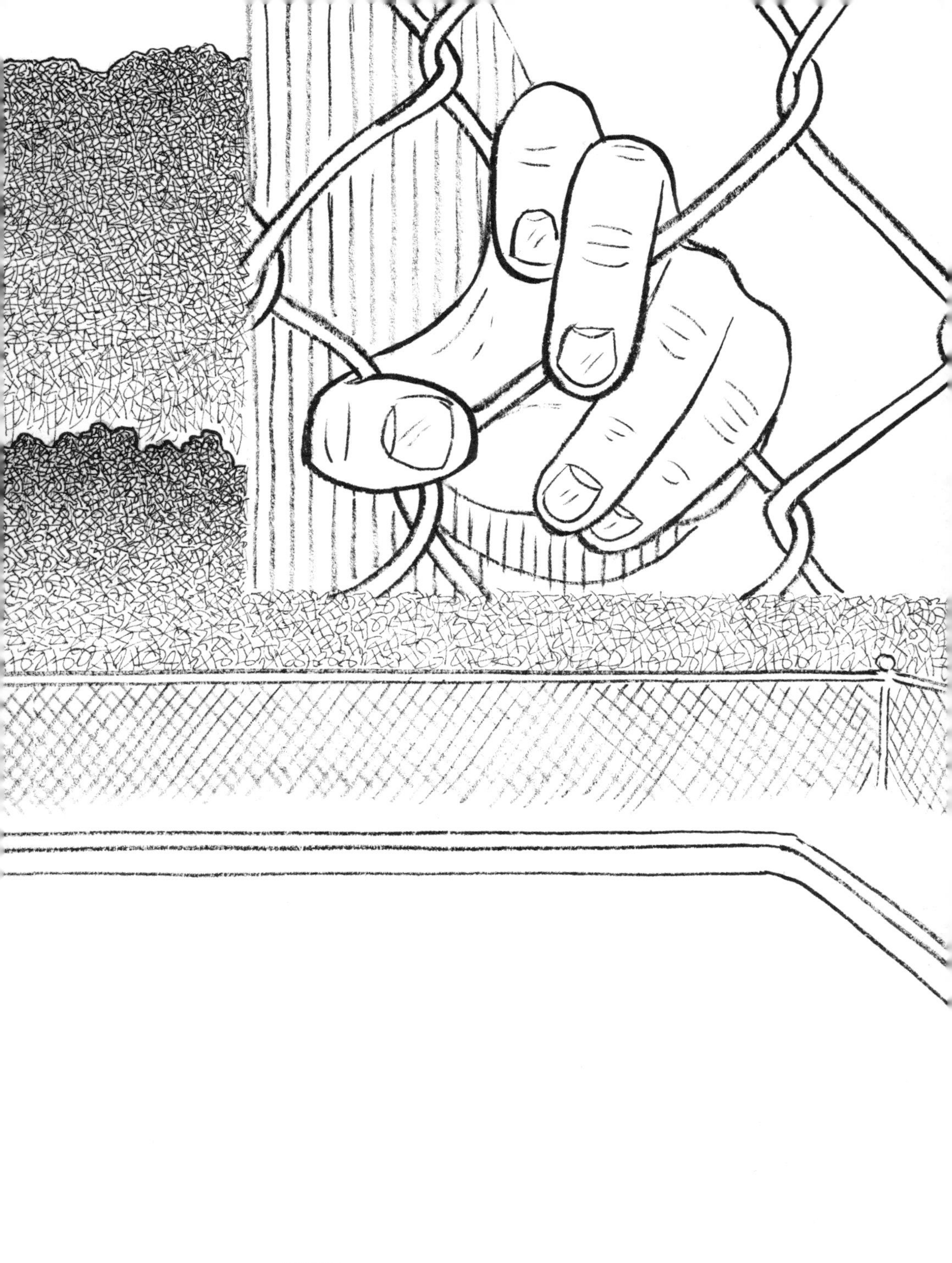

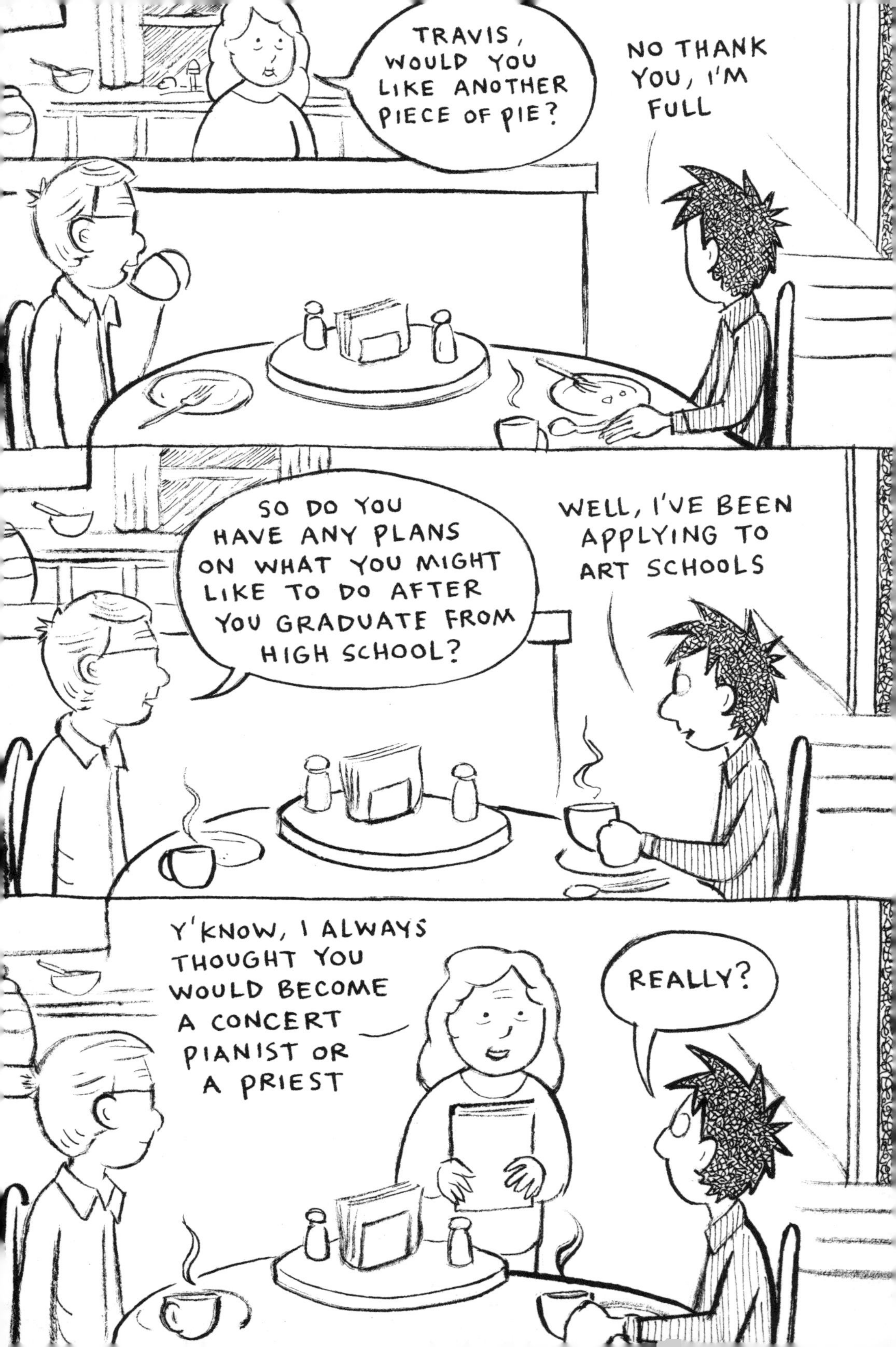
TRAVIS, WOULD YOU LIKE ANOTHER PIECE OF PIE?
NO THANK YOU, I'M FULL
SO DO YOU HAVE ANY PLANS ON WHAT YOU MIGHT LIKE TO DO AFTER YOU GRADUATE FROM HIGH SCHOOL?
WELL, I'VE BEEN APPLYING TO ART SCHOOLS
Y'KNOW, I ALWAYS THOUGHT YOU WOULD BECOME A CONCERT PIANIST OR A PRIEST
REALLY?

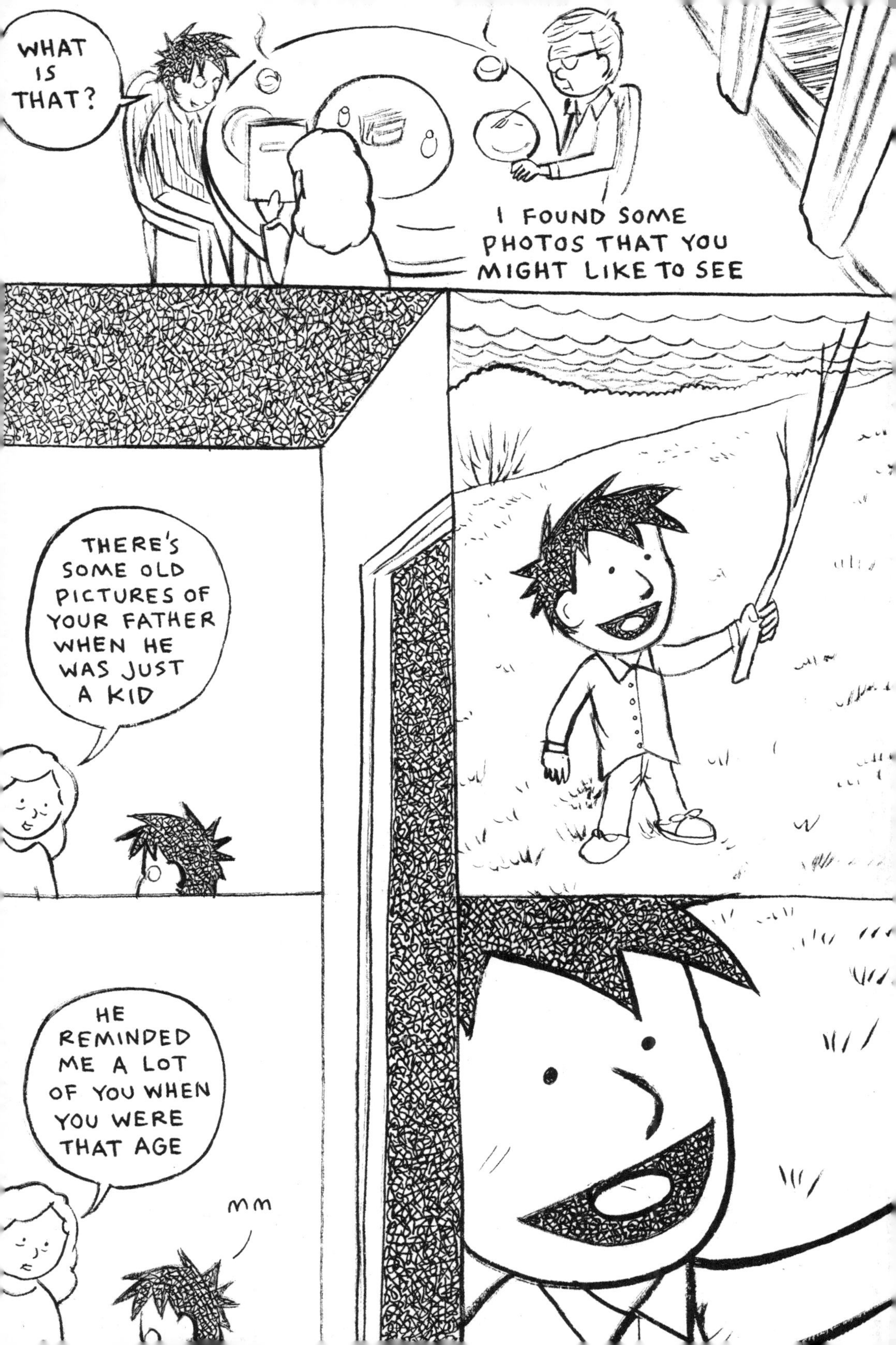
WHAT IS THAT?
I FOUND SOME PHOTOS THAT YOU MIGHT LIKE TO SEE
THERE'S SOME OLD PICTURES OF YOUR FATHER WHEN HE WAS JUST A KID
HE REMINDED ME A LOT OF YOU WHEN YOU WERE THAT AGE
MM

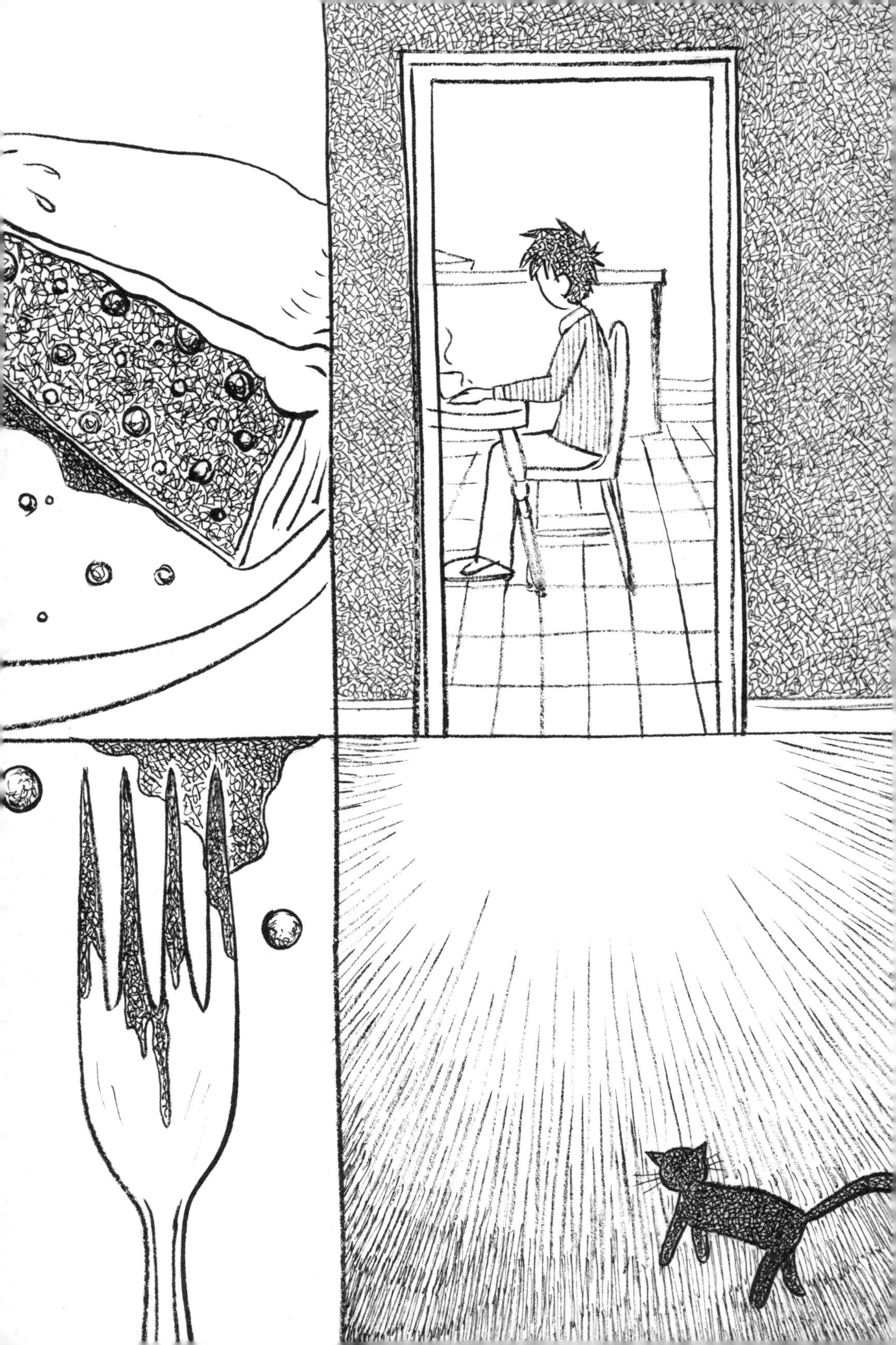

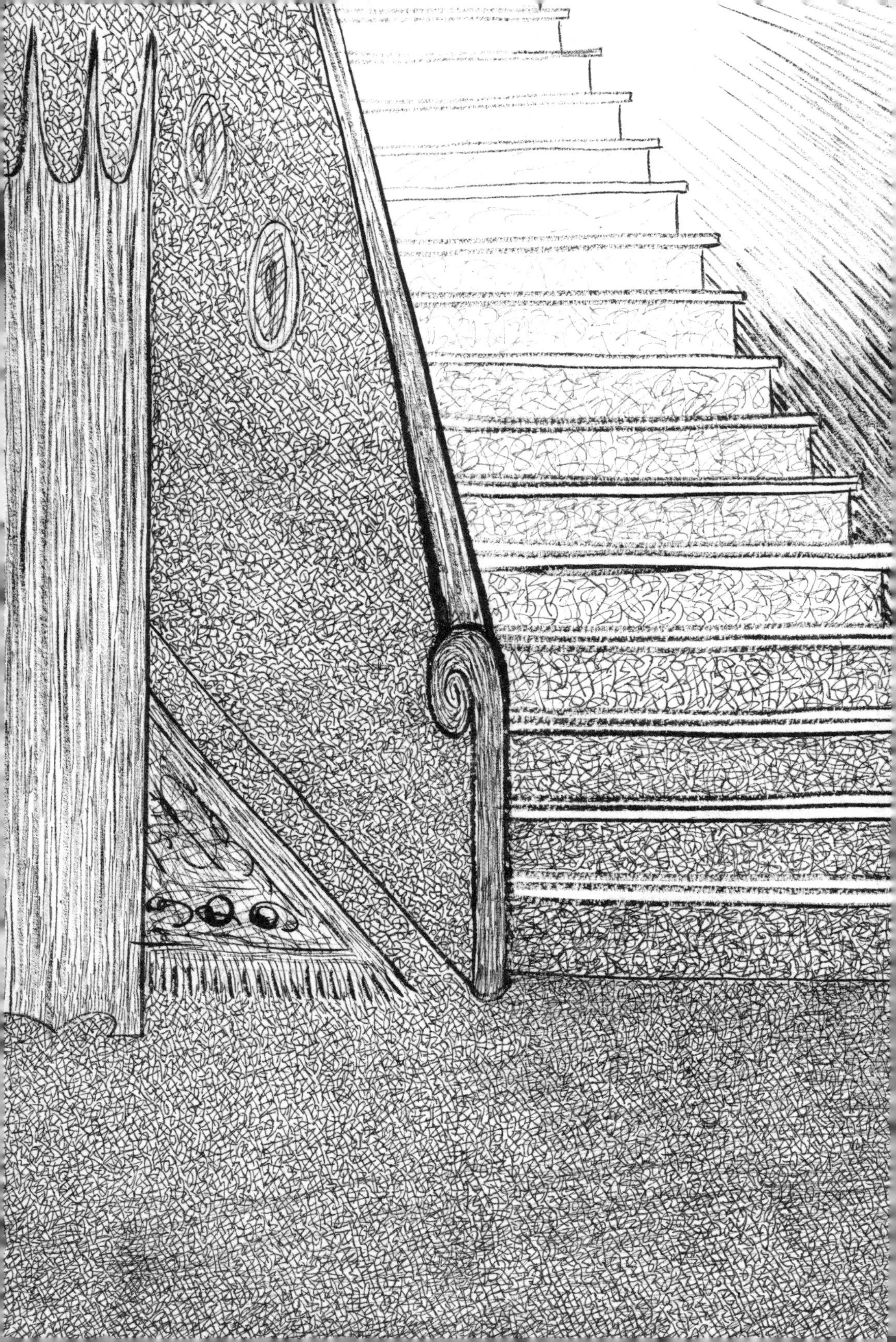

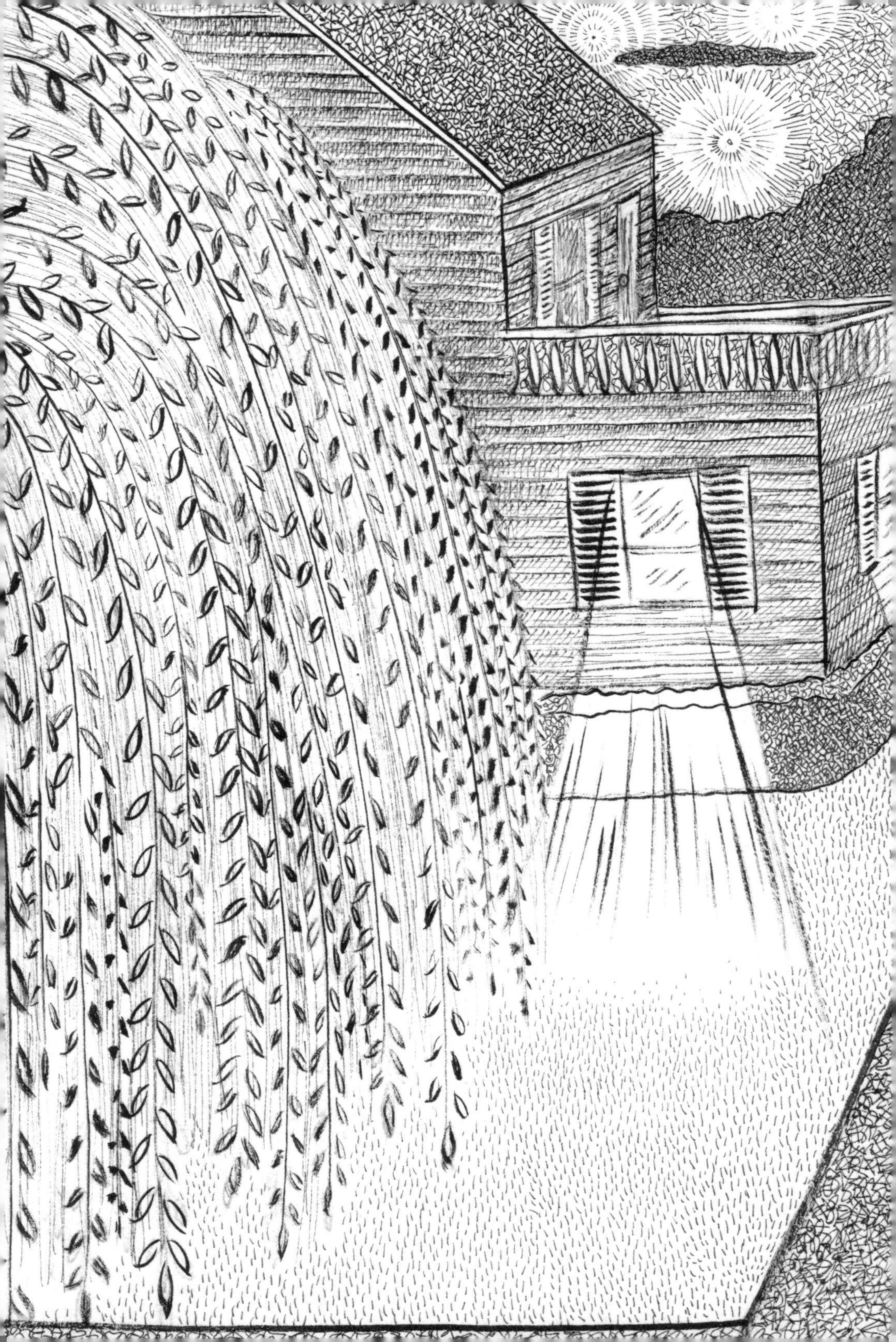

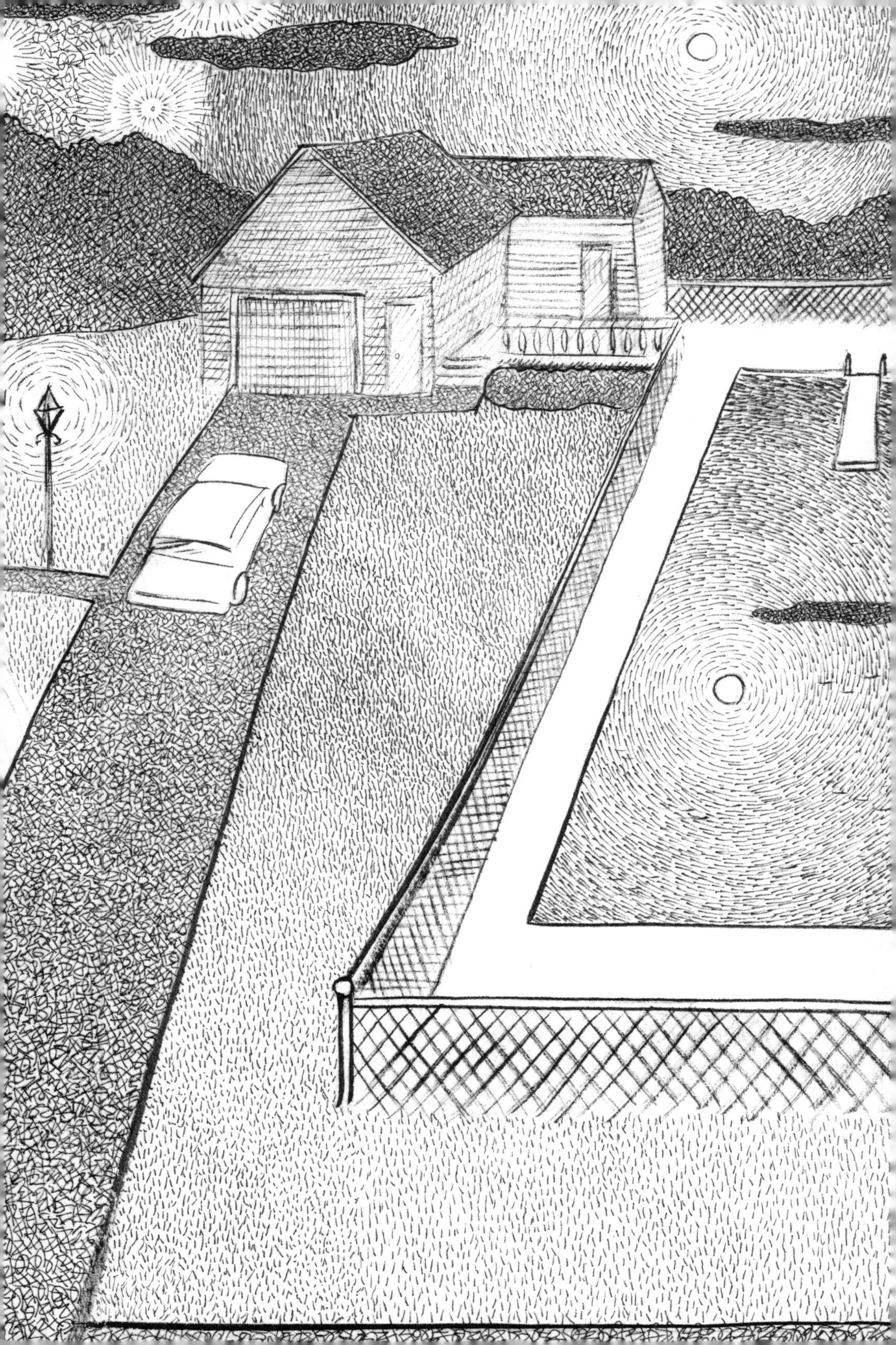

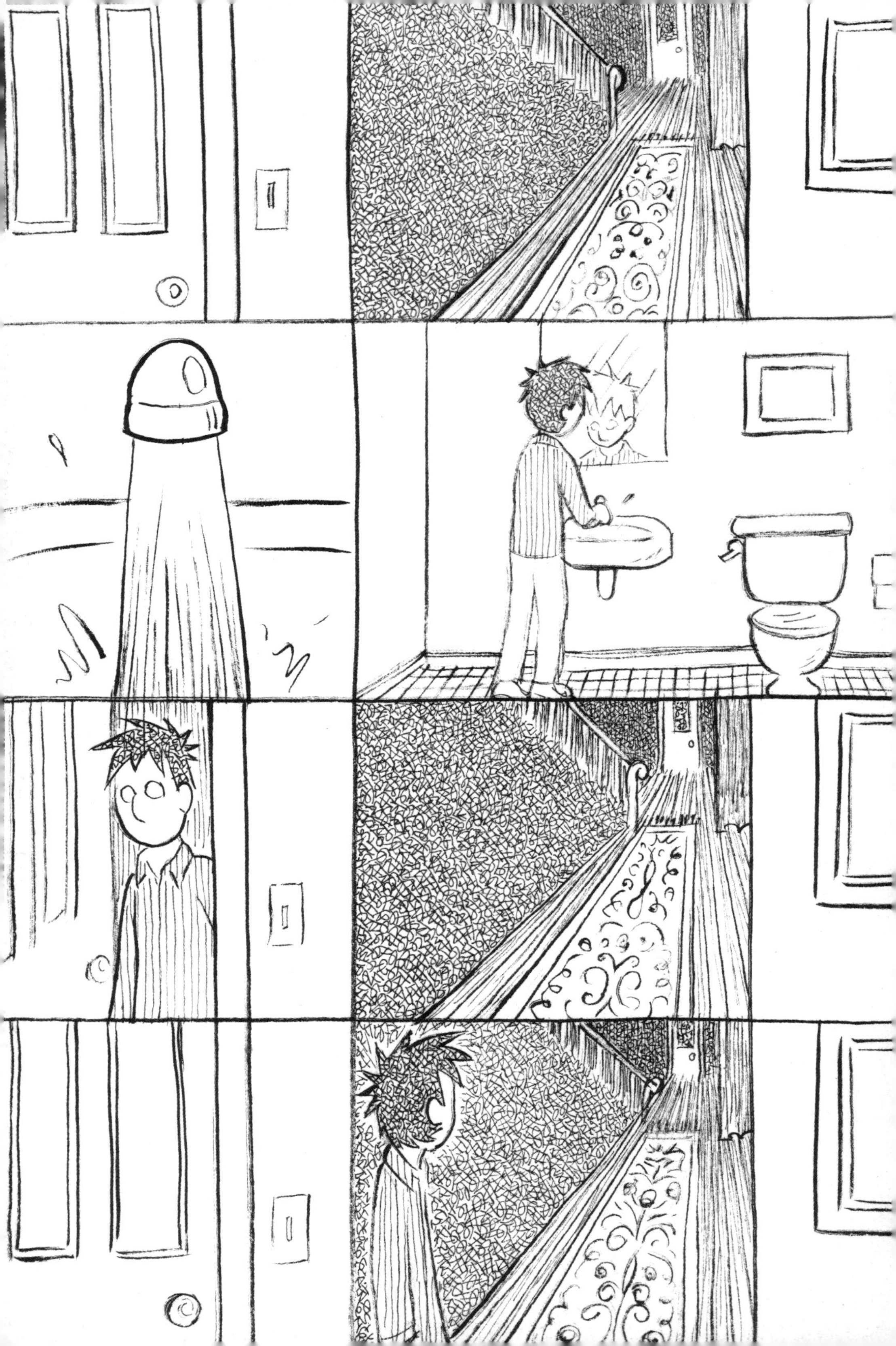

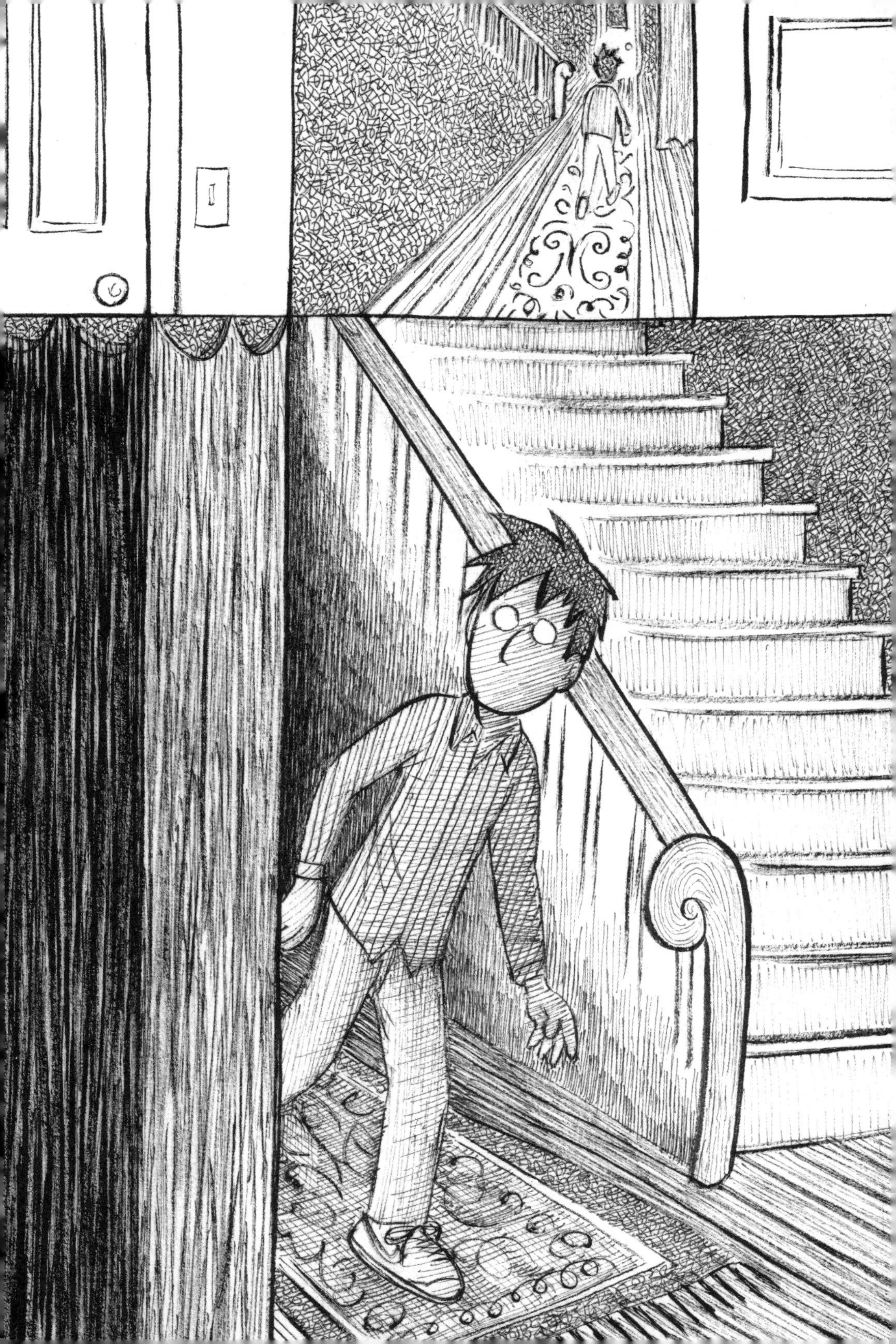

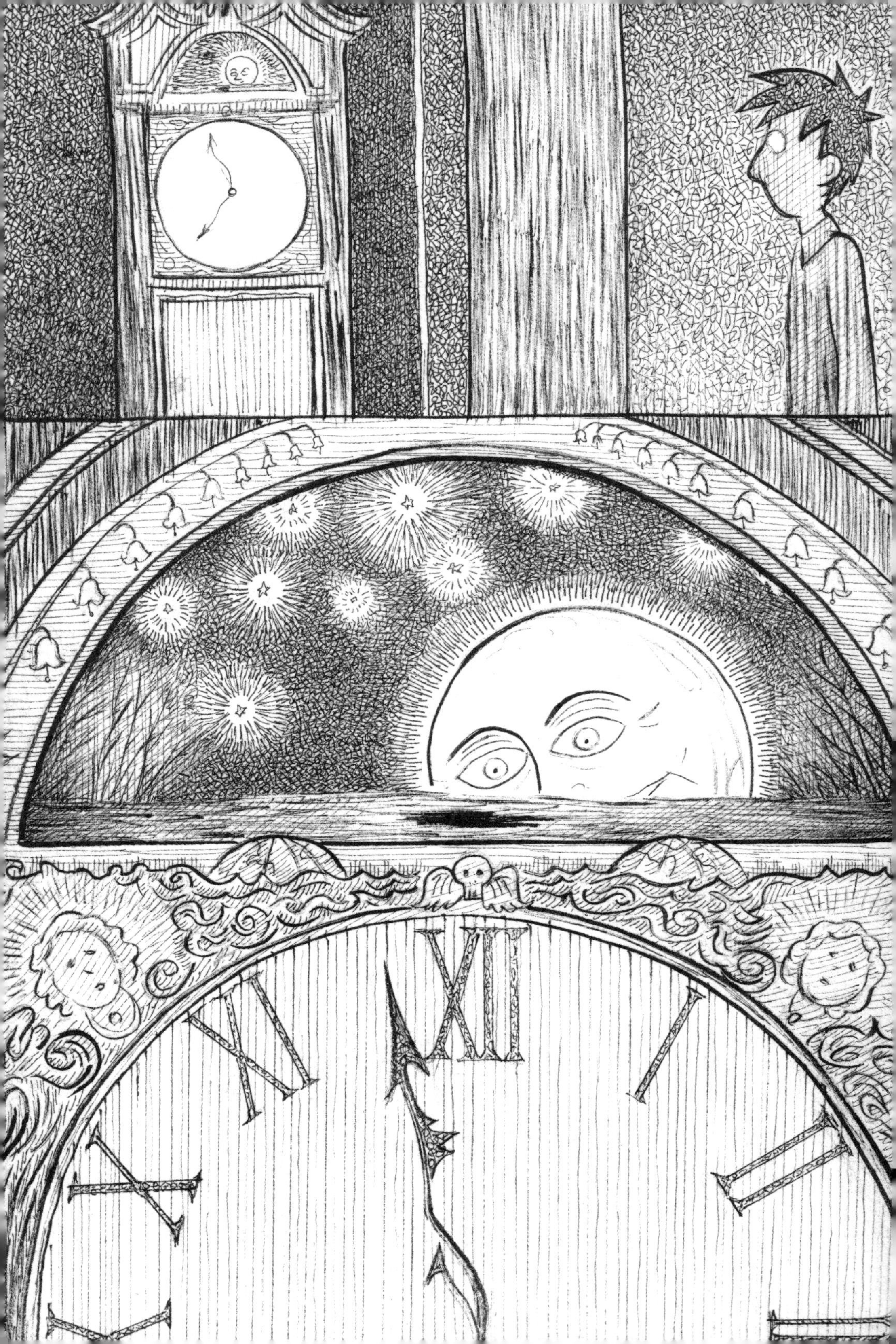

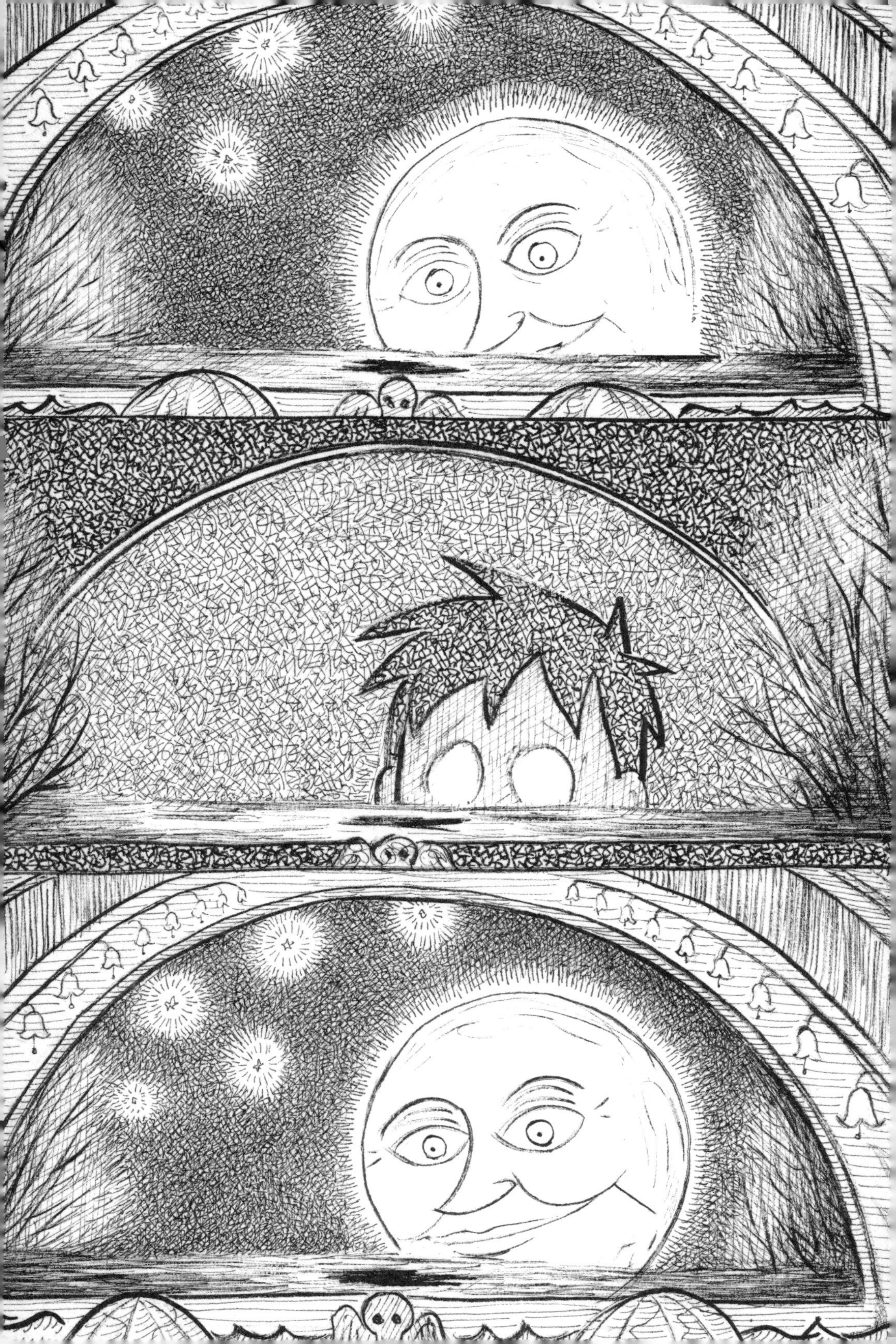

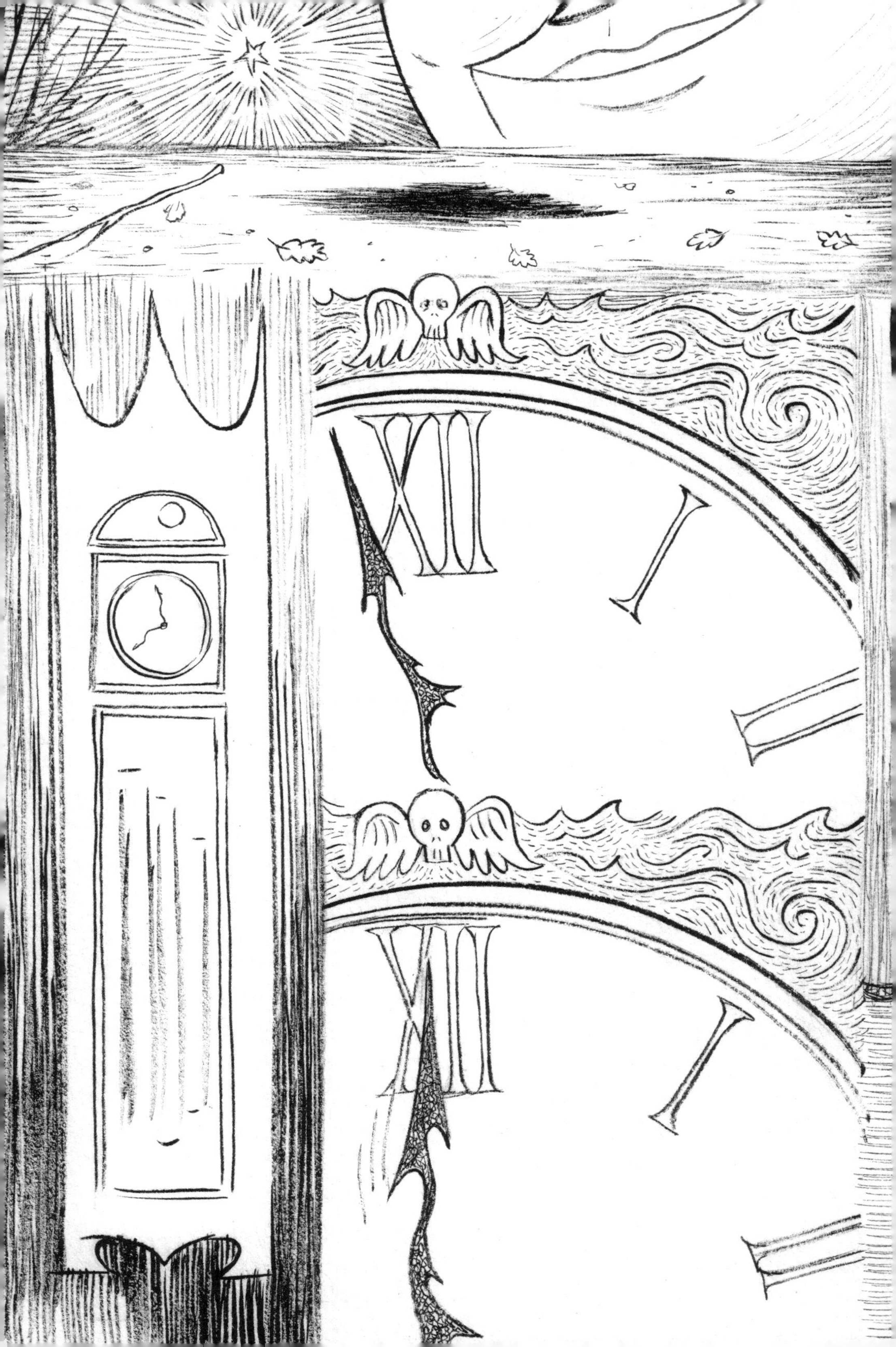
XII
I
VIII
I

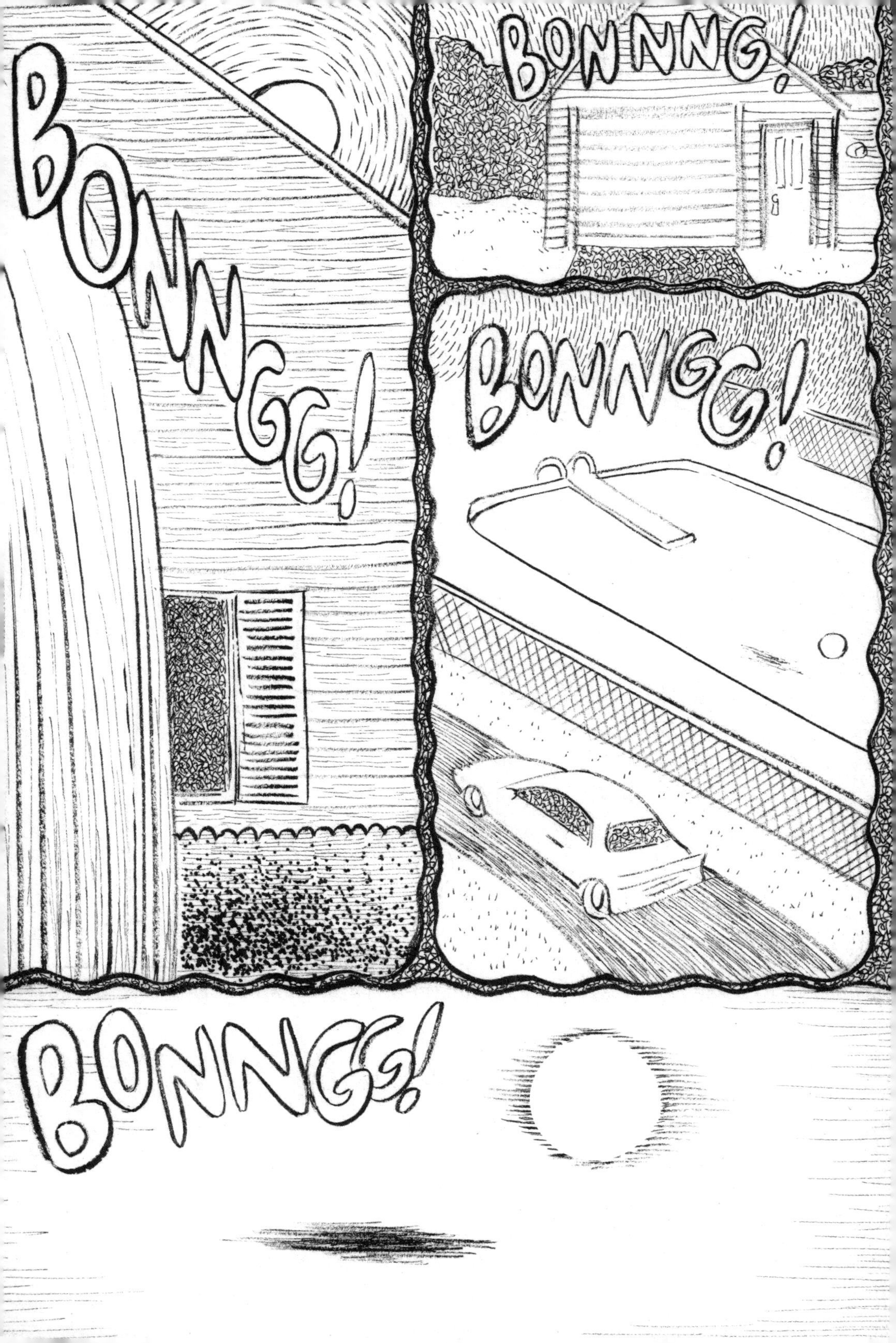
BONNGG!
BONNNG!
BONNGG!
BONNGG!

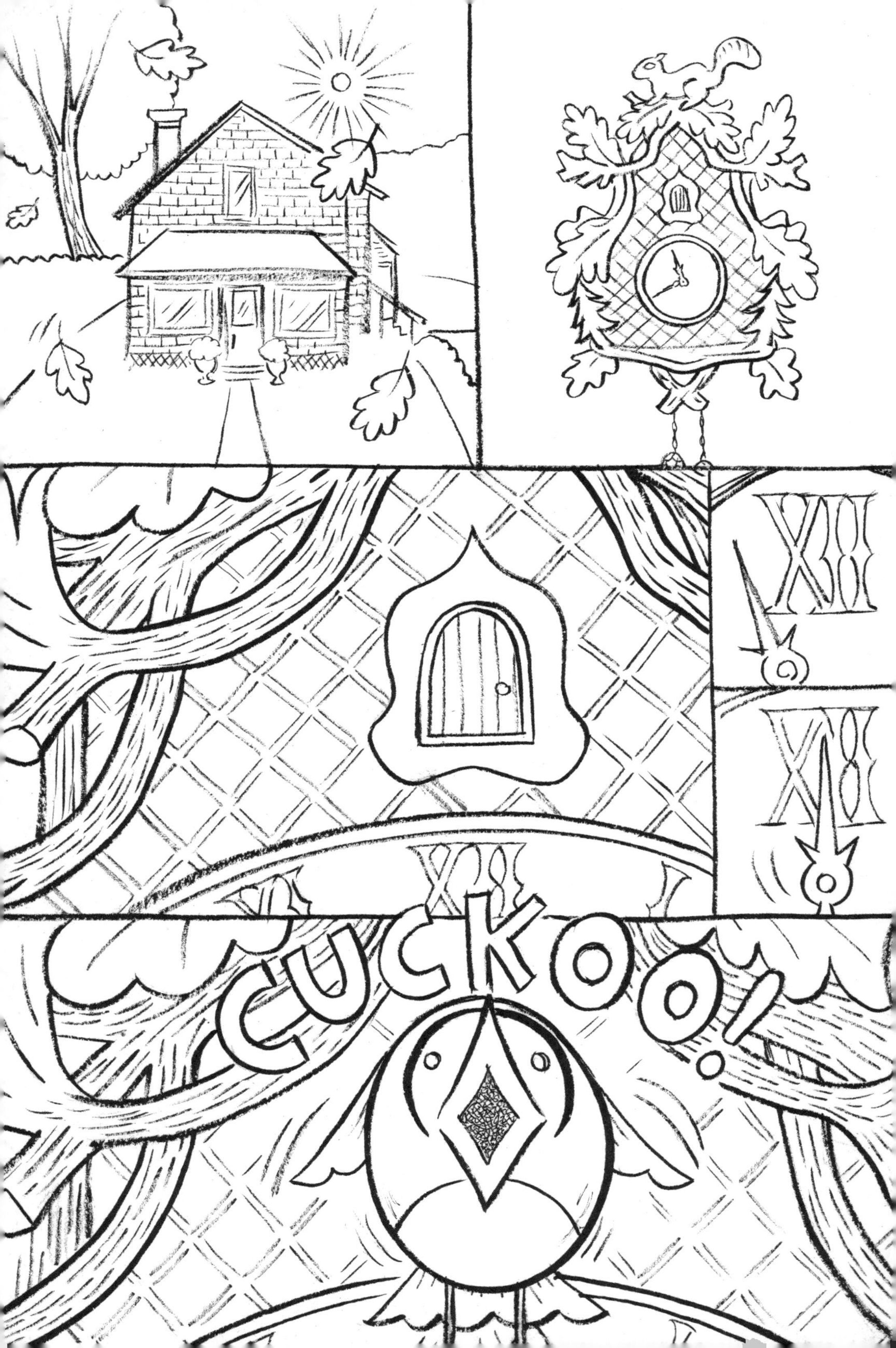
CUCKOO!

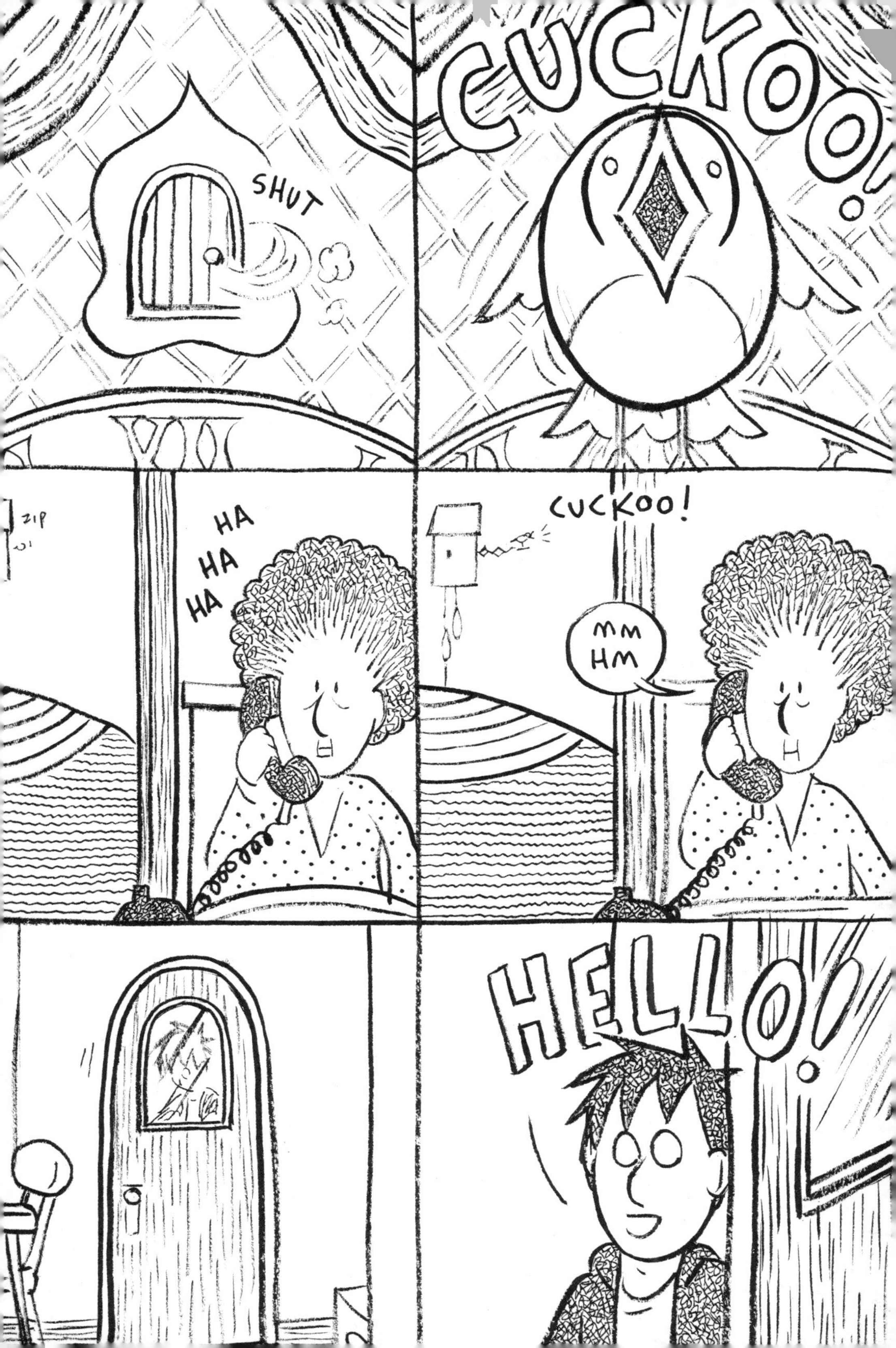
SHUT
CUCKOO!
zip
HA
HA
HA
CUCKOO!
MM HM
HELLO!

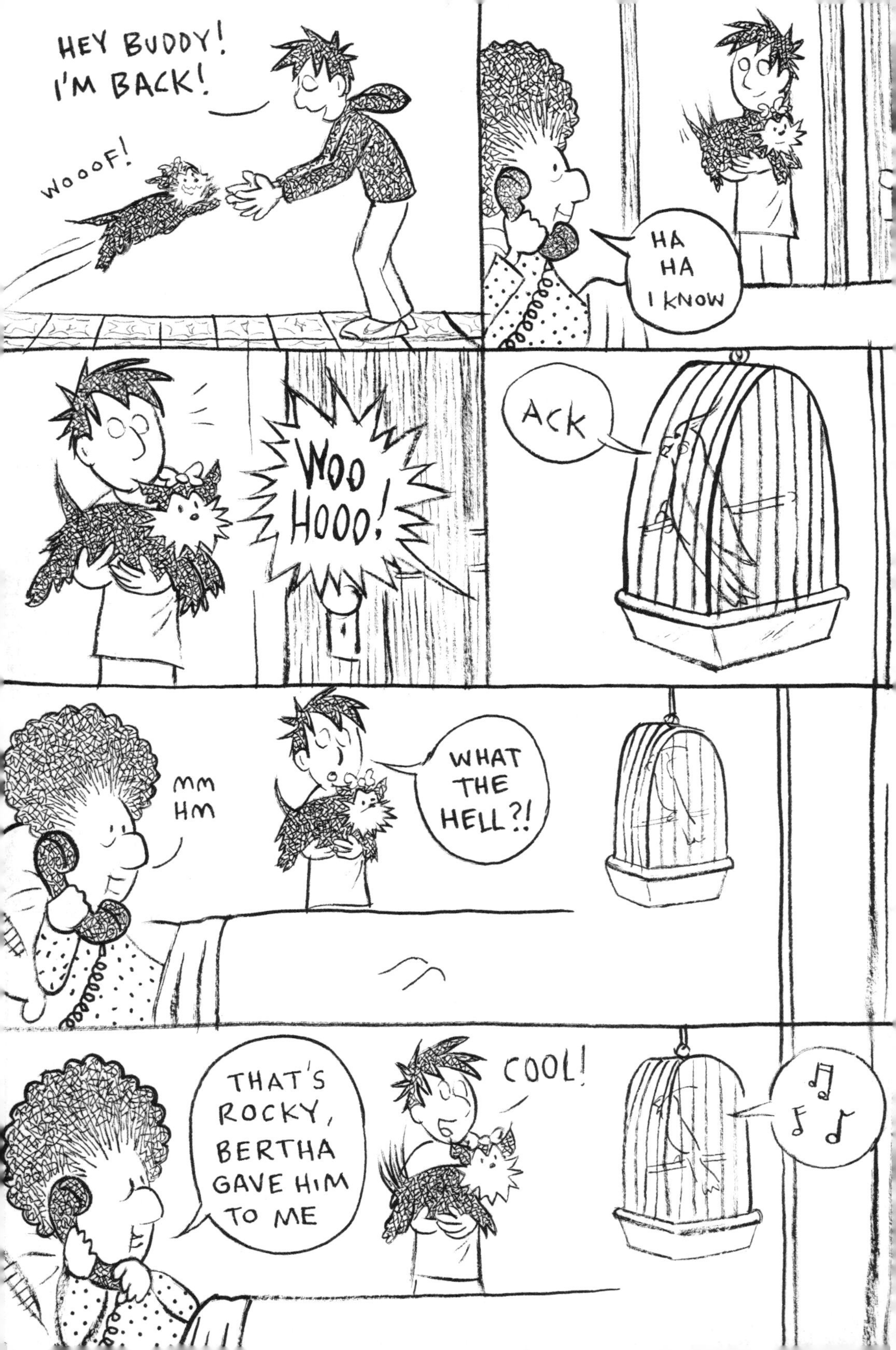
HEY BUDDY! I'M BACK!
WOOOF!
HA HA I KNOW
WOO HOOO!
ACK
MM HM
WHAT THE HELL?!
THAT'S ROCKY, BERTHA GAVE HIM TO ME
COOL!

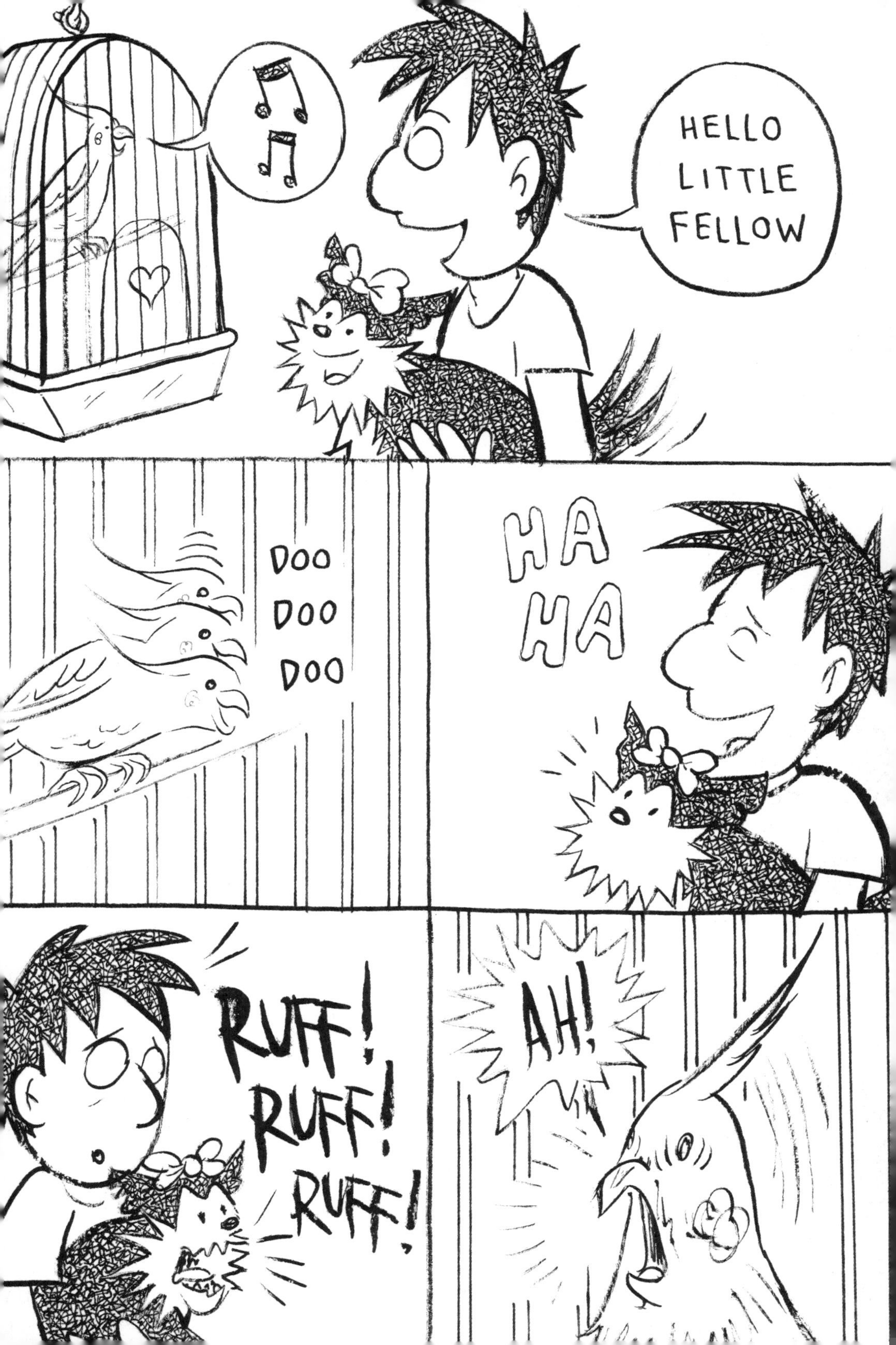
HELLO LITTLE FELLOW
DOO DOO DOO
HA HA HA
RUFF! RUFF! RUFF!
AH!

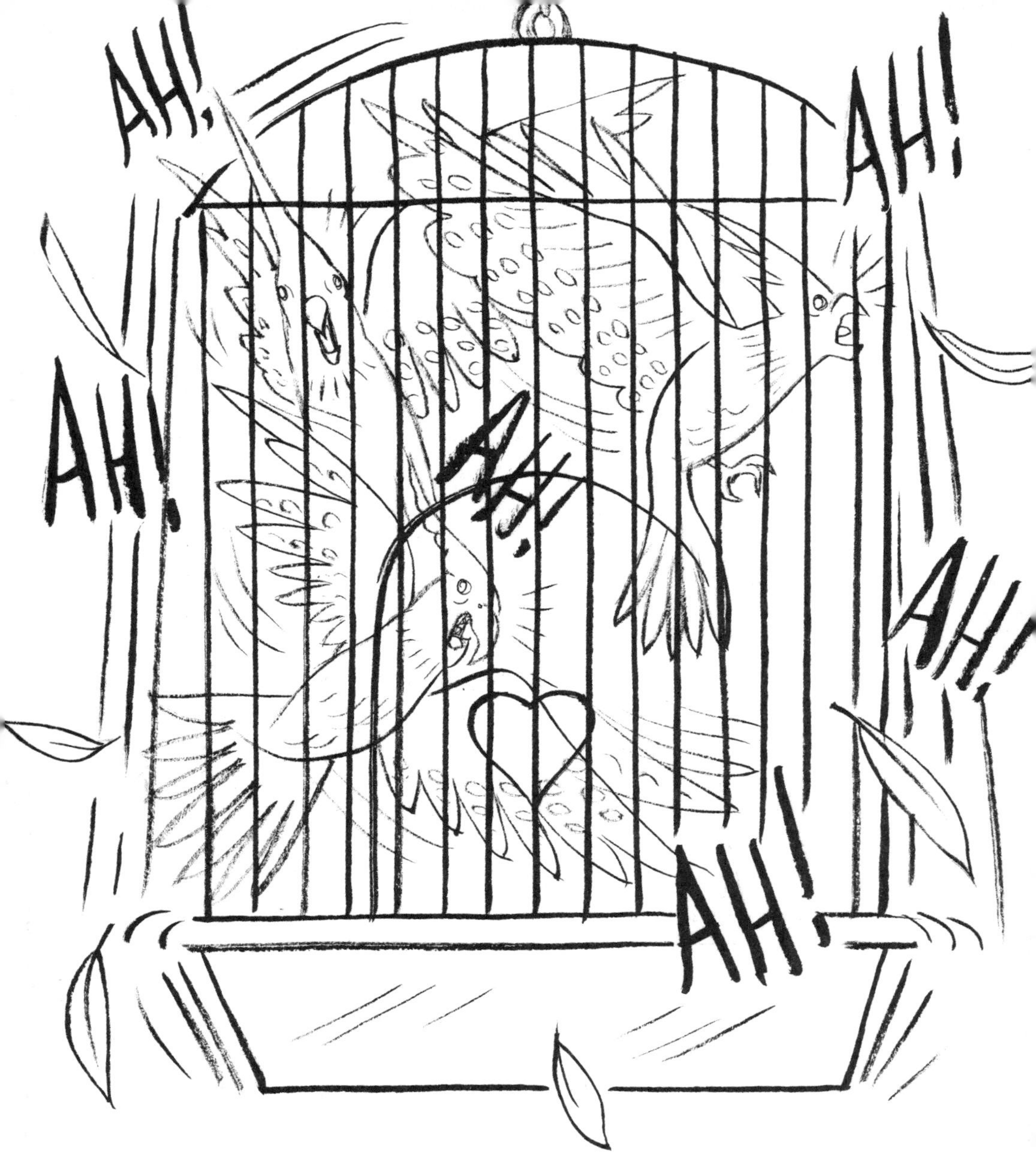
AH!
AH!
AH!
AH!
AH!
AH!

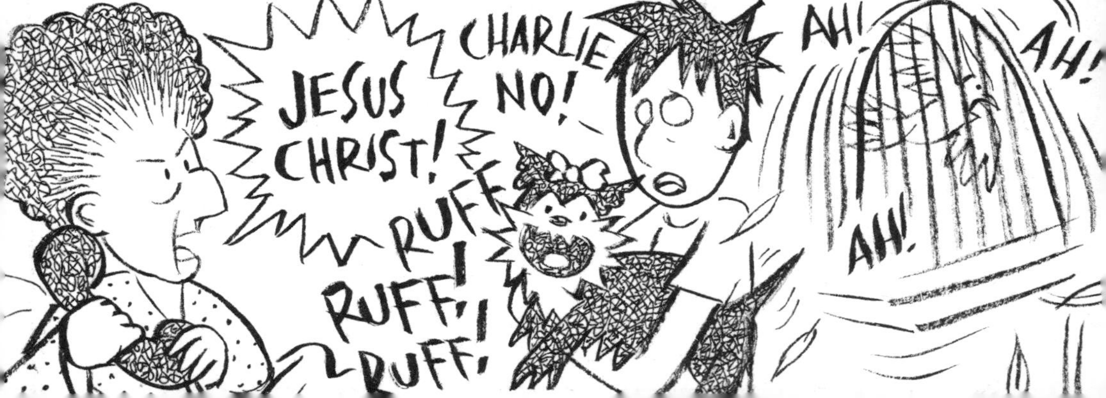
JESUS CHRIST!
CHARLIE NO!
RUFF! RUFF! RUFF!
AH!
AH!
AH!

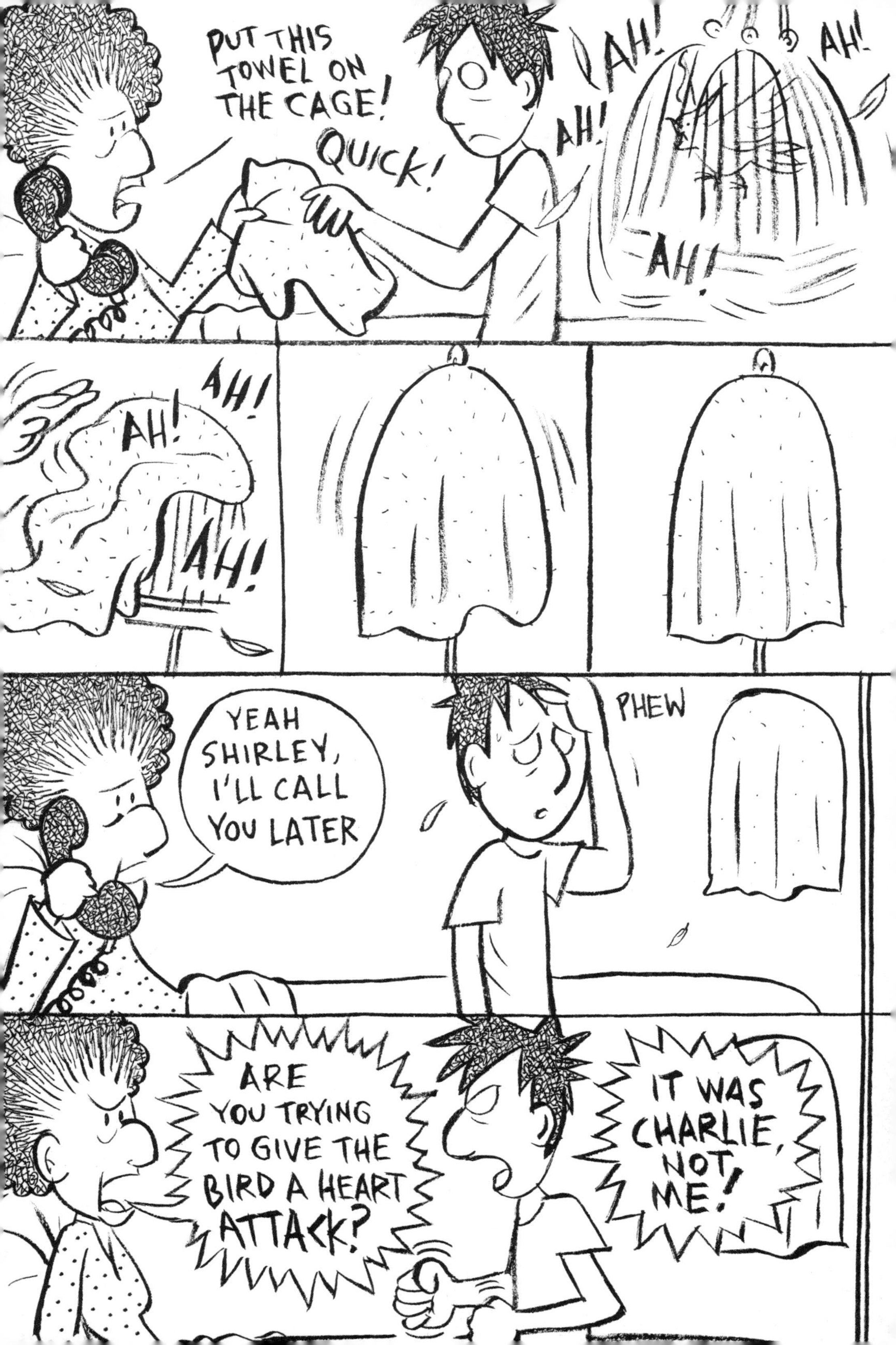
PUT THIS TOWEL ON THE CAGE!
QUICK!
AH!
AH!
AH!
AH!
AH!
AH!
AH!
YEAH SHIRLEY, I'LL CALL YOU LATER
PHEW
ARE YOU TRYING TO GIVE THE BIRD A HEART ATTACK?
IT WAS CHARLIE, NOT ME!

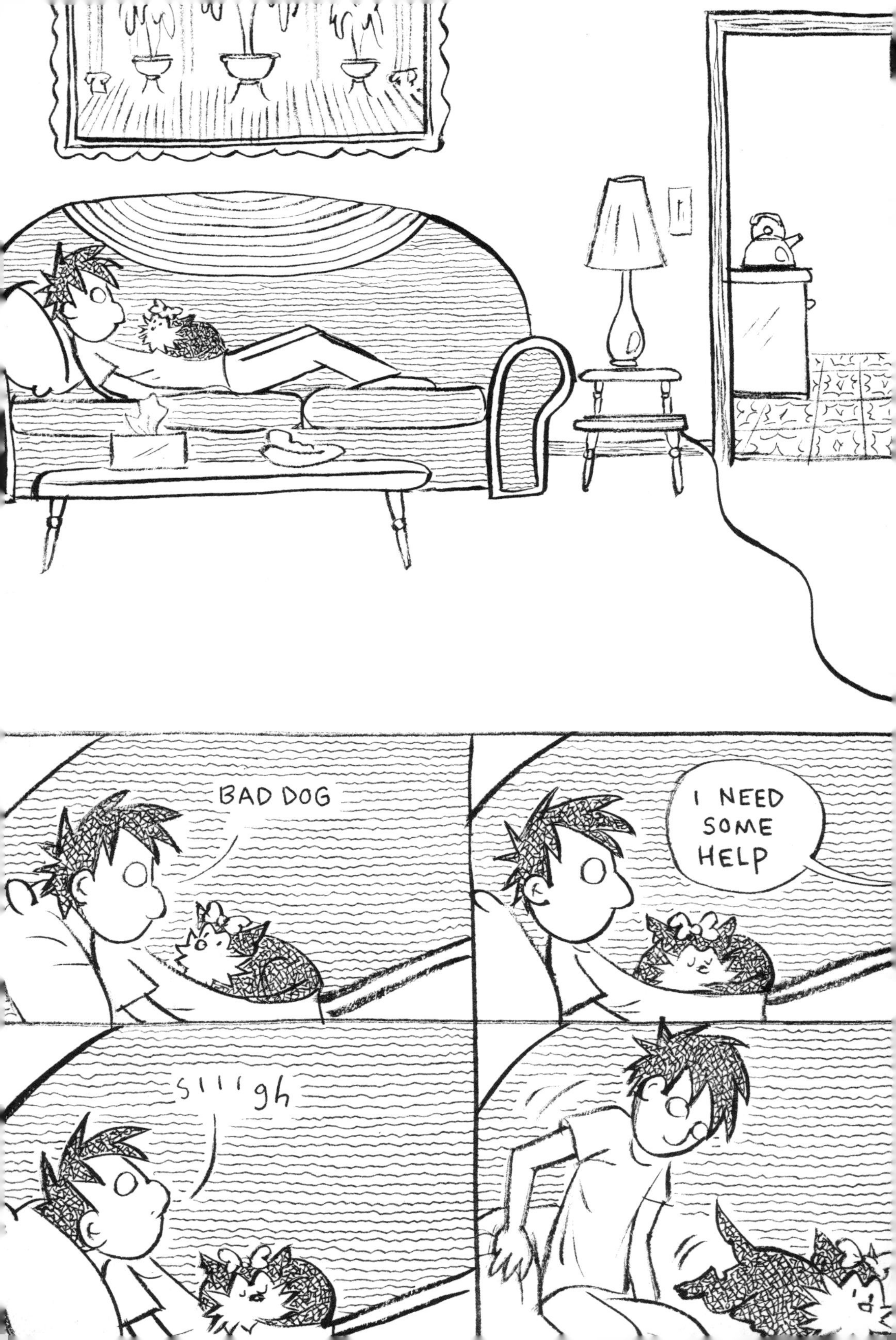
BAD DOG
I NEED SOME HELP
siiigh

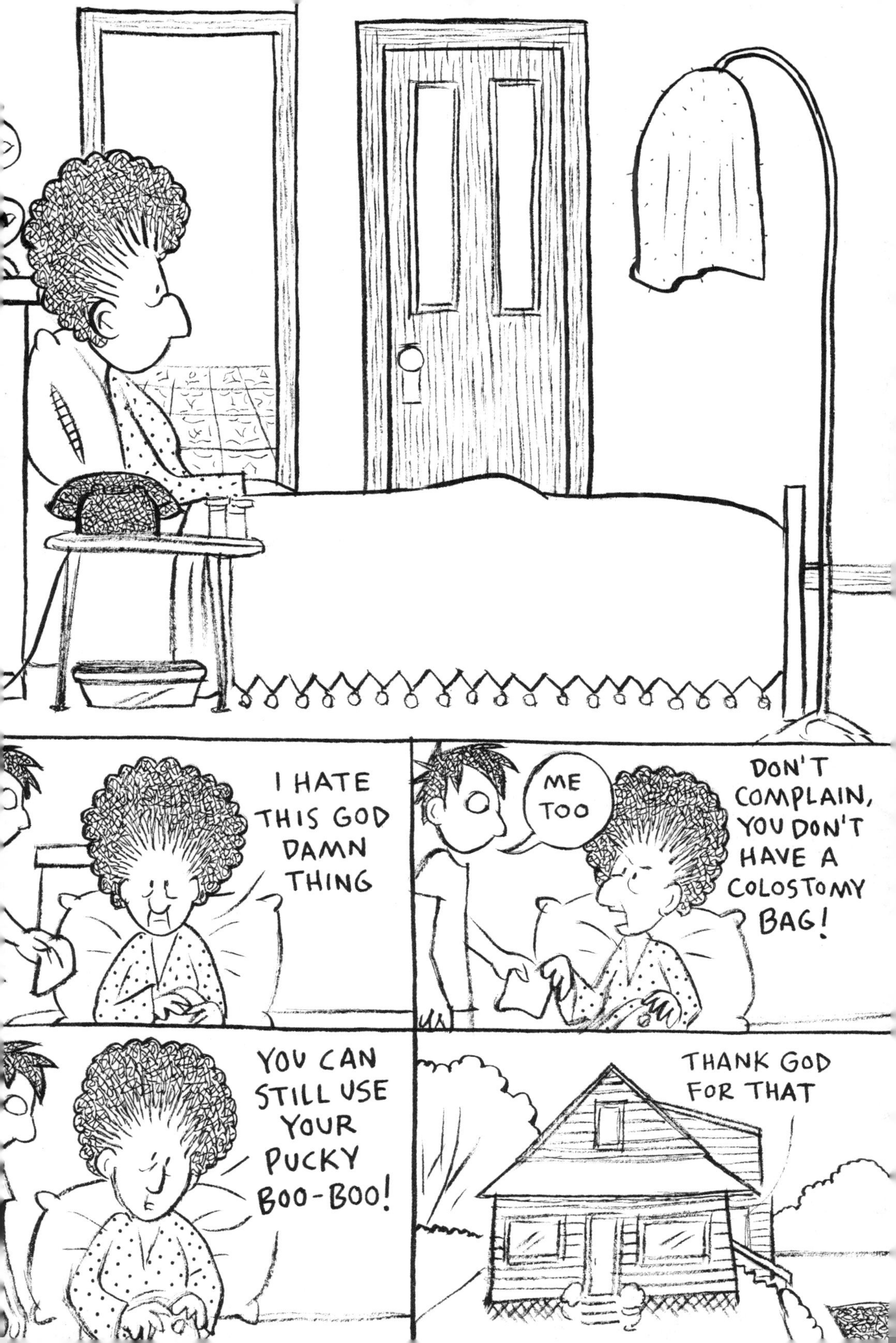
I HATE THIS GOD DAMN THING
ME TOO
DON'T COMPLAIN, YOU DON'T HAVE A COLOSTOMY BAG!
YOU CAN STILL USE YOUR PUCKY BOO-BOO!
THANK GOD FOR THAT

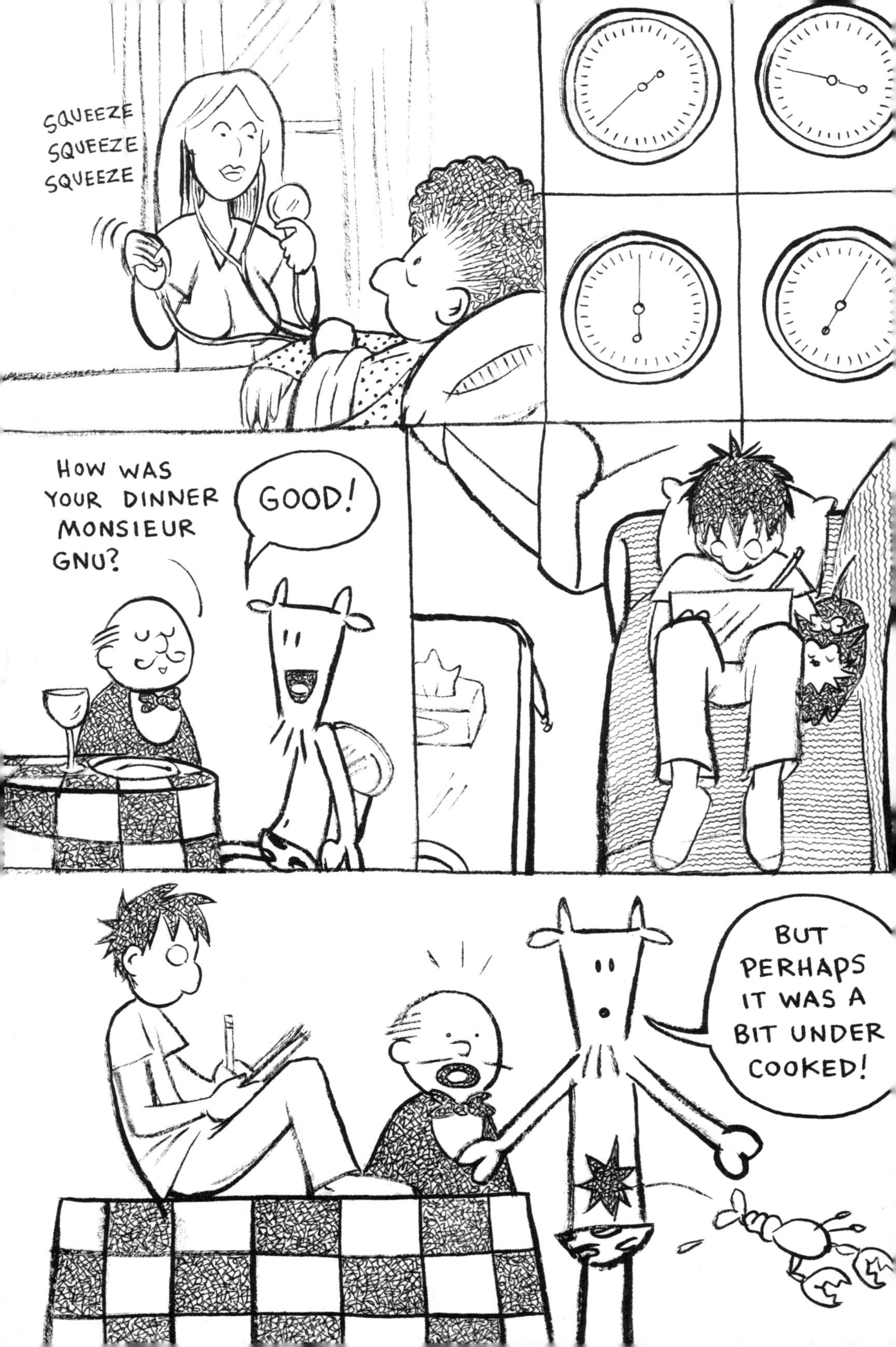
SQUEEZE
SQUEEZE
SQUEEZE
HOW WAS YOUR DINNER MONSIEUR GNU?
GOOD!
BUT PERHAPS IT WAS A BIT UNDER COOKED!

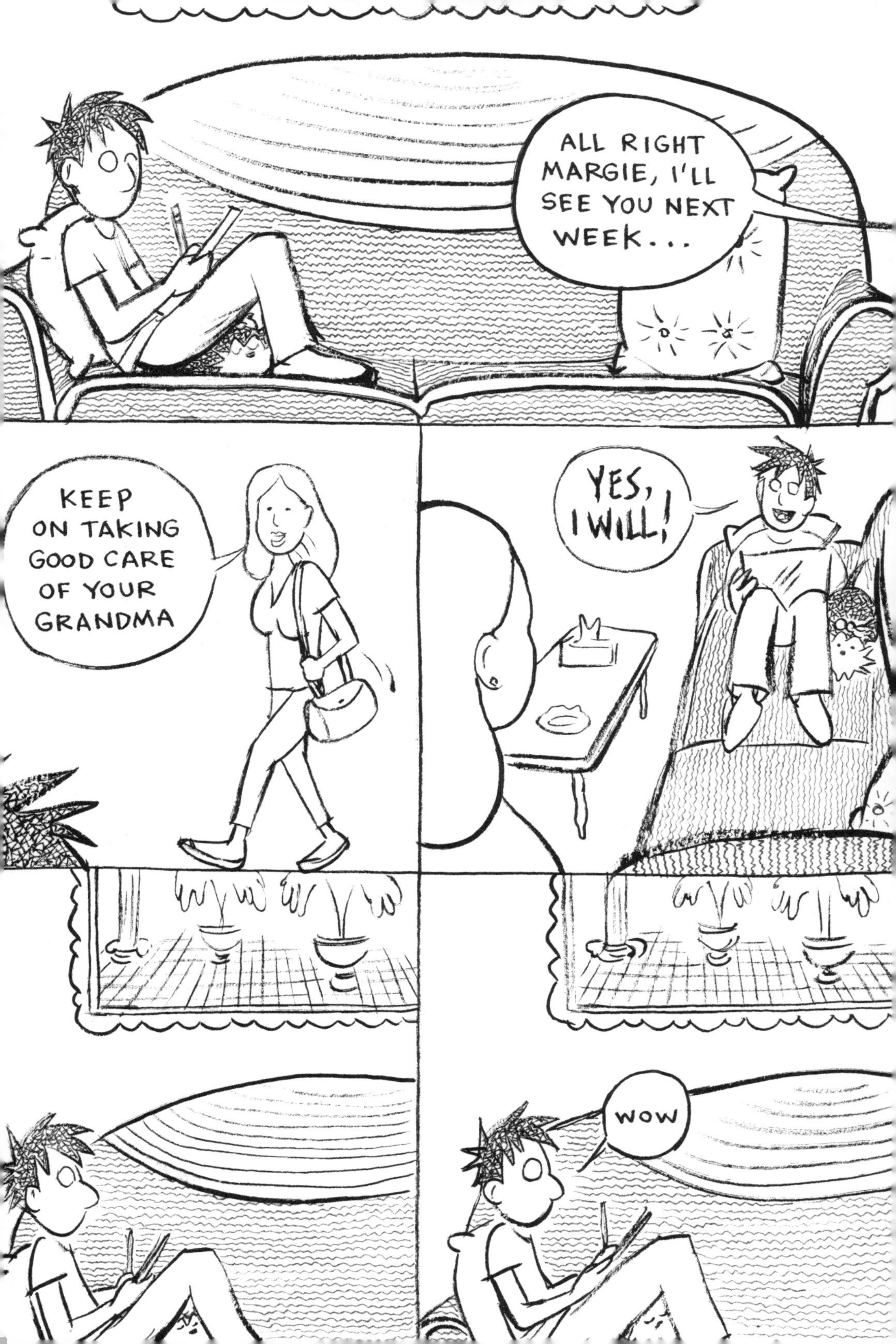
ALL RIGHT MARGIE, I'LL SEE YOU NEXT WEEK...
KEEP ON TAKING GOOD CARE OF YOUR GRANDMA
YES, I WILL!
WOW

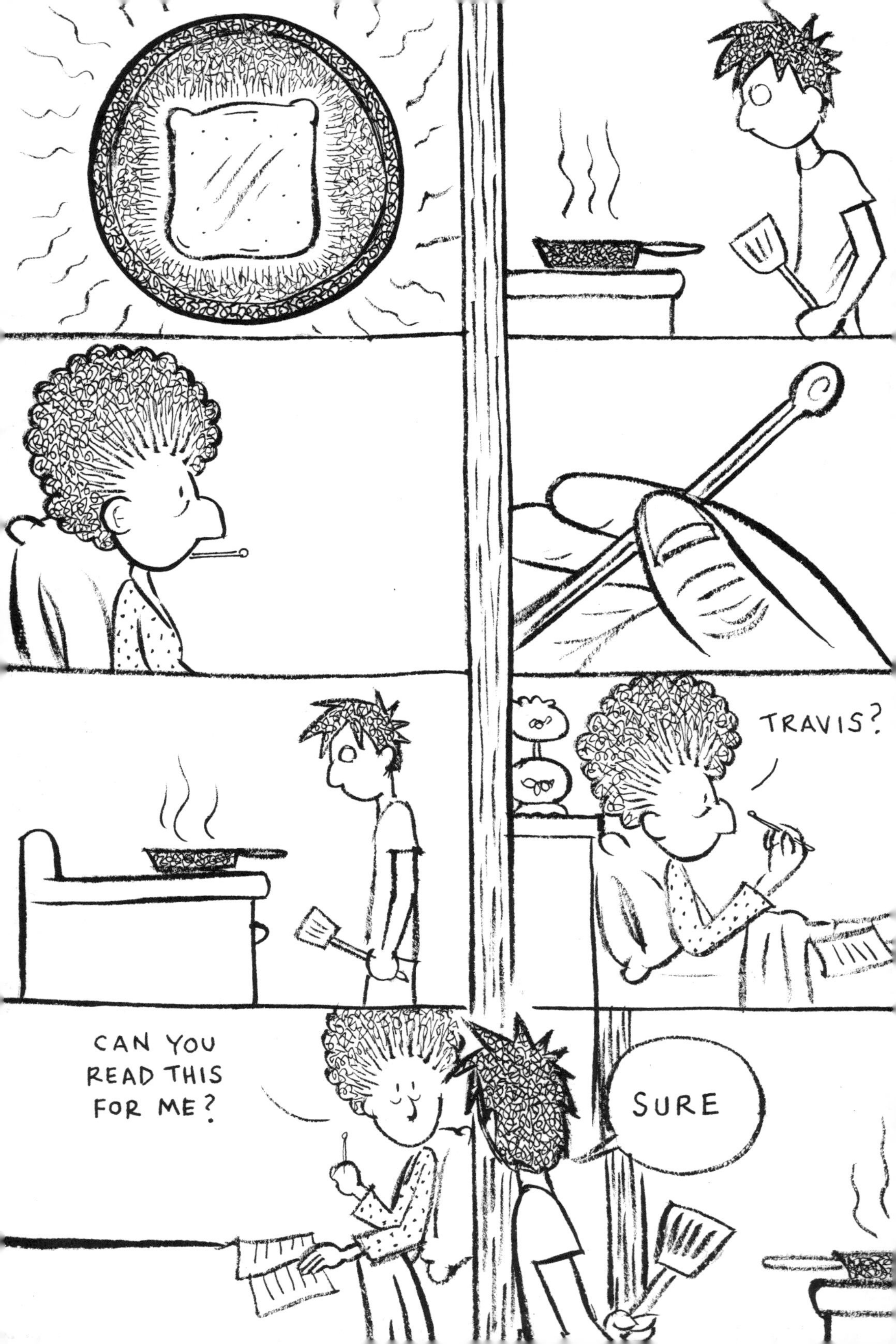
TRAVIS?
CAN YOU READ THIS FOR ME?
SURE

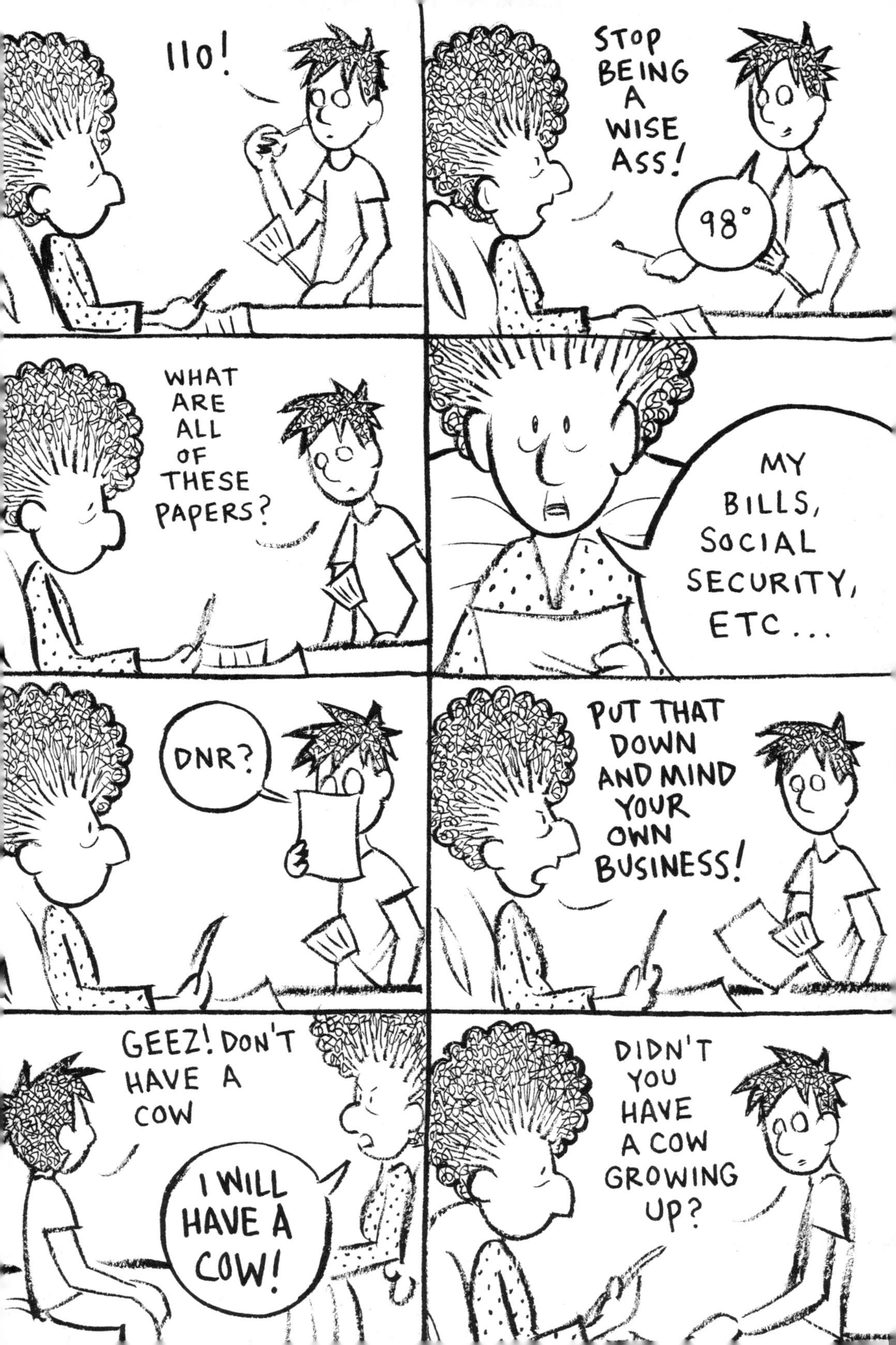
110!
STOP BEING A WISE ASS!
98°
WHAT ARE ALL OF THESE PAPERS?
MY BILLS, SOCIAL SECURITY, ETC...
DNR?
PUT THAT DOWN AND MIND YOUR OWN BUSINESS!
GEEZ! DON'T HAVE A COW
I WILL HAVE A COW!
DIDN'T YOU HAVE A COW GROWING UP?

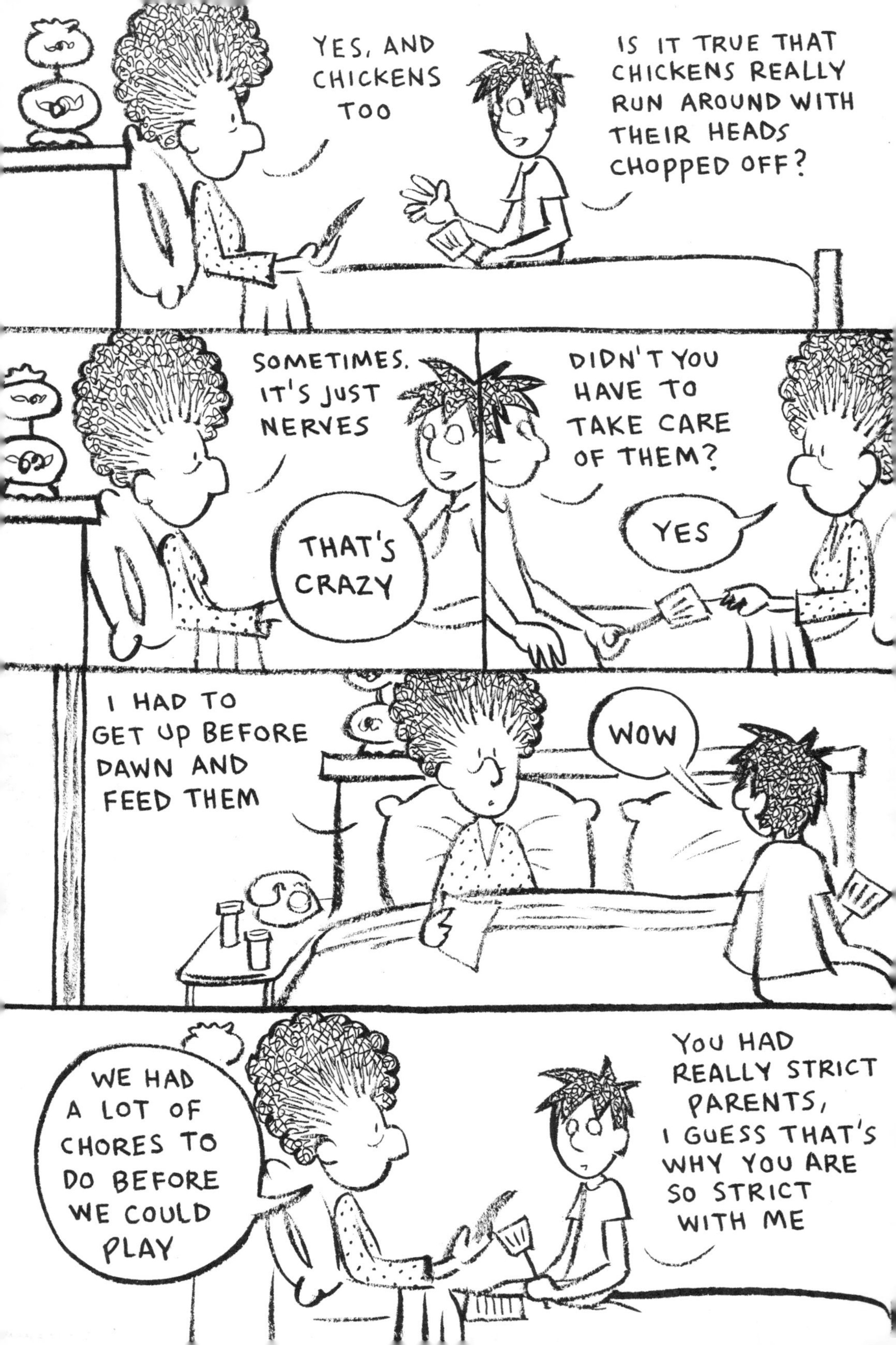
IS IT TRUE THAT CHICKENS REALLY RUN AROUND WITH THEIR HEADS CHOPPED OFF?
YES, AND CHICKENS TOO
SOMETIMES. IT'S JUST NERVES
THAT'S CRAZY
DIDN'T YOU HAVE TO TAKE CARE OF THEM?
YES
I HAD TO GET UP BEFORE DAWN AND FEED THEM
WOW
WE HAD A LOT OF CHORES TO DO BEFORE WE COULD PLAY
YOU HAD REALLY STRICT PARENTS, I GUESS THAT'S WHY YOU ARE SO STRICT WITH ME

I'M NOT STRICT!
YOU JUST MADE ME READ YOUR THERMOMETER!
OH, BIG DEAL!
IT STRAINED MY SORE EYES
GOOD, MAYBE YOU'LL GO BLIND AND WON'T BE ABLE TO DRAW ANY-MORE!
HA HA
THAT'S NOT VERY NICE!
SNIF SNIF
WHAT?
I SMELL SMOKE
MY GRILLED CHEESE!

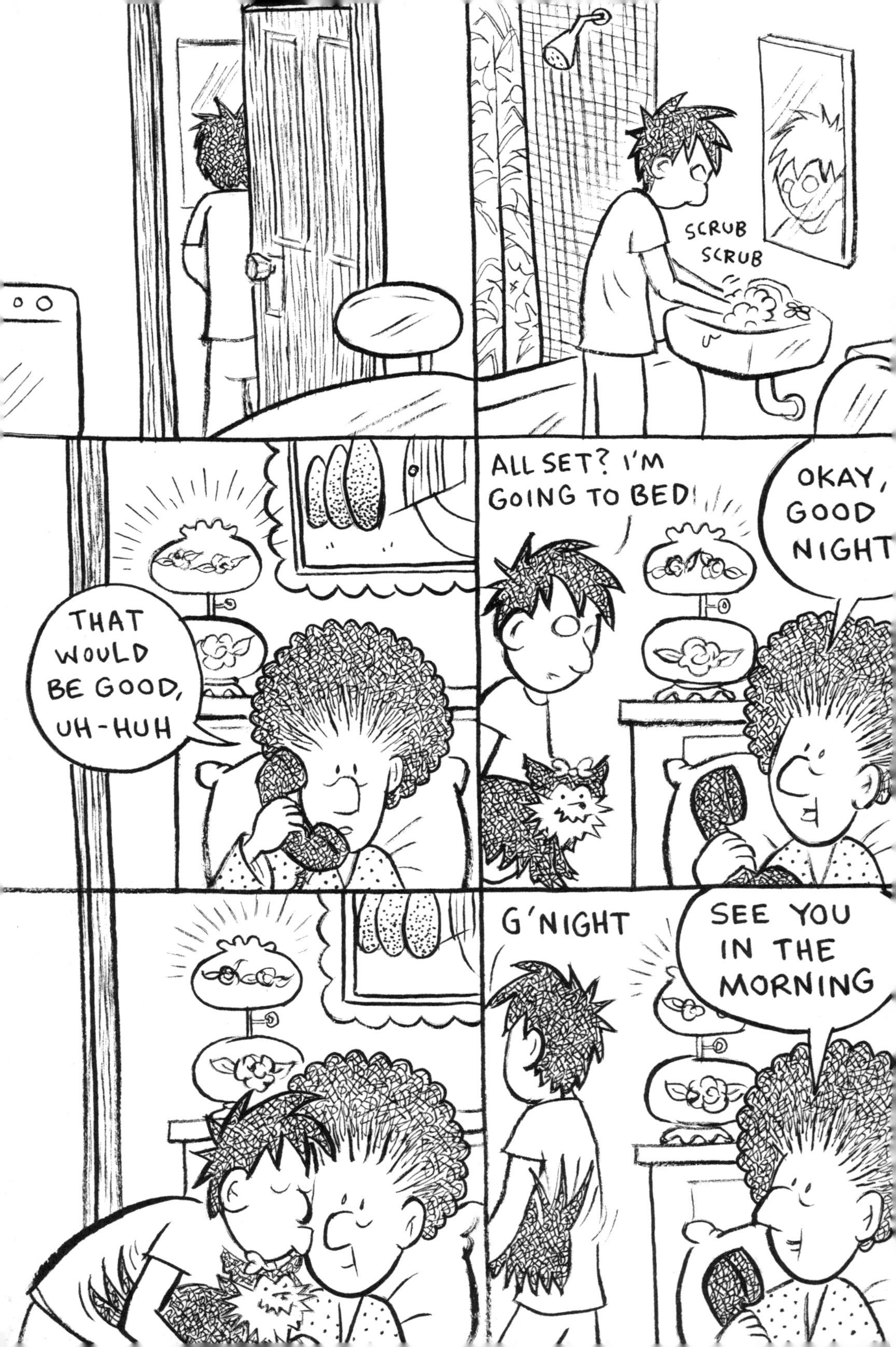
SCRUB
SCRUB
THAT WOULD BE GOOD, UH-HUH
ALL SET? I'M GOING TO BED
OKAY, GOOD NIGHT
G'NIGHT
SEE YOU IN THE MORNING

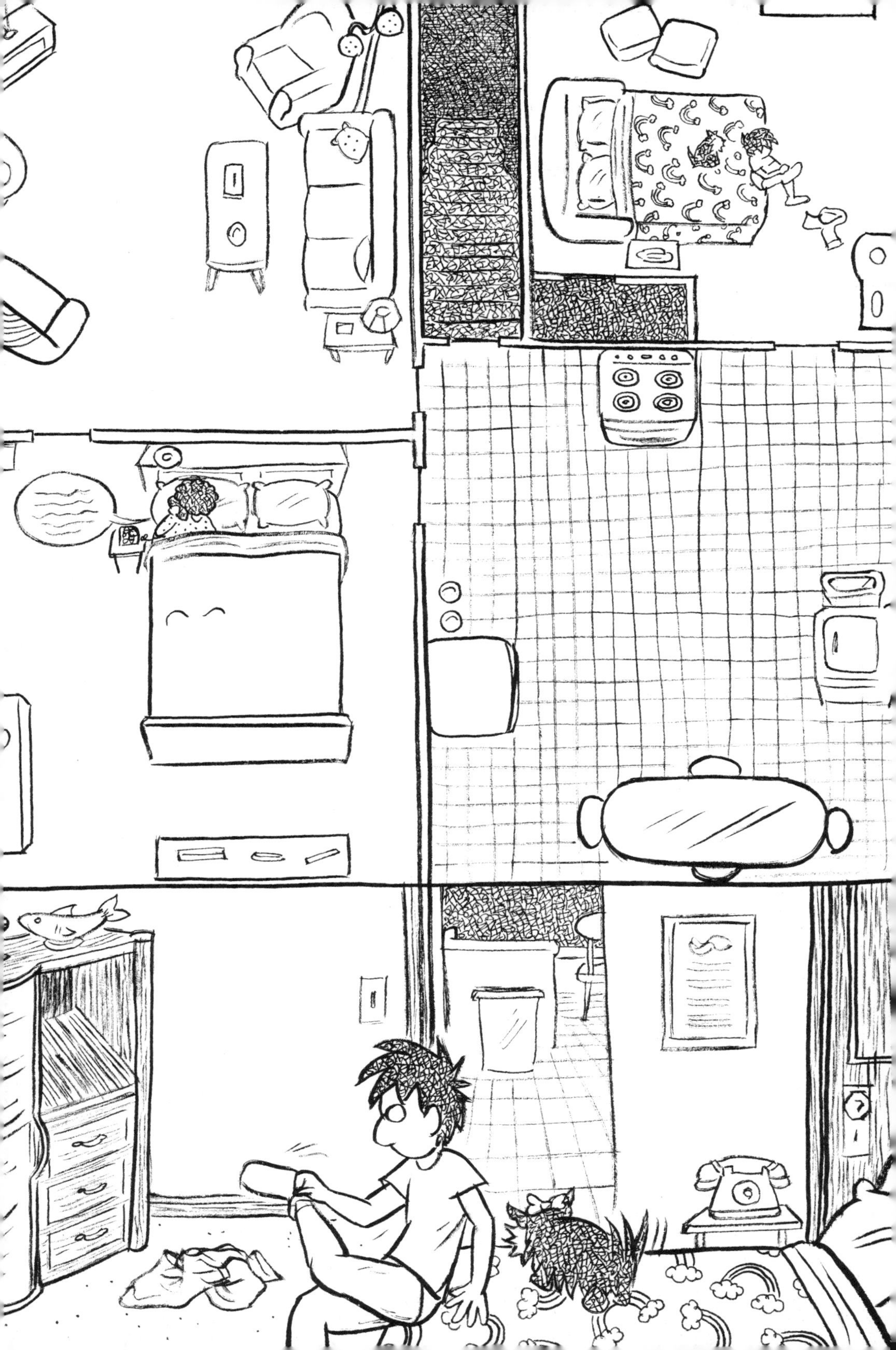

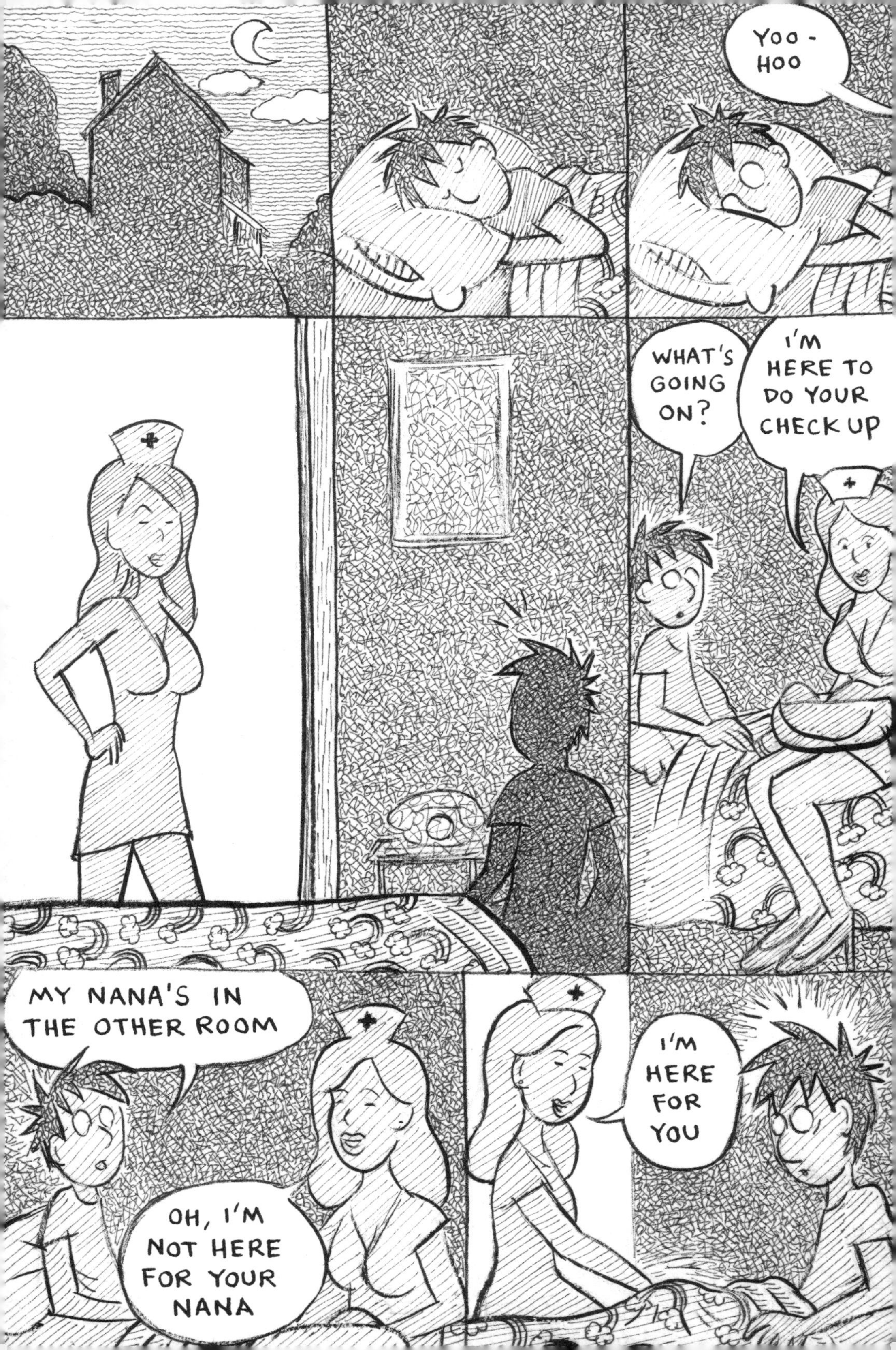
YOO - HOO
WHAT'S GOING ON?
I'M HERE TO DO YOUR CHECK UP
MY NANA'S IN THE OTHER ROOM
OH, I'M NOT HERE FOR YOUR NANA
I'M HERE FOR YOU

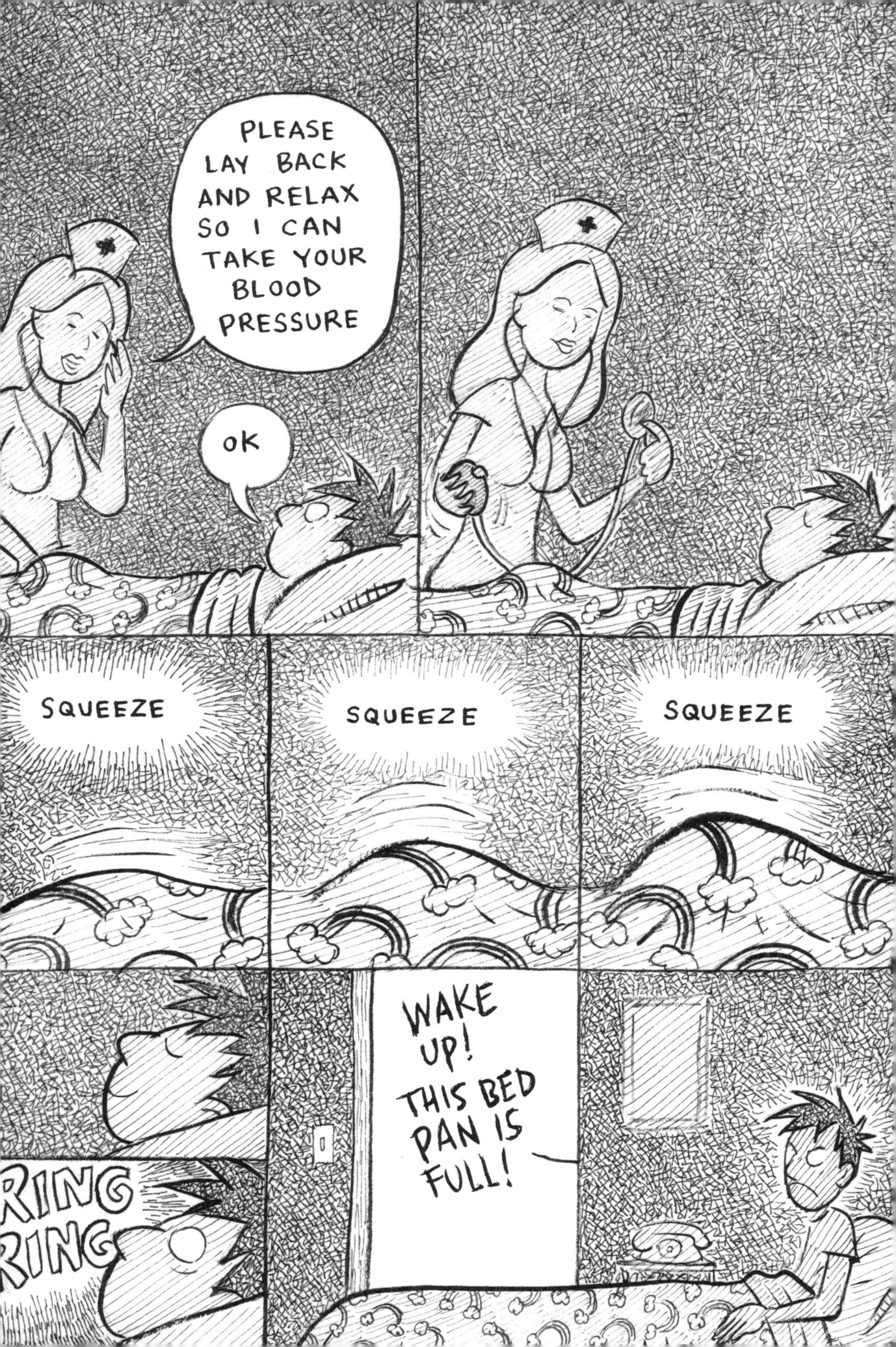
PLEASE LAY BACK AND RELAX SO I CAN TAKE YOUR BLOOD PRESSURE
OK
SQUEEZE
SQUEEZE
SQUEEZE
RING RING
WAKE UP! THIS BED PAN IS FULL!

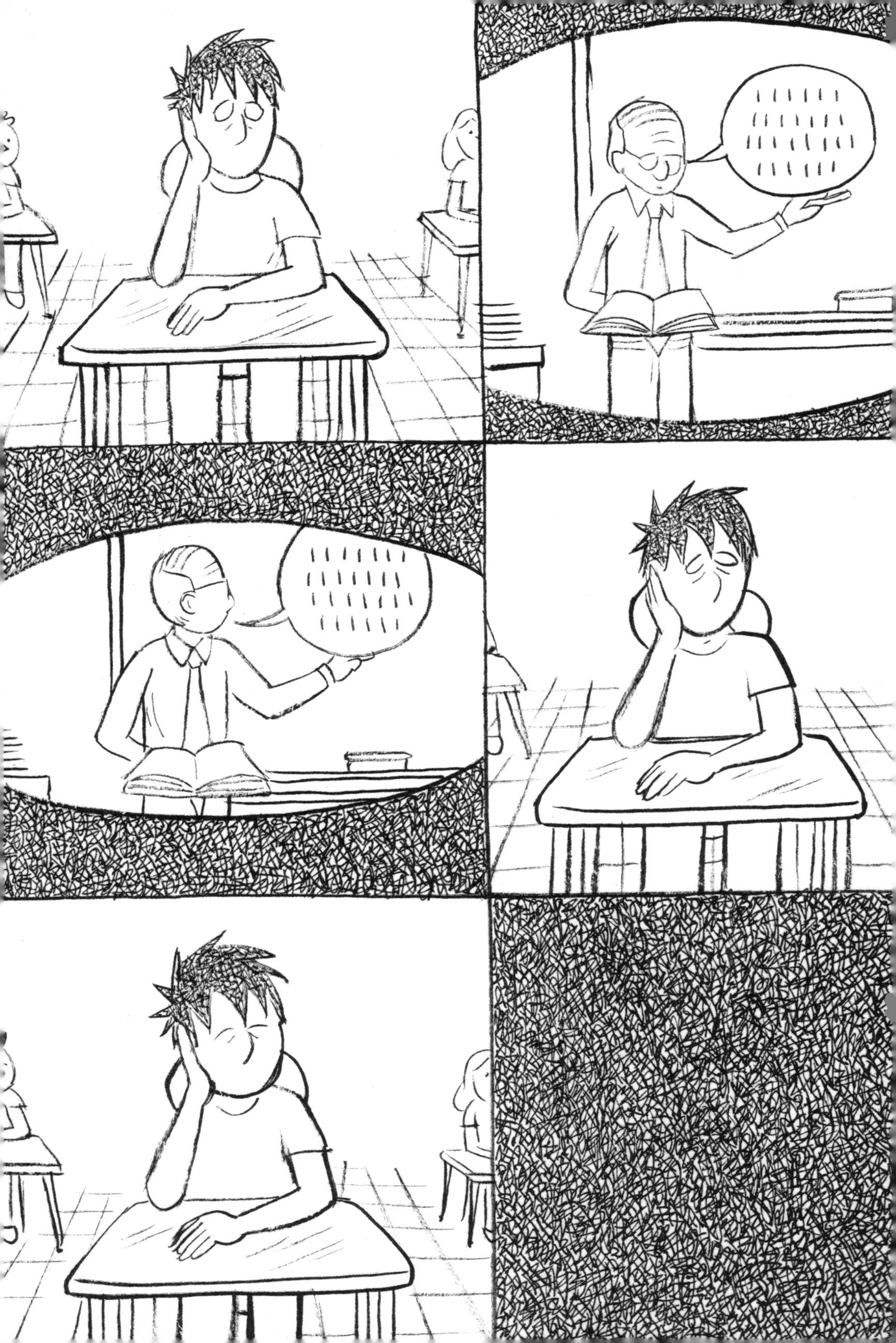

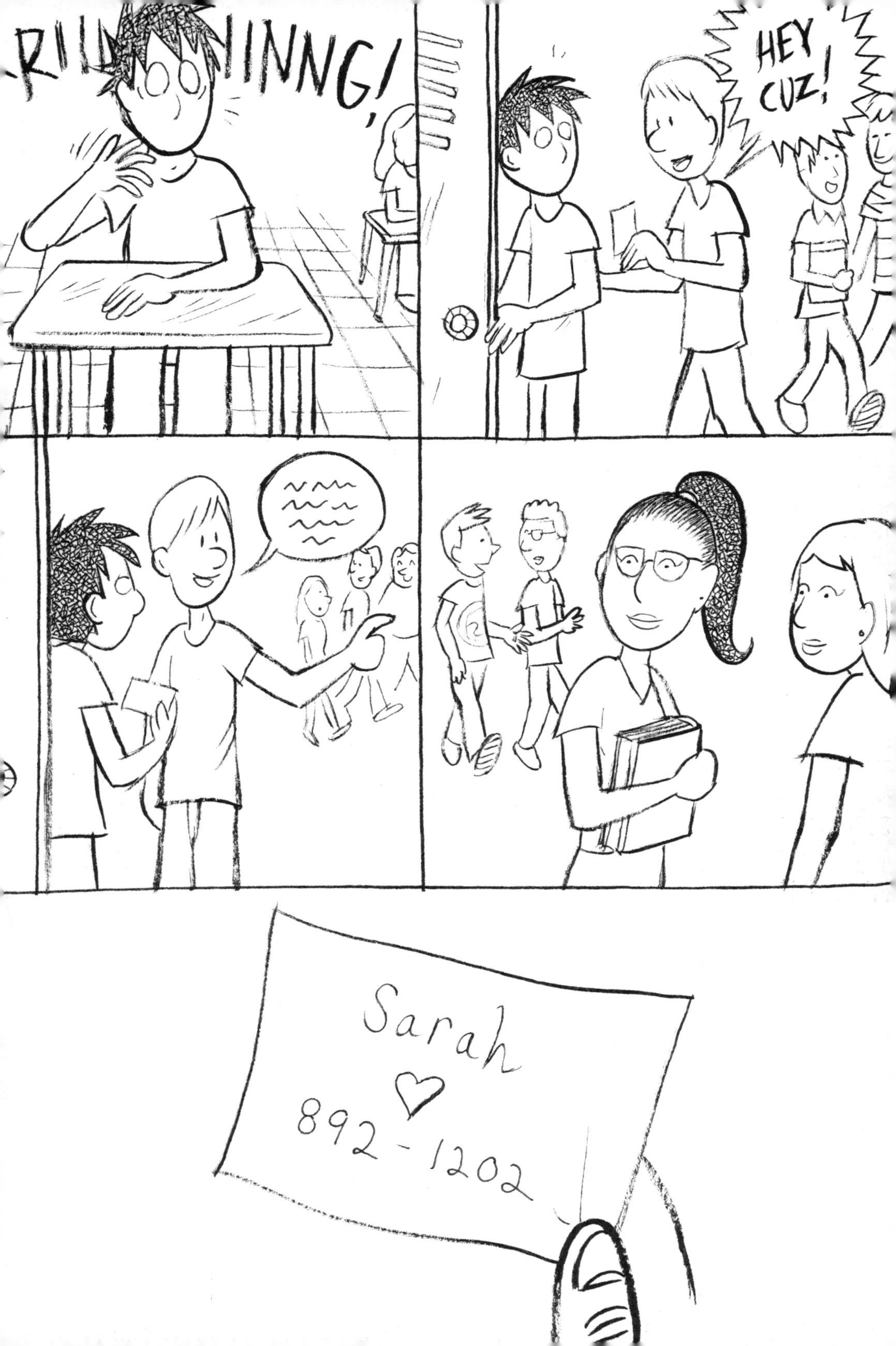
RIIIIIIINNG!
HEY CUZ!
Sarah
892-1202

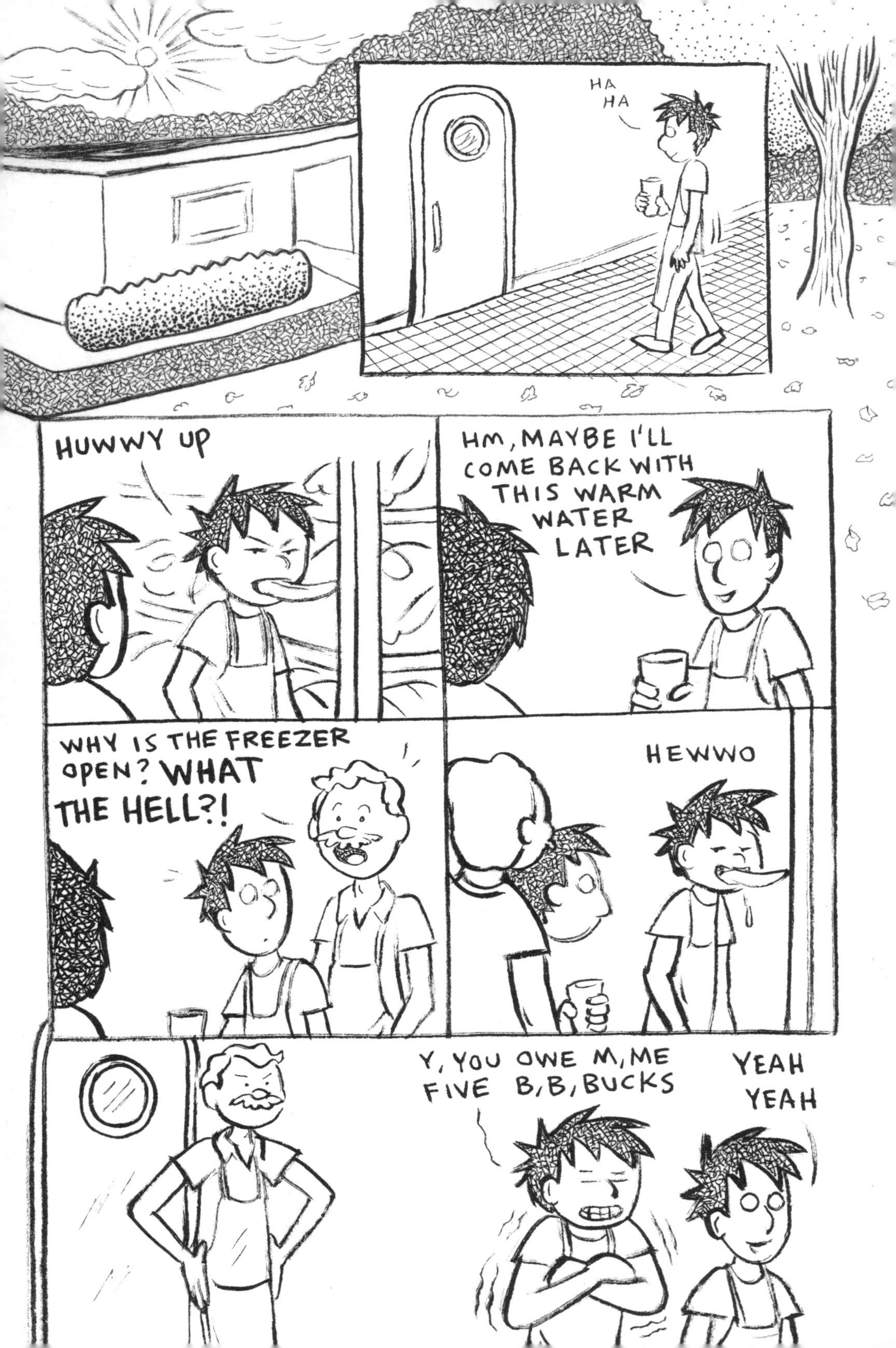
HA
HA
HUWWY UP
HM, MAYBE I'LL COME BACK WITH THIS WARM WATER LATER
WHY IS THE FREEZER OPEN? WHAT THE HELL?!
HEWWO
Y, YOU OWE M, ME FIVE B, B, BUCKS
YEAH YEAH

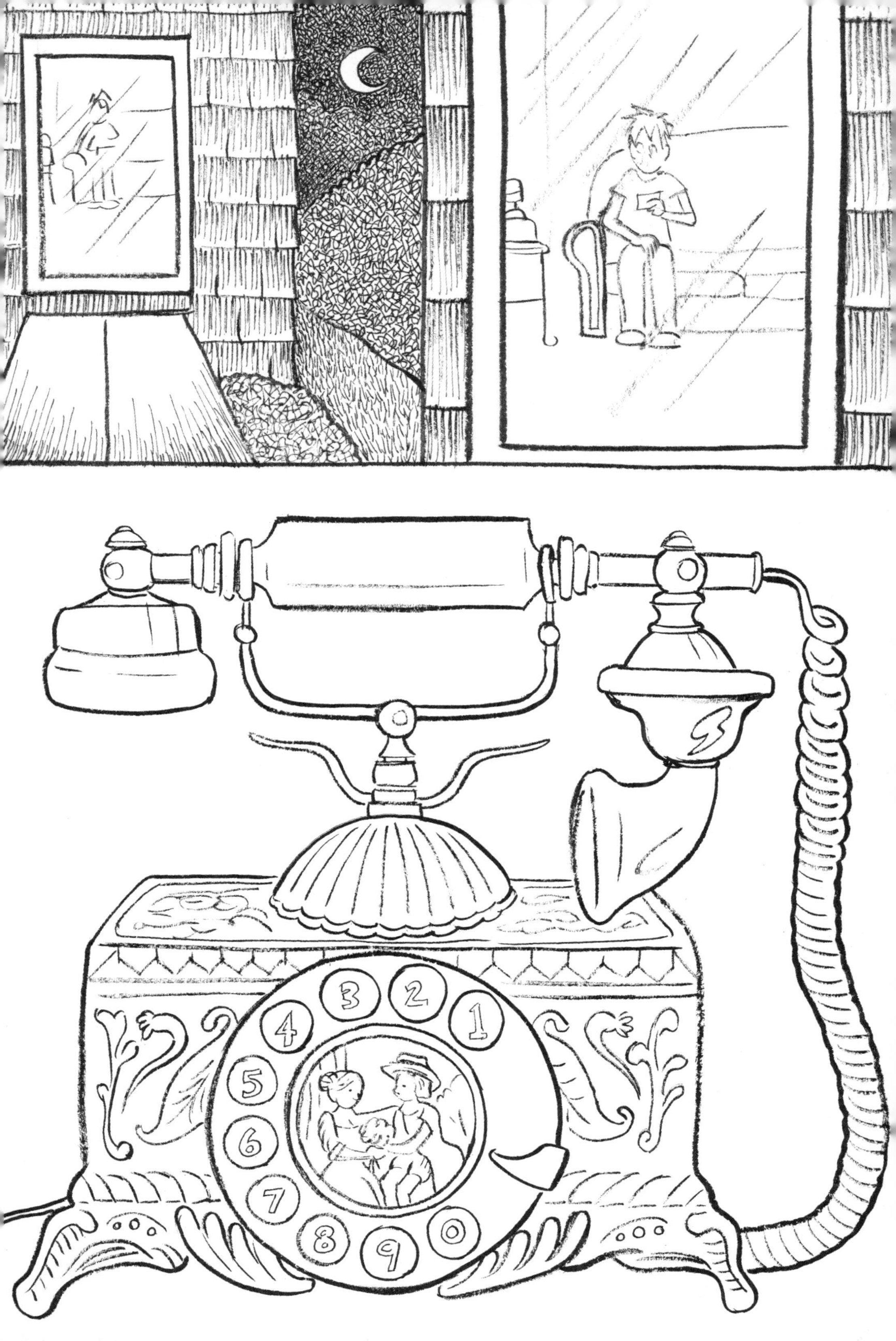

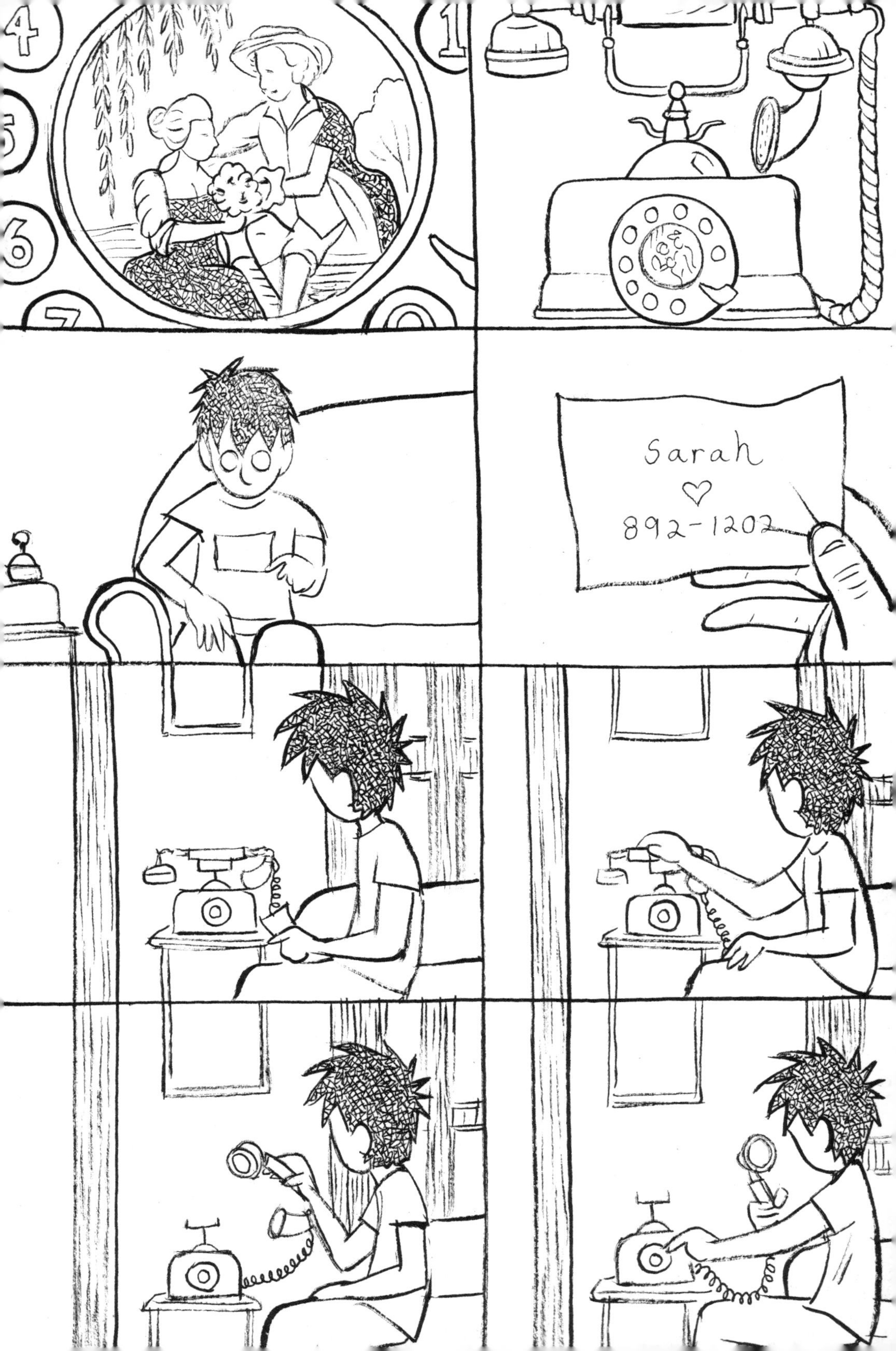
Sarah
892-1202

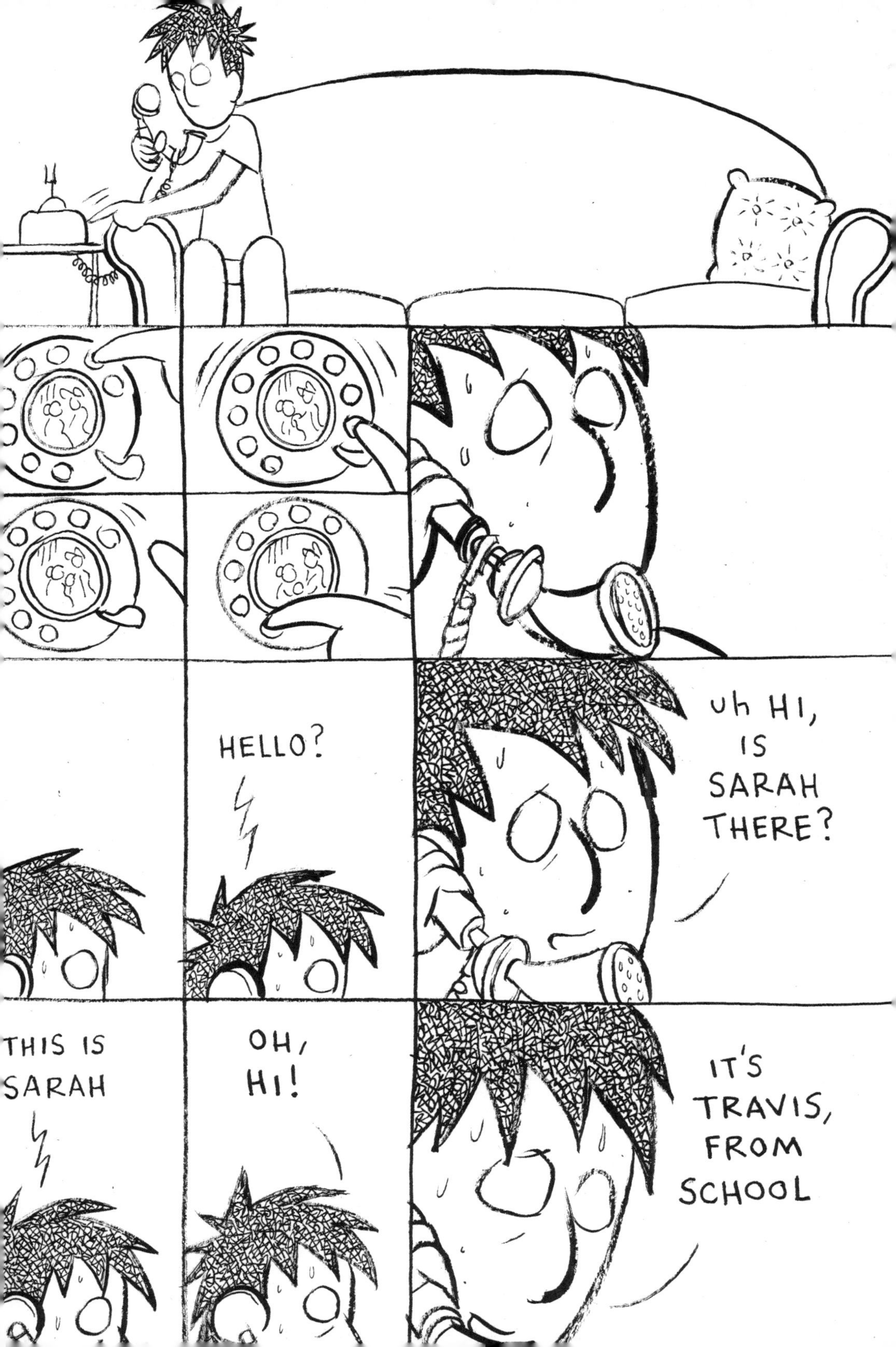
HELLO?
uh HI, IS SARAH THERE?
THIS IS SARAH
OH, HI!
IT'S TRAVIS, FROM SCHOOL

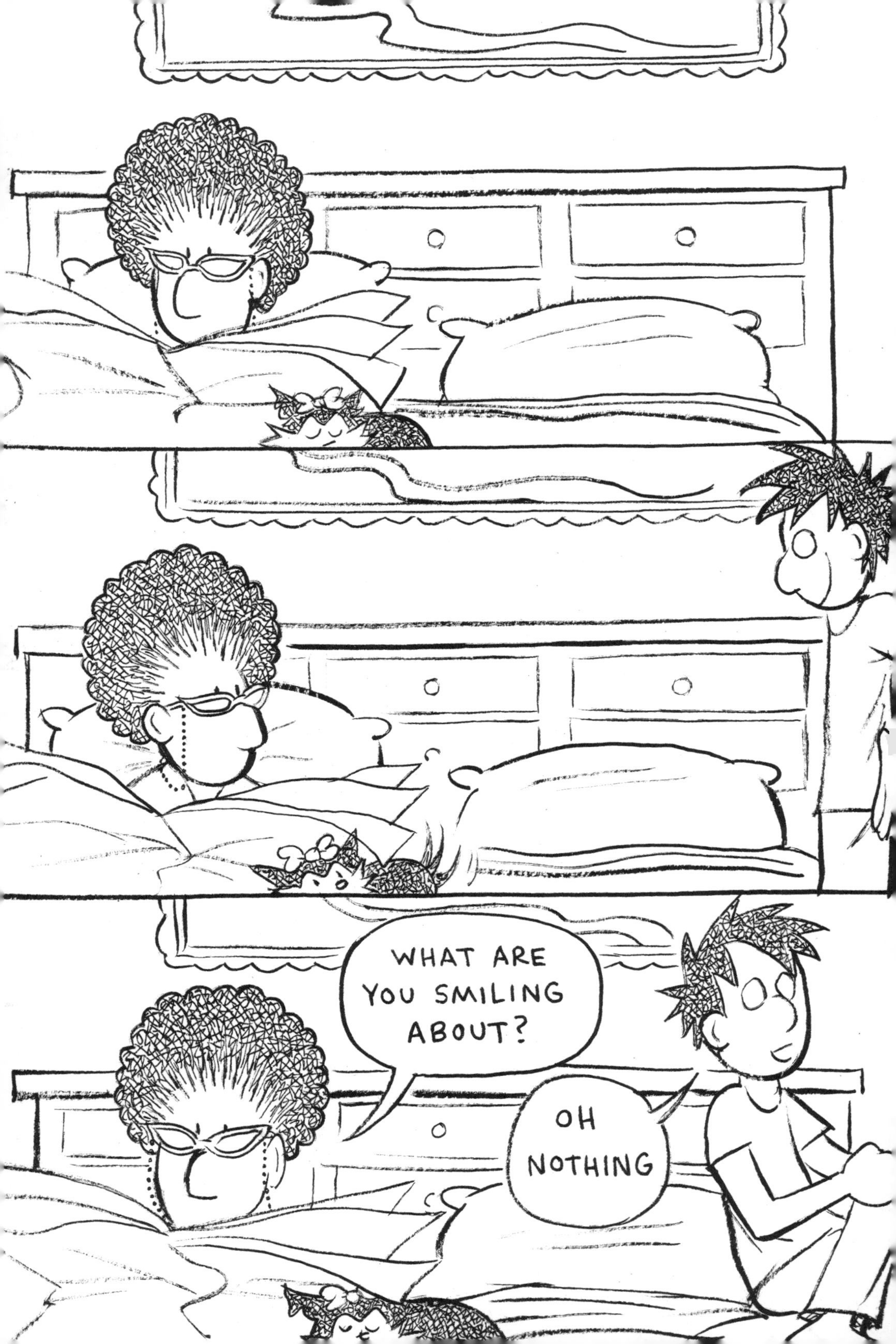
WHAT ARE YOU SMILING ABOUT?
OH NOTHING

CAN I GET YOU ANY-THING?
LIKE WHAT?
SOMETHING TO EAT OR DRINK?
I'M GOOD
GOOD FOR WHAT? HA HA
GOOD ENOUGH TO WIPE THAT SMIRK OFF YOUR FACE!
I'D LIKE TO SEE YOU TRY!
SMOOCH
HAHAHA
WISE ASS

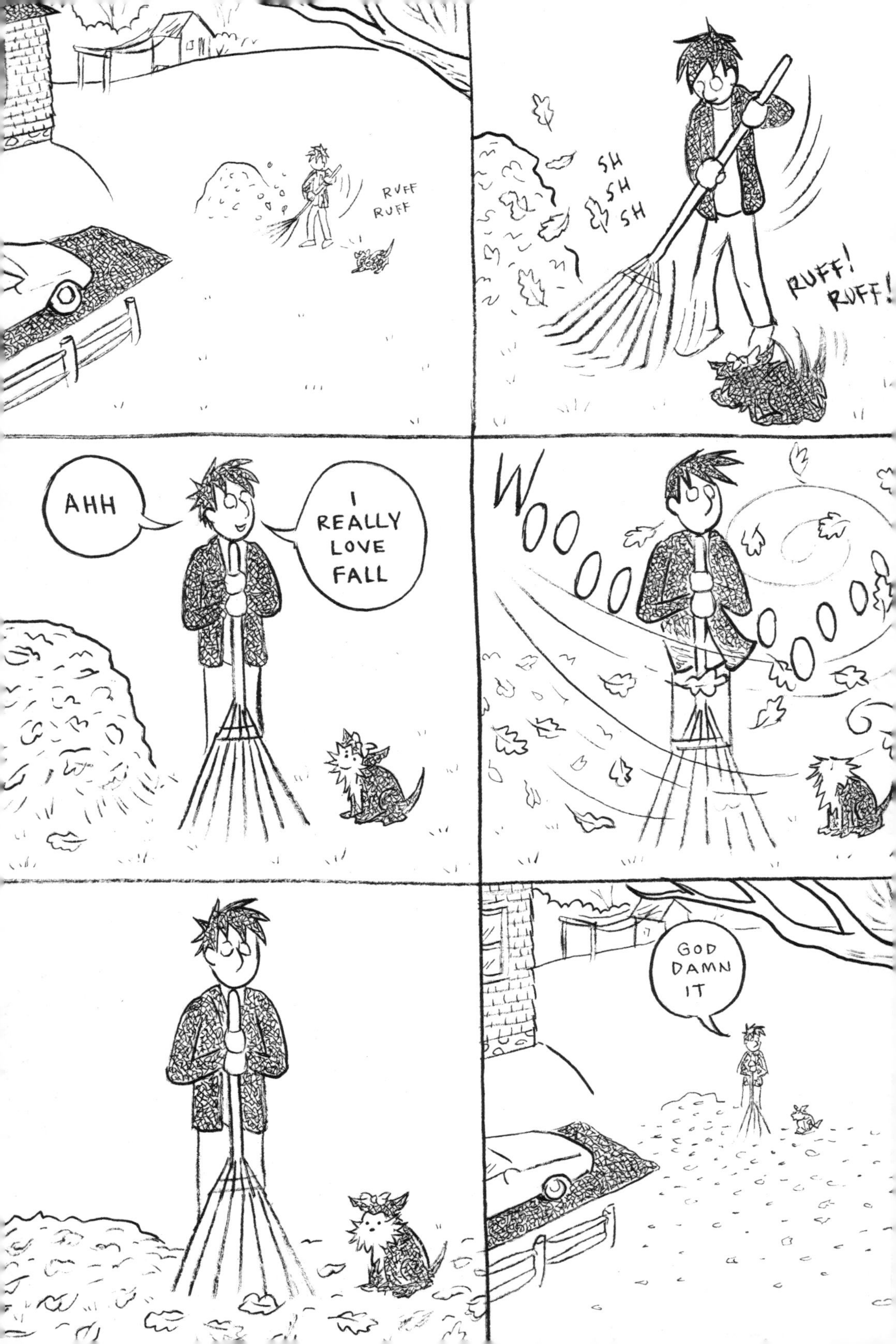
RUFF
RUFF
SH
SH
SH
RUFF!
RUFF!
AHH
I REALLY LOVE FALL
WOOOOOOOOOOO
GOD DAMN IT

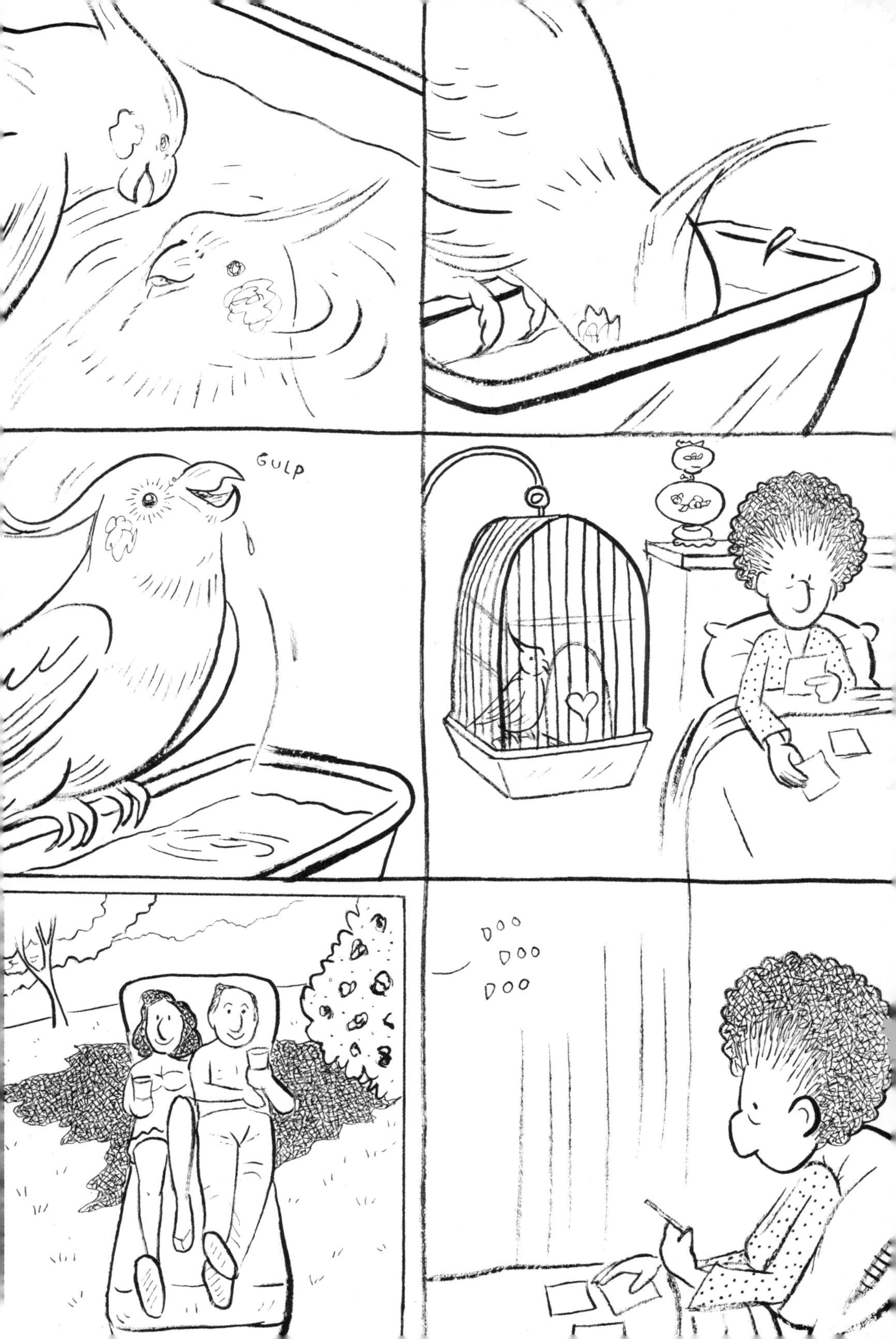
GULP
DOO
DOO
DOO

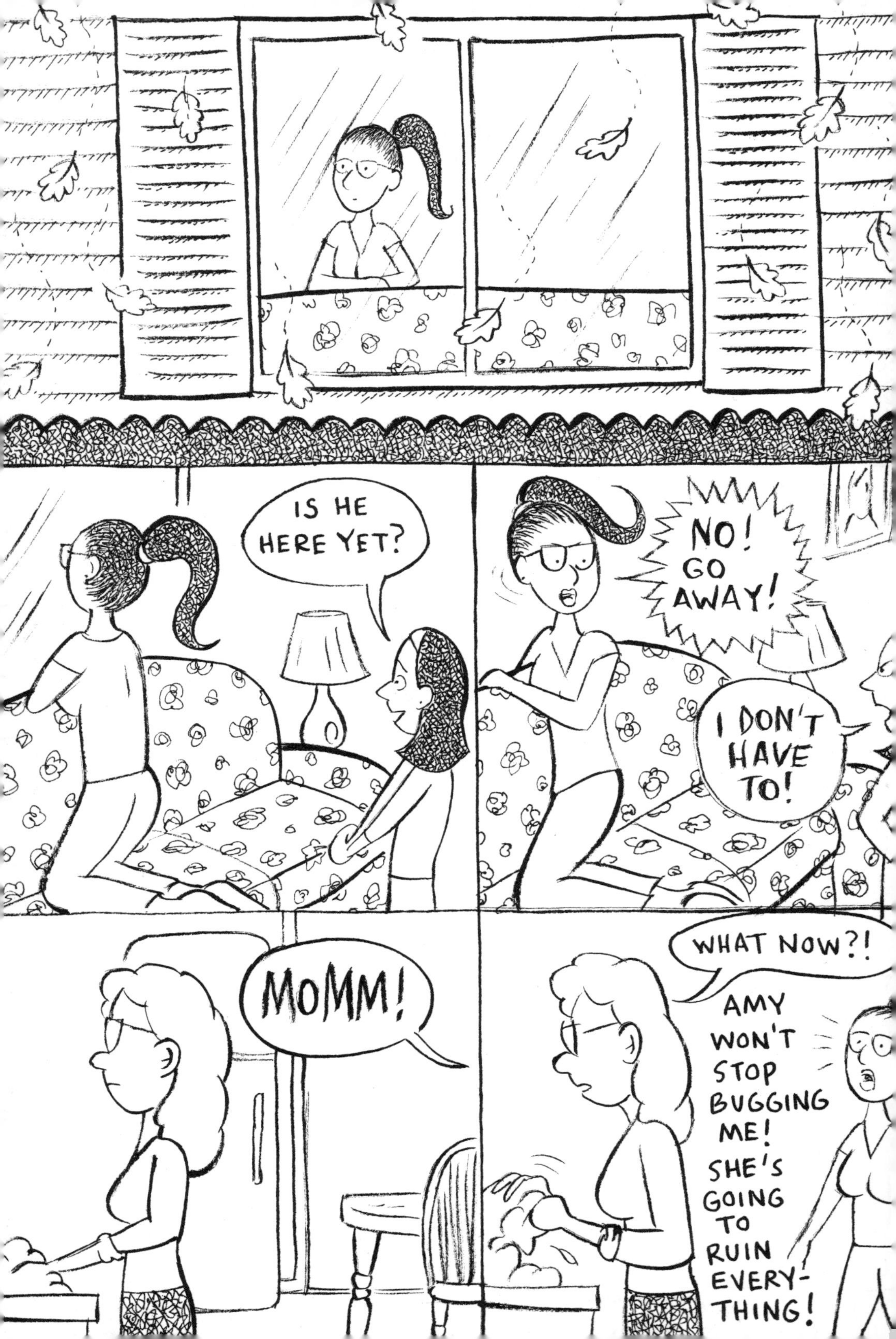
IS HE HERE YET?
NO! GO AWAY!
I DON'T HAVE TO!
MOMM!
WHAT NOW?!
AMY WON'T STOP BUGGING ME! SHE'S GOING TO RUIN EVERY-THING!

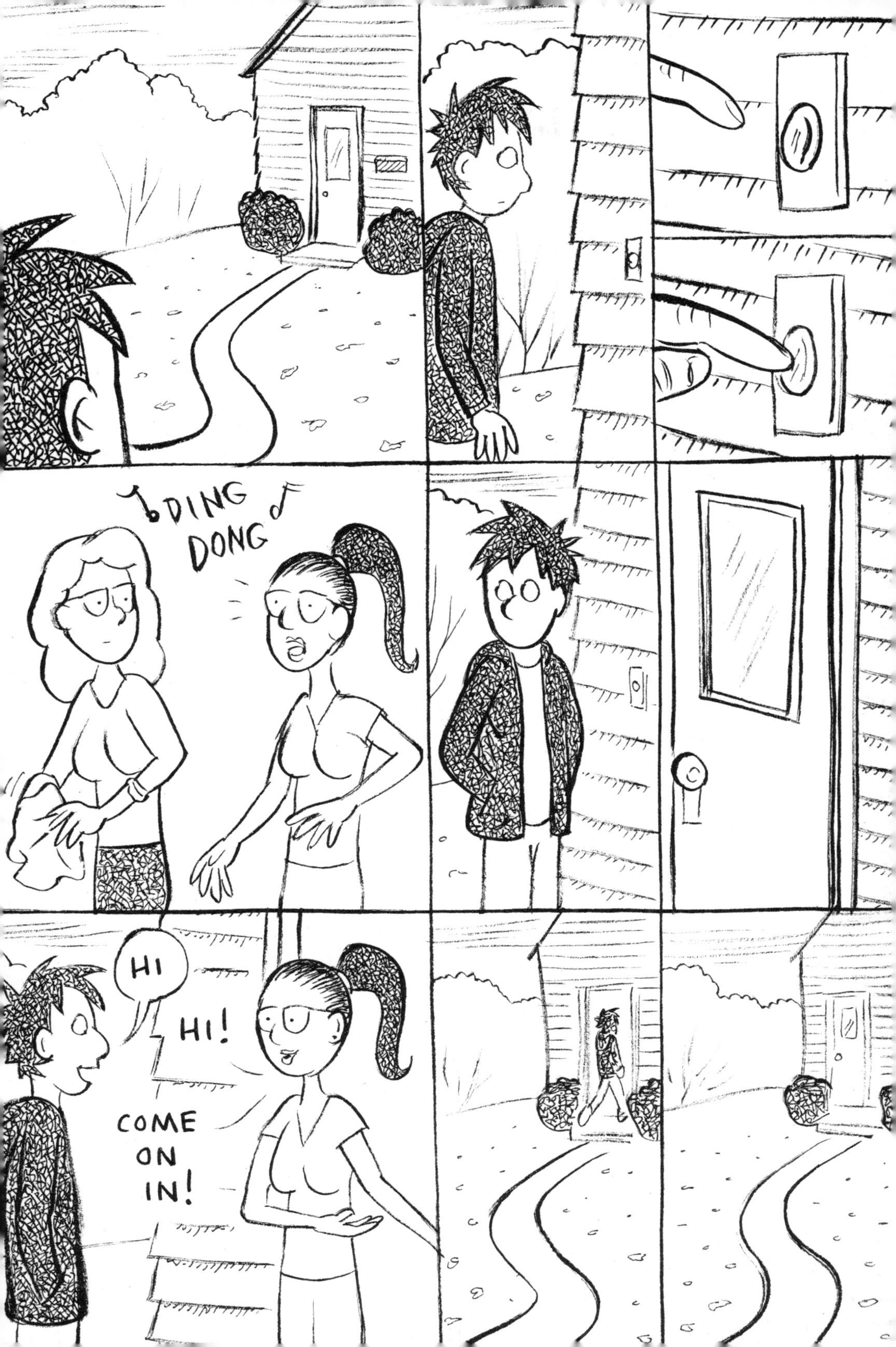
DING DONG
HI
HI!
COME ON IN!

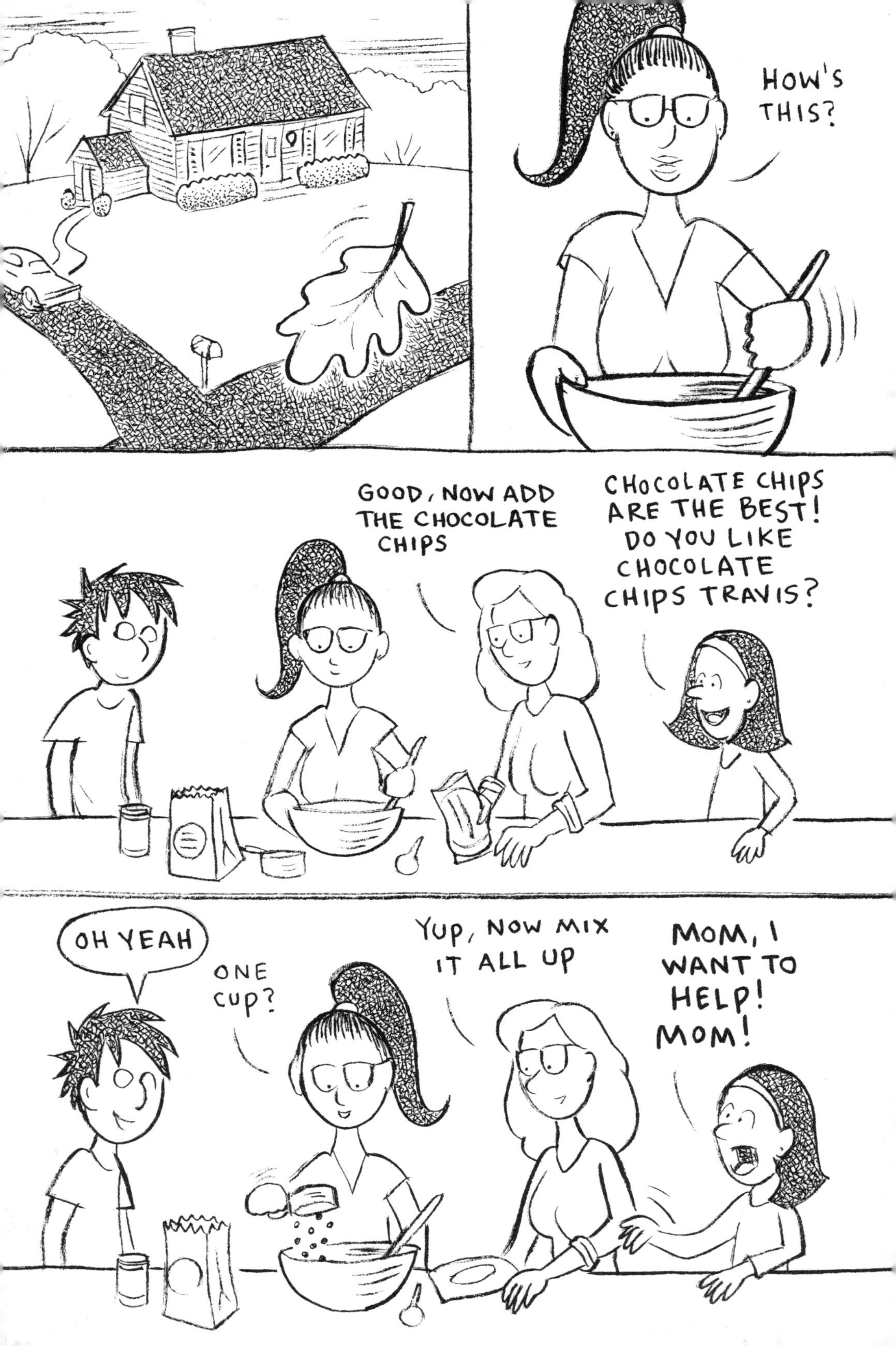
HOW'S THIS?
GOOD, NOW ADD THE CHOCOLATE CHIPS
CHOCOLATE CHIPS ARE THE BEST! DO YOU LIKE CHOCOLATE CHIPS TRAVIS?
OH YEAH
ONE CUP?
YUP, NOW MIX IT ALL UP
MOM, I WANT TO HELP! MOM!

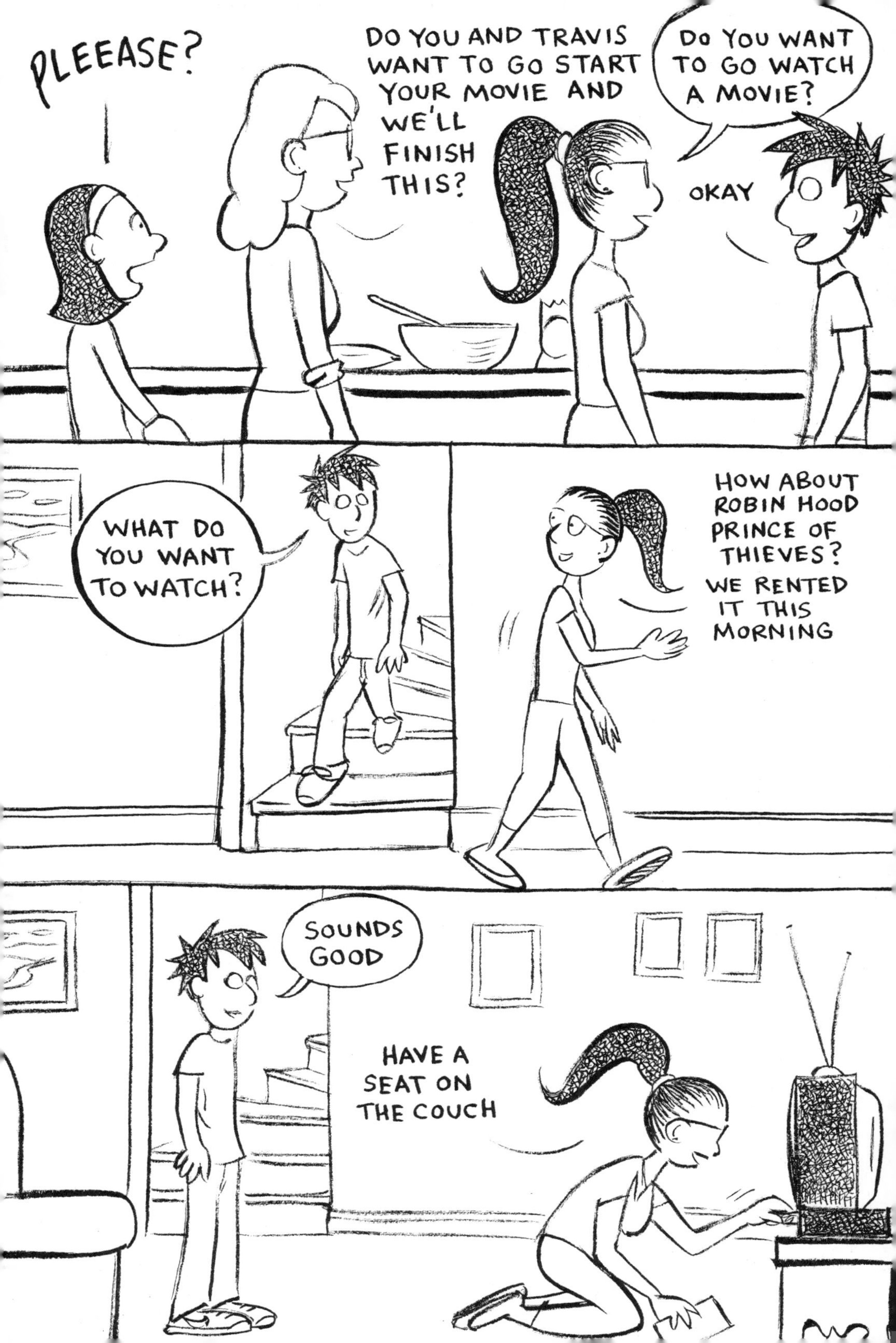
PLEEASE?
DO YOU AND TRAVIS WANT TO GO START YOUR MOVIE AND WE'LL FINISH THIS?
DO YOU WANT TO GO WATCH A MOVIE?
OKAY
WHAT DO YOU WANT TO WATCH?
HOW ABOUT ROBIN HOOD PRINCE OF THIEVES?
WE RENTED IT THIS MORNING
SOUNDS GOOD
HAVE A SEAT ON THE COUCH

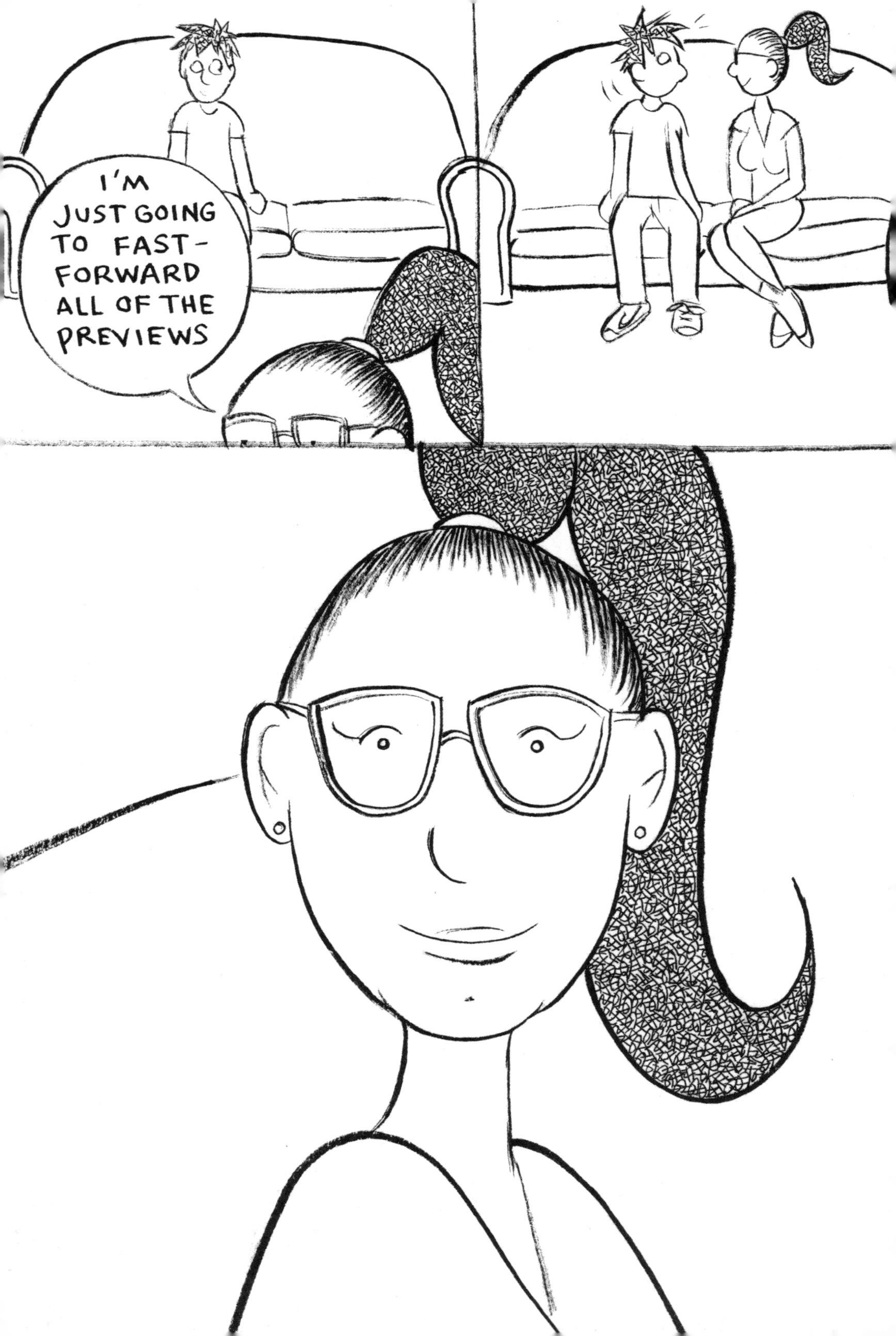
I'M JUST GOING TO FAST-FORWARD ALL OF THE PREVIEWS

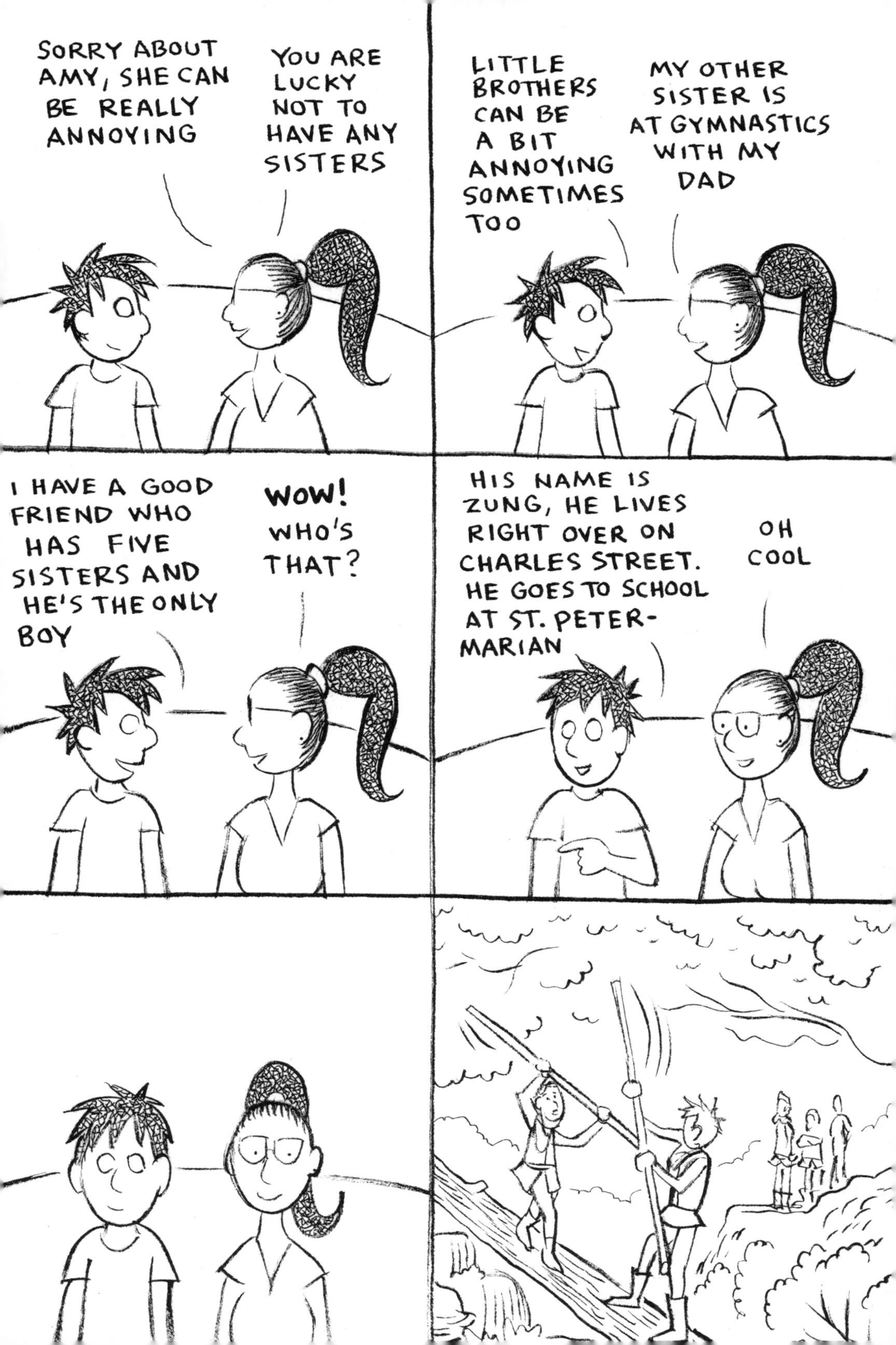

SORRY ABOUT AMY, SHE CAN BE REALLY ANNOYING
YOU ARE LUCKY NOT TO HAVE ANY SISTERS
LITTLE BROTHERS CAN BE A BIT ANNOYING SOMETIMES TOO
MY OTHER SISTER IS AT GYMNASTICS WITH MY DAD
I HAVE A GOOD FRIEND WHO HAS FIVE SISTERS AND HE'S THE ONLY BOY
WOW! WHO'S THAT?
HIS NAME IS ZUNG, HE LIVES RIGHT OVER ON CHARLES STREET. HE GOES TO SCHOOL AT ST. PETER-MARIAN
OH COOL

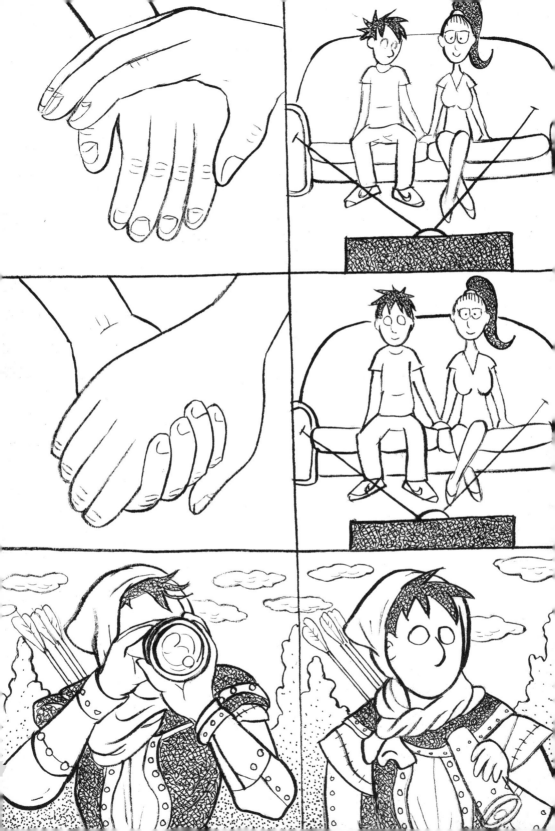

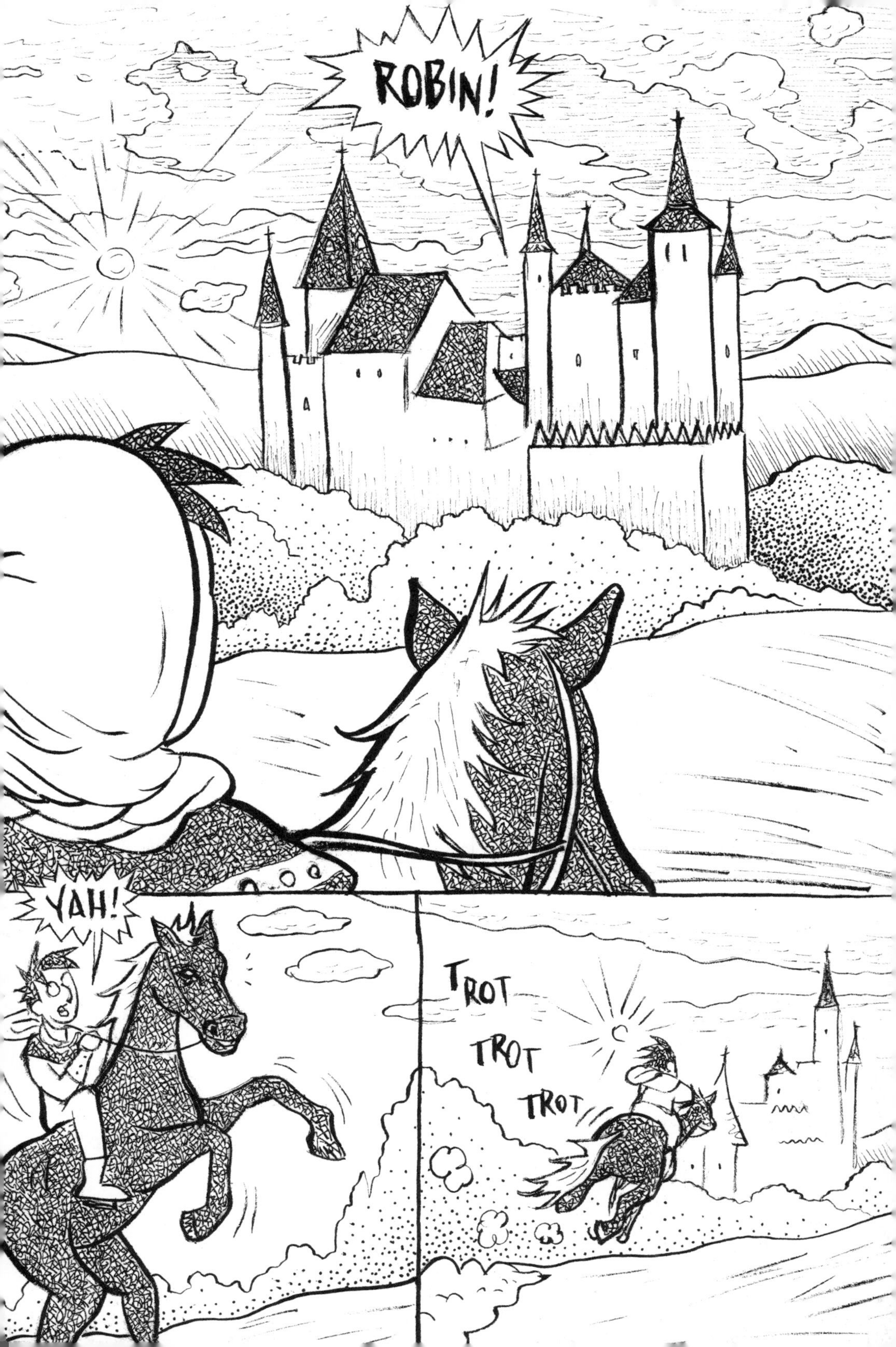
ROBIN!
YAH!
TROT
TROT
TROT

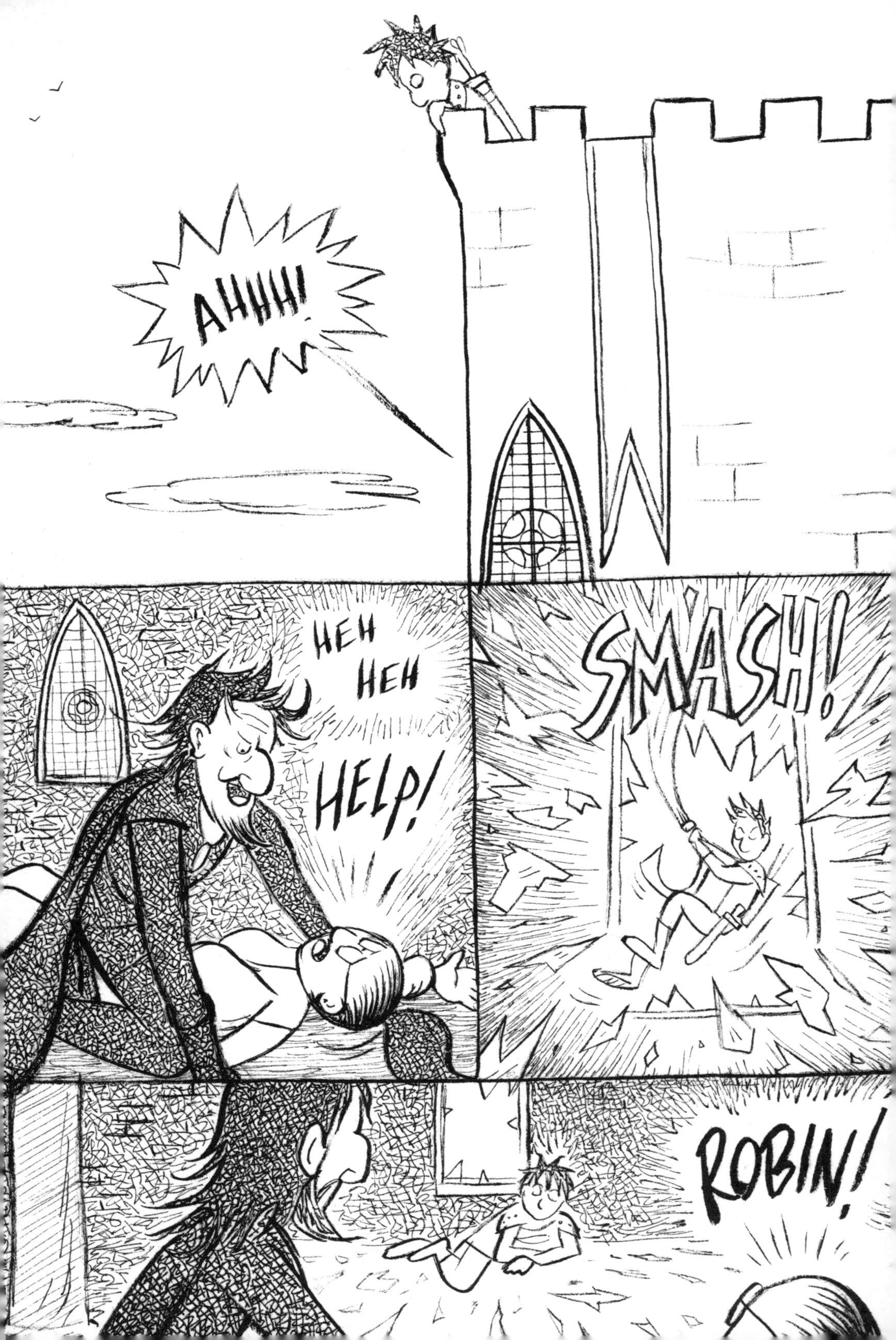
AHHH!
HEH HEH
HELP!
SMASH!
ROBIN!

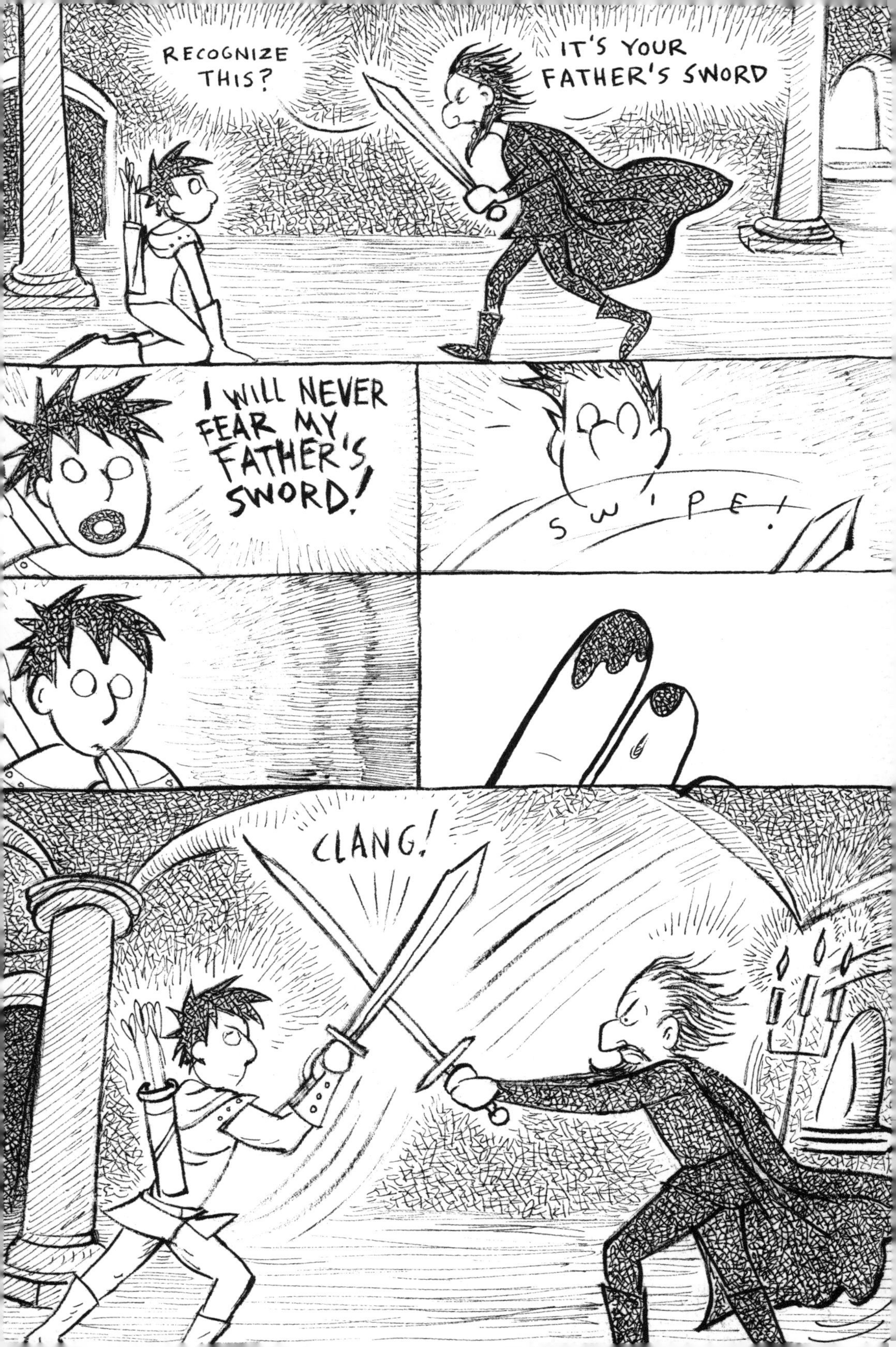
RECOGNIZE THIS?
IT'S YOUR FATHER'S SWORD
I WILL NEVER FEAR MY FATHER'S SWORD!
SWIPE!
CLANG!

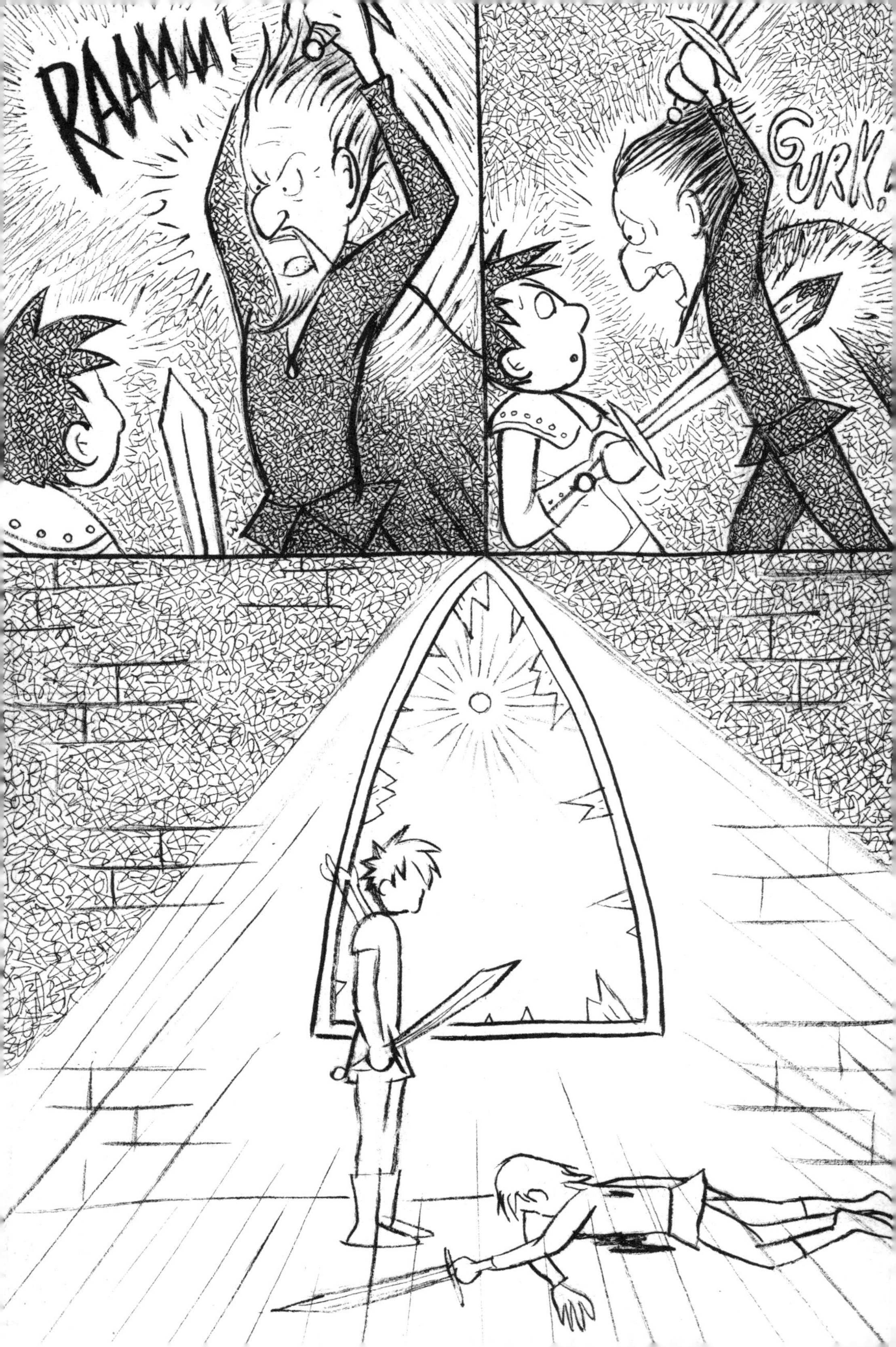
RAAAAA!
GURK!

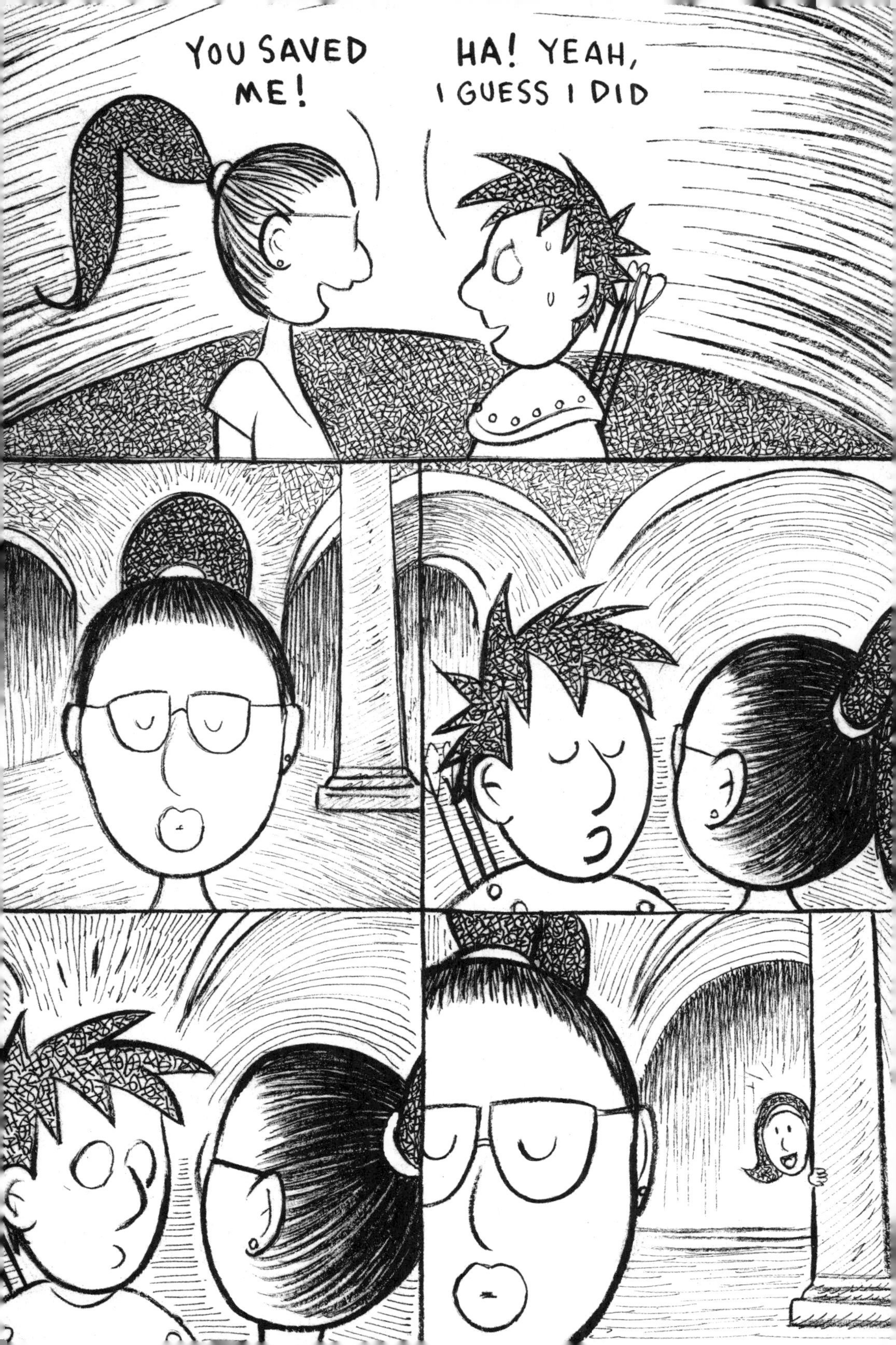
YOU SAVED ME!
HA! YEAH, I GUESS I DID

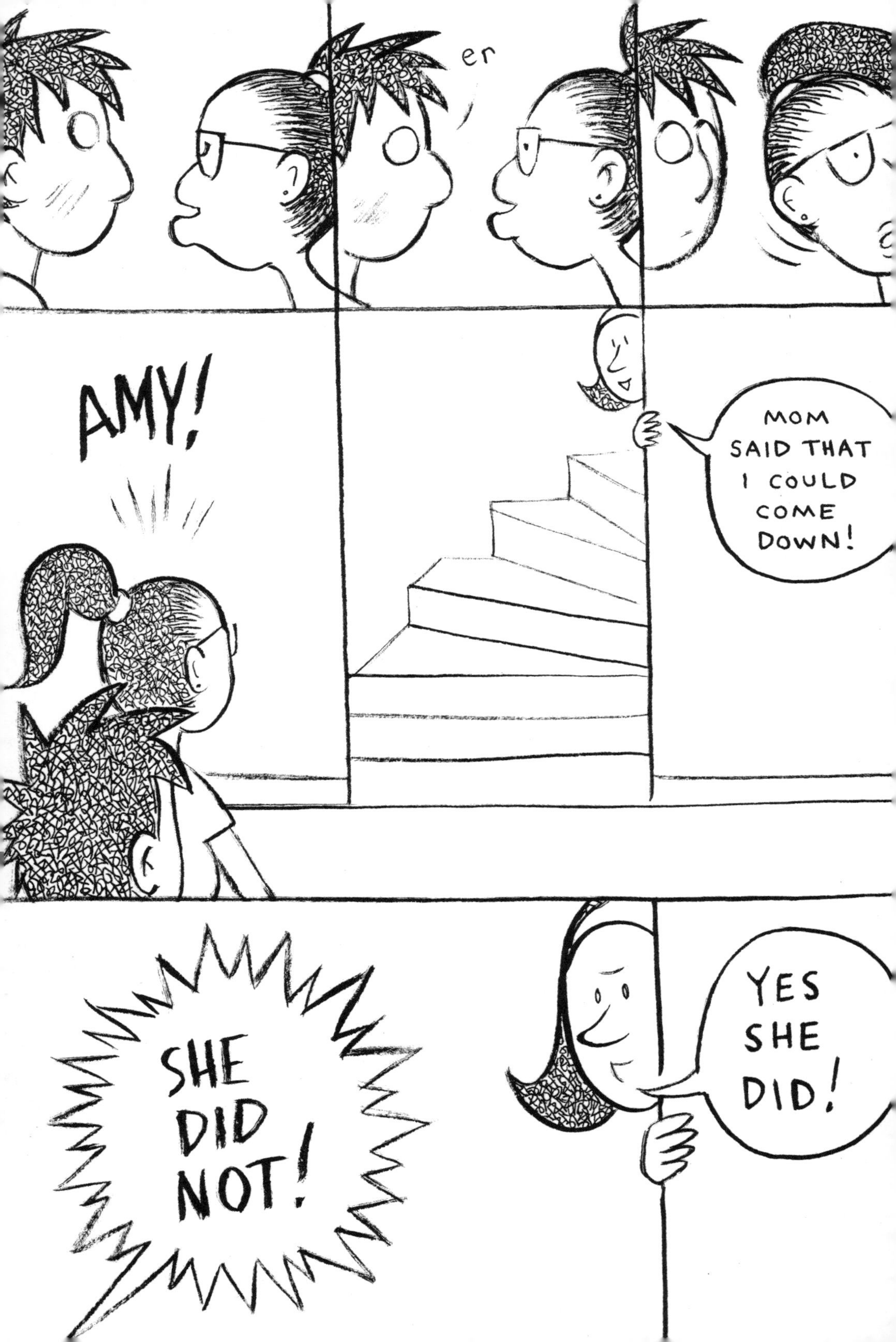
er
AMY!
MOM SAID THAT I COULD COME DOWN!
SHE DID NOT!
YES SHE DID!

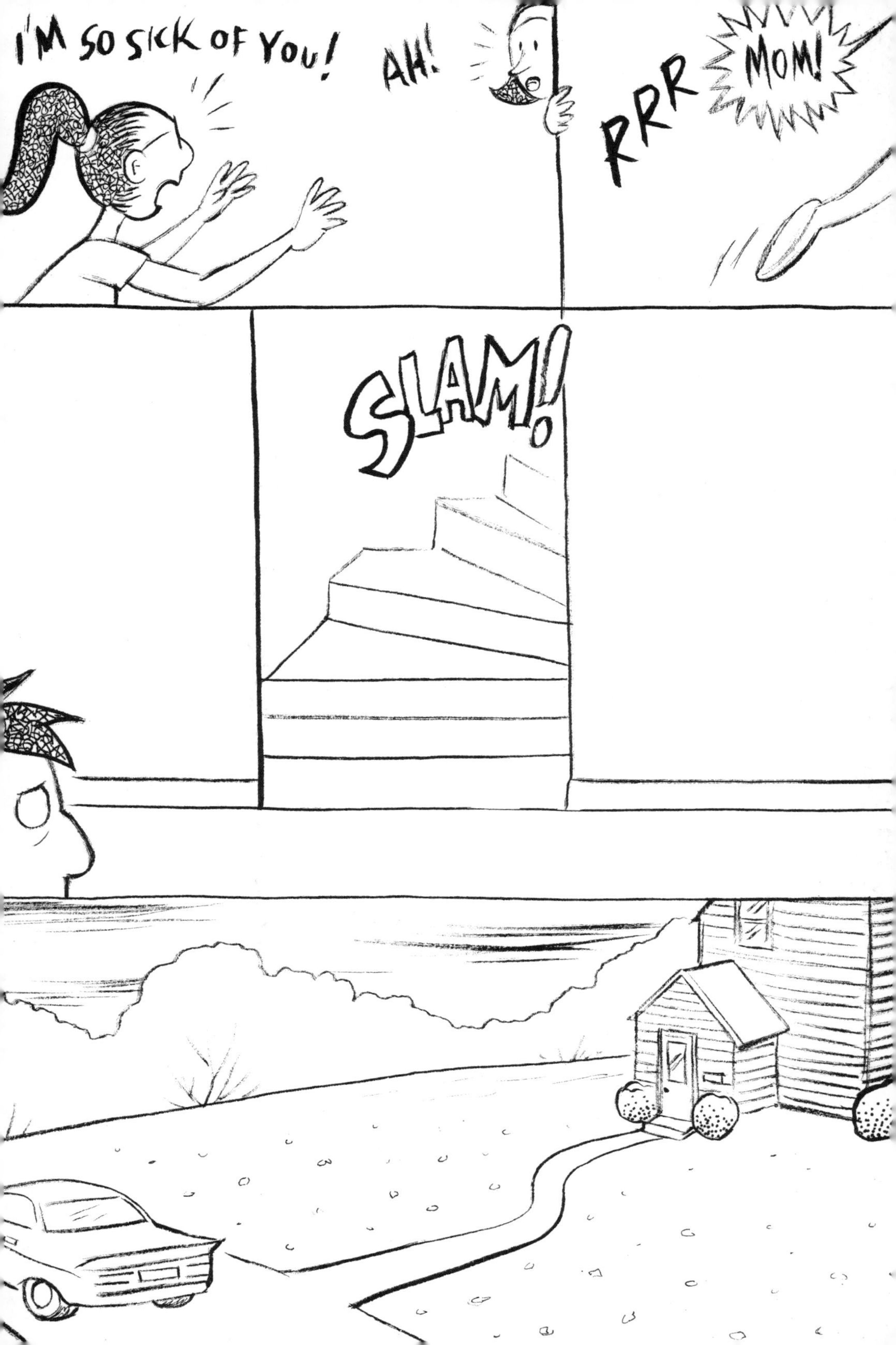
I'M SO SICK OF YOU!
AH!
RRR
MOM!
SLAM!

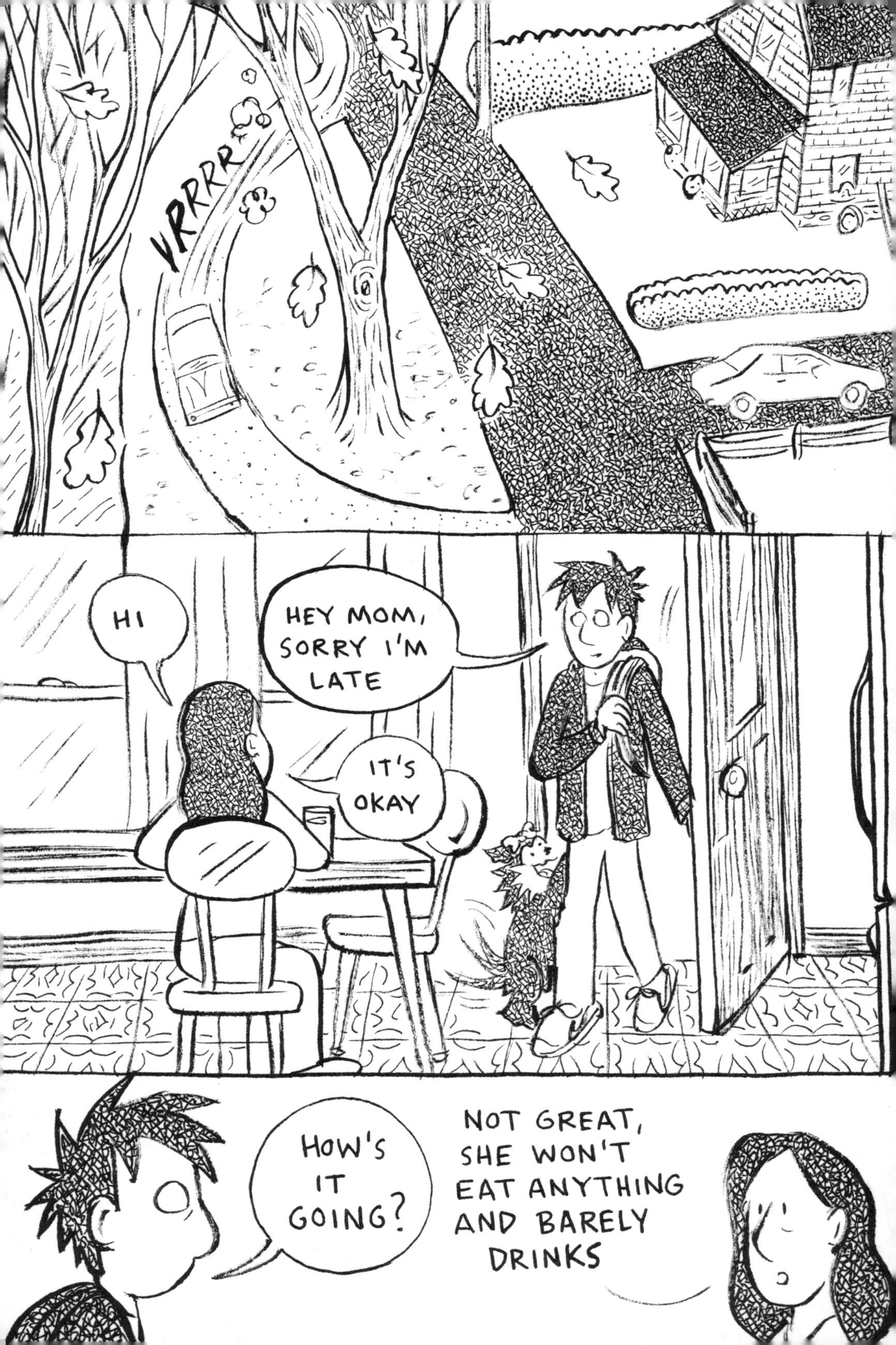
VRRRR
HI
HEY MOM, SORRY I'M LATE
IT'S OKAY
HOW'S IT GOING?
NOT GREAT, SHE WON'T EAT ANYTHING AND BARELY DRINKS

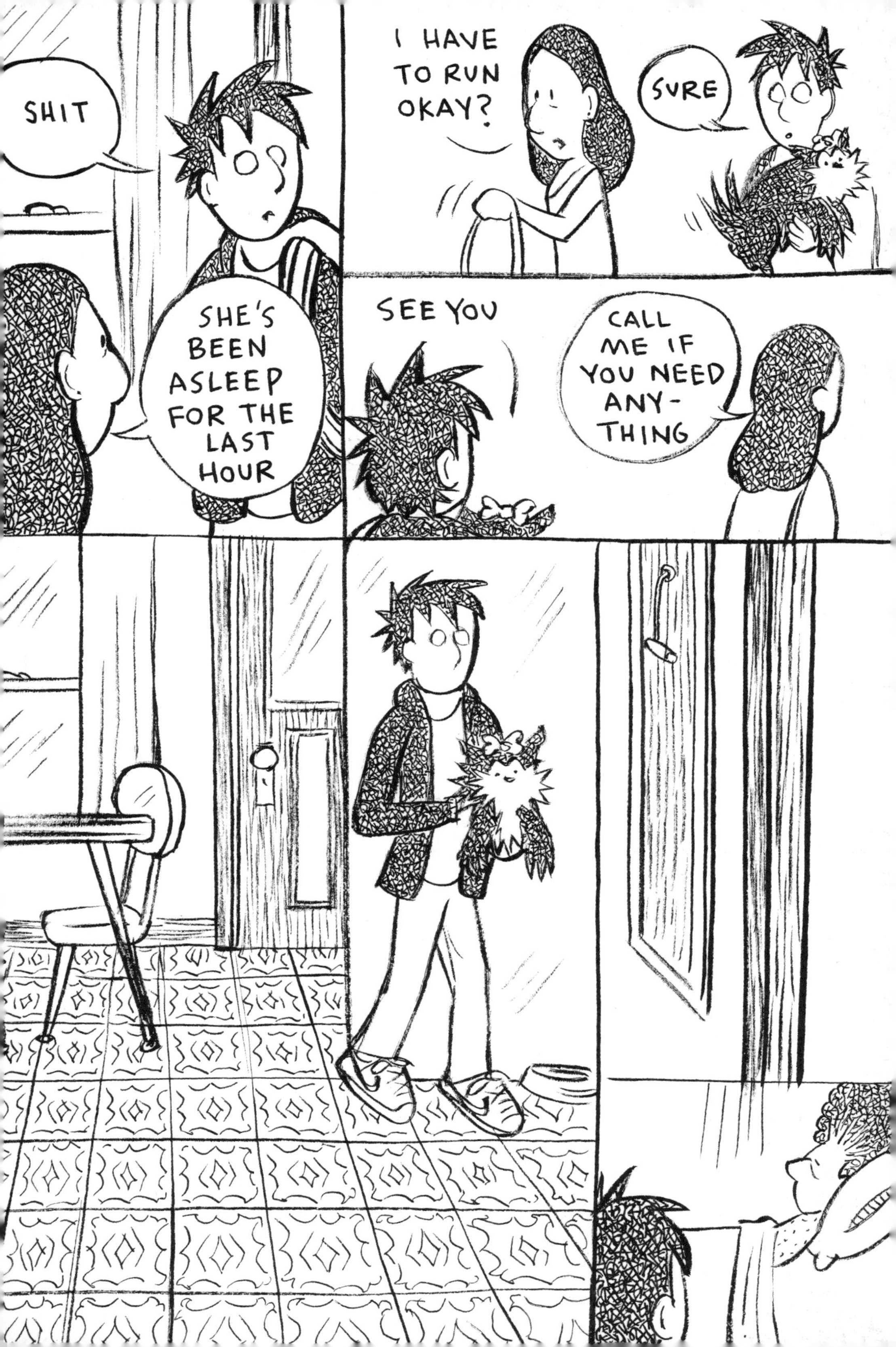
SHIT
SHE'S BEEN ASLEEP FOR THE LAST HOUR
I HAVE TO RUN OKAY?
SURE
SEE YOU
CALL ME IF YOU NEED ANY-THING

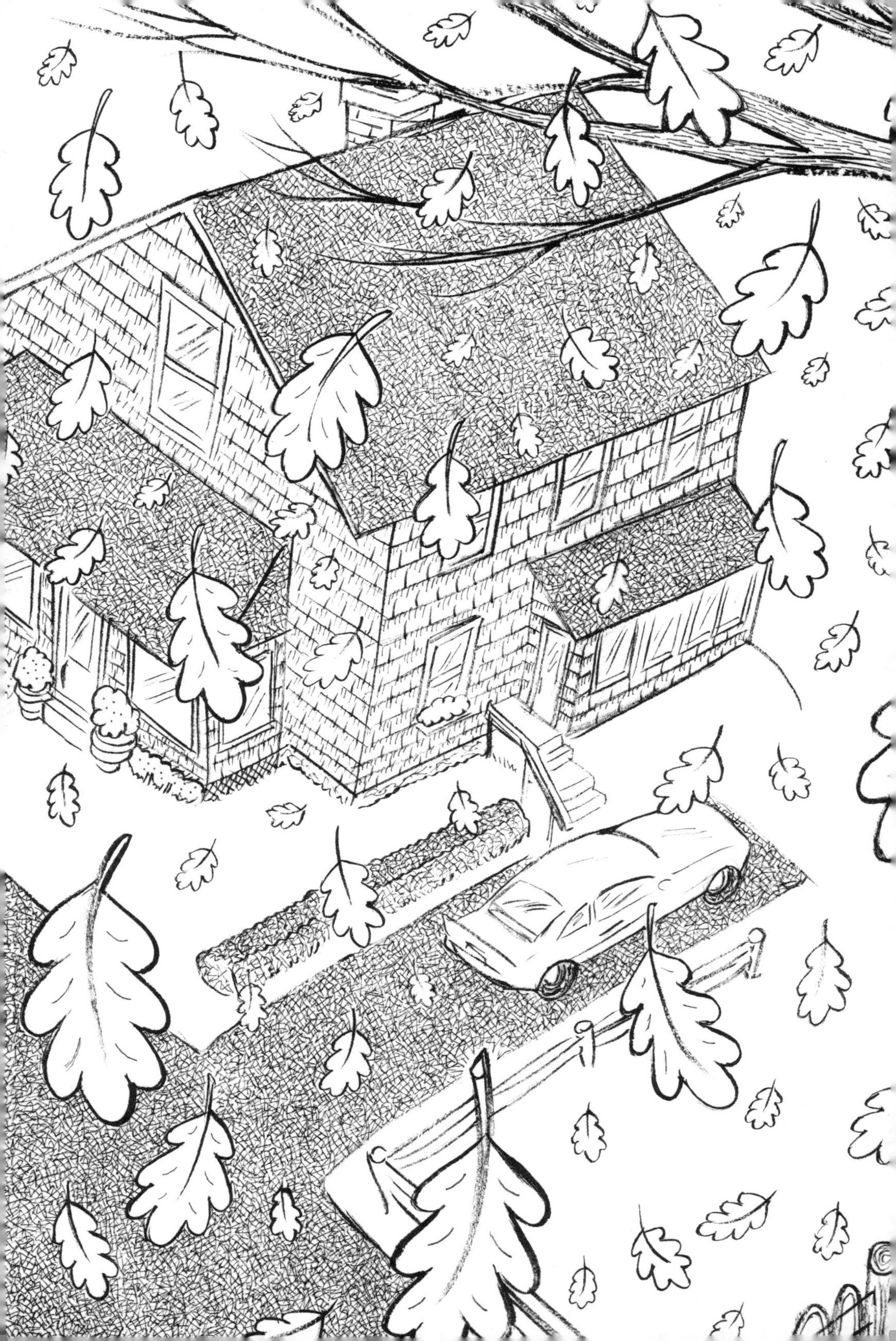

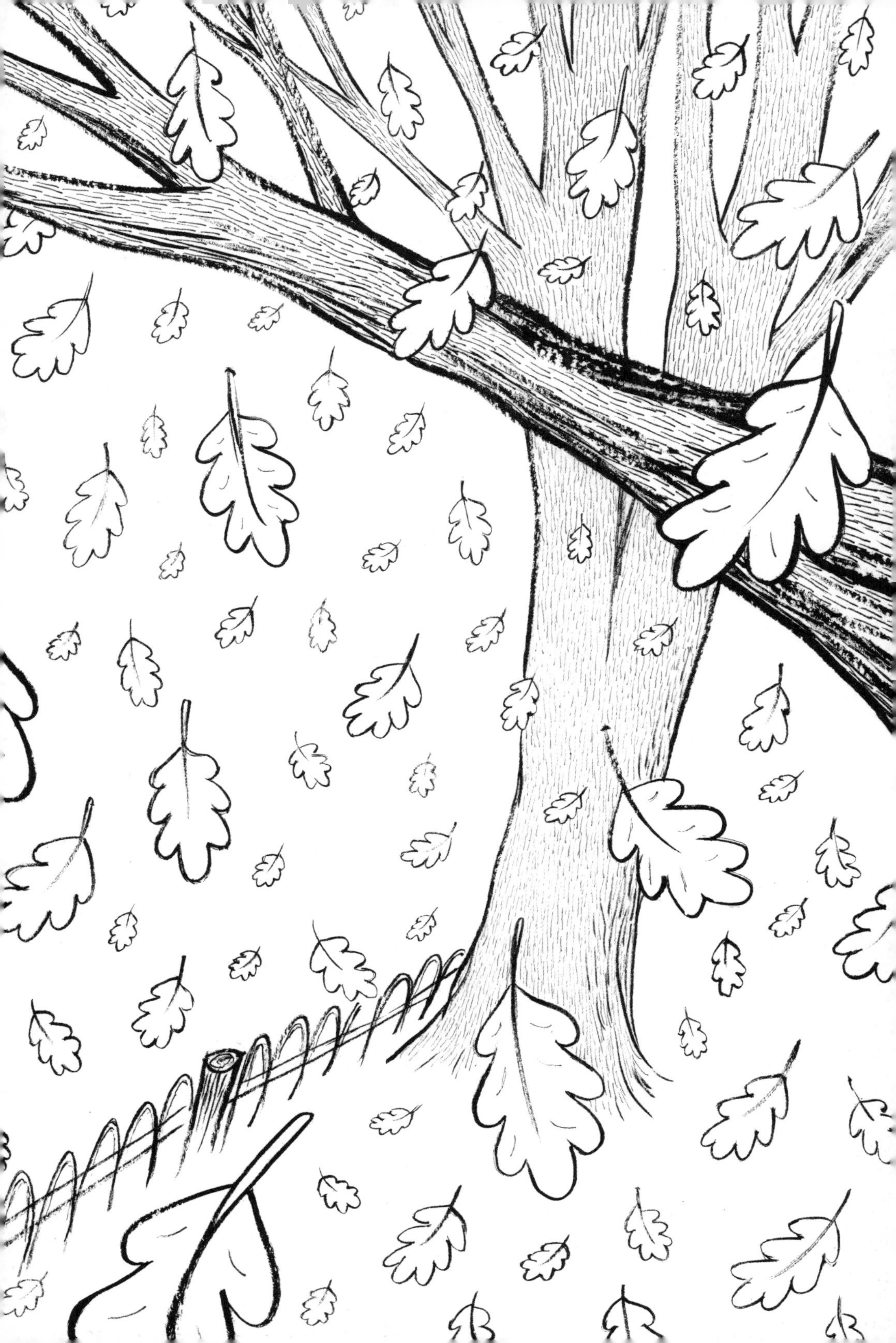

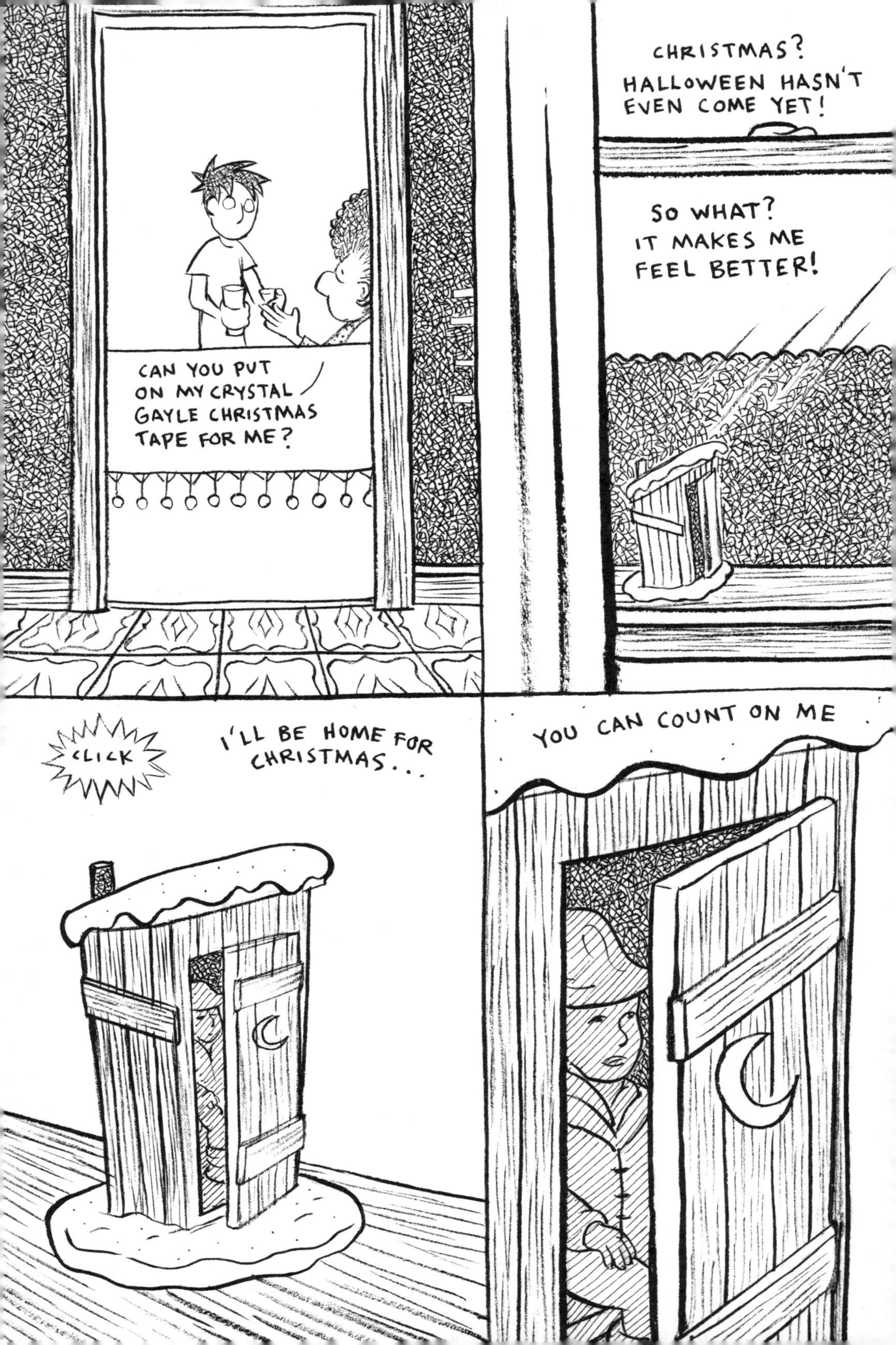
CAN YOU PUT ON MY CRYSTAL GAYLE CHRISTMAS TAPE FOR ME?
CHRISTMAS? HALLOWEEN HASN'T EVEN COME YET!
SO WHAT? IT MAKES ME FEEL BETTER!
CLICK
I'LL BE HOME FOR CHRISTMAS...
YOU CAN COUNT ON ME

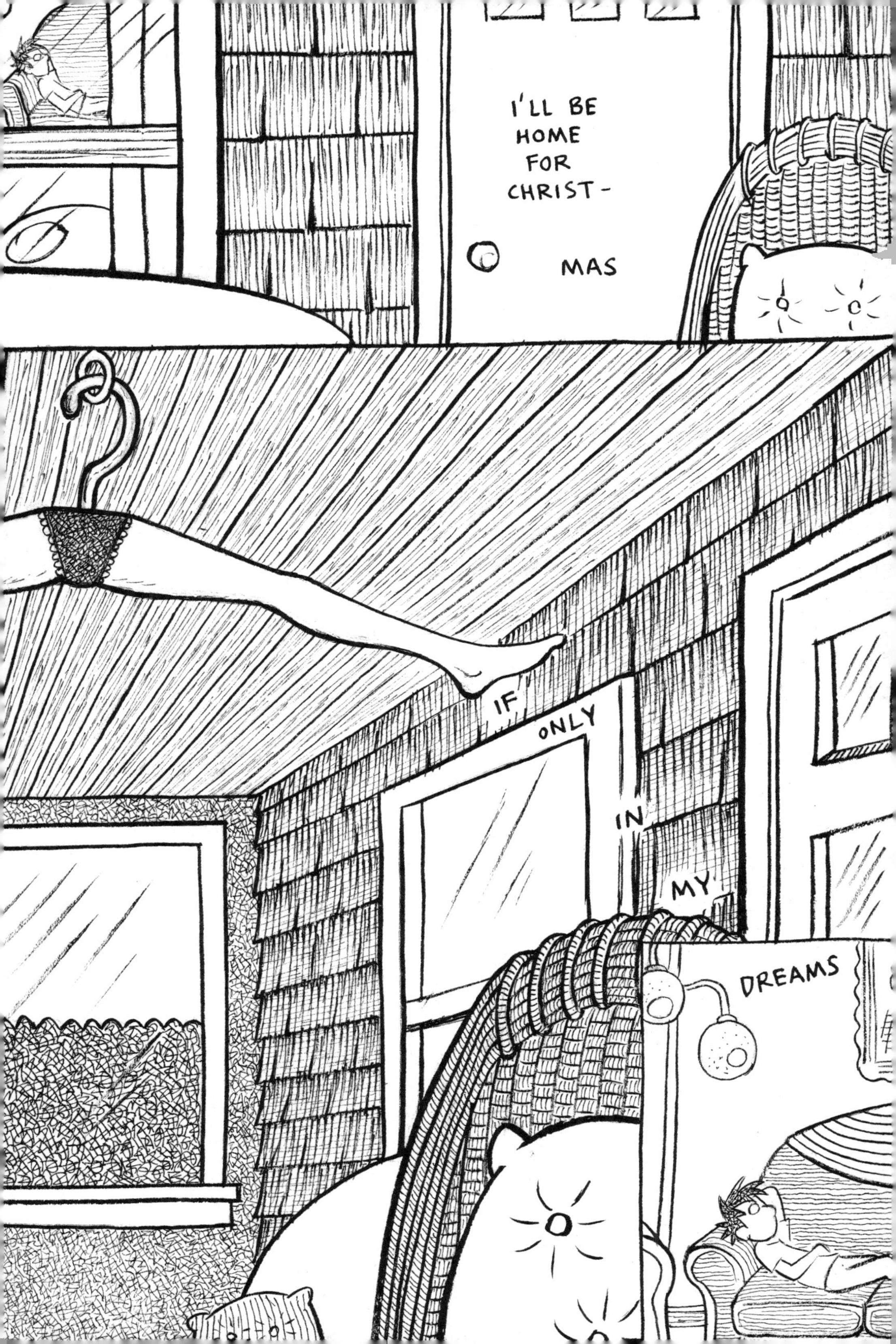
I'LL BE HOME FOR CHRIST-
MAS
IF ONLY IN MY DREAMS

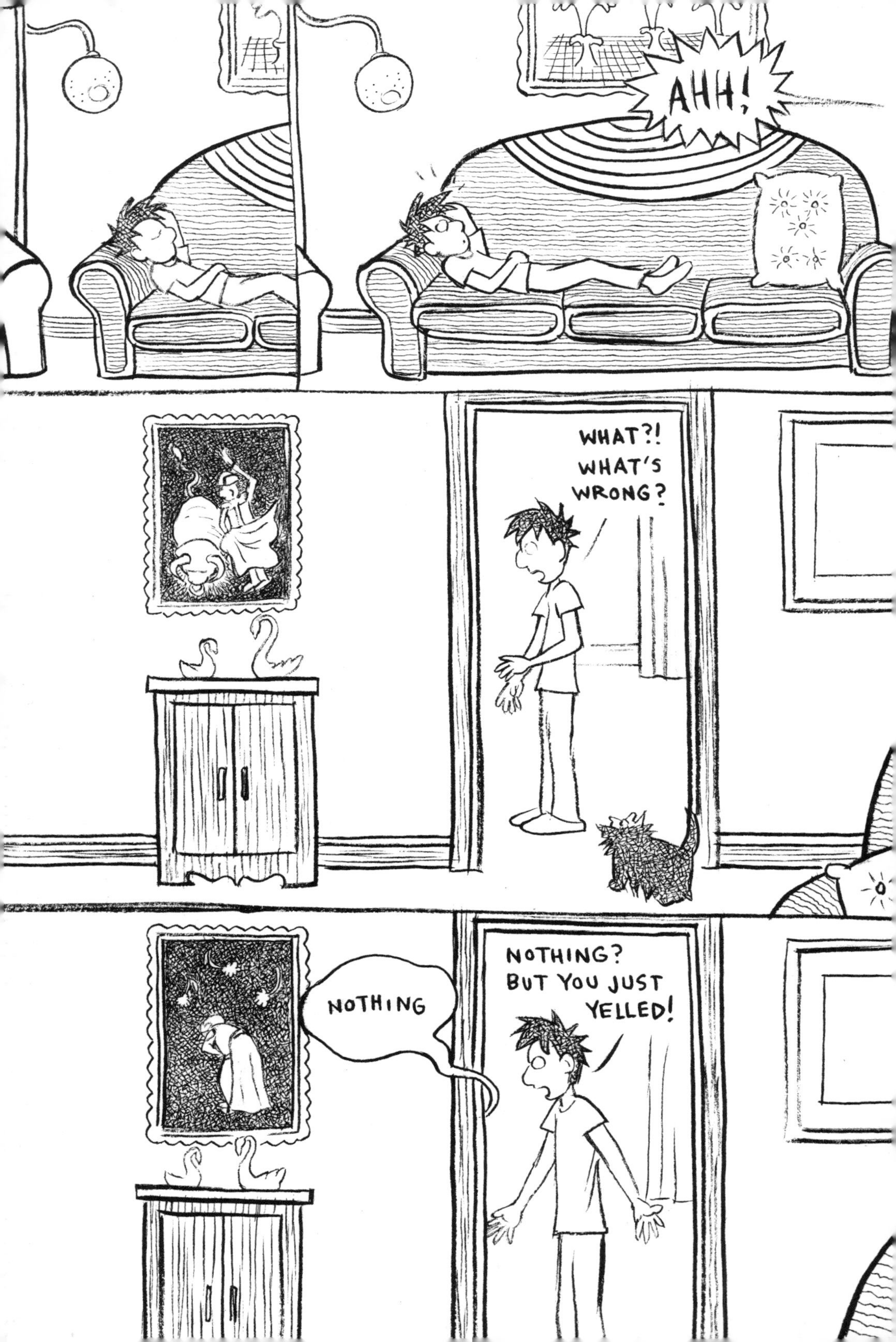
AHH!
WHAT?! WHAT'S WRONG?
NOTHING
NOTHING? BUT YOU JUST YELLED!

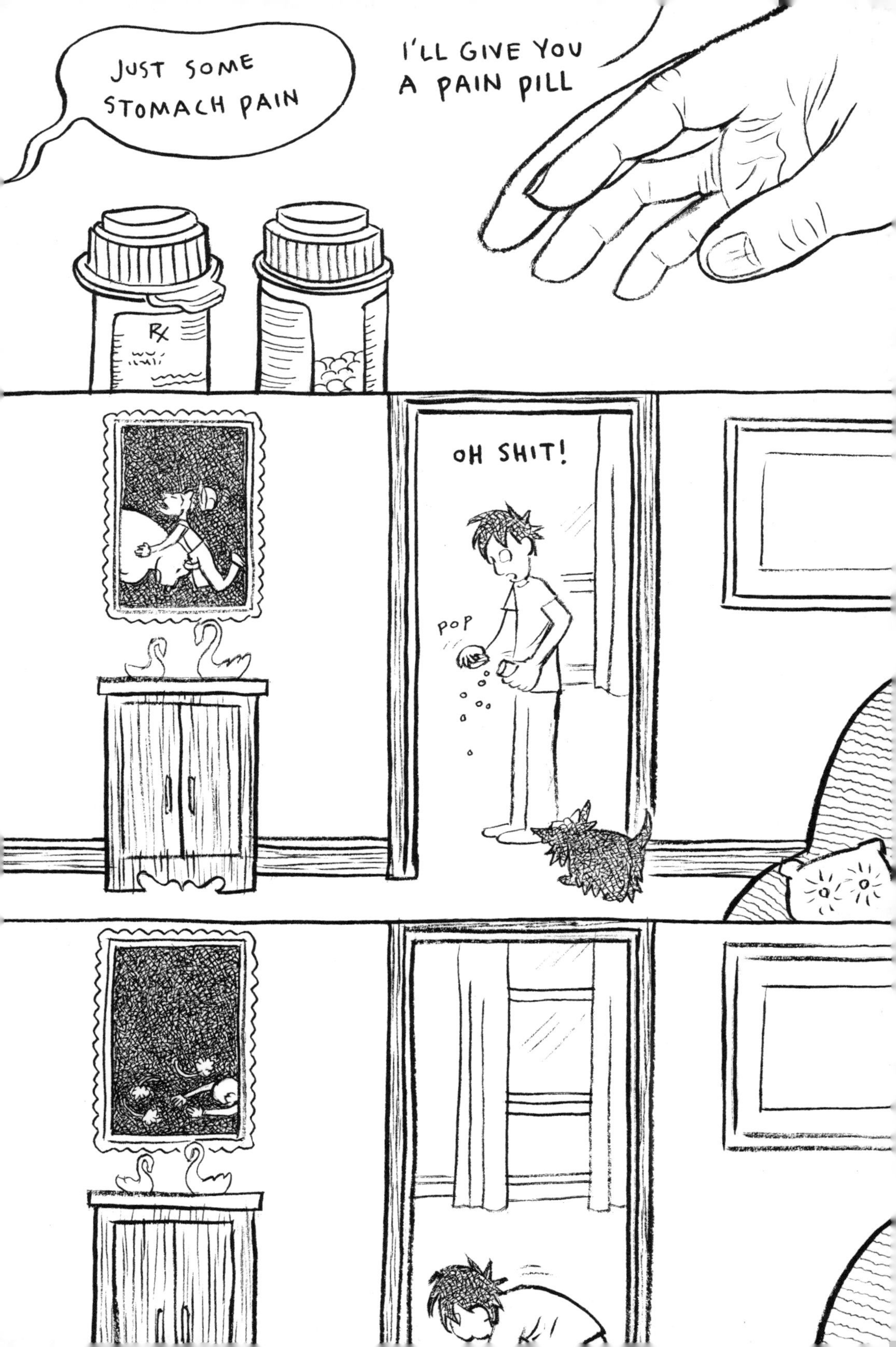
JUST SOME STOMACH PAIN
I'LL GIVE YOU A PAIN PILL
Rx
OH SHIT!
POP

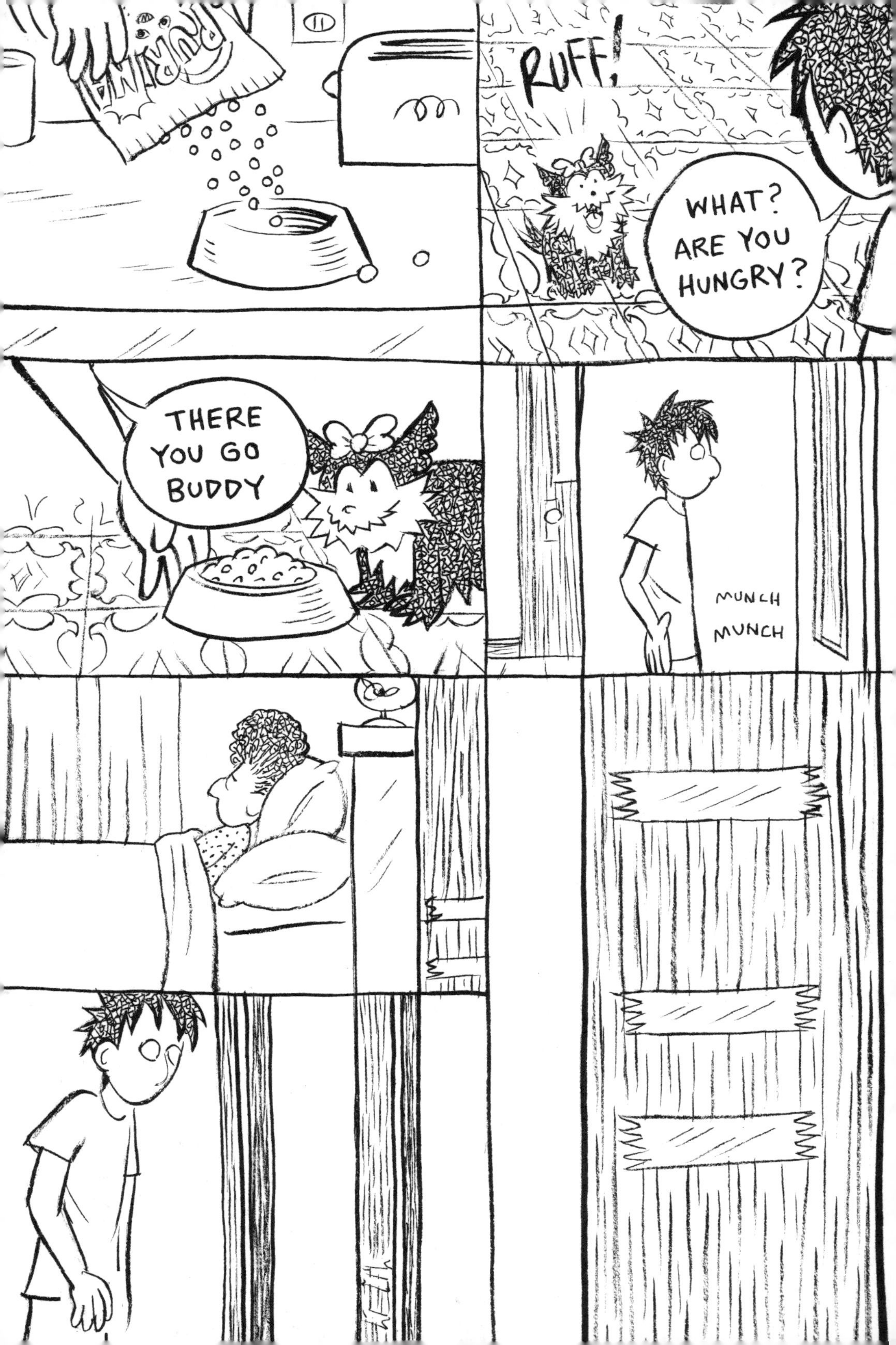
RUFF!
WHAT? ARE YOU HUNGRY?
THERE YOU GO BUDDY
MUNCH
MUNCH

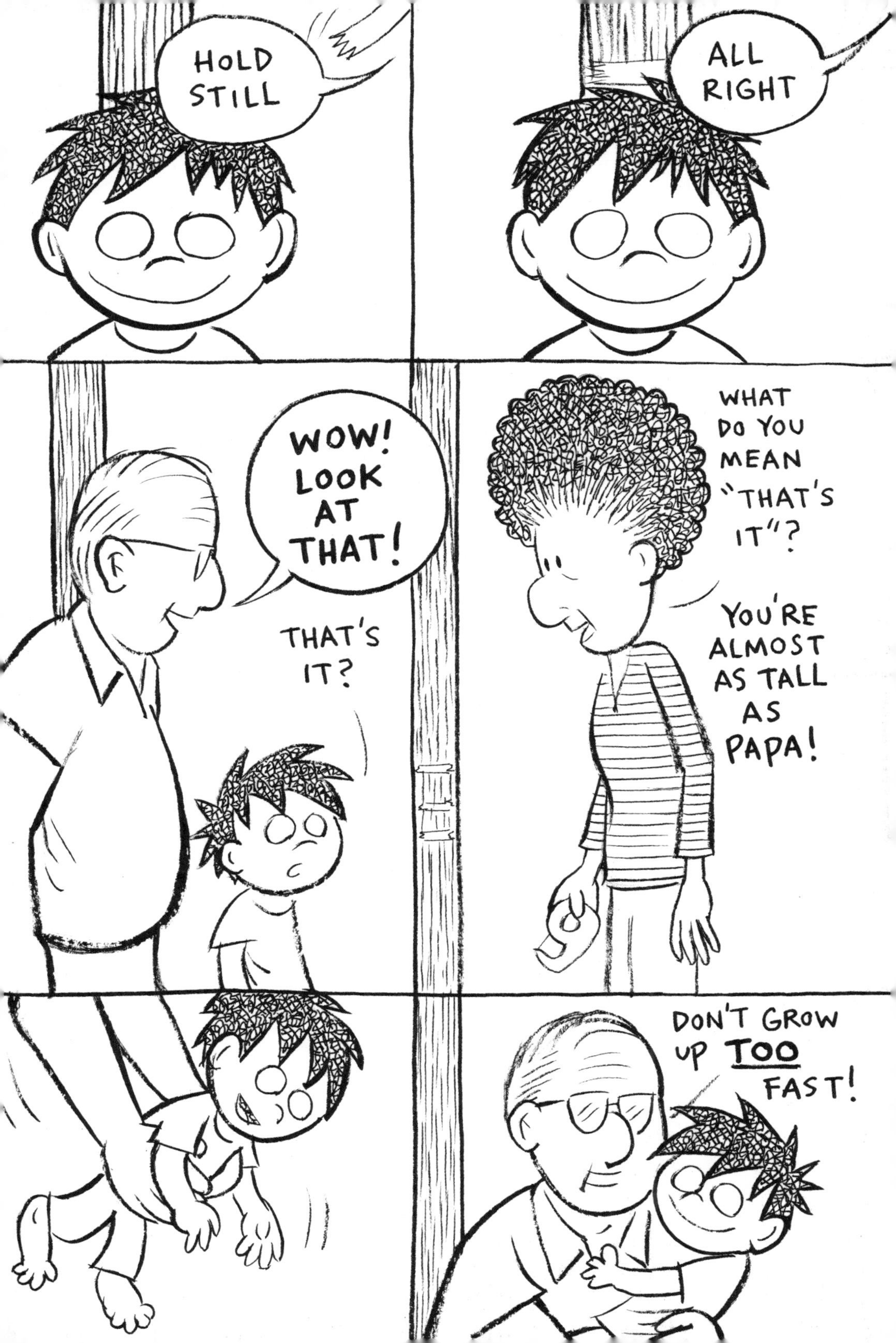
HOLD STILL
ALL RIGHT
WOW! LOOK AT THAT!
THAT'S IT?
WHAT DO YOU MEAN "THAT'S IT"?
YOU'RE ALMOST AS TALL AS PAPA!
DON'T GROW UP TOO FAST!

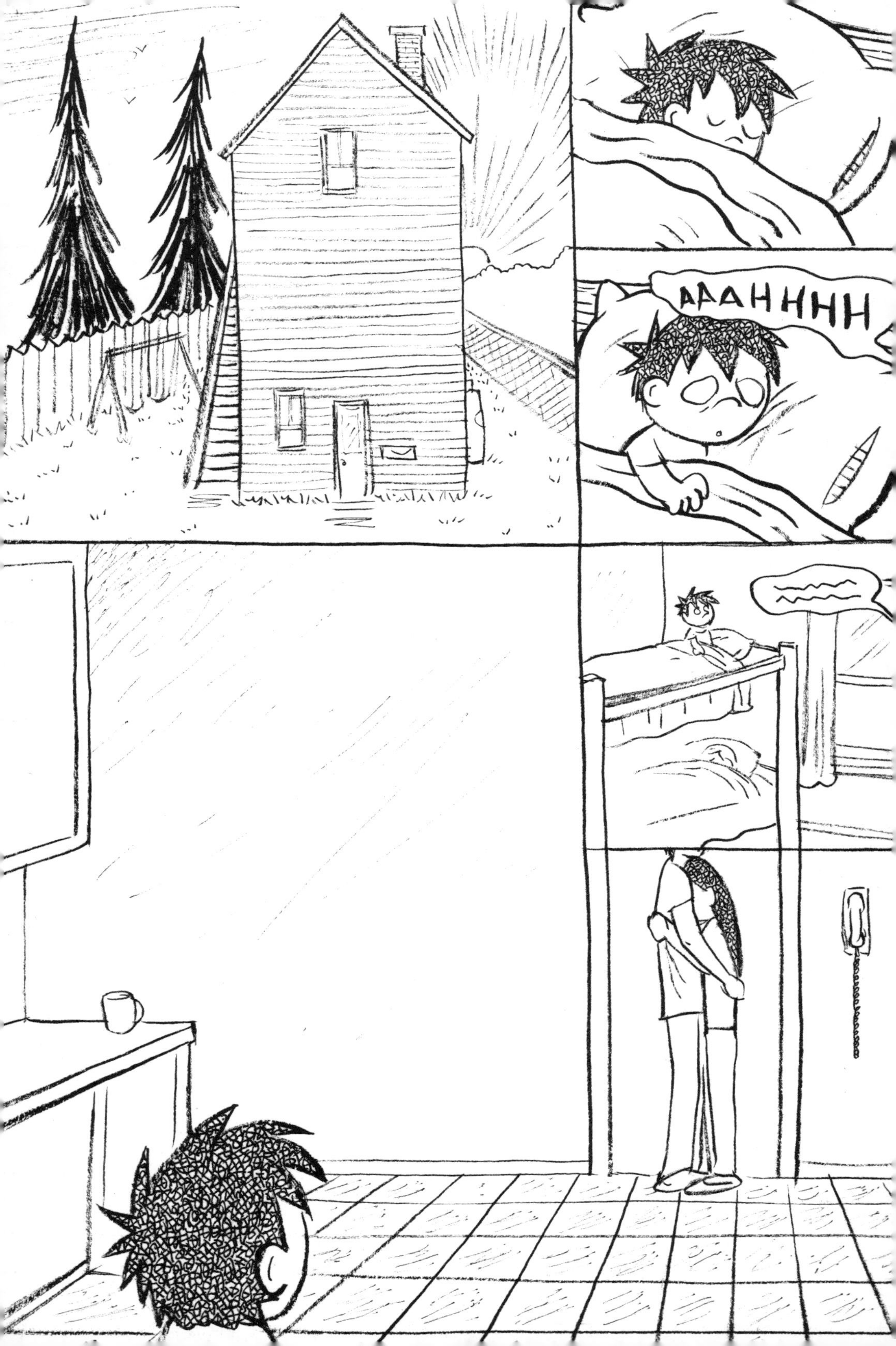
AAAHHHH

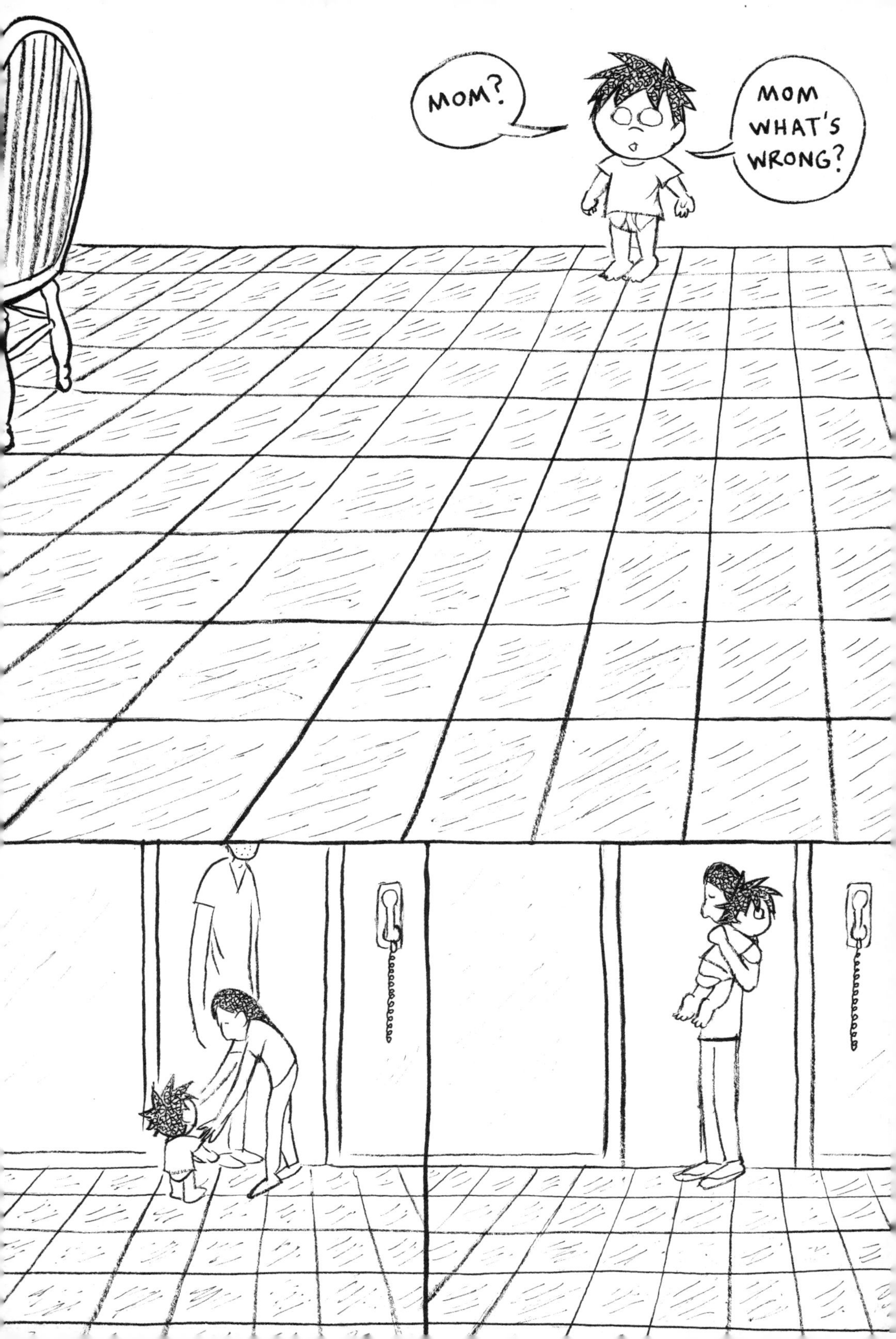
MOM?
MOM WHAT'S WRONG?

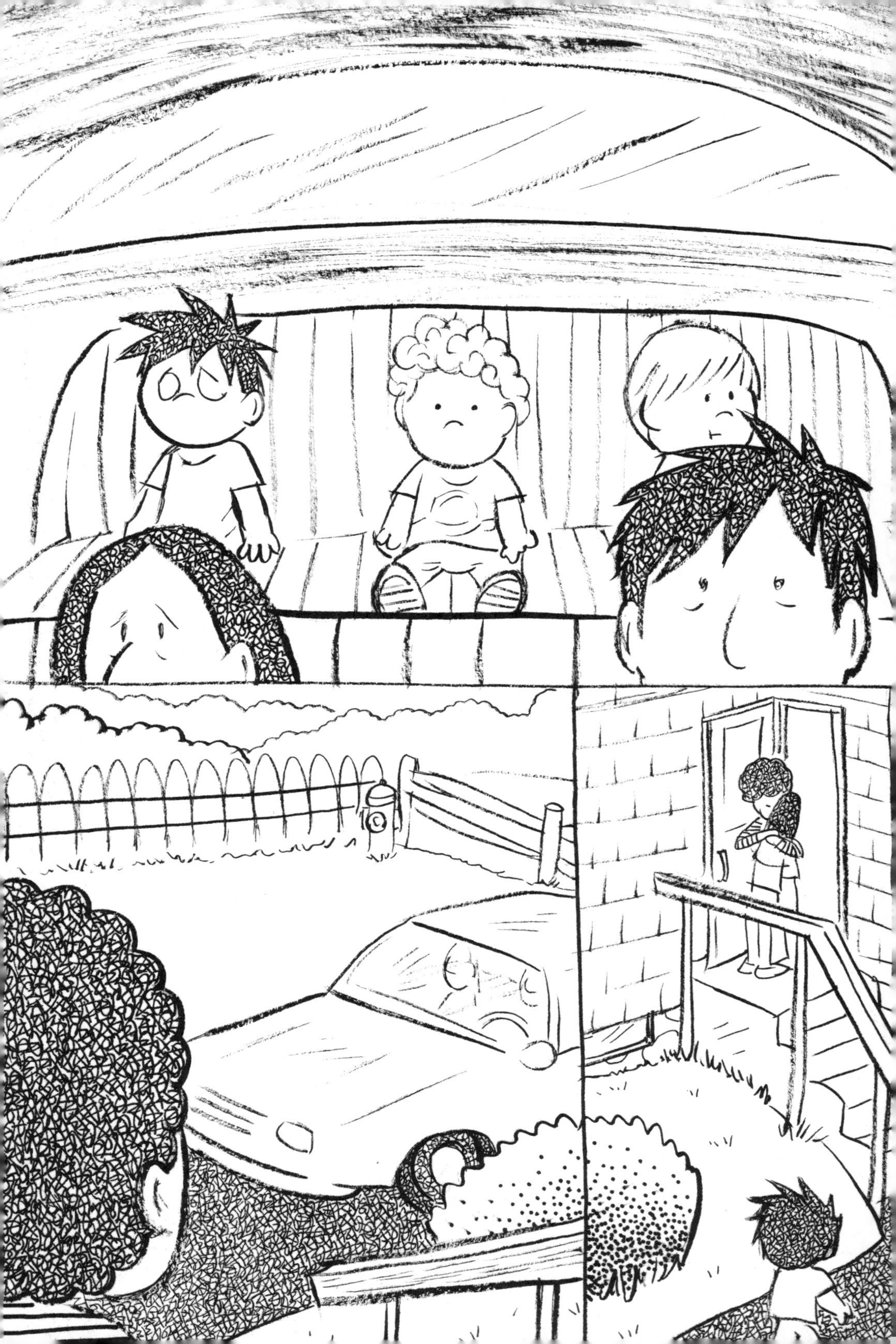

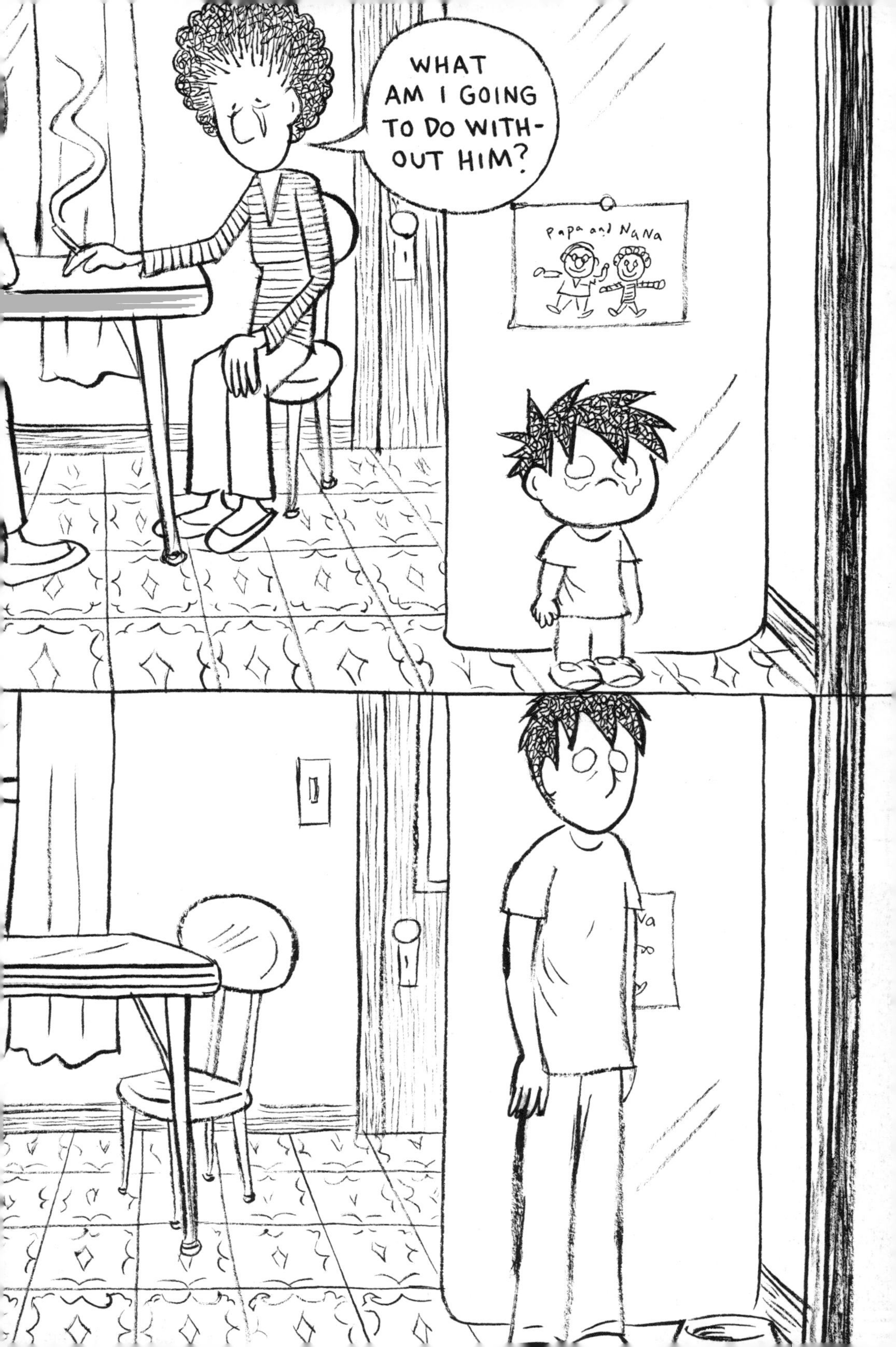
WHAT AM I GOING TO DO WITH-OUT HIM?
Papa and NaNa

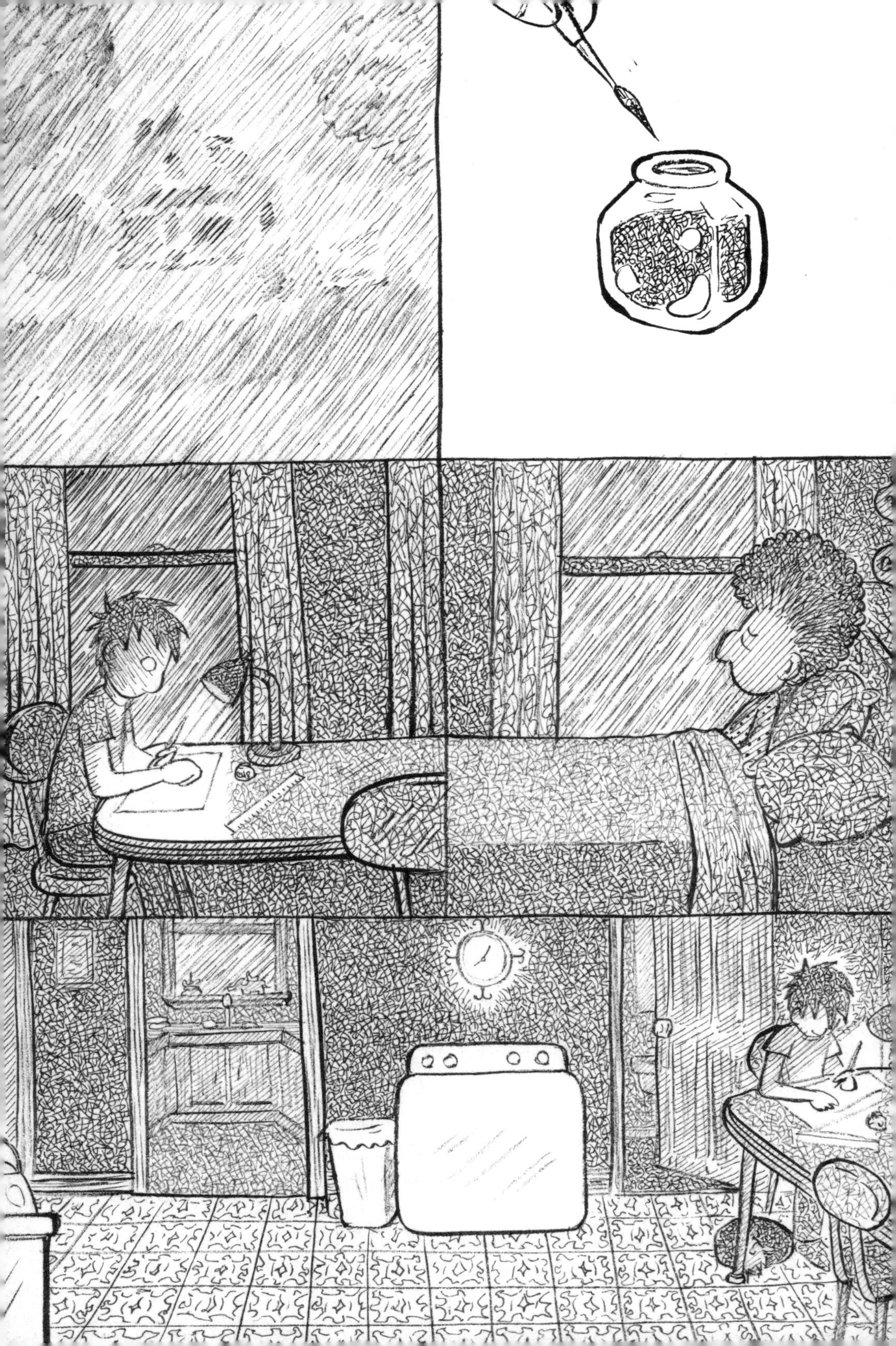

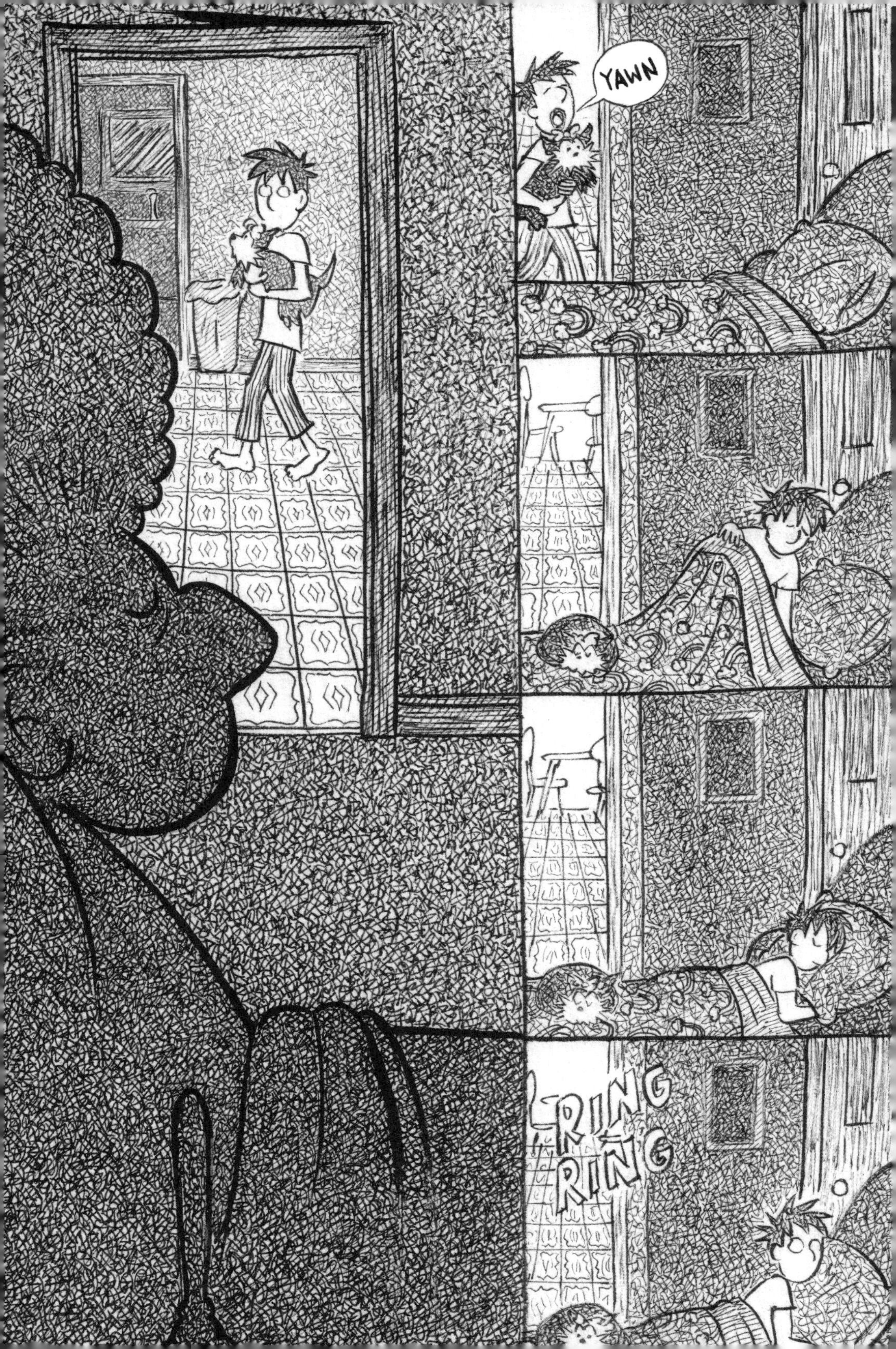
YAWN
RING
RING

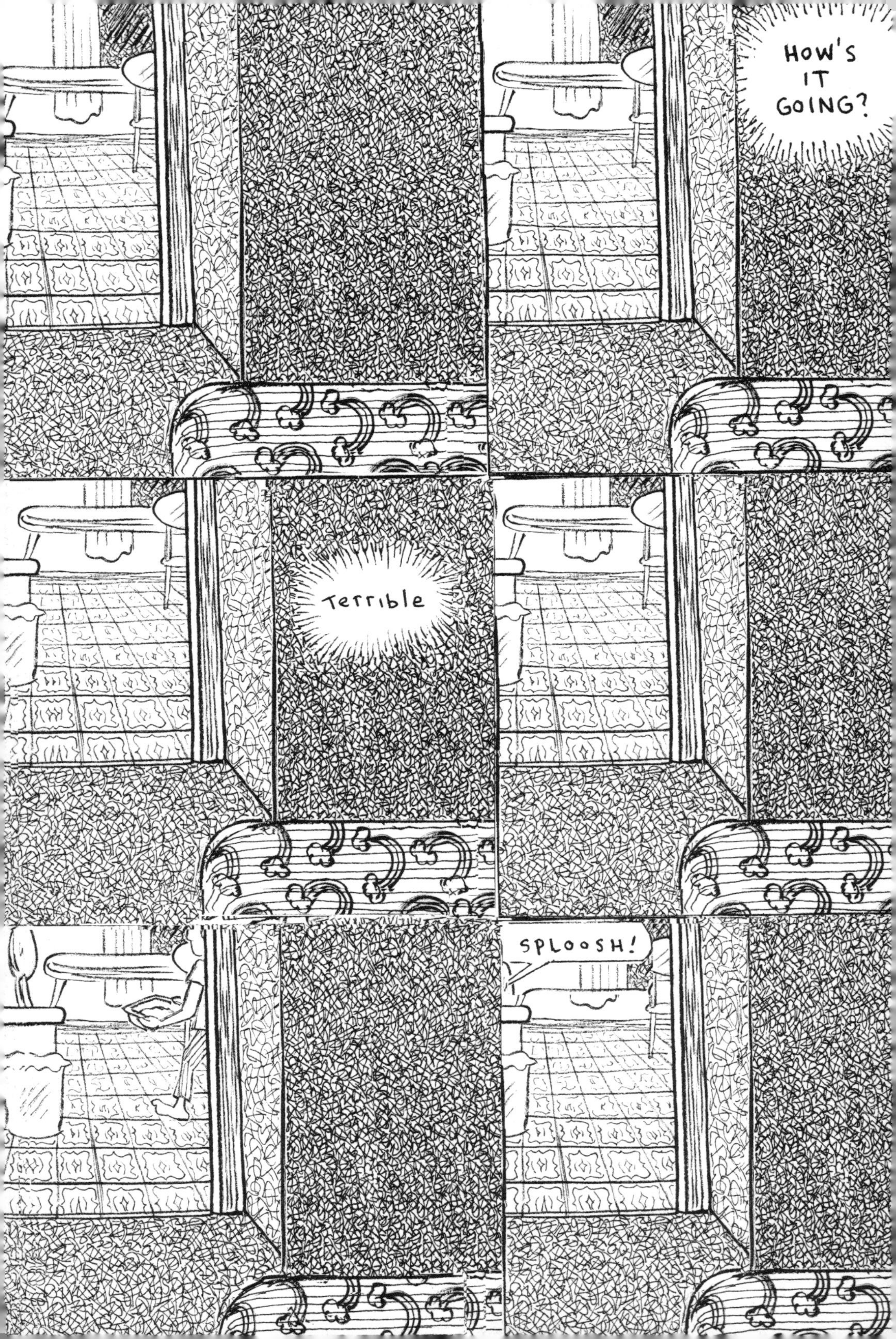
HOW'S IT GOING?
Terrible
SPLOOSH!

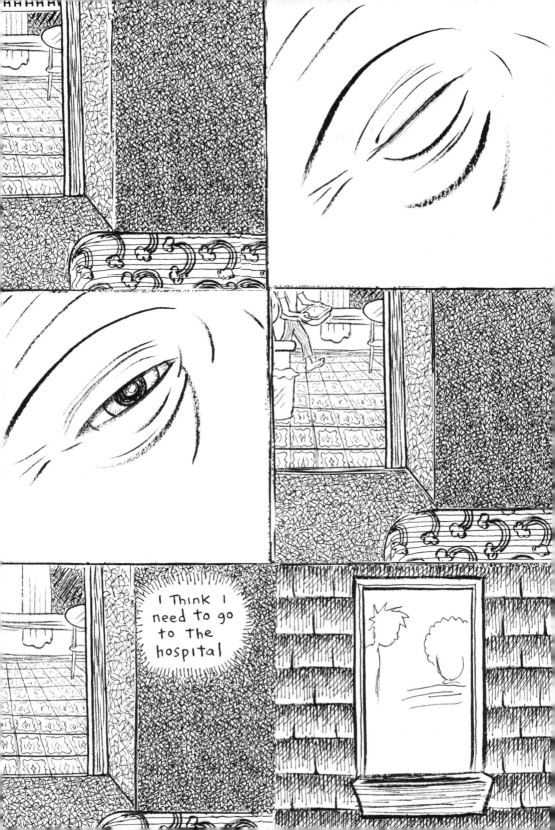

I think I
need to go
to the
hospital

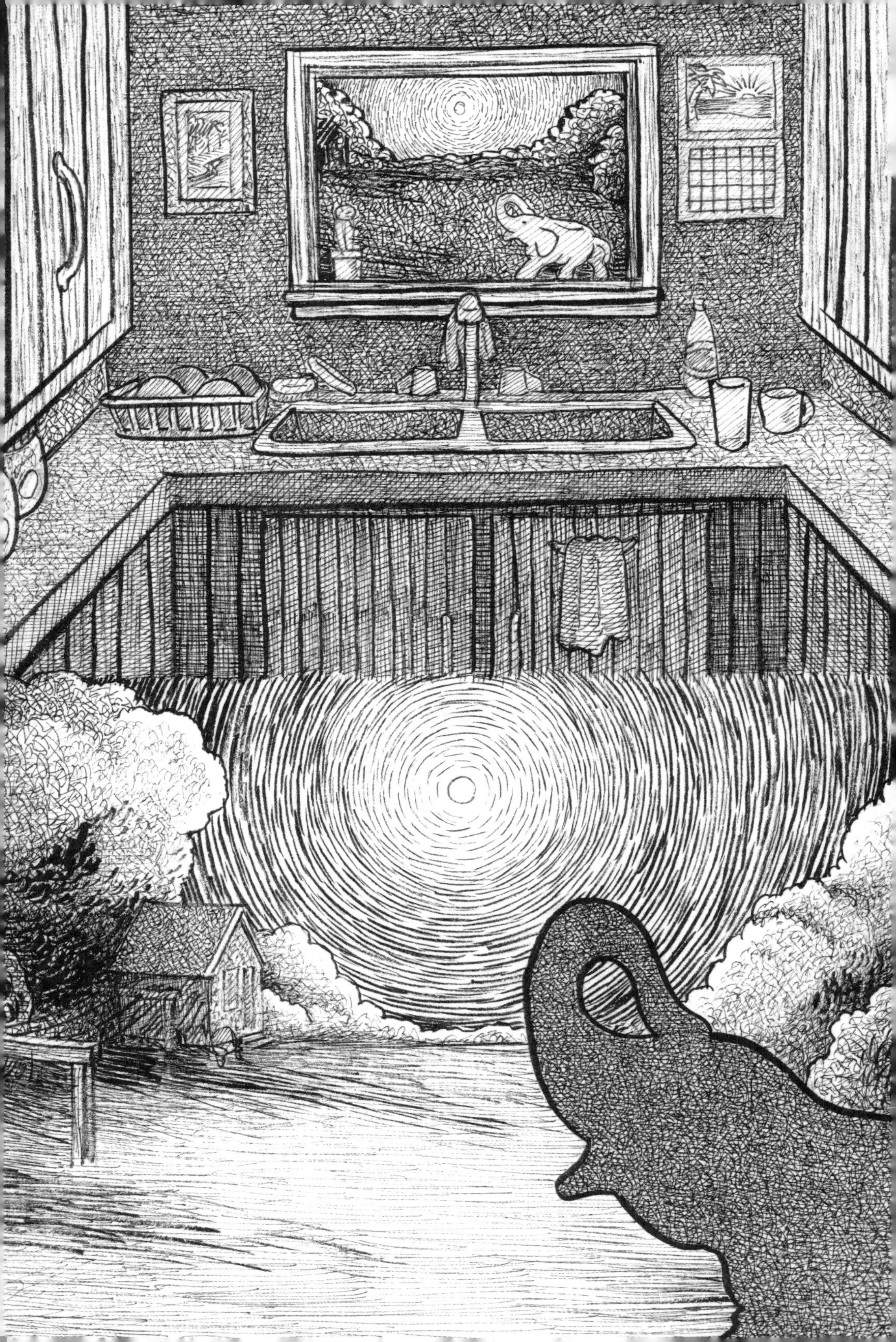

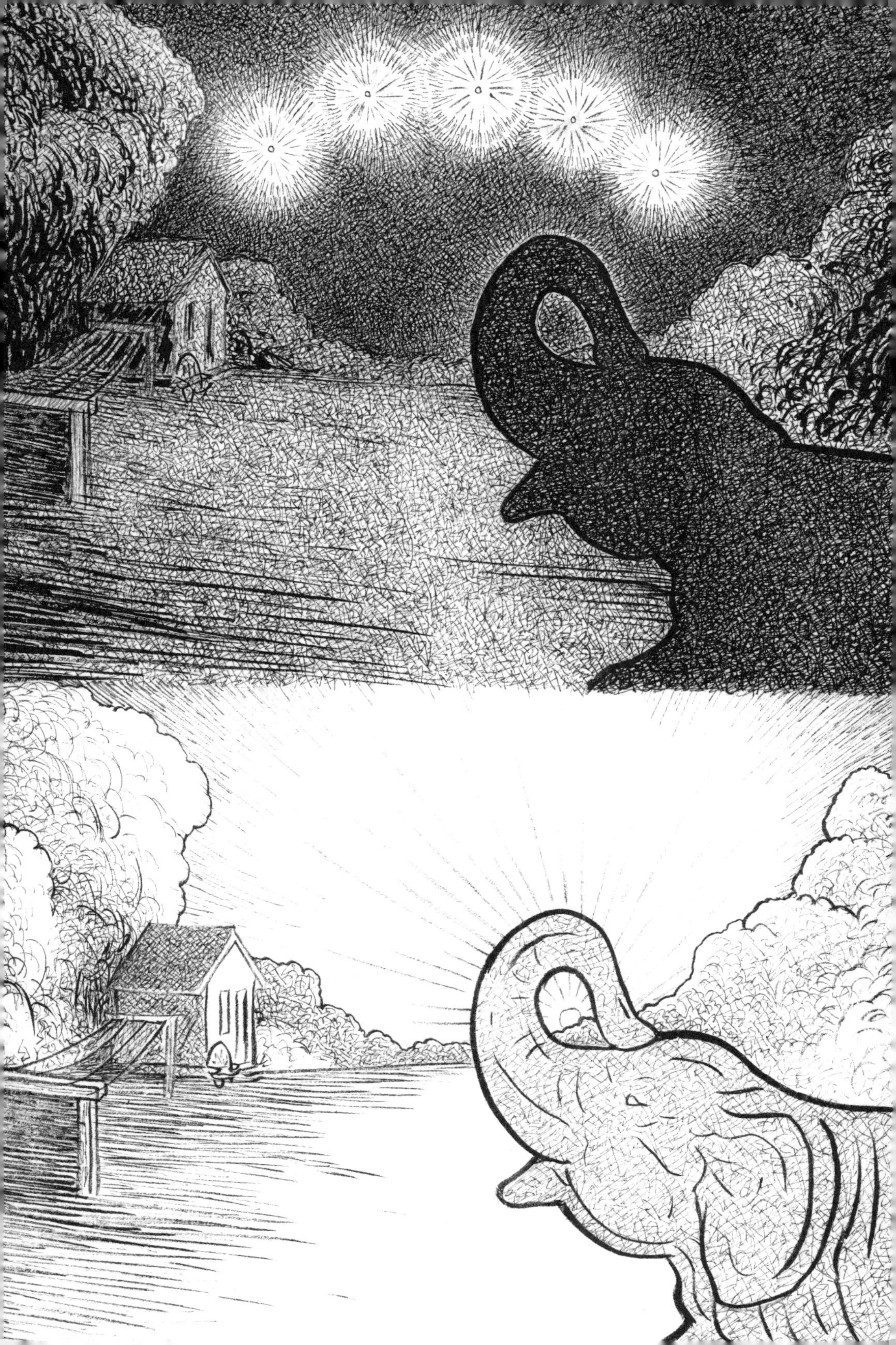

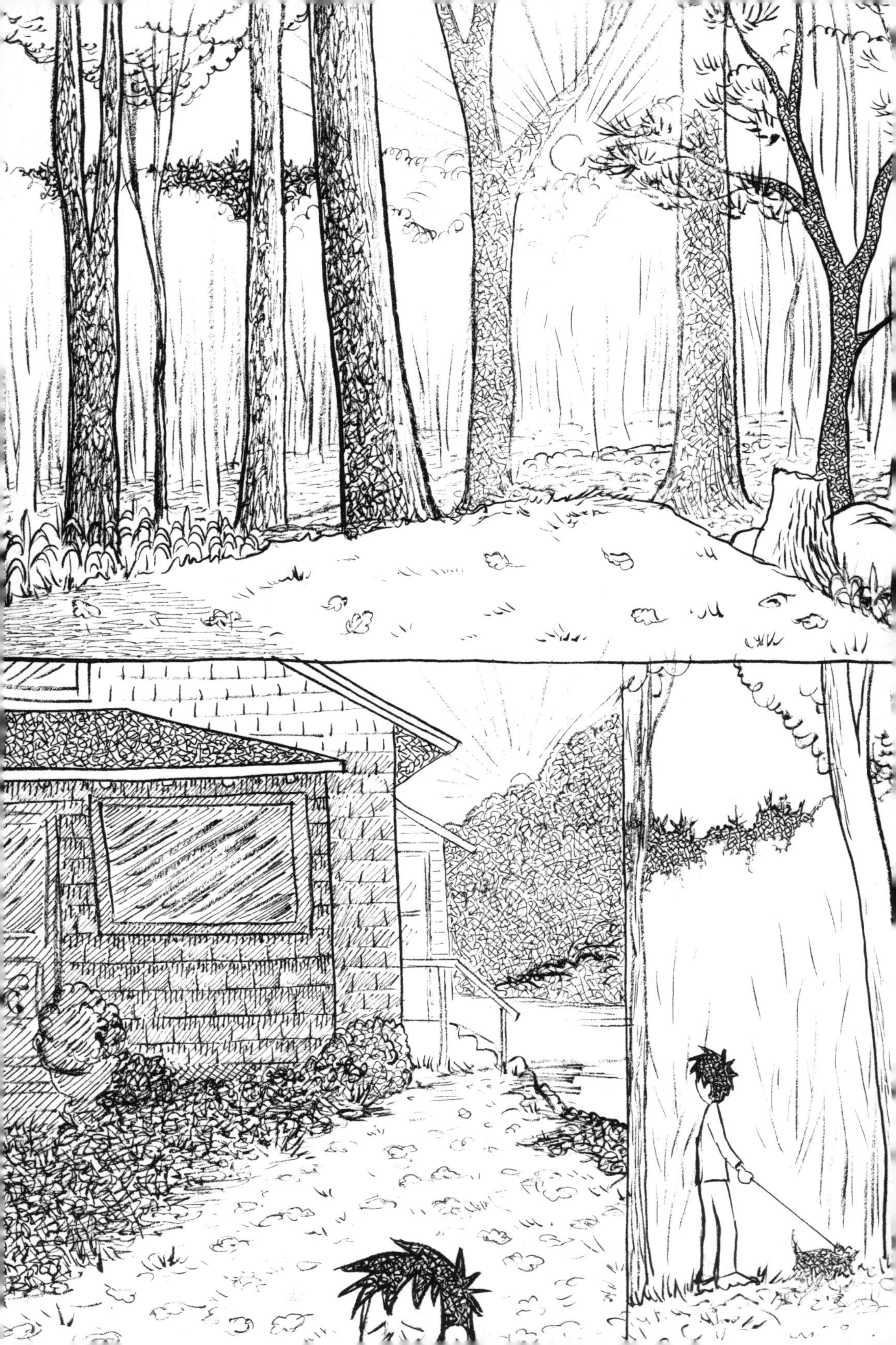

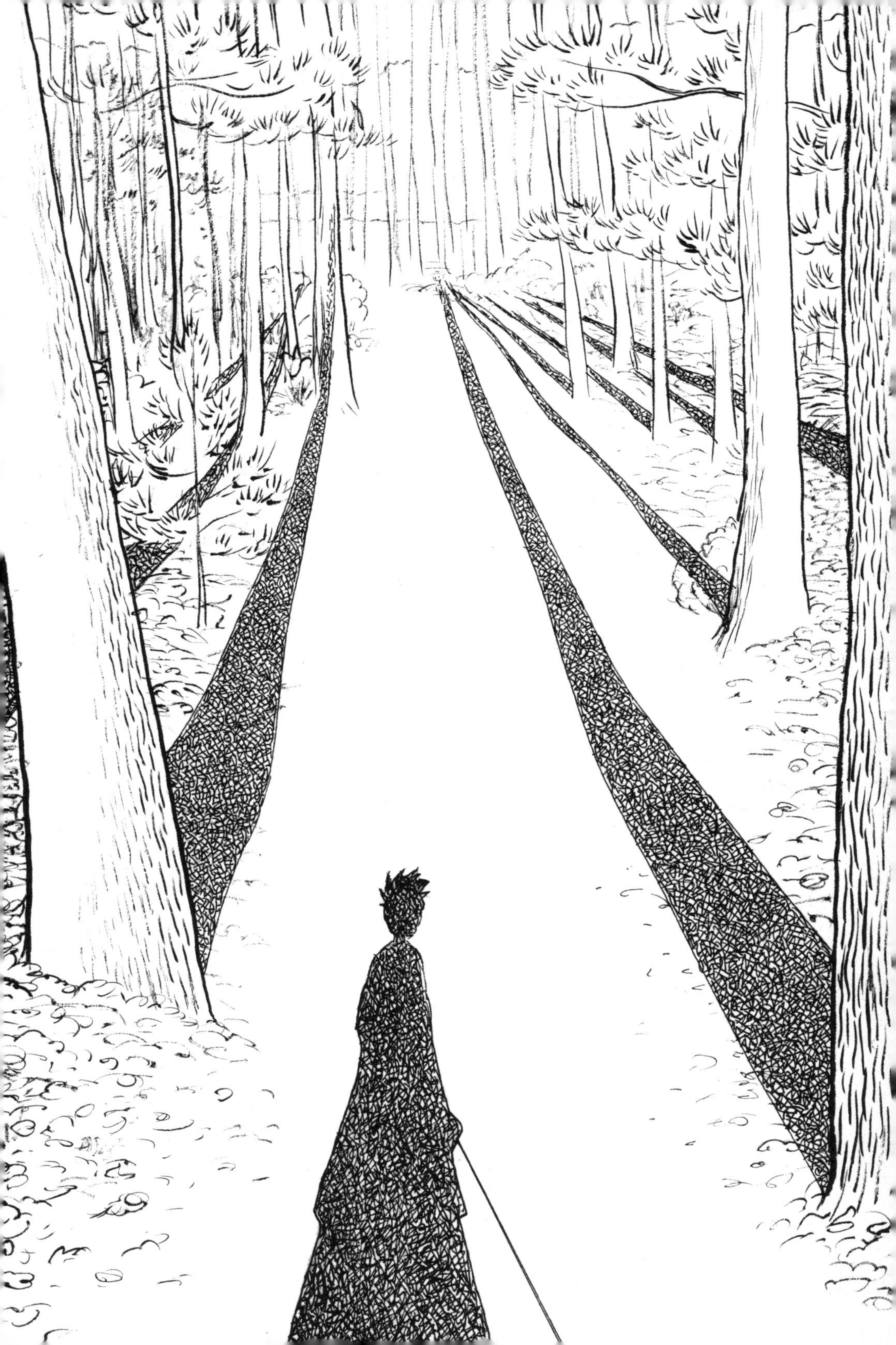

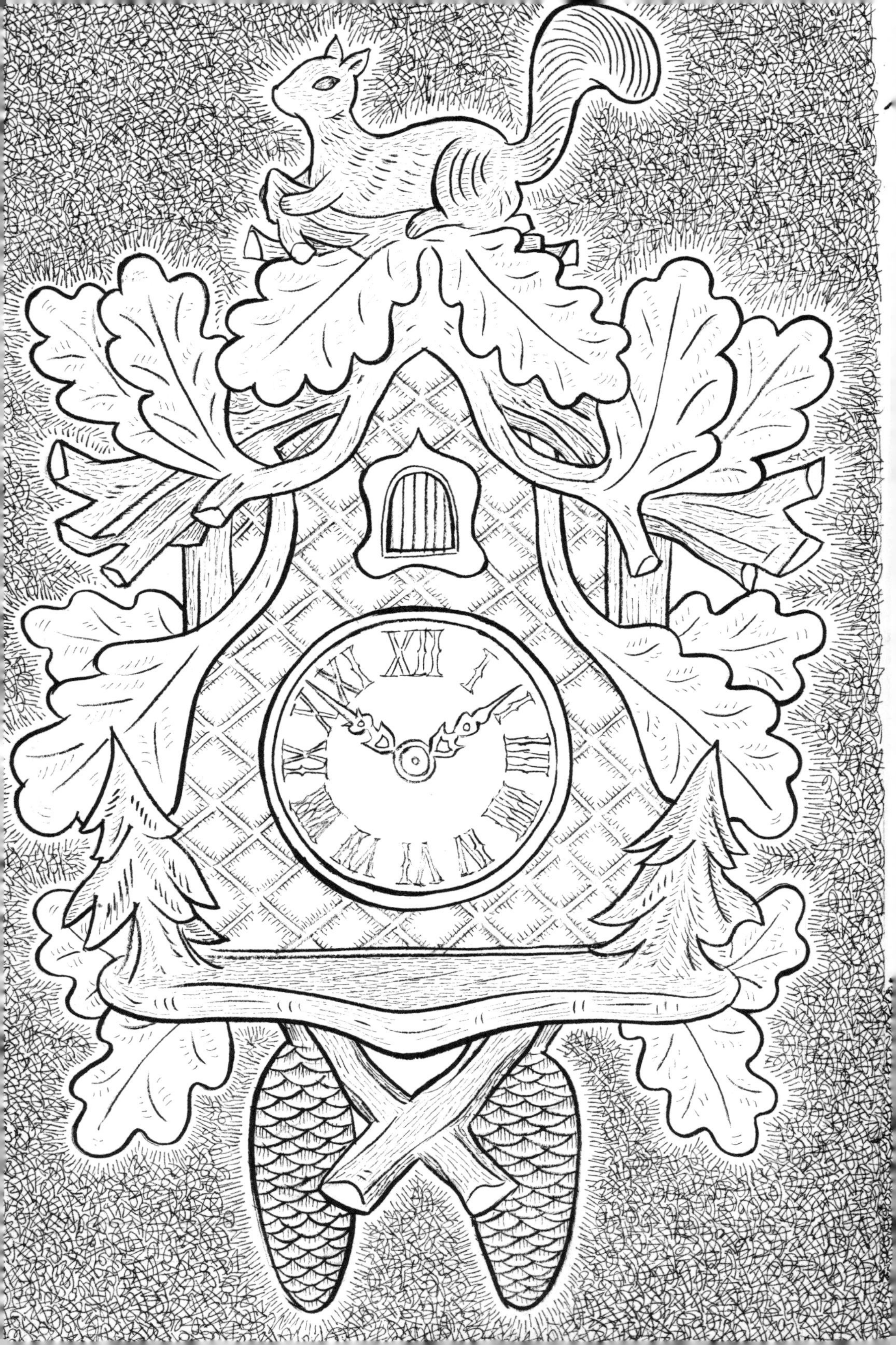
XII
I
II
III
IIII
V
VI
VII
VIII
IX
X
XI

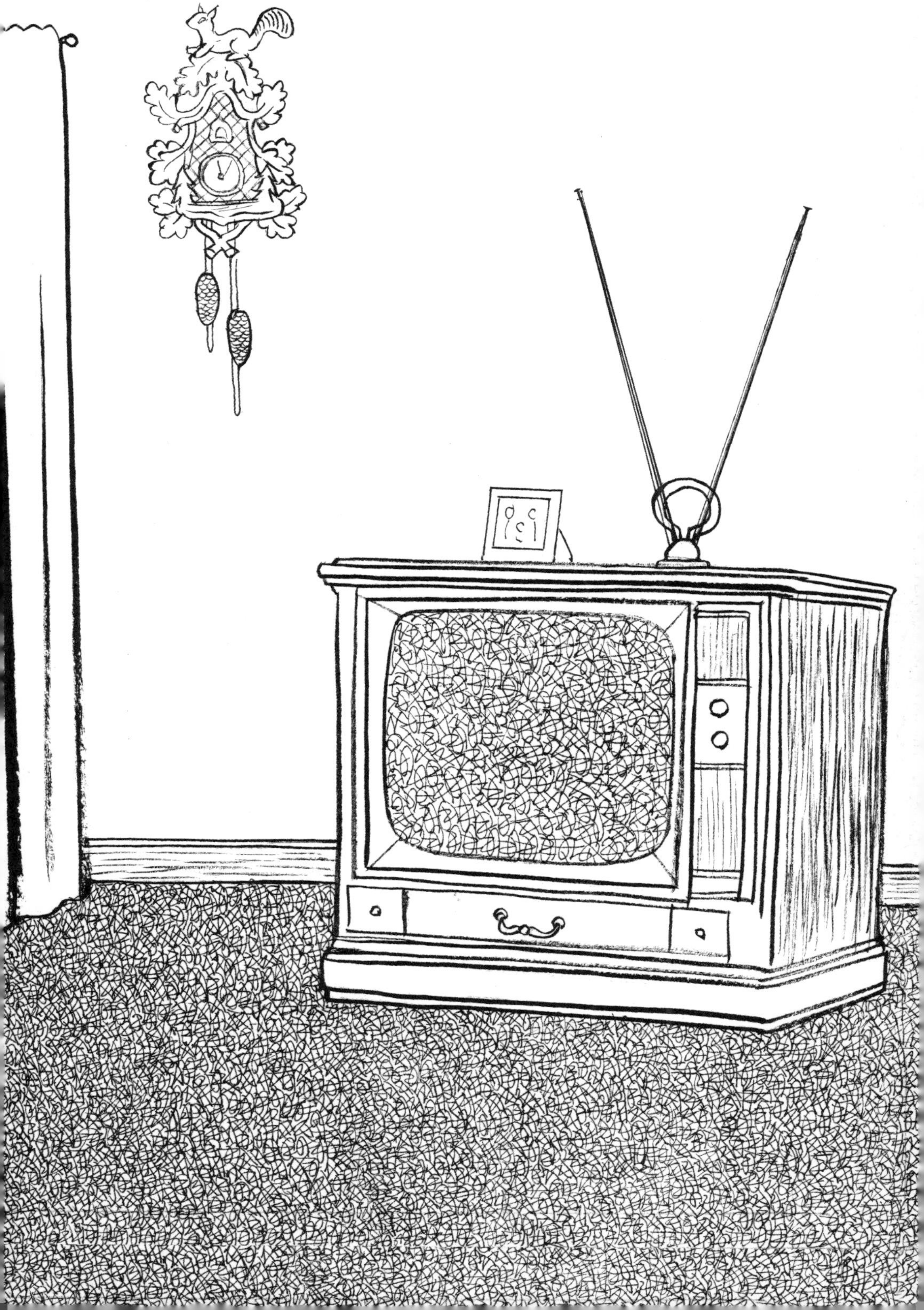

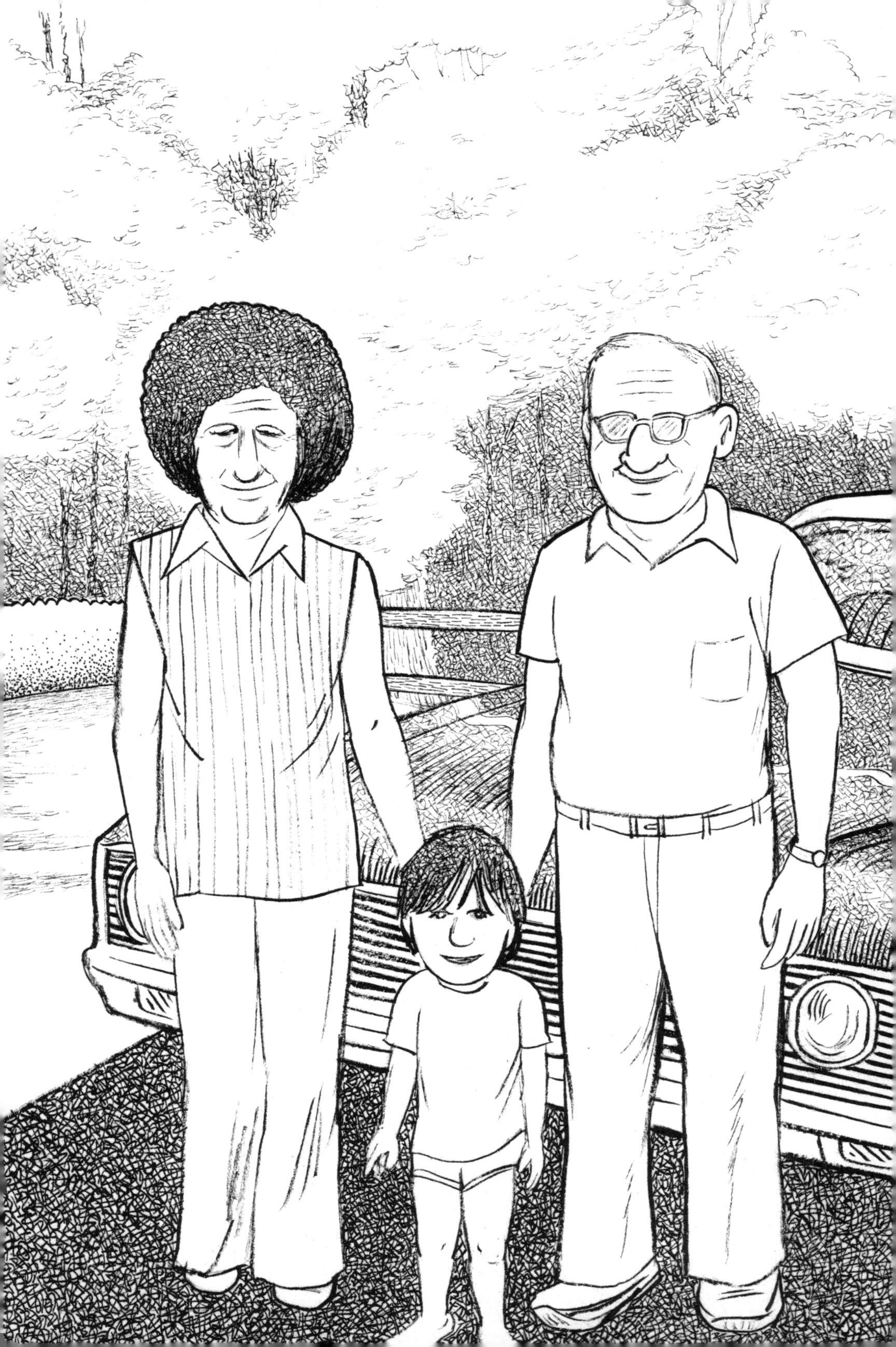

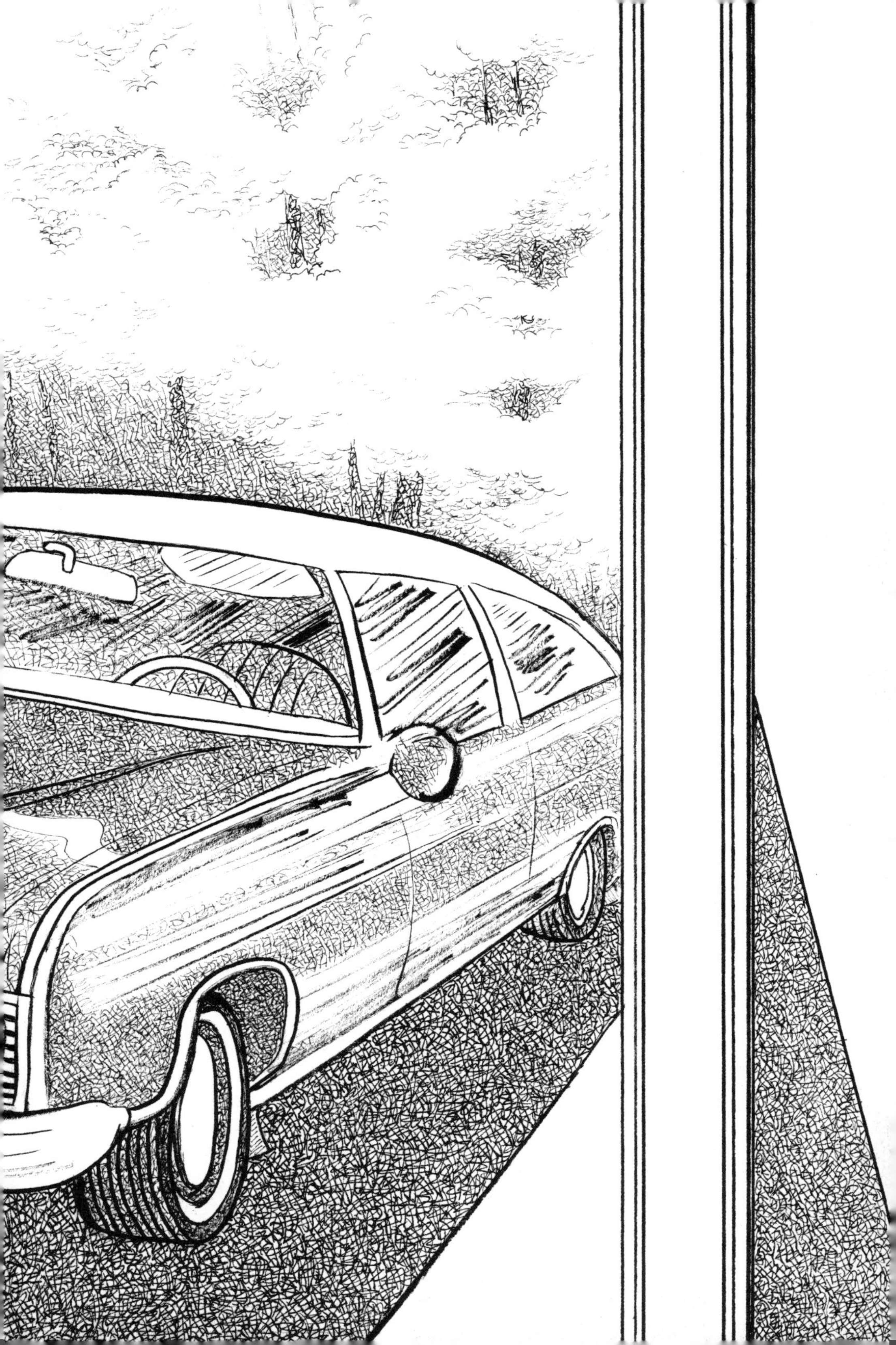

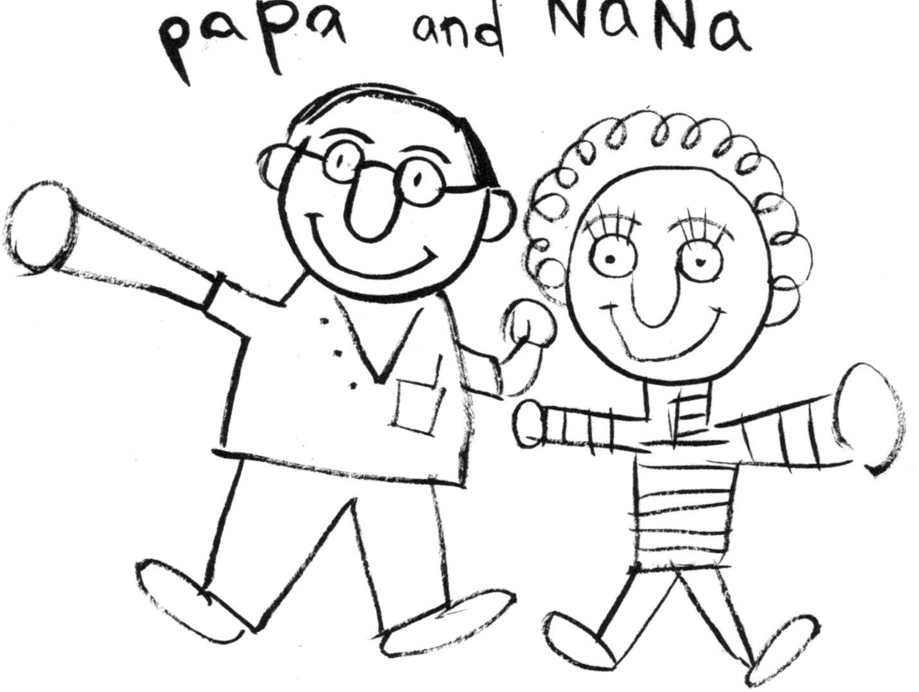
papa and NaNa
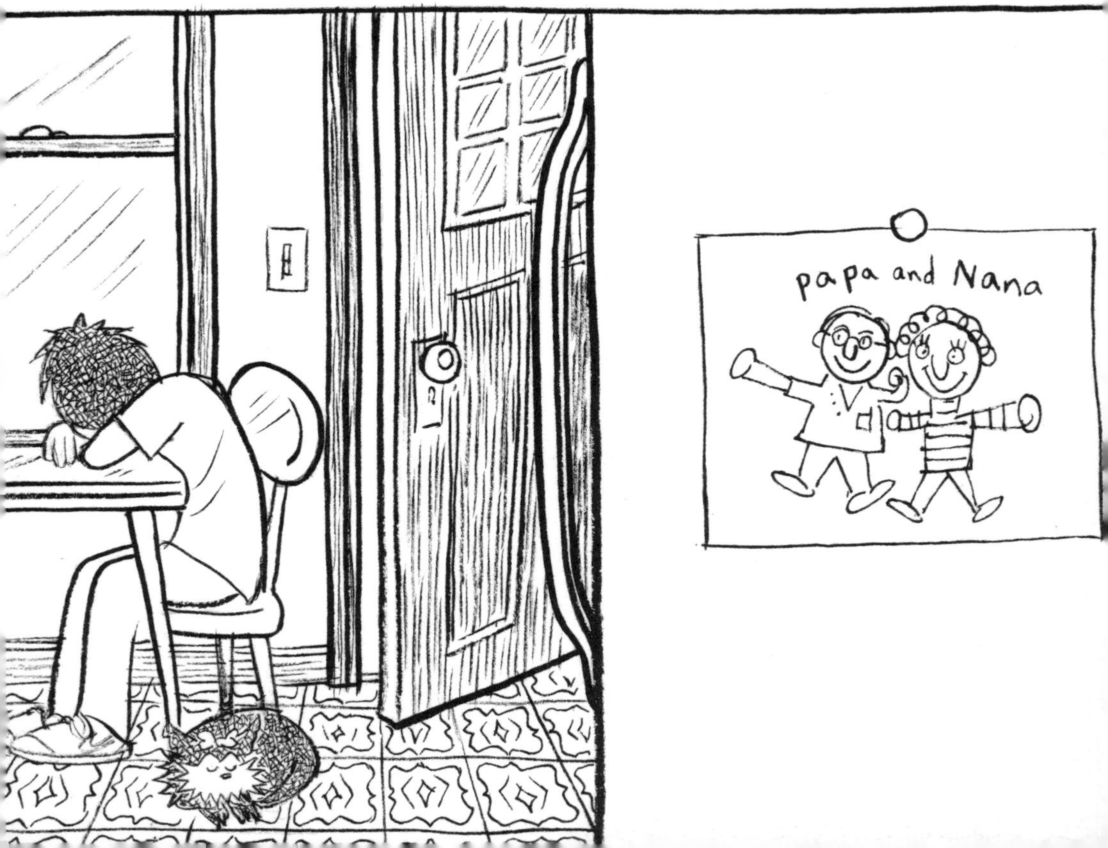
papa and Nana

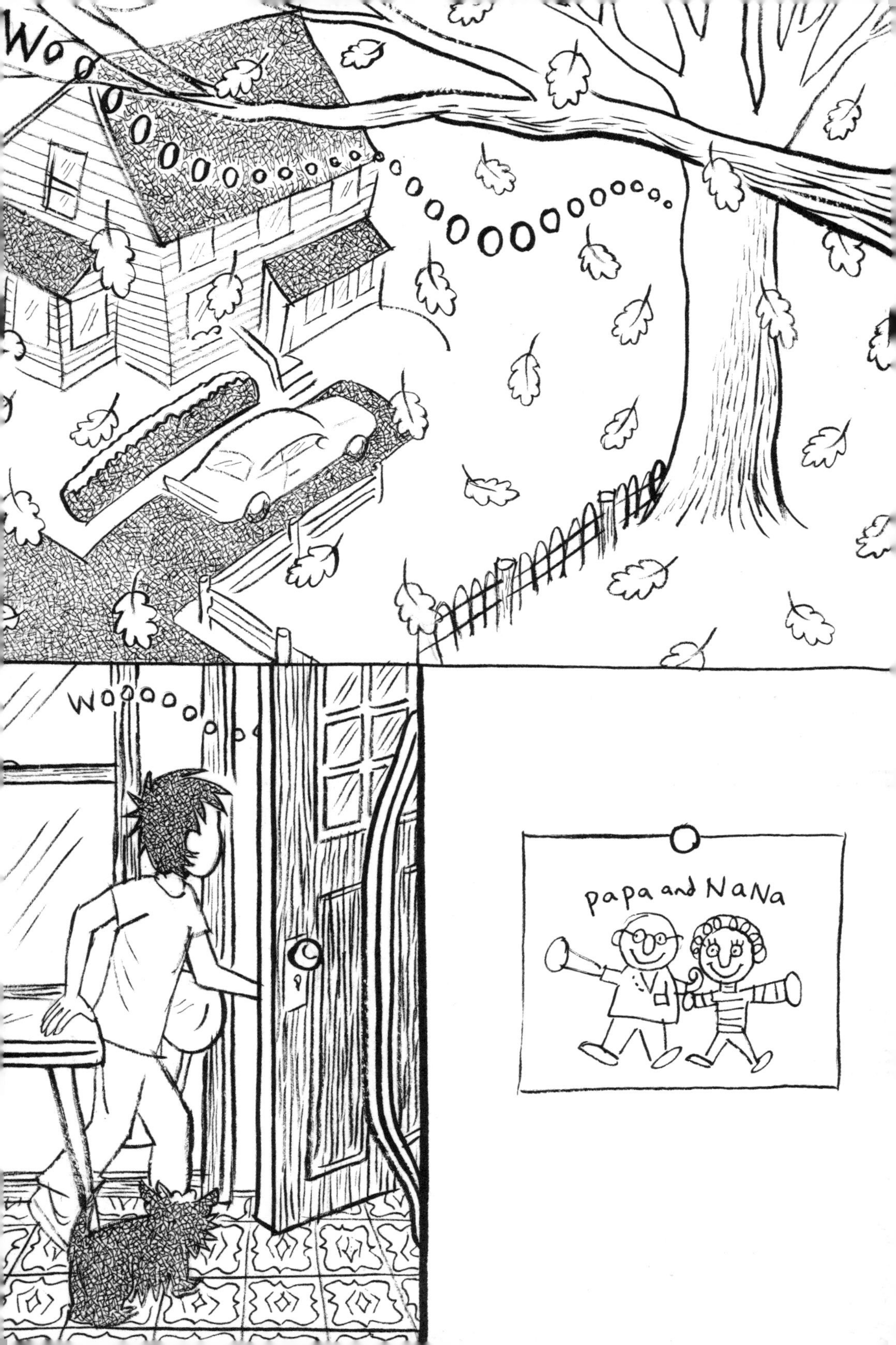
Wooooooooooooooooooooooooooooooo
Woooooooo
papa and NaNa

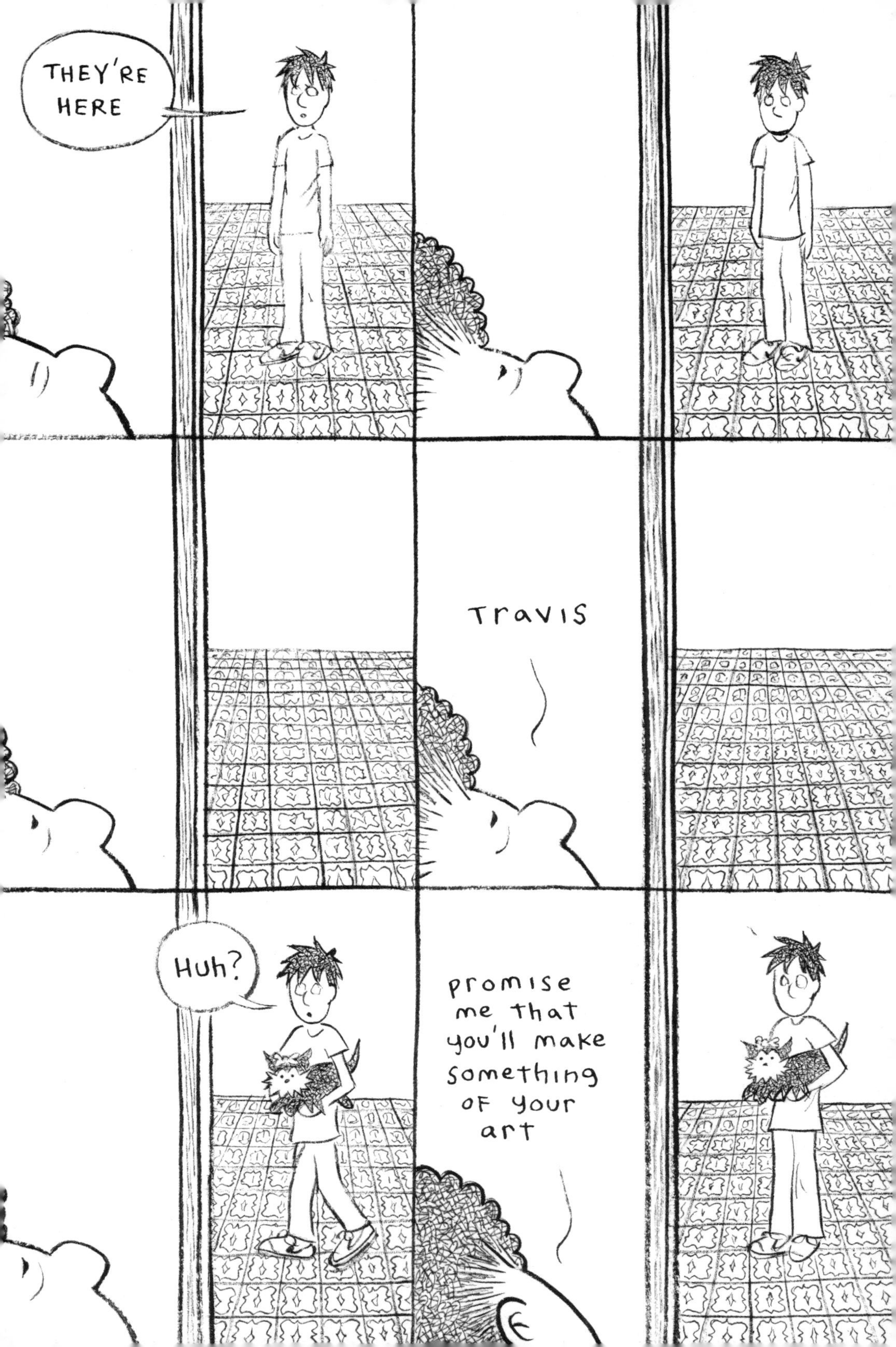
THEY'RE HERE
Travis
Huh?
promise me that you'll make something of your art

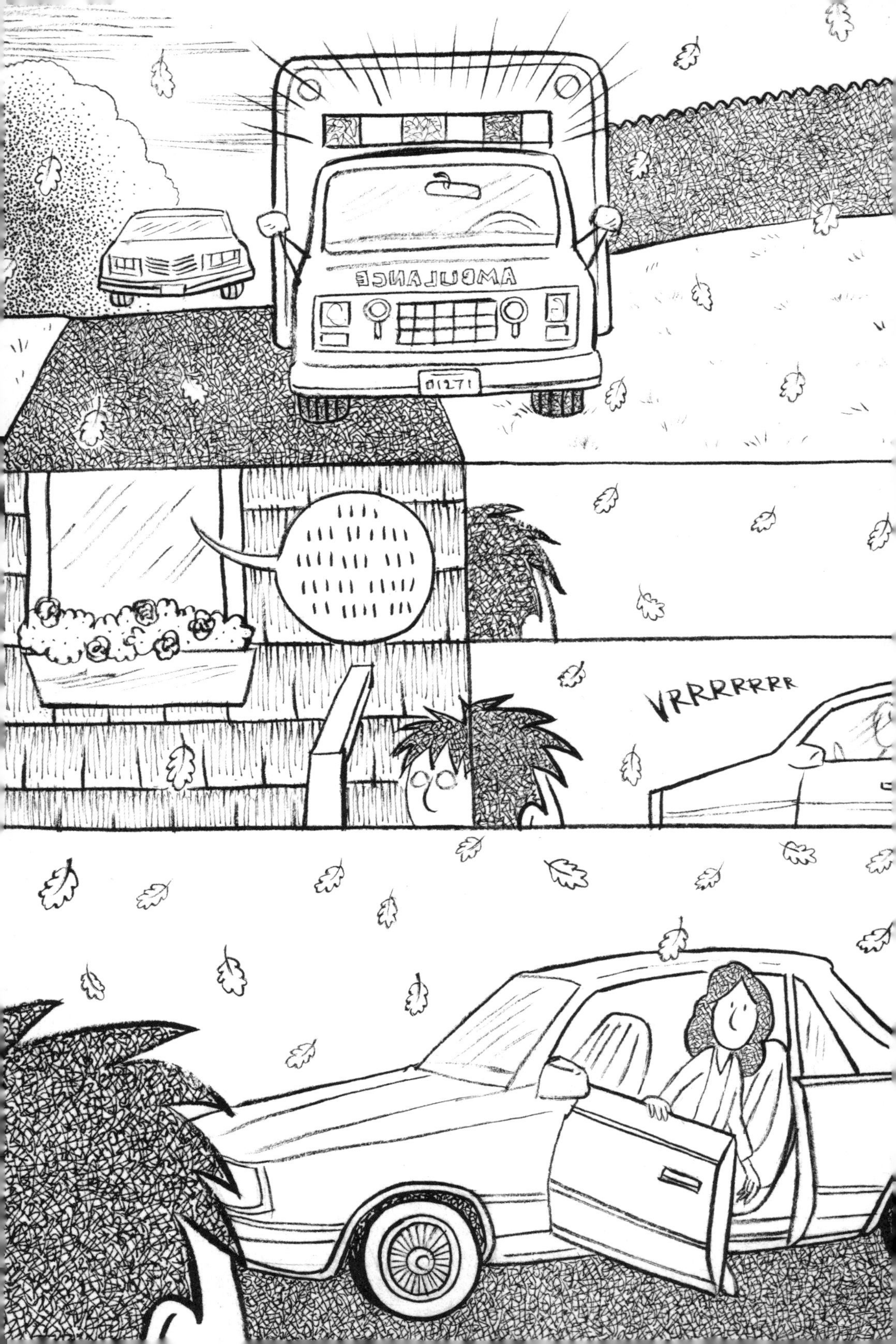
VRRRRRRR

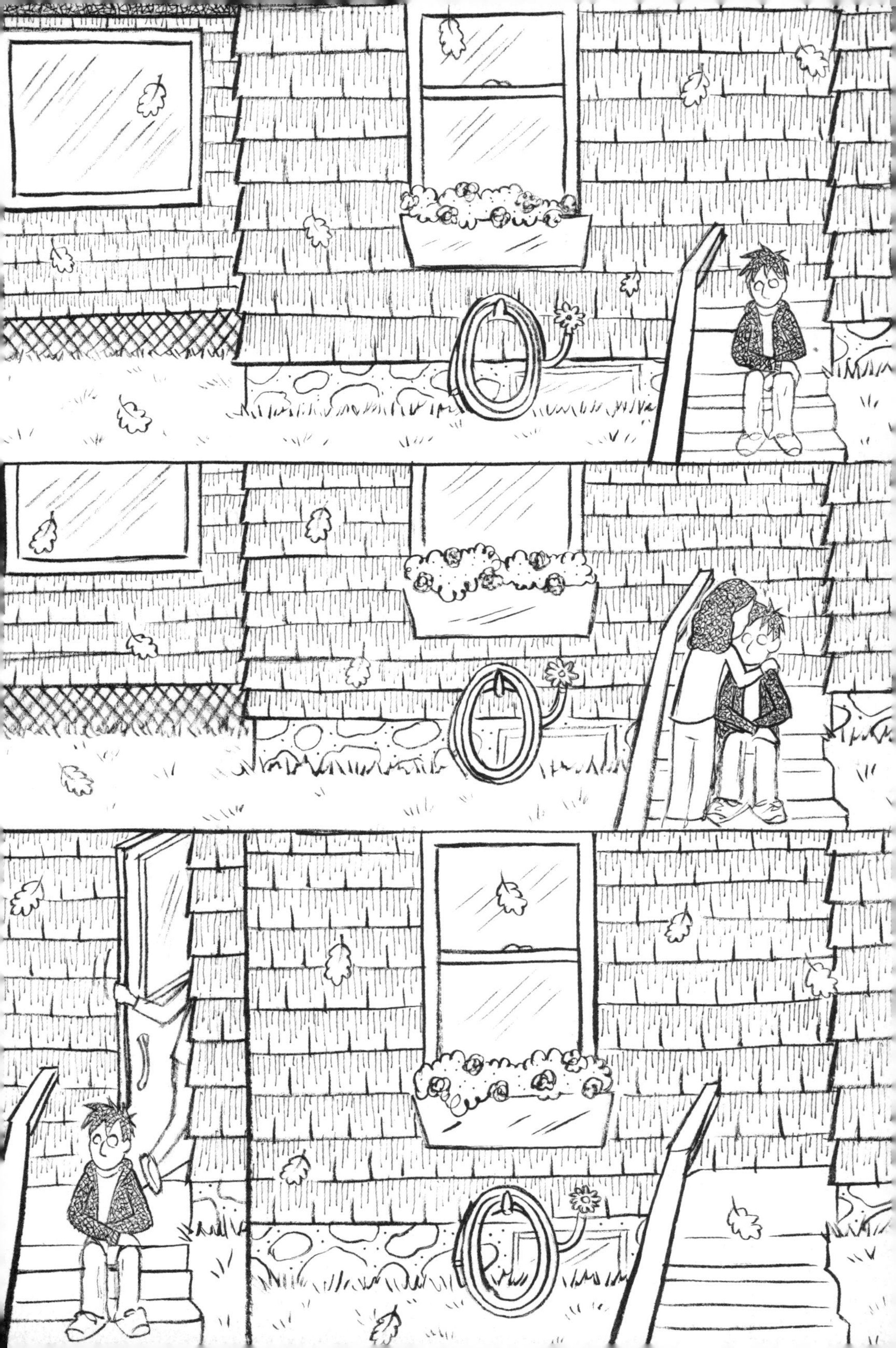

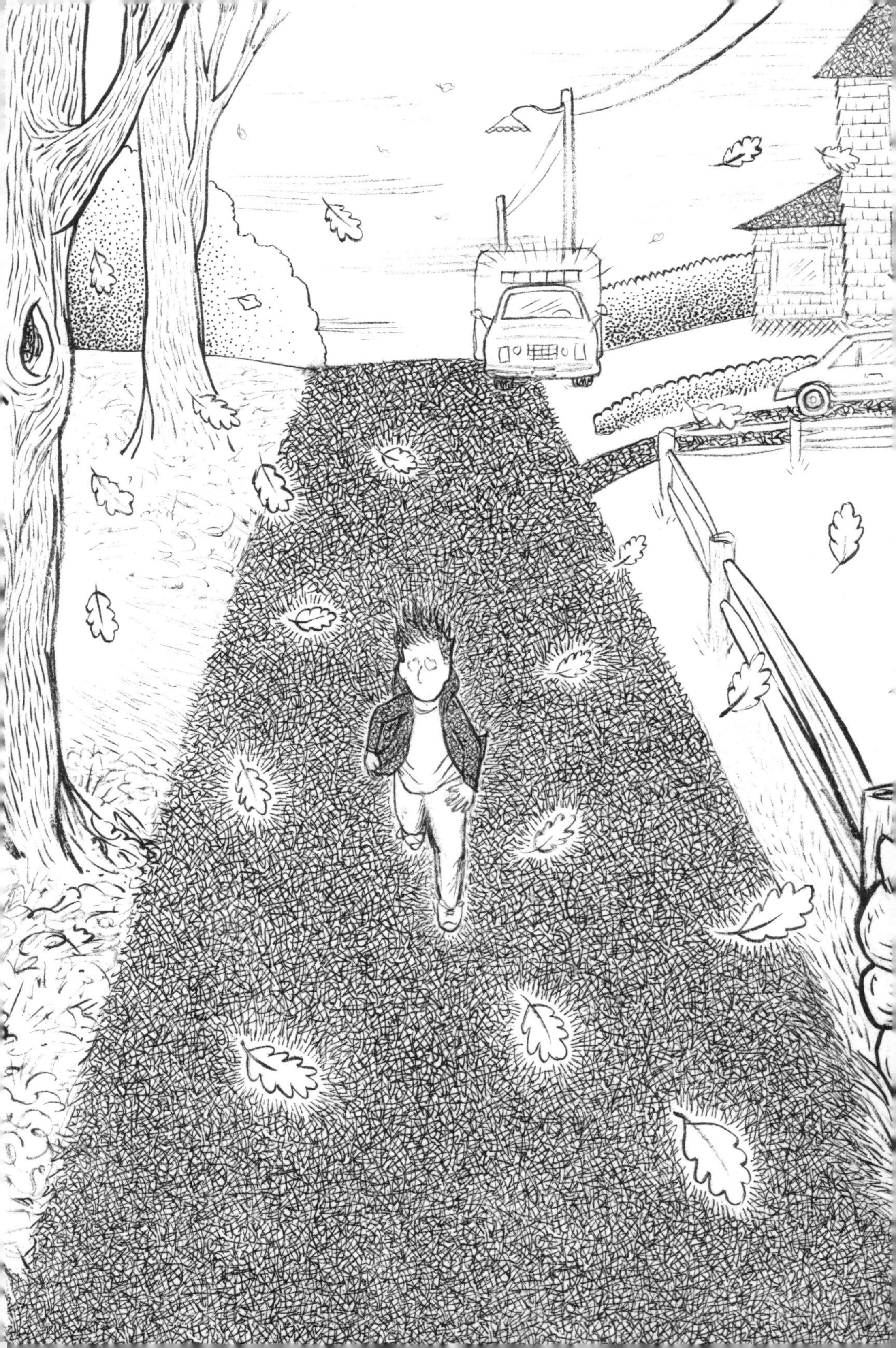

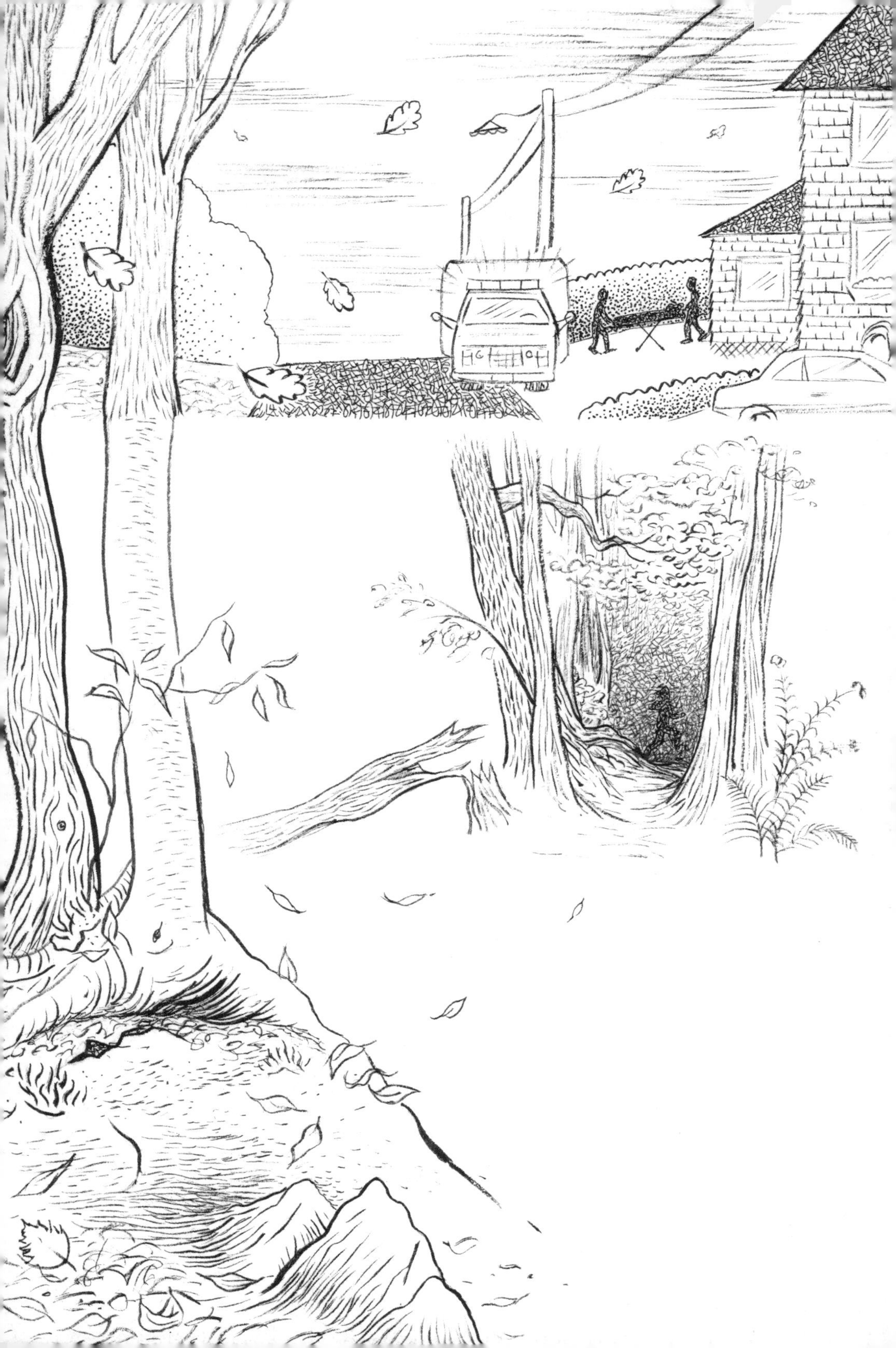

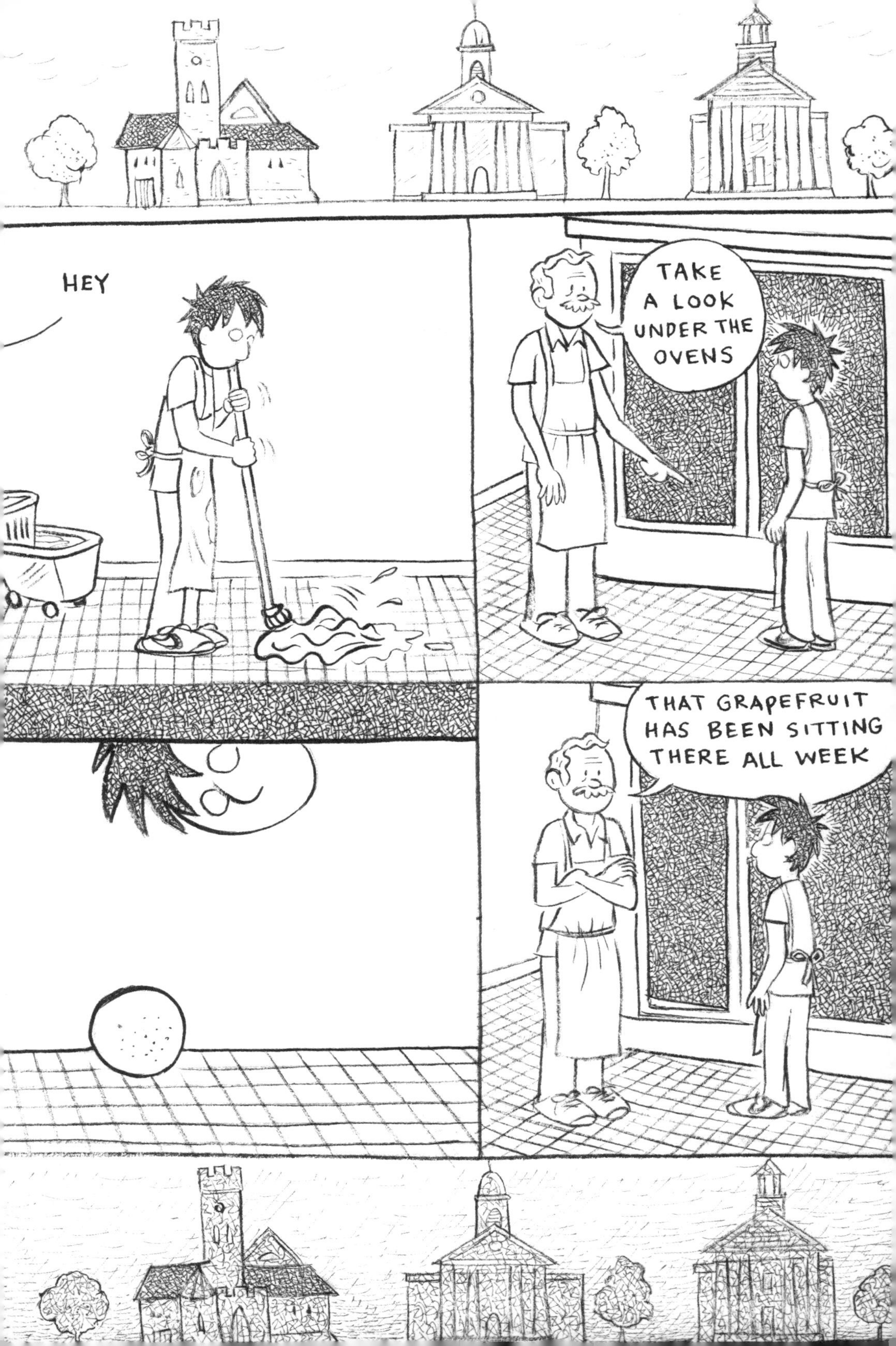
HEY
TAKE A LOOK UNDER THE OVENS
THAT GRAPEFRUIT HAS BEEN SITTING THERE ALL WEEK

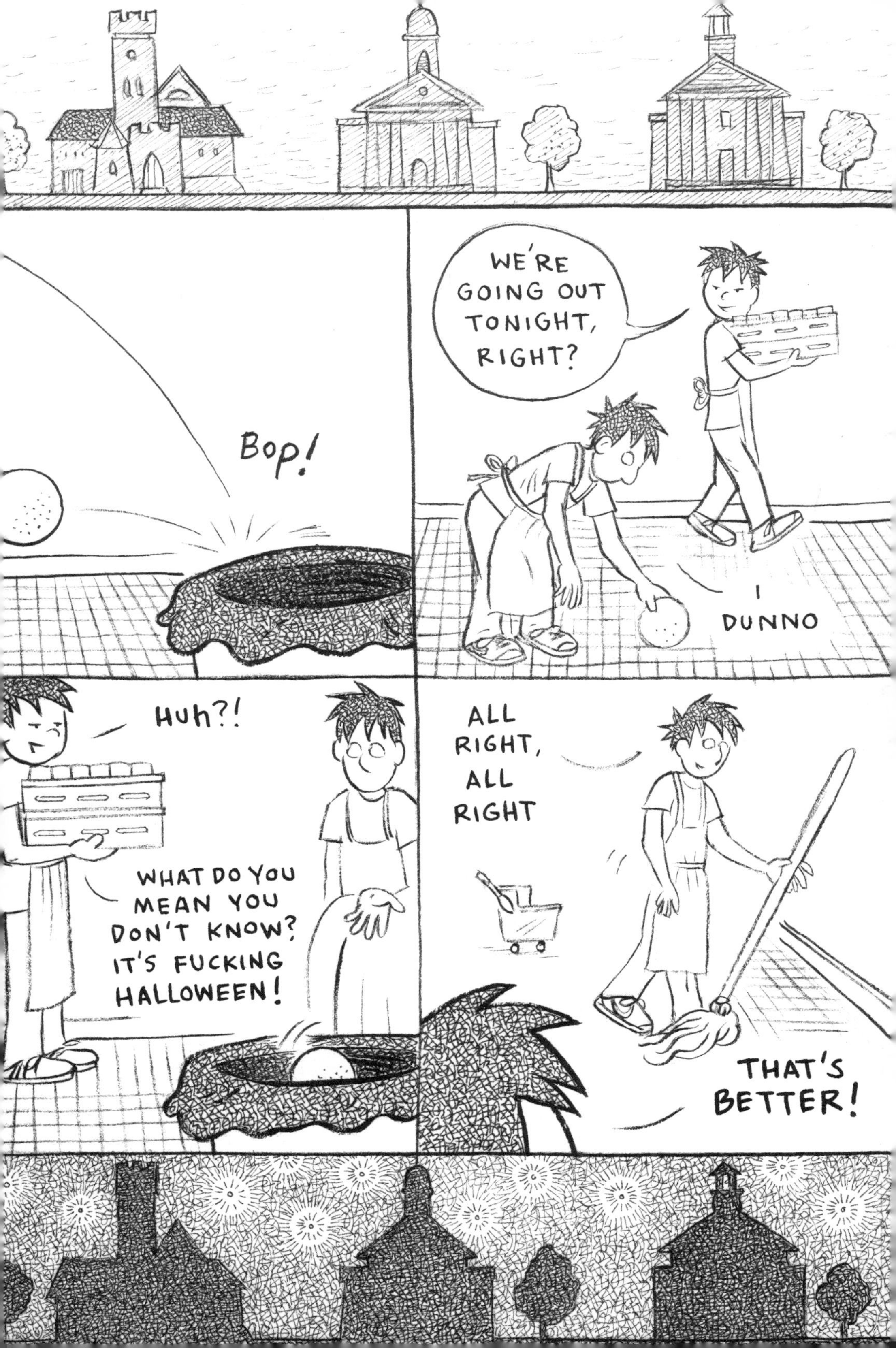
Bop!
WE'RE GOING OUT TONIGHT, RIGHT?
I DUNNO
Huh?!
WHAT DO YOU MEAN YOU DON'T KNOW? IT'S FUCKING HALLOWEEN!
ALL RIGHT, ALL RIGHT
THAT'S BETTER!

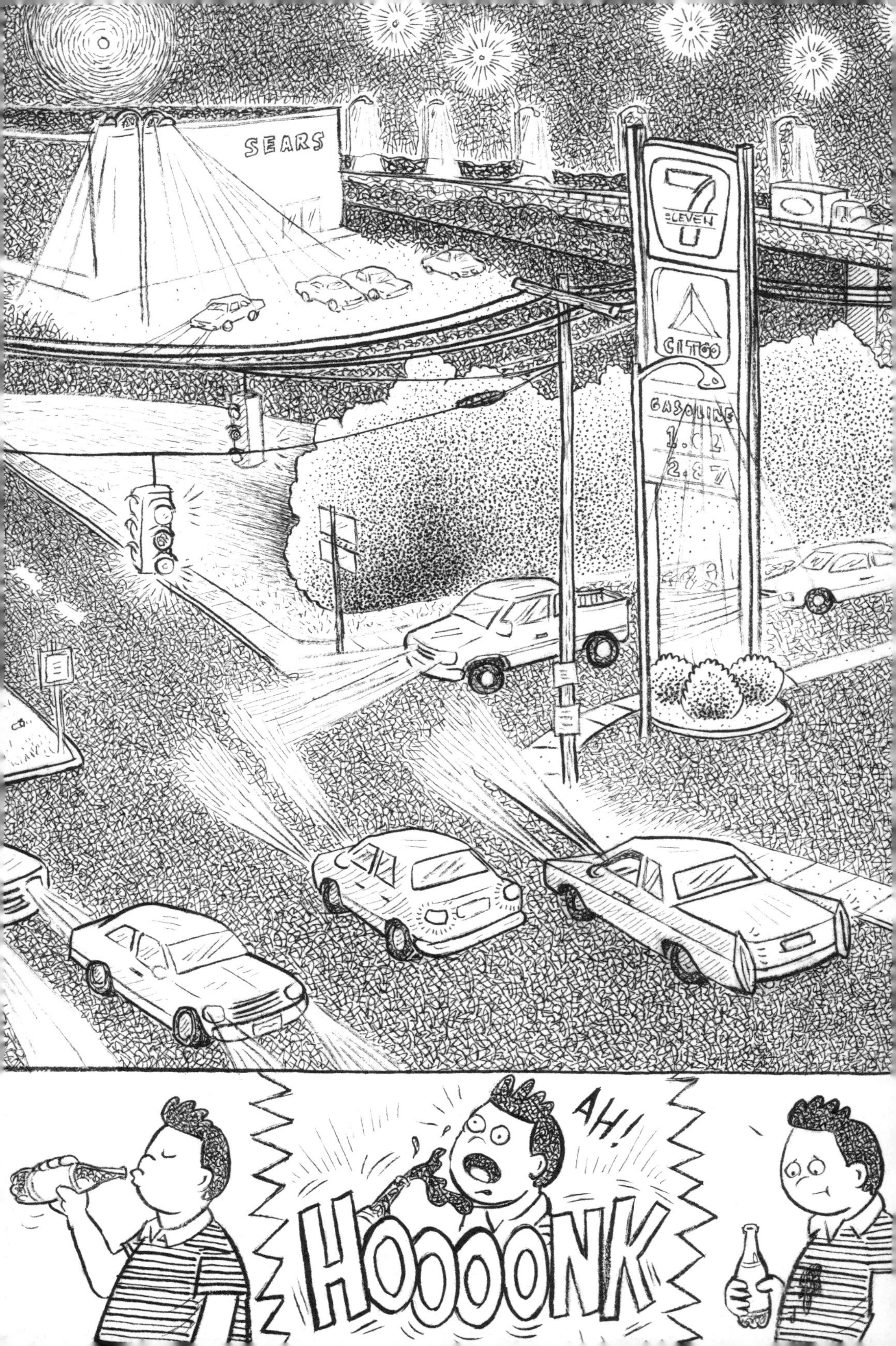
SEARS
7 ELEVEN
CITGO
GASOLINE
HOOOONK
AH!

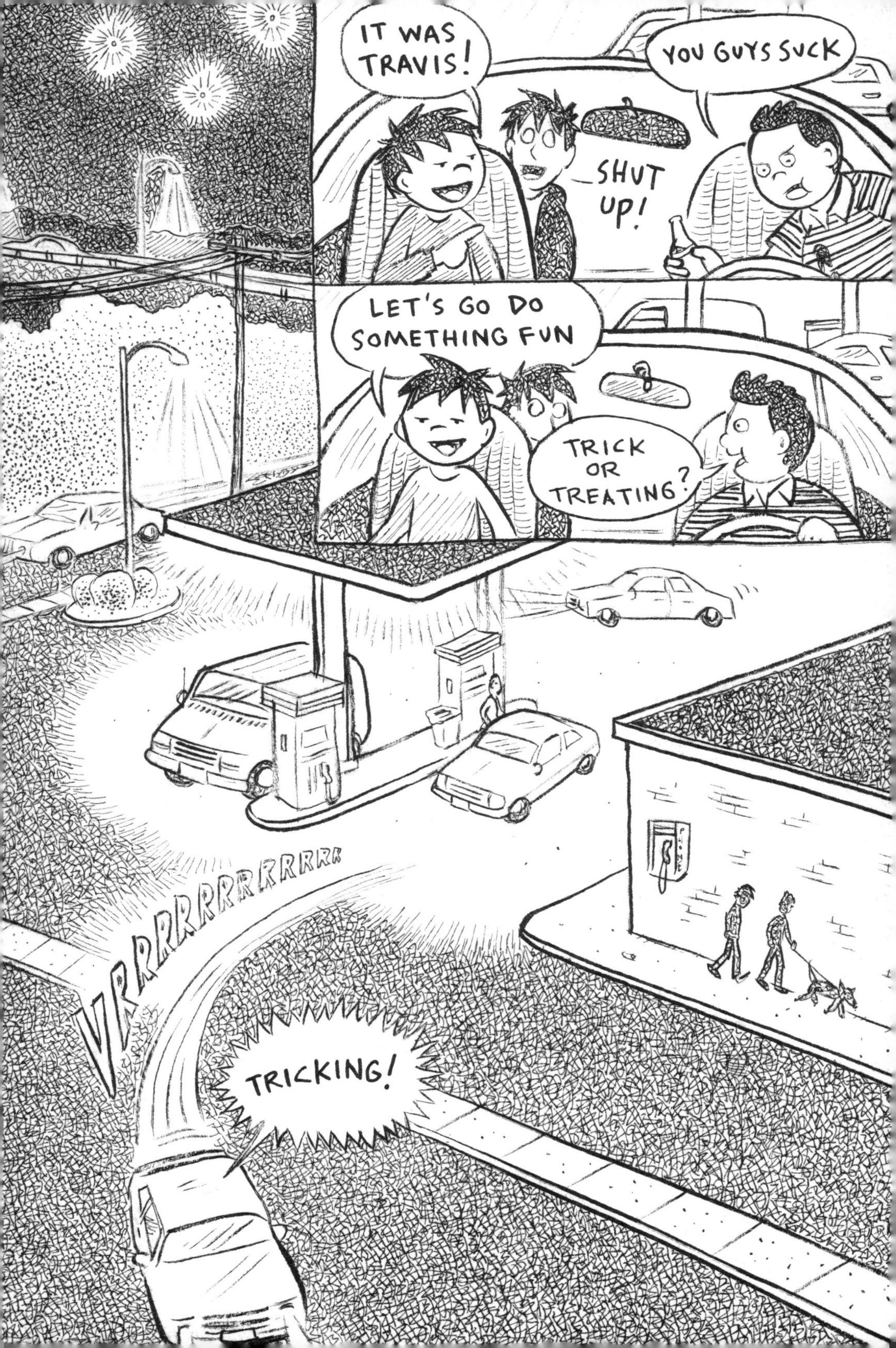
IT WAS TRAVIS!
SHUT UP!
YOU GUYS SUCK
LET'S GO DO SOMETHING FUN
TRICK OR TREATING?
VRRRRRRRRRRRRRRR
TRICKING!

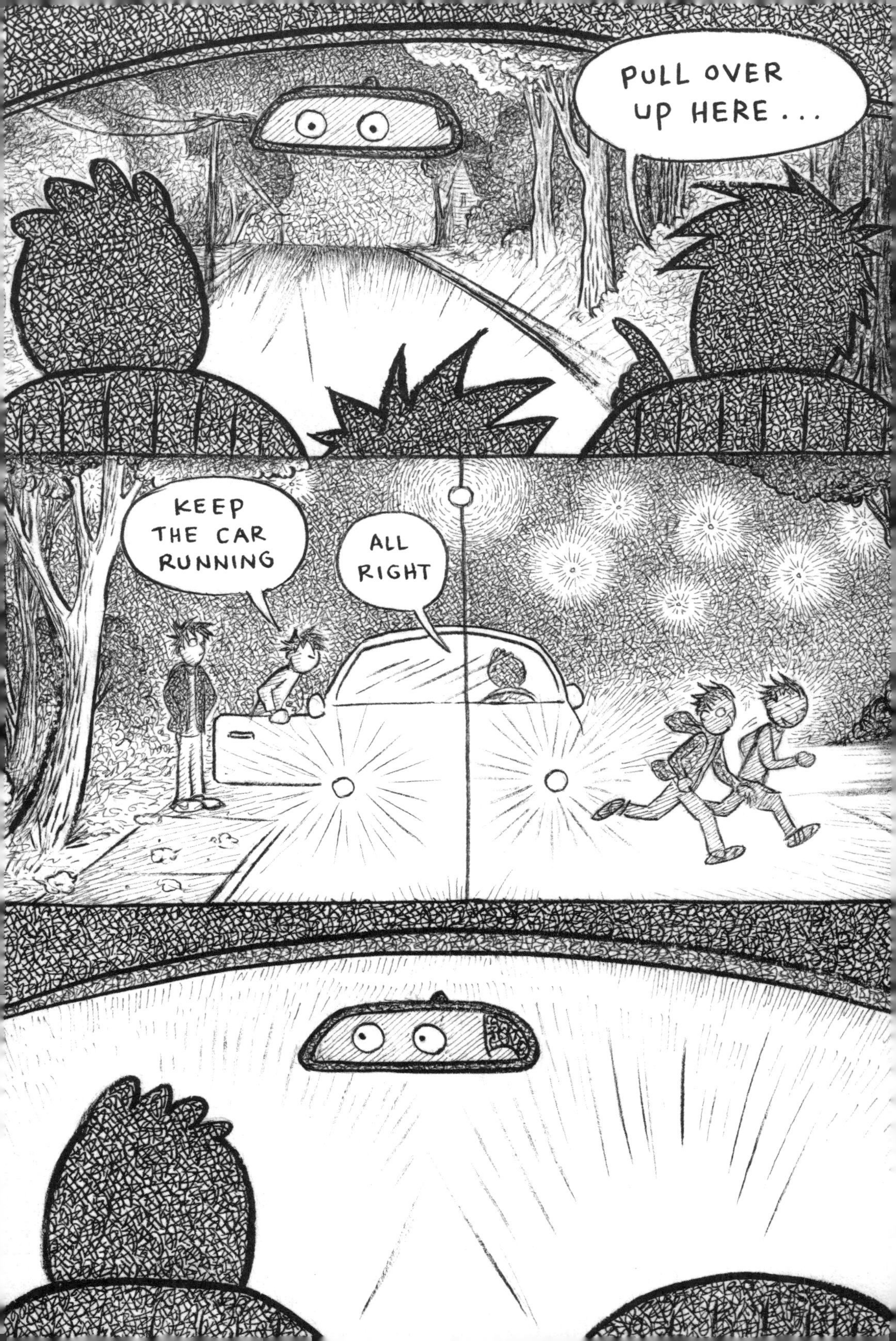
PULL OVER UP HERE . . .
KEEP THE CAR RUNNING
ALL RIGHT

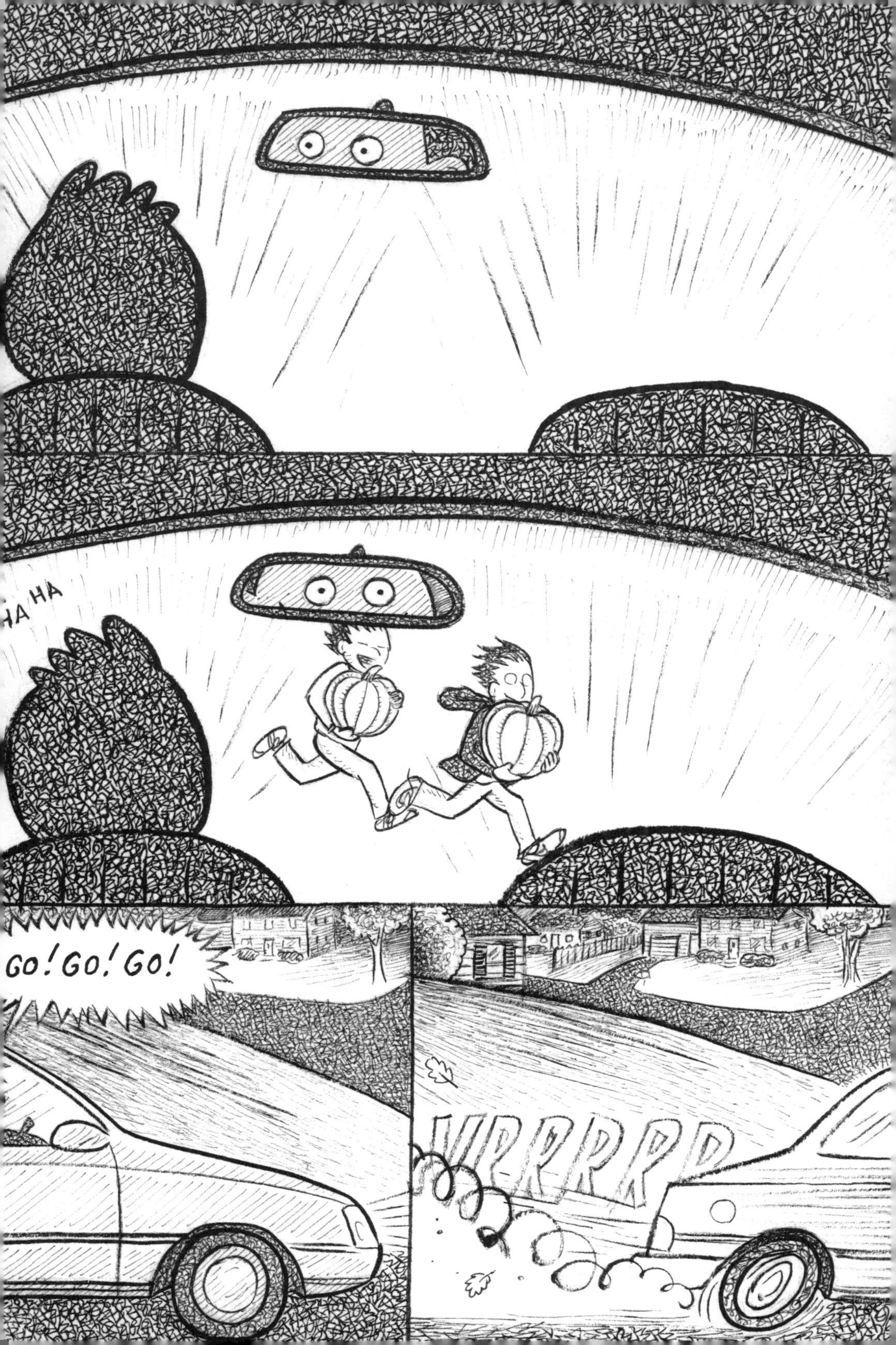
HA HA
GO! GO! GO!
VRRRRR

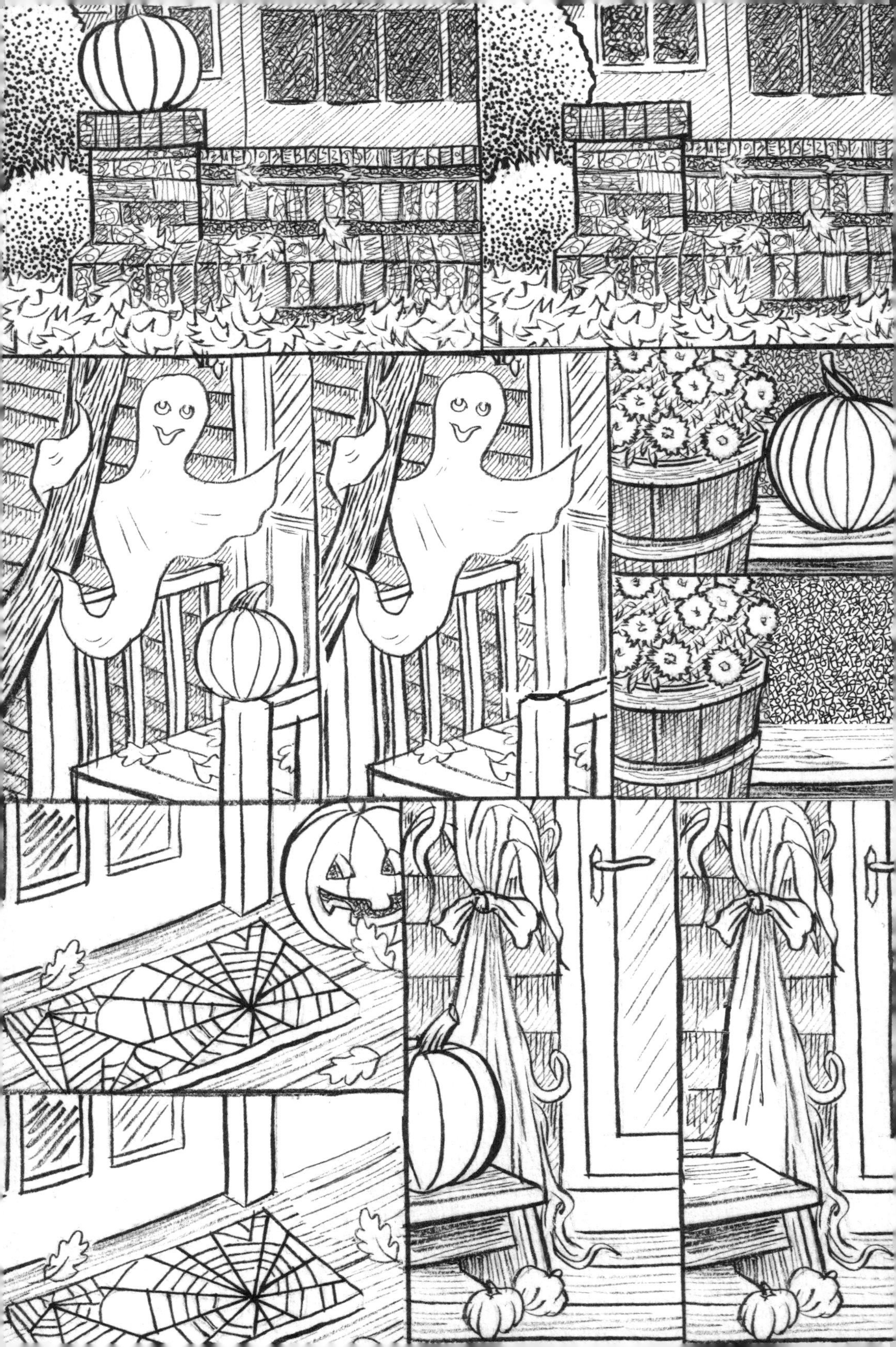

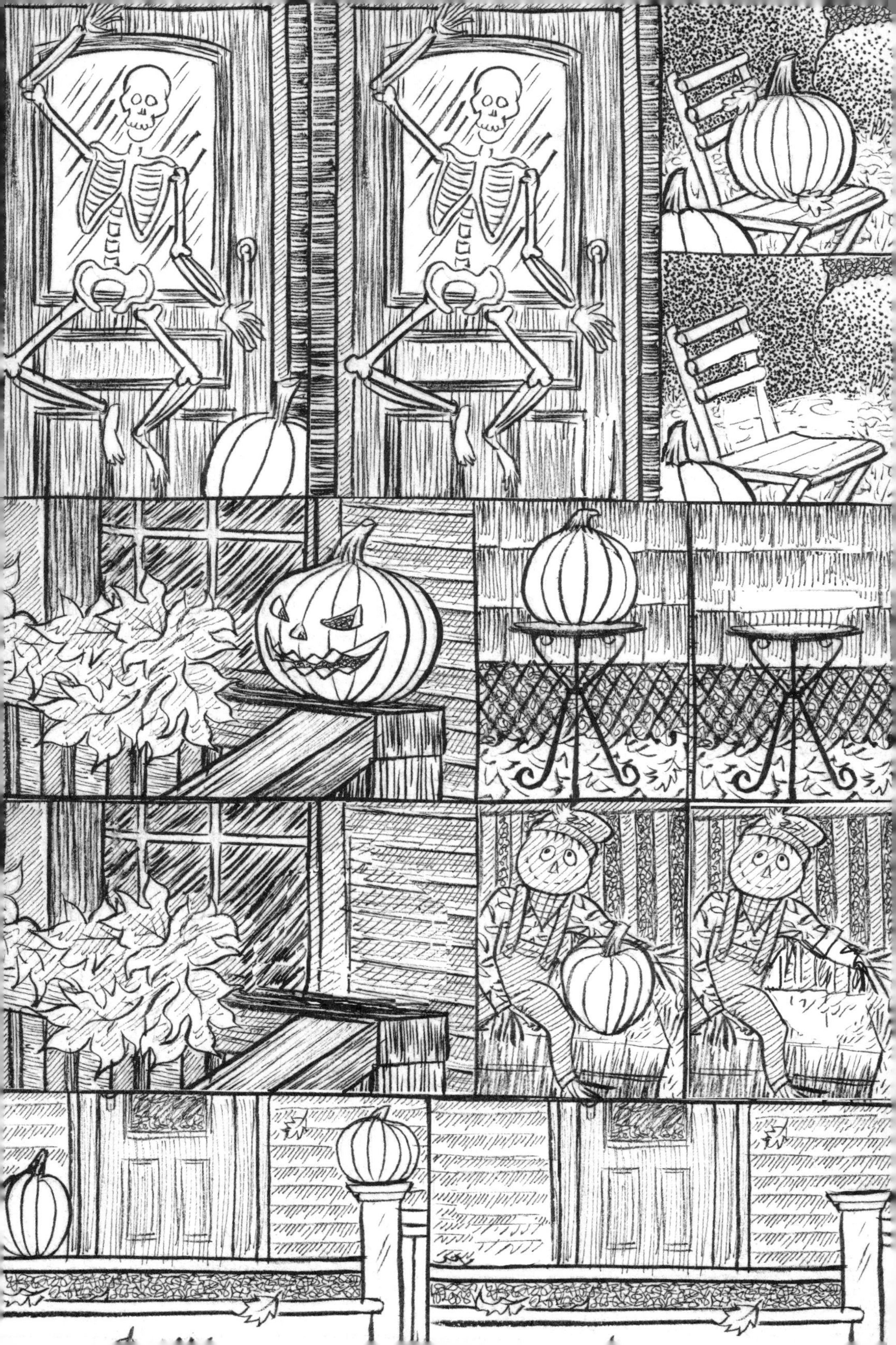

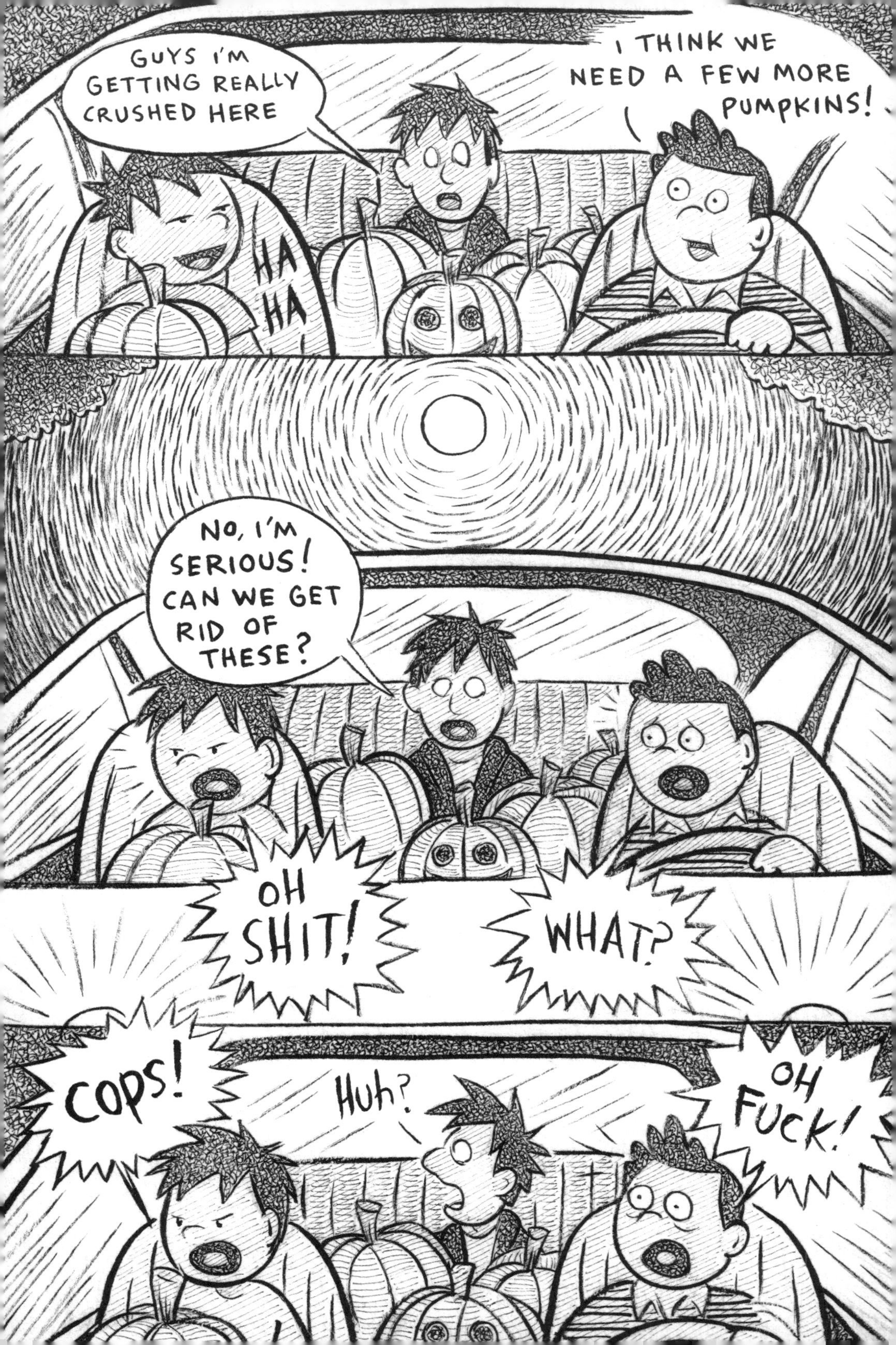
GUYS I'M GETTING REALLY CRUSHED HERE
I THINK WE NEED A FEW MORE PUMPKINS!
HA HA
NO, I'M SERIOUS! CAN WE GET RID OF THESE?
OH SHIT!
WHAT?
COPS!
Huh?
OH FUCK!

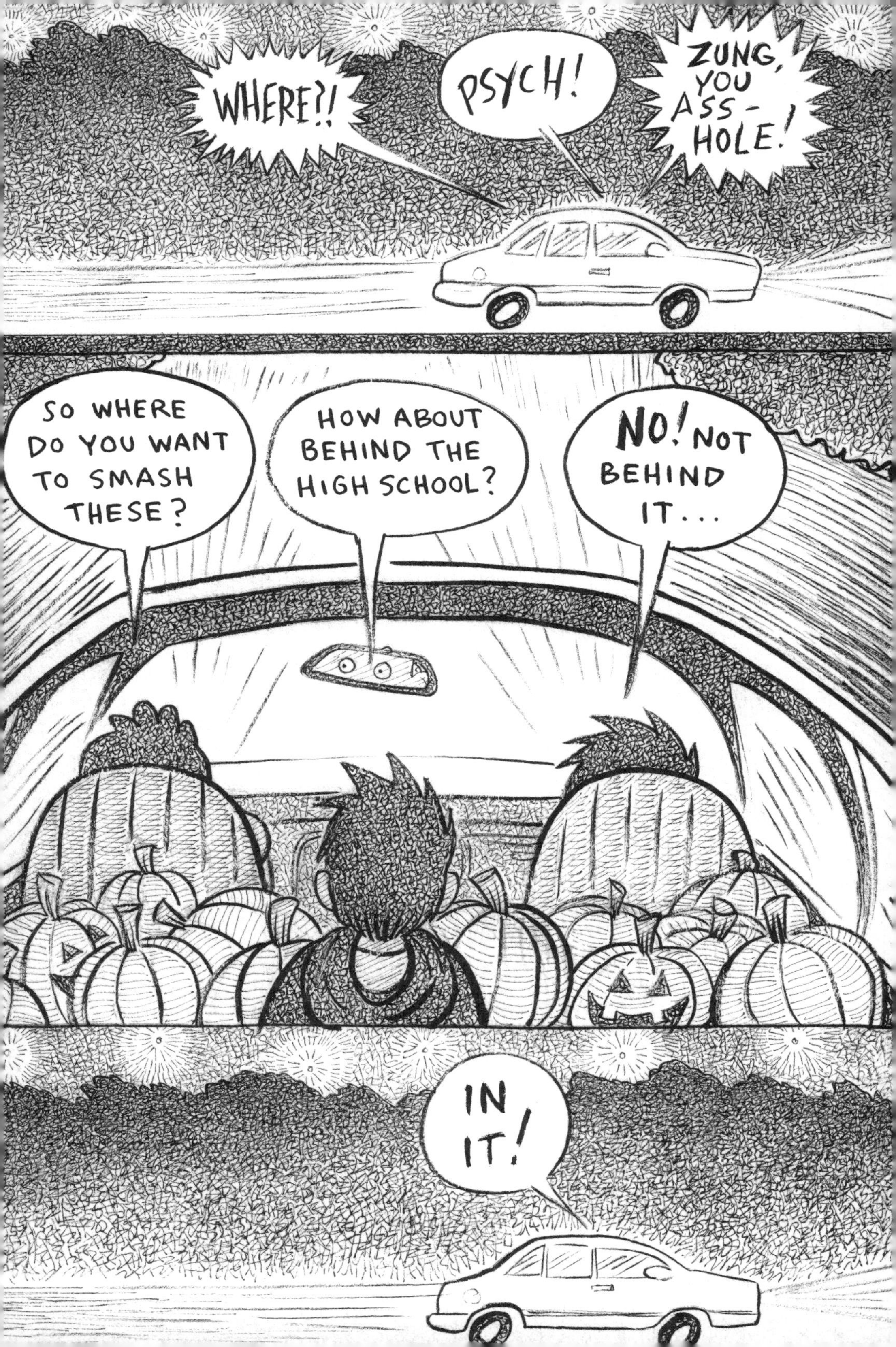
WHERE?!
PSYCH!
ZUNG, YOU ASS-HOLE!
SO WHERE DO YOU WANT TO SMASH THESE?
HOW ABOUT BEHIND THE HIGH SCHOOL?
NO! NOT BEHIND IT...
IN IT!

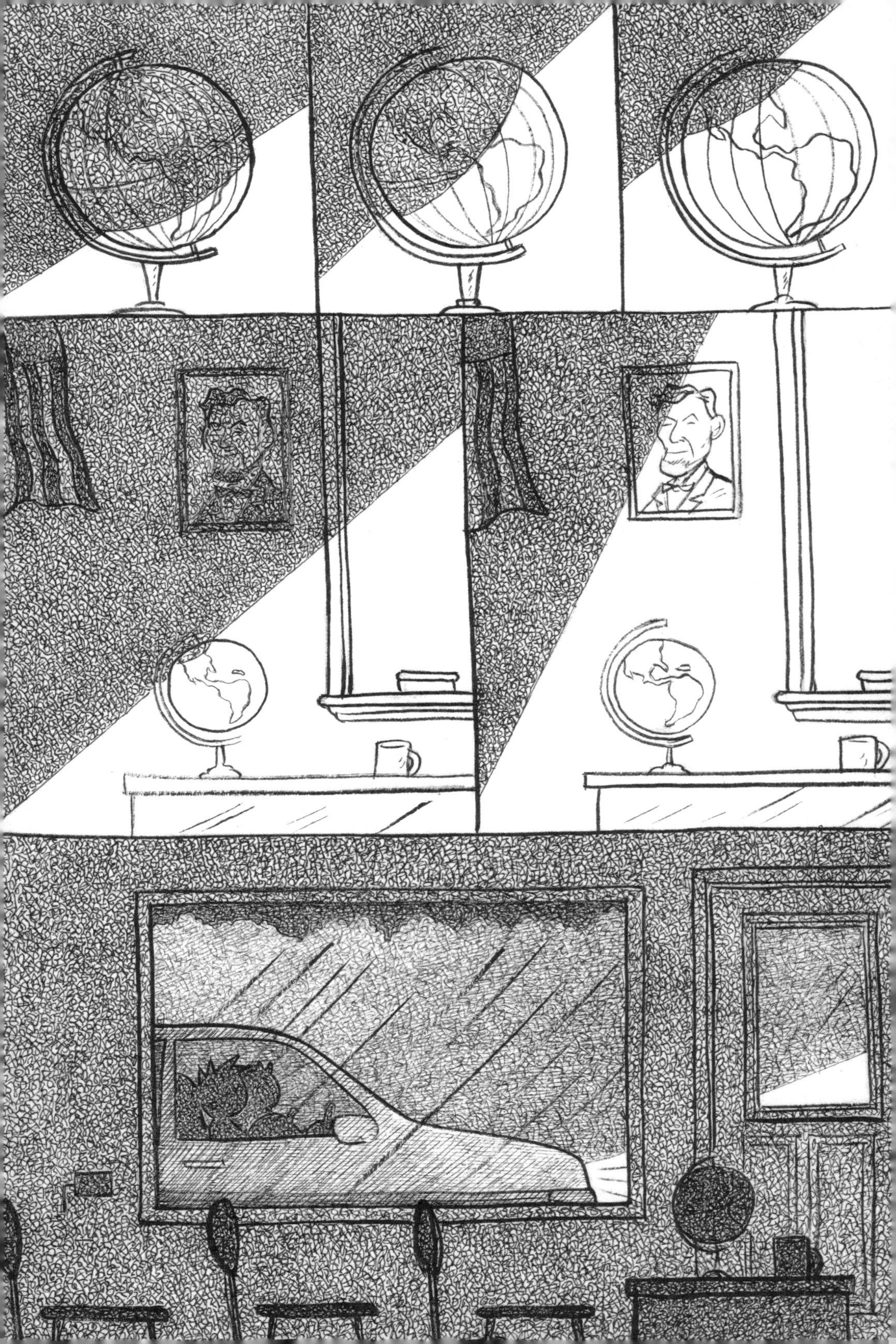

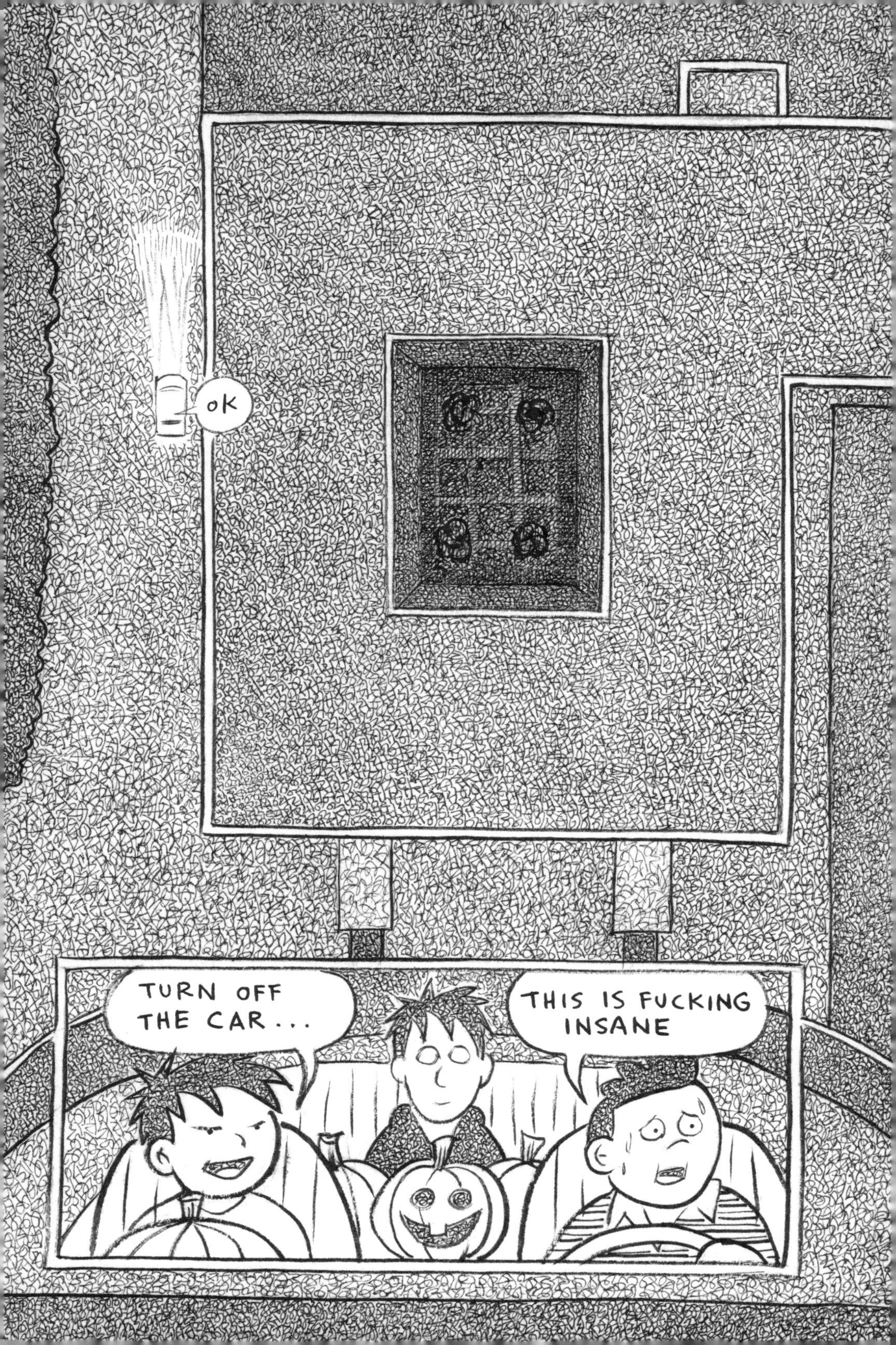
OK
TURN OFF THE CAR...
THIS IS FUCKING INSANE

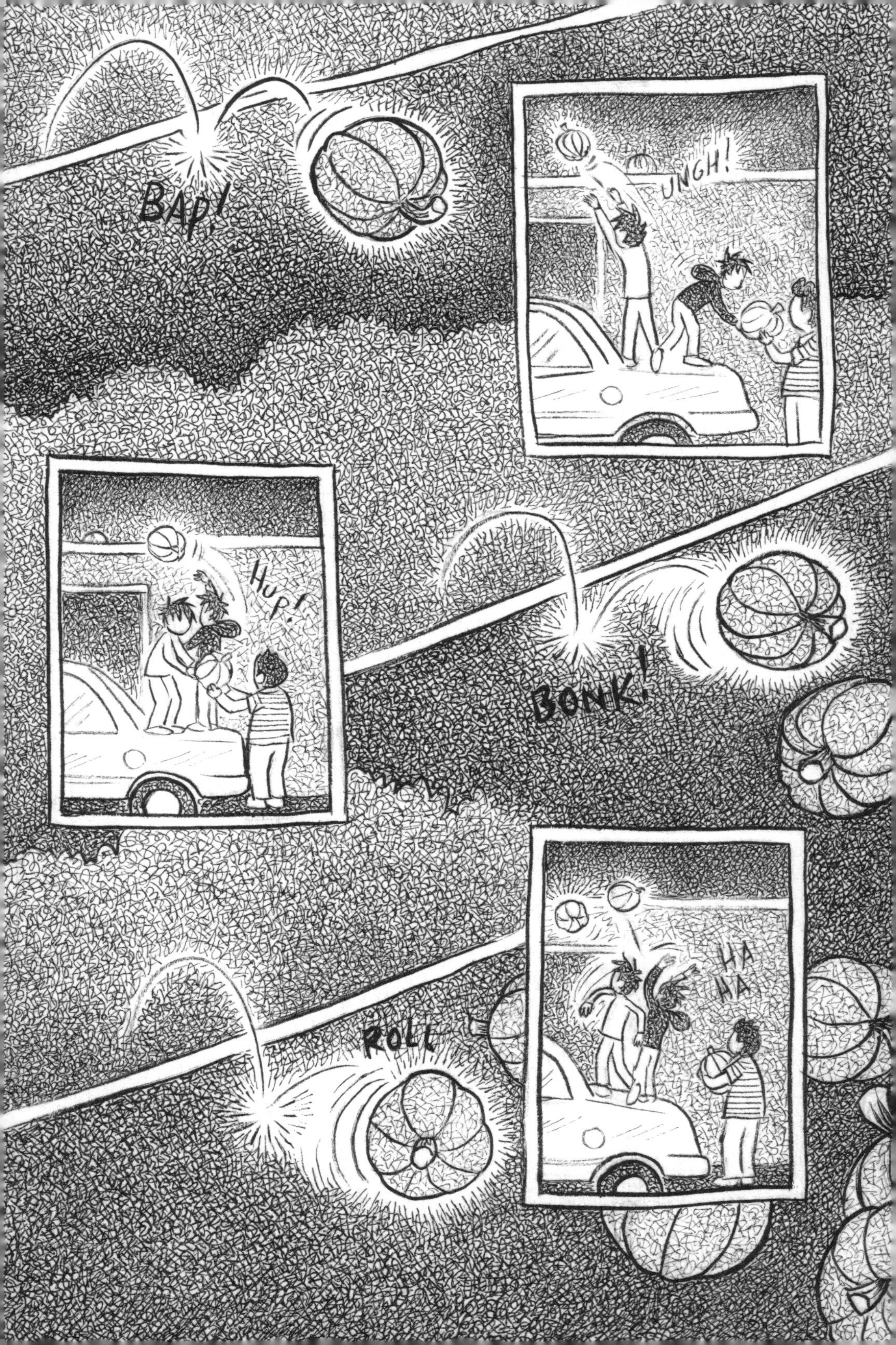
BAP!
UNGH!
HUP!
BONK!
ROLL
HA
HA

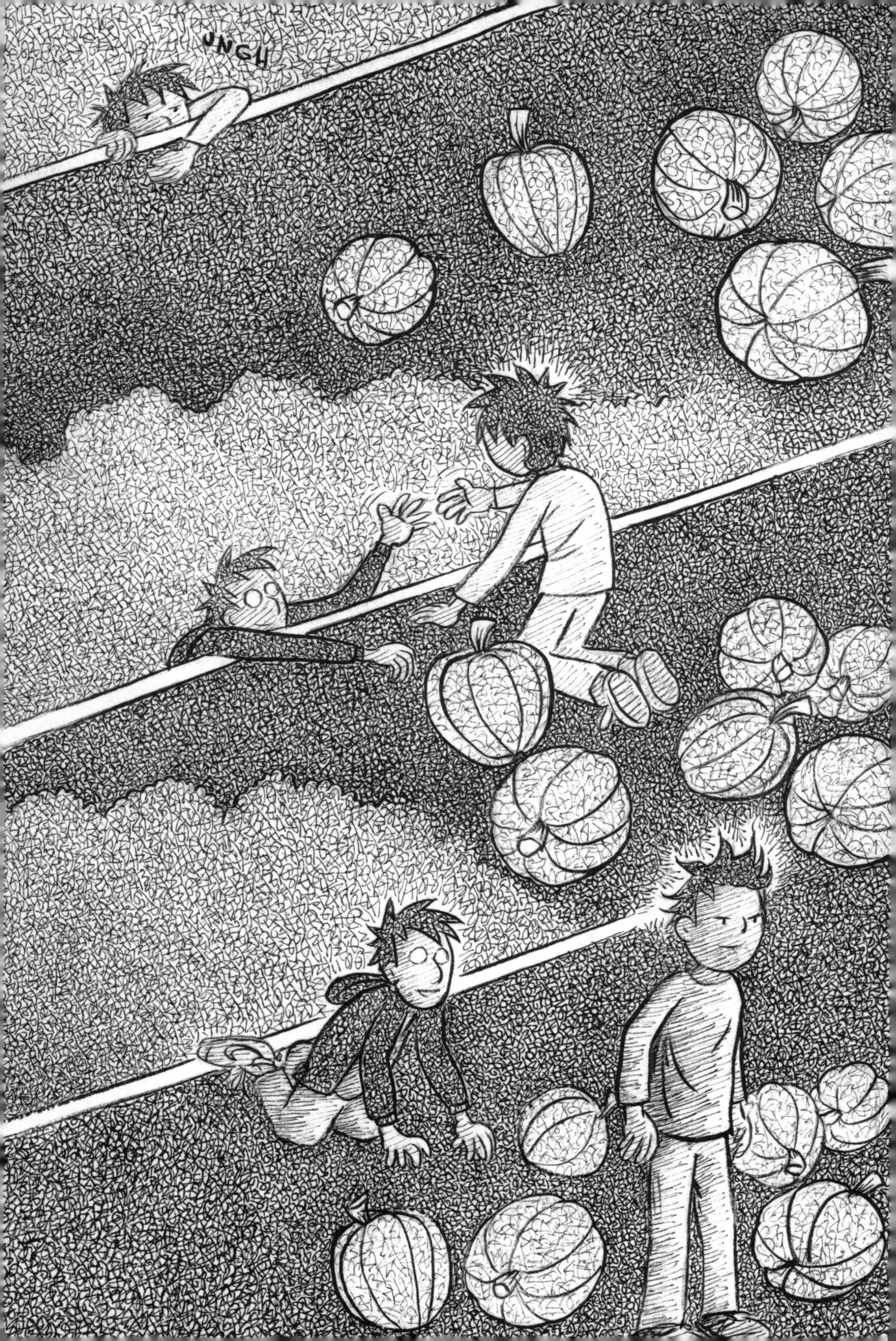
UNGH

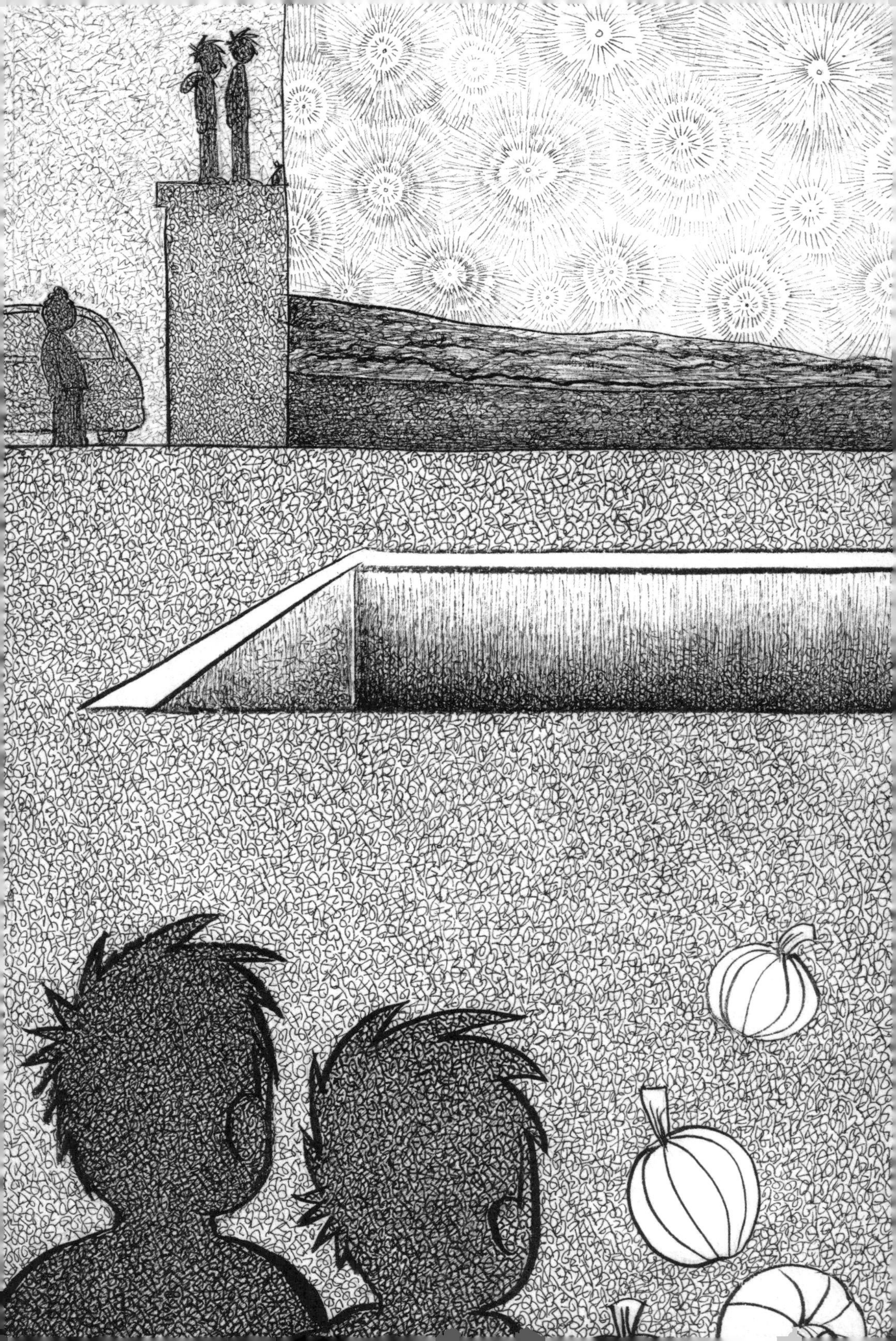

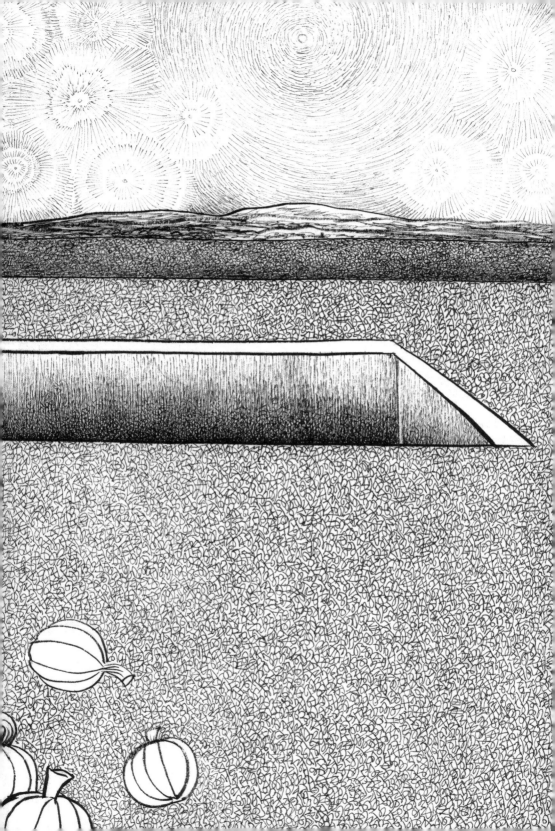

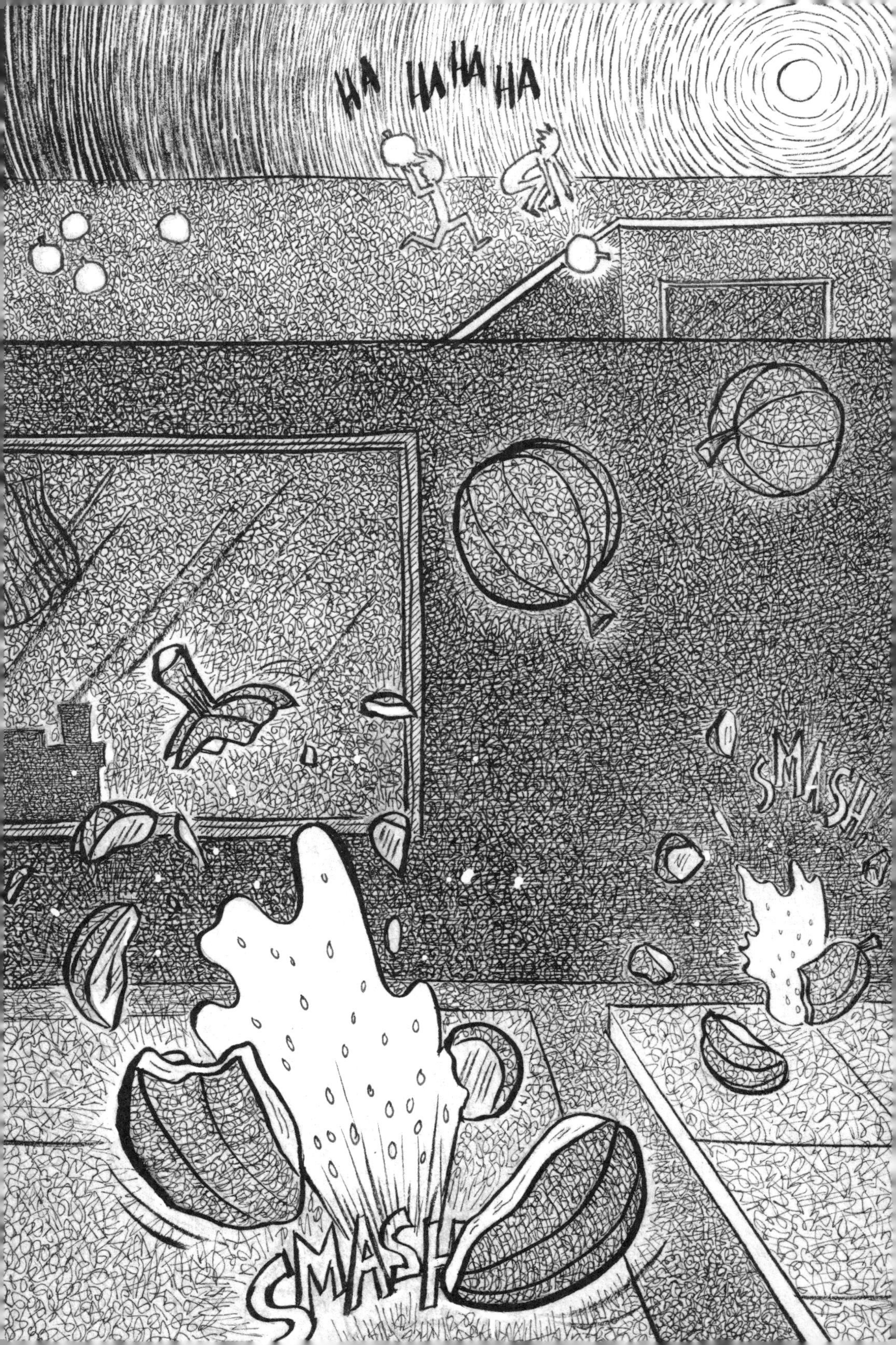

HA HAHAHA
SMASH
SMASH

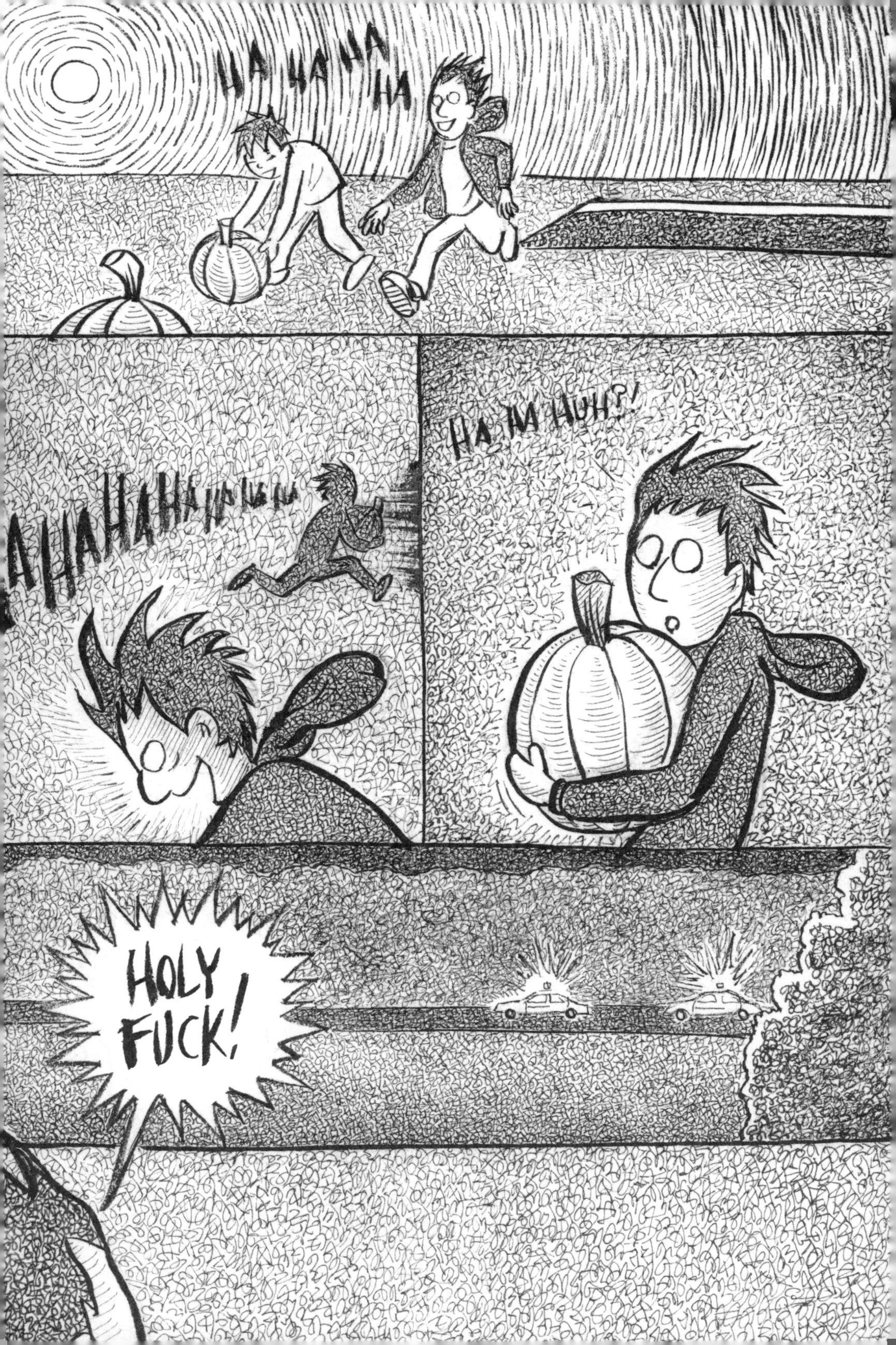

HA HA HA HA
AHAHAHAHA
HA HA HUH?!
HOLY FUCK!

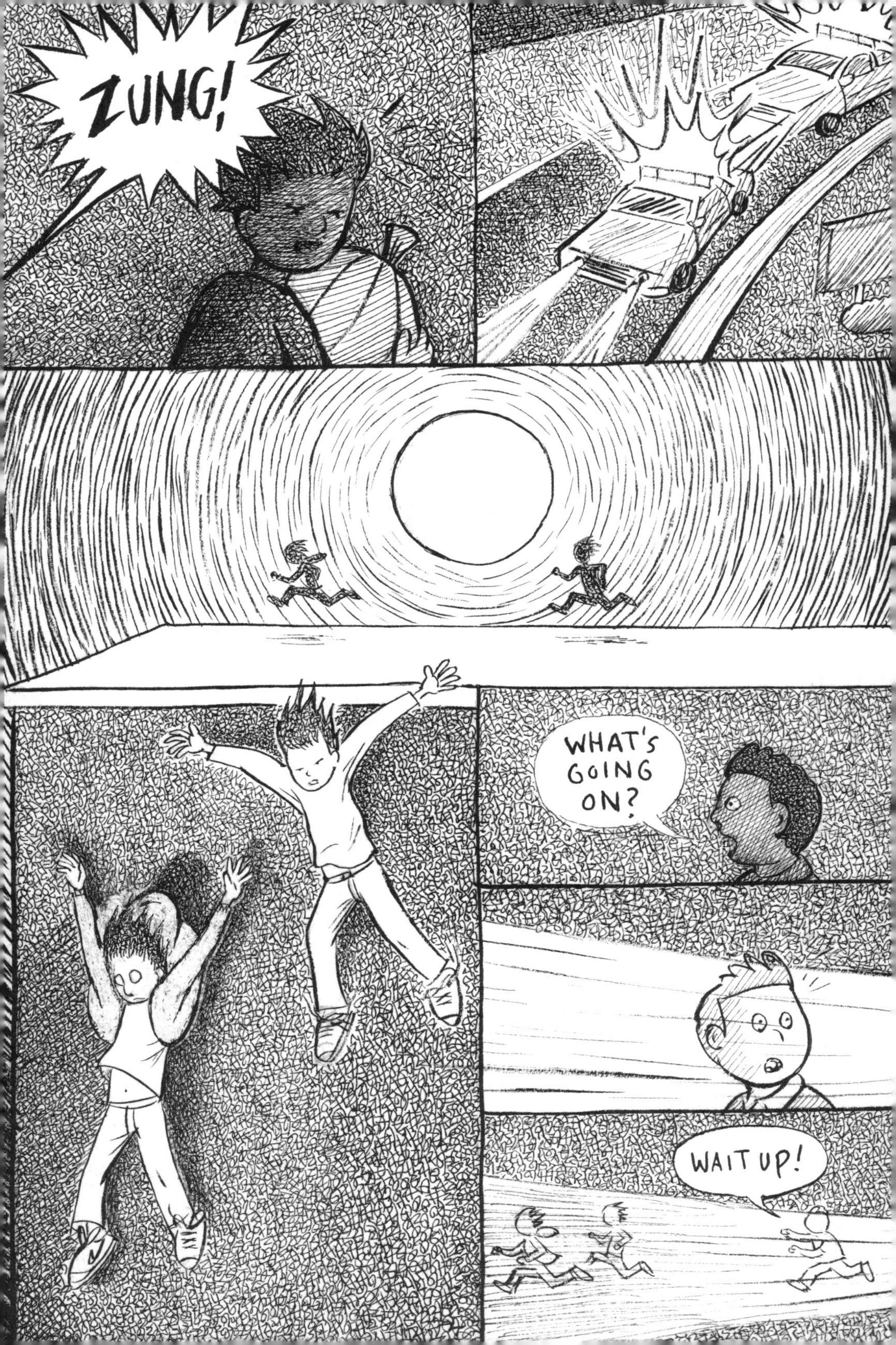
ZUNG!
WHAT'S GOING ON?
WAIT UP!

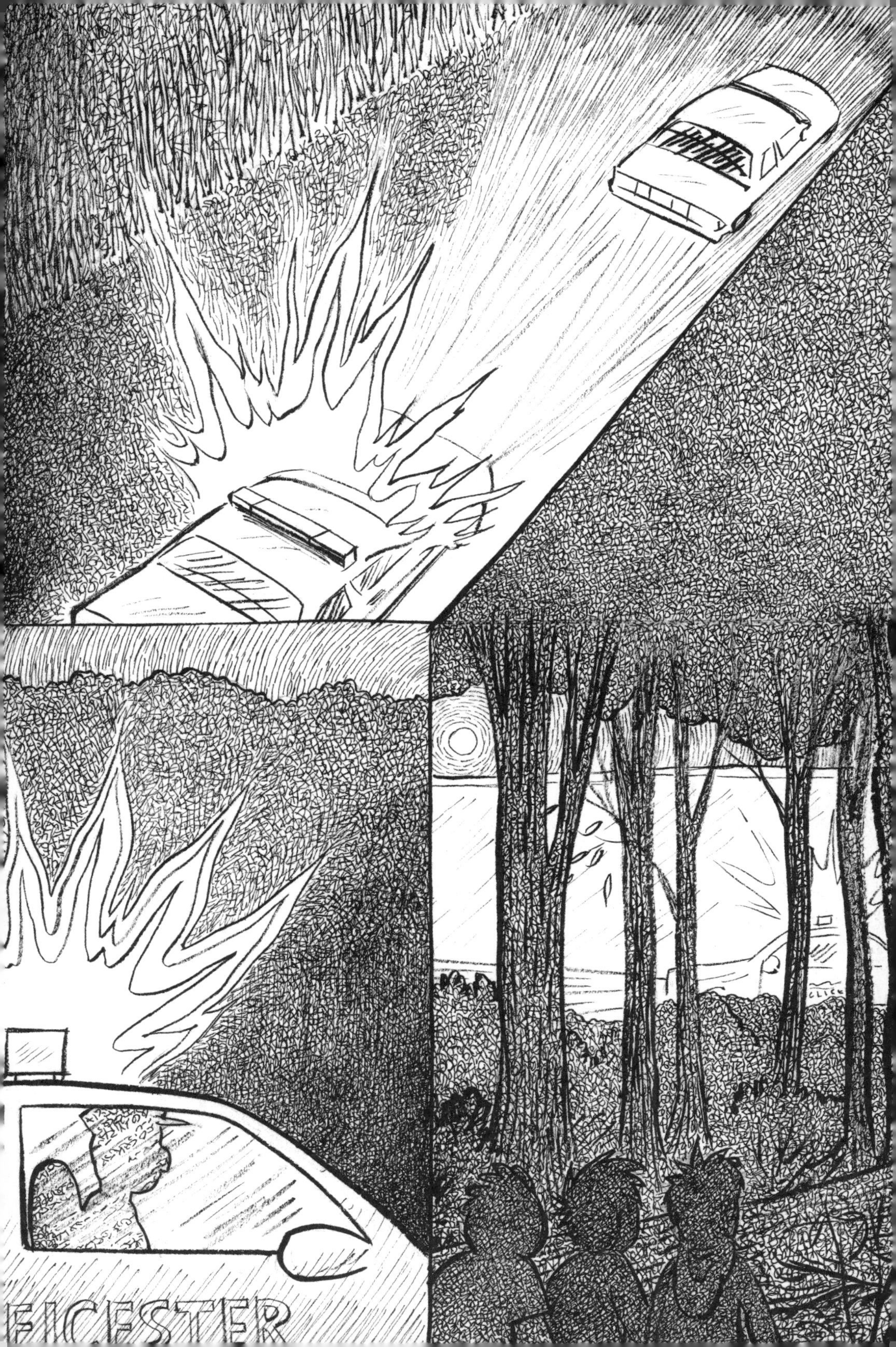

CLICK
EICESTER

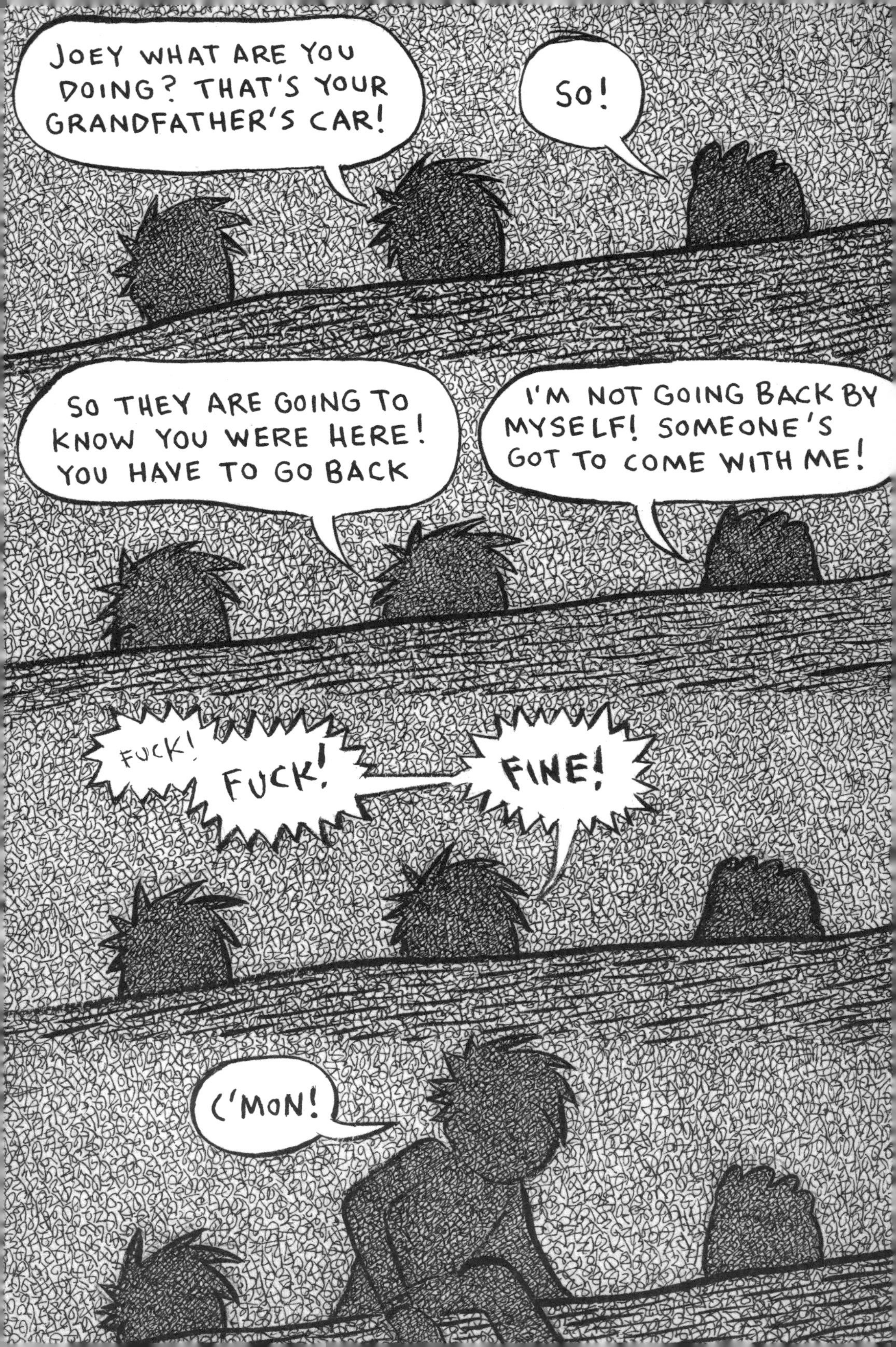
JOEY WHAT ARE YOU DOING? THAT'S YOUR GRANDFATHER'S CAR!
SO!
SO THEY ARE GOING TO KNOW YOU WERE HERE! YOU HAVE TO GO BACK
I'M NOT GOING BACK BY MYSELF! SOMEONE'S GOT TO COME WITH ME!
FUCK!
FUCK!
FINE!
C'MON!

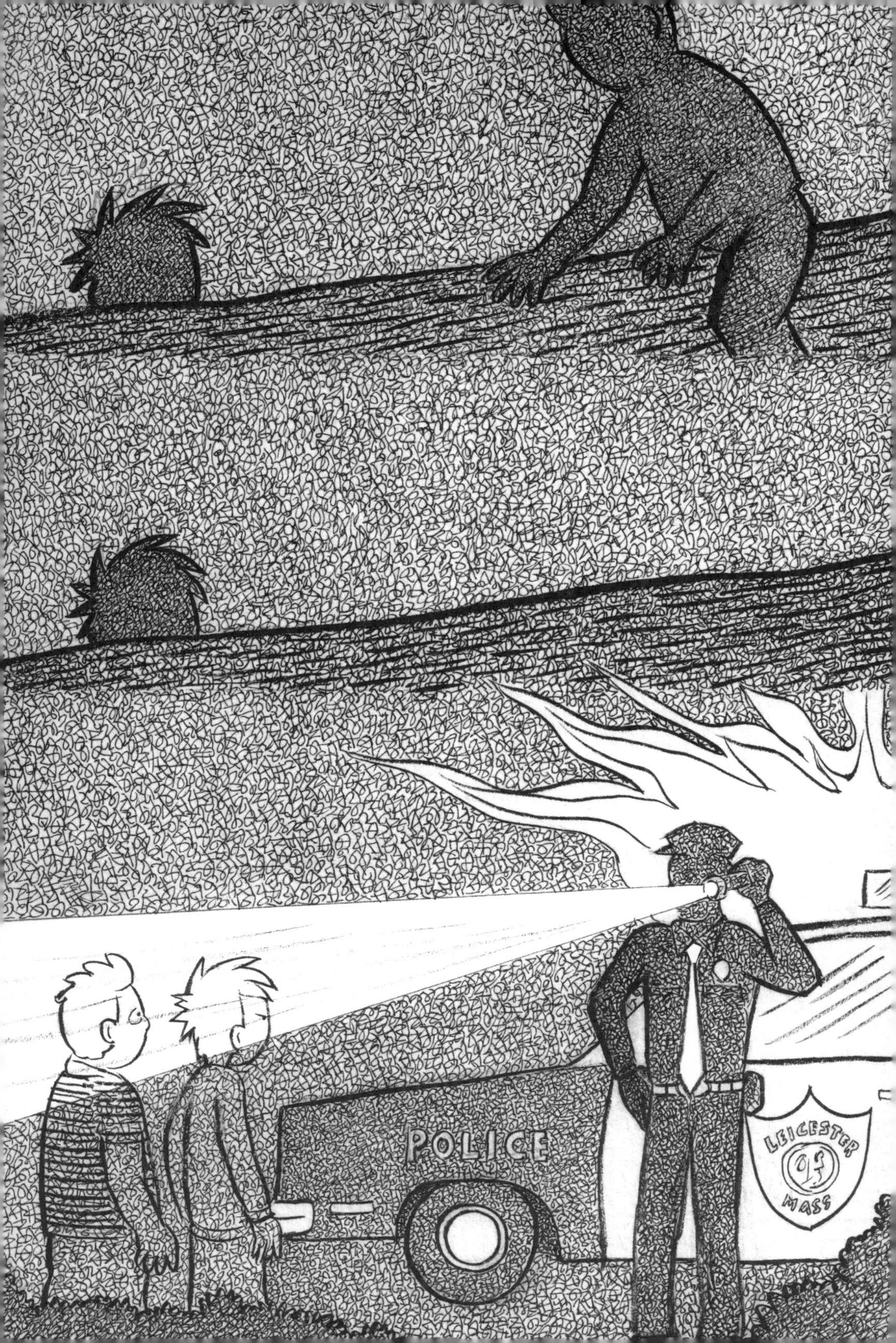
POLICE
LEICESTER
MASS

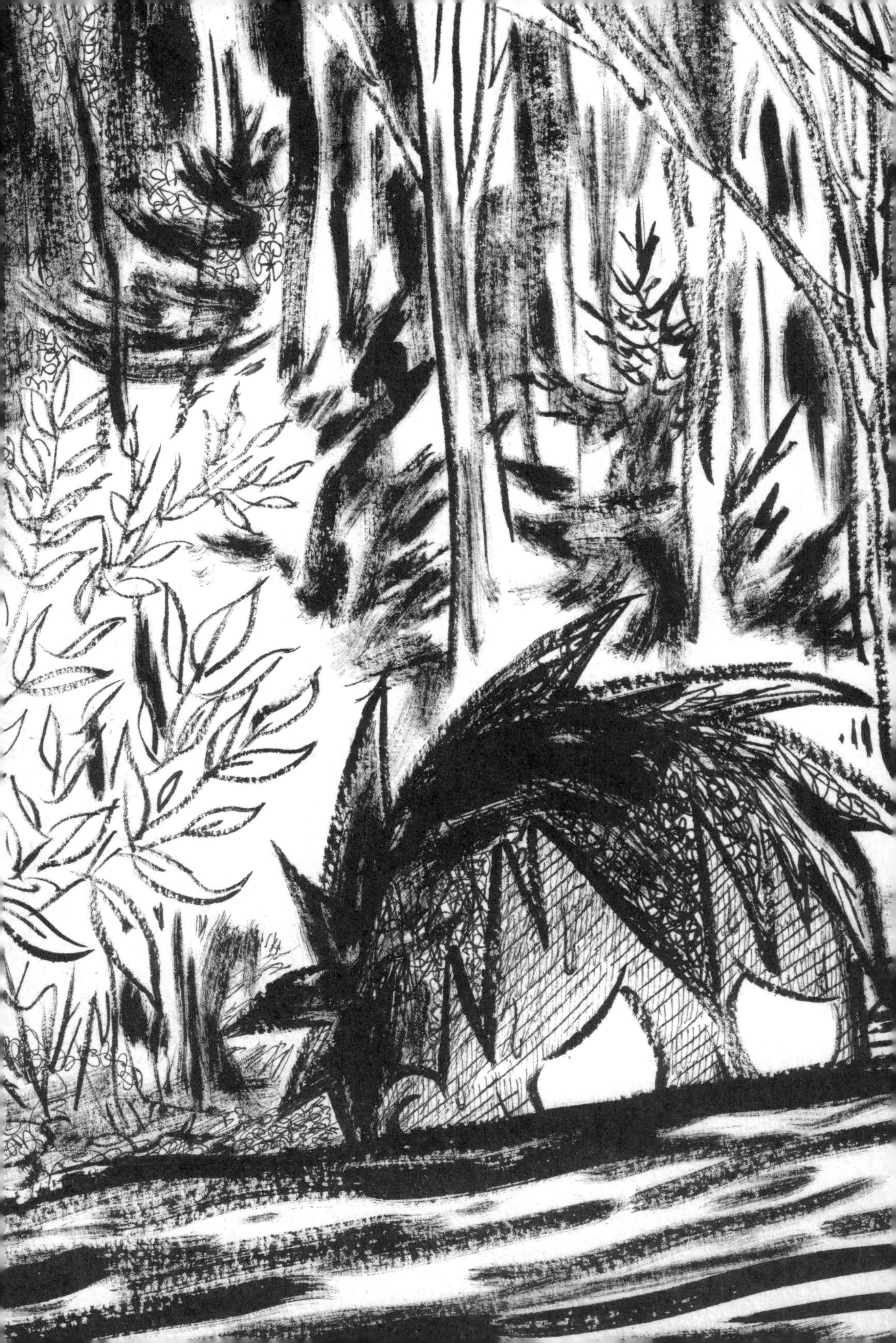

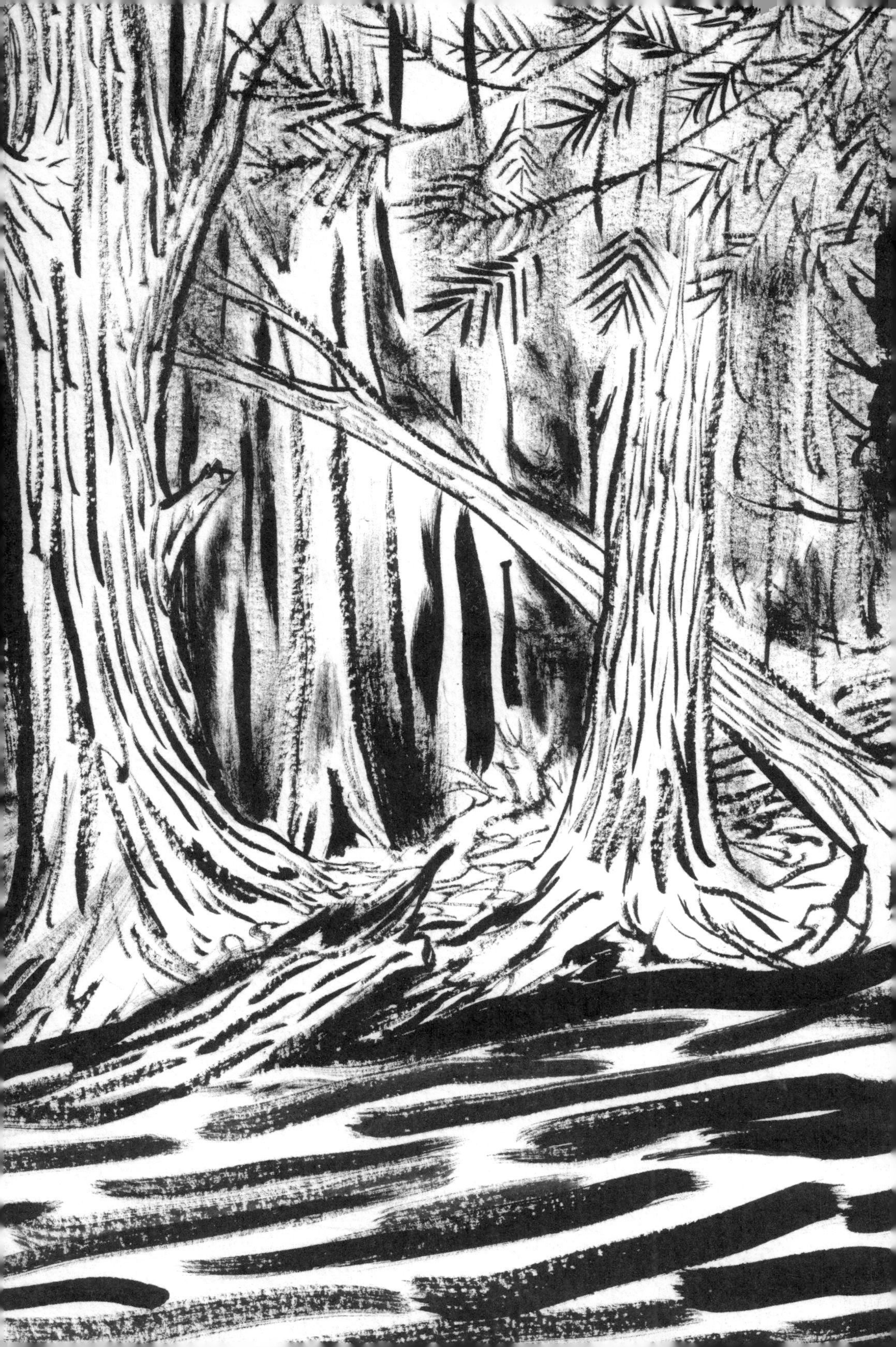

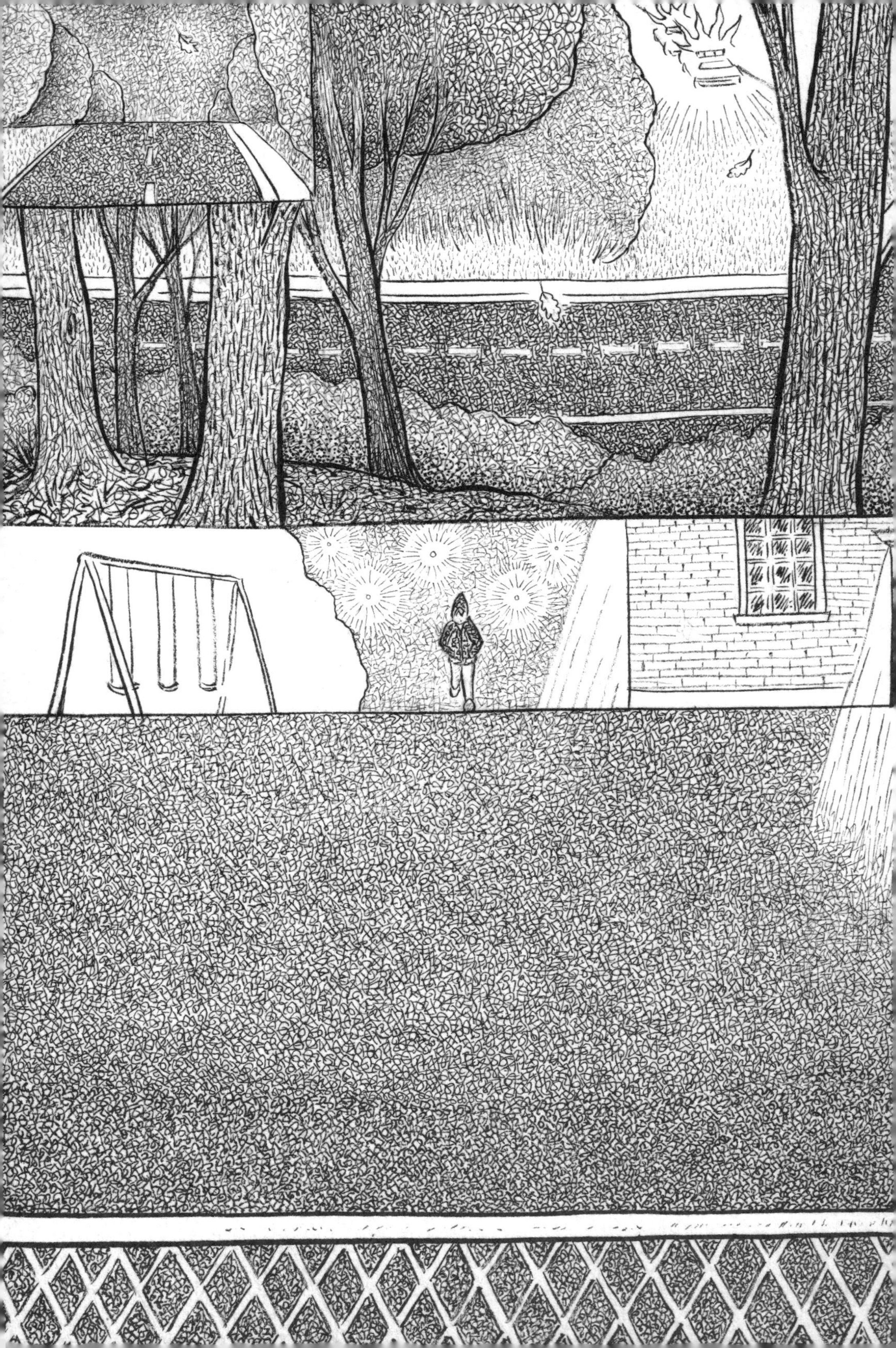

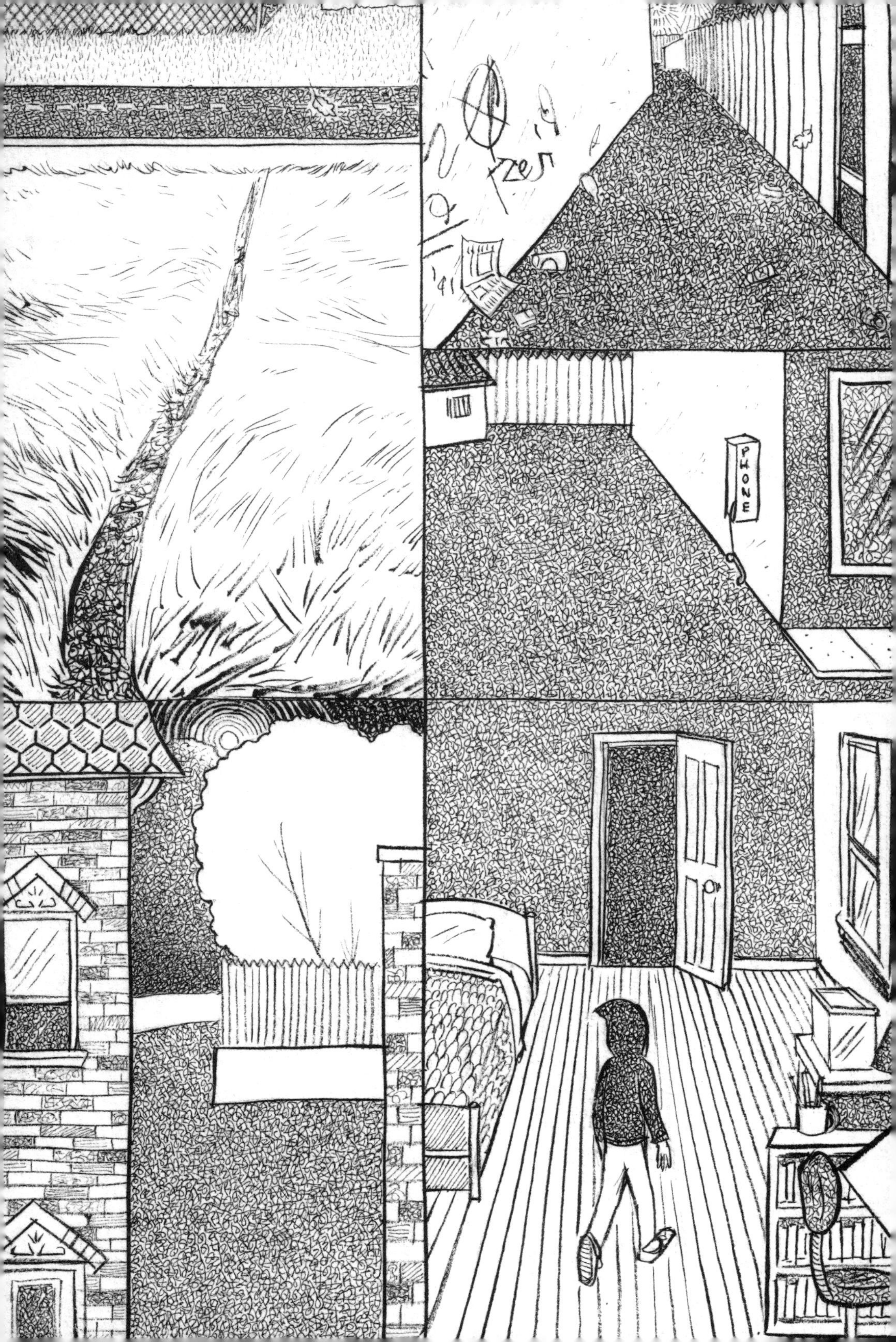
PHONE

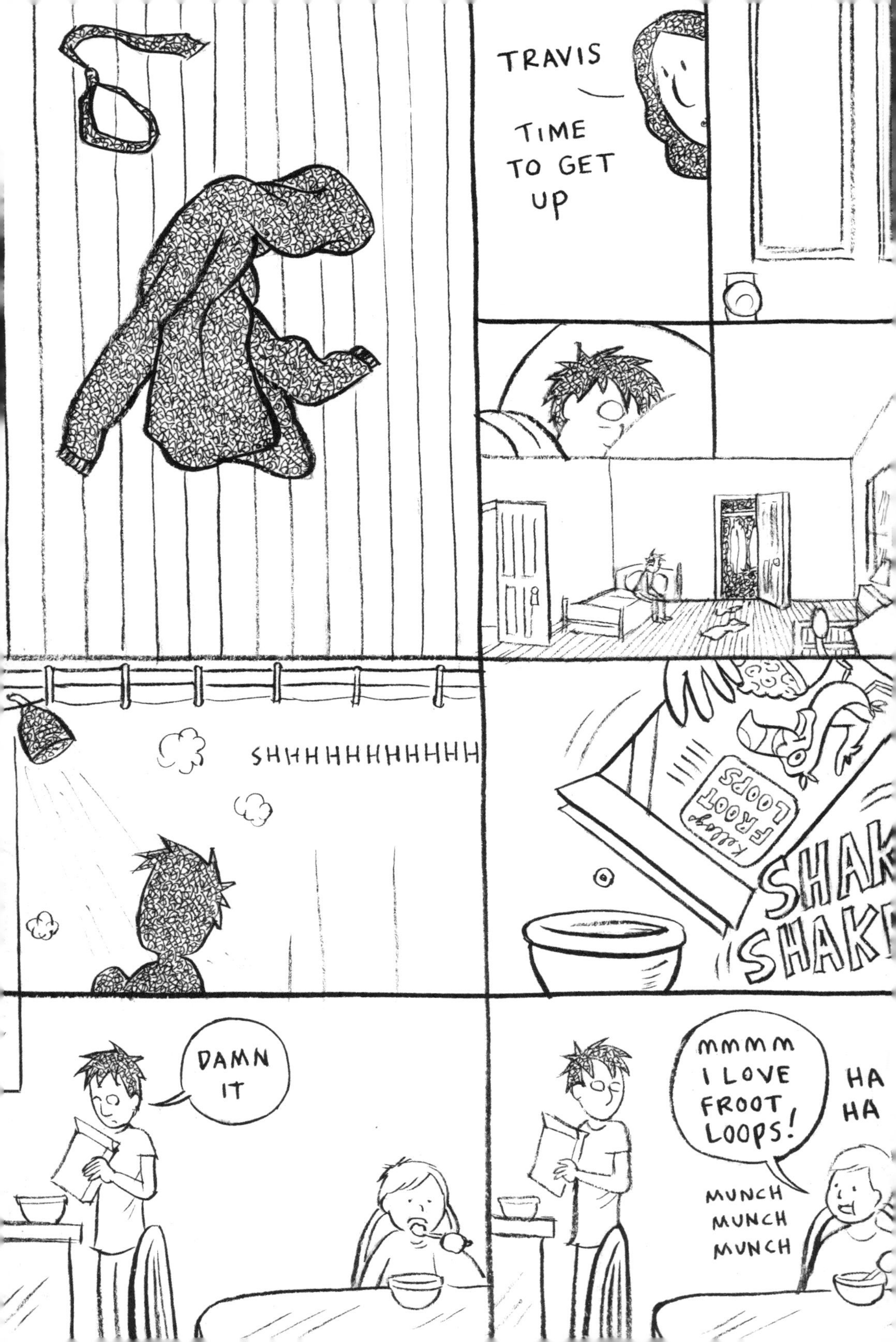
TRAVIS
TIME TO GET UP
SHHHHHHHHHHH
FROOT LOOPS
SHAK
SHAK
DAMN IT
MMMM I LOVE FROOT LOOPS!
HA HA
MUNCH MUNCH MUNCH

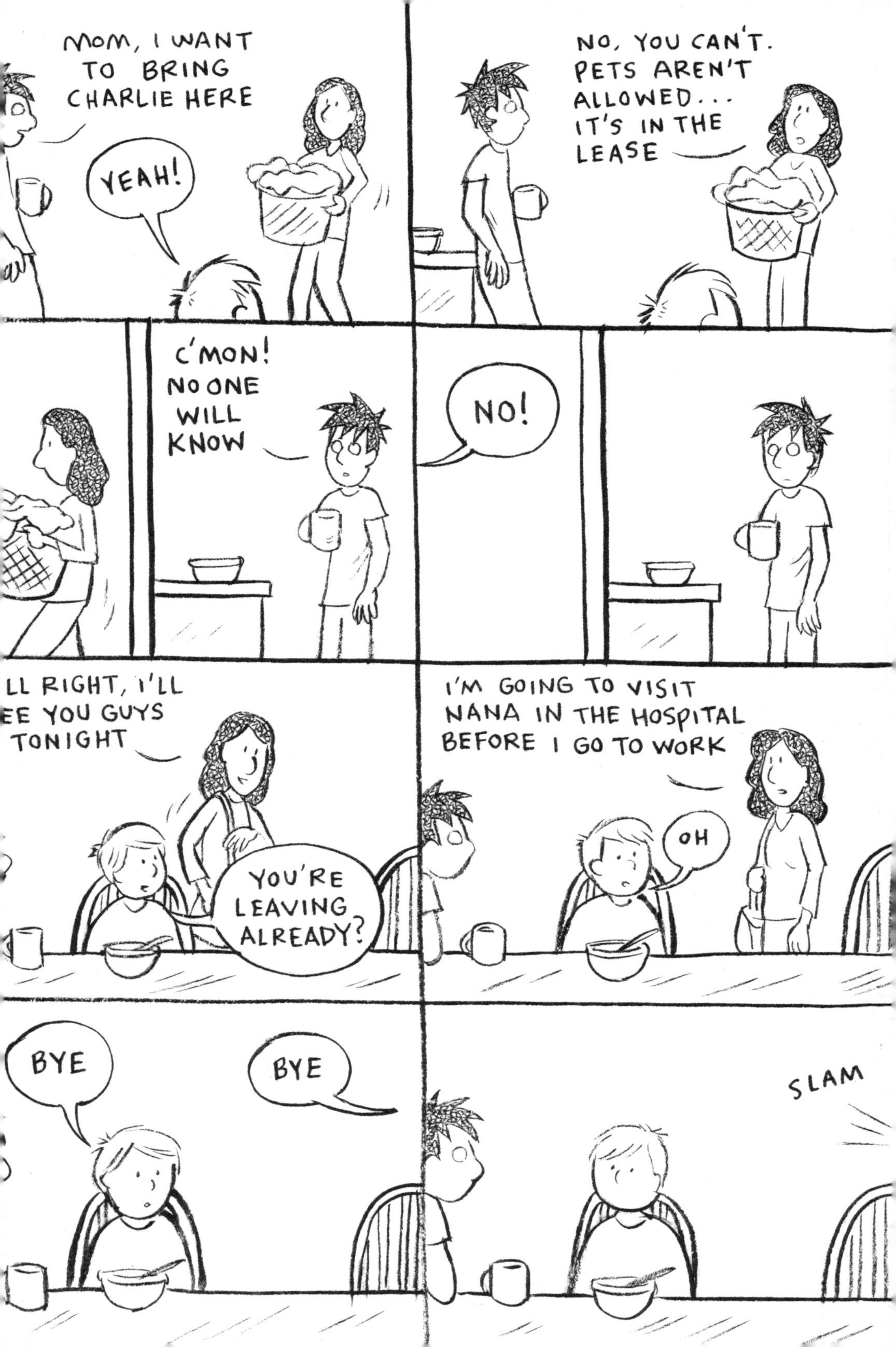
MOM, I WANT TO BRING CHARLIE HERE
YEAH!
NO, YOU CAN'T. PETS AREN'T ALLOWED... IT'S IN THE LEASE
C'MON! NO ONE WILL KNOW
NO!
LL RIGHT, I'LL EE YOU GUYS TONIGHT
YOU'RE LEAVING ALREADY?
I'M GOING TO VISIT NANA IN THE HOSPITAL BEFORE I GO TO WORK
OH
BYE
BYE
SLAM

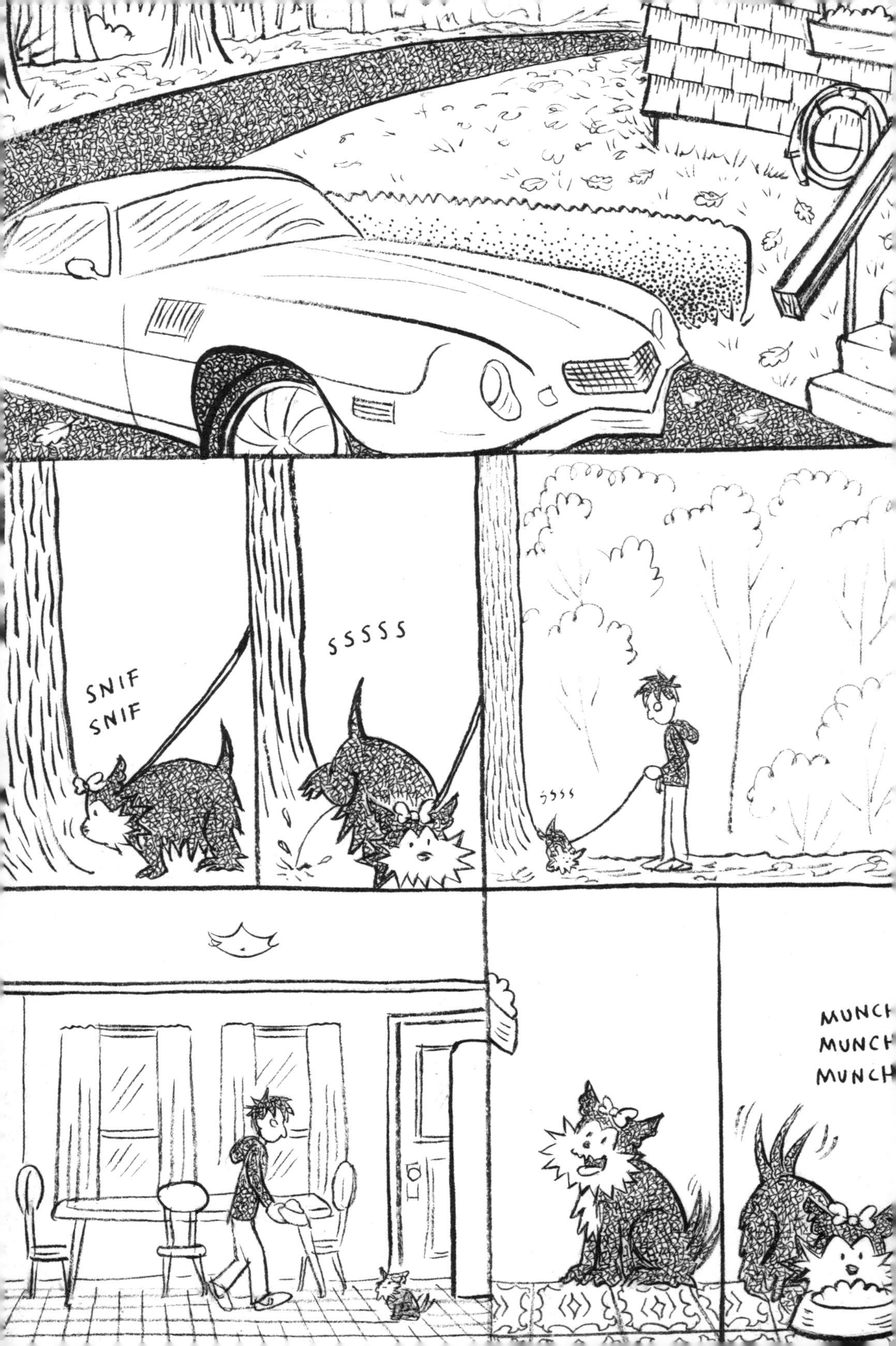
SNIF
SNIF
SSSSS
SSSS
MUNCH
MUNCH
MUNCH

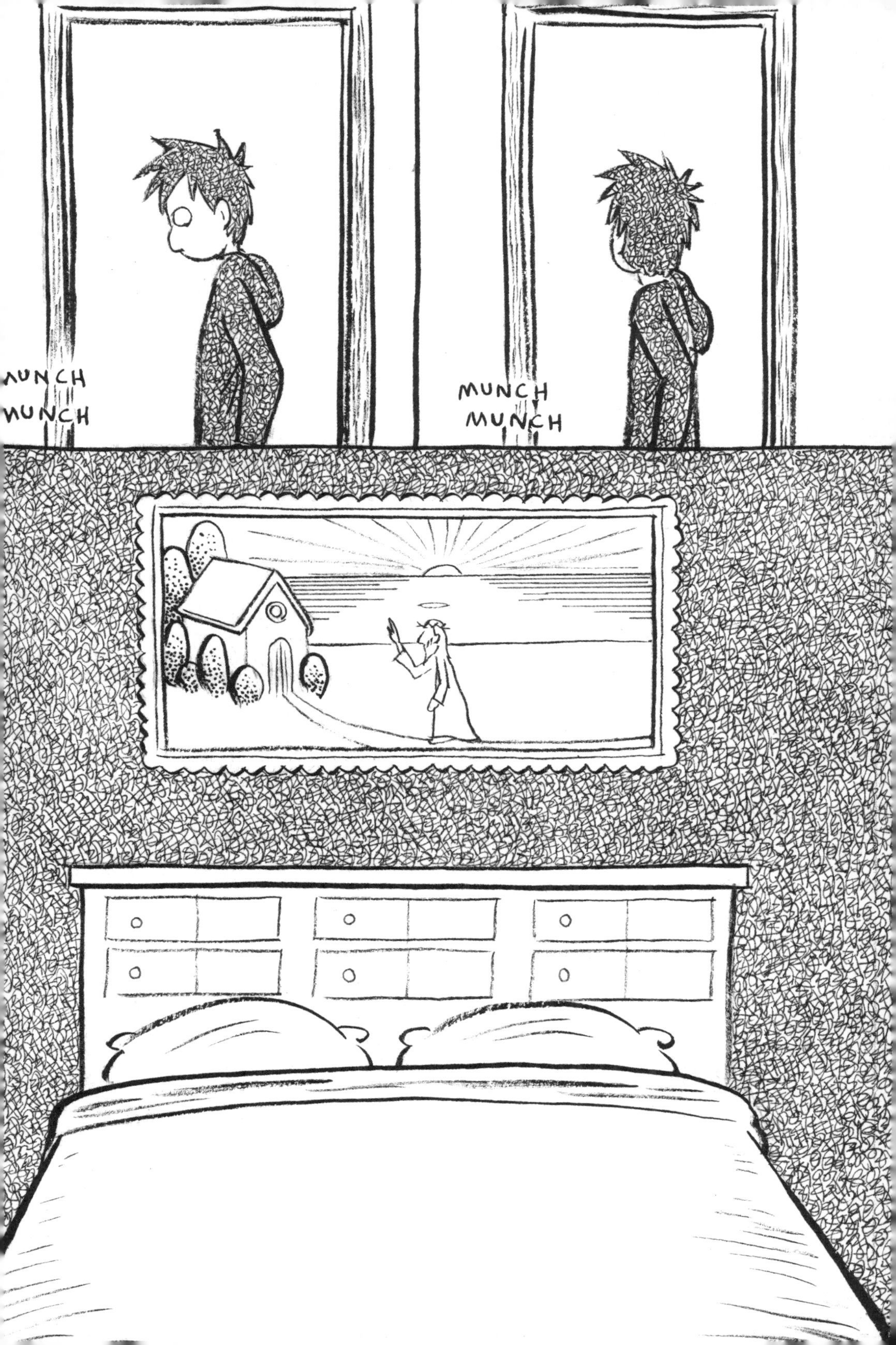
MUNCH
MUNCH
MUNCH
MUNCH

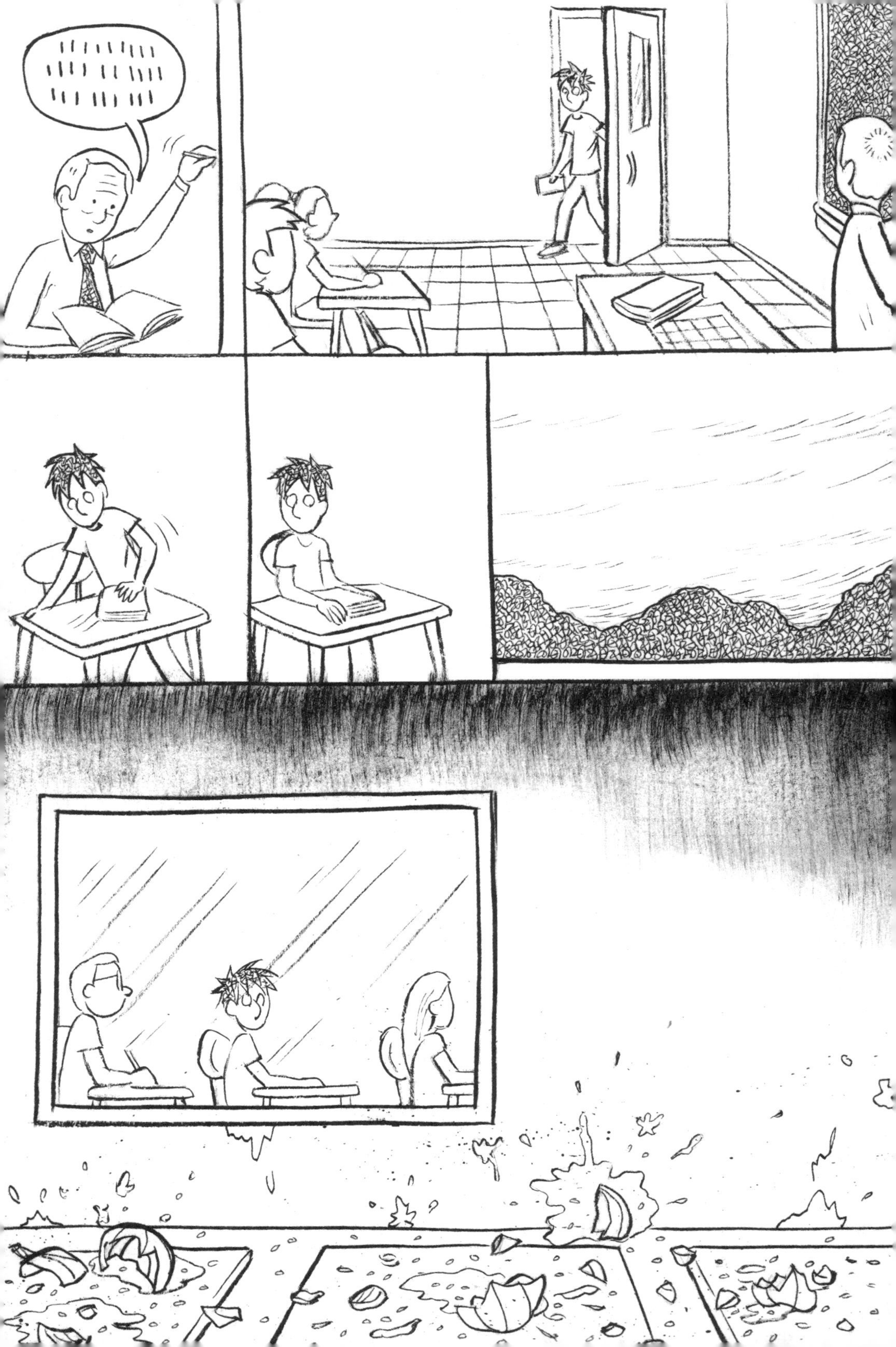

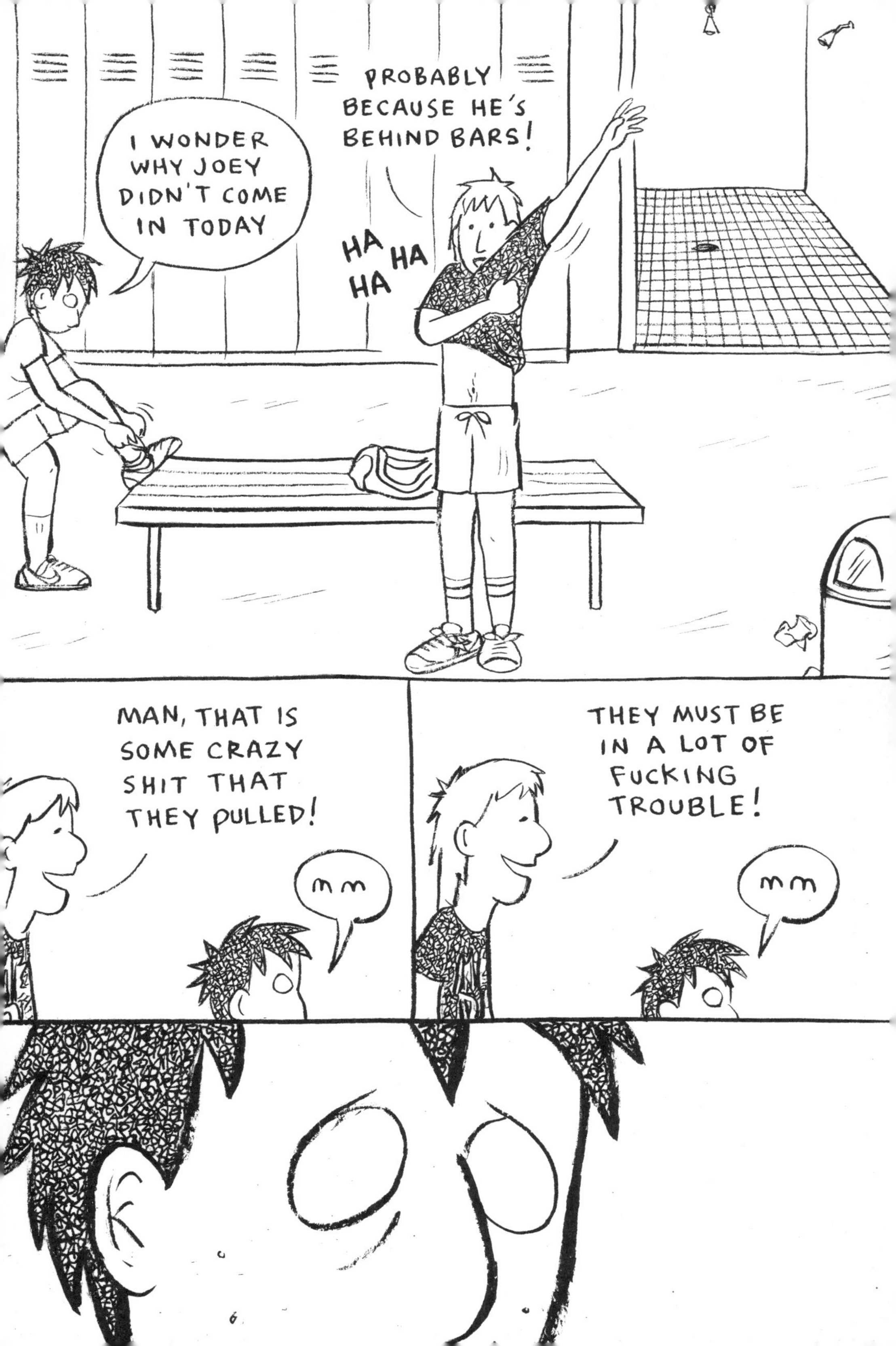
I WONDER WHY JOEY DIDN'T COME IN TODAY
PROBABLY BECAUSE HE'S BEHIND BARS!
HA HA HA
MAN, THAT IS SOME CRAZY SHIT THAT THEY PULLED!
mm
THEY MUST BE IN A LOT OF FUCKING TROUBLE!
mm

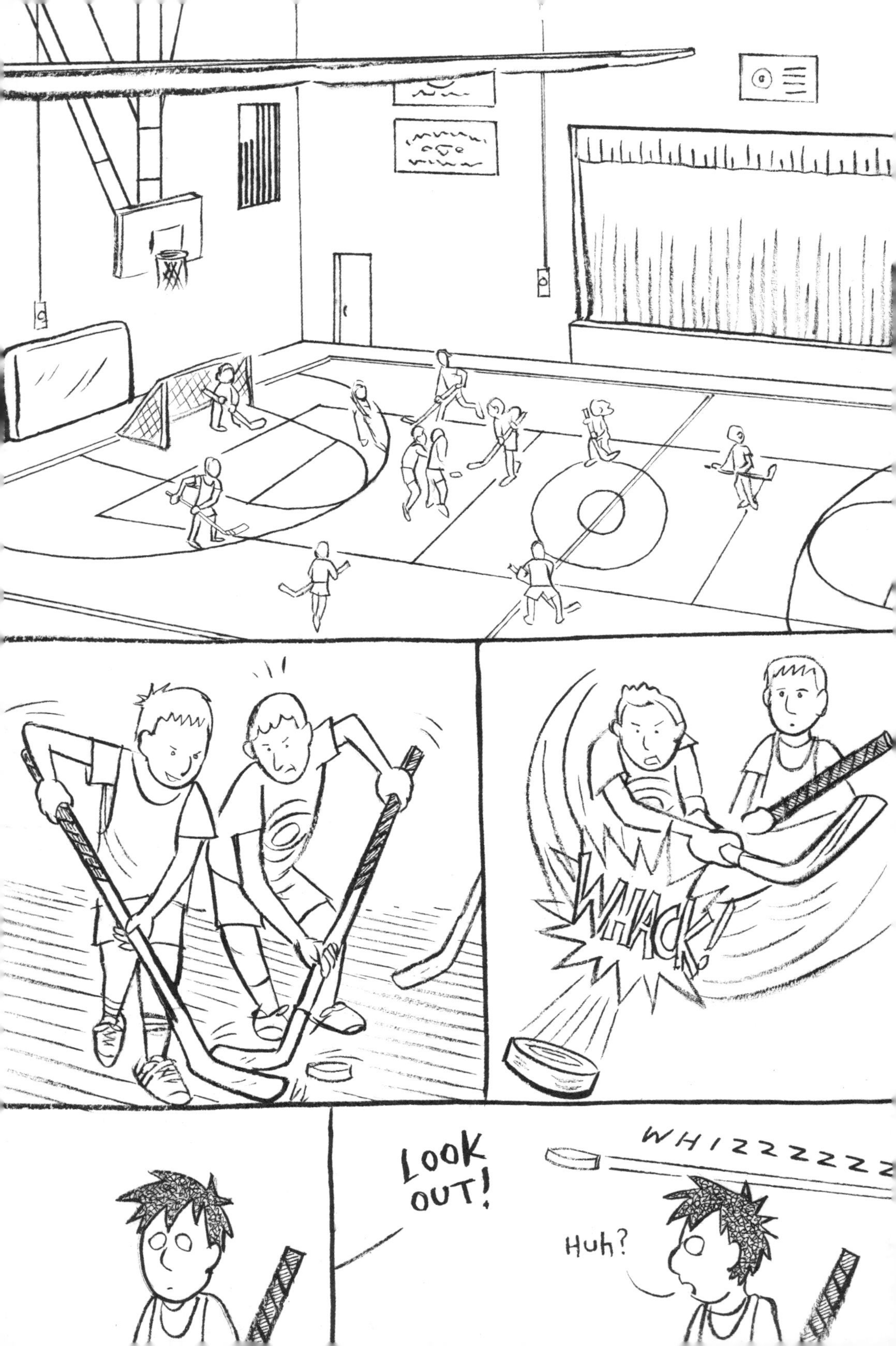
WHACK!
LOOK OUT!
WHIZZZZZZZ
Huh?

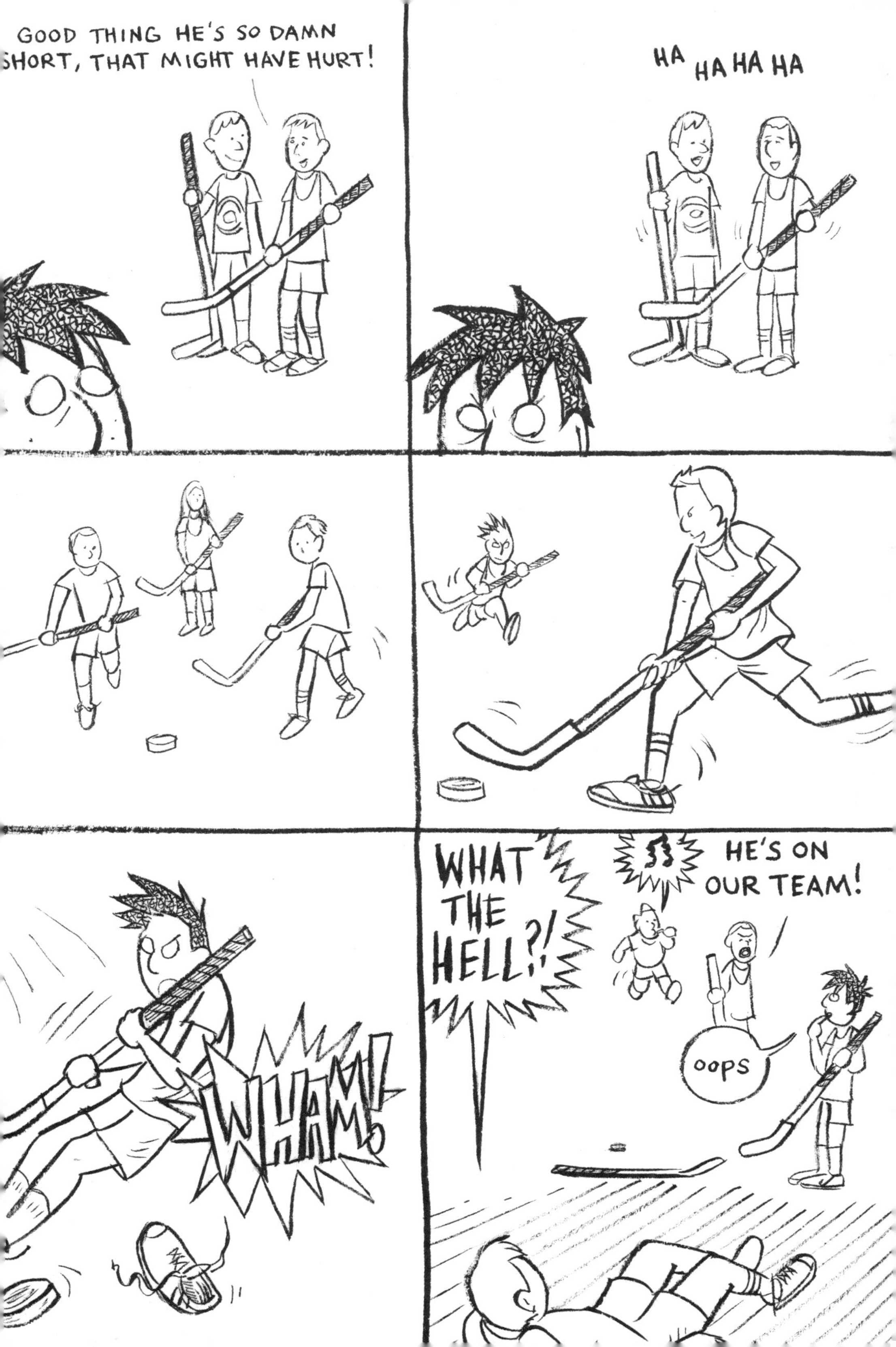
GOOD THING HE'S SO DAMN SHORT, THAT MIGHT HAVE HURT!
HA HA HA HA
WHAM!
WHAT THE HELL?!
HE'S ON OUR TEAM!
OOPS

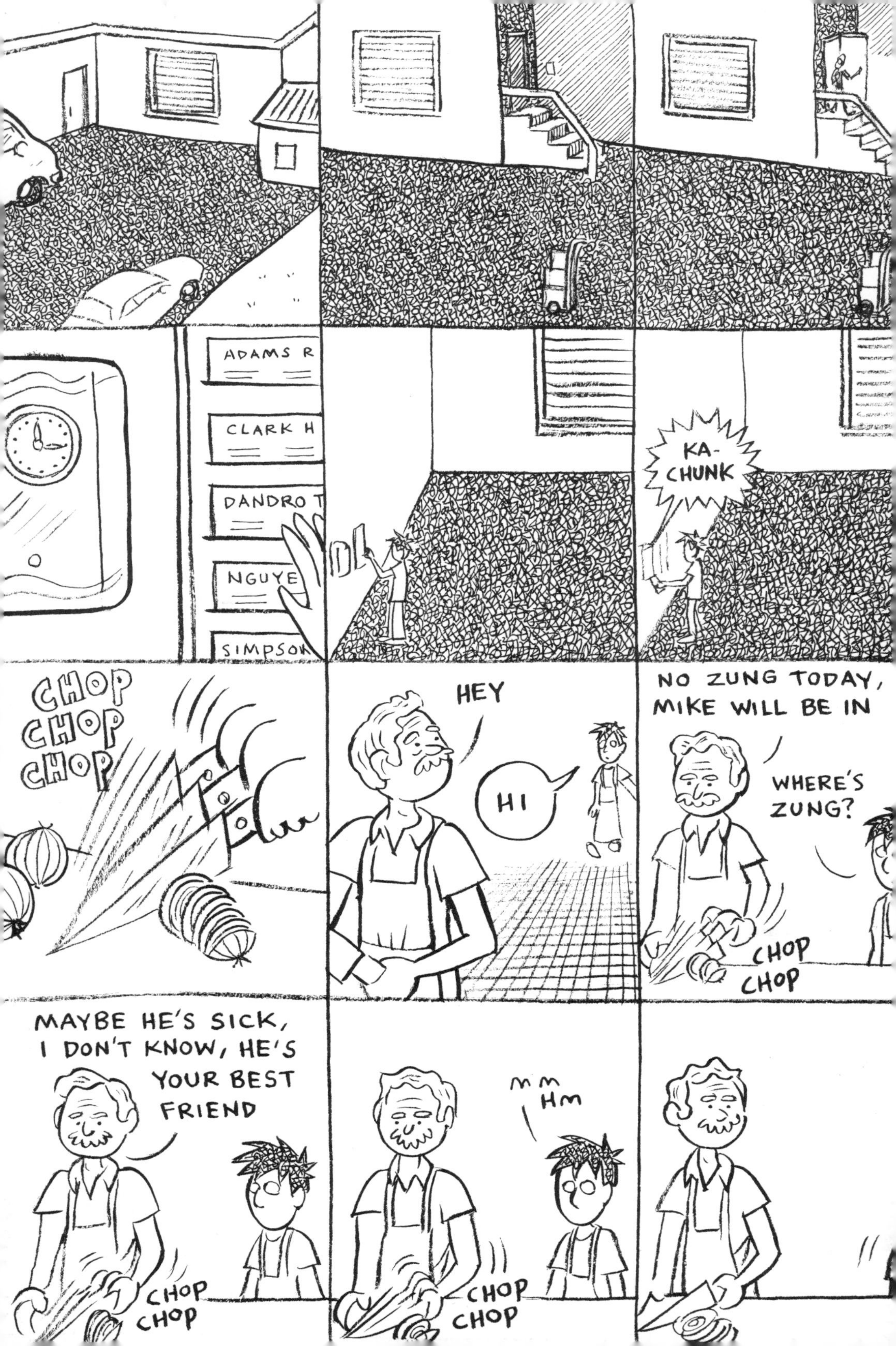
ADAMS R
CLARK H
DANDRO T
NGUYE
SIMPSON
KA-CHUNK
CHOP CHOP CHOP
HEY
HI
NO ZUNG TODAY, MIKE WILL BE IN
WHERE'S ZUNG?
CHOP CHOP
MAYBE HE'S SICK, I DON'T KNOW, HE'S YOUR BEST FRIEND
CHOP CHOP
MM HM
CHOP CHOP

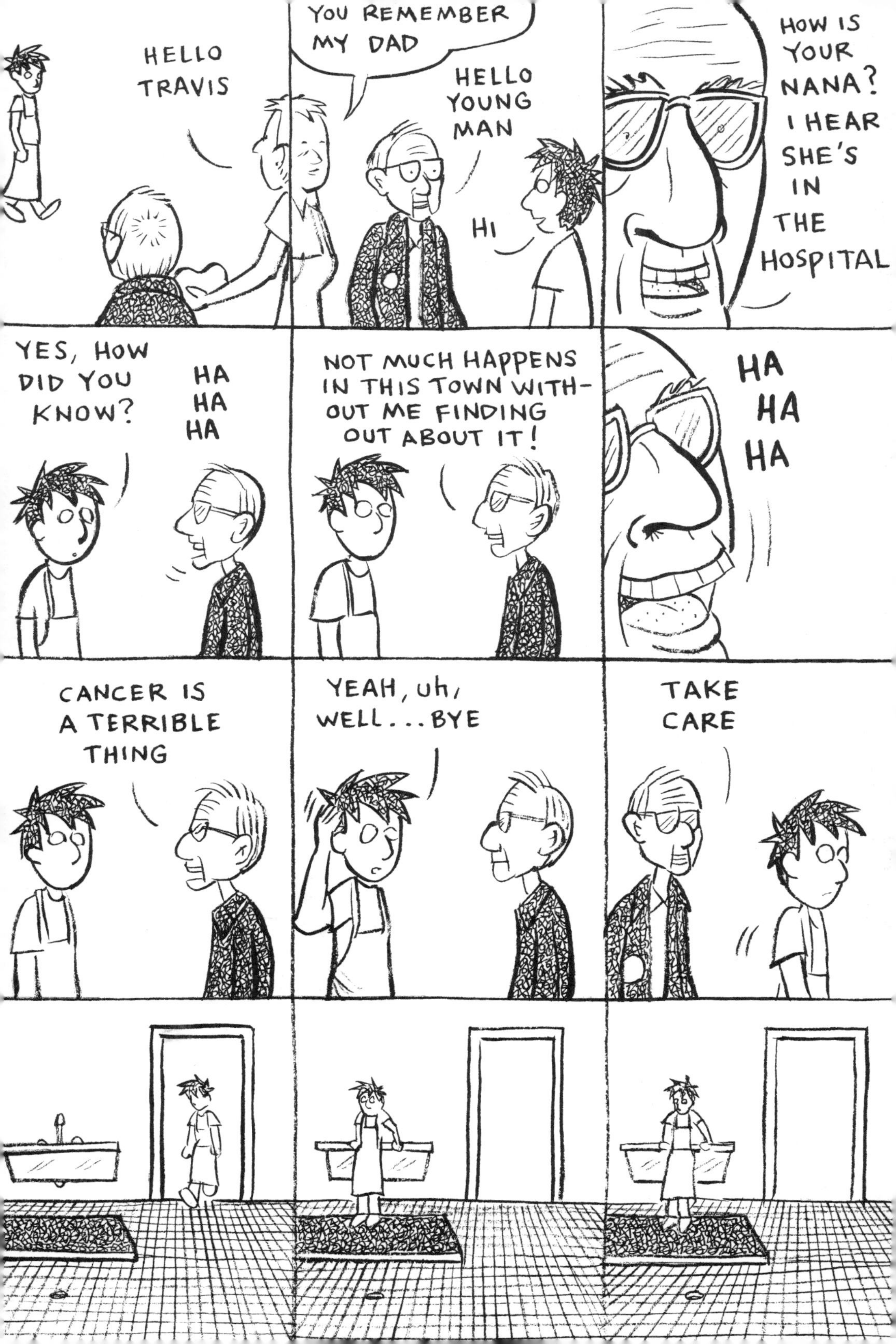
HELLO TRAVIS
YOU REMEMBER MY DAD
HELLO YOUNG MAN
HI
HOW IS YOUR NANA? I HEAR SHE'S IN THE HOSPITAL
YES, HOW DID YOU KNOW?
HA HA HA
NOT MUCH HAPPENS IN THIS TOWN WITH-OUT ME FINDING OUT ABOUT IT!
HA HA HA
CANCER IS A TERRIBLE THING
YEAH, uh, WELL... BYE
TAKE CARE

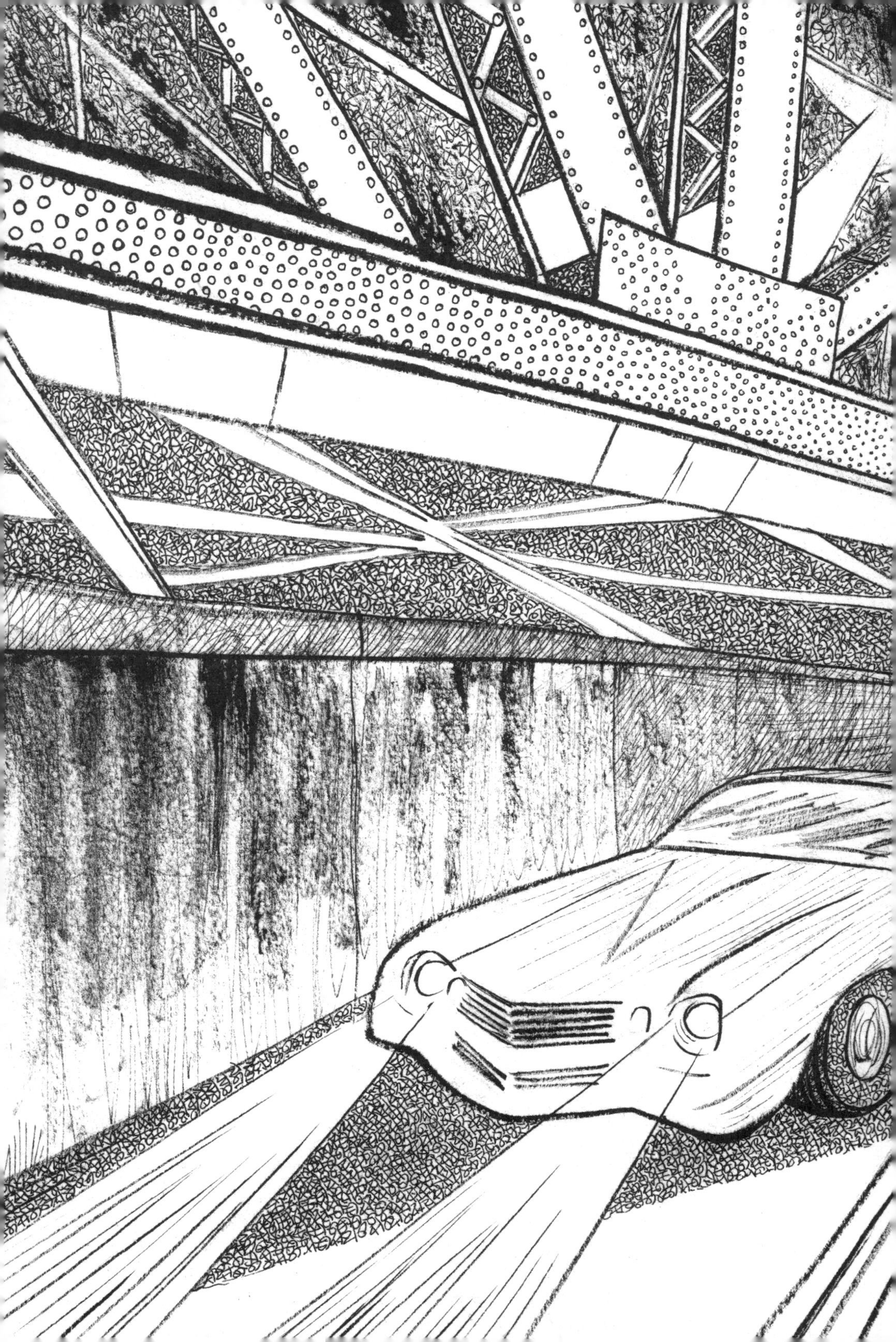

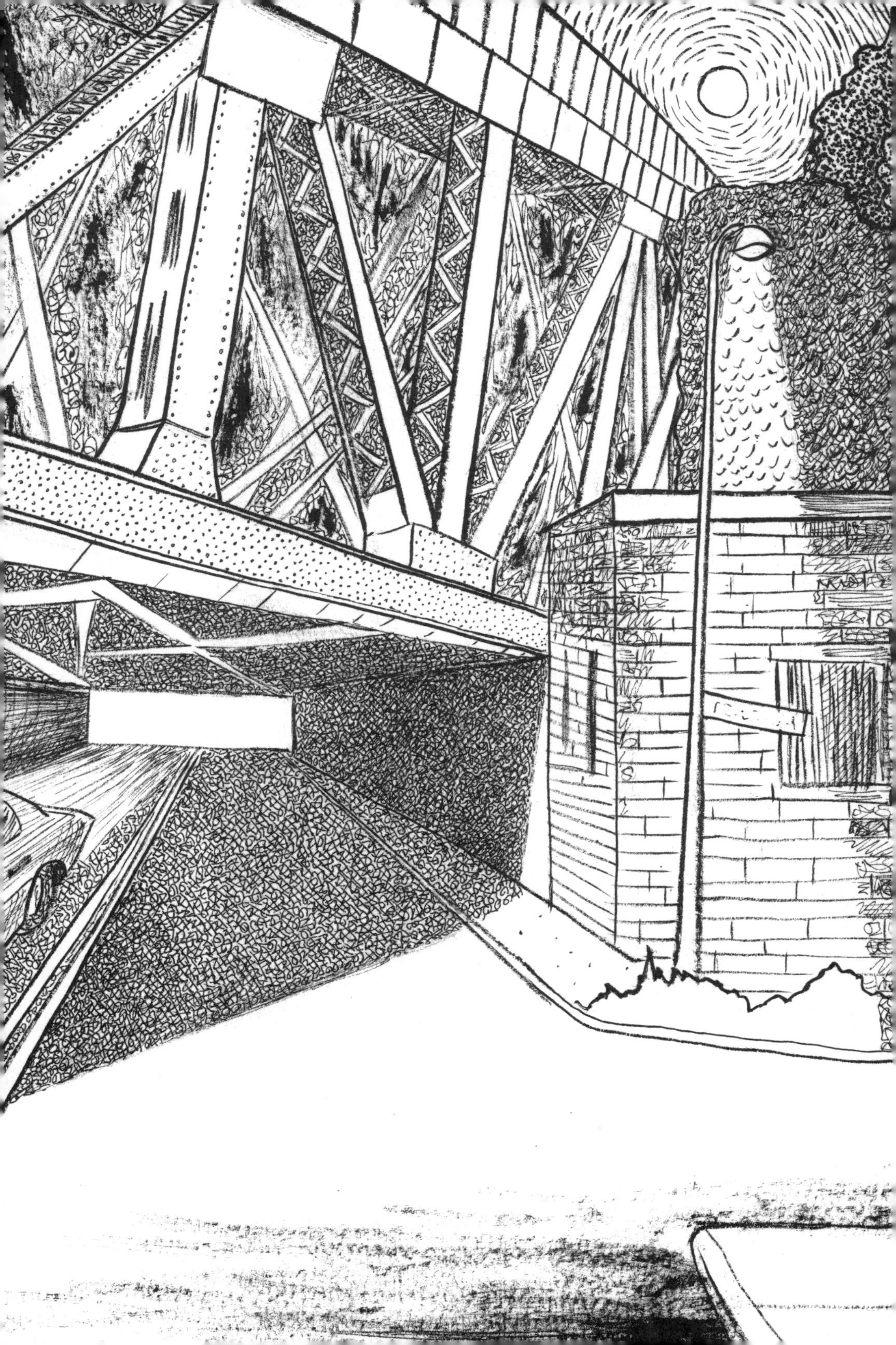

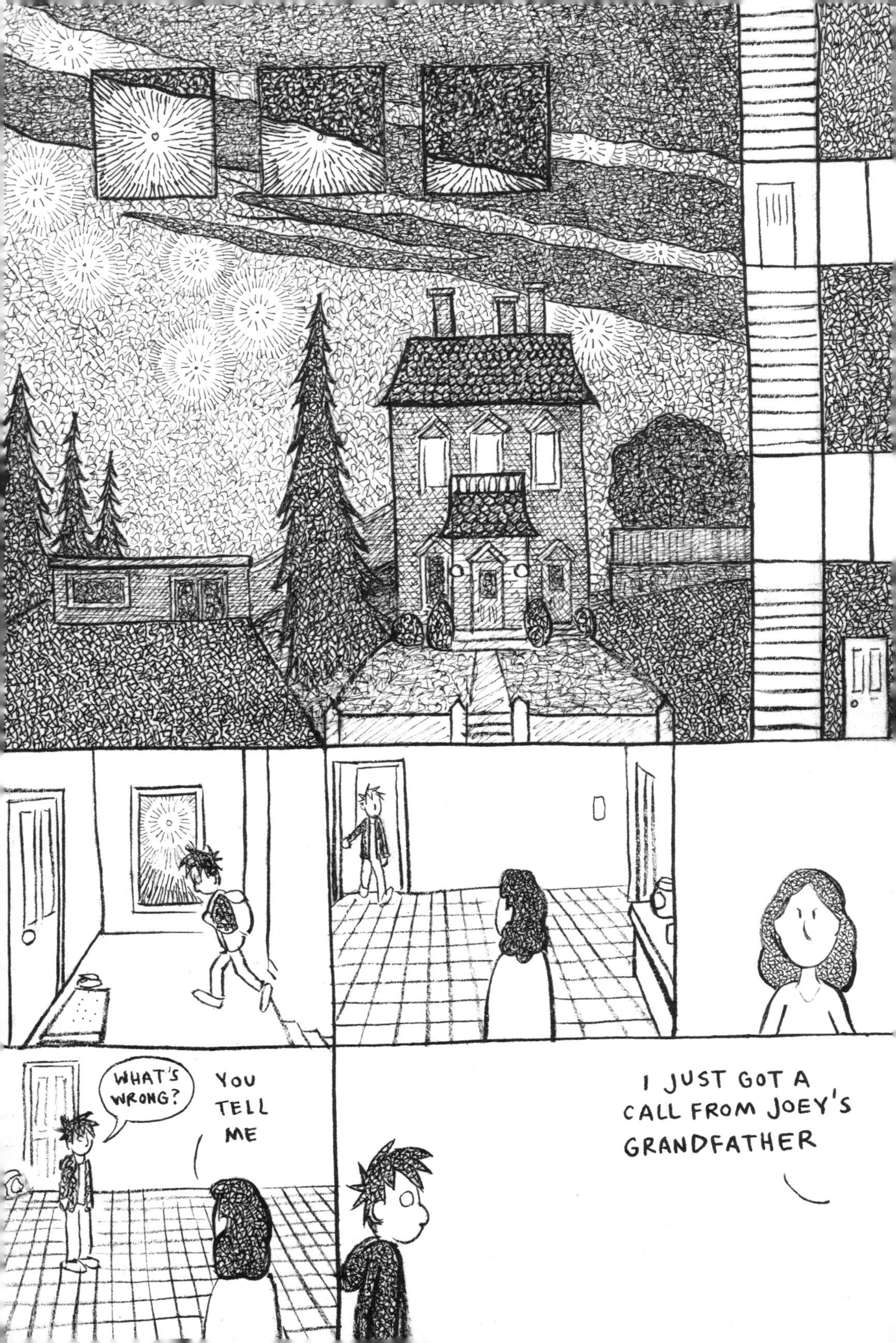
WHAT'S WRONG?
YOU TELL ME
I JUST GOT A CALL FROM JOEY'S GRANDFATHER

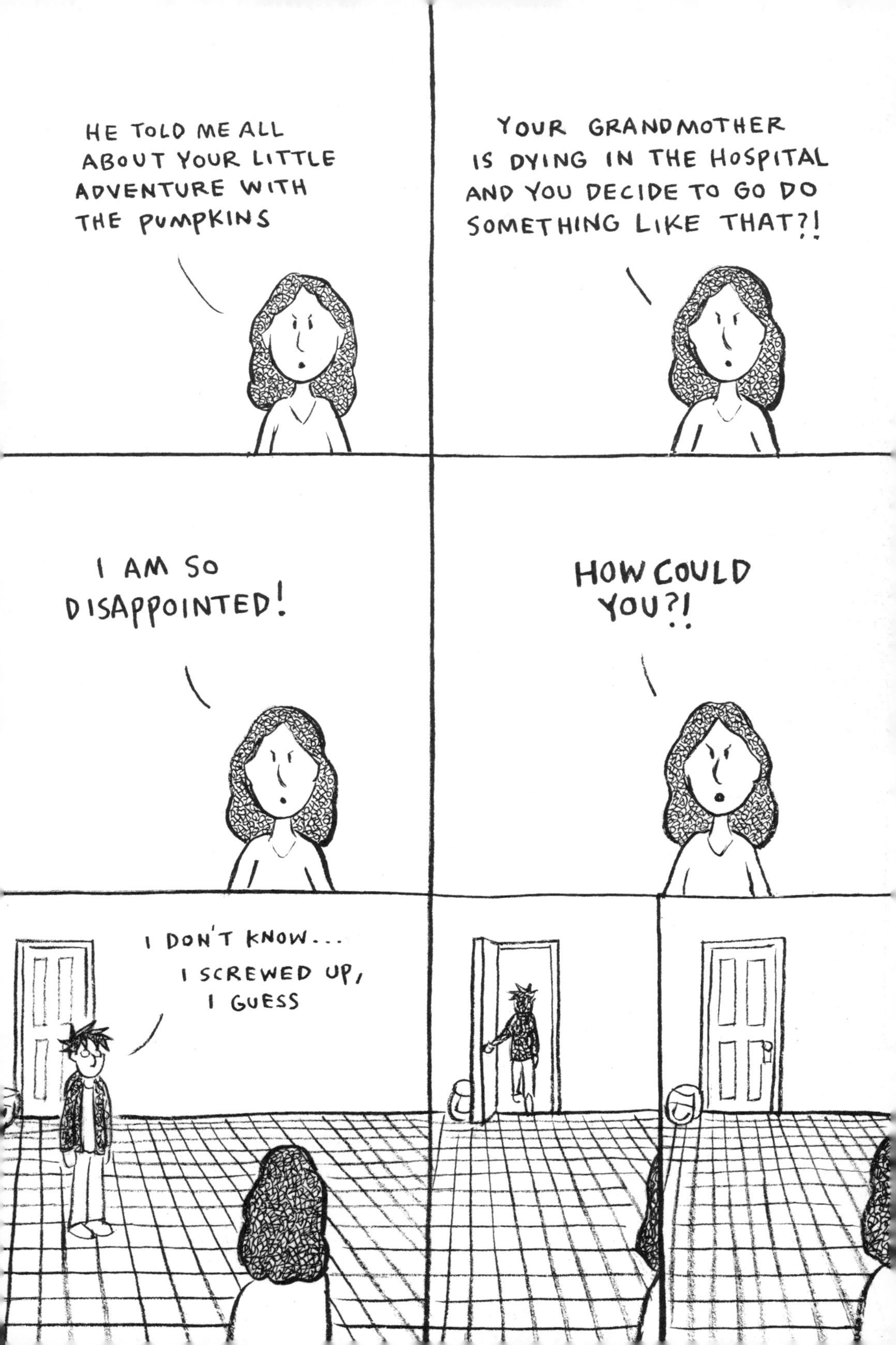
HE TOLD ME ALL ABOUT YOUR LITTLE ADVENTURE WITH THE PUMPKINS
YOUR GRANDMOTHER IS DYING IN THE HOSPITAL AND YOU DECIDE TO GO DO SOMETHING LIKE THAT?!
I AM SO DISAPPOINTED!
HOW COULD YOU?!
I DON'T KNOW... I SCREWED UP, I GUESS

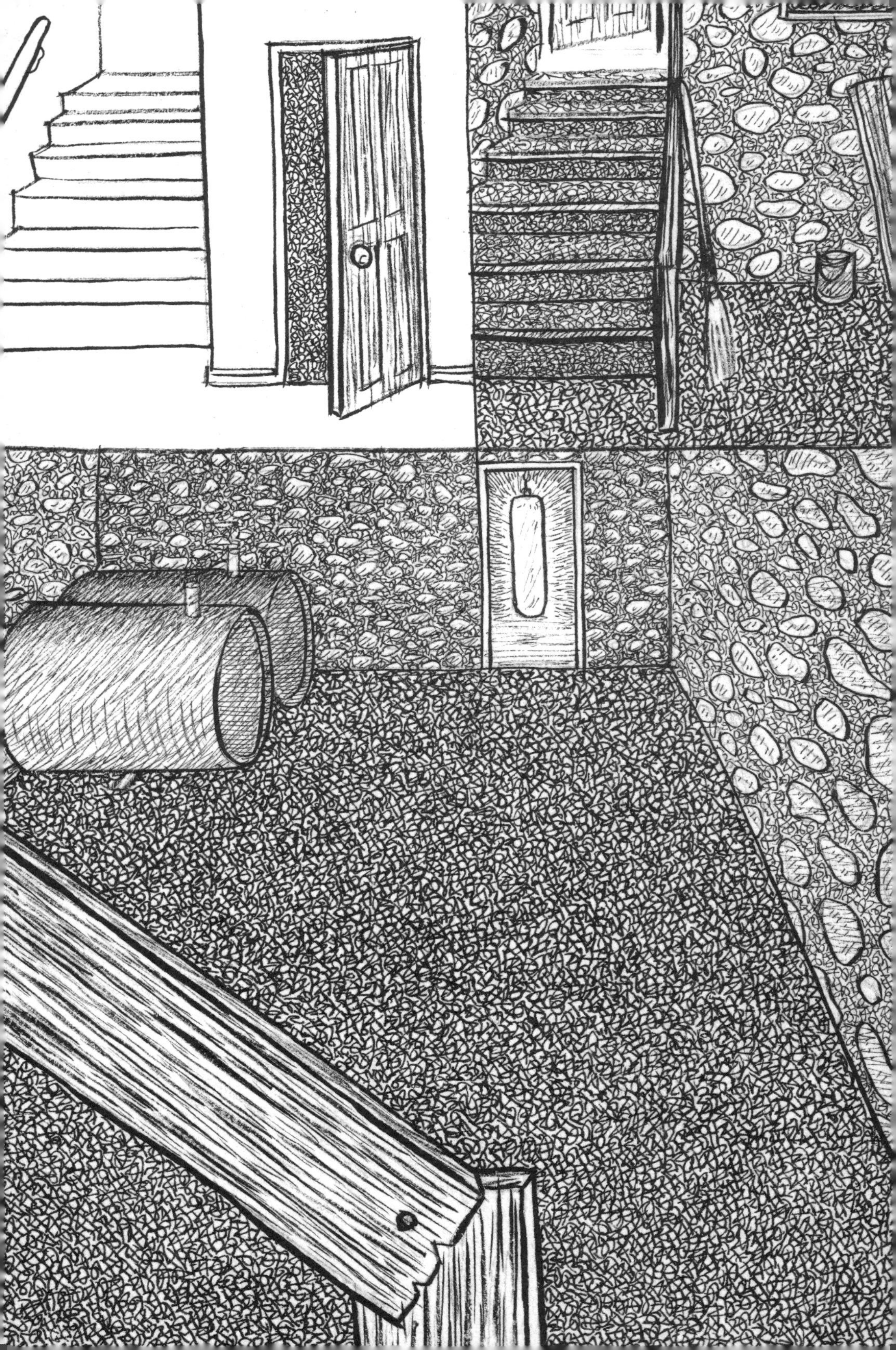

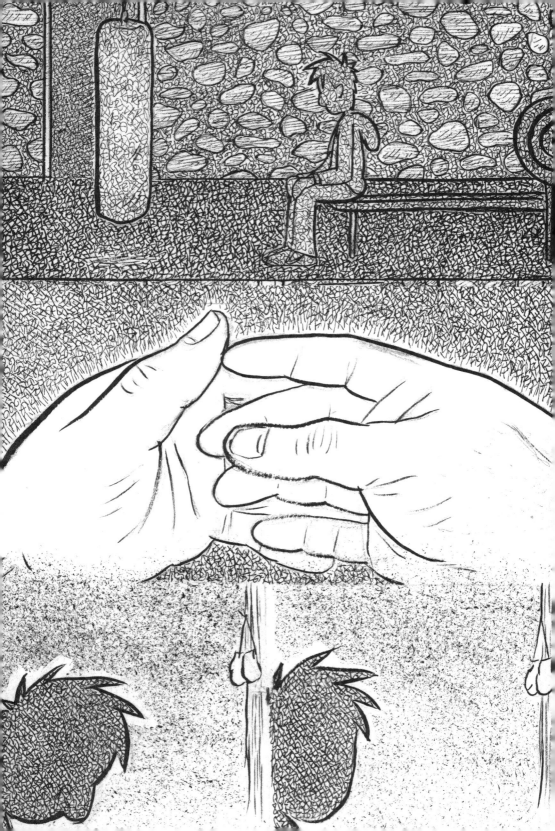

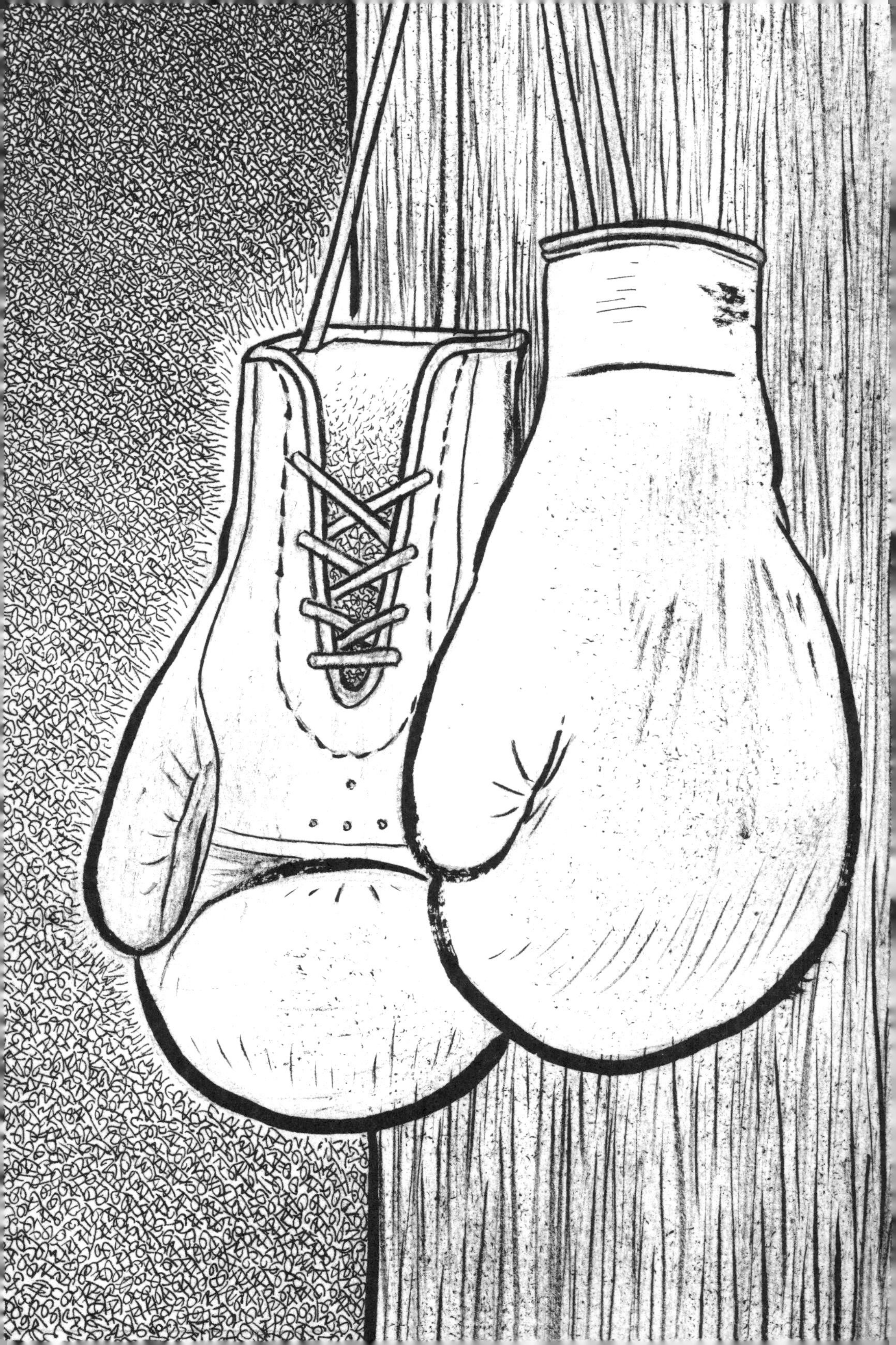

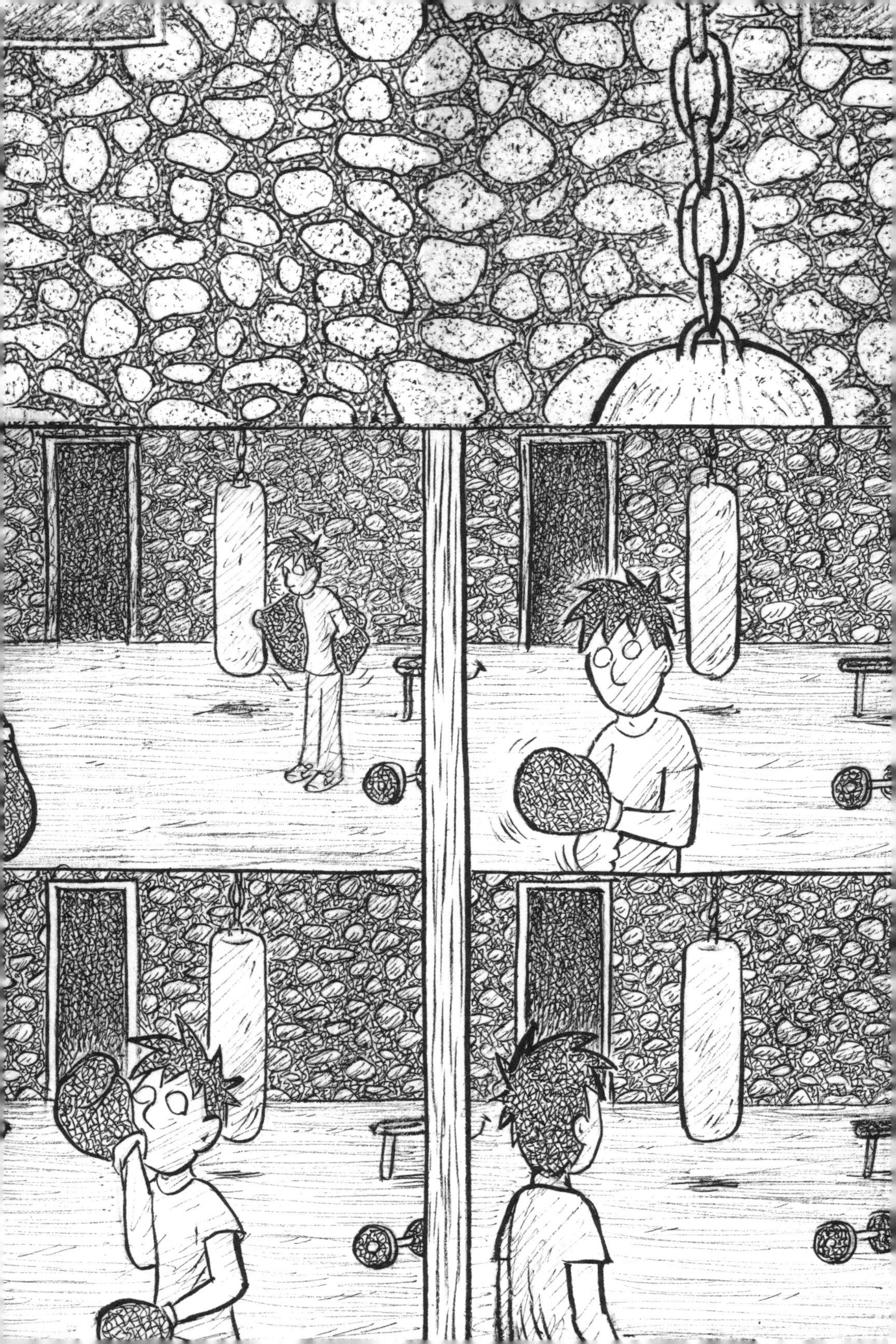

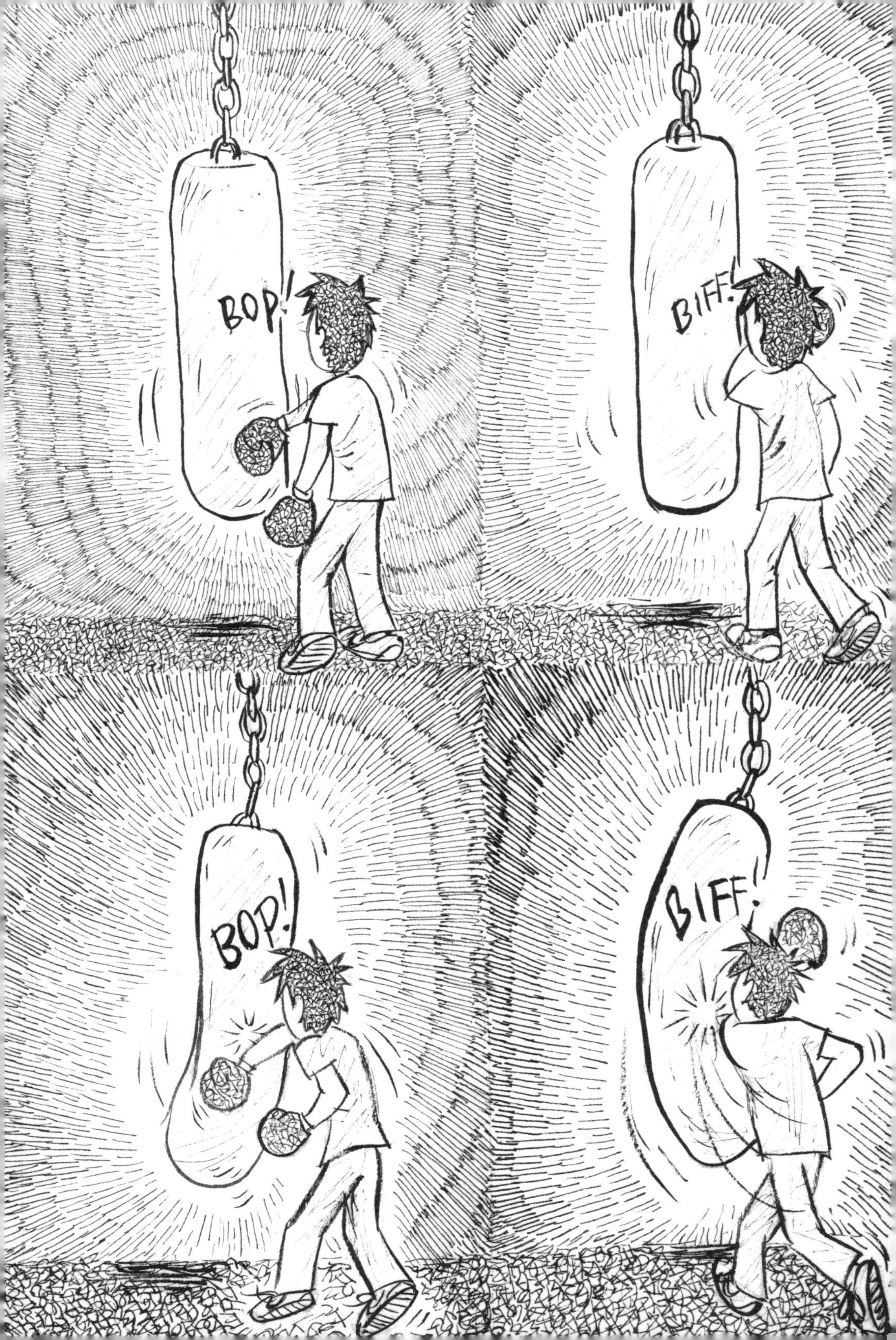
BOP!
BIFF!
BOP!
BIFF!

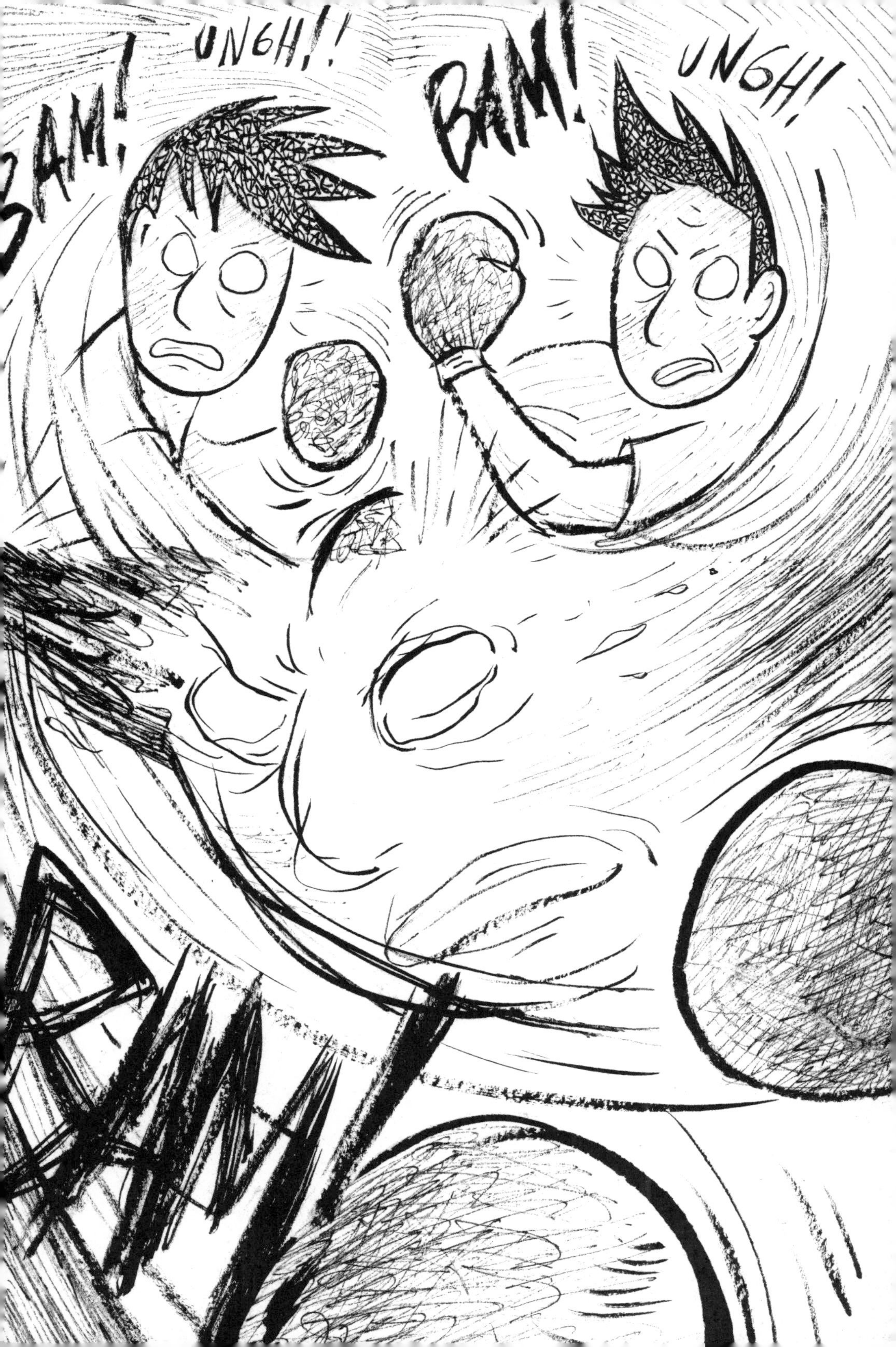
BAM!
UNGH!!
BAM!
UNGH!

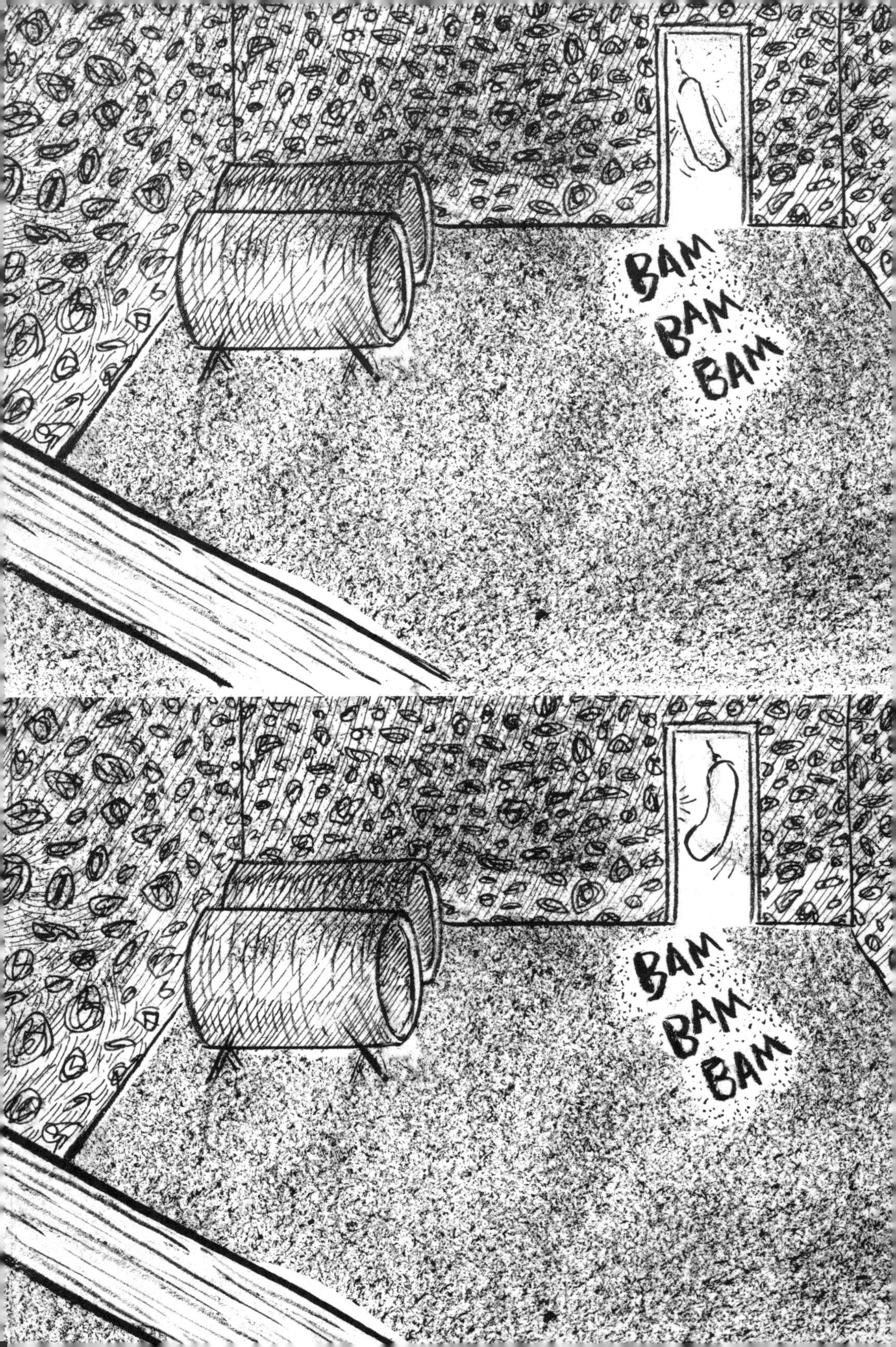
BAM
BAM
BAM
BAM
BAM
BAM

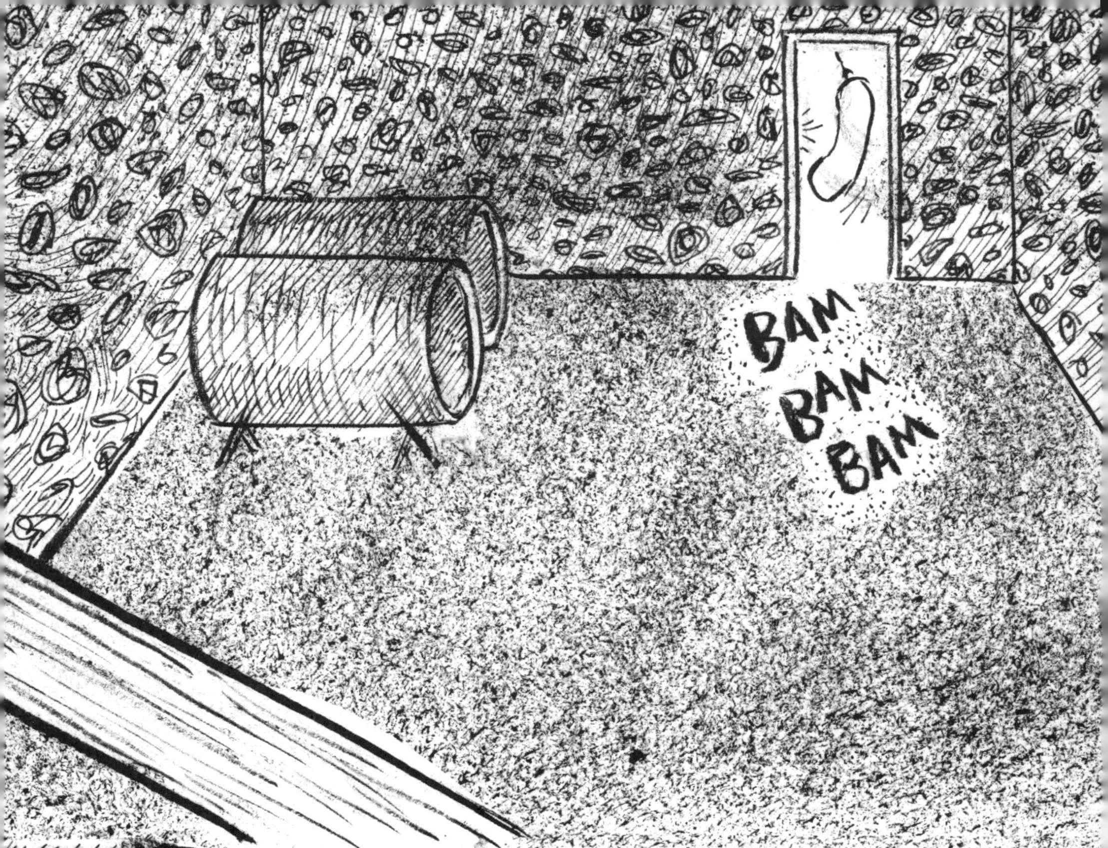
BAM
BAM
BAM
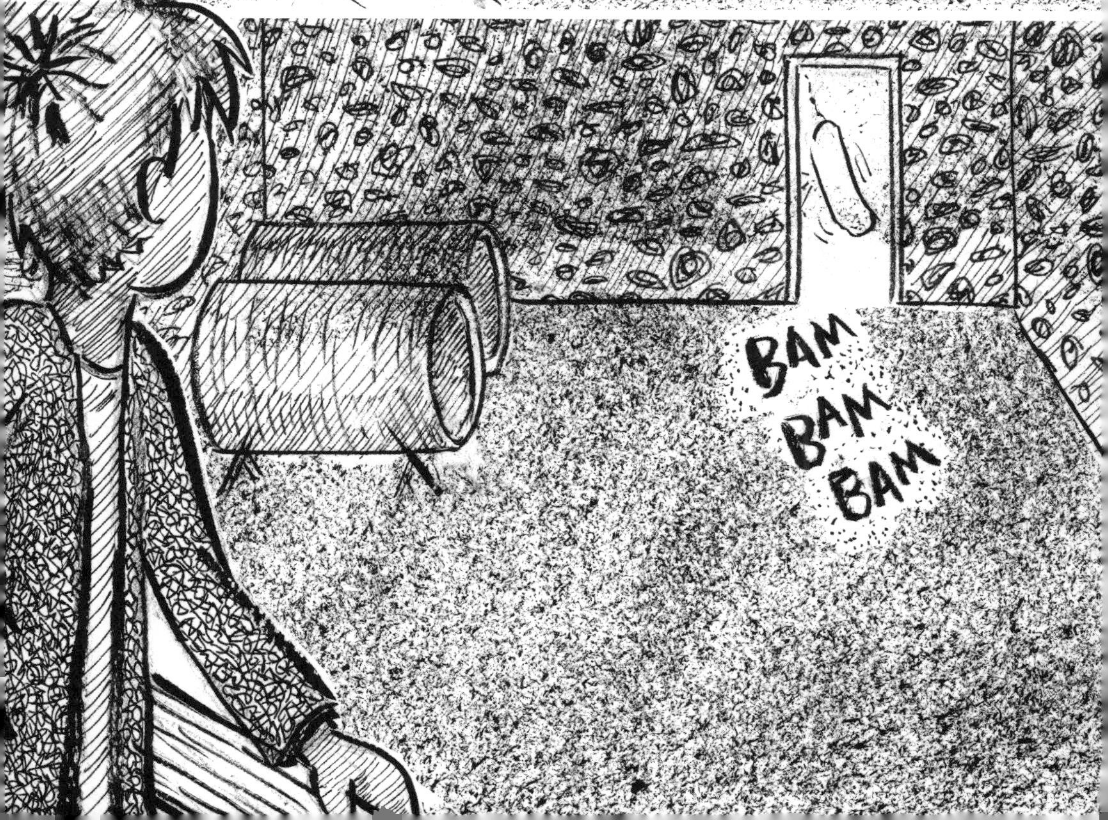
BAM
BAM
BAM

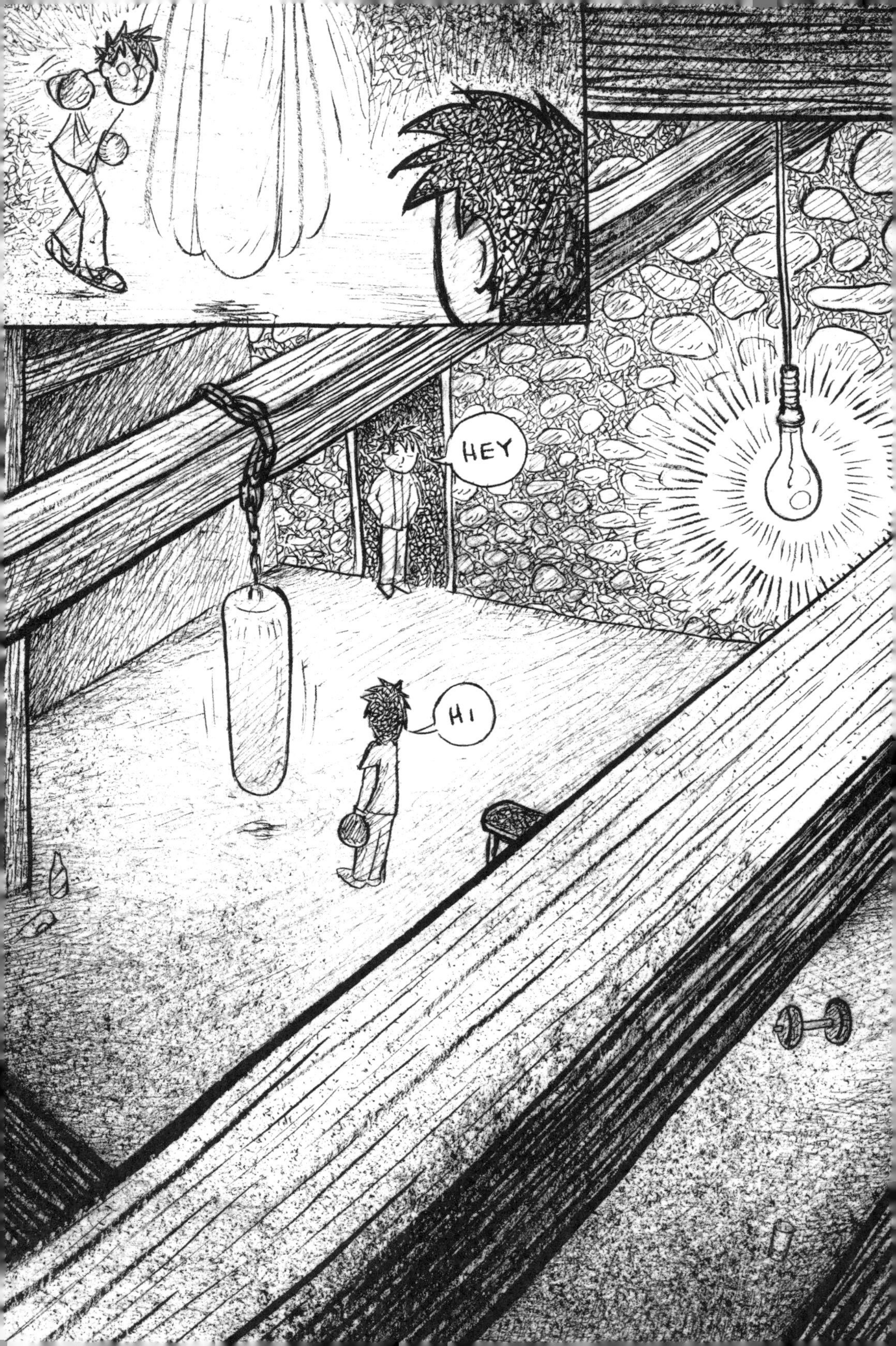
HEY
HI

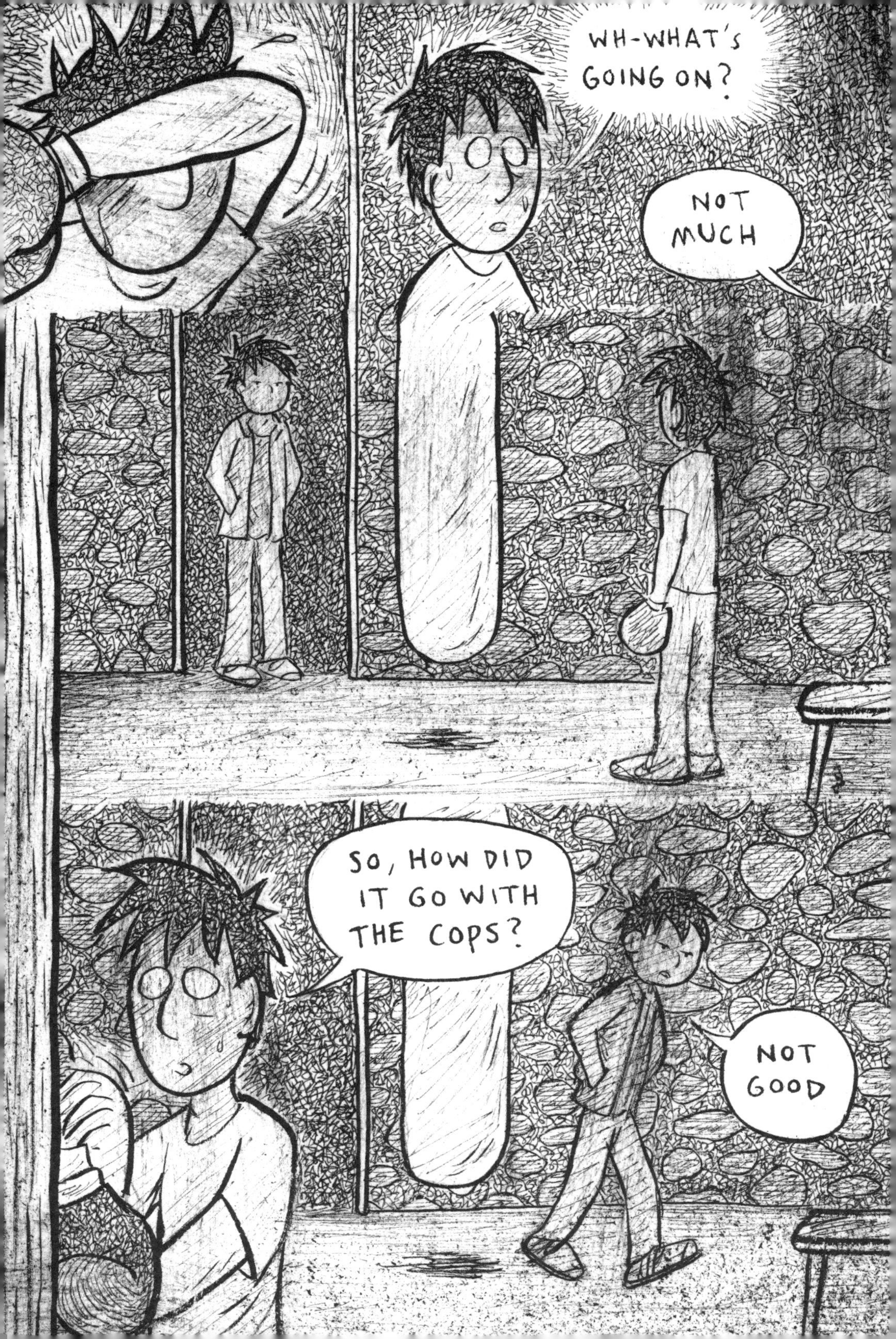
WH-WHAT'S GOING ON?
NOT MUCH
SO, HOW DID IT GO WITH THE COPS?
NOT GOOD

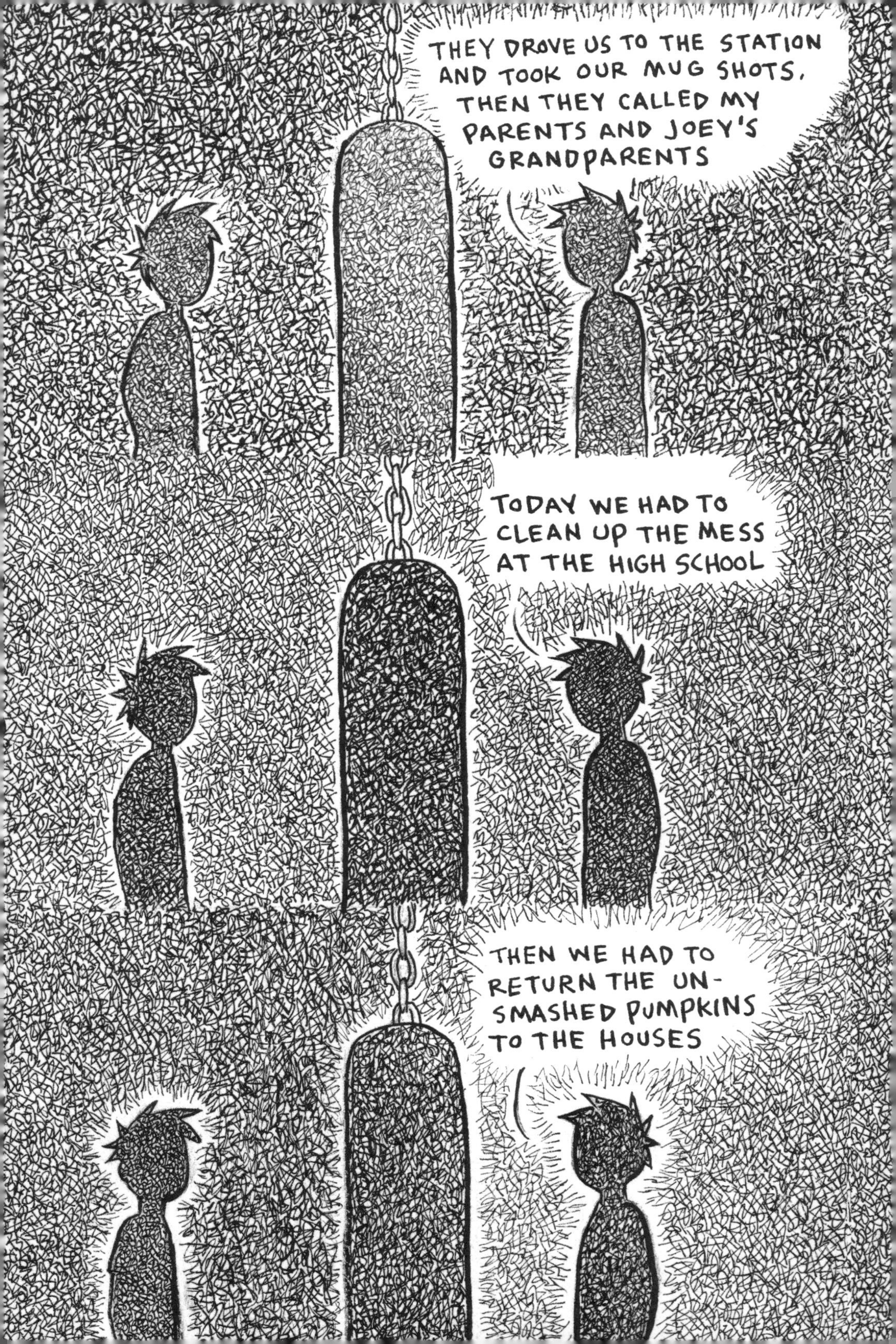
THEY DROVE US TO THE STATION AND TOOK OUR MUG SHOTS, THEN THEY CALLED MY PARENTS AND JOEY'S GRANDPARENTS
TODAY WE HAD TO CLEAN UP THE MESS AT THE HIGH SCHOOL
THEN WE HAD TO RETURN THE UN-SMASHED PUMPKINS TO THE HOUSES

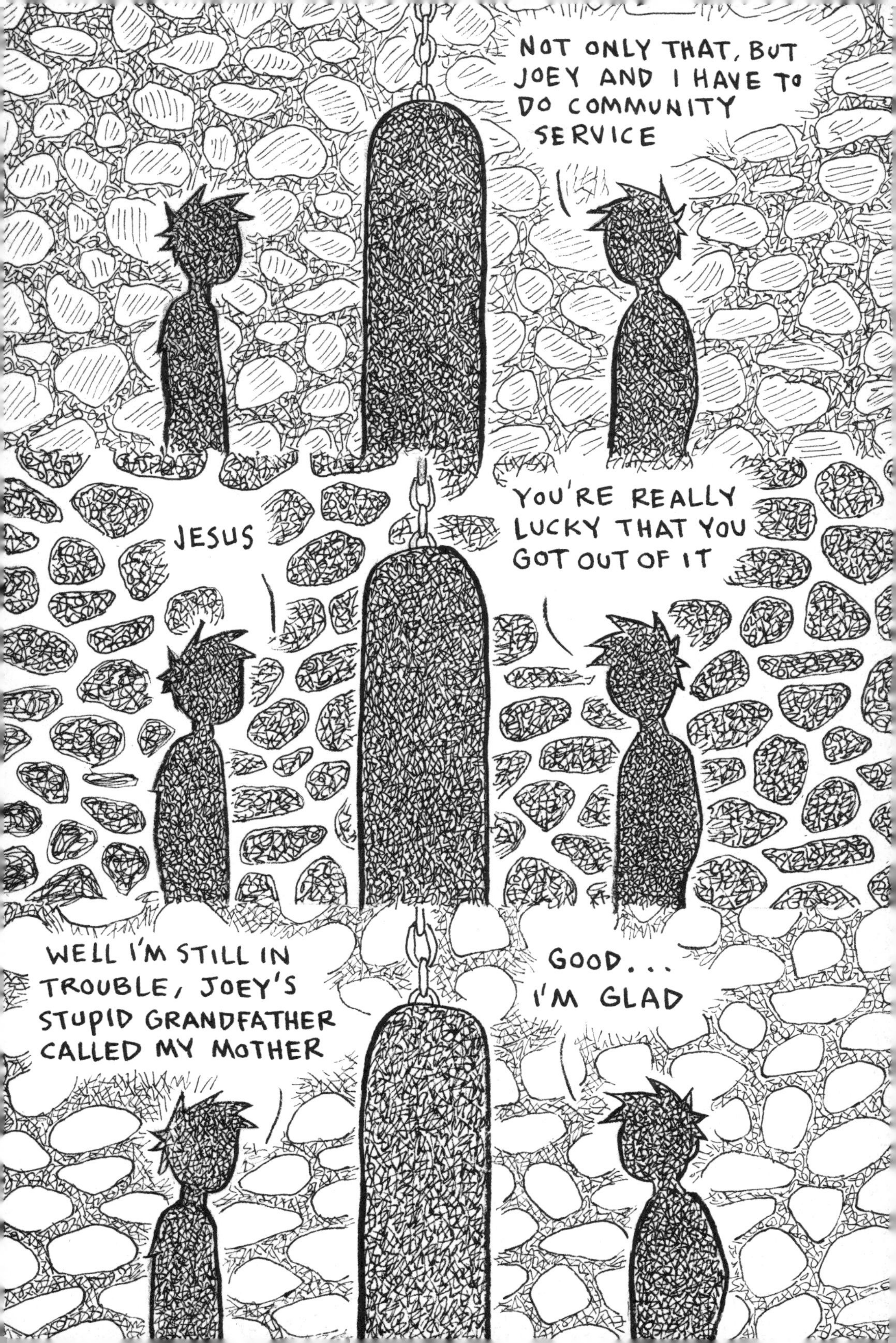
NOT ONLY THAT, BUT JOEY AND I HAVE TO DO COMMUNITY SERVICE
JESUS
YOU'RE REALLY LUCKY THAT YOU GOT OUT OF IT
WELL I'M STILL IN TROUBLE, JOEY'S STUPID GRANDFATHER CALLED MY MOTHER
GOOD... I'M GLAD

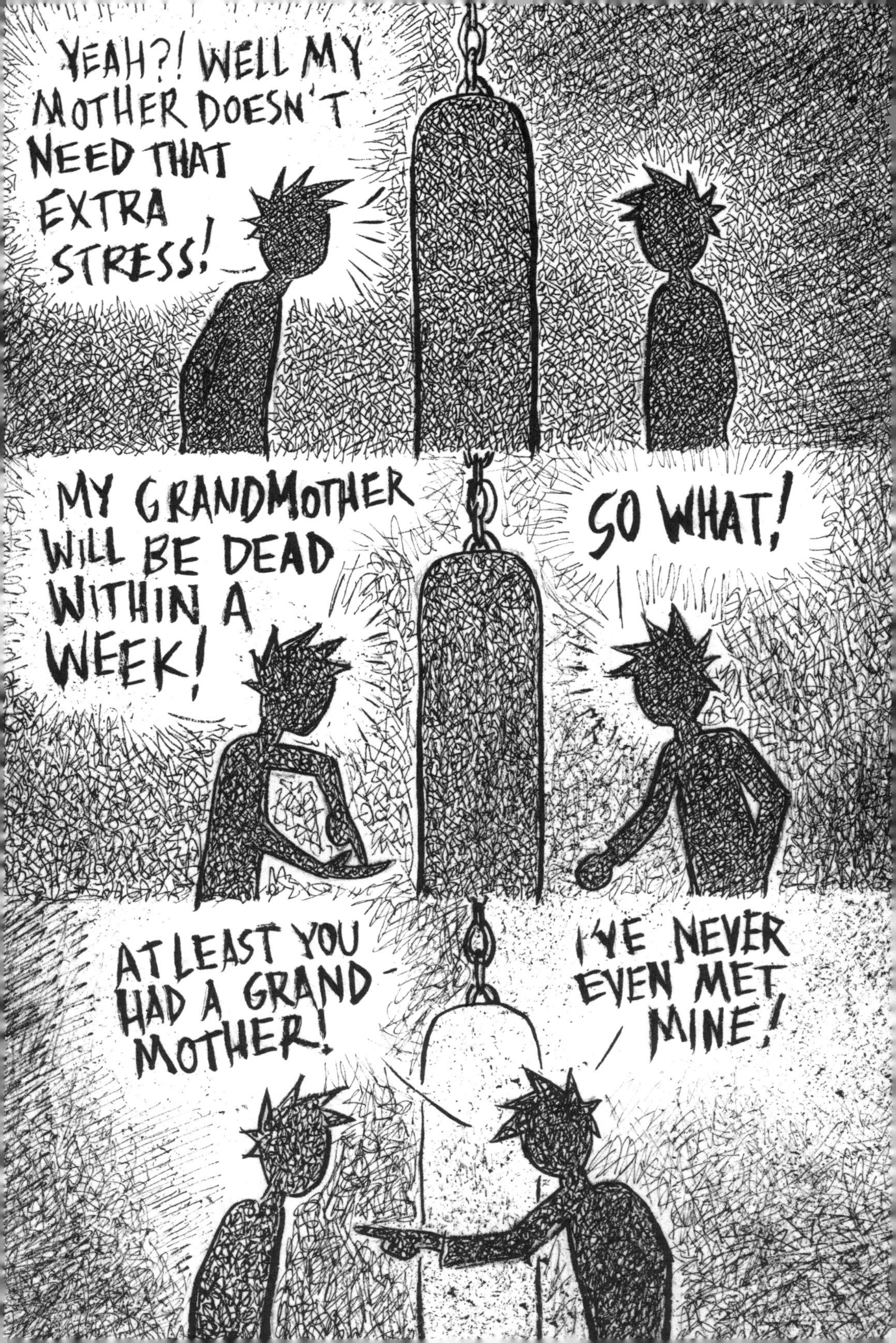
YEAH?! WELL MY MOTHER DOESN'T NEED THAT EXTRA STRESS!
MY GRANDMOTHER WILL BE DEAD WITHIN A WEEK!
SO WHAT!
AT LEAST YOU HAD A GRANDMOTHER!
I'VE NEVER EVEN MET MINE!

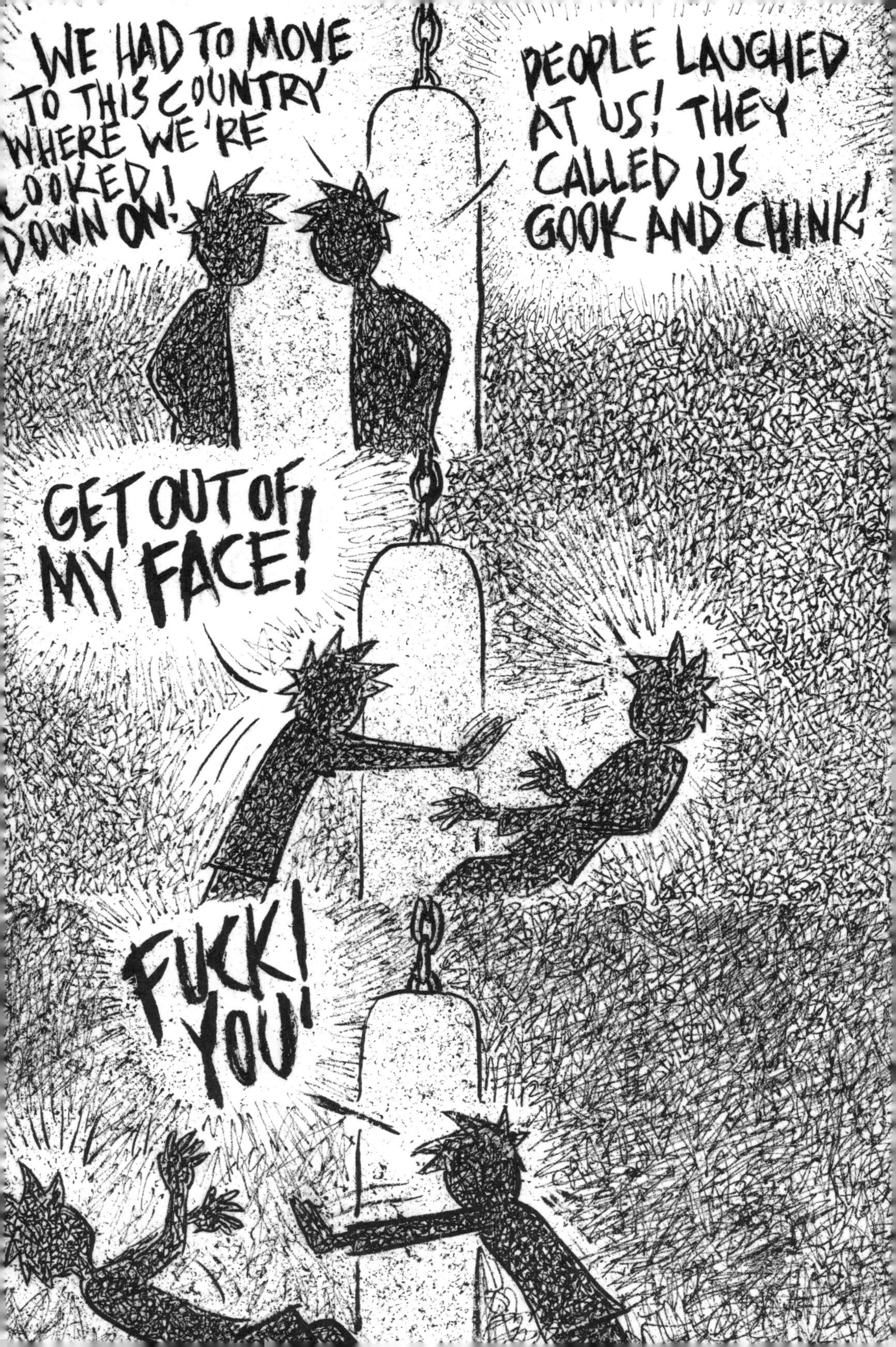
WE HAD TO MOVE TO THIS COUNTRY WHERE WE'RE LOOKED DOWN ON!
PEOPLE LAUGHED AT US! THEY CALLED US GOOK AND CHINK!
GET OUT OF MY FACE!
FUCK YOU!

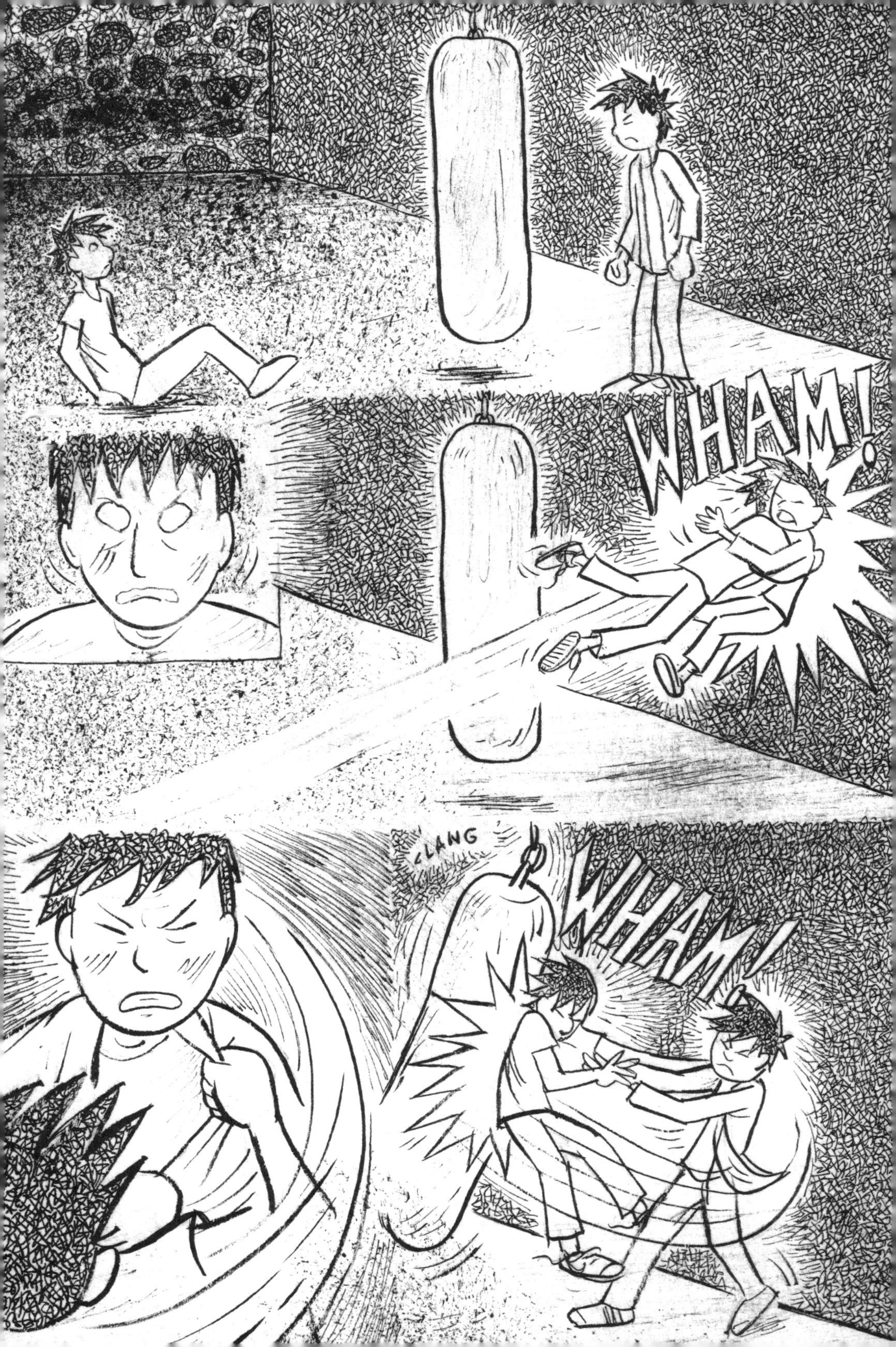
WHAM!
CLANG
WHAM!

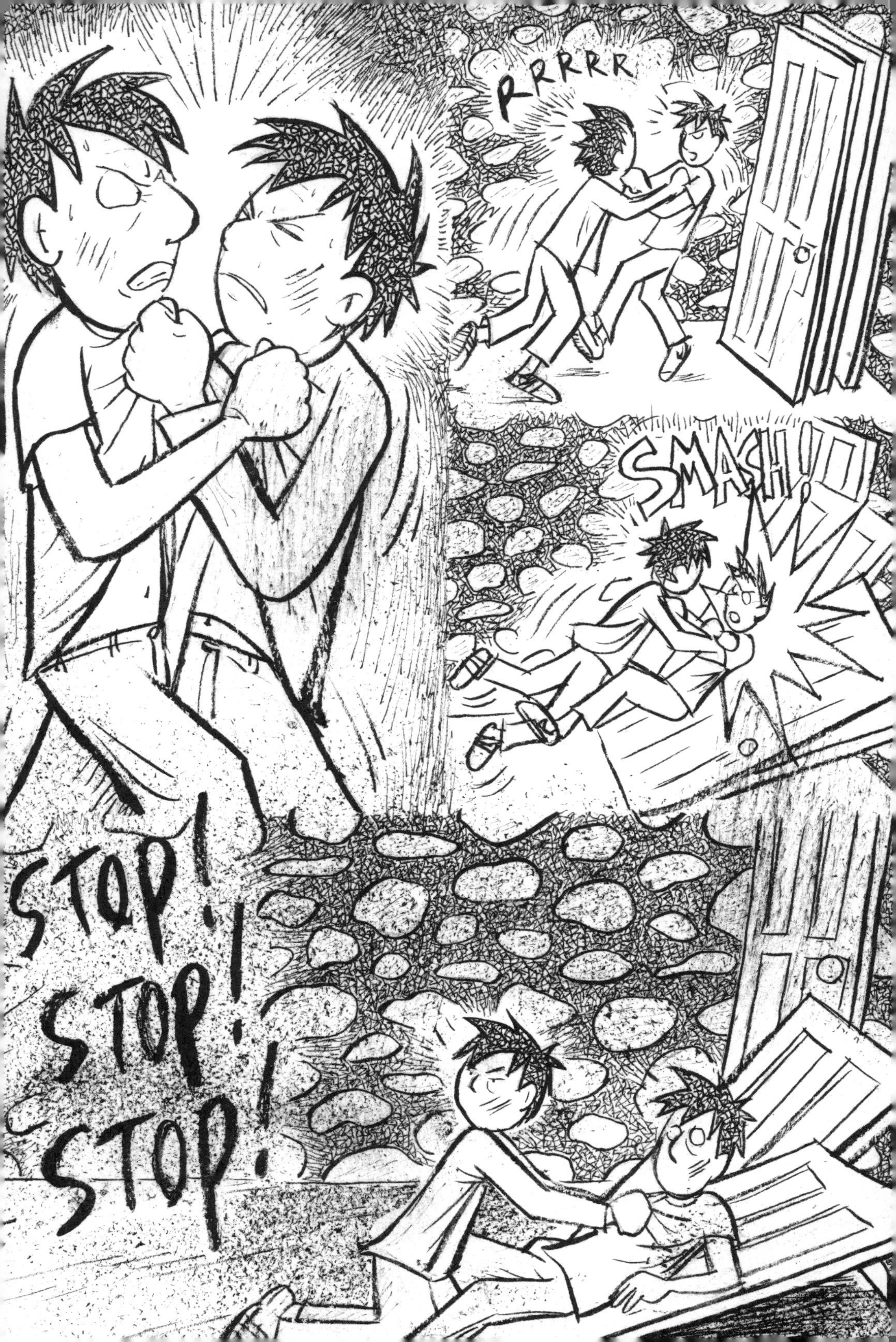
RRRRR
SMASH!
STOP!
STOP!
STOP!

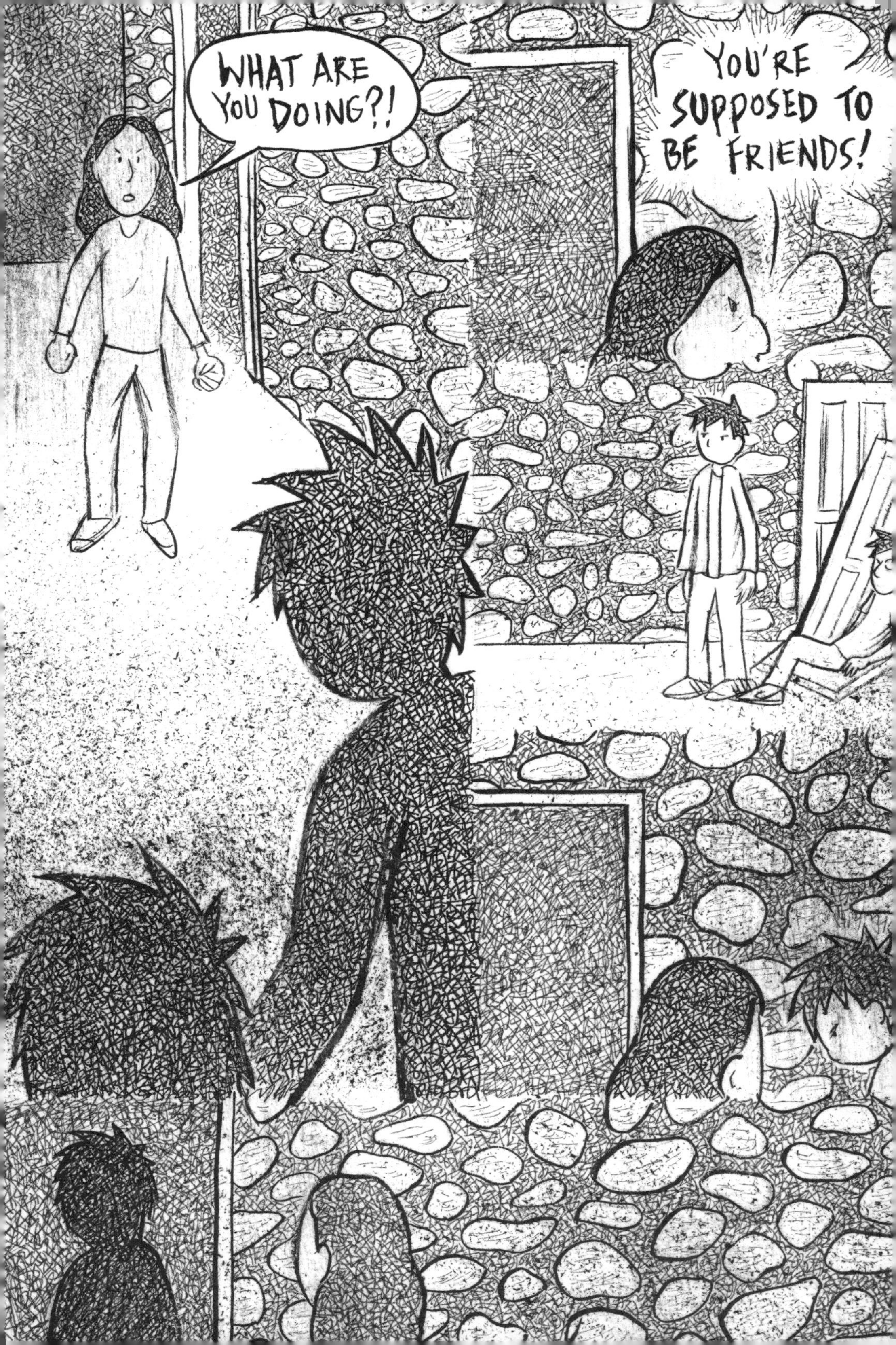
WHAT ARE YOU DOING?!
YOU'RE SUPPOSED TO BE FRIENDS!

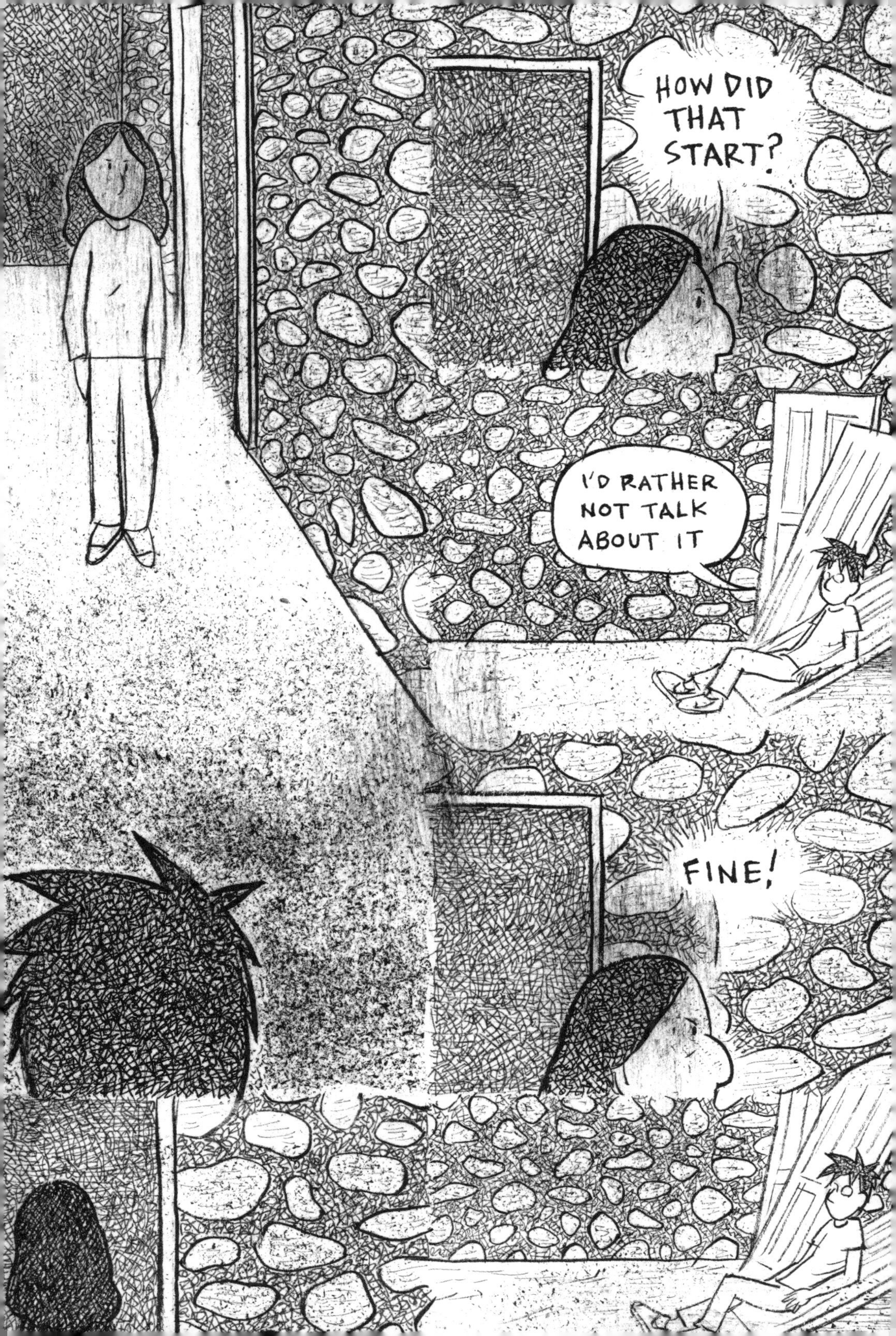
HOW DID THAT START?
I'D RATHER NOT TALK ABOUT IT
FINE!

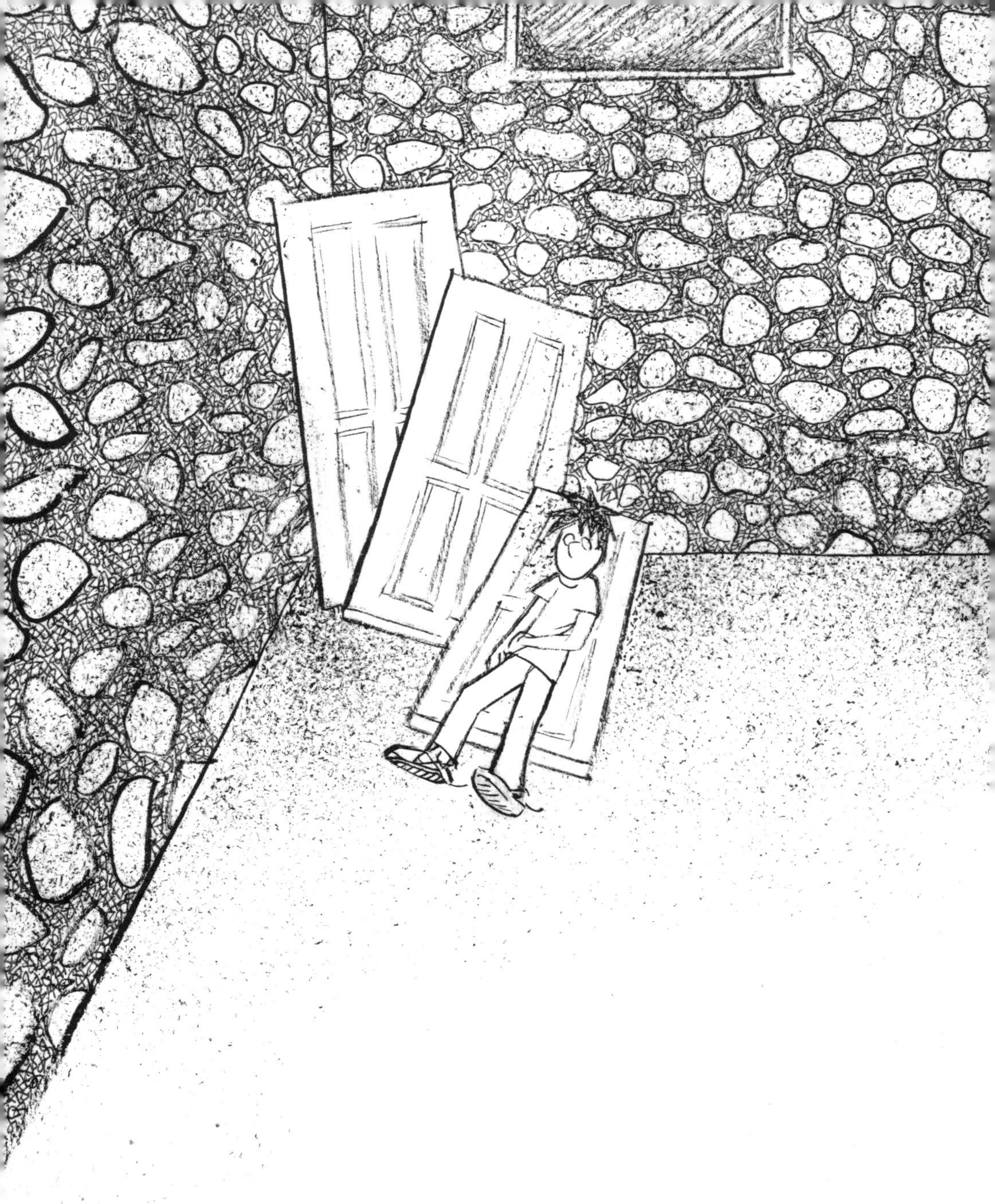

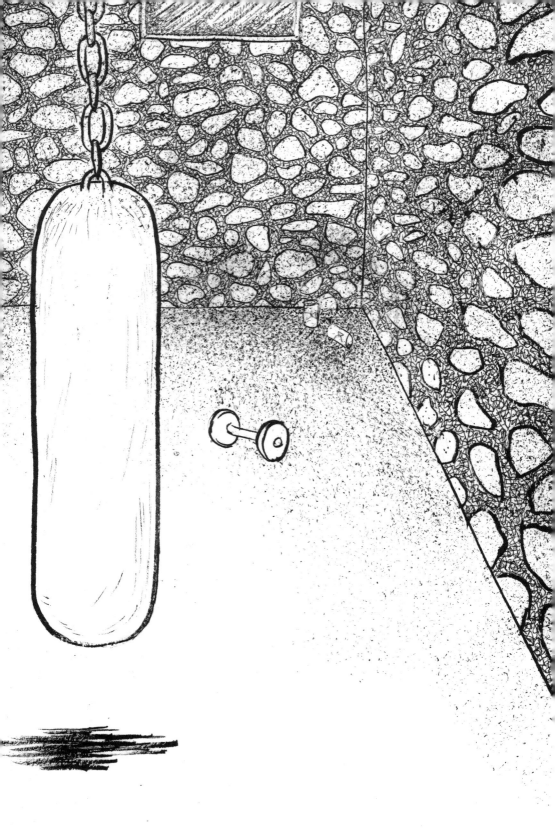

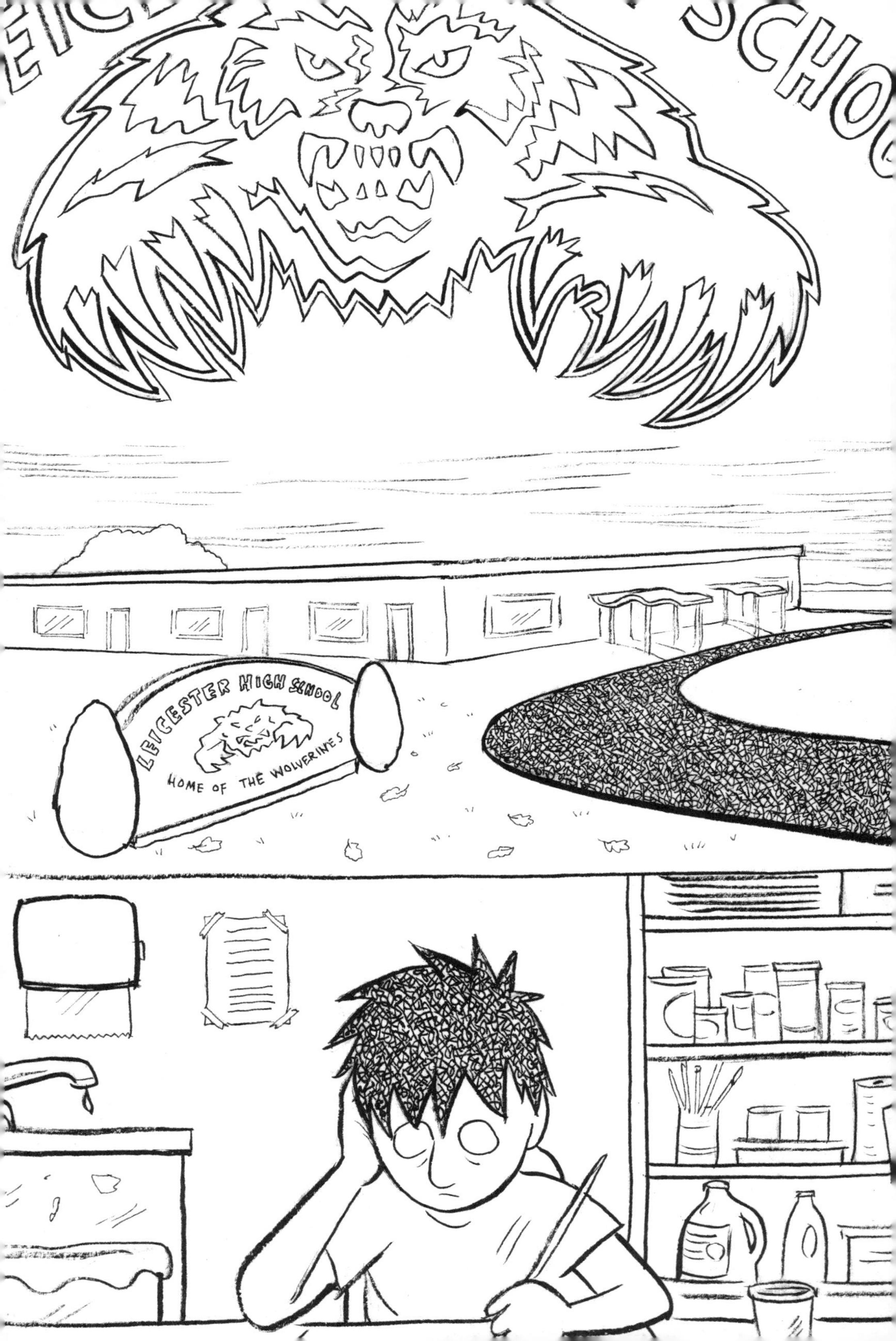

EICE
SCHOO
LEICESTER HIGH SCHOOL
HOME OF THE WOLVERINES

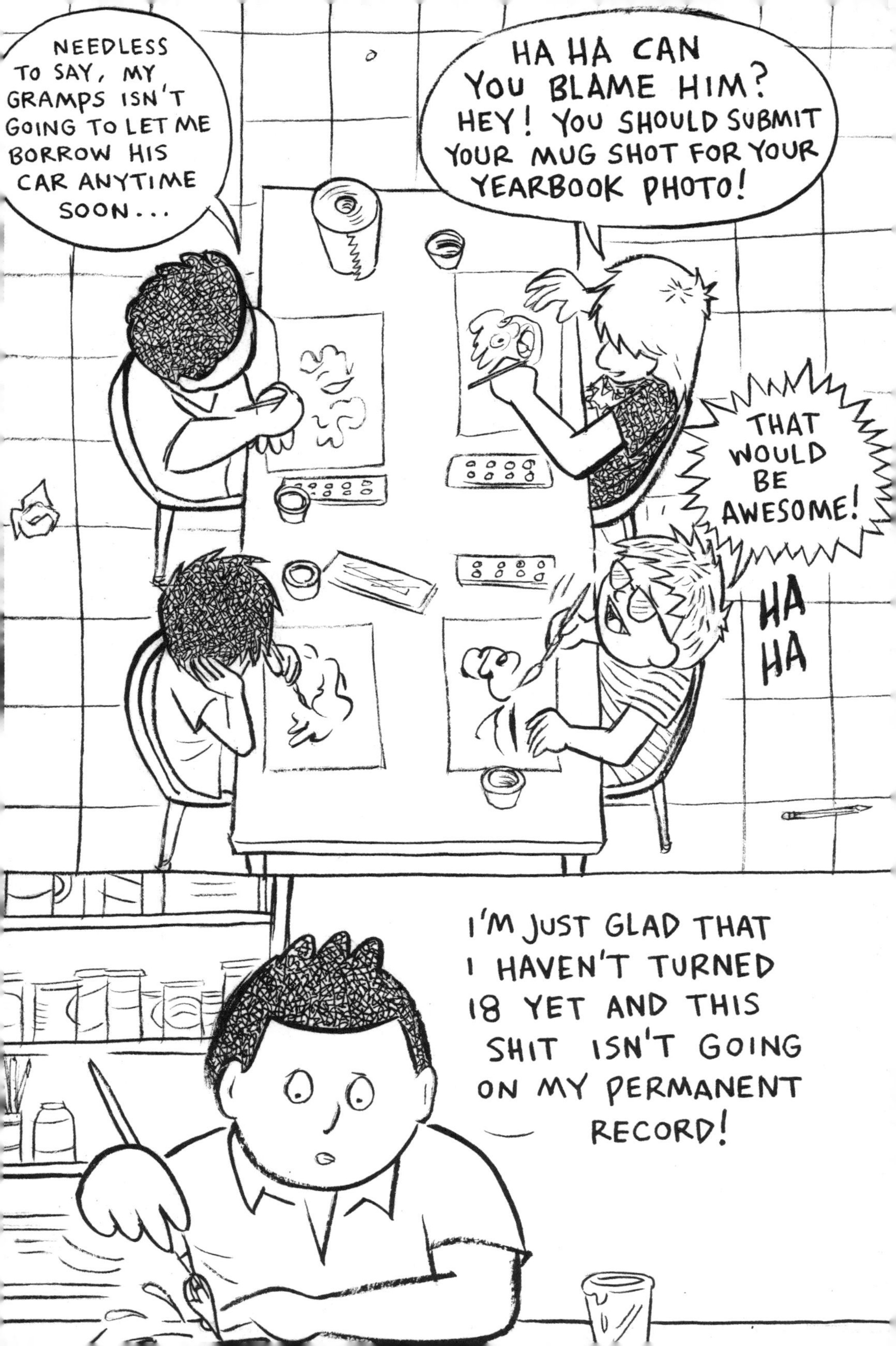
NEEDLESS TO SAY, MY GRAMPS ISN'T GOING TO LET ME BORROW HIS CAR ANYTIME SOON...
HA HA CAN YOU BLAME HIM? HEY! YOU SHOULD SUBMIT YOUR MUG SHOT FOR YOUR YEARBOOK PHOTO!
THAT WOULD BE AWESOME!
HA HA
I'M JUST GLAD THAT I HAVEN'T TURNED 18 YET AND THIS SHIT ISN'T GOING ON MY PERMANENT RECORD!

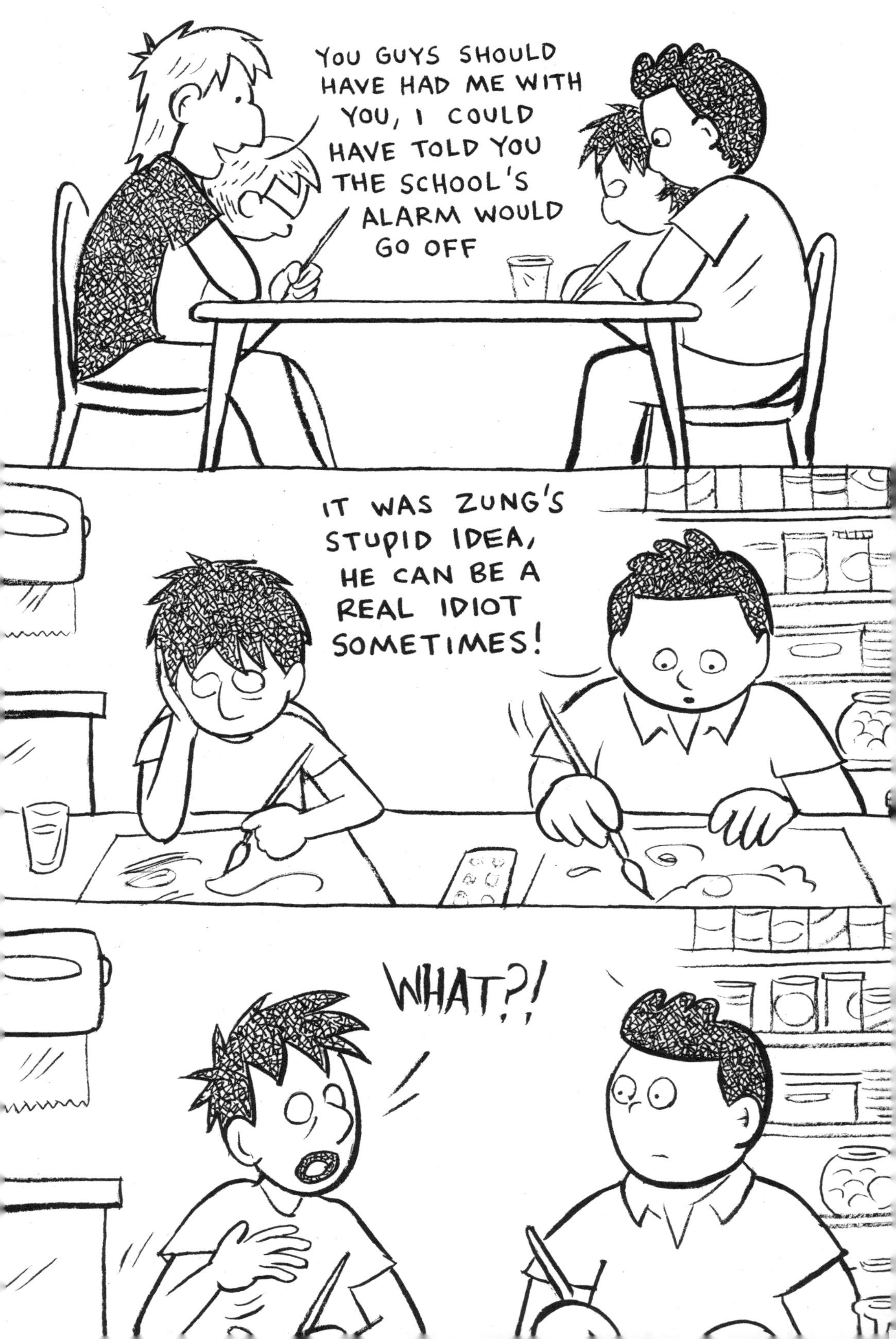
YOU GUYS SHOULD HAVE HAD ME WITH YOU, I COULD HAVE TOLD YOU THE SCHOOL'S ALARM WOULD GO OFF
IT WAS ZUNG'S STUPID IDEA, HE CAN BE A REAL IDIOT SOMETIMES!
WHAT?!

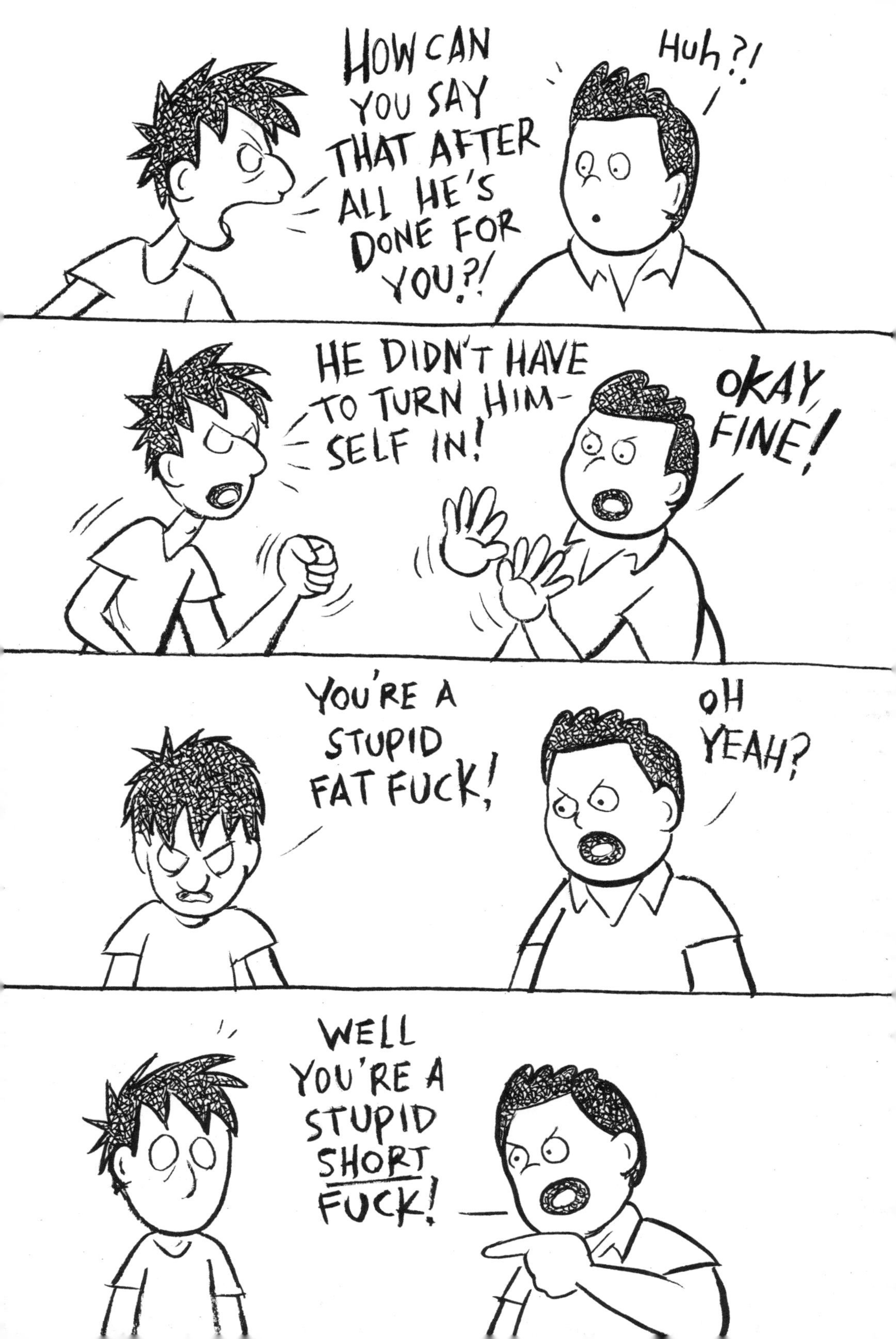
HOW CAN YOU SAY THAT AFTER ALL HE'S DONE FOR YOU?!
Huh?!
HE DIDN'T HAVE TO TURN HIM-SELF IN!
OKAY FINE!
YOU'RE A STUPID FAT FUCK!
OH YEAH?
WELL YOU'RE A STUPID SHORT FUCK!

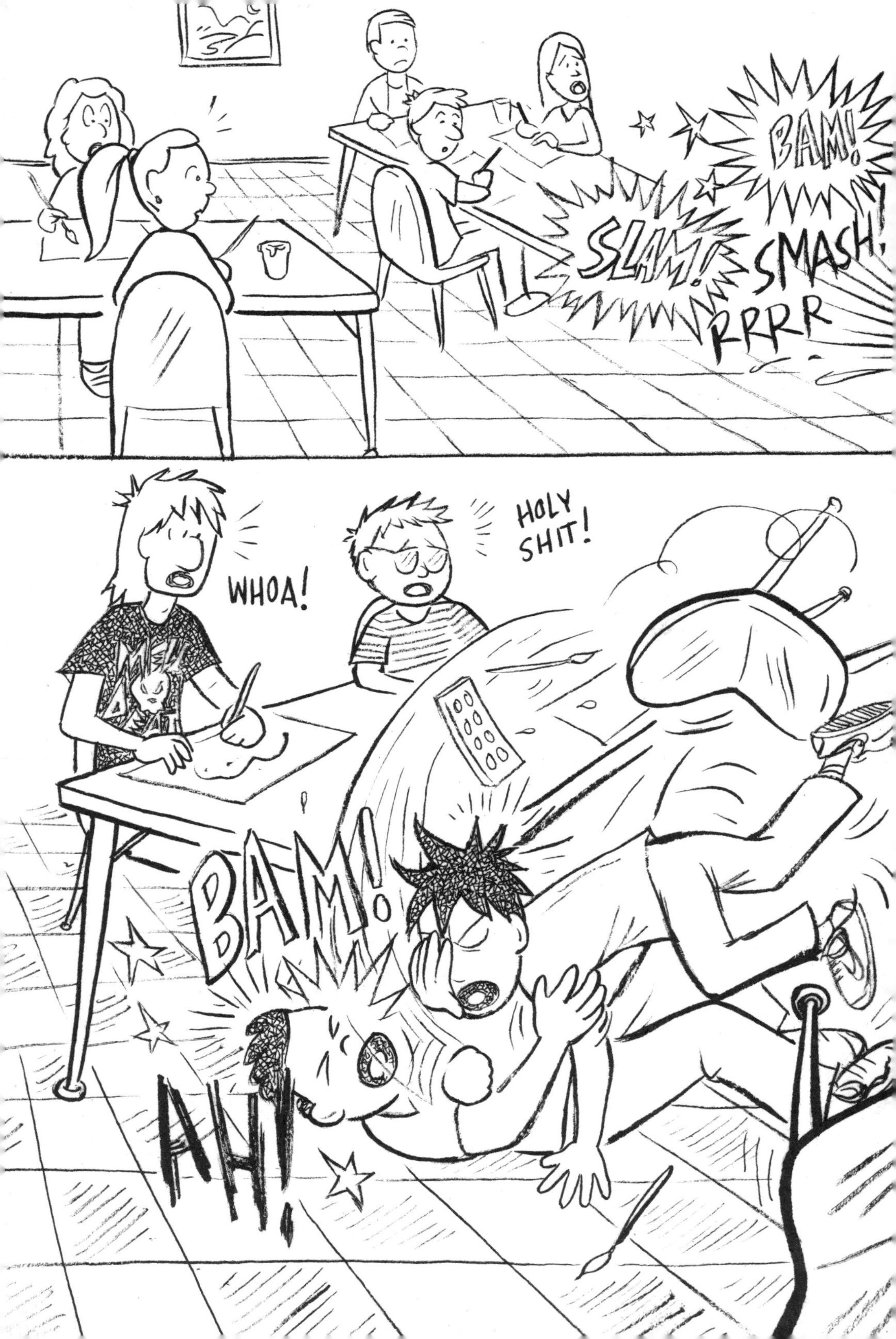
BAM!
SLAM!
SMASH!
RRRR
WHOA!
HOLY SHIT!
BAM!
AH!

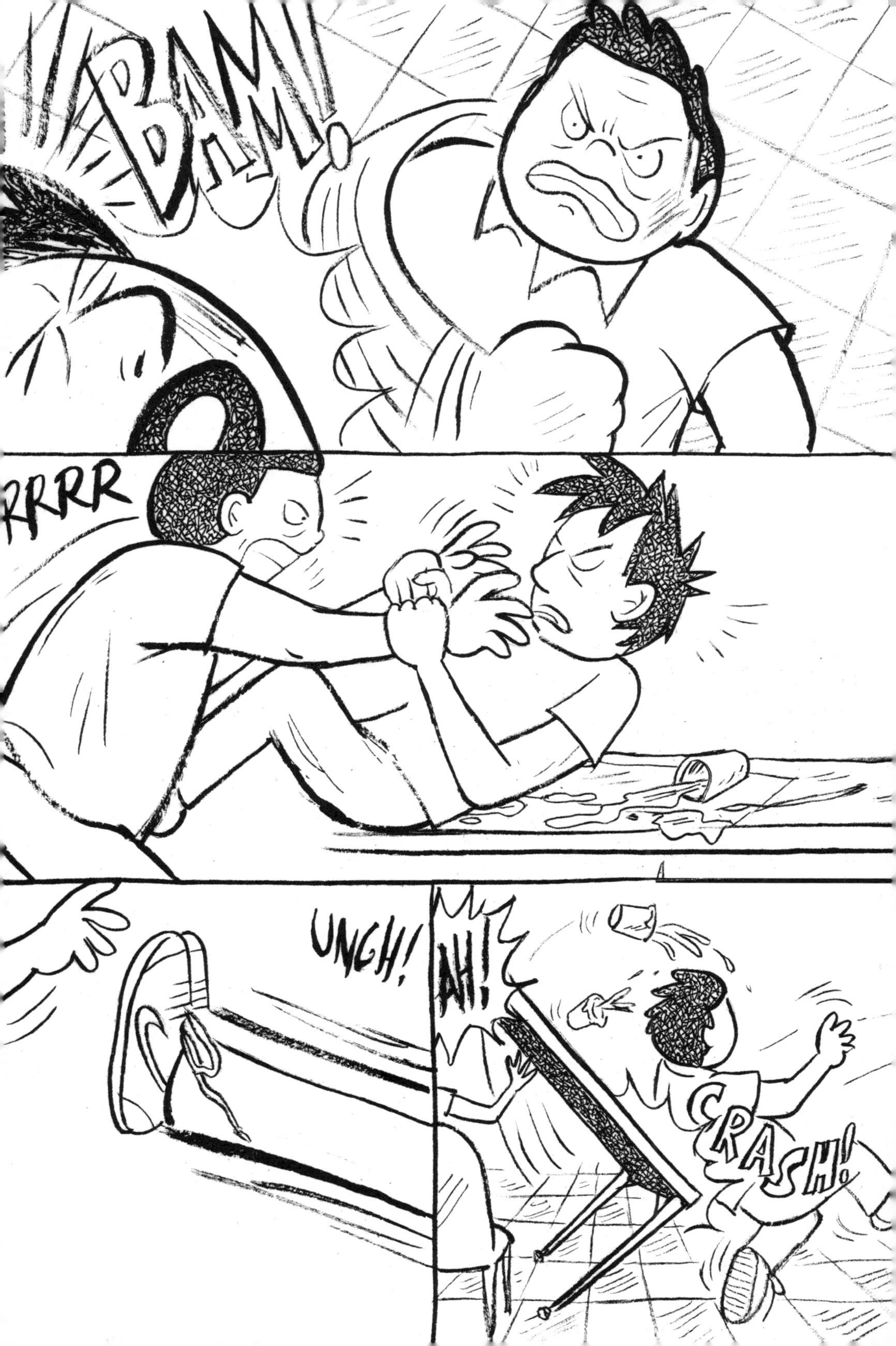
BAM!
RRRR
UNGH!
AH!
CRASH!

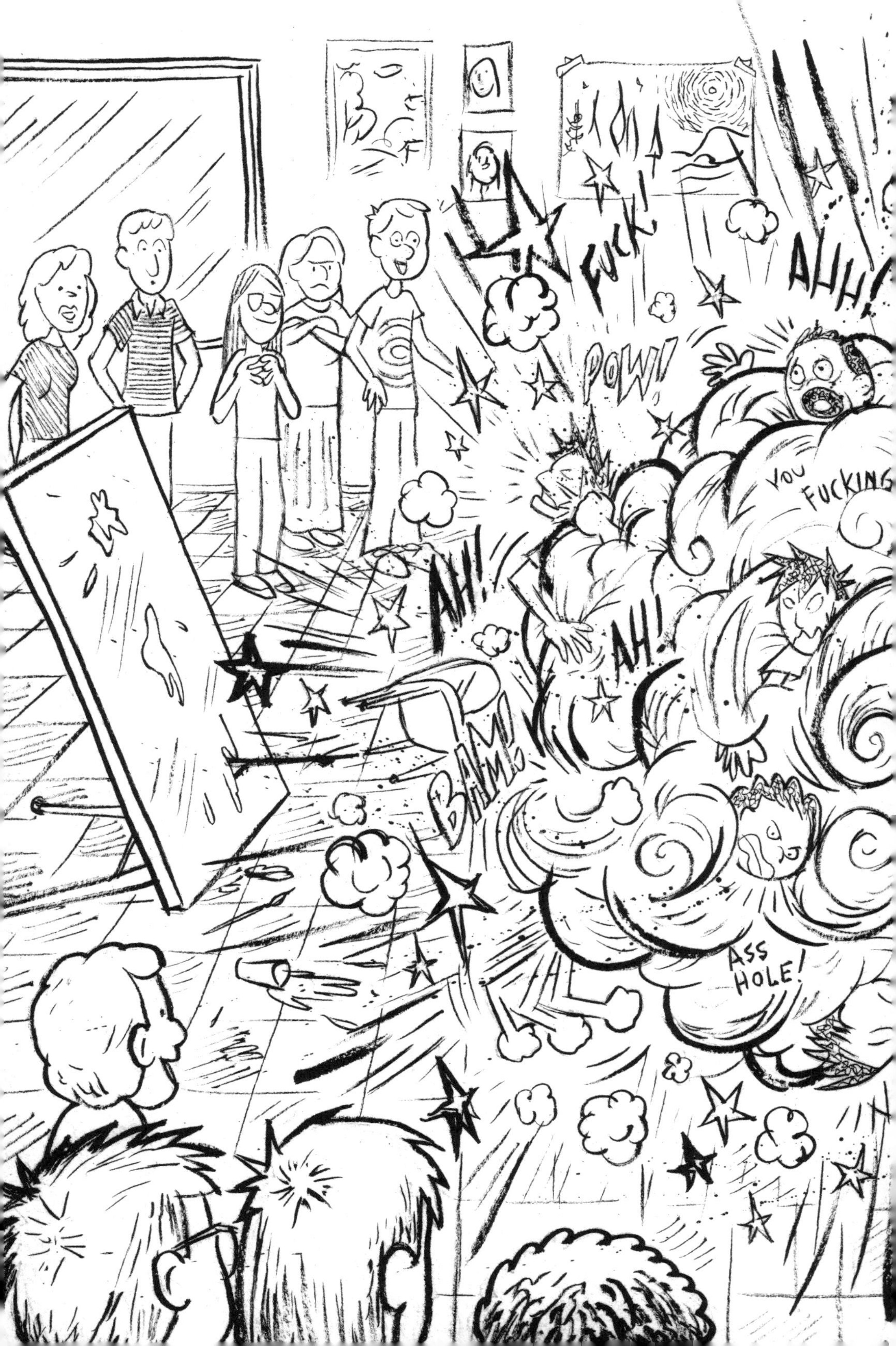
FUCK!
AHH!
POW!
YOU FUCKING
AH!
AH!
BAM!
ASS HOLE!

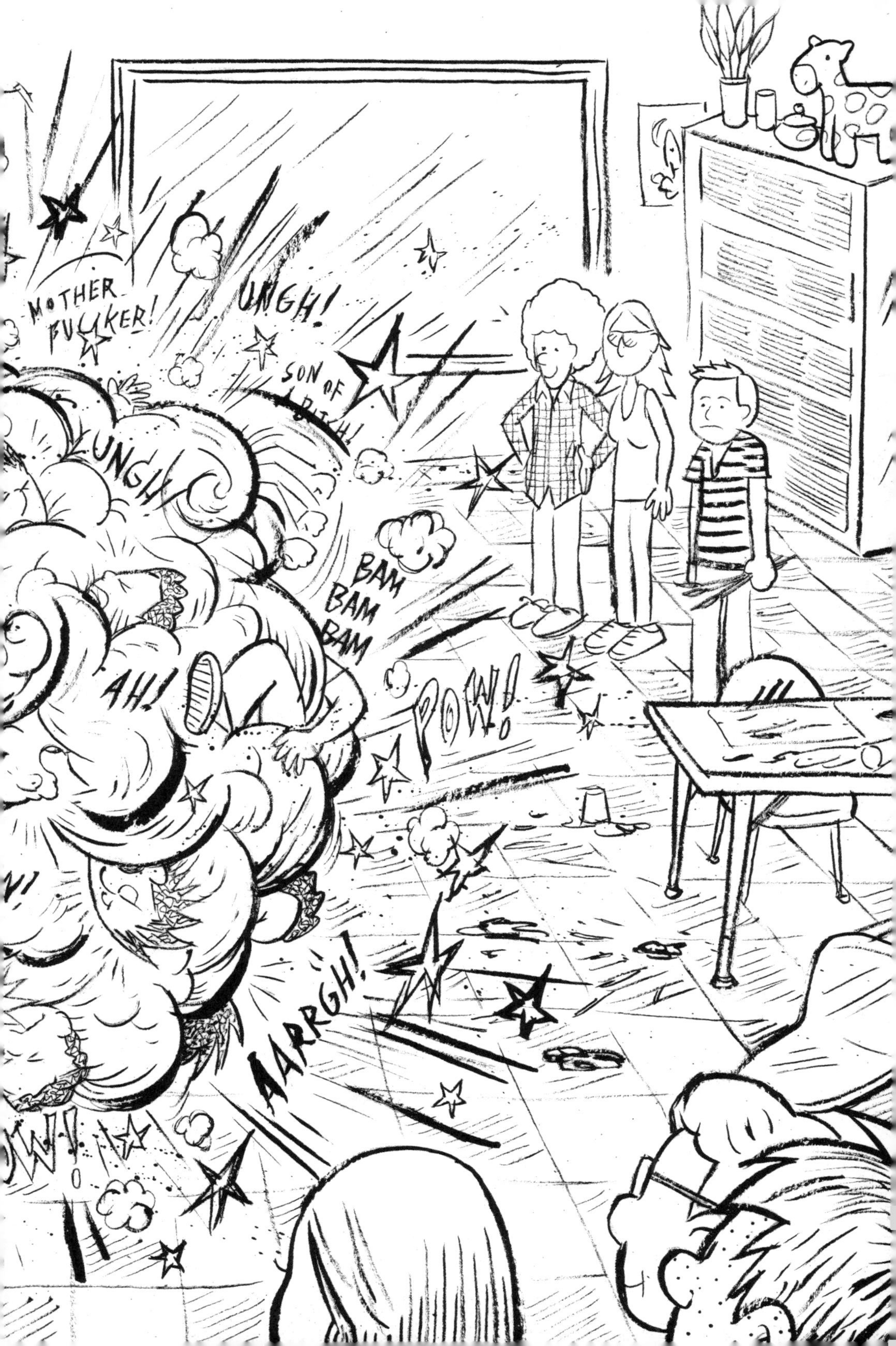
MOTHER FUCKER!
UNGH!
SON OF A BITCH!
UNGH
BAM BAM BAM
AH!
POW!
AARGH!

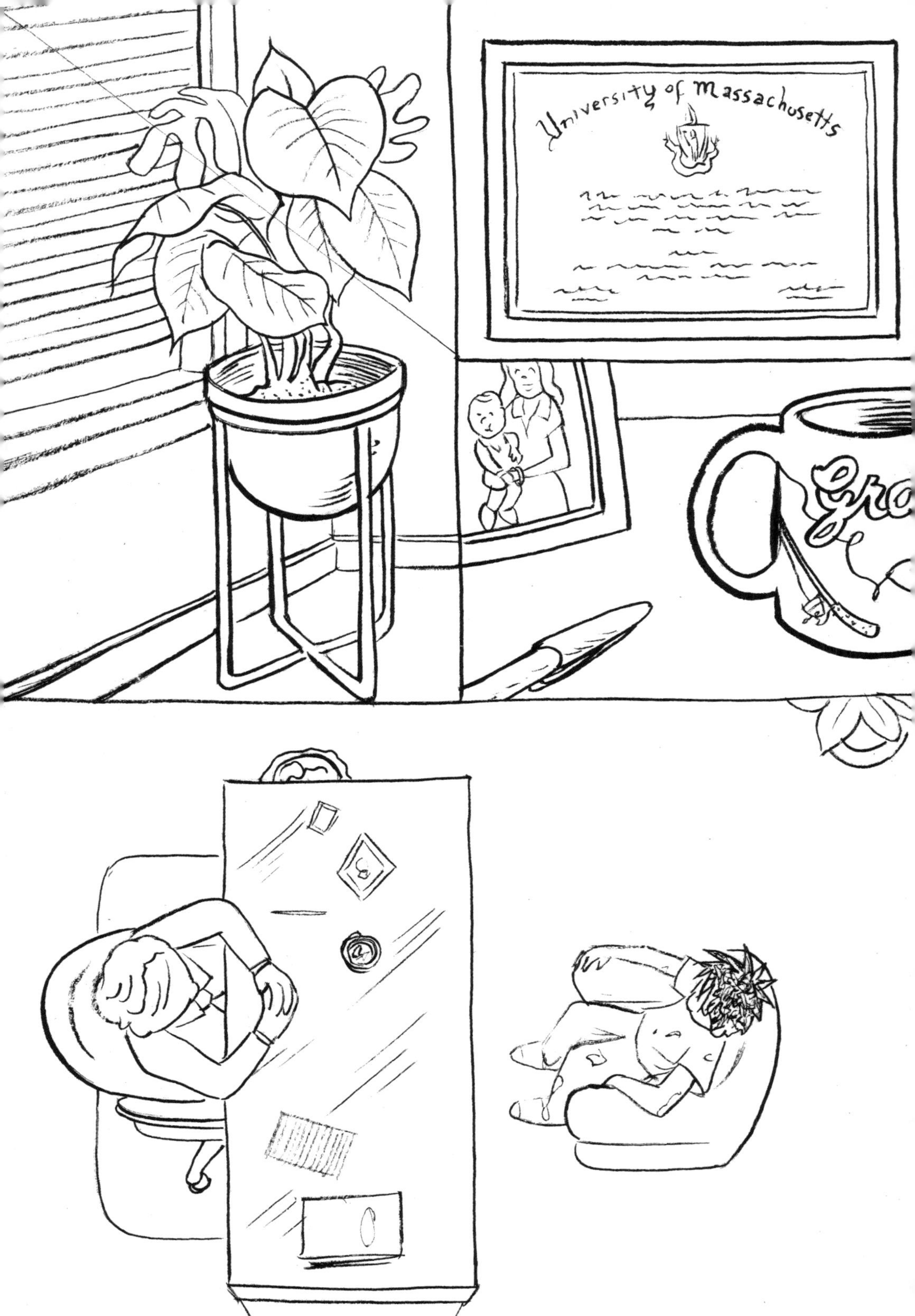
University of Massachusetts
Gro

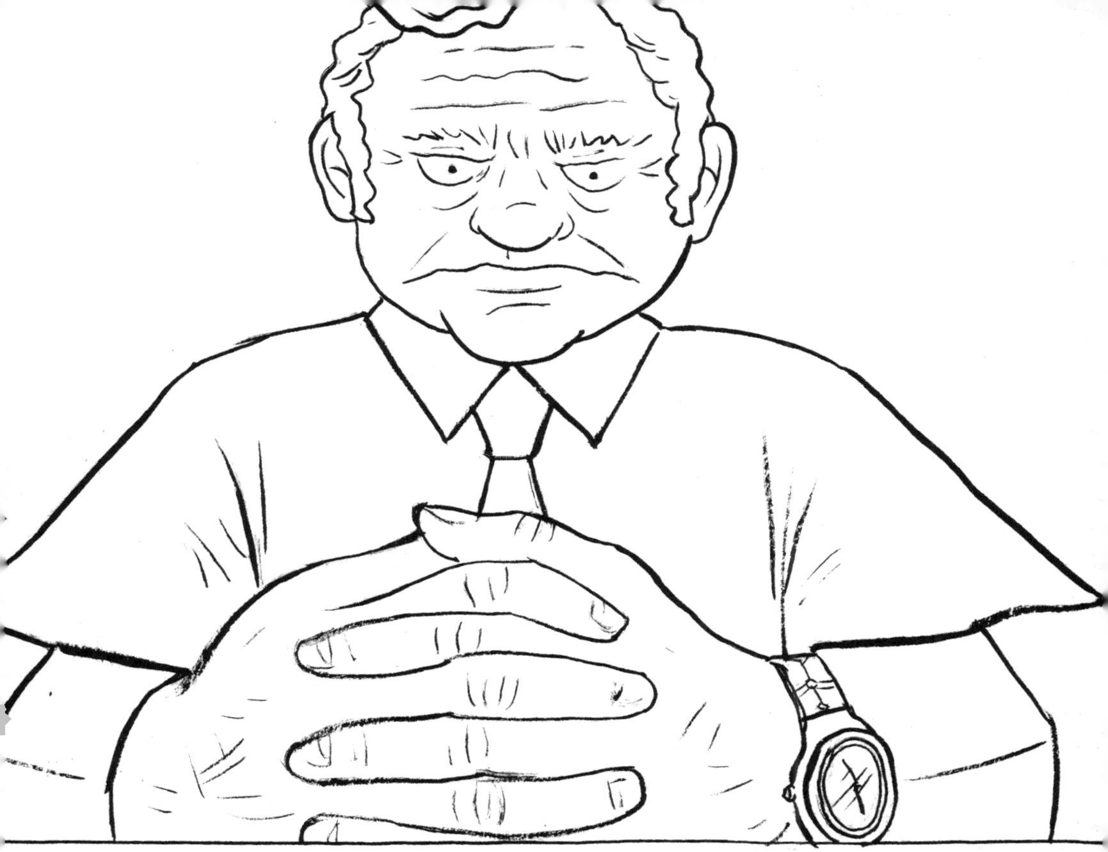

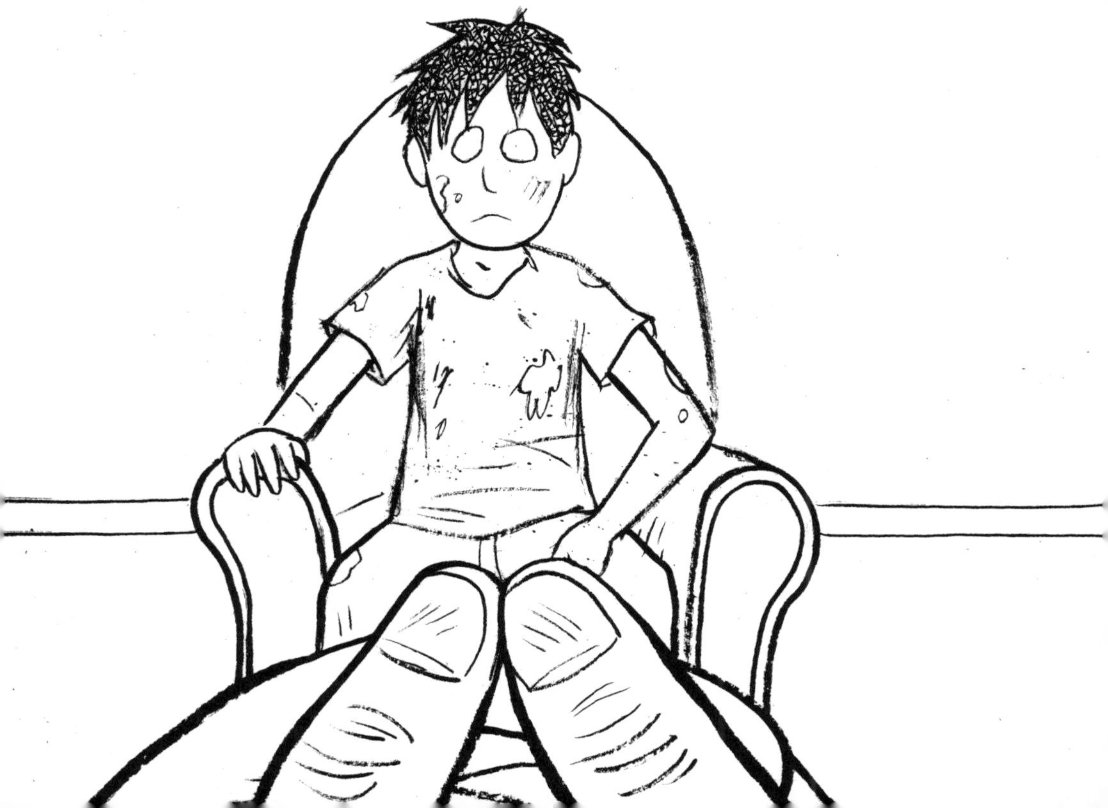

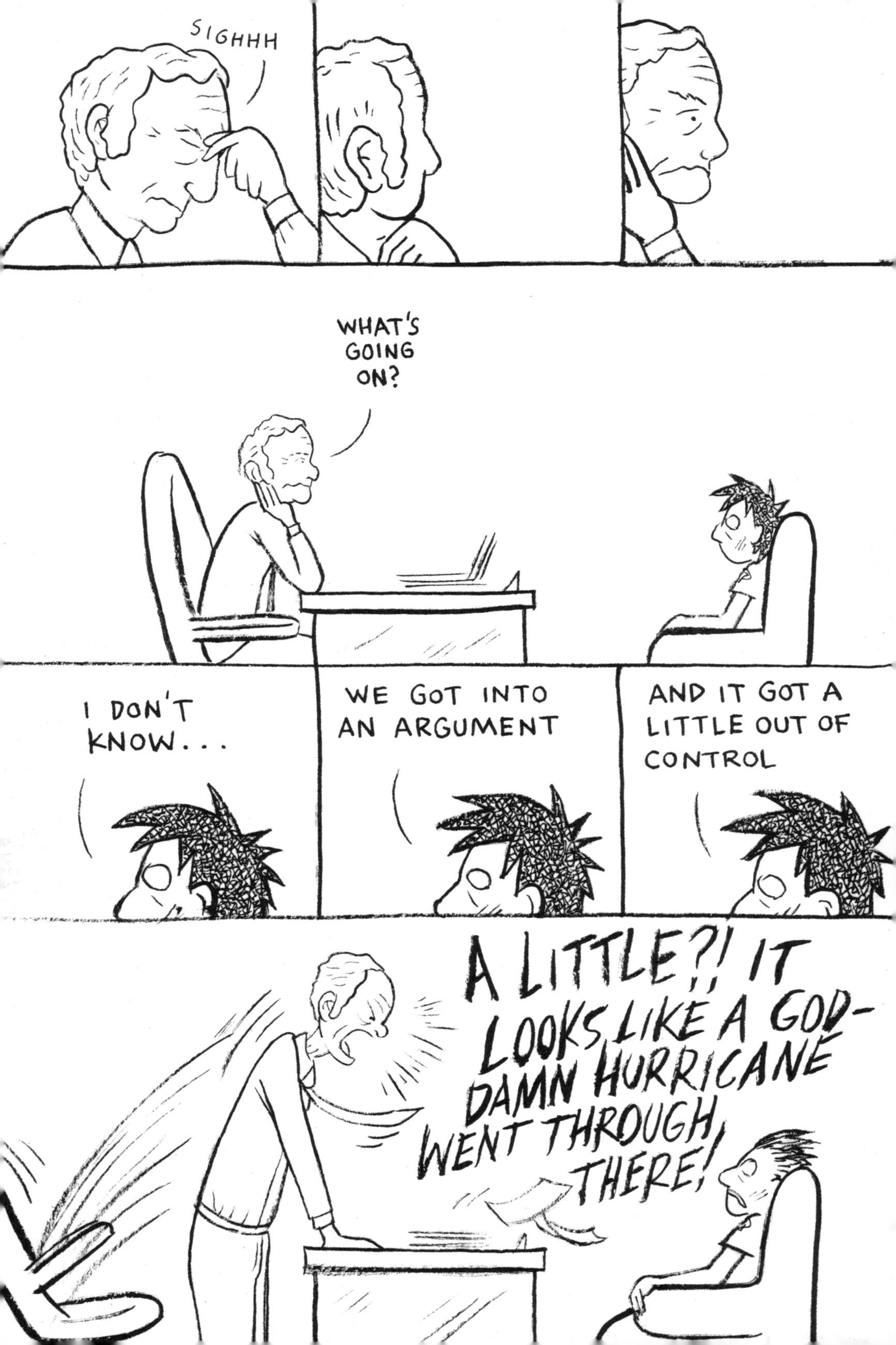
SIGHHH
WHAT'S GOING ON?
I DON'T KNOW...
WE GOT INTO AN ARGUMENT
AND IT GOT A LITTLE OUT OF CONTROL
A LITTLE?! IT LOOKS LIKE A GOD-DAMN HURRICANE WENT THROUGH THERE!

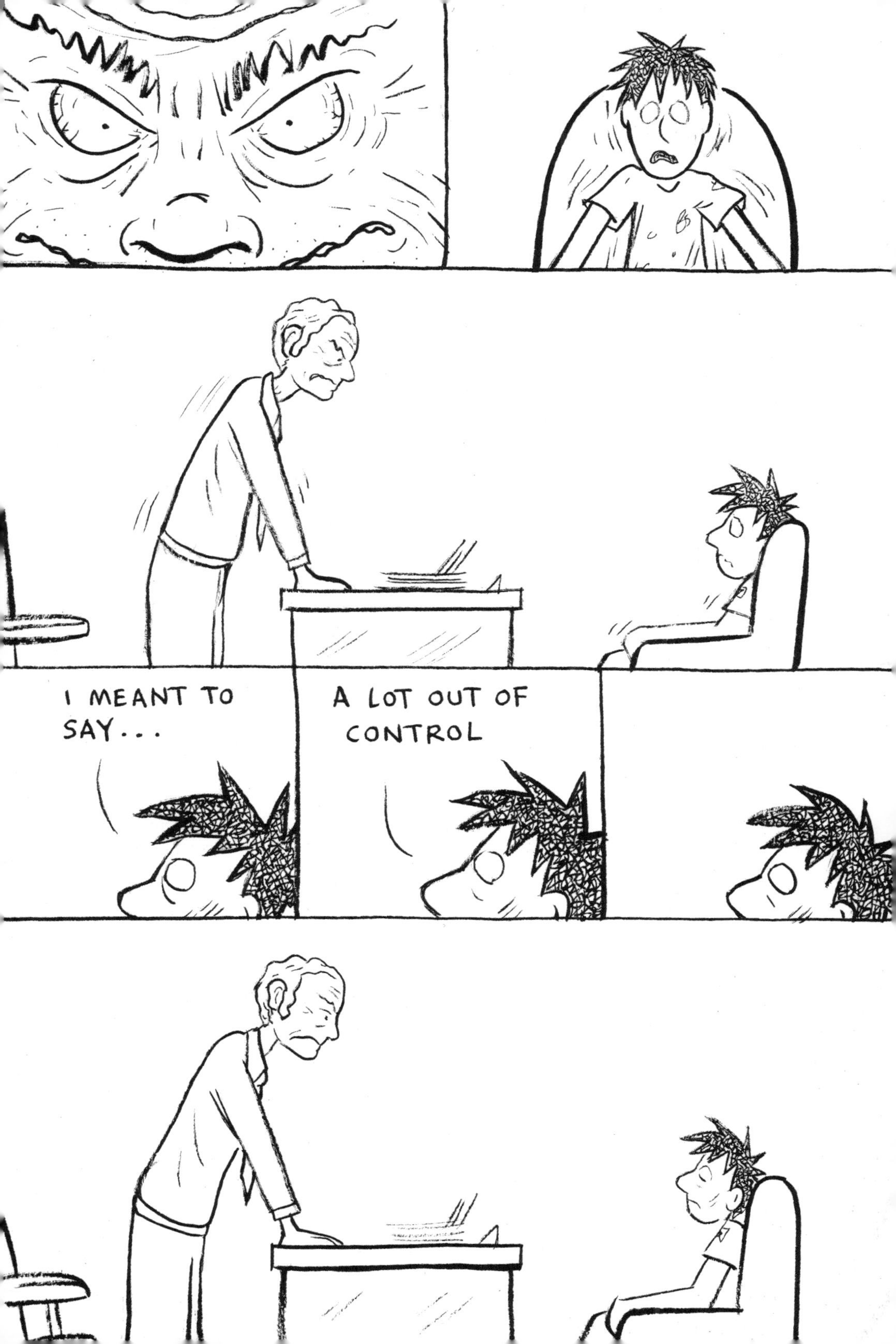
I MEANT TO SAY...
A LOT OUT OF CONTROL

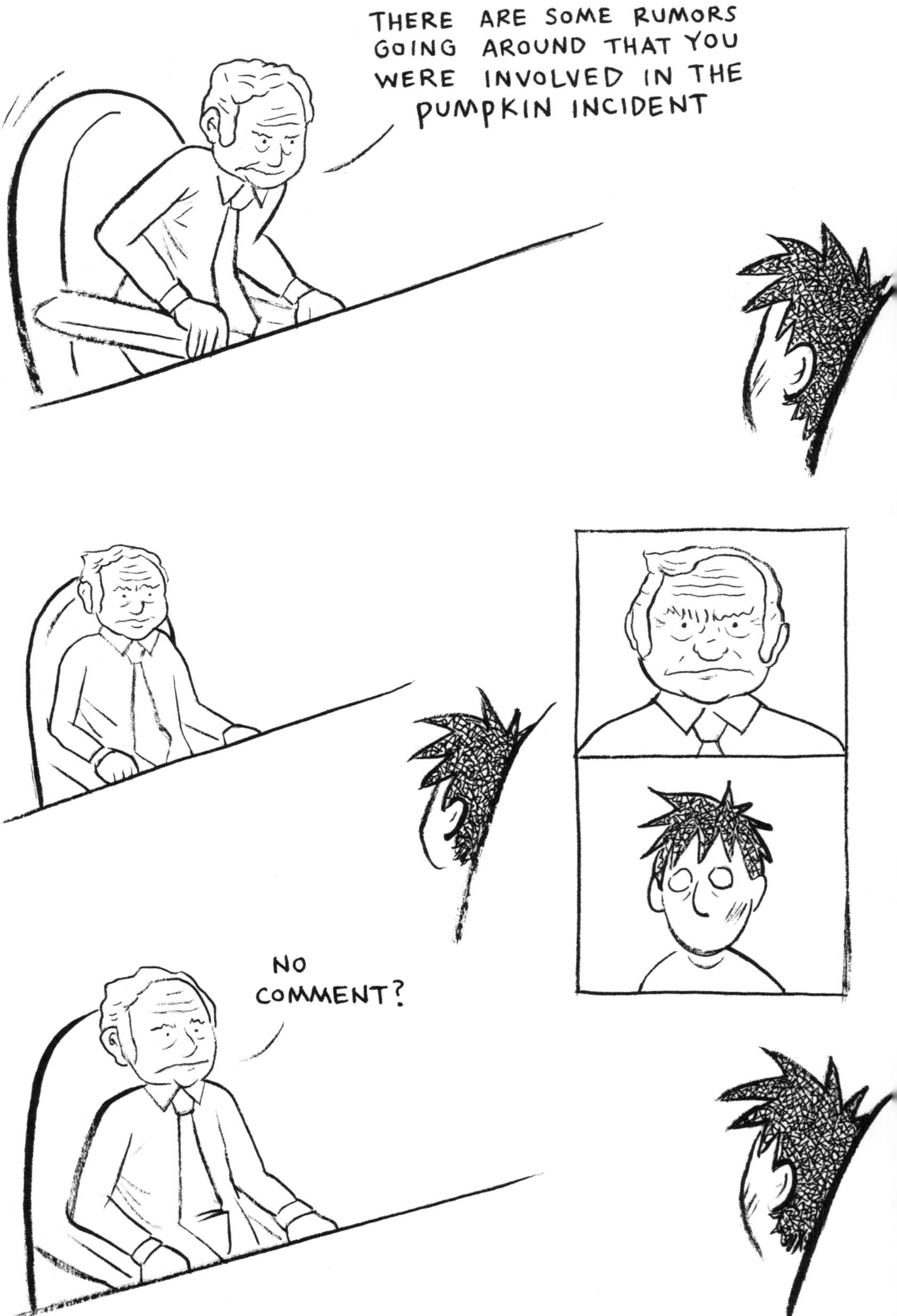
THERE ARE SOME RUMORS GOING AROUND THAT YOU WERE INVOLVED IN THE PUMPKIN INCIDENT
NO COMMENT?

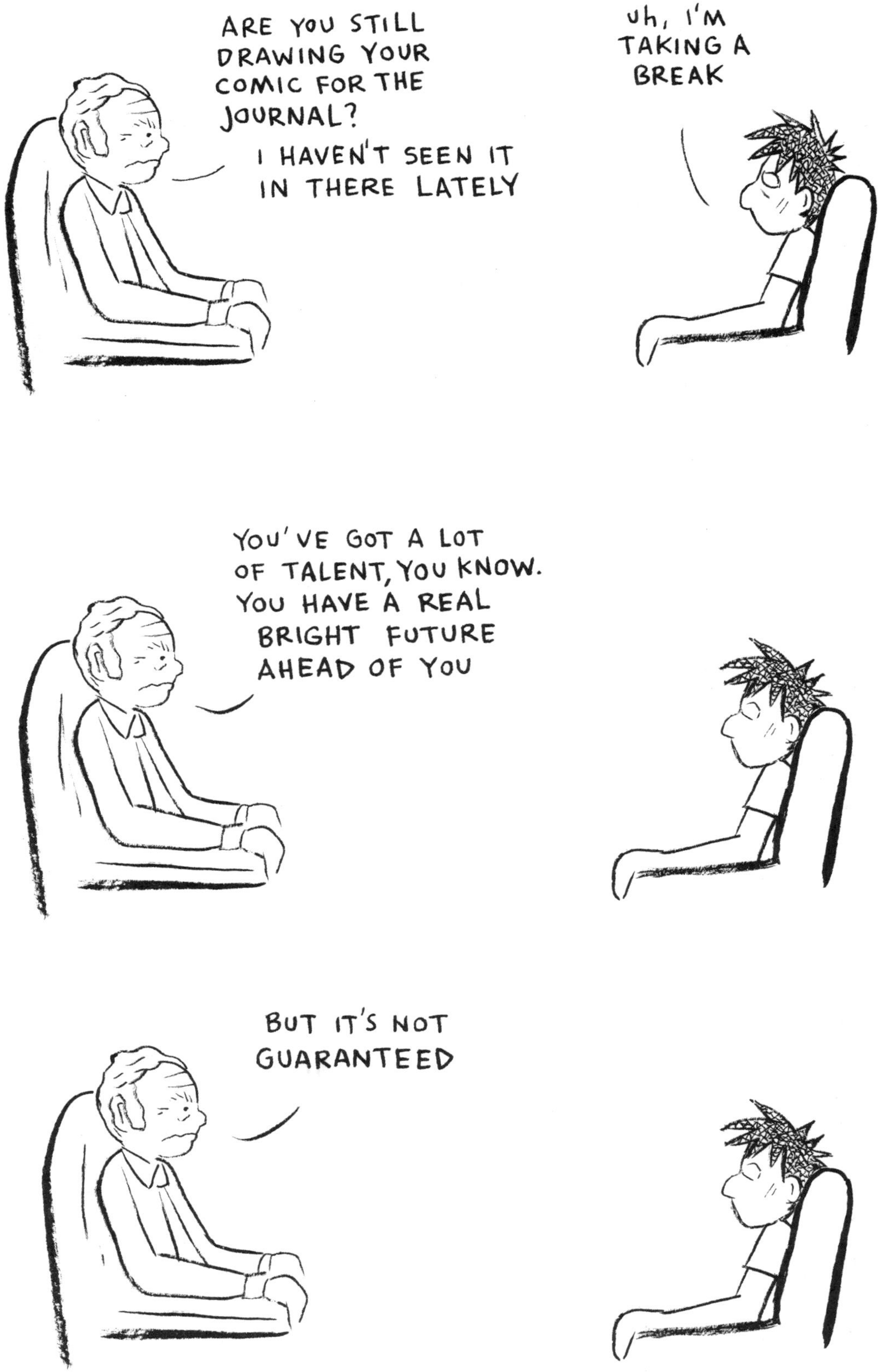
ARE YOU STILL DRAWING YOUR COMIC FOR THE JOURNAL?
I HAVEN'T SEEN IT IN THERE LATELY
uh, I'M TAKING A BREAK
YOU'VE GOT A LOT OF TALENT, YOU KNOW. YOU HAVE A REAL BRIGHT FUTURE AHEAD OF YOU
BUT IT'S NOT GUARANTEED

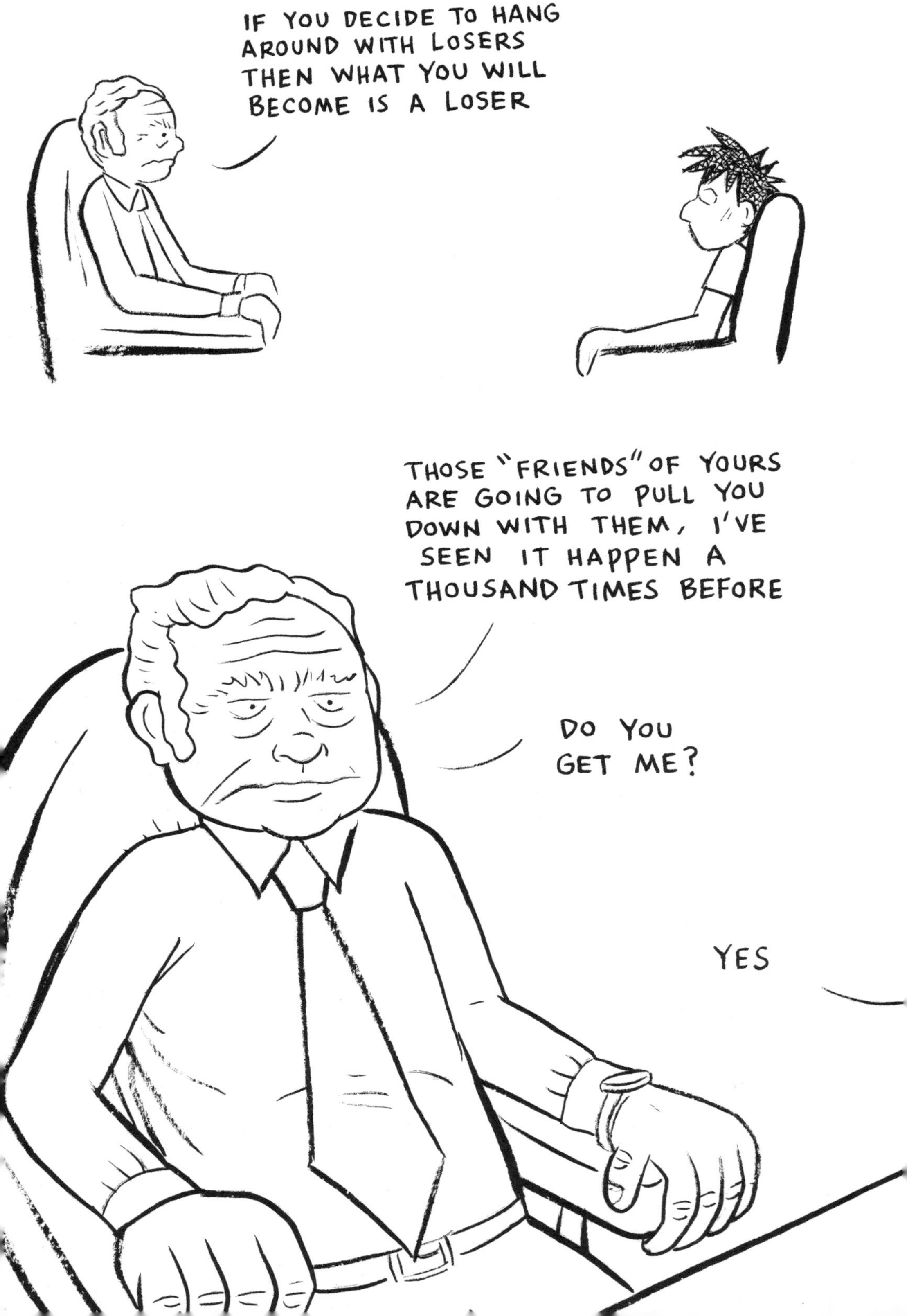
IF YOU DECIDE TO HANG AROUND WITH LOSERS THEN WHAT YOU WILL BECOME IS A LOSER
THOSE "FRIENDS" OF YOURS ARE GOING TO PULL YOU DOWN WITH THEM, I'VE SEEN IT HAPPEN A THOUSAND TIMES BEFORE
DO YOU GET ME?
YES

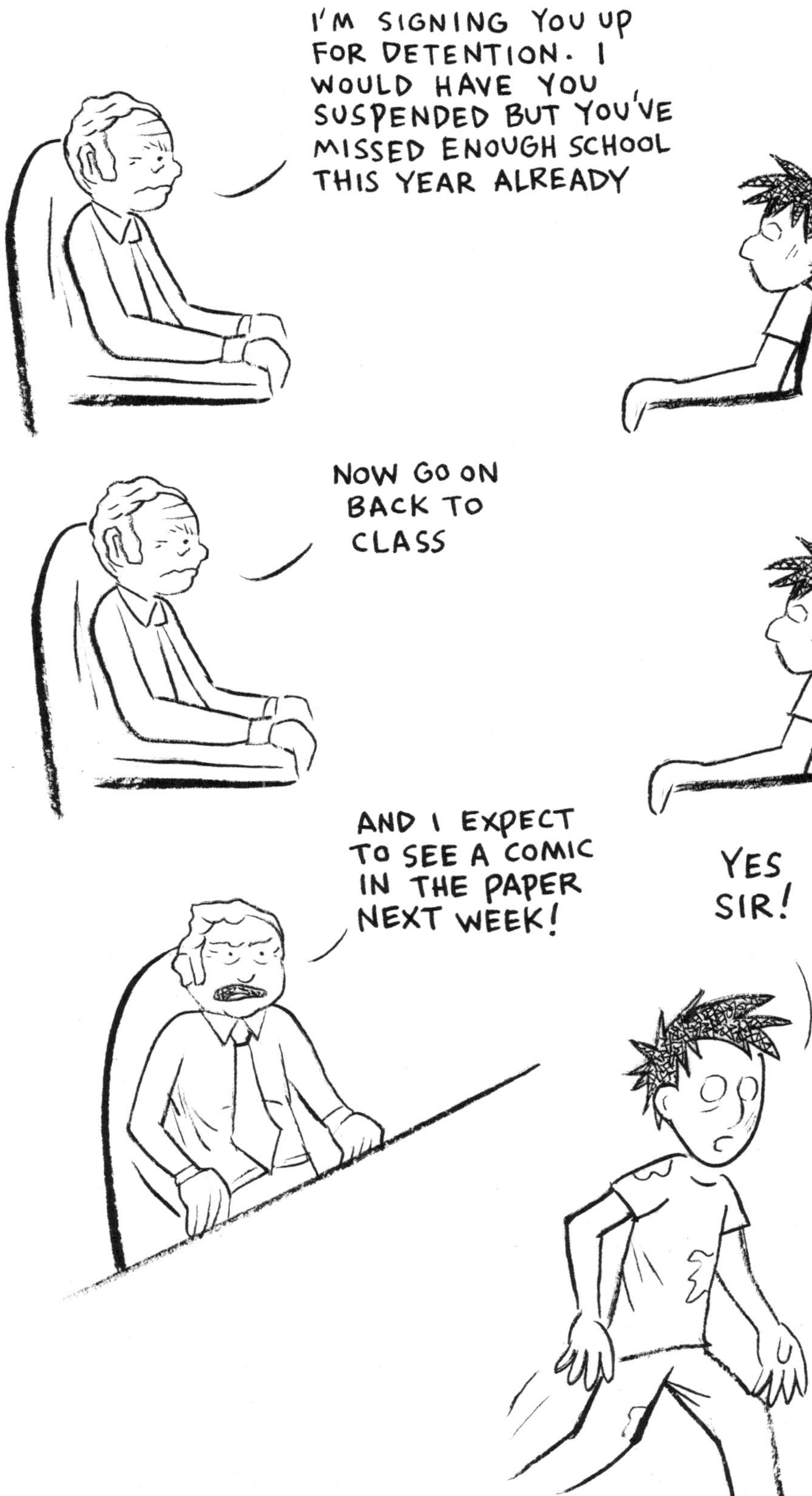
I'M SIGNING YOU UP FOR DETENTION. I WOULD HAVE YOU SUSPENDED BUT YOU'VE MISSED ENOUGH SCHOOL THIS YEAR ALREADY
NOW GO ON BACK TO CLASS
AND I EXPECT TO SEE A COMIC IN THE PAPER NEXT WEEK!
YES SIR!

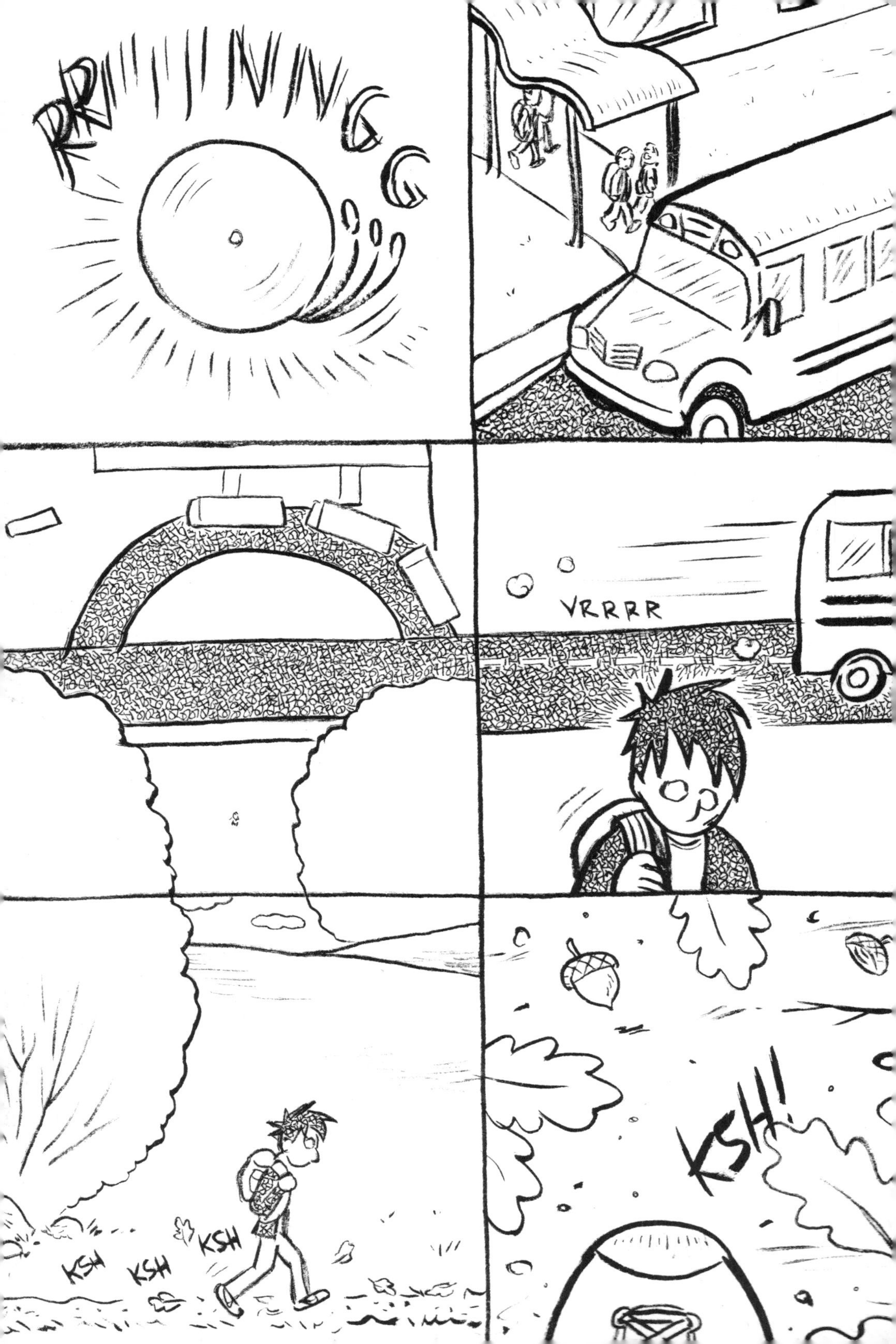
RRIIINNGG
VRRRR
KSH
KSH
KSH
KSH!

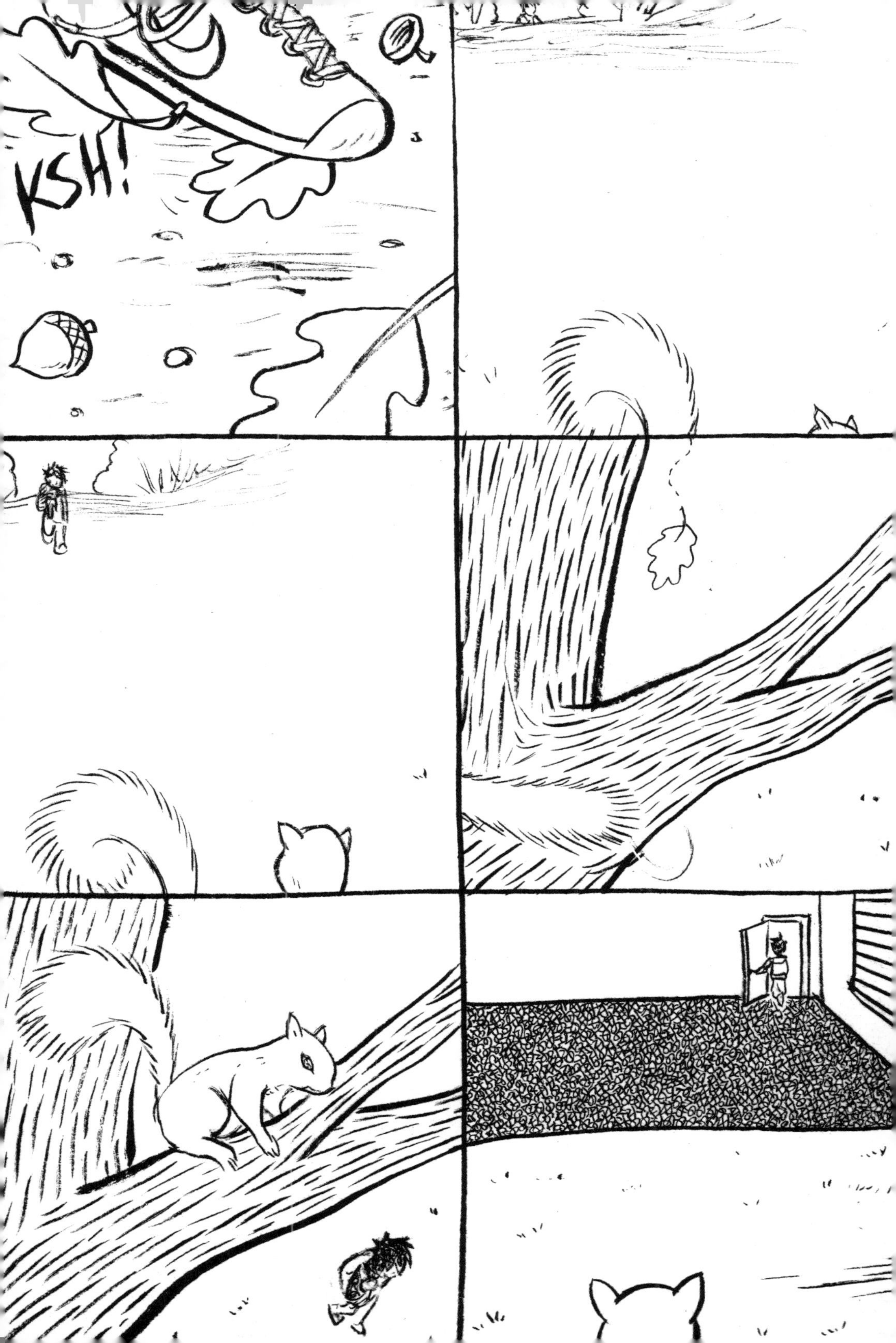
KSH!

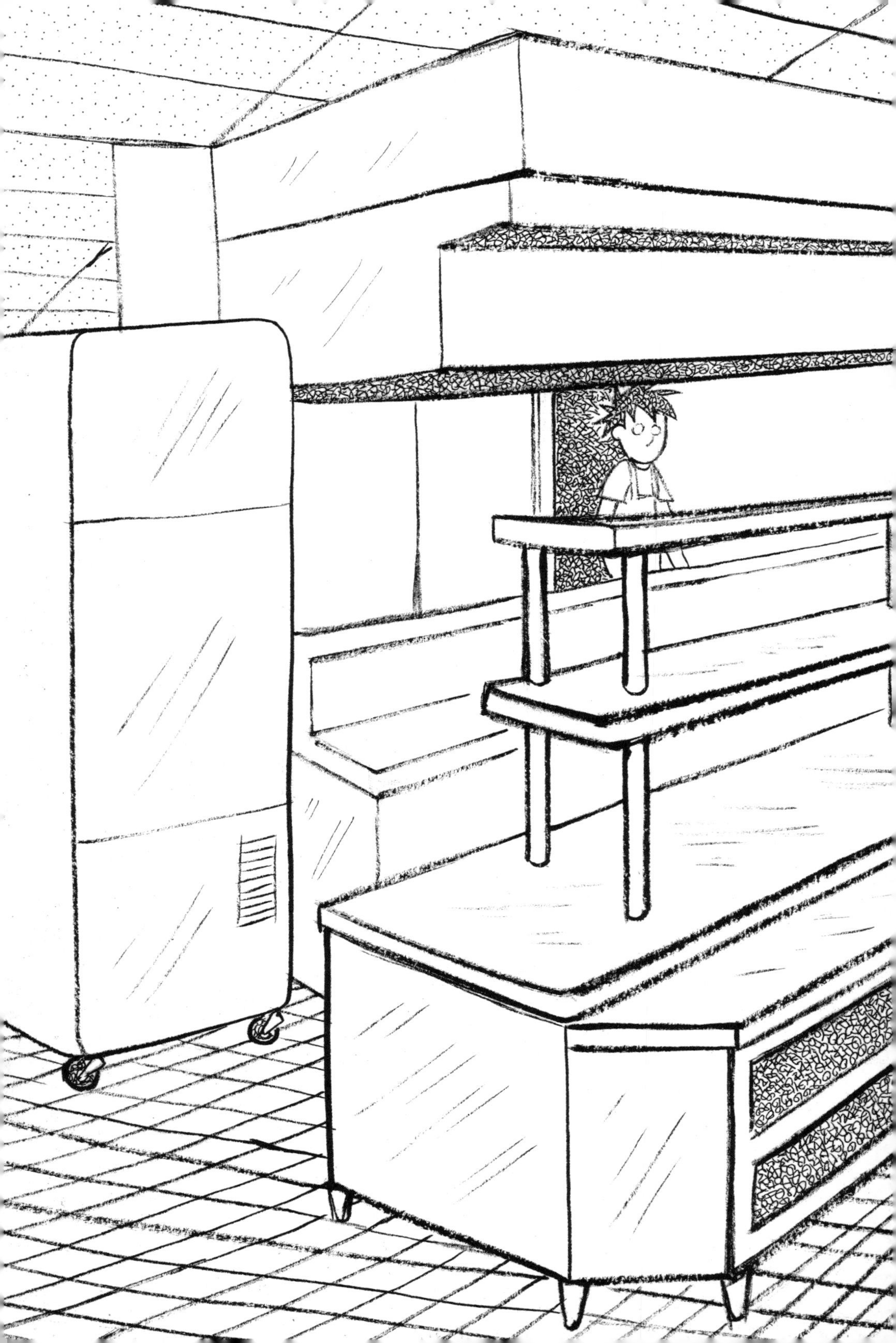

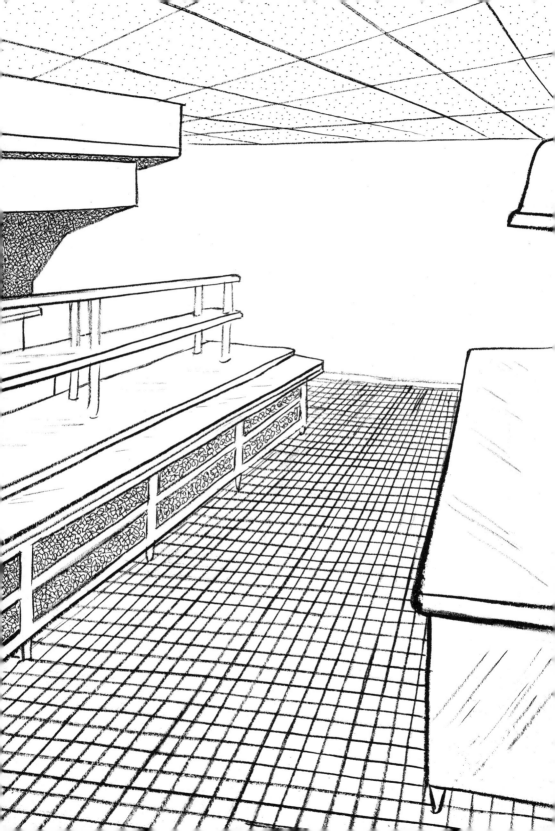

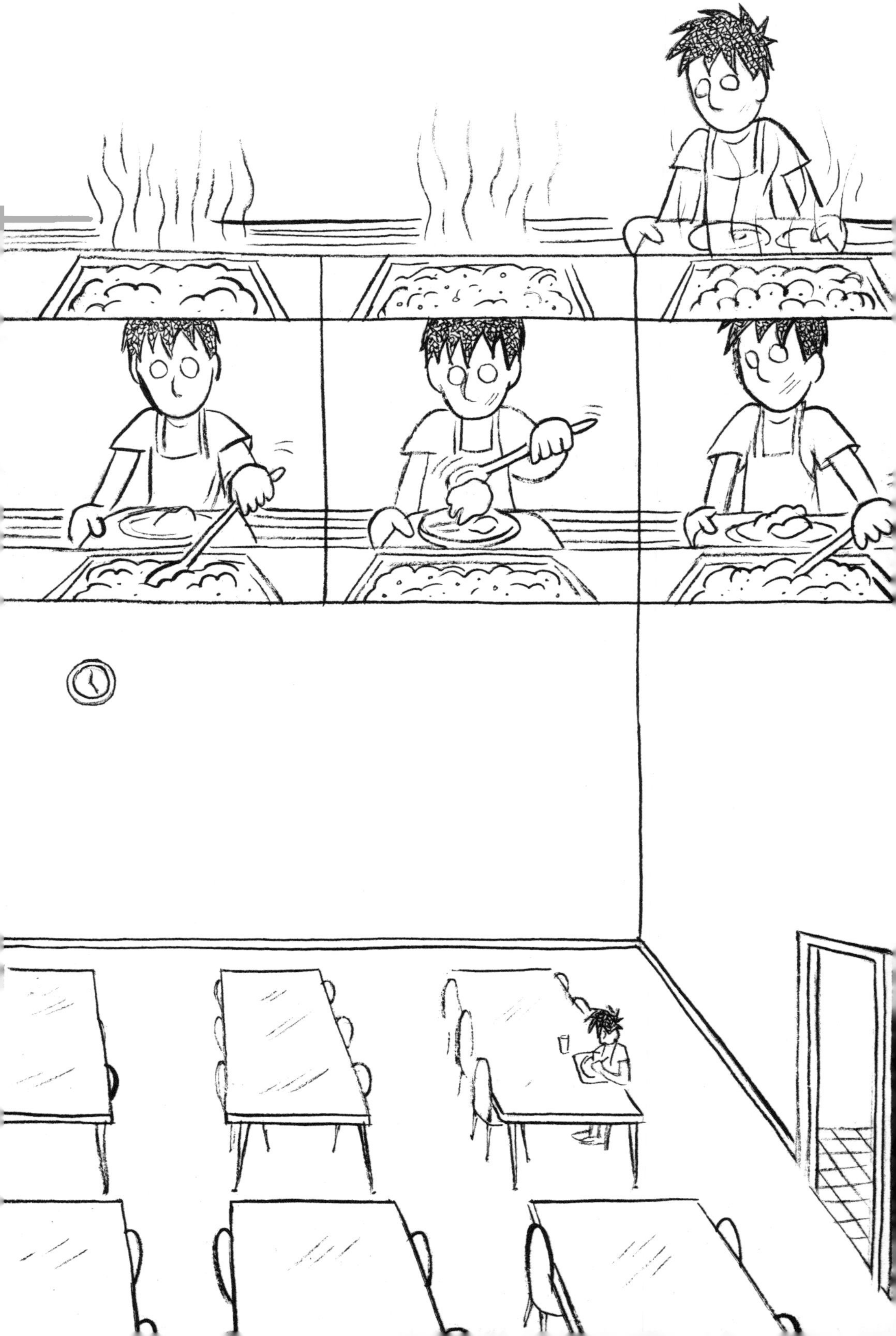

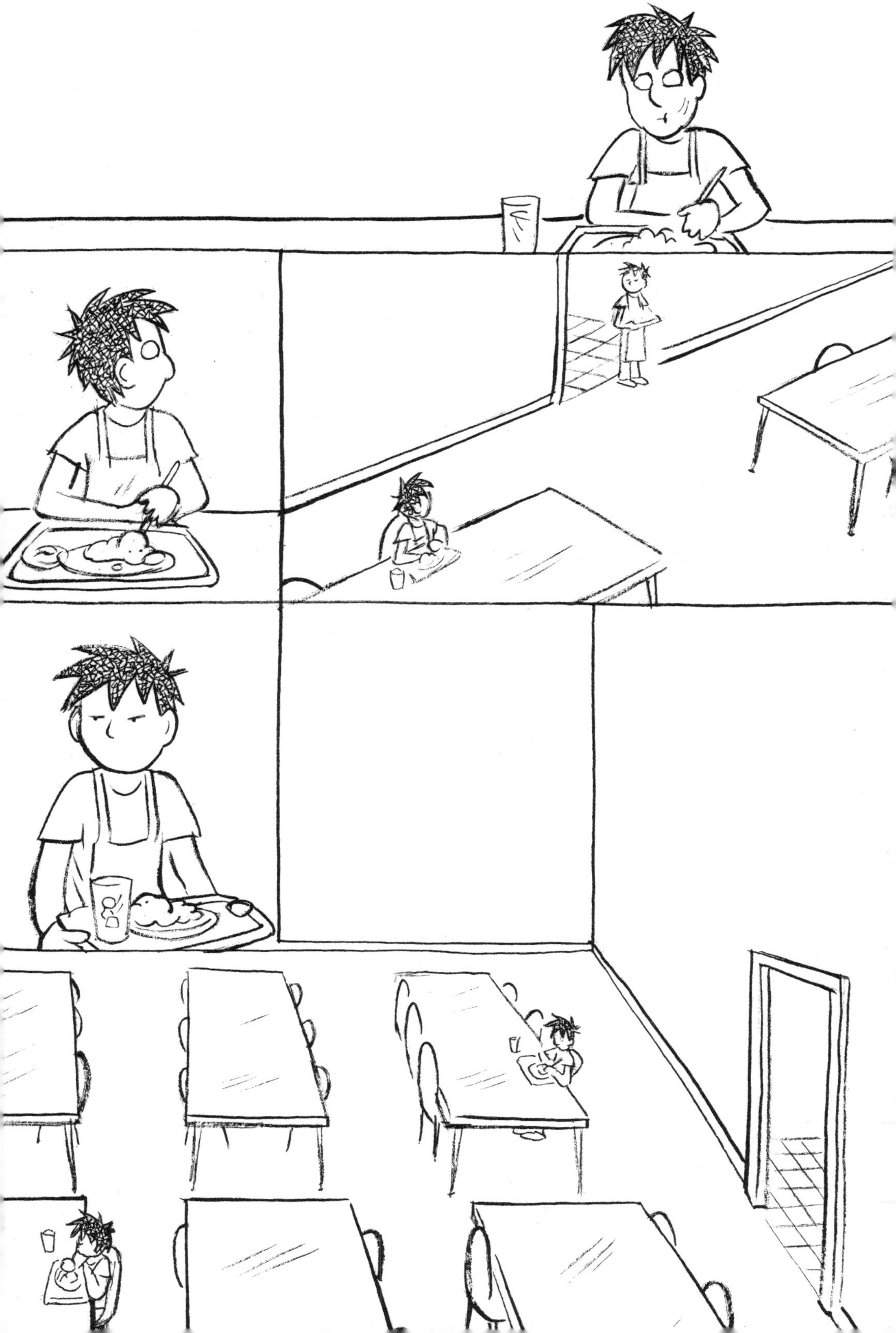

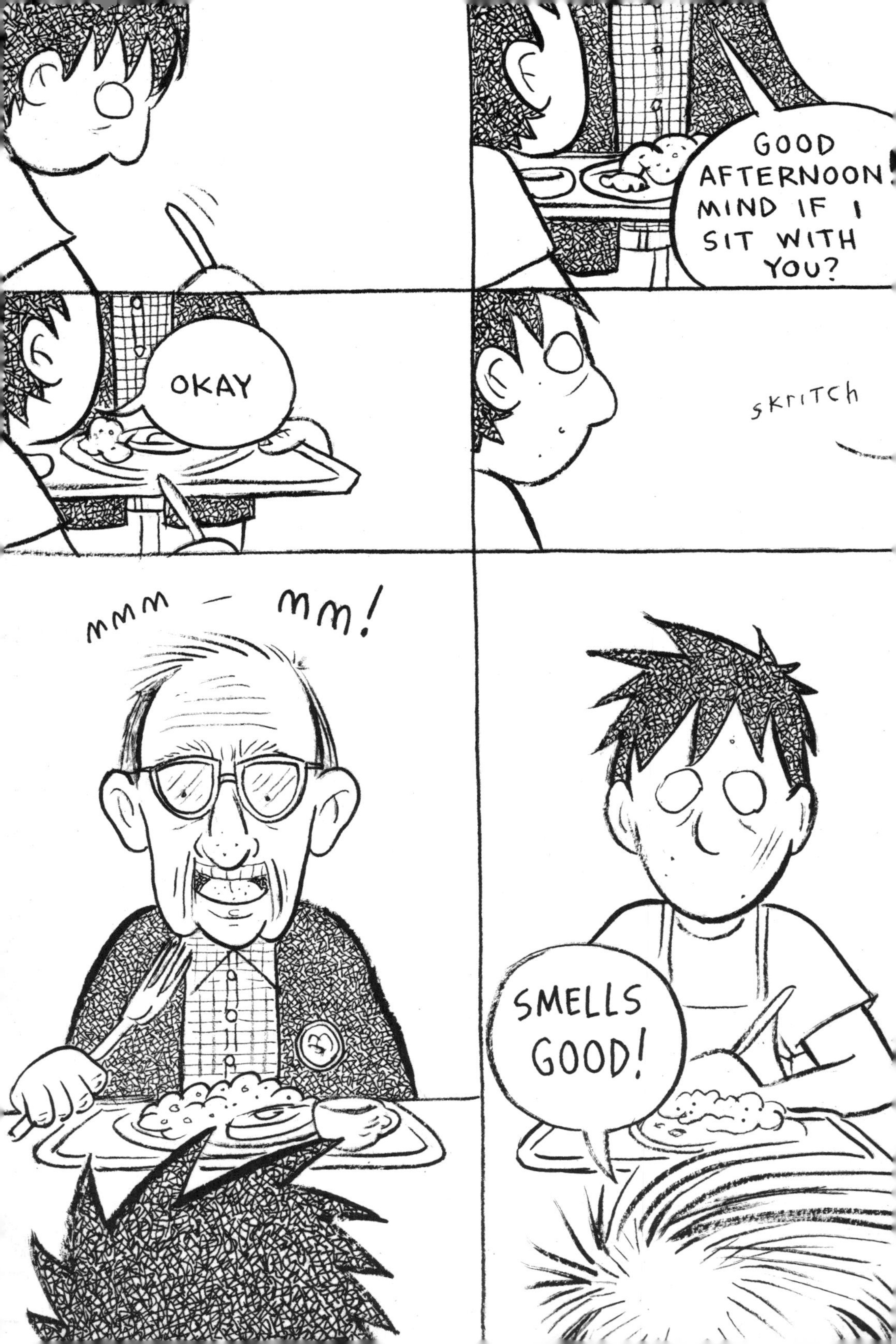
GOOD AFTERNOON! MIND IF I SIT WITH YOU?
OKAY
skritch
mmm - mm!
SMELLS GOOD!

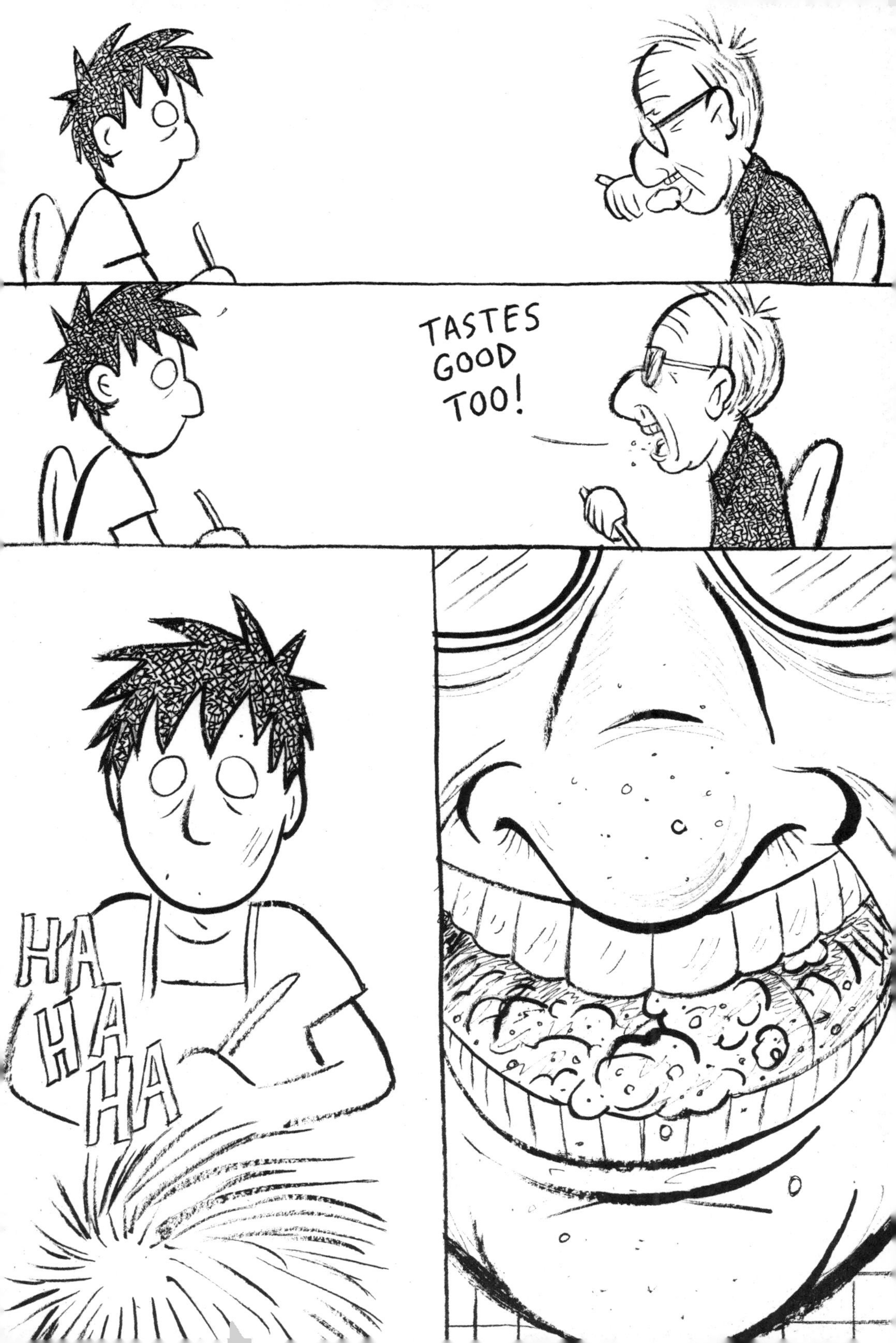
TASTES GOOD TOO!
HA HA HA HA

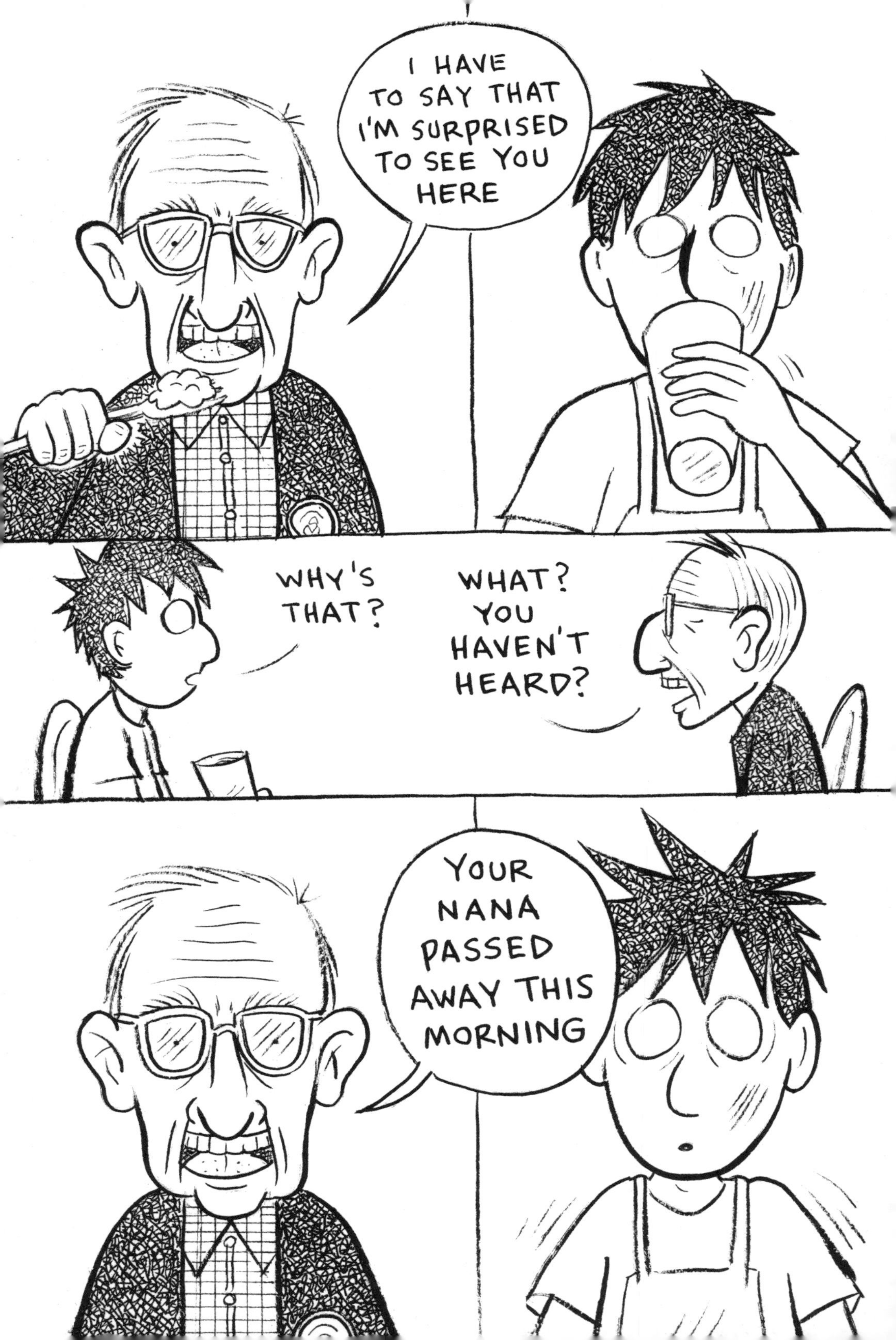

I HAVE TO SAY THAT I'M SURPRISED TO SEE YOU HERE
WHY'S THAT?
WHAT? YOU HAVEN'T HEARD?
YOUR NANA PASSED AWAY THIS MORNING

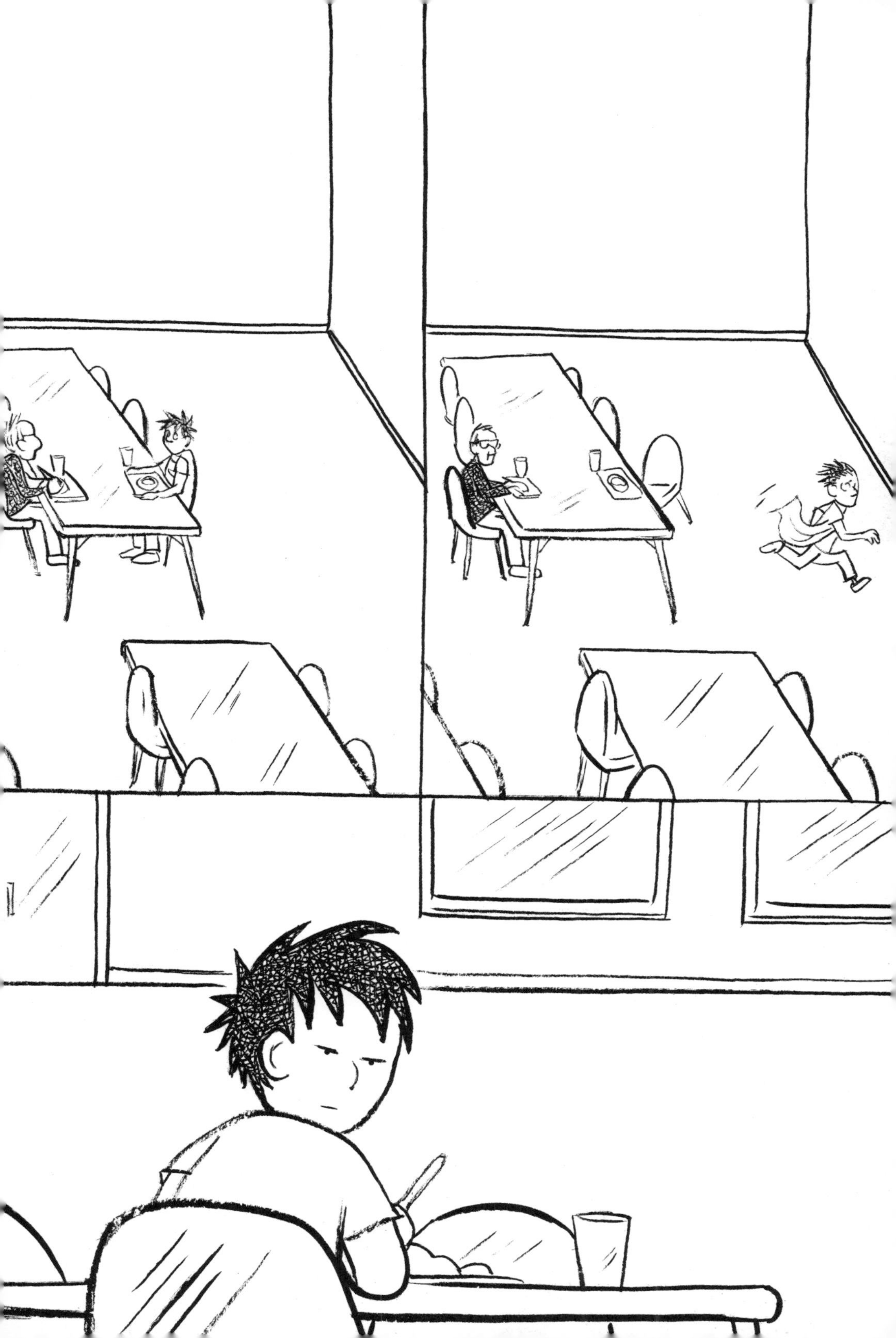

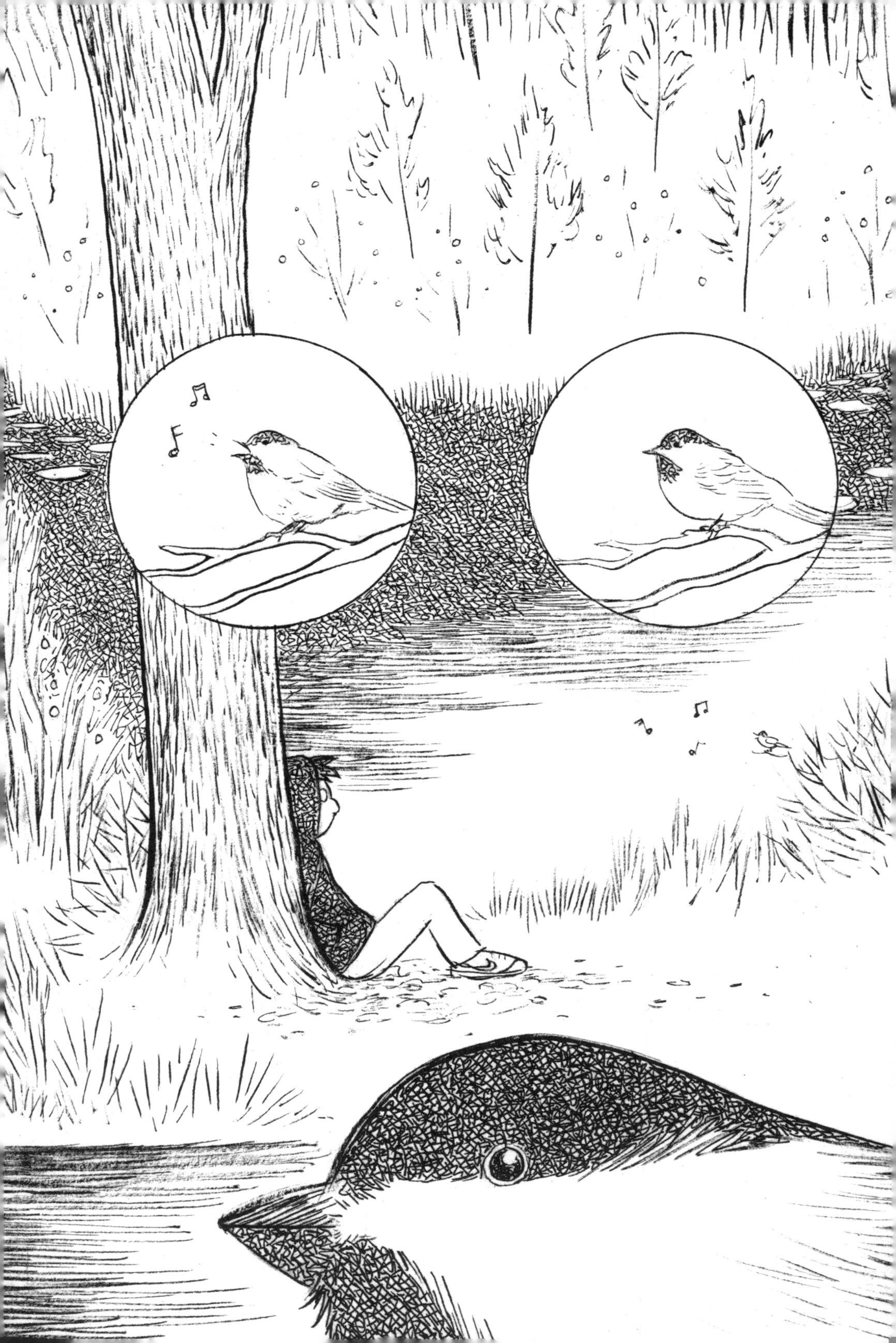

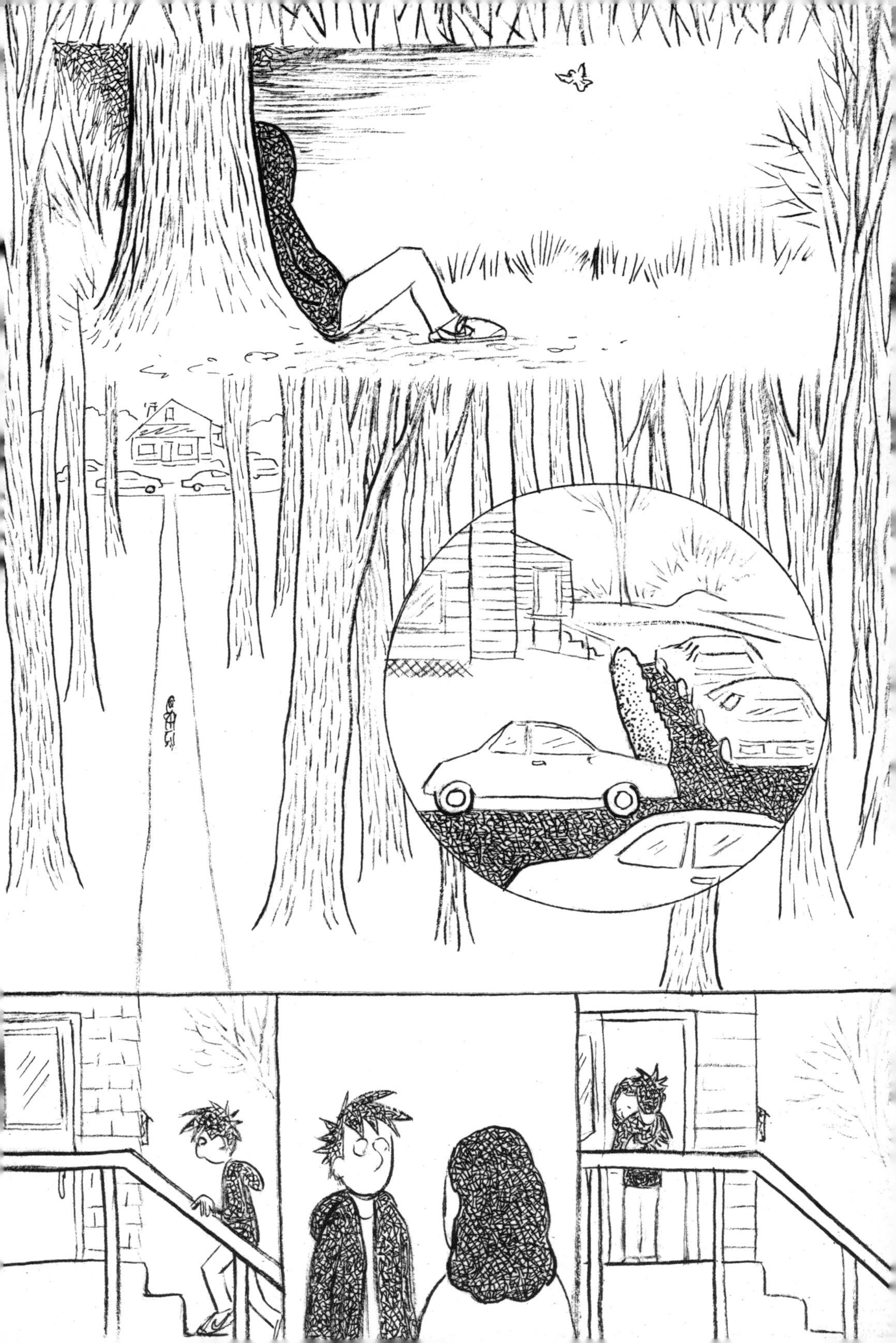

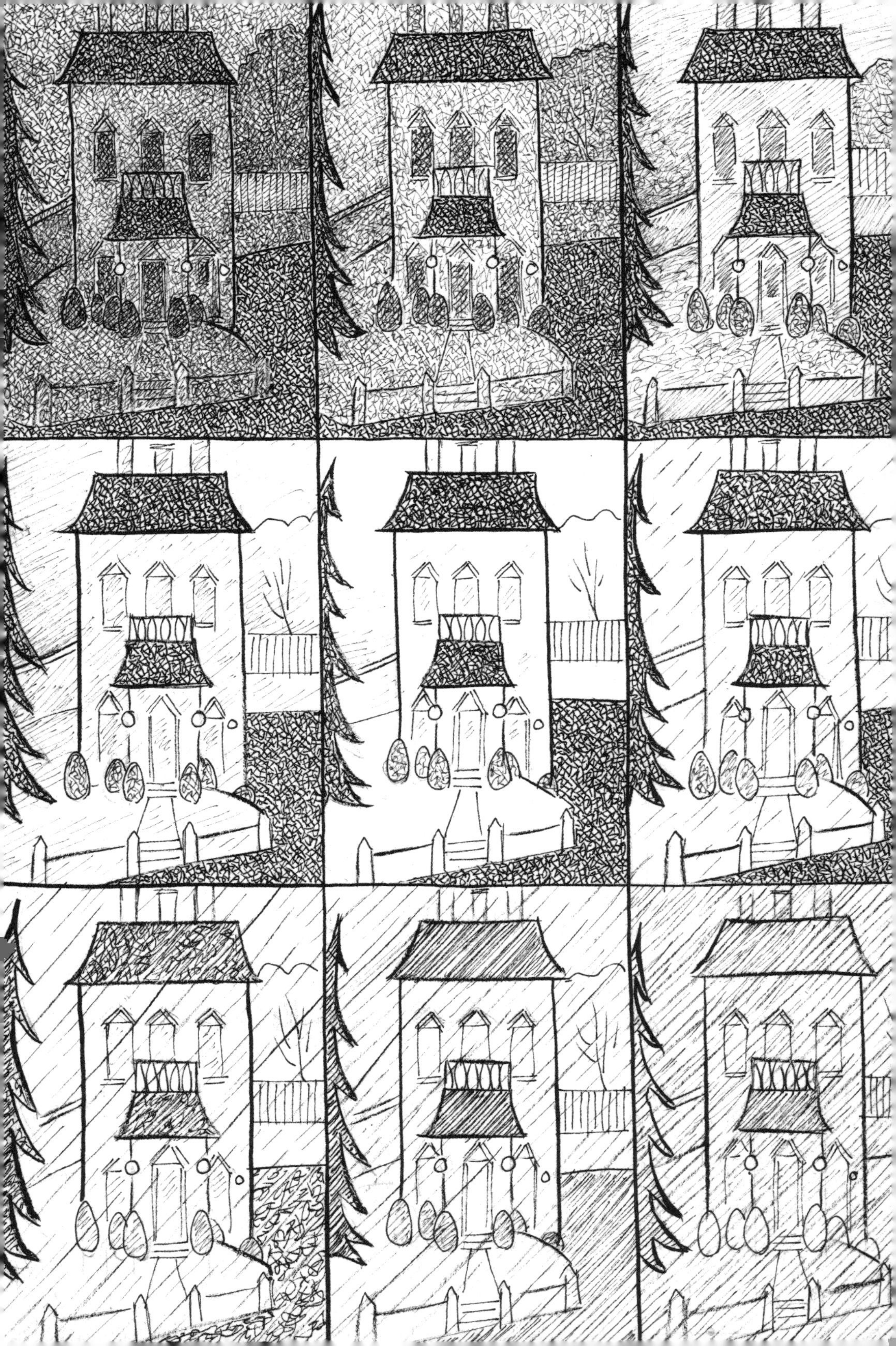

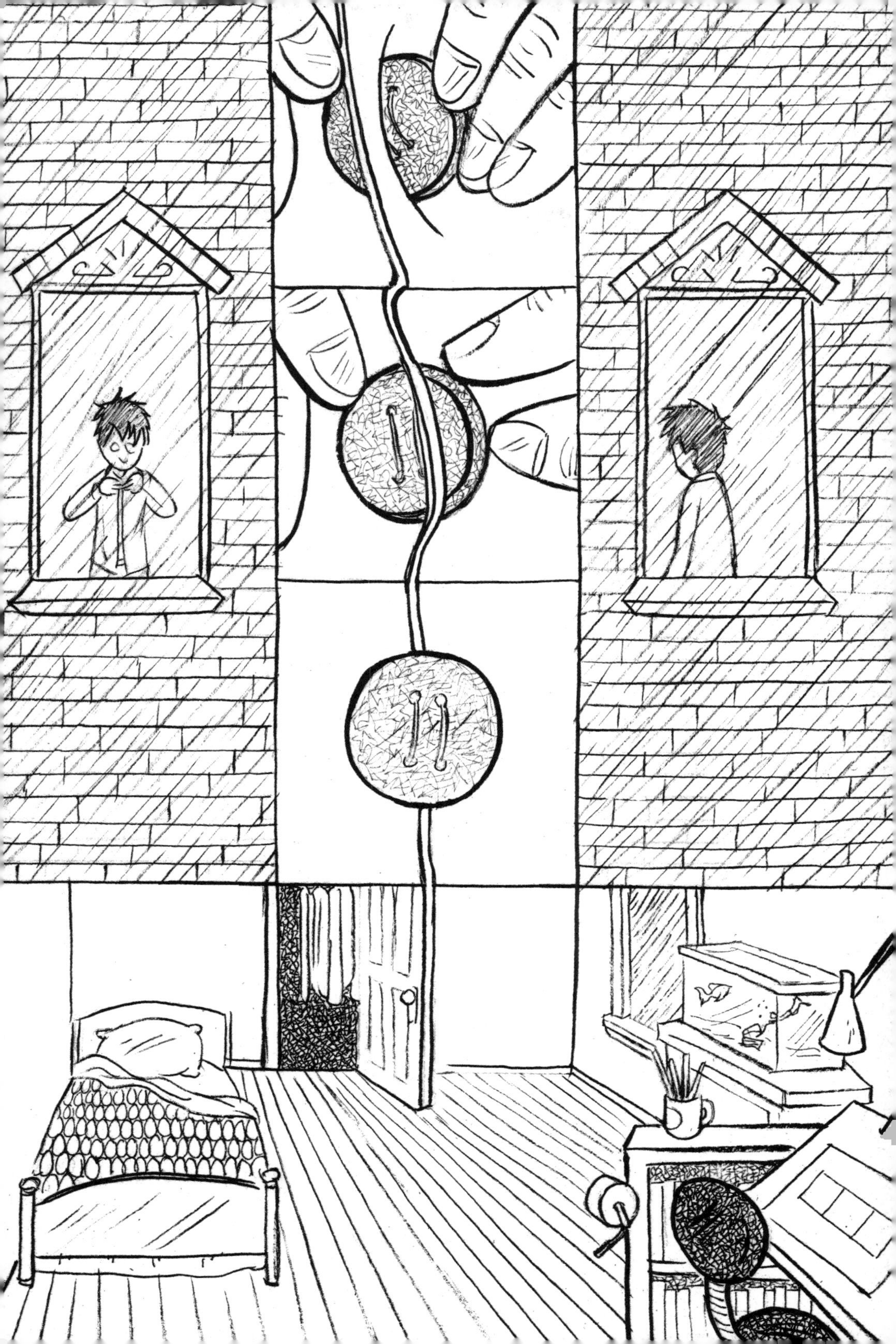

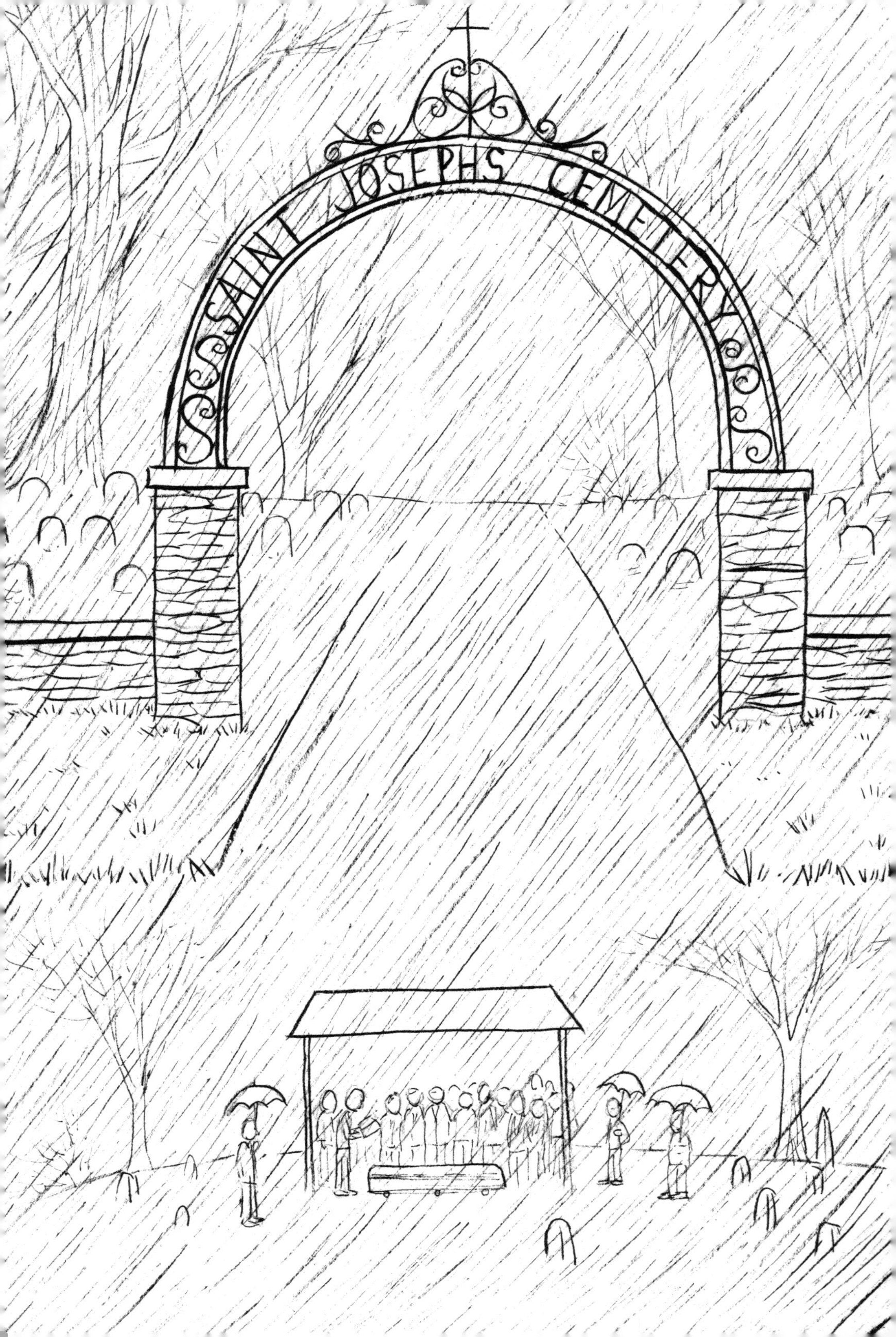
SAINT JOSEPHS CEMETERY

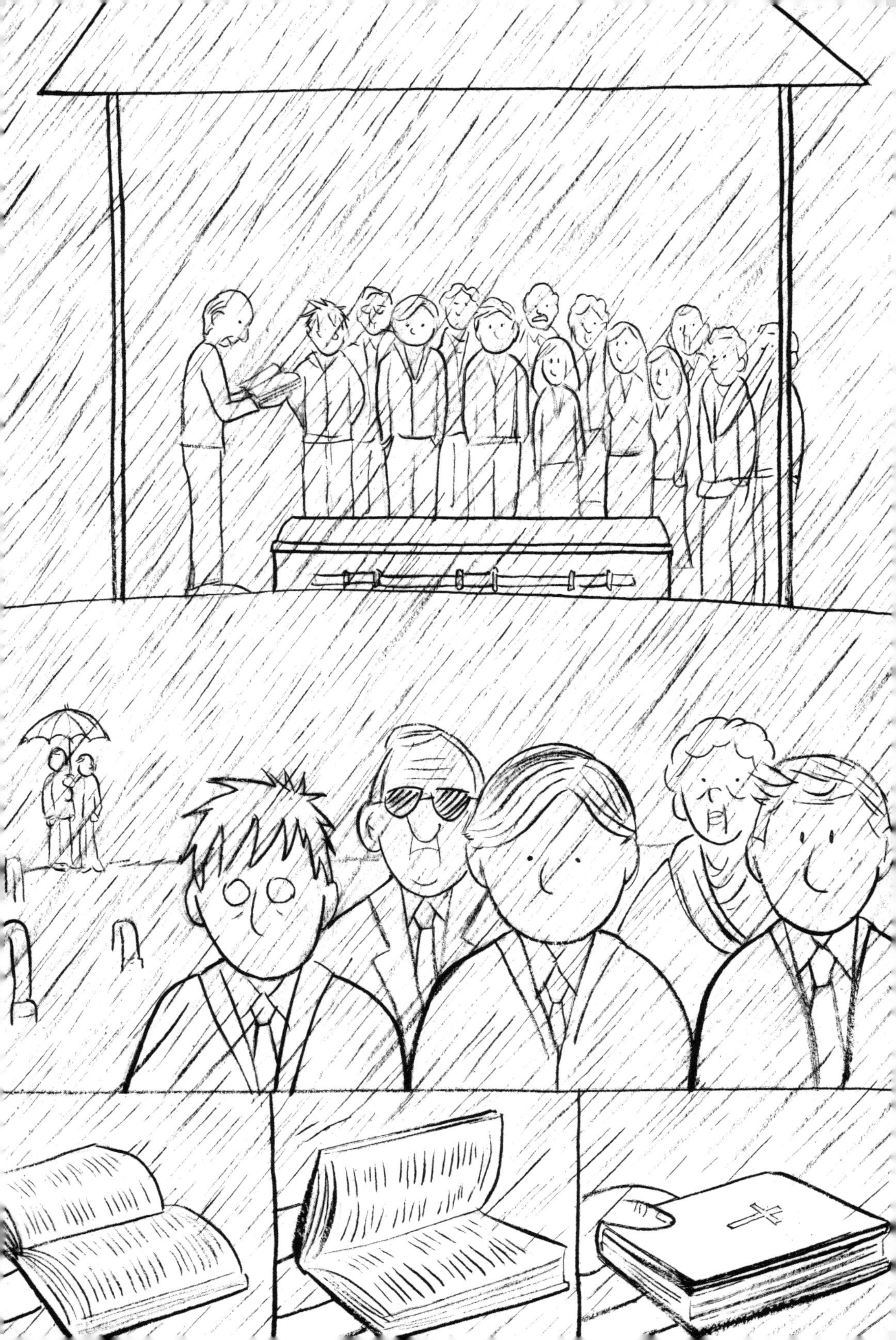

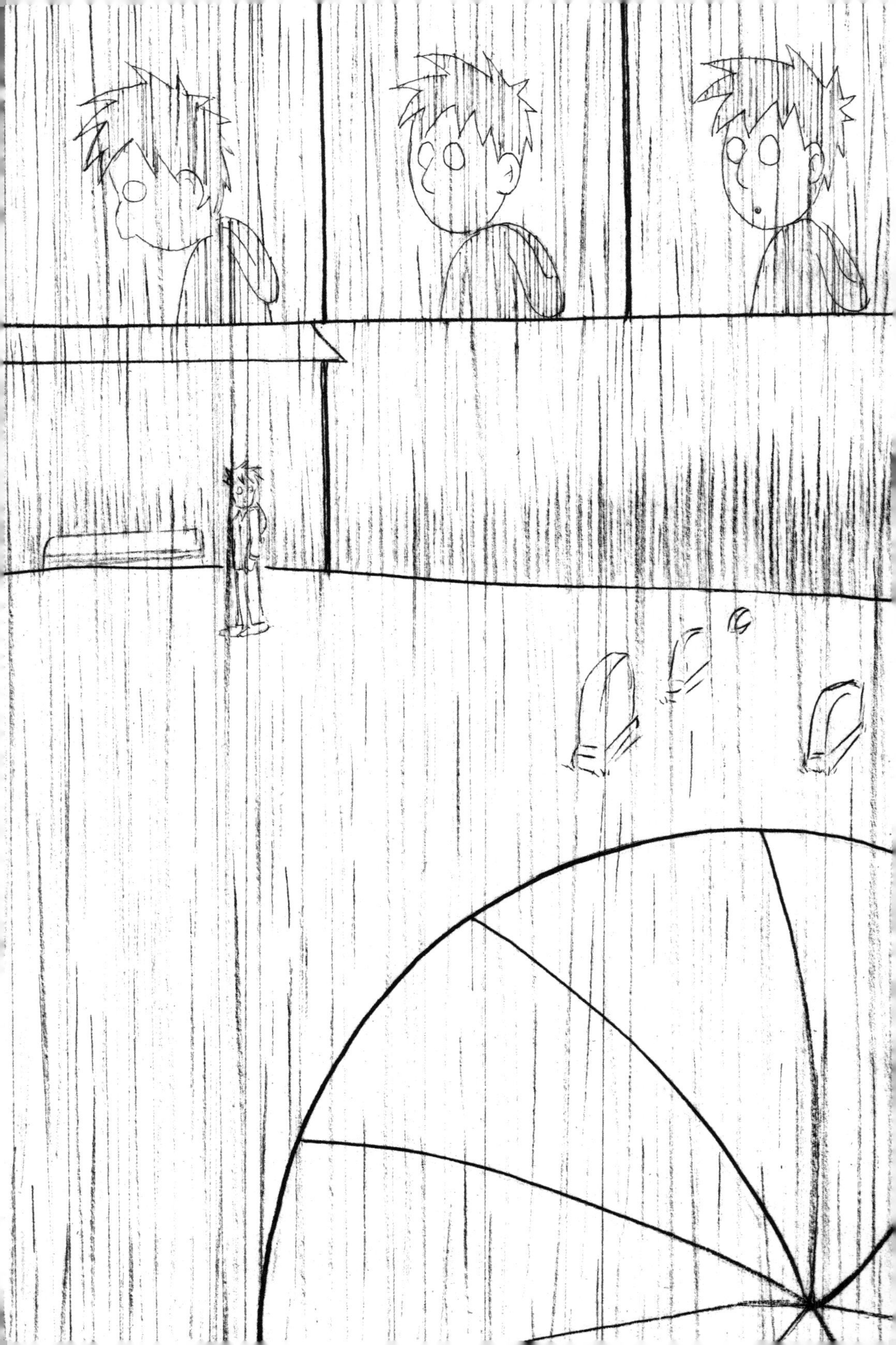

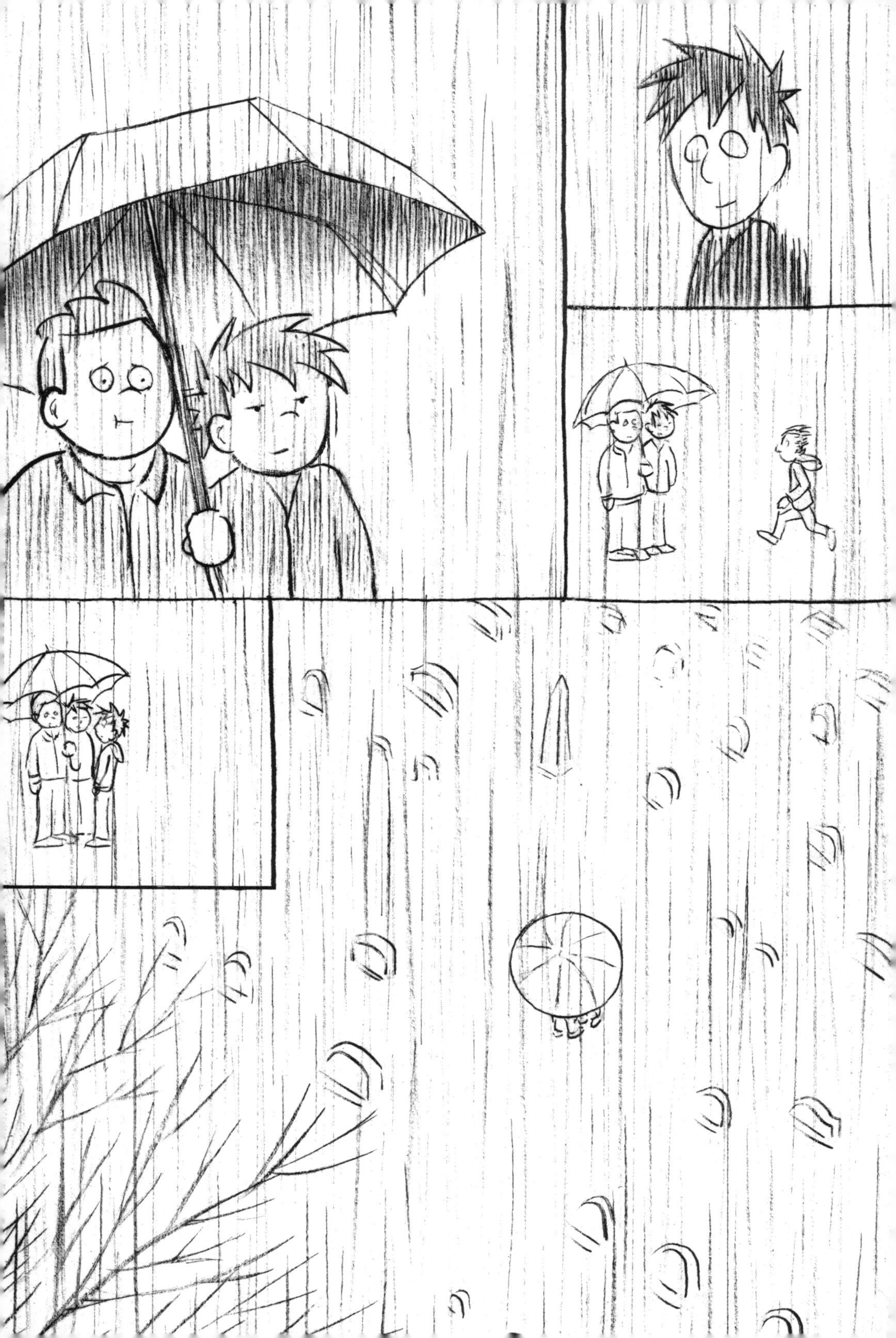

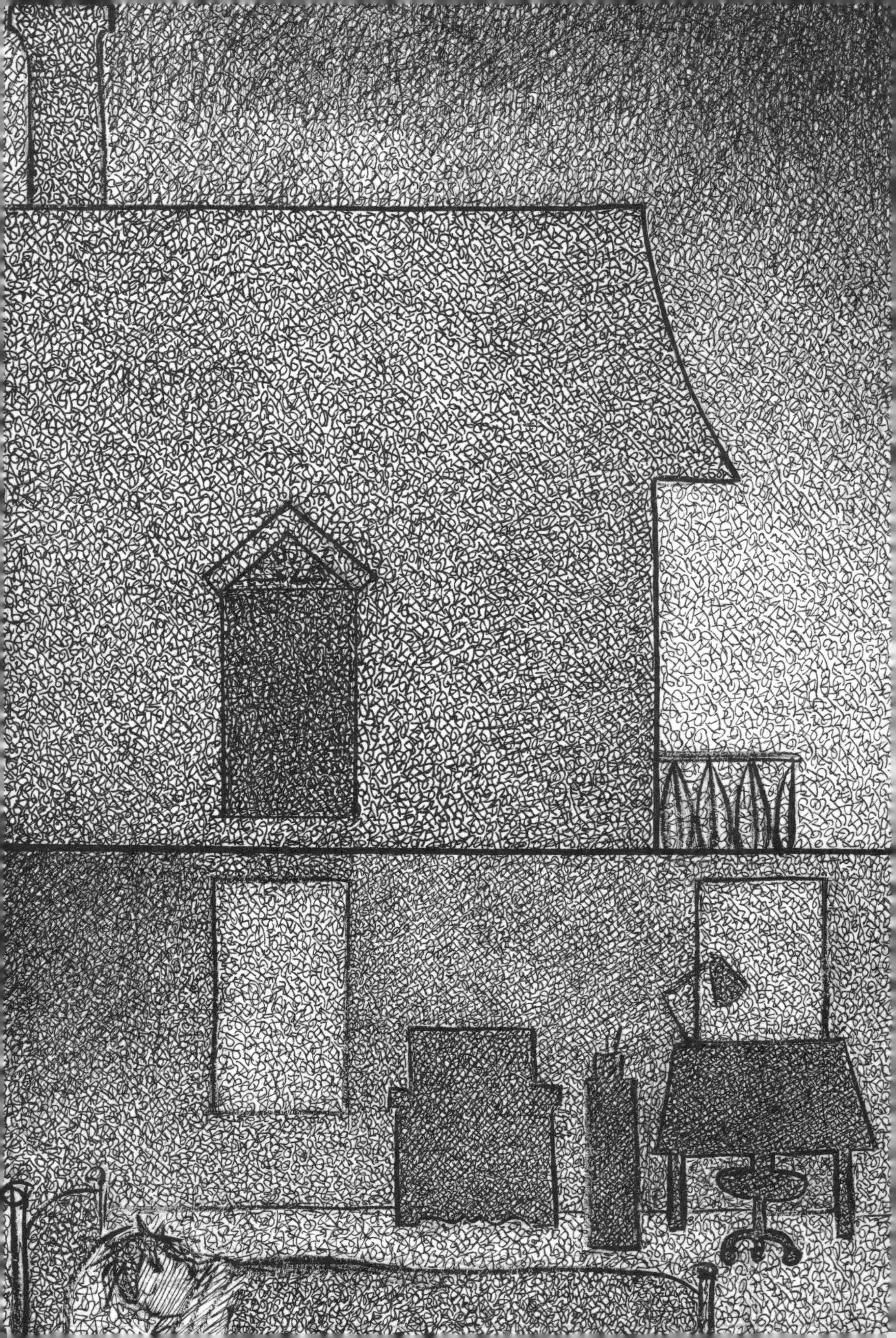

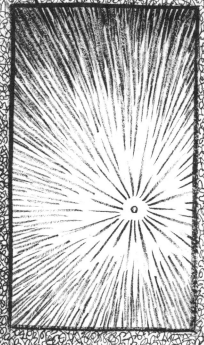

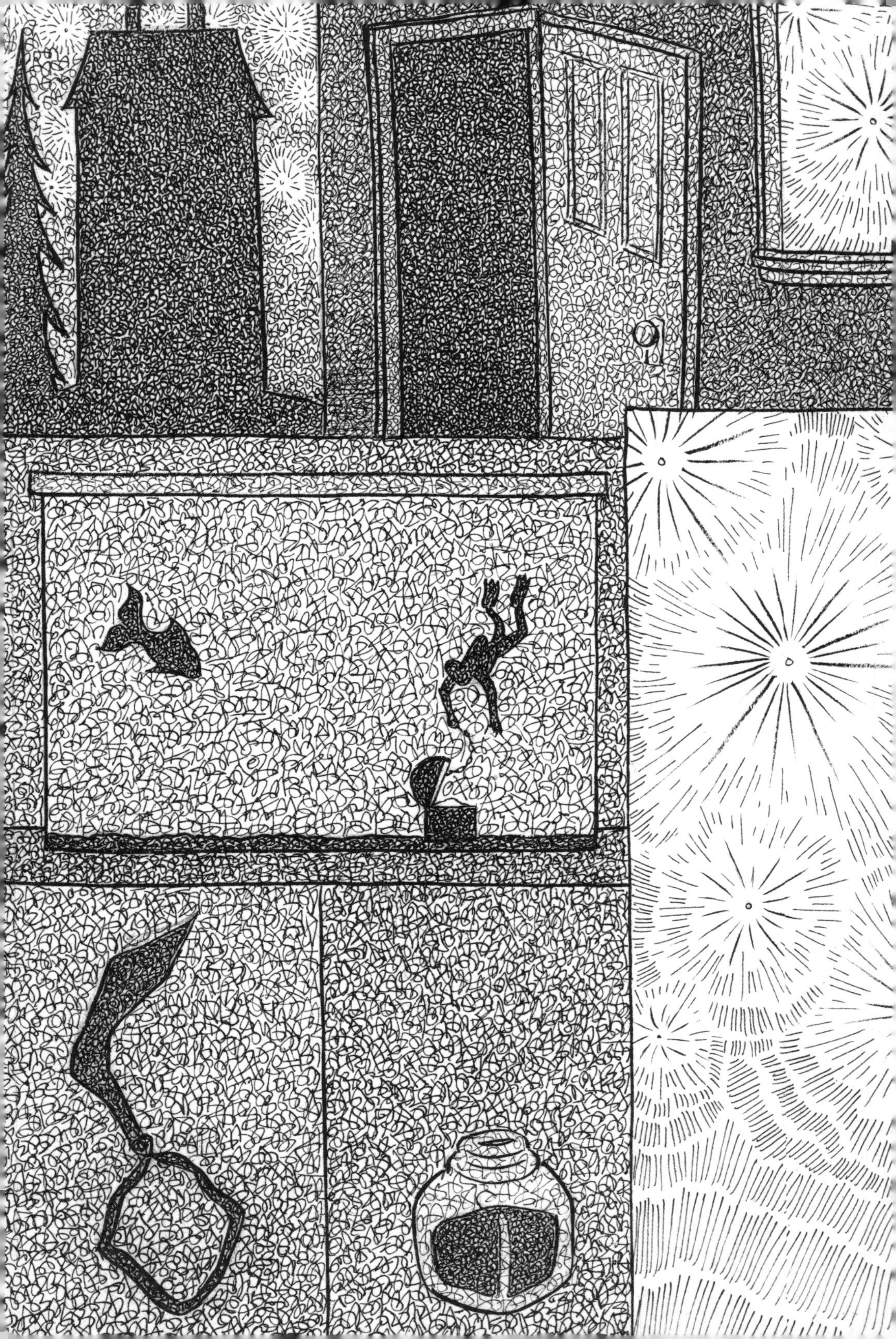

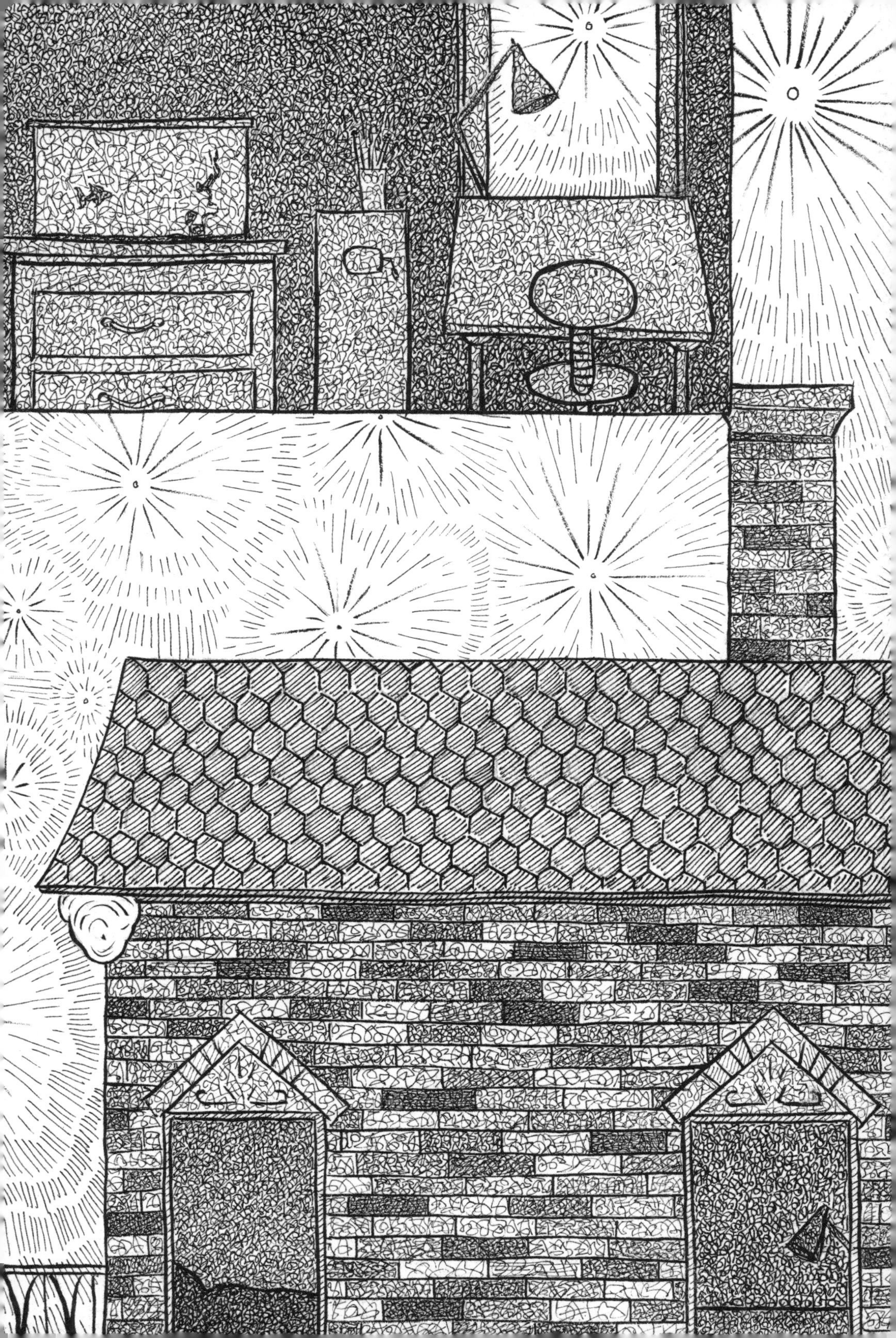

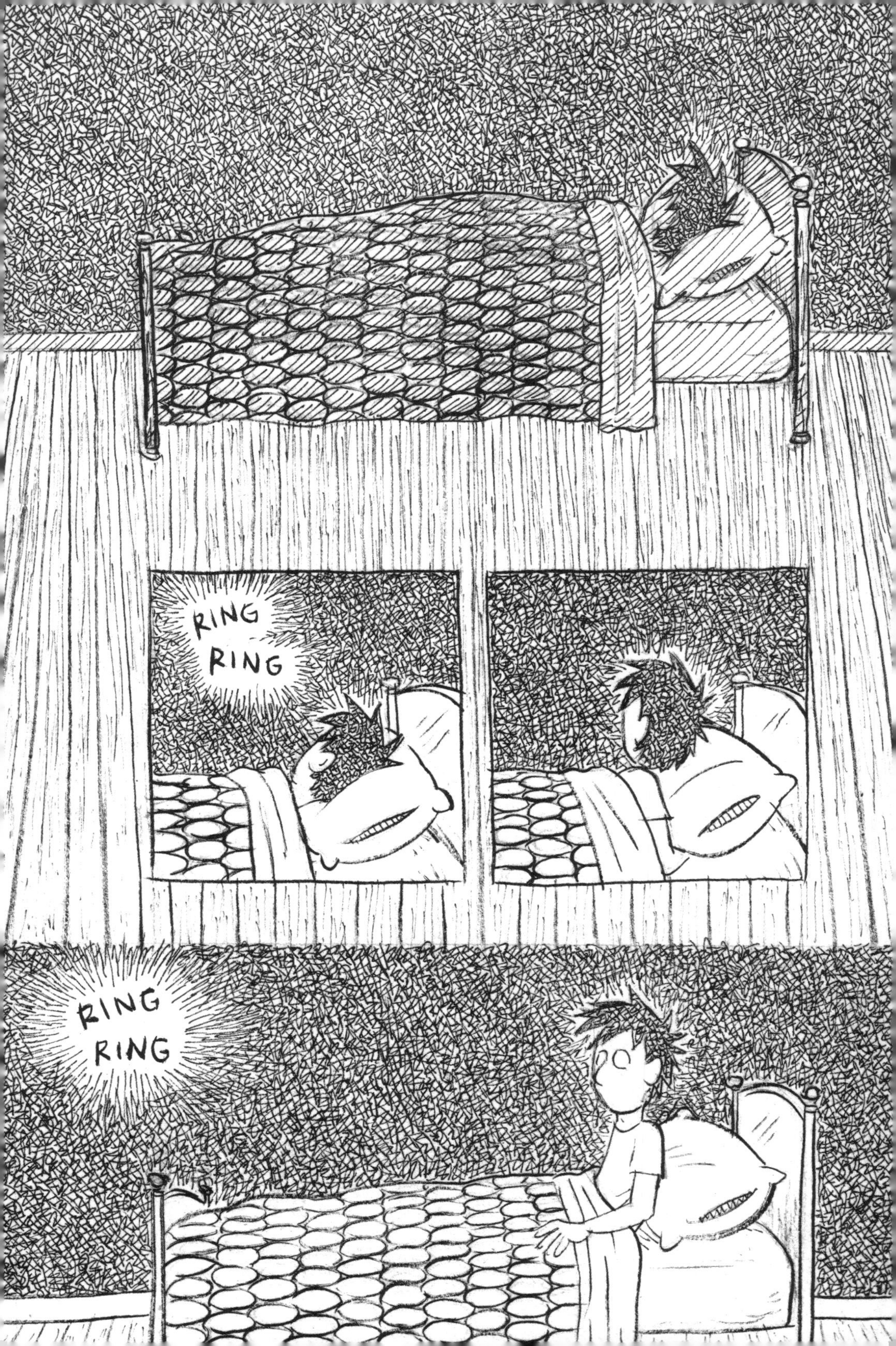
RING
RING
RING
RING

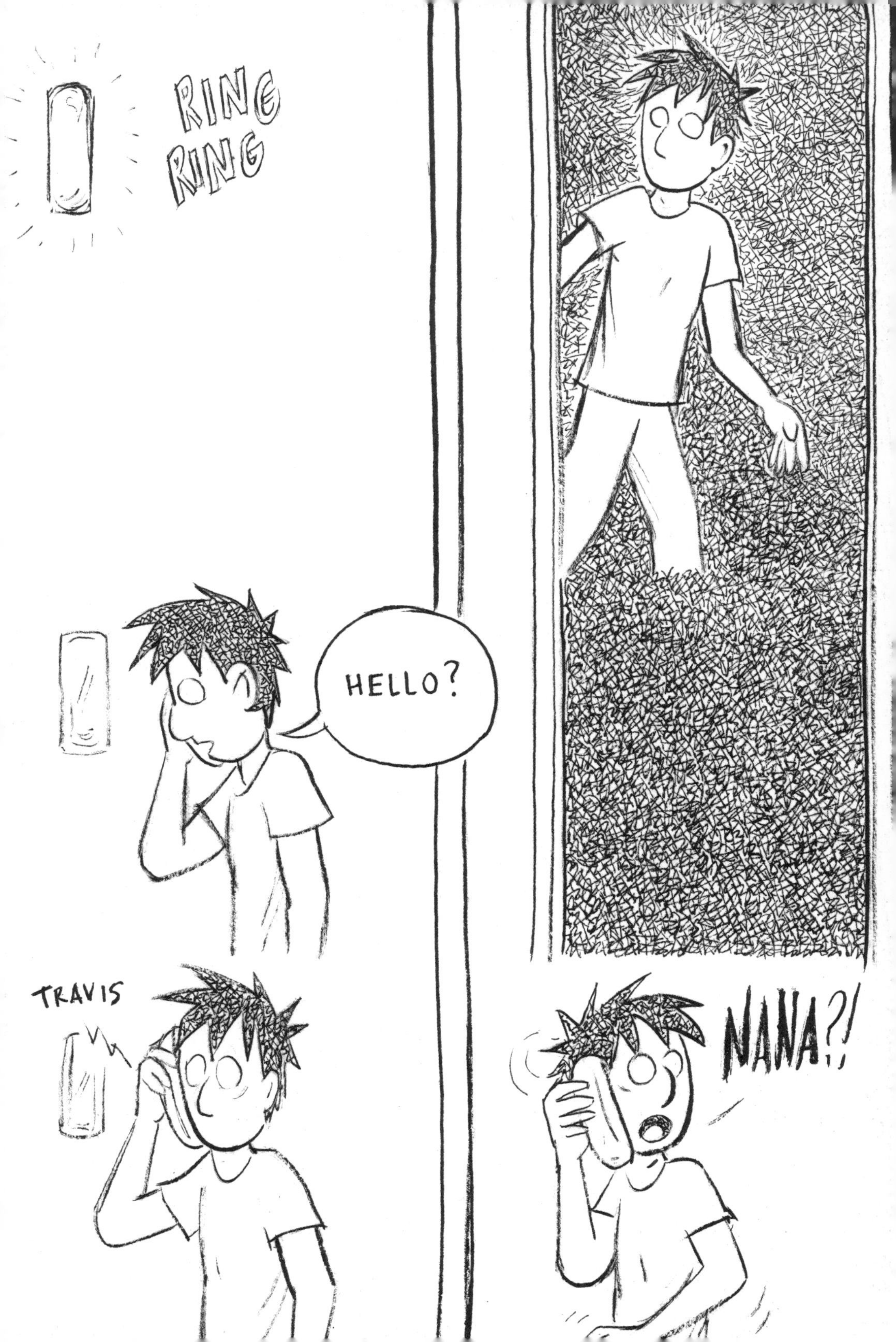
RING
RING
HELLO?
TRAVIS
NANA?!

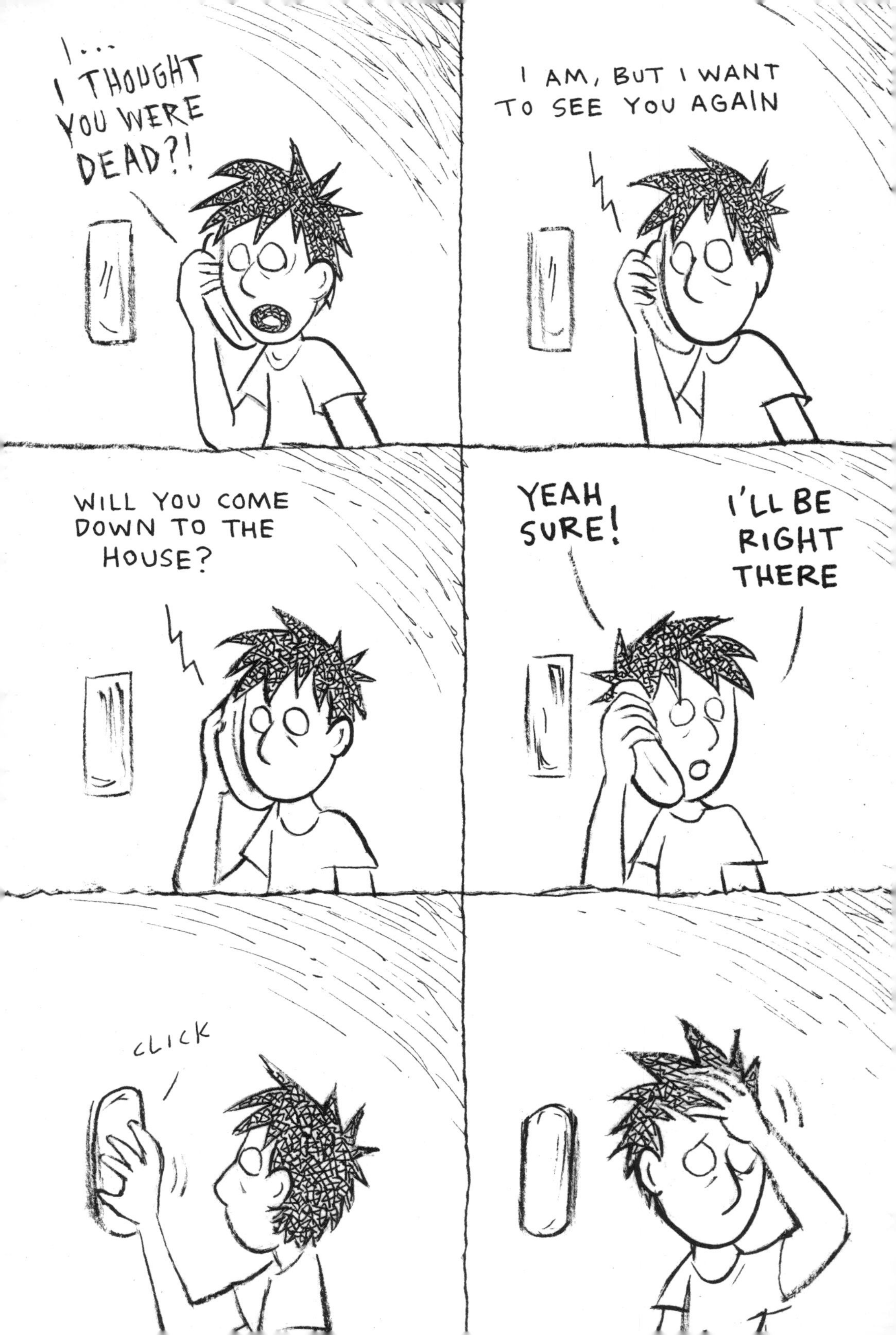
I...
I THOUGHT YOU WERE DEAD?!
I AM, BUT I WANT TO SEE YOU AGAIN
WILL YOU COME DOWN TO THE HOUSE?
YEAH SURE!
I'LL BE RIGHT THERE
CLICK

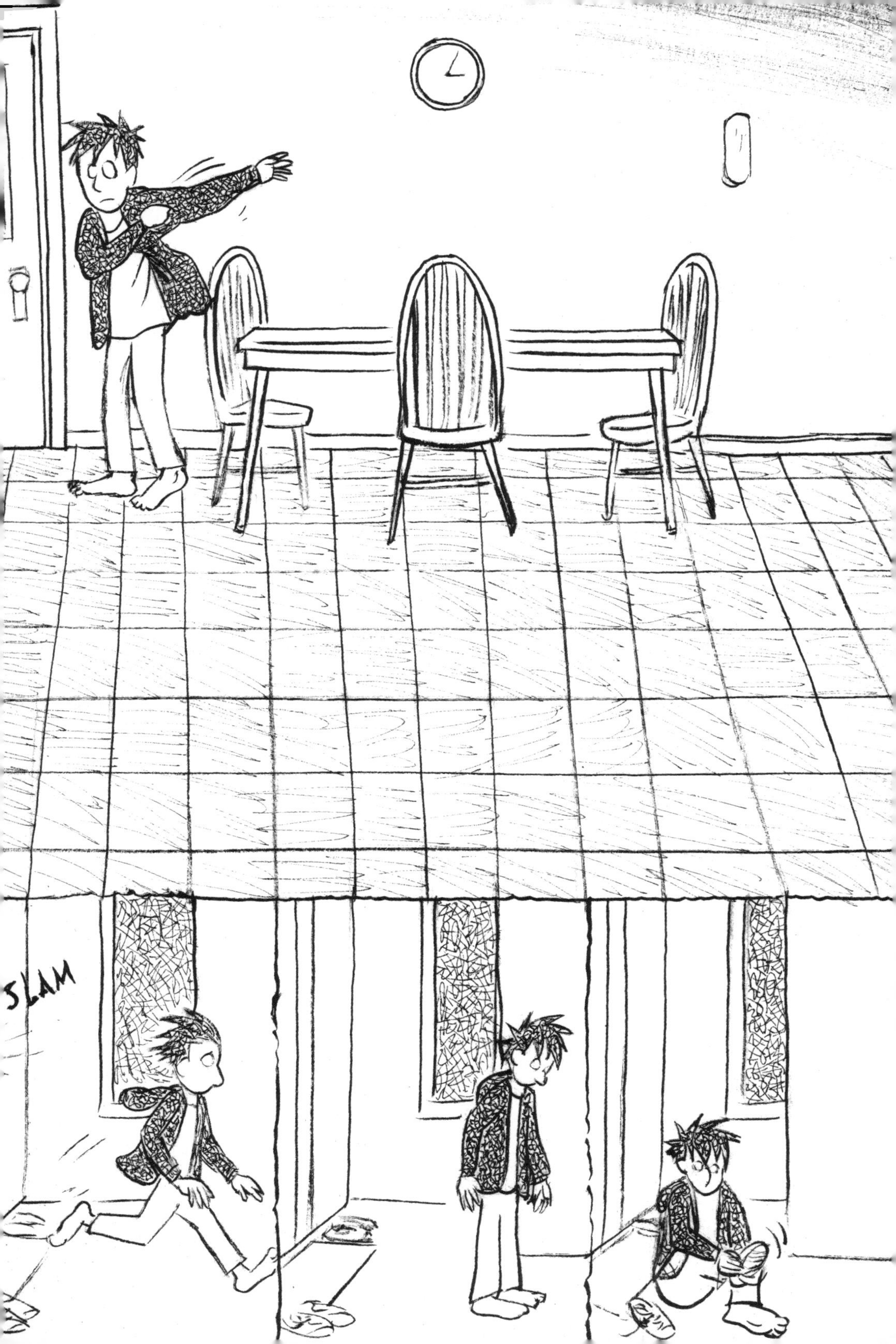
SLAM

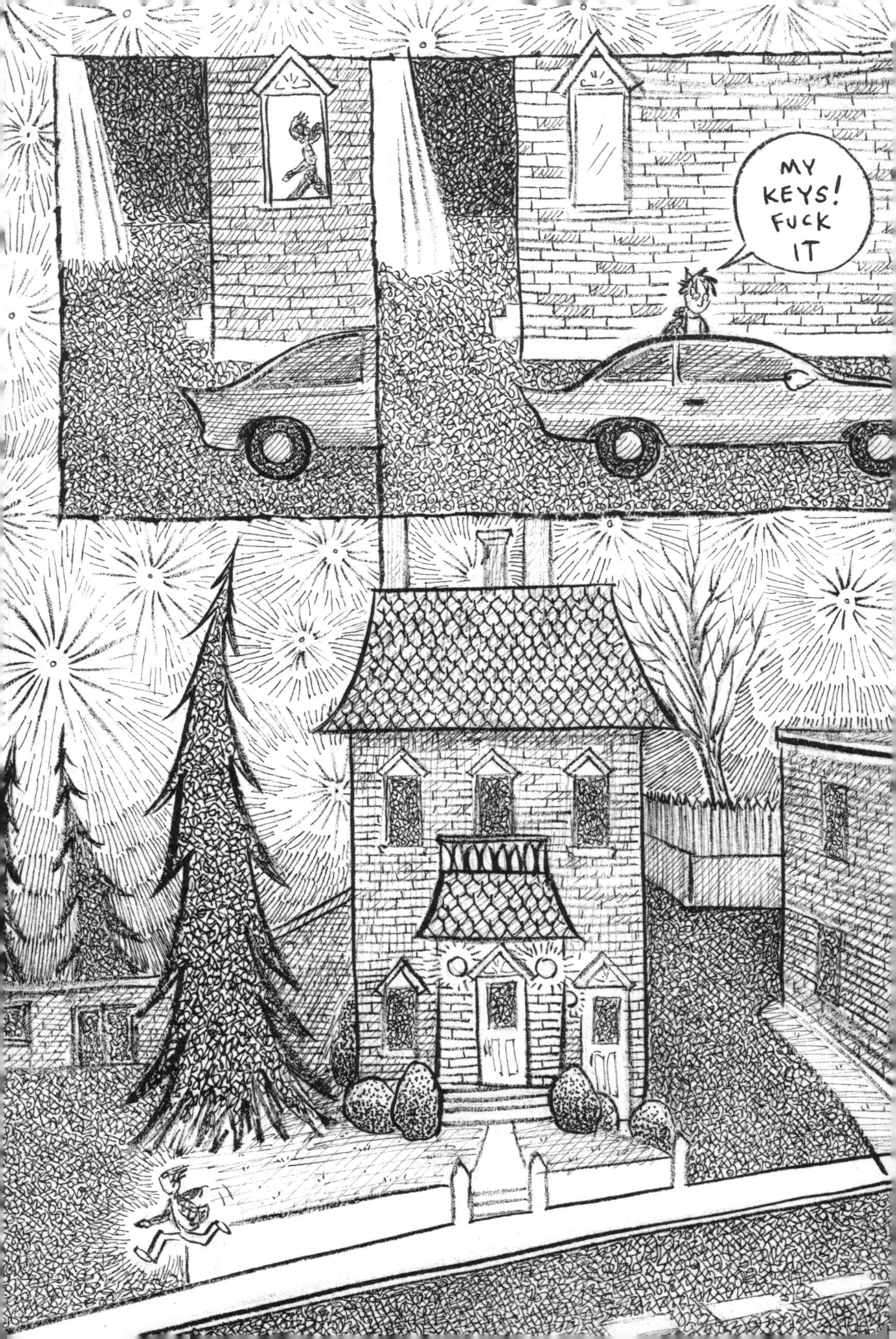
MY KEYS! FUCK IT

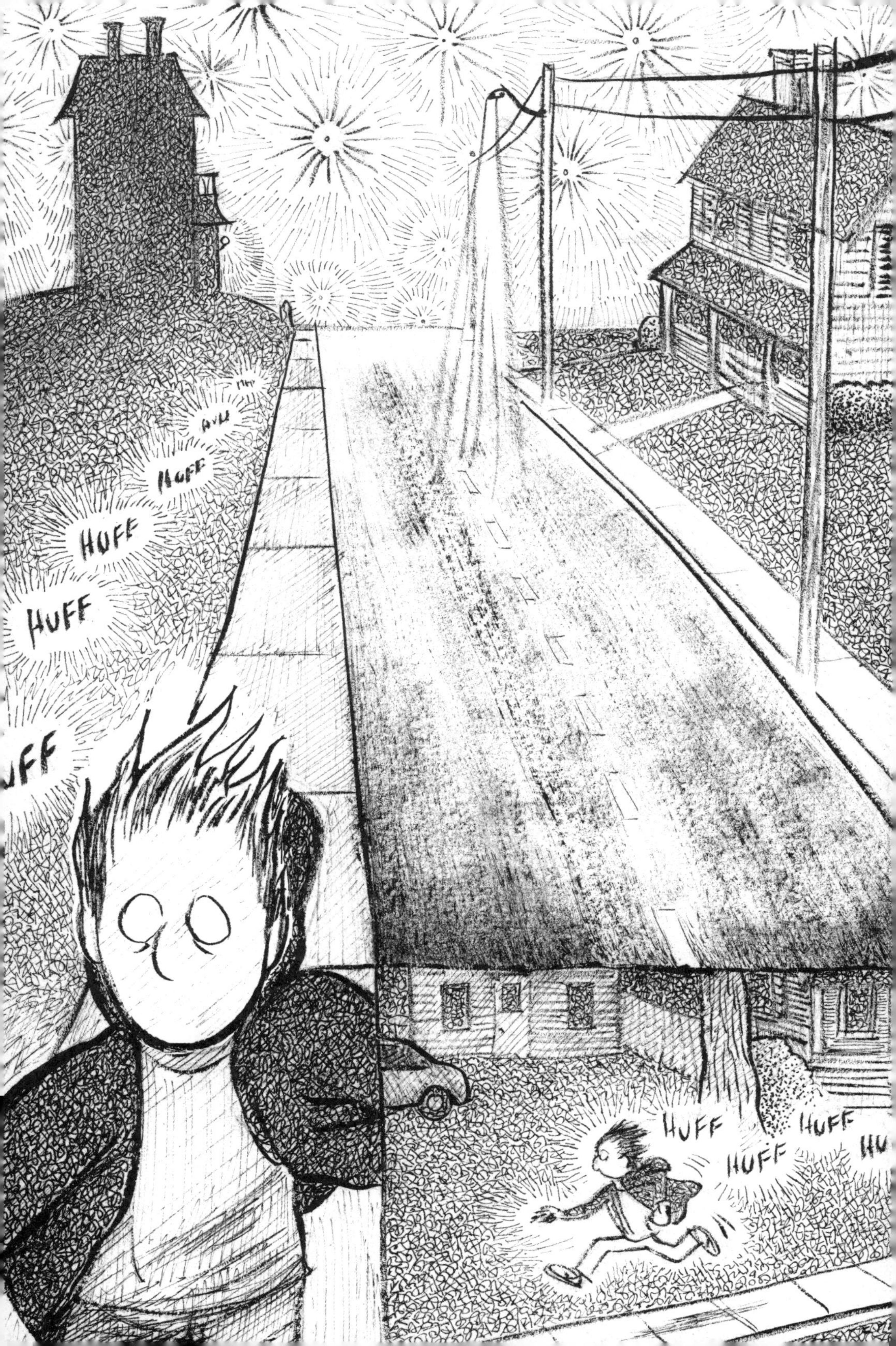
HUFF
HUFF
HUFF
HUFF
UFF
HUFF
HUFF
HUFF

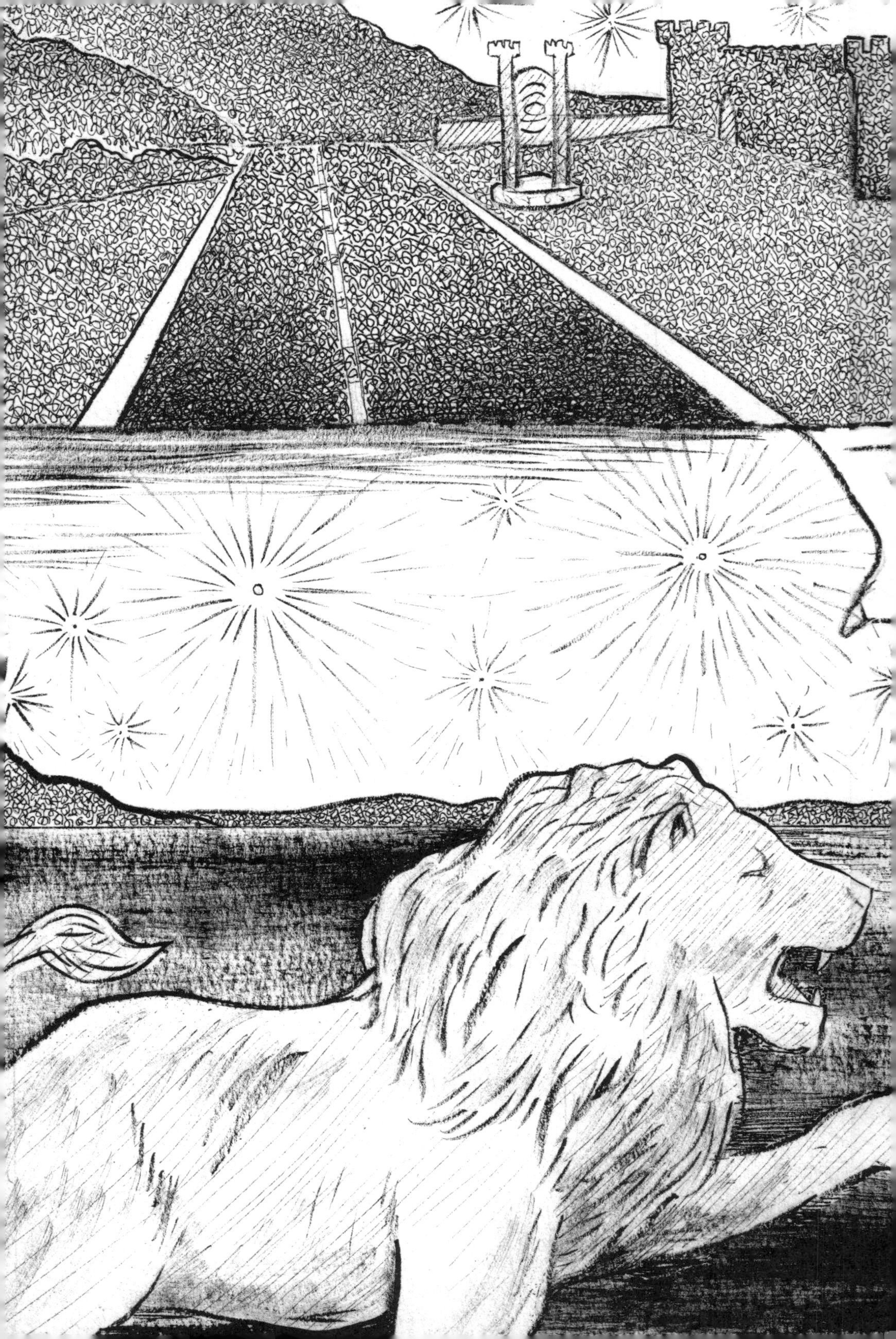

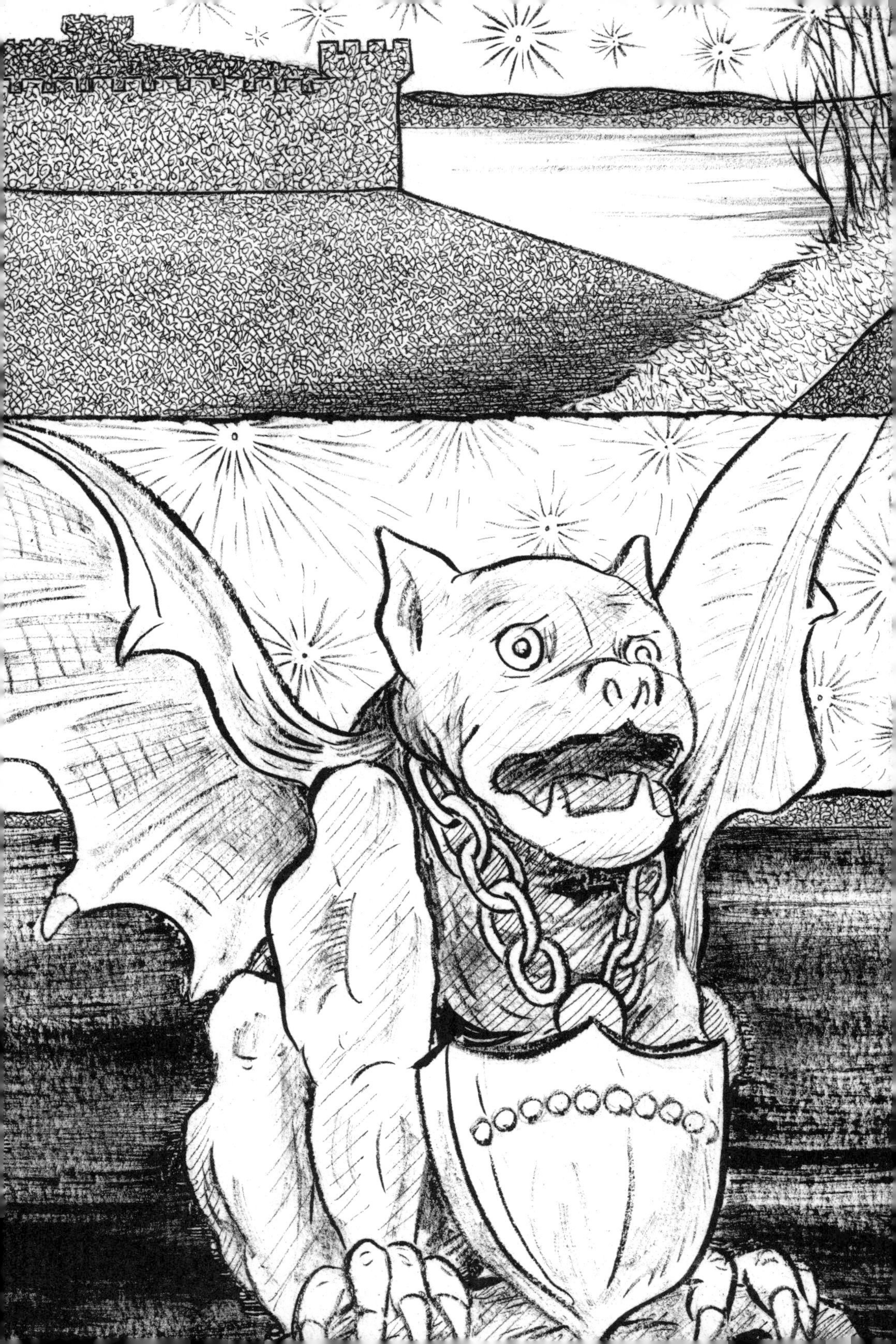

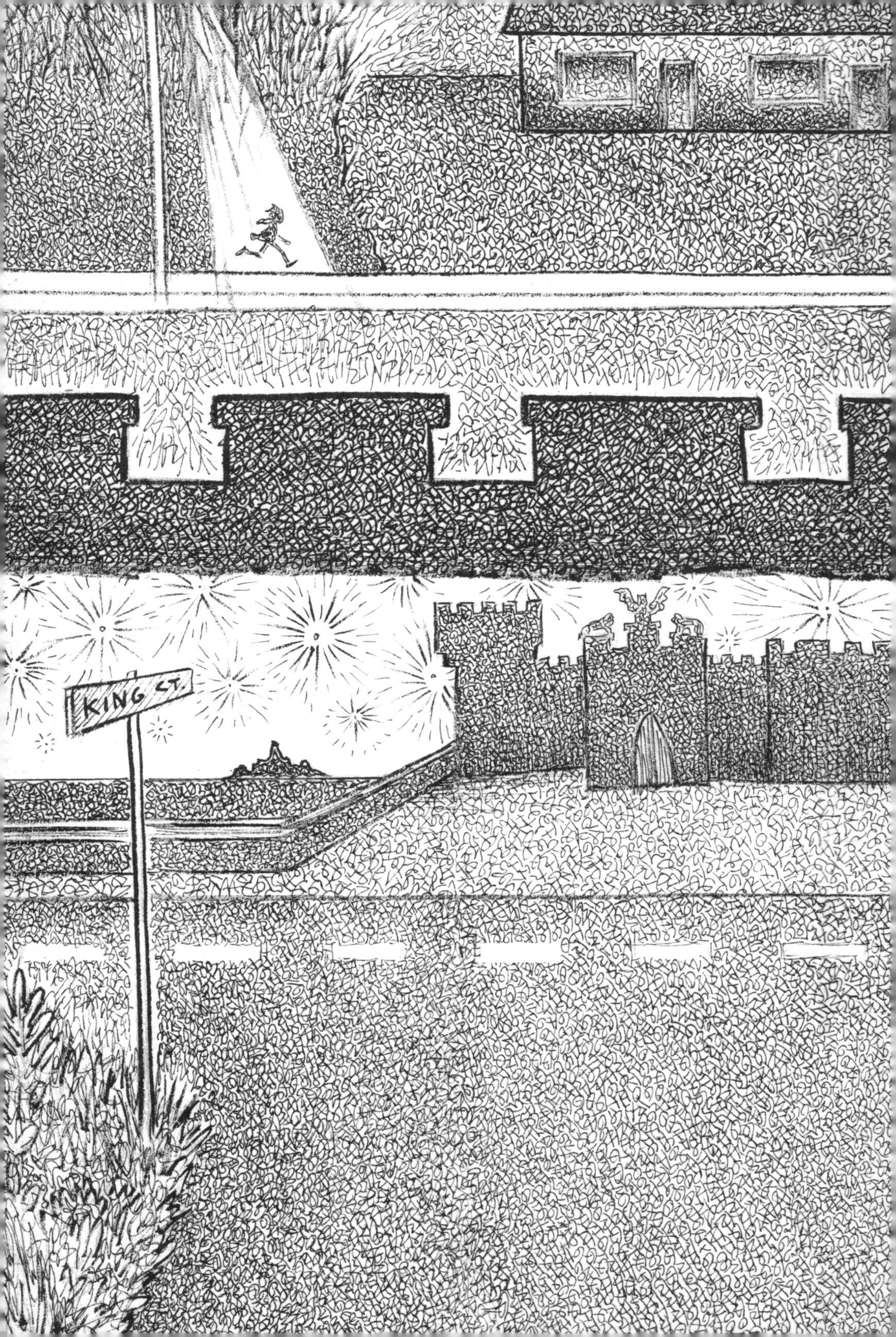
KING ST.

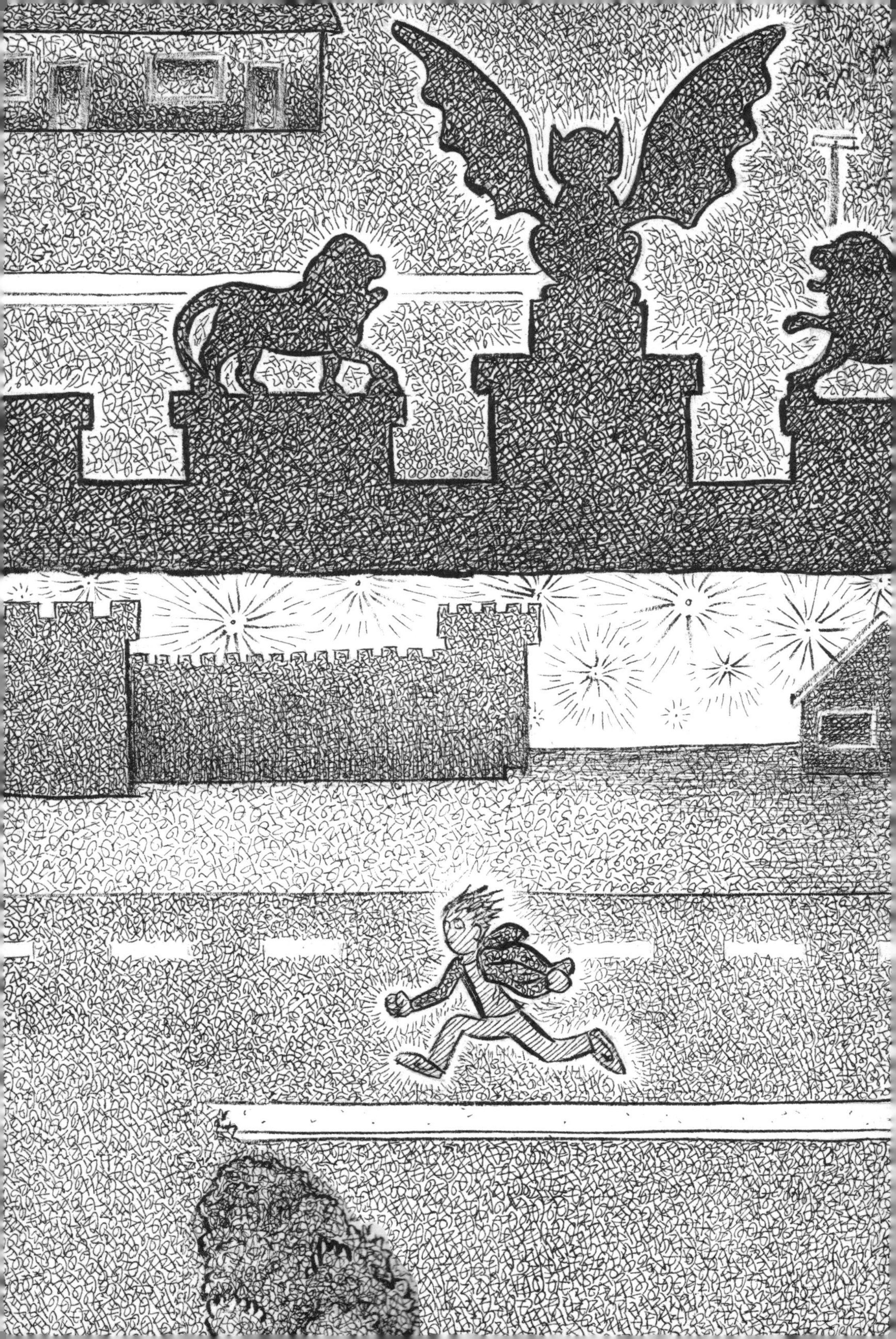

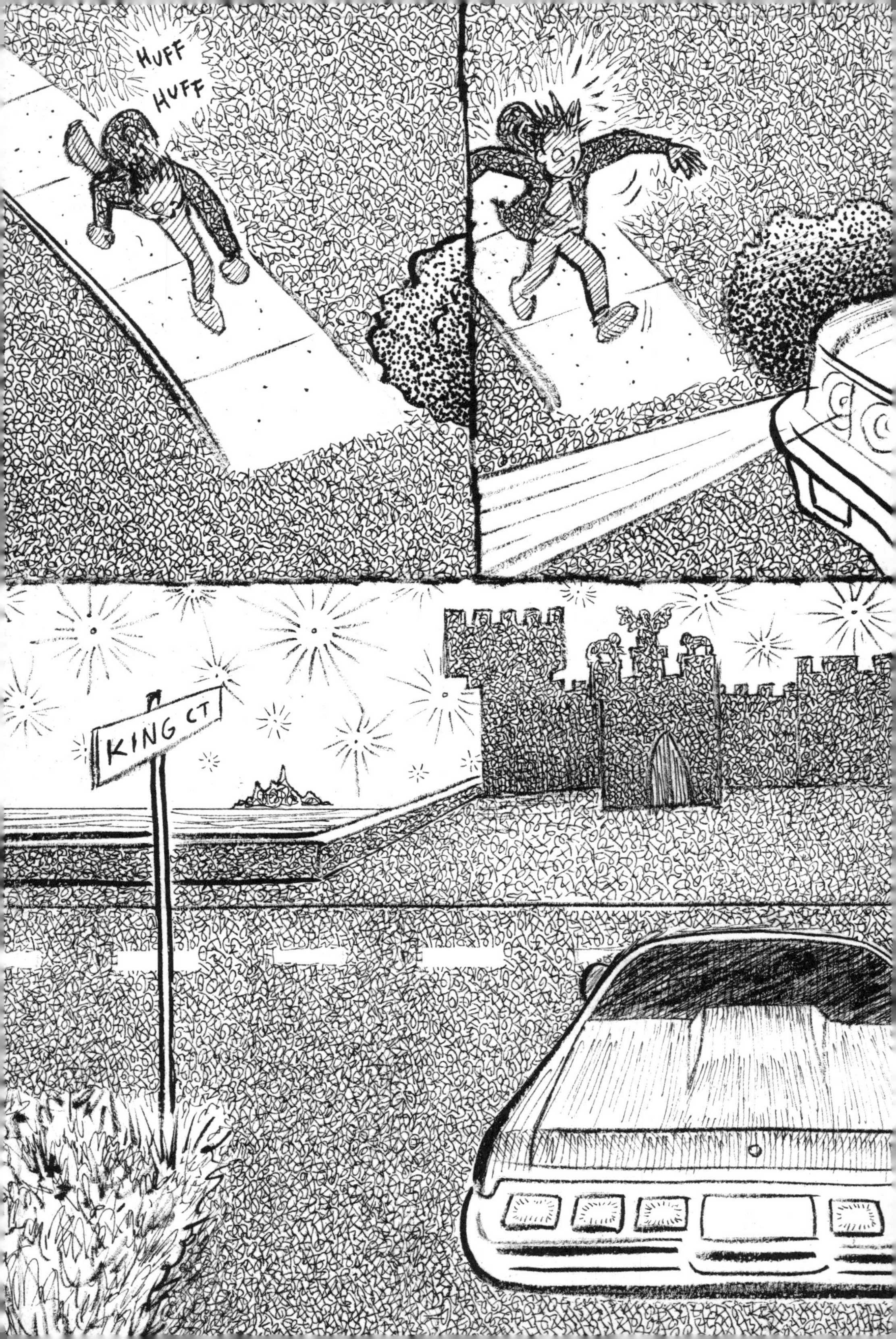
HUFF
HUFF
KING CT

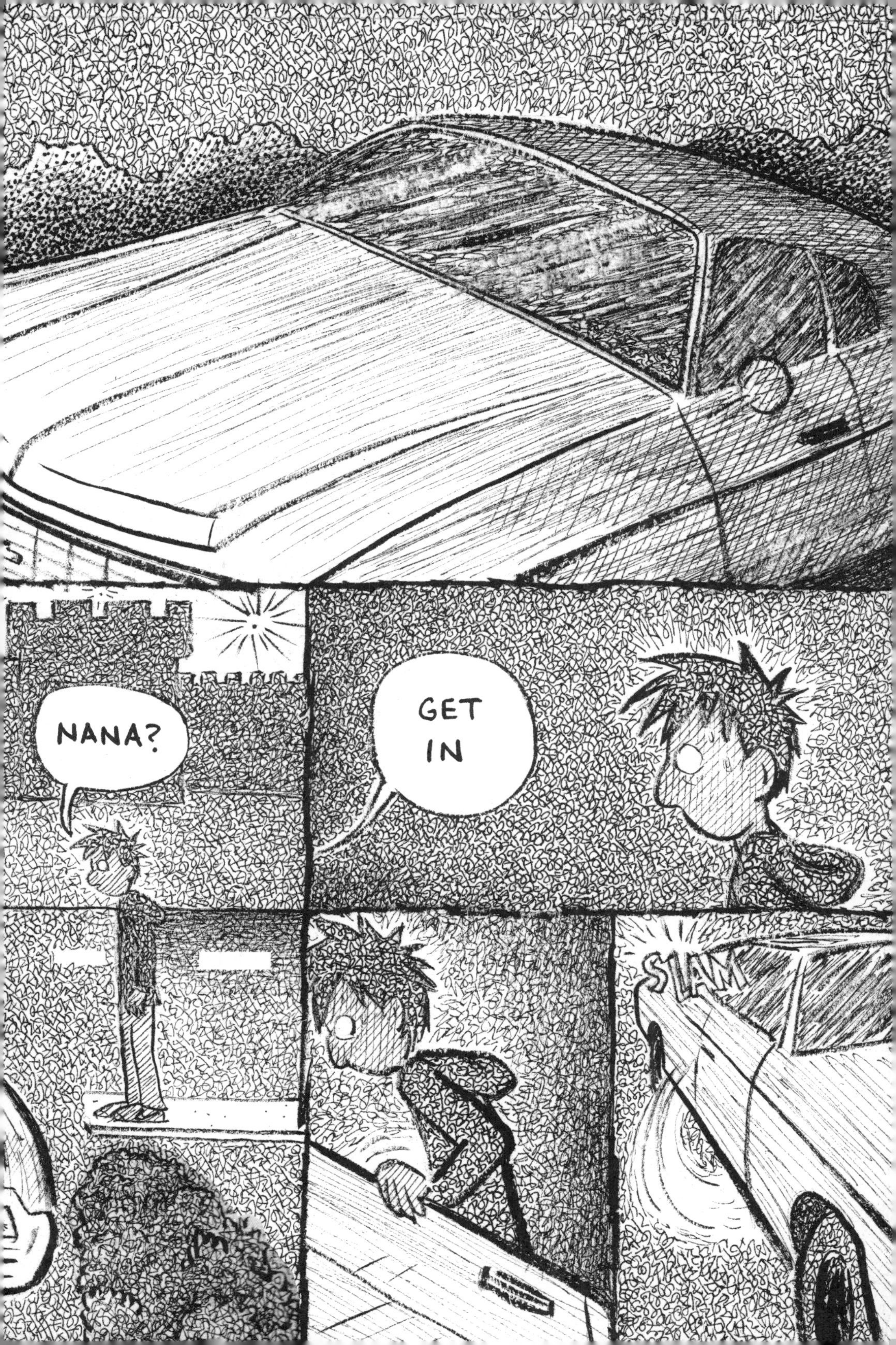
NANA?
GET IN
SLAM

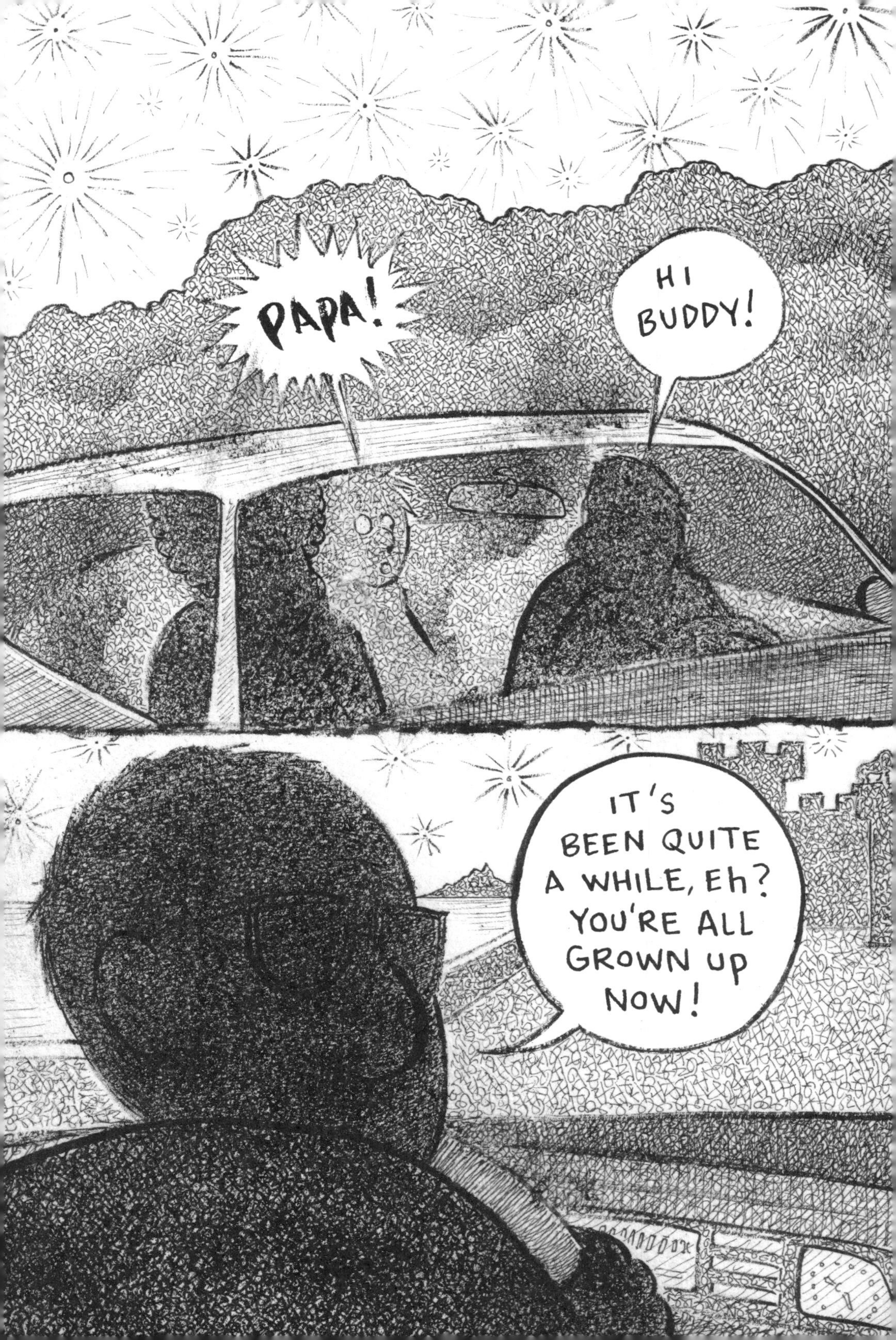
PAPA!
HI BUDDY!
IT'S BEEN QUITE A WHILE, Eh? YOU'RE ALL GROWN UP NOW!

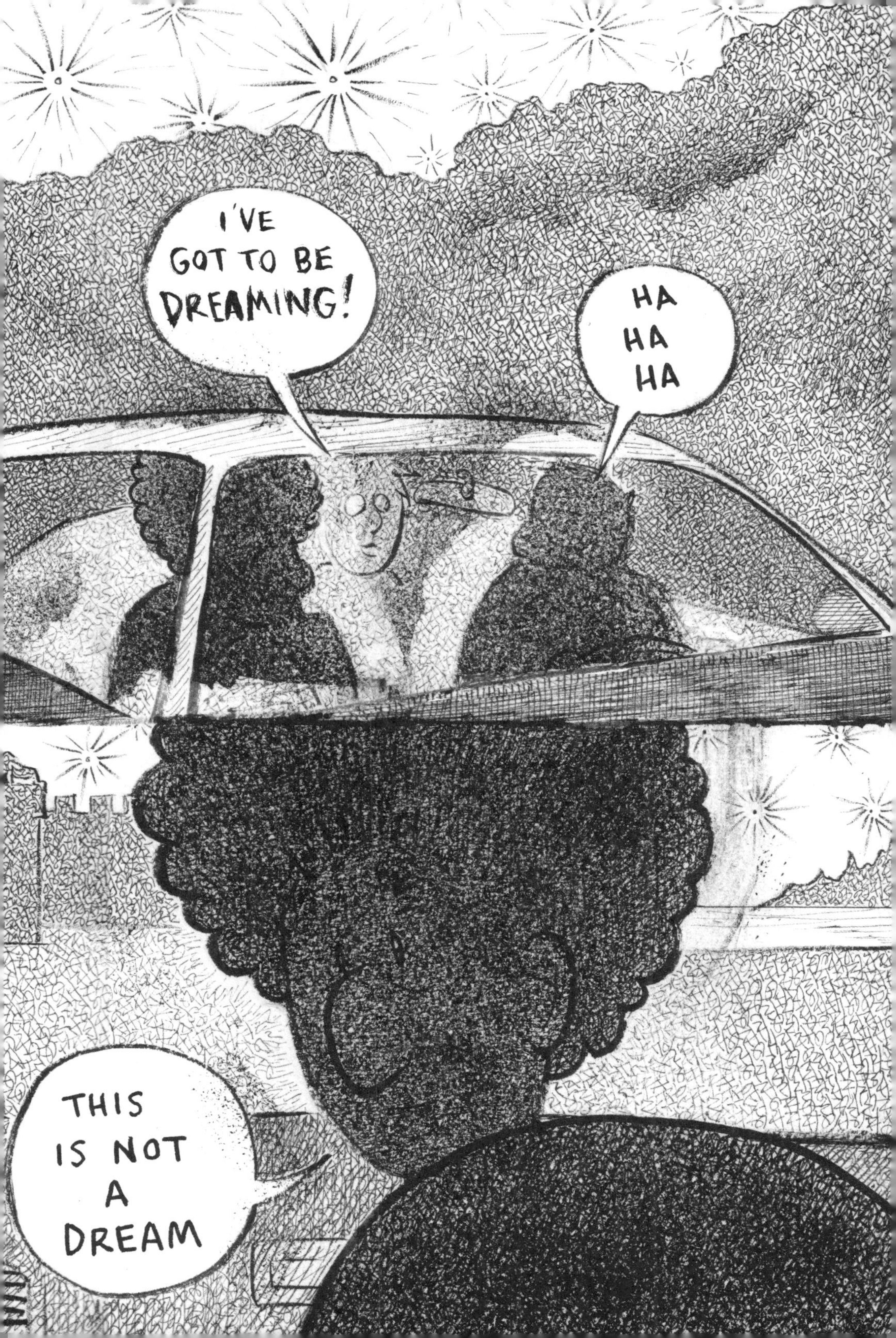
I'VE GOT TO BE DREAMING!
HA HA HA
THIS IS NOT A DREAM

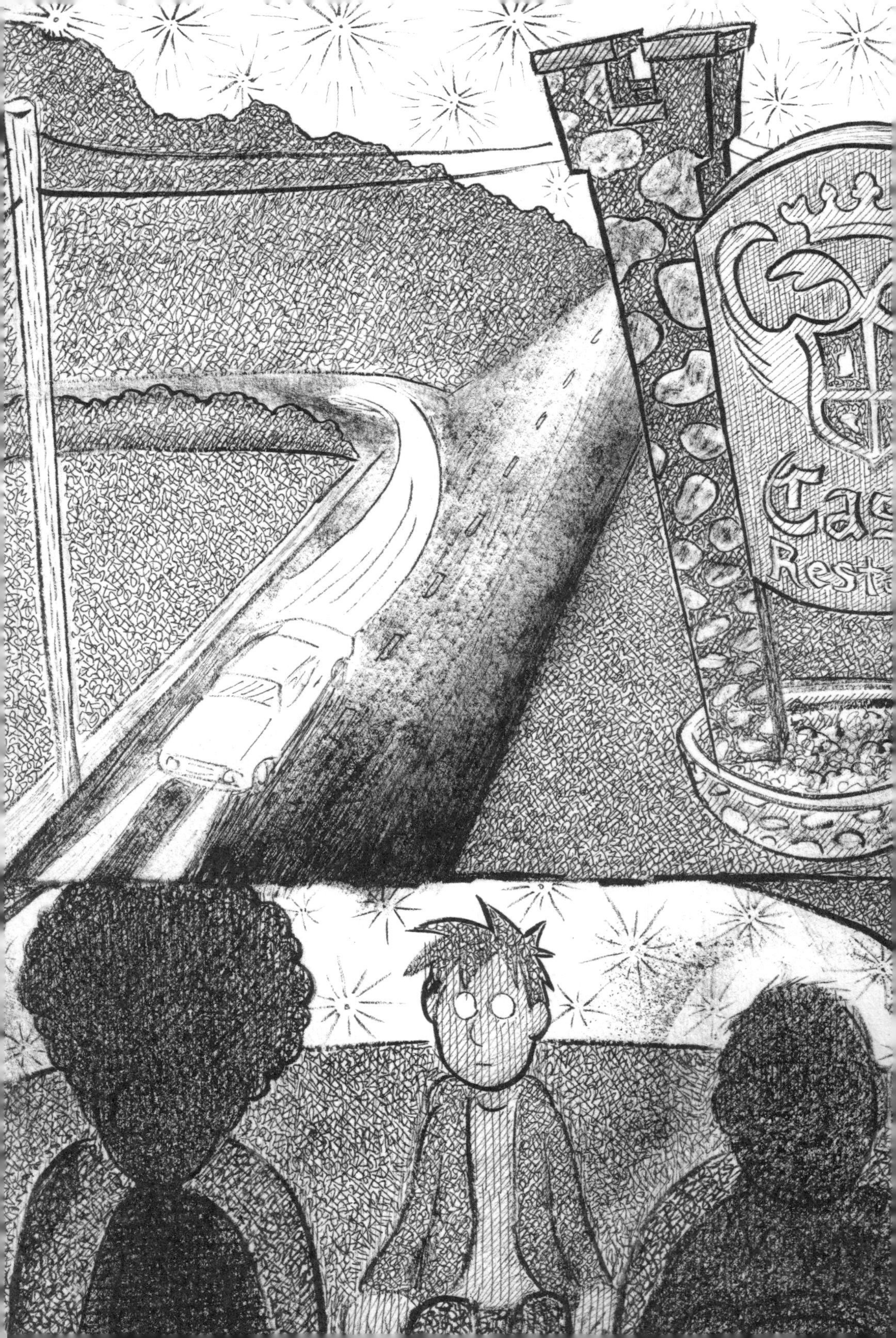
Cas
Resta

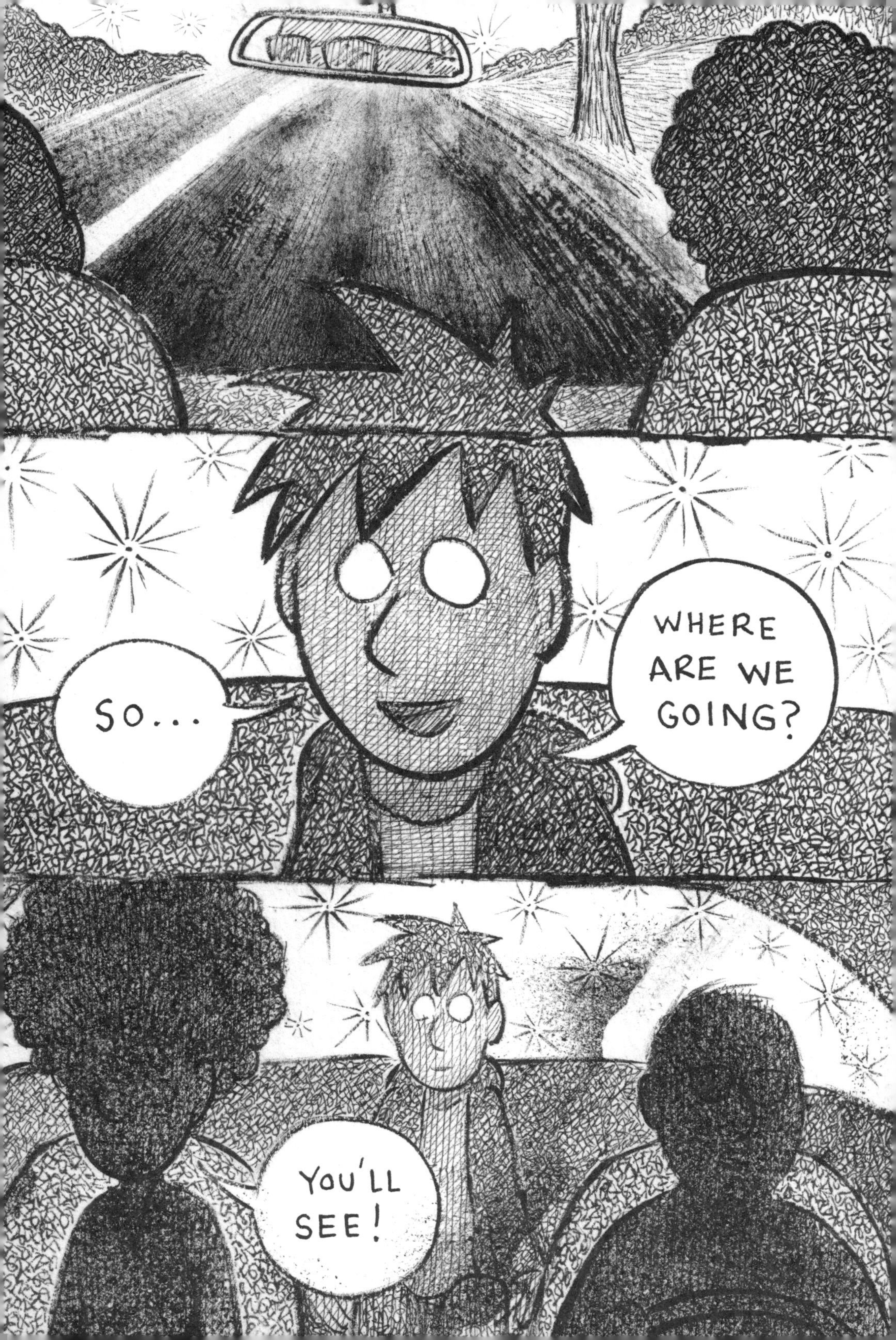
SO...
WHERE ARE WE GOING?
YOU'LL SEE!

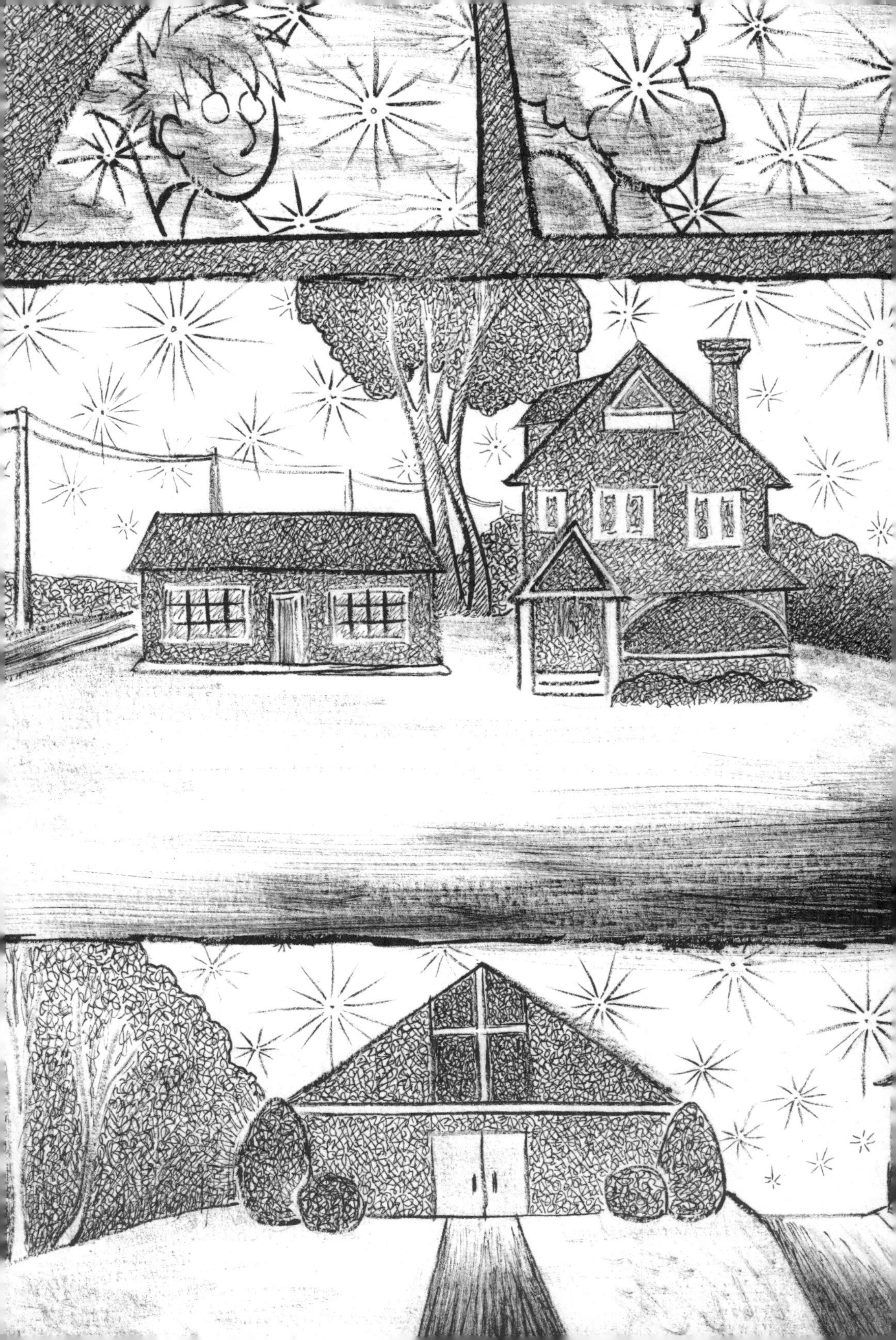

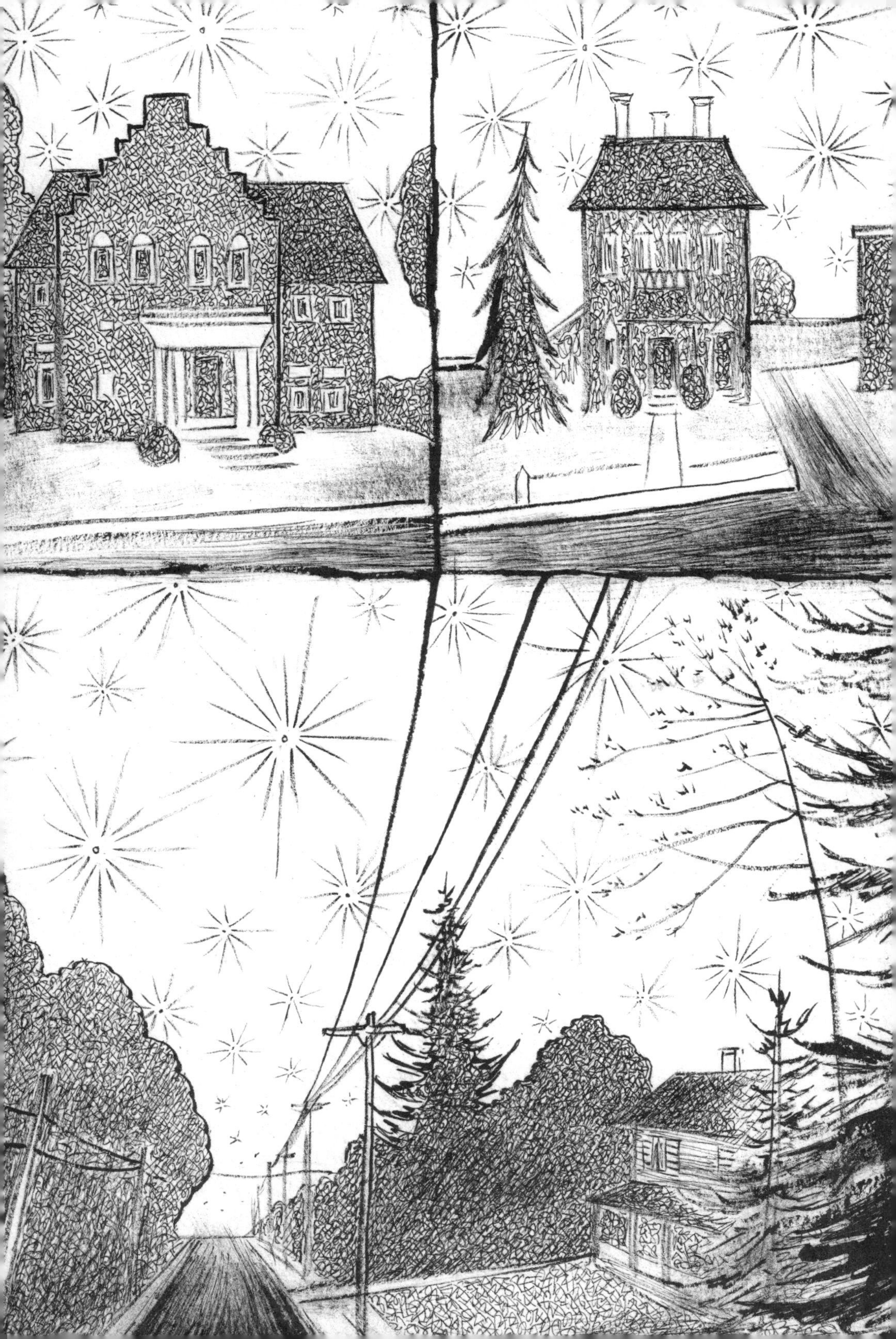

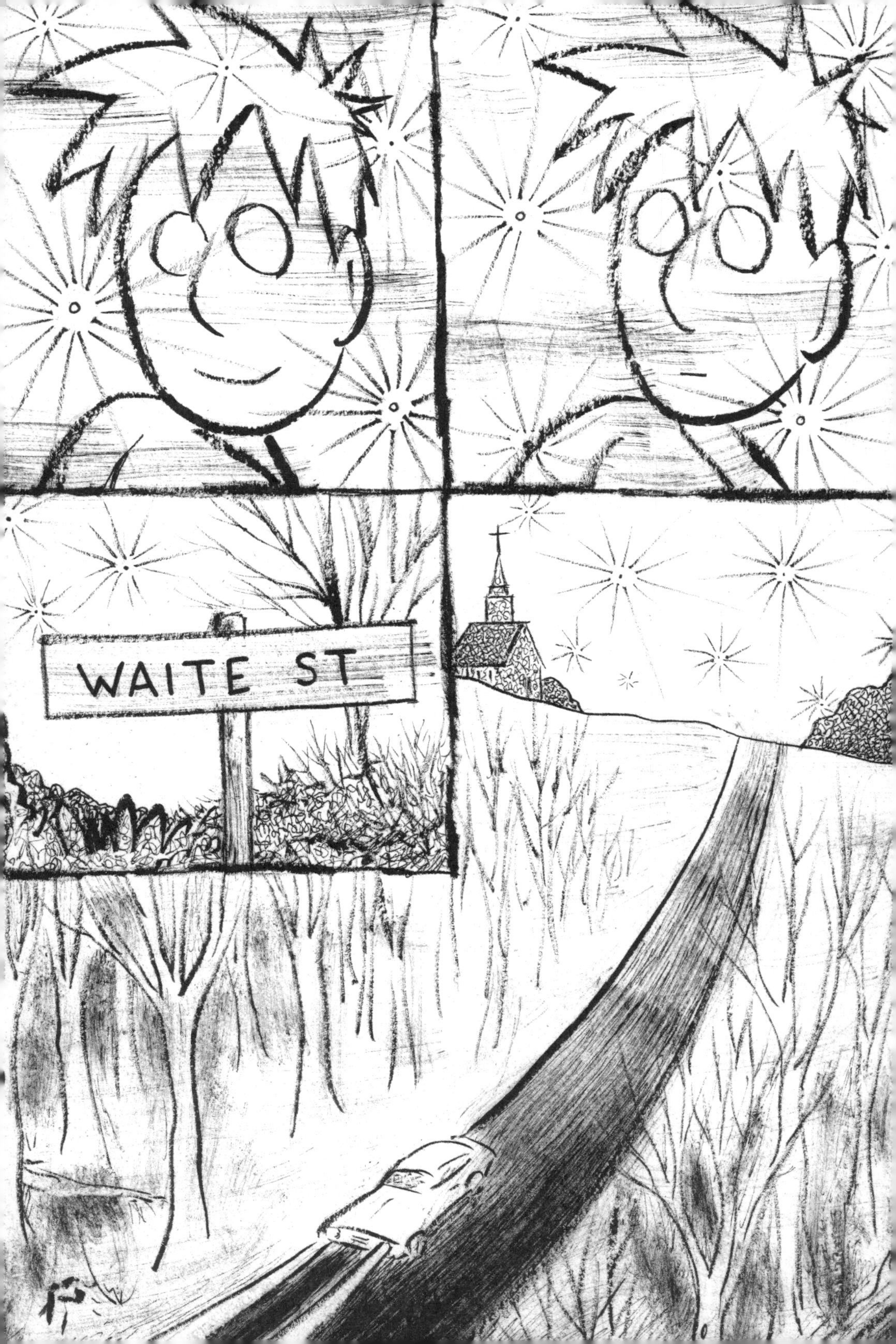
WAITE ST

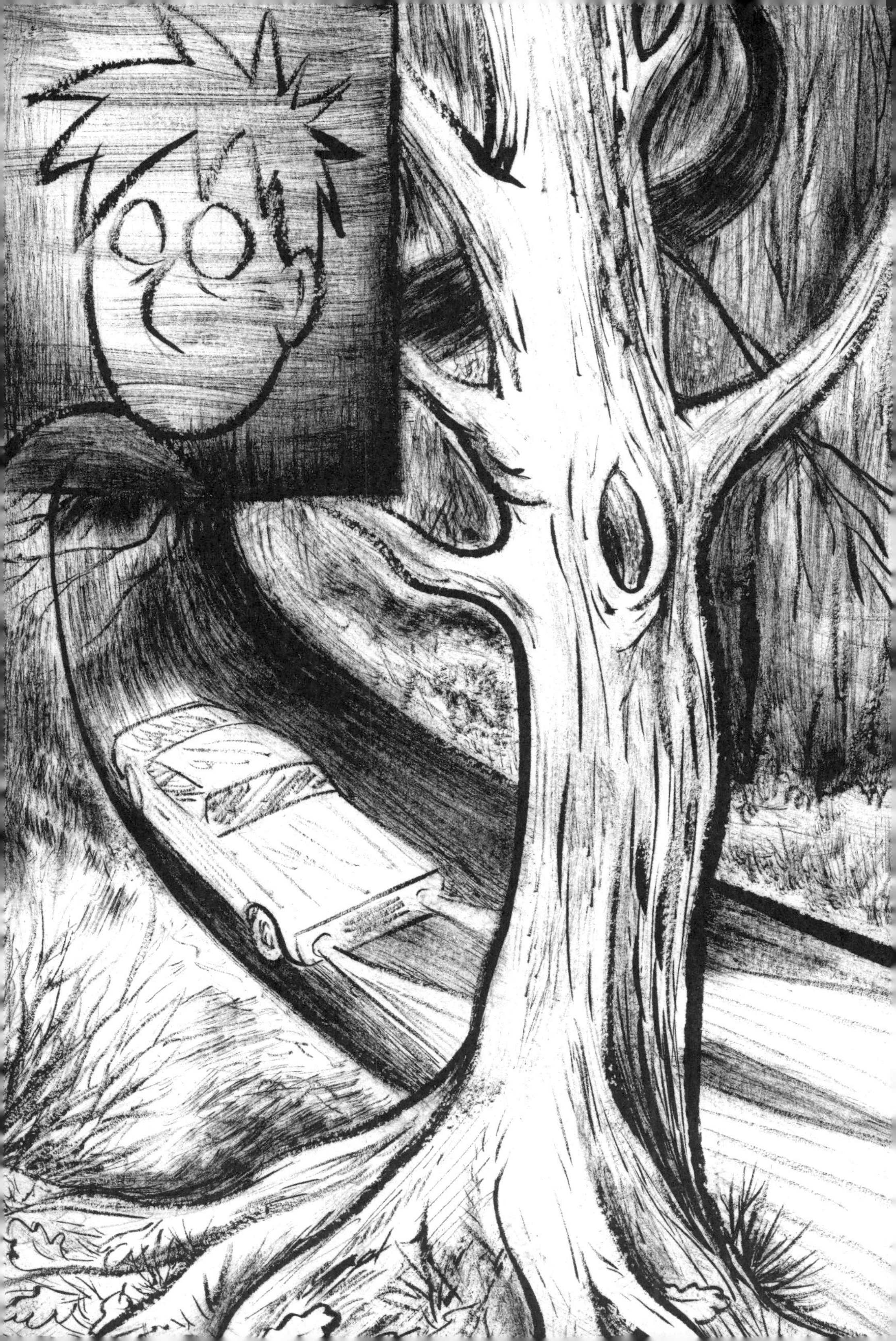

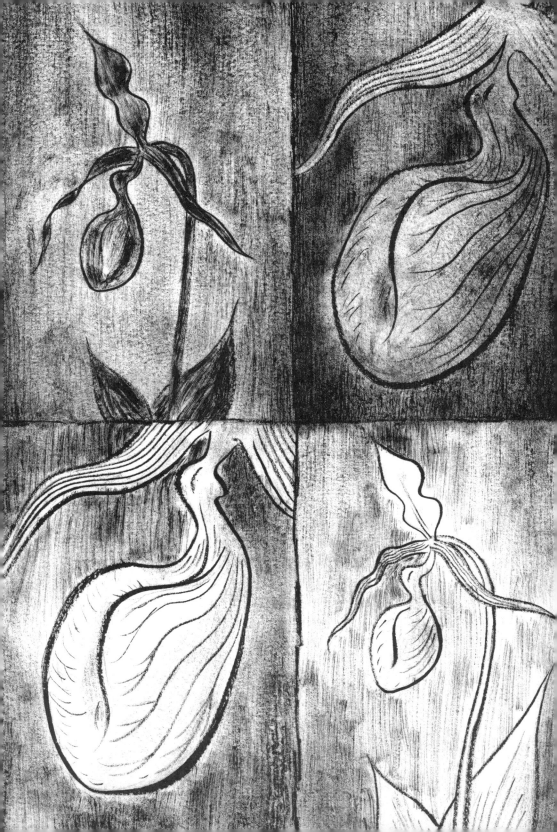

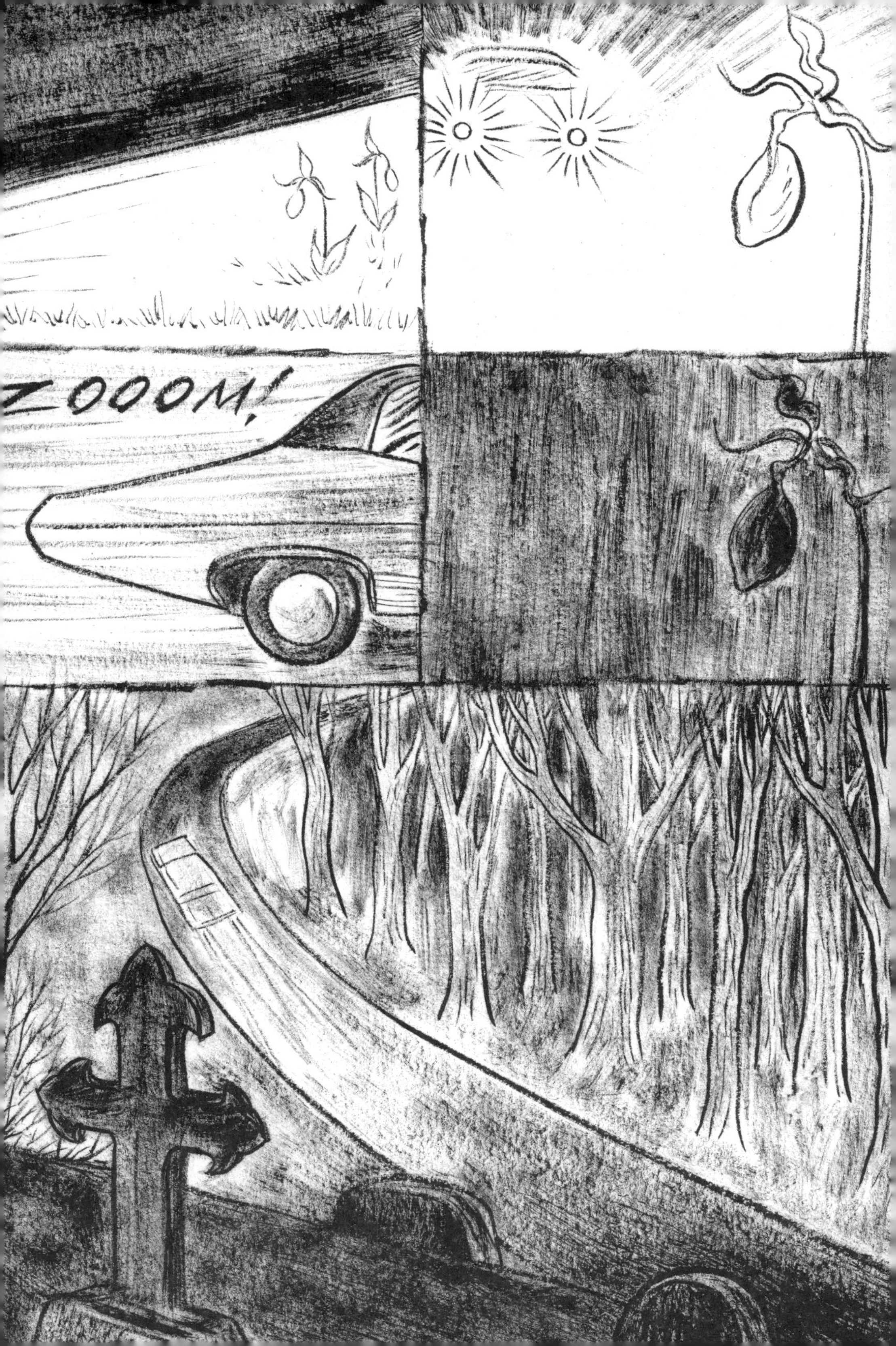
ZOOOM!

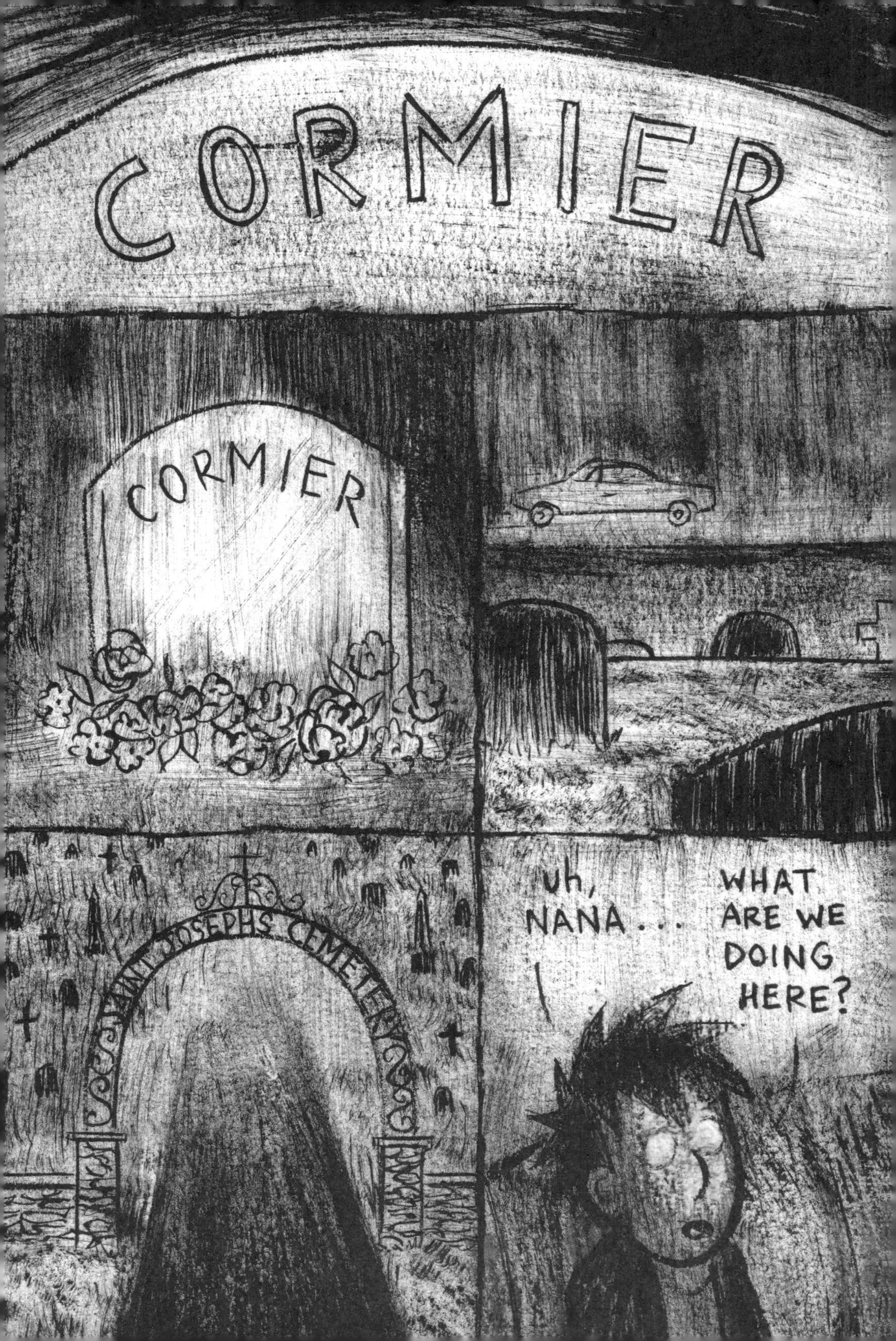
CORMIER
CORMIER
SAINT JOSEPHS CEMETERY
uh, NANA...
WHAT ARE WE DOING HERE?

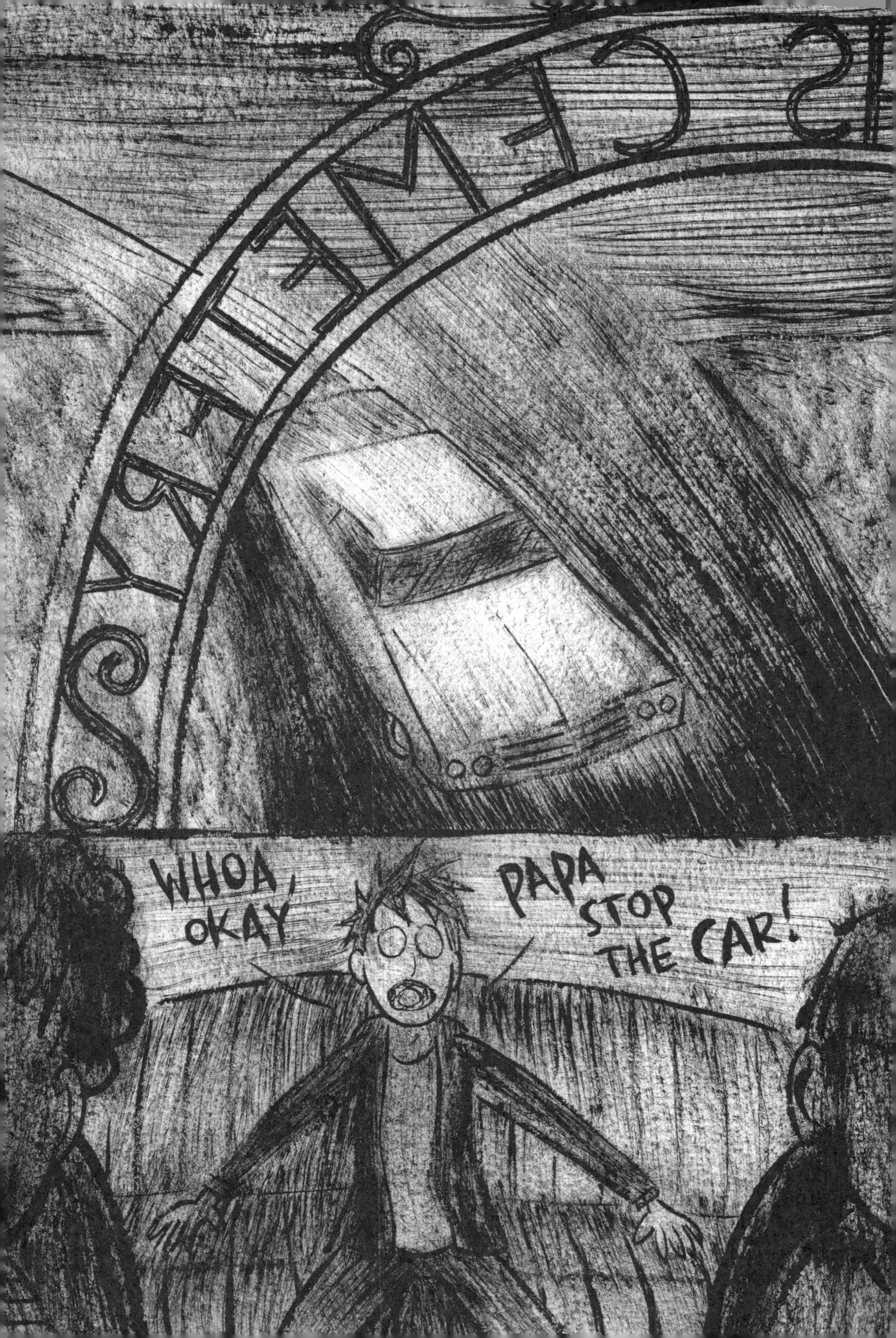
WHOA, OKAY
PAPA STOP THE CAR!

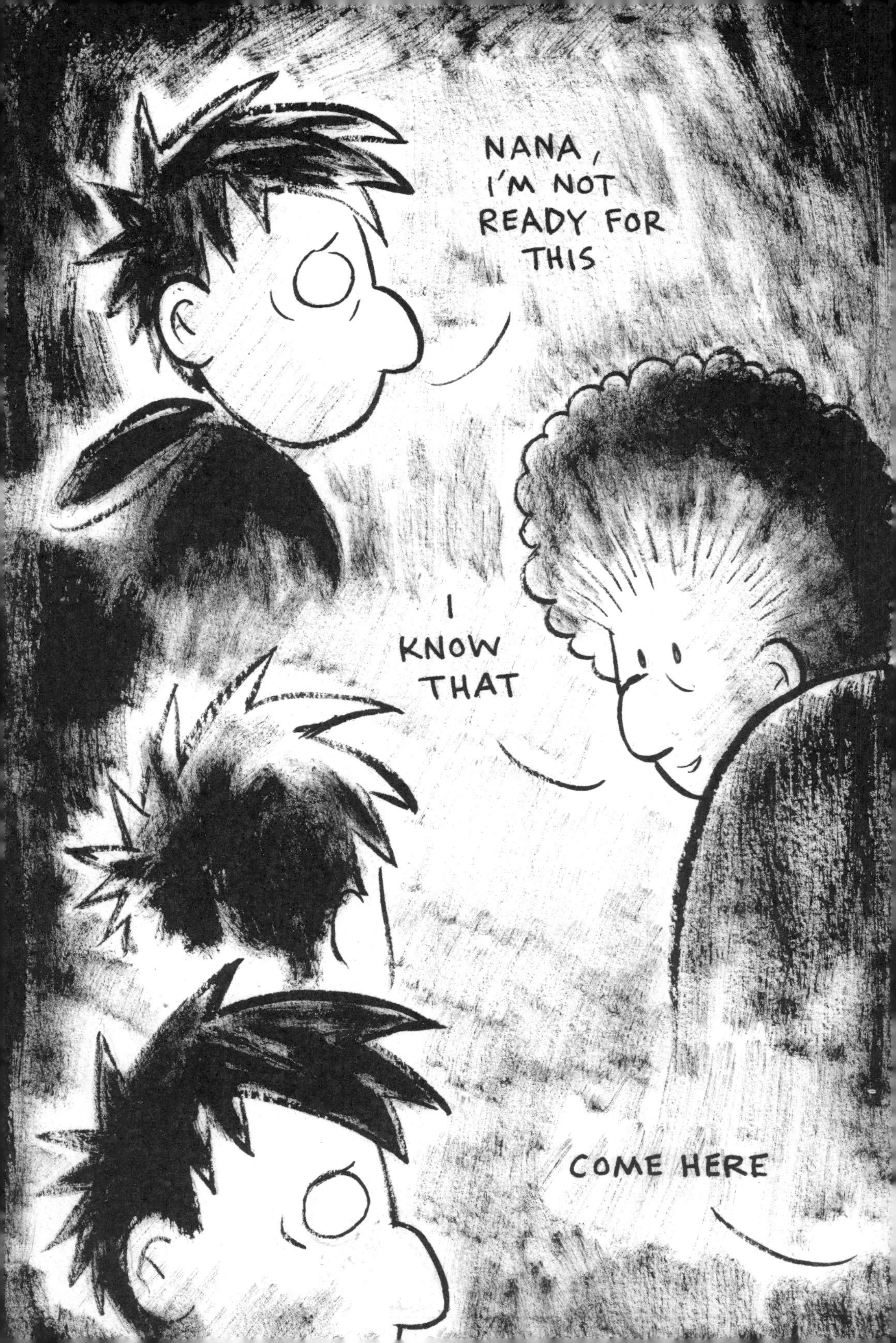
NANA, I'M NOT READY FOR THIS
I KNOW THAT
COME HERE

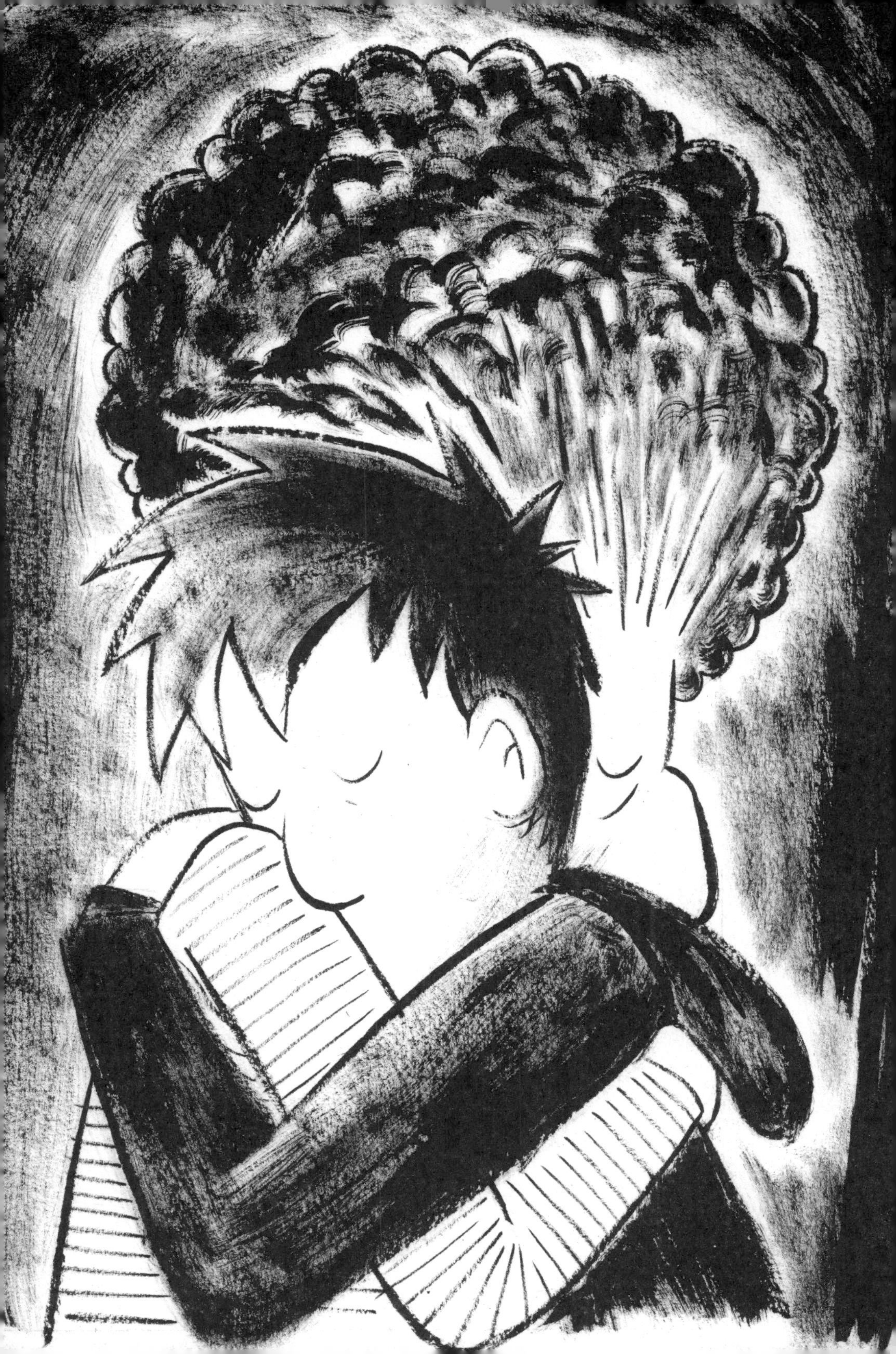

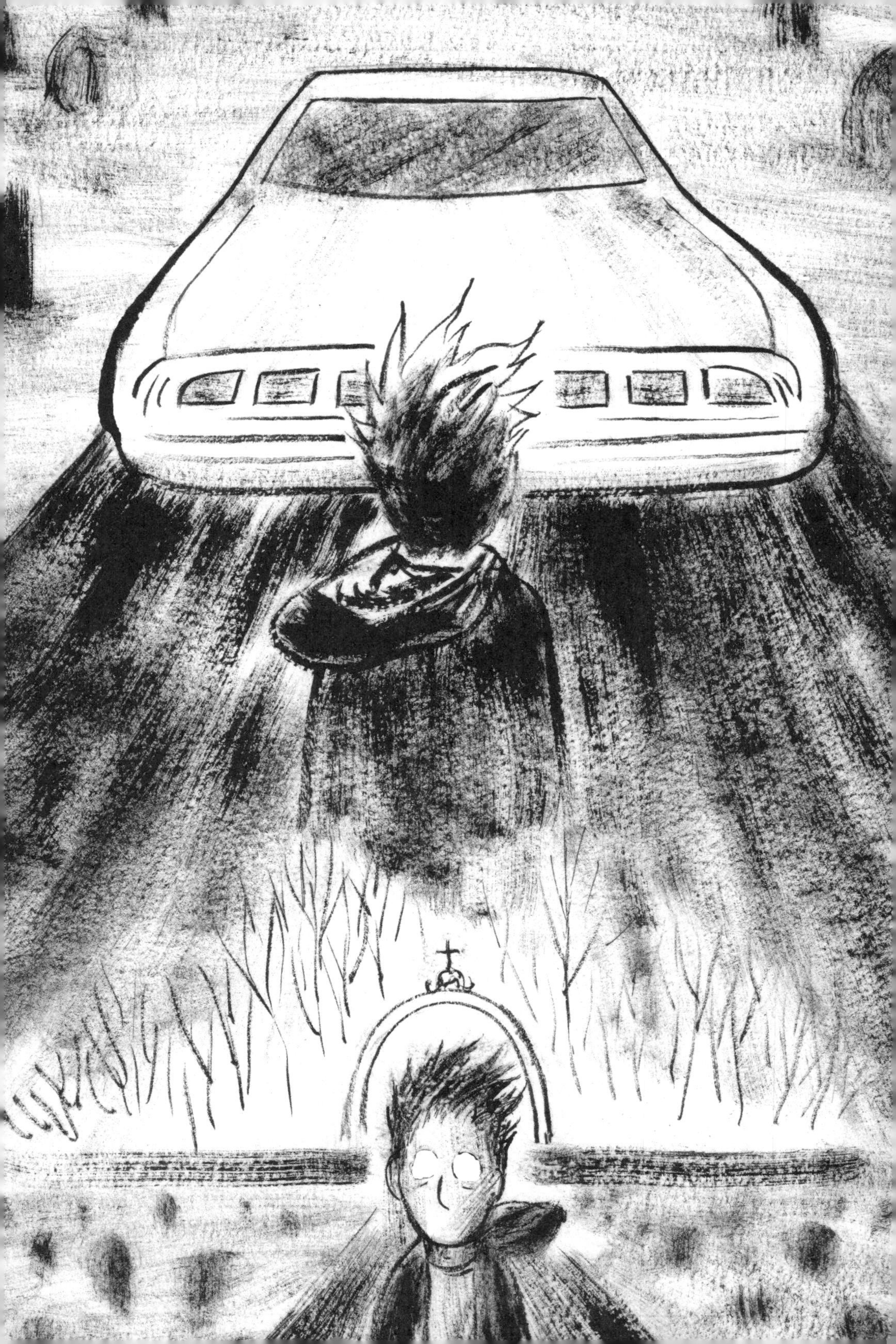

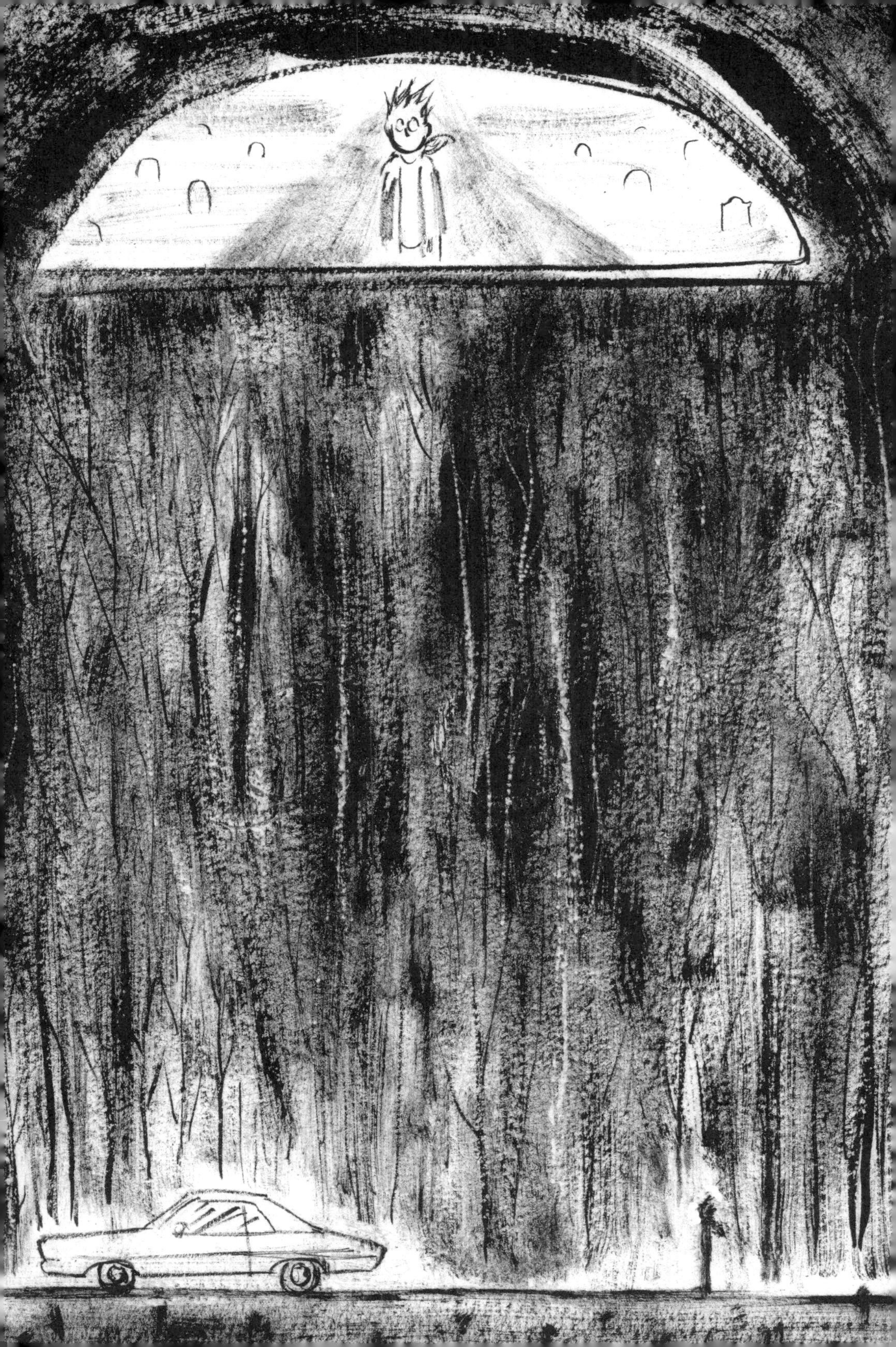

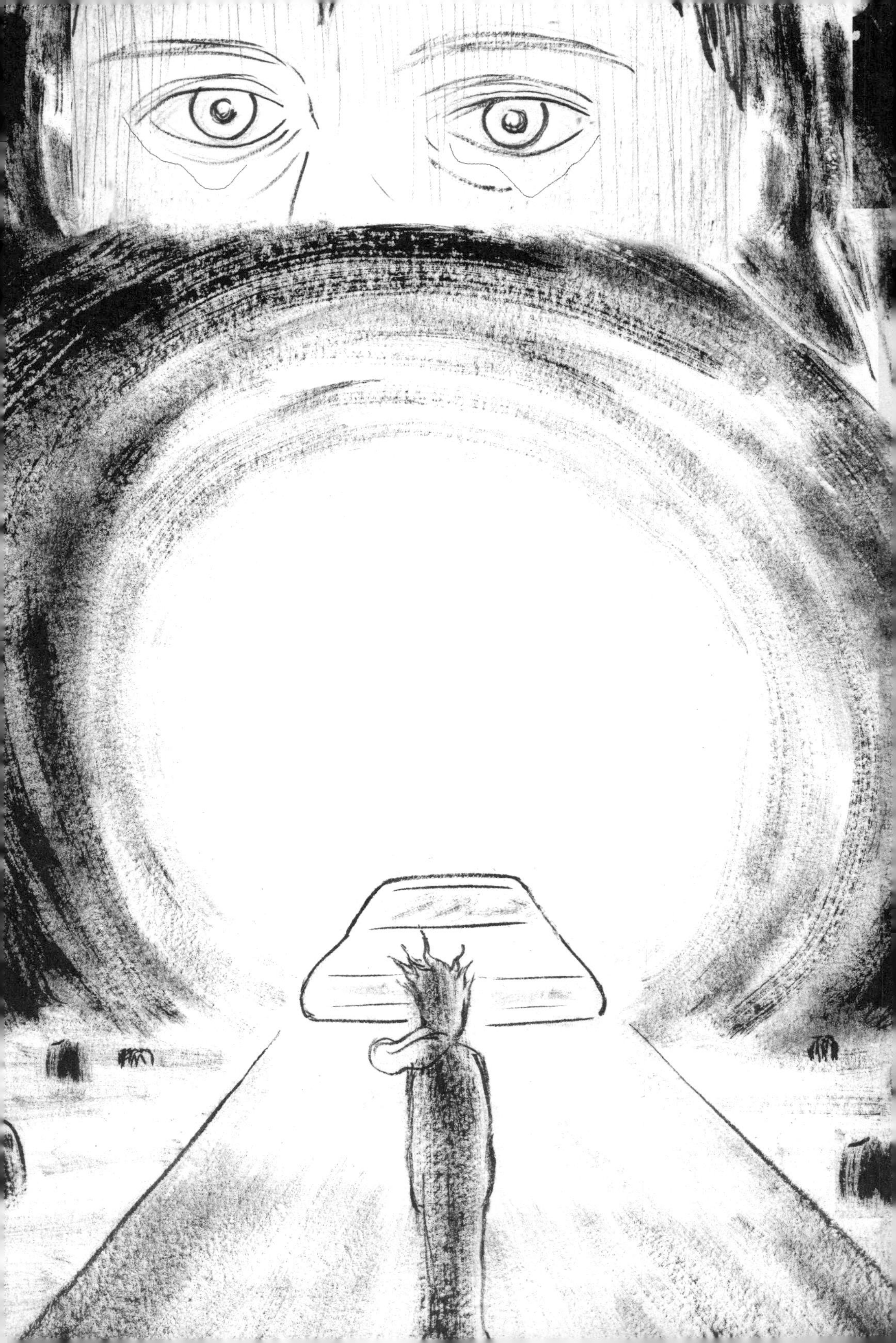

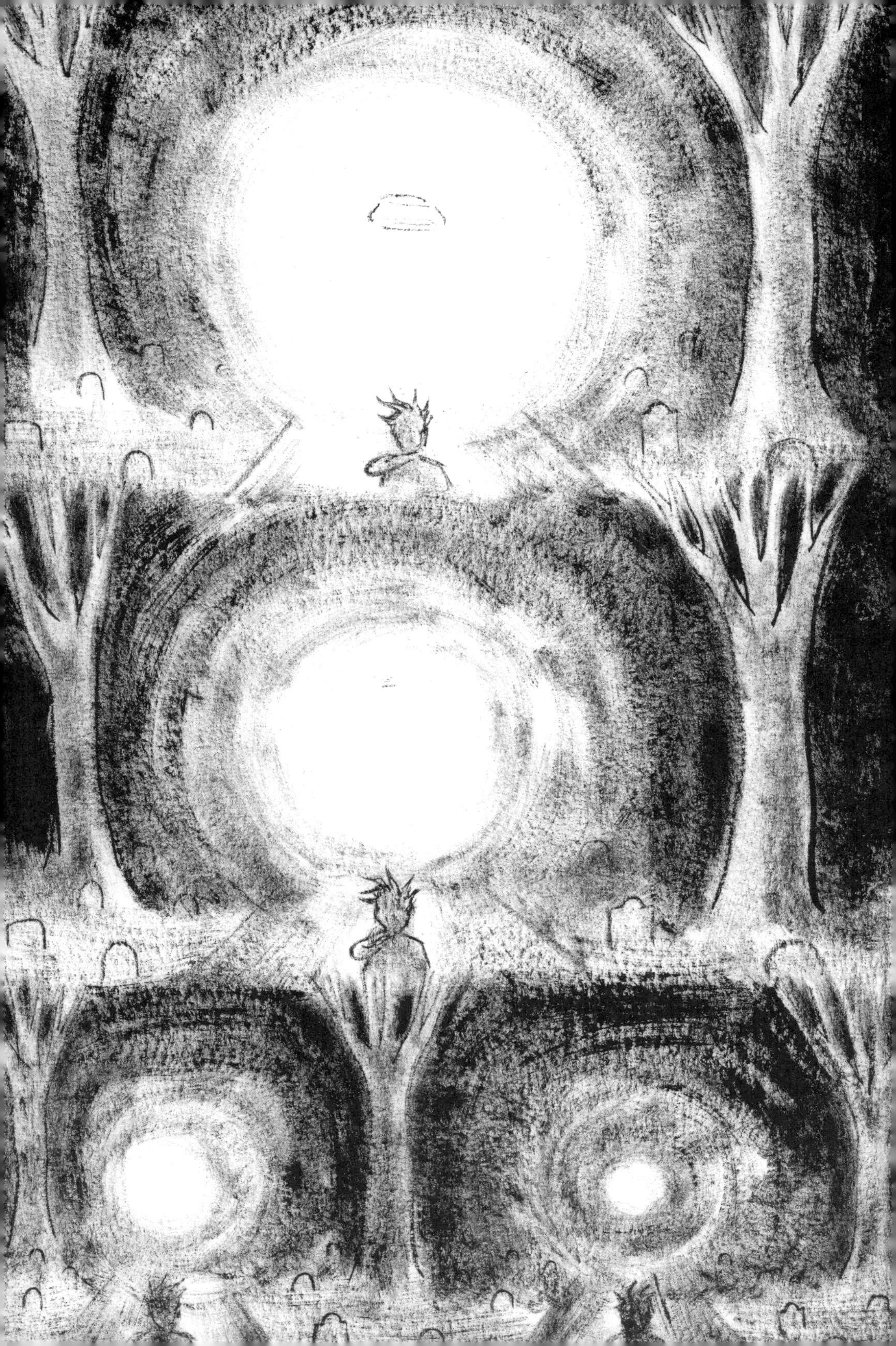

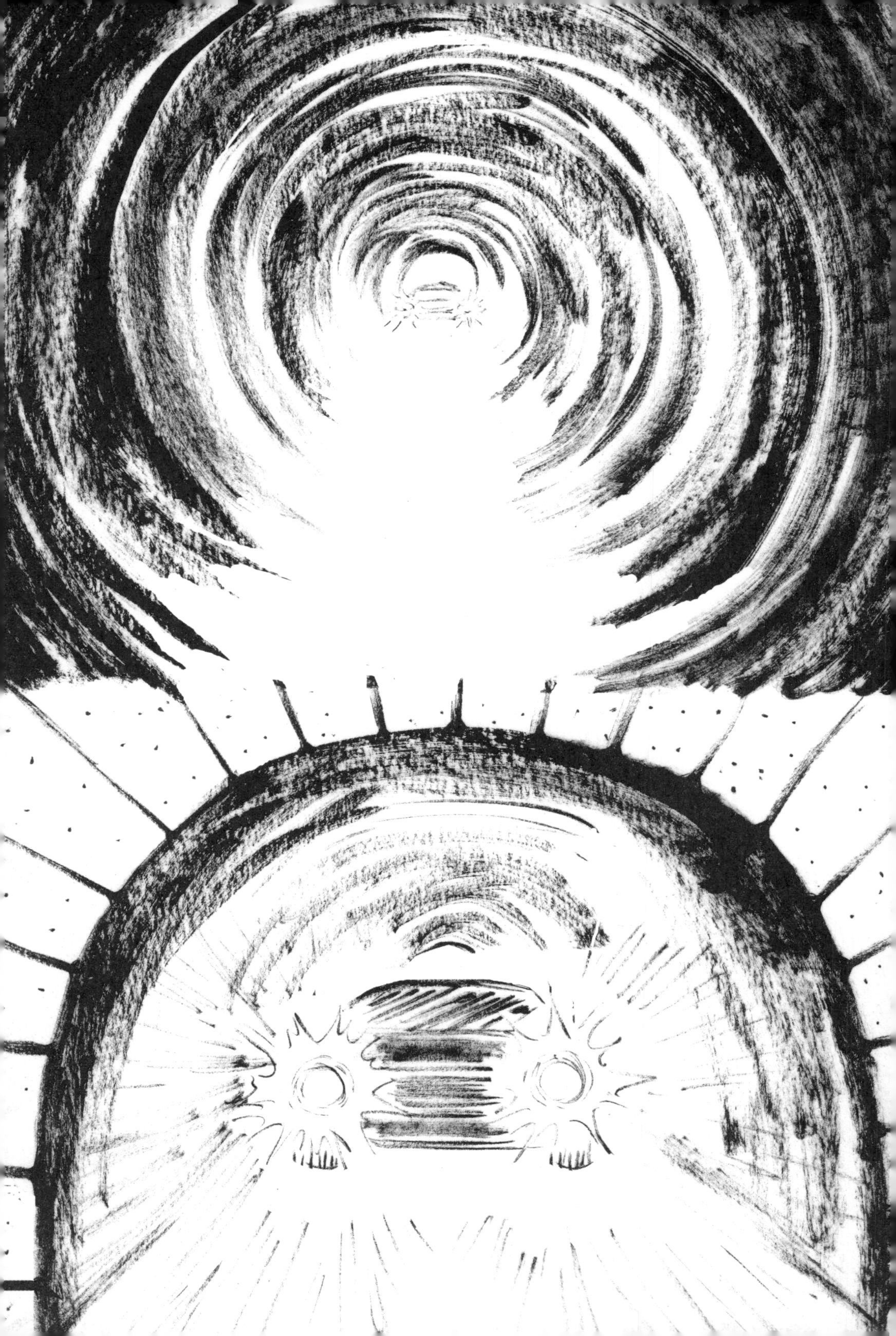

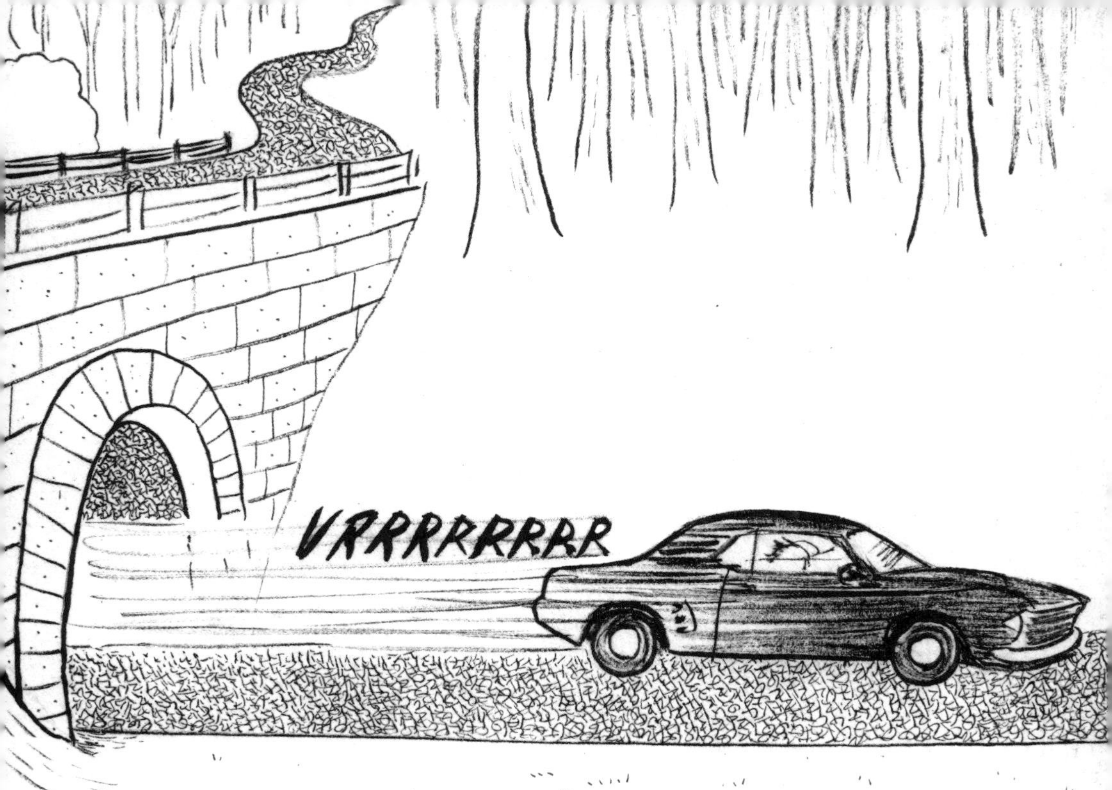
VRRRRRRRR

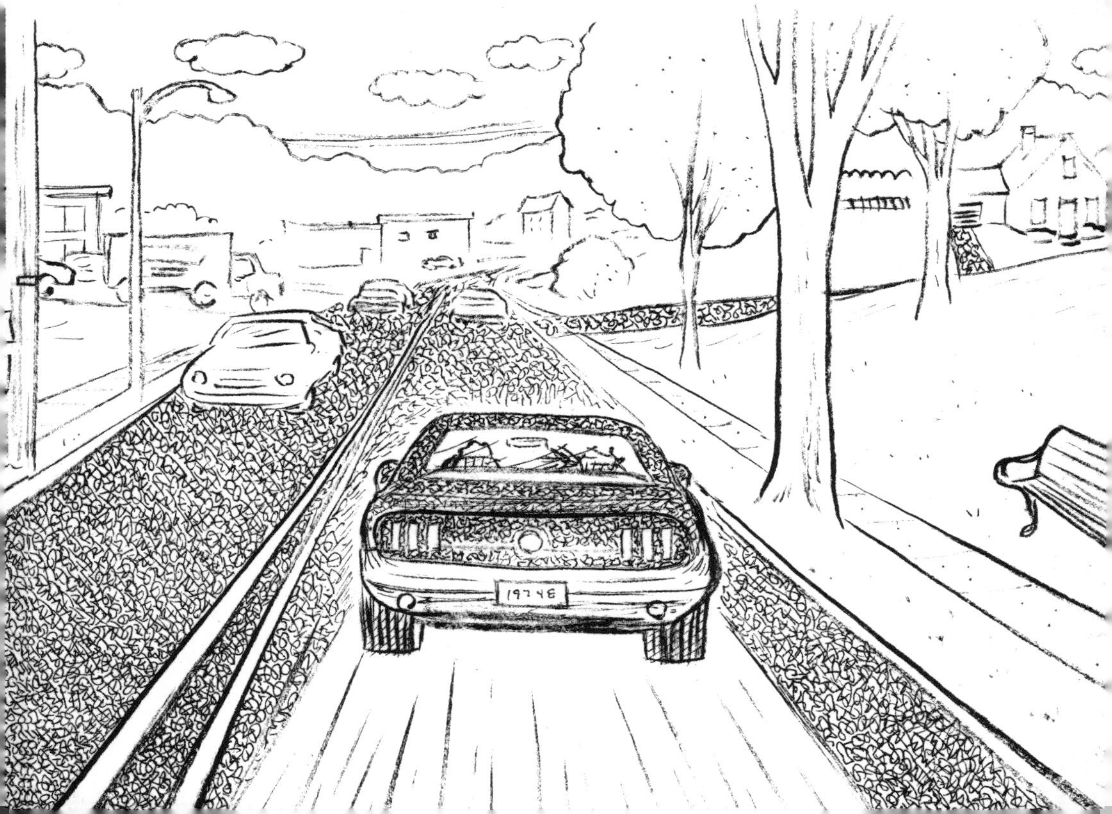

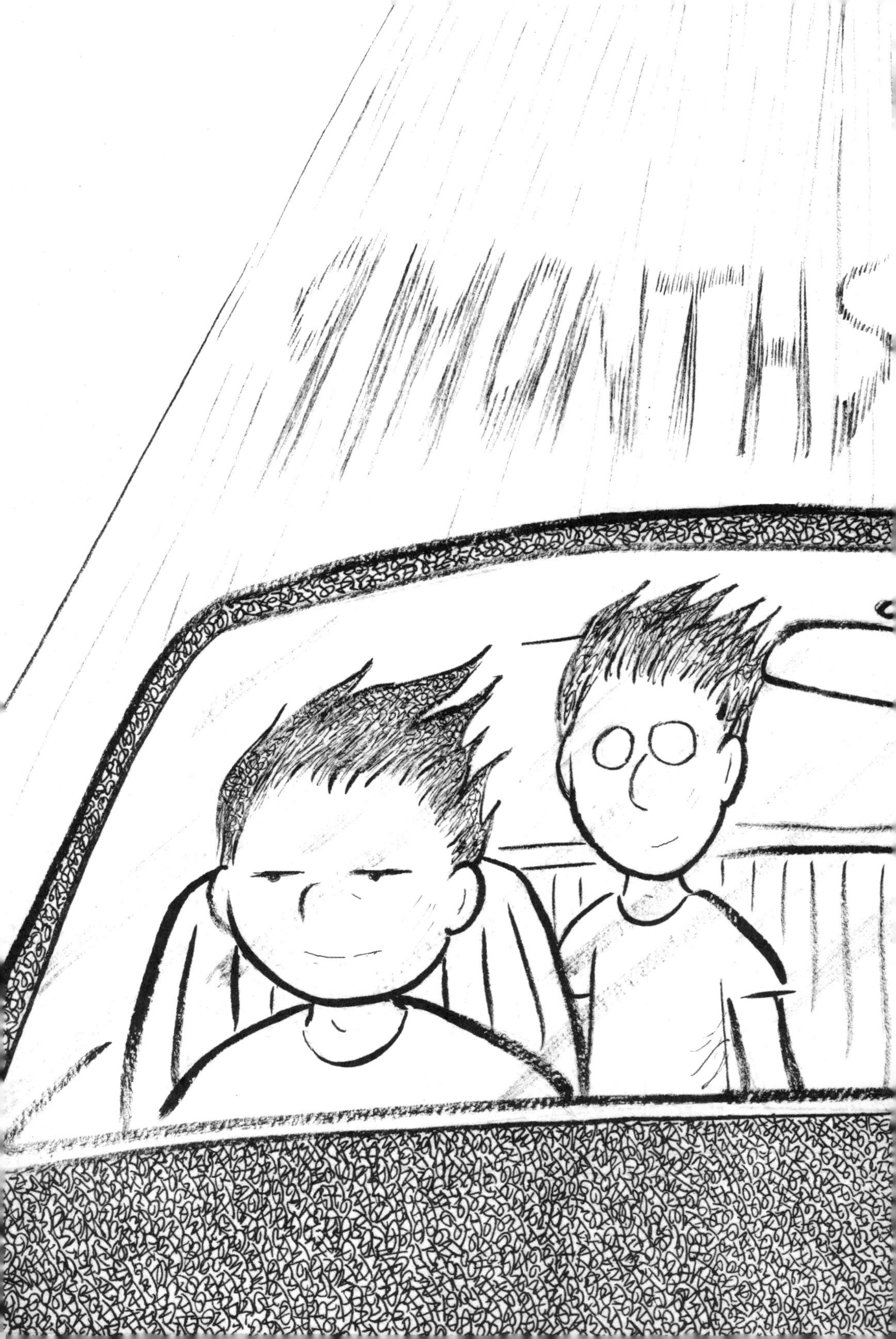
2 MONTHS

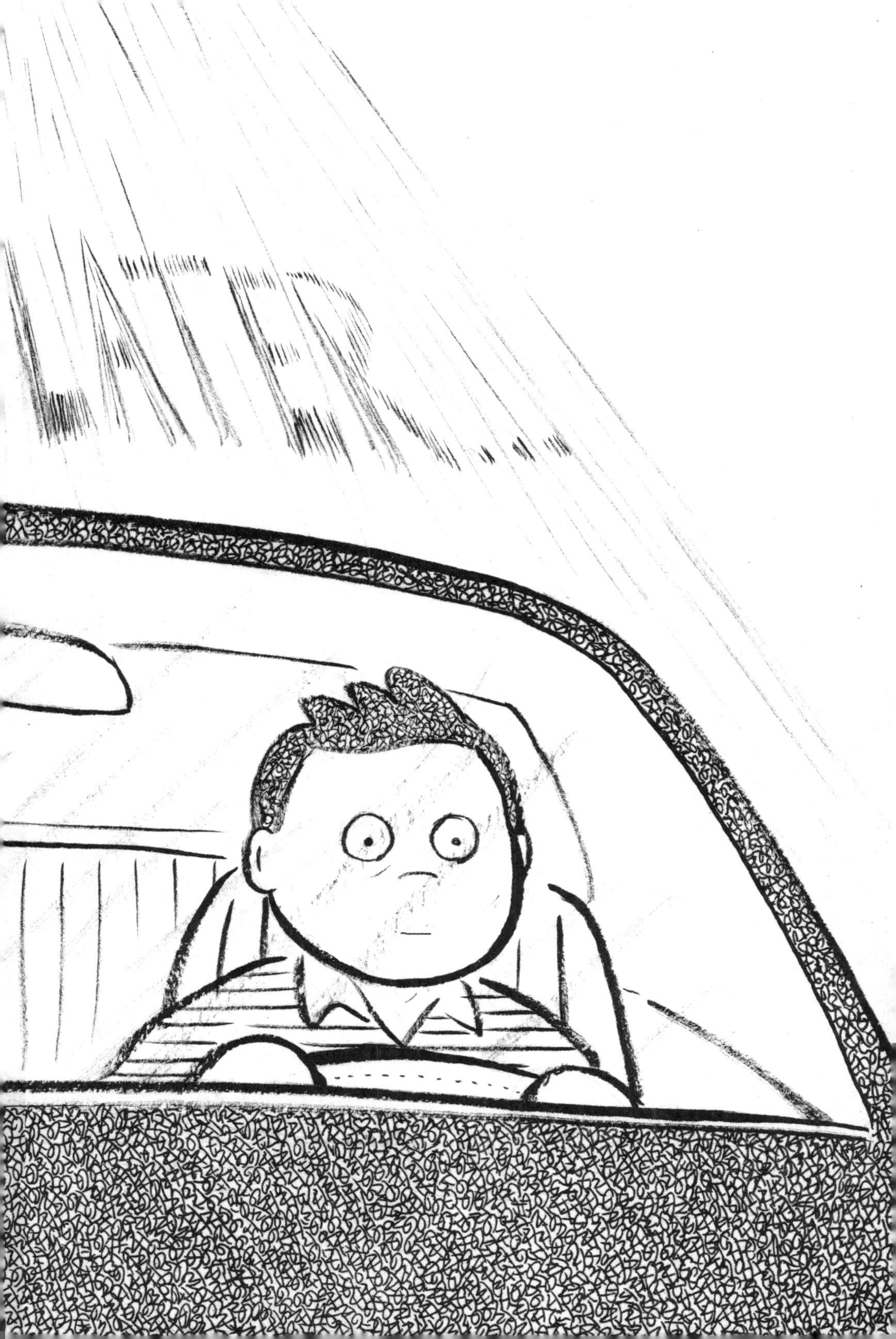
LATER...

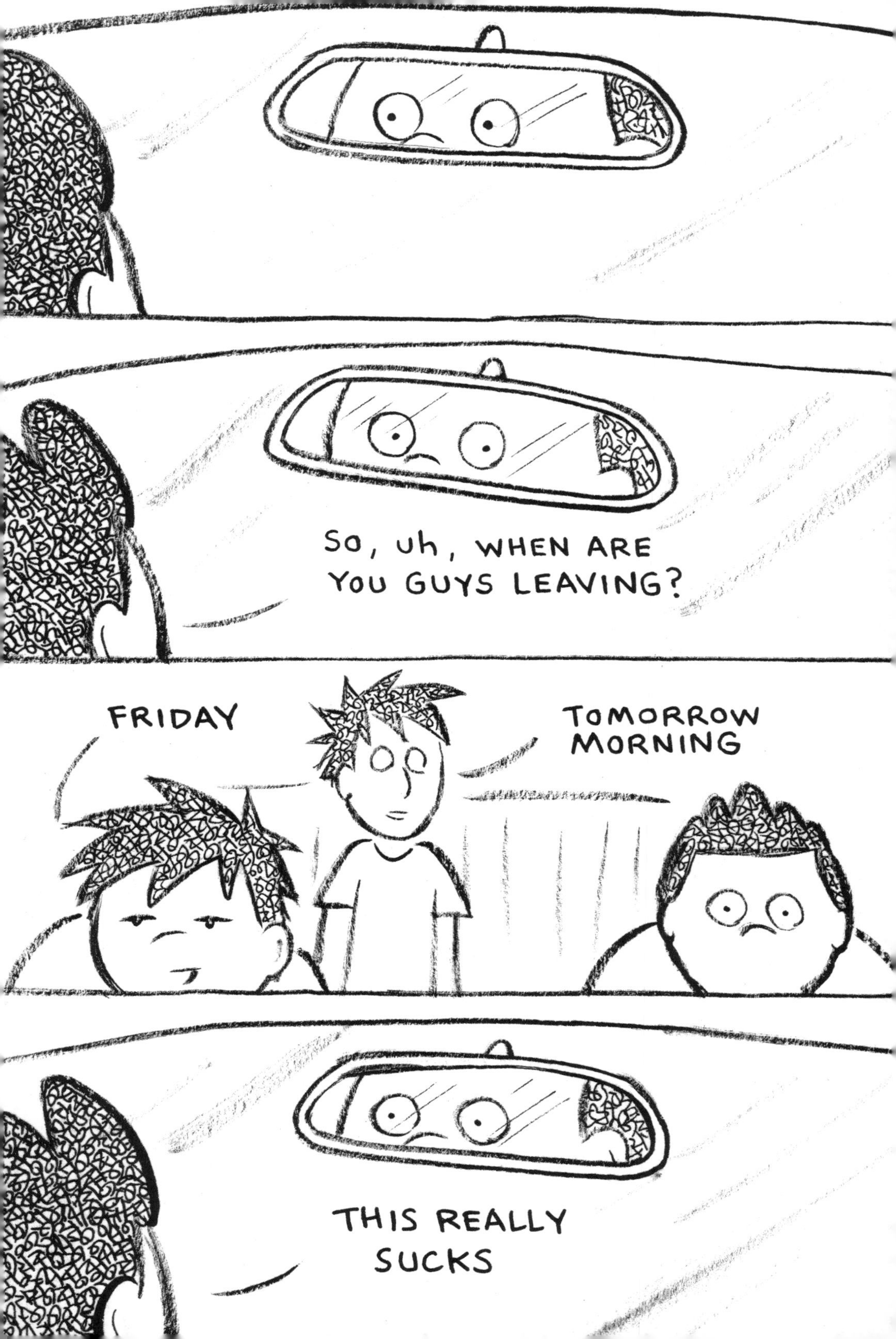
So, uh, WHEN ARE YOU GUYS LEAVING?
FRIDAY
TOMORROW MORNING
THIS REALLY SUCKS

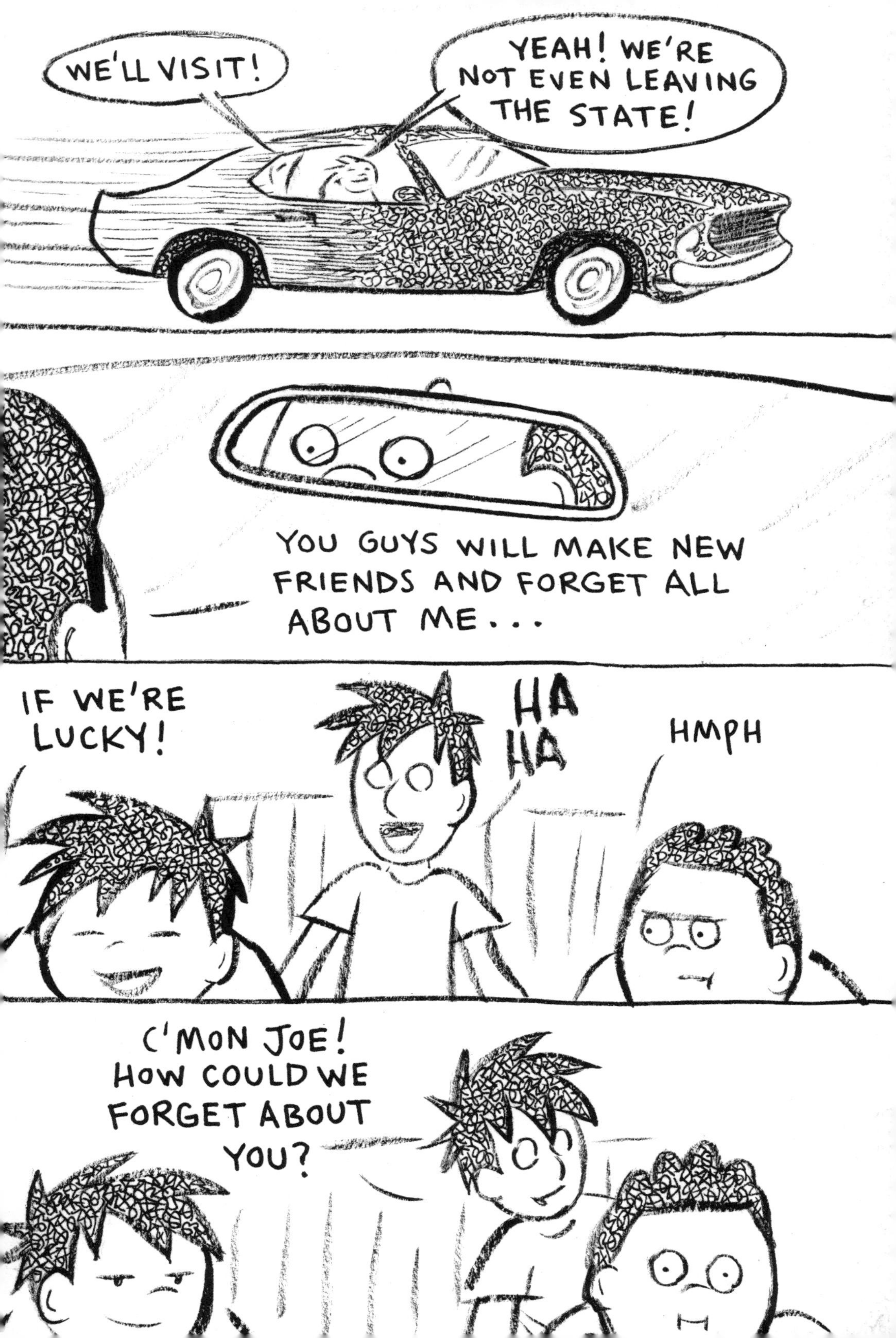
WE'LL VISIT!
YEAH! WE'RE NOT EVEN LEAVING THE STATE!
YOU GUYS WILL MAKE NEW FRIENDS AND FORGET ALL ABOUT ME...
IF WE'RE LUCKY!
HA HA
HMPH
C'MON JOE! HOW COULD WE FORGET ABOUT YOU?

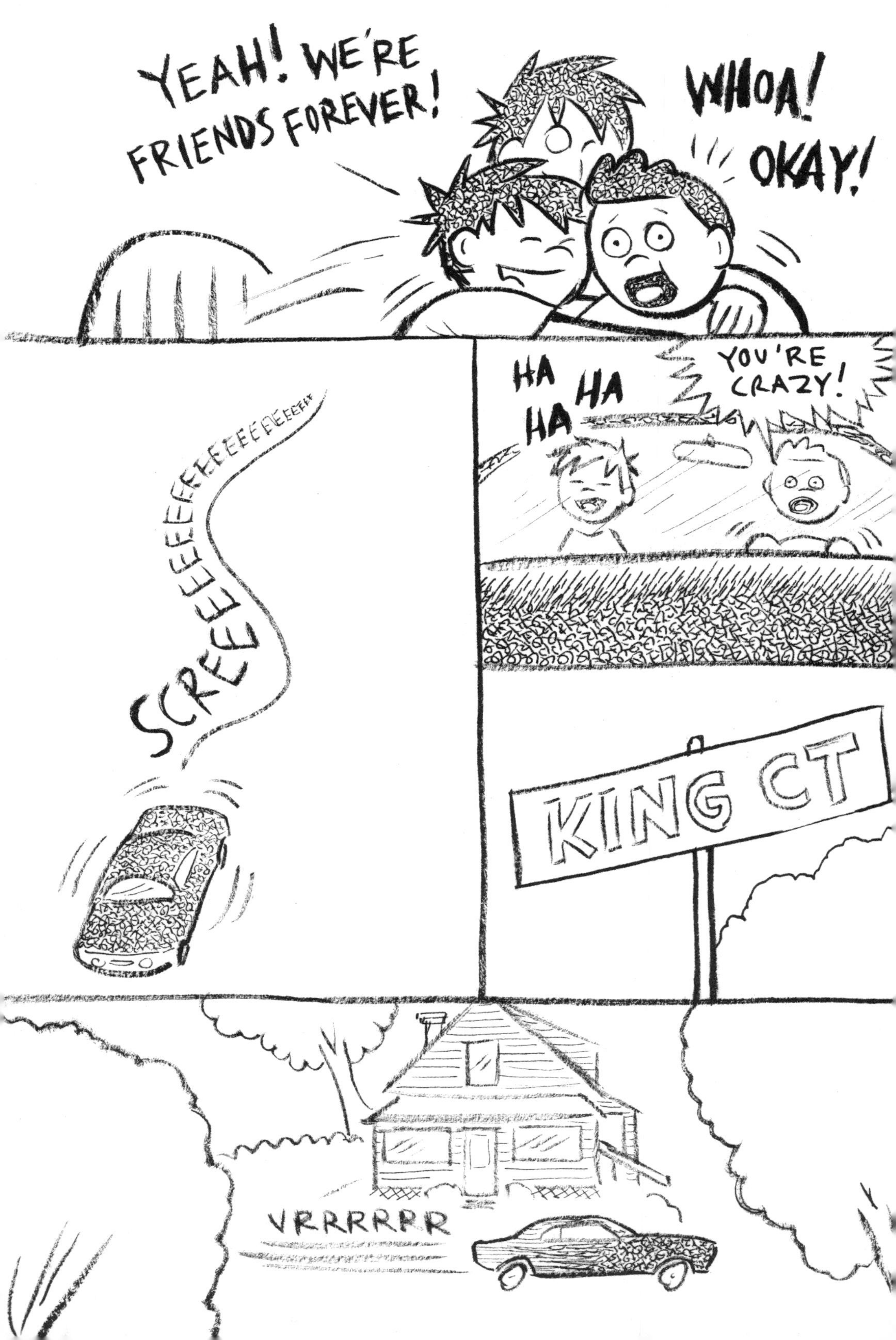
YEAH! WE'RE FRIENDS FOREVER!
WHOA! OKAY!
HA HA HA
YOU'RE CRAZY!
SCREEEEEEEEEEEEEEEEEEEEE
KING CT
VRRRRRR

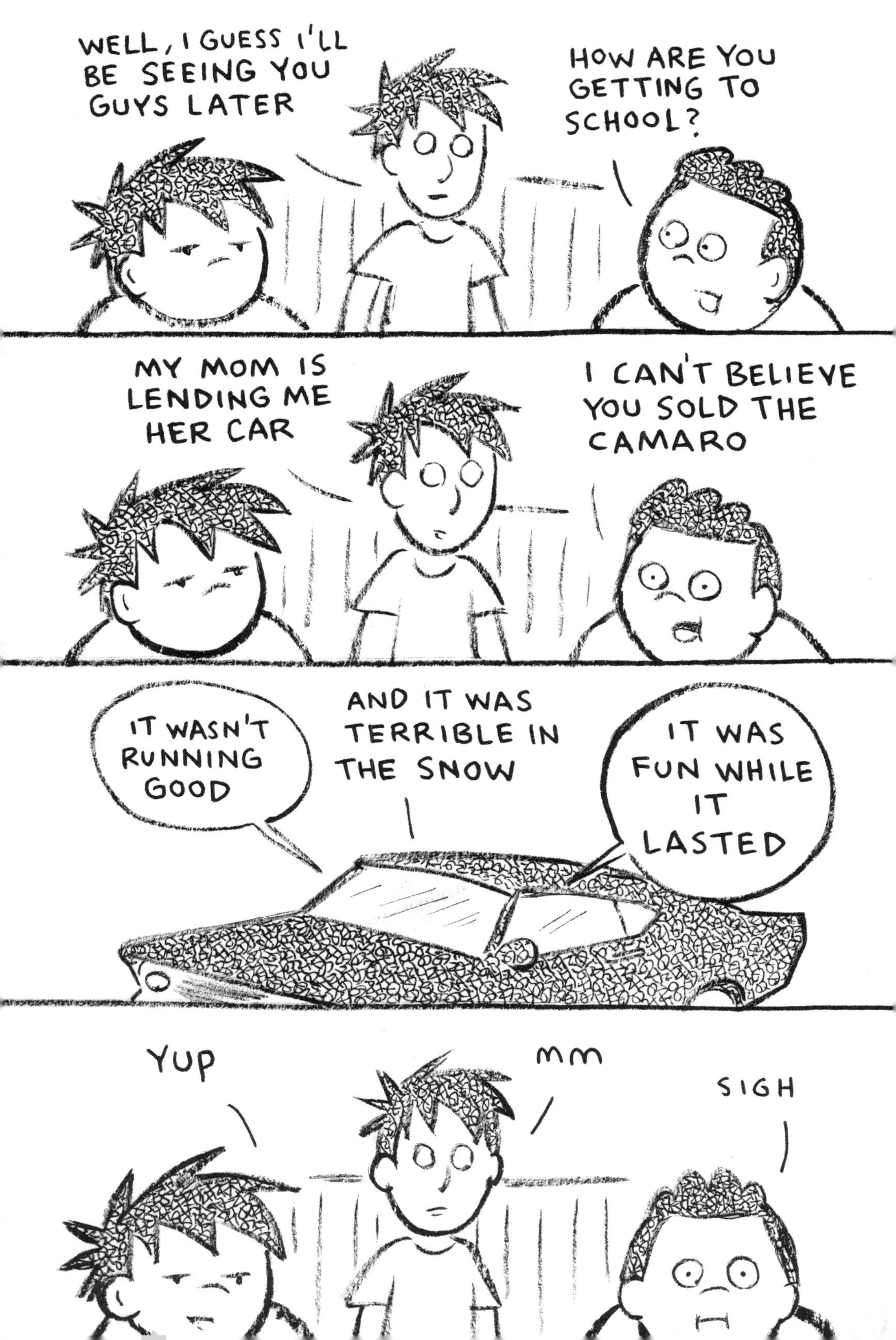
WELL, I GUESS I'LL BE SEEING YOU GUYS LATER
HOW ARE YOU GETTING TO SCHOOL?
MY MOM IS LENDING ME HER CAR
I CAN'T BELIEVE YOU SOLD THE CAMARO
IT WASN'T RUNNING GOOD
AND IT WAS TERRIBLE IN THE SNOW
IT WAS FUN WHILE IT LASTED
YUP
MM
SIGH

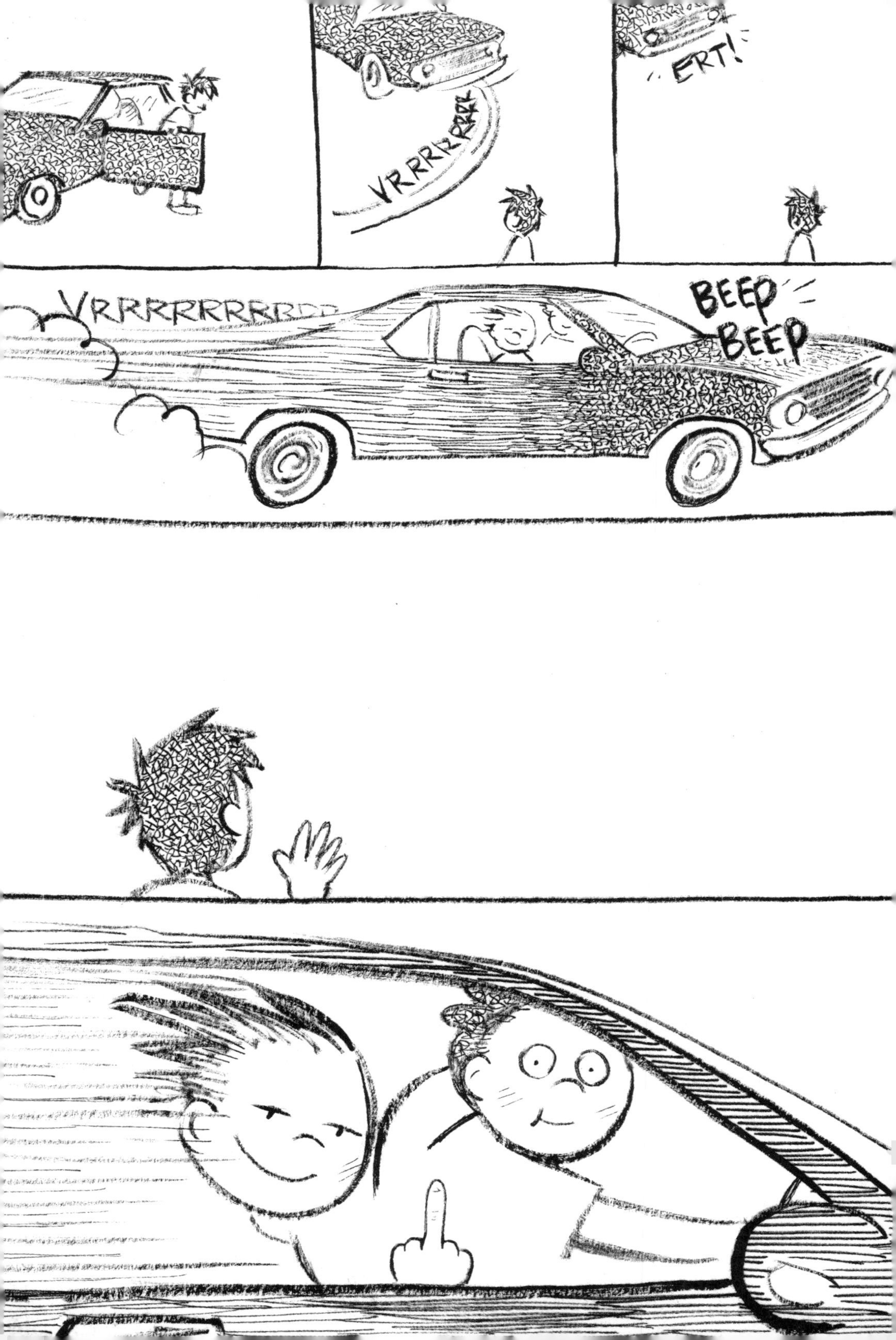
VRRRRRRRK
ERT!
VRRRRRRRRRR
BEEP
BEEP

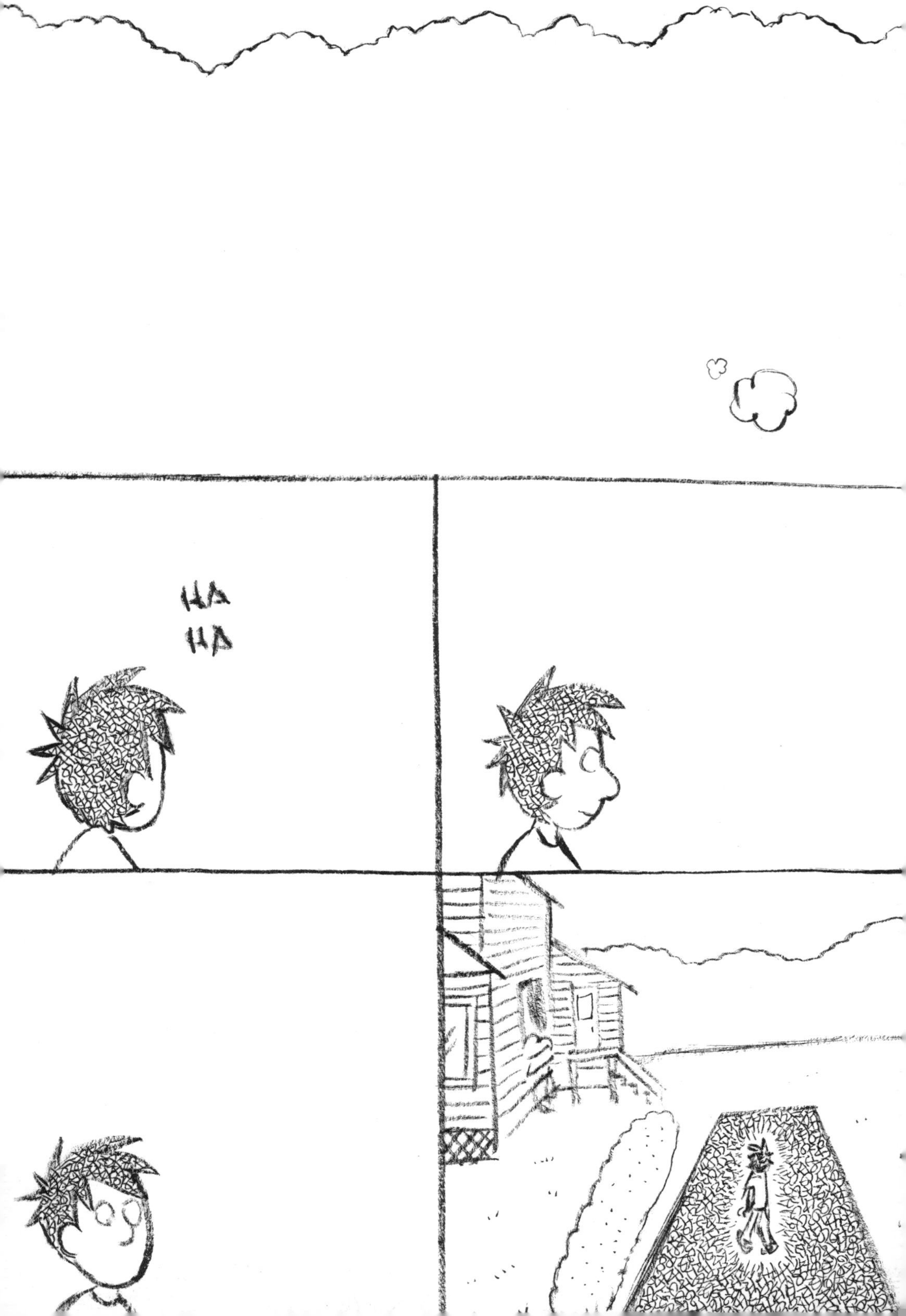
HA
HA

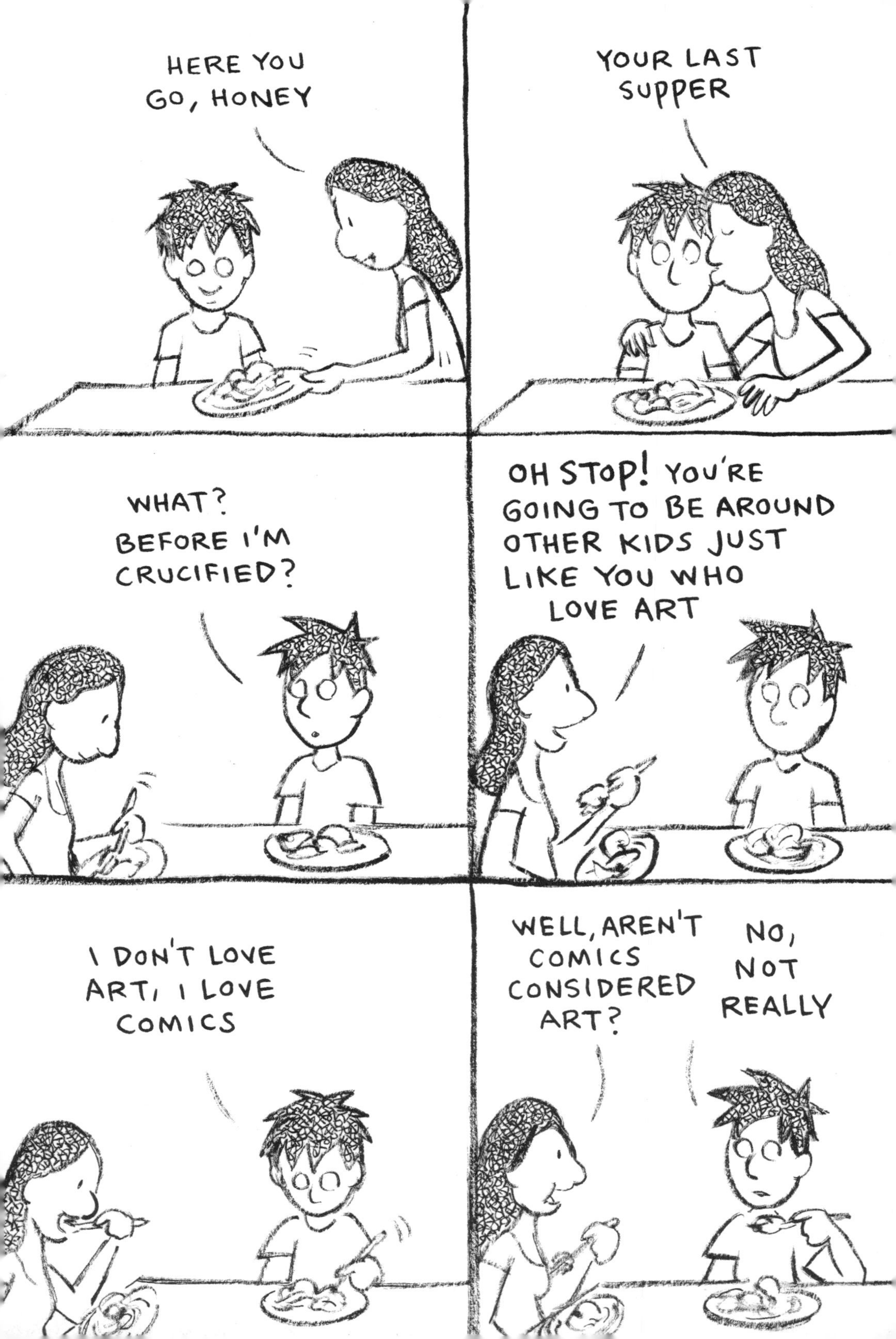
HERE YOU GO, HONEY
YOUR LAST SUPPER
WHAT? BEFORE I'M CRUCIFIED?
OH STOP! YOU'RE GOING TO BE AROUND OTHER KIDS JUST LIKE YOU WHO LOVE ART
I DON'T LOVE ART, I LOVE COMICS
WELL, AREN'T COMICS CONSIDERED ART?
NO, NOT REALLY

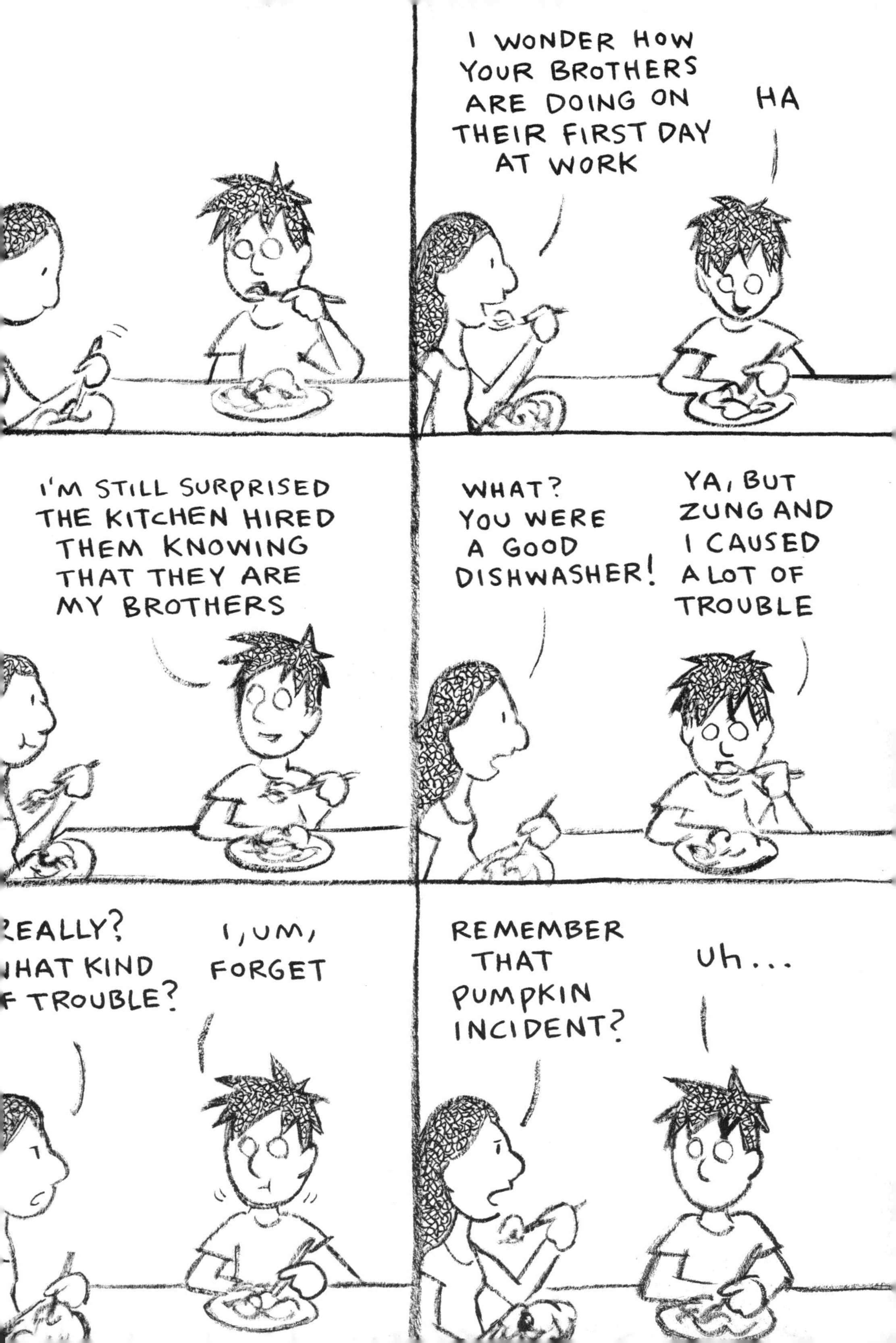
I WONDER HOW YOUR BROTHERS ARE DOING ON THEIR FIRST DAY AT WORK
HA
I'M STILL SURPRISED THE KITCHEN HIRED THEM KNOWING THAT THEY ARE MY BROTHERS
WHAT? YOU WERE A GOOD DISHWASHER!
YA, BUT ZUNG AND I CAUSED A LOT OF TROUBLE
EALLY? HAT KIND F TROUBLE?
I, UM, FORGET
REMEMBER THAT PUMPKIN INCIDENT?
Uh...

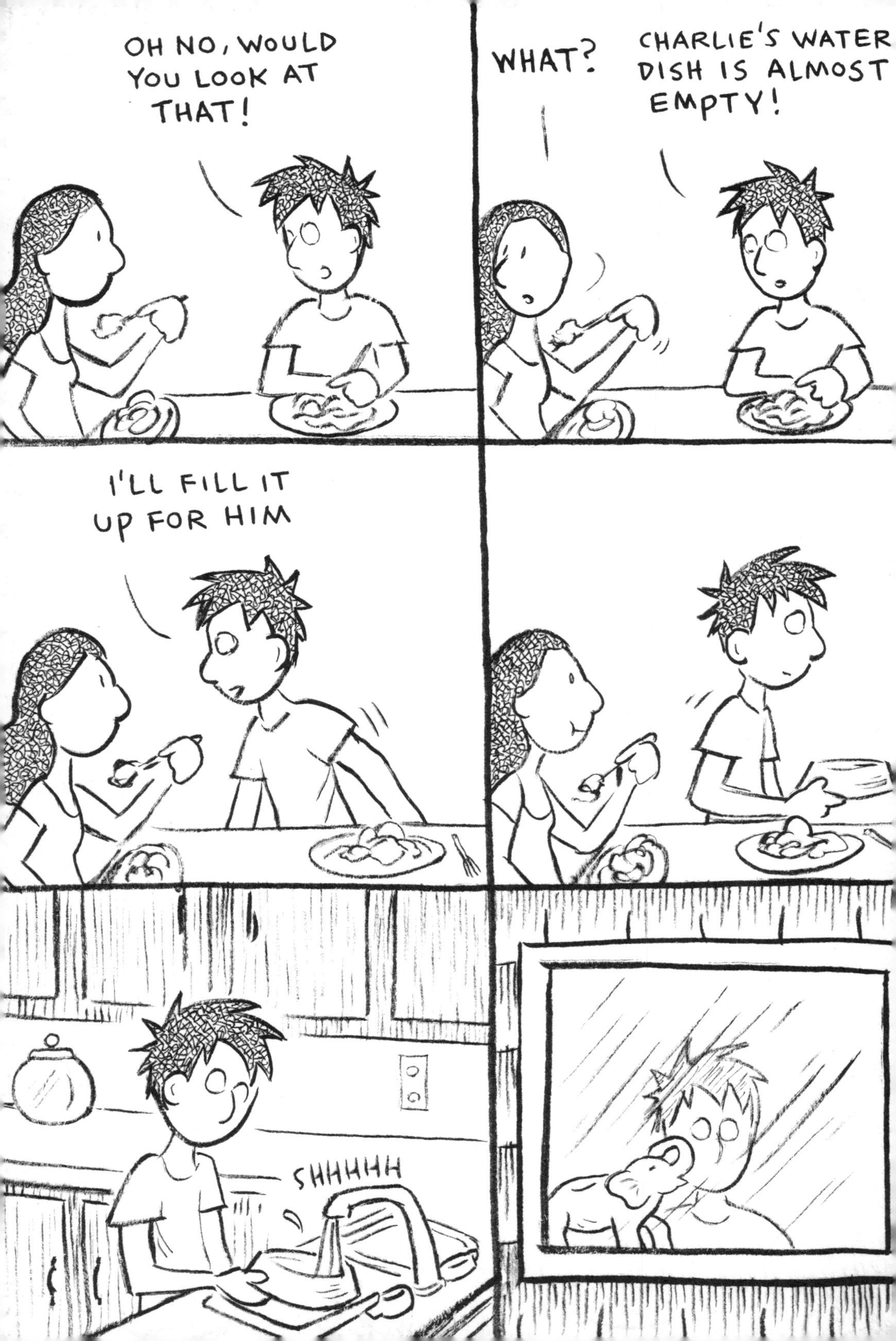
OH NO, WOULD YOU LOOK AT THAT!
WHAT?
CHARLIE'S WATER DISH IS ALMOST EMPTY!
I'LL FILL IT UP FOR HIM
SHHHHH

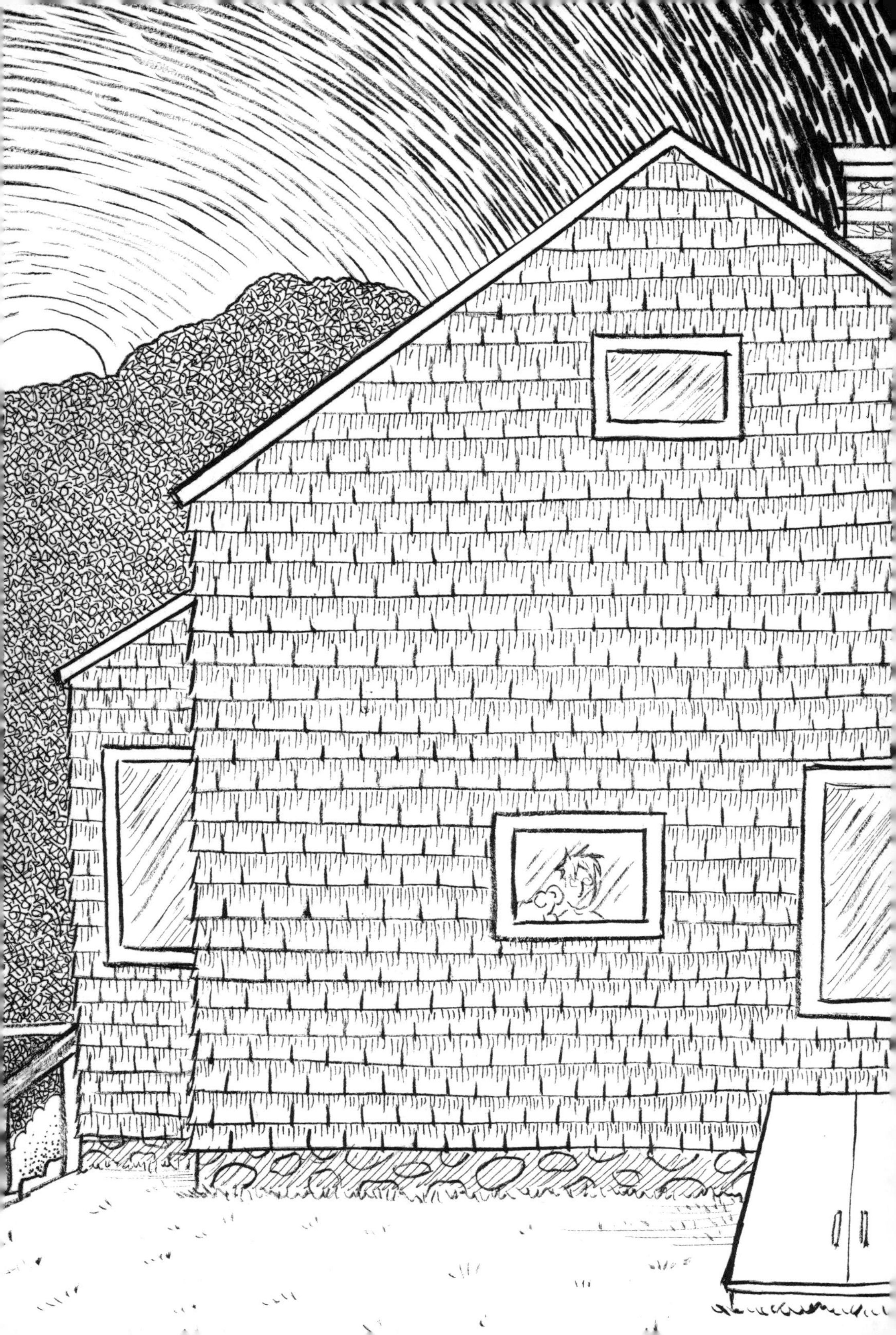

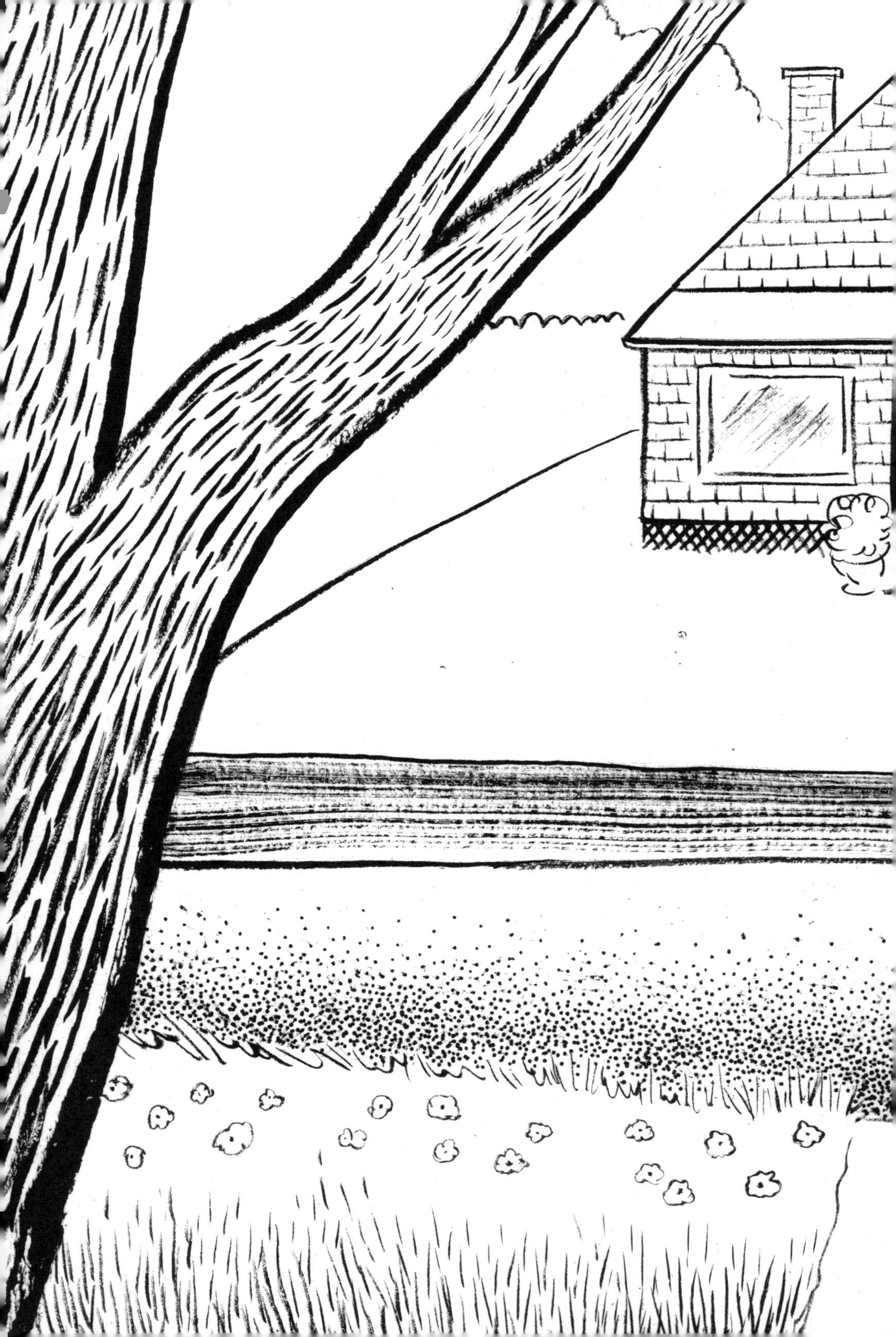

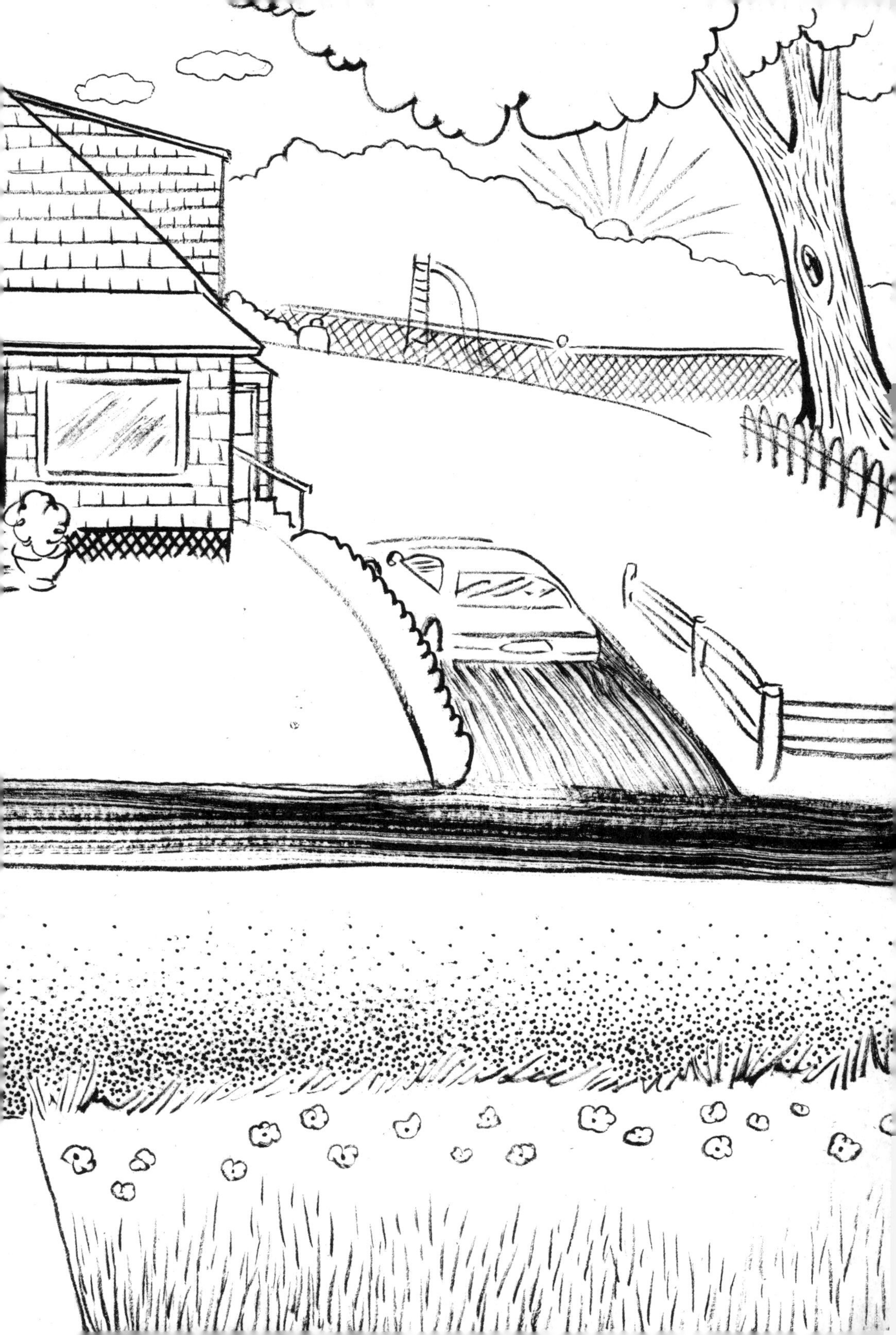

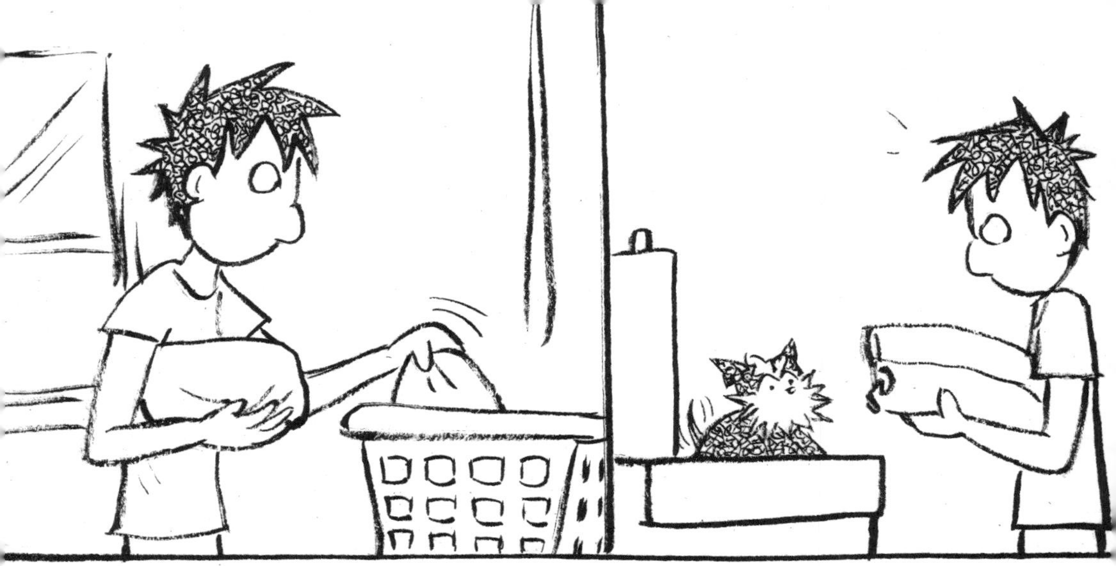
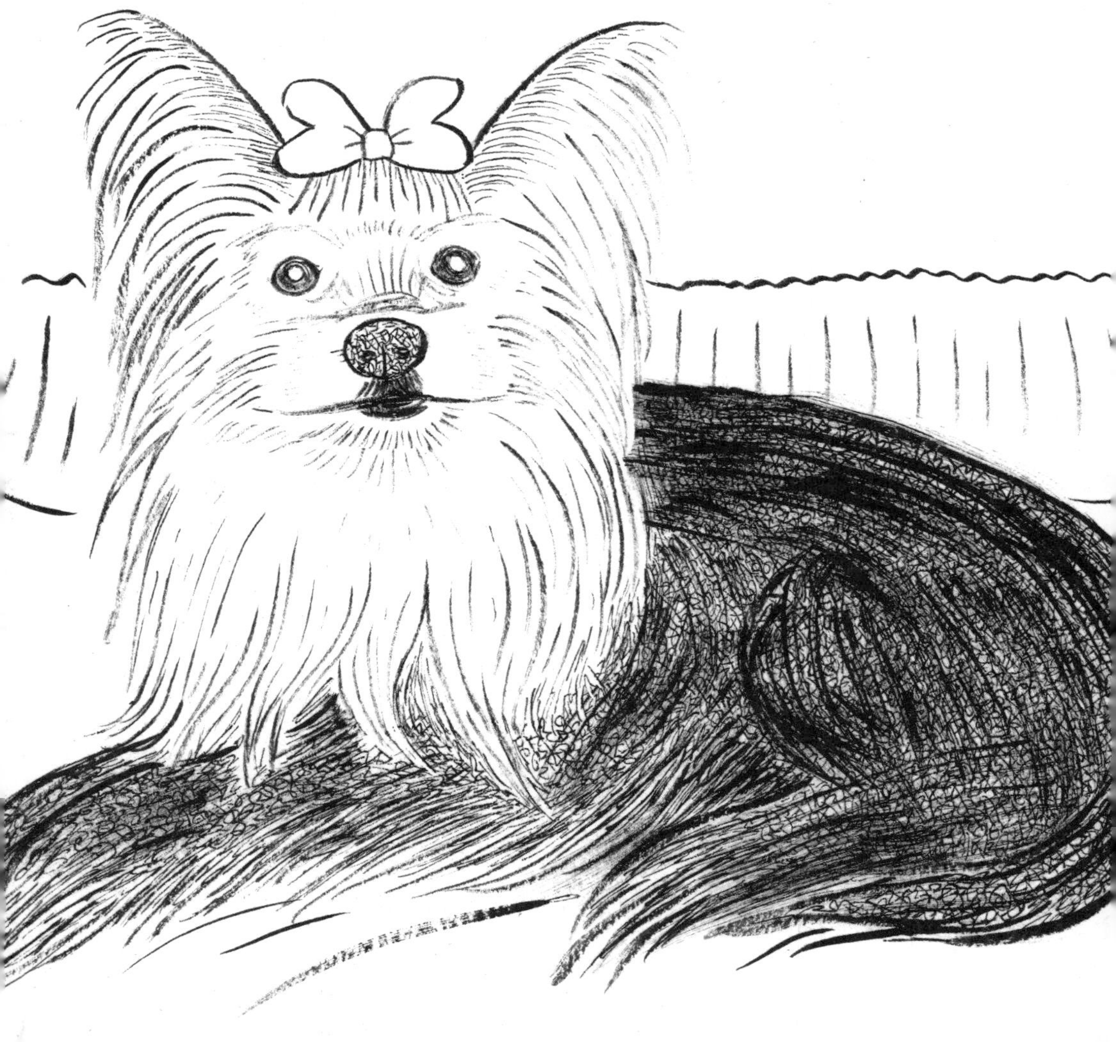

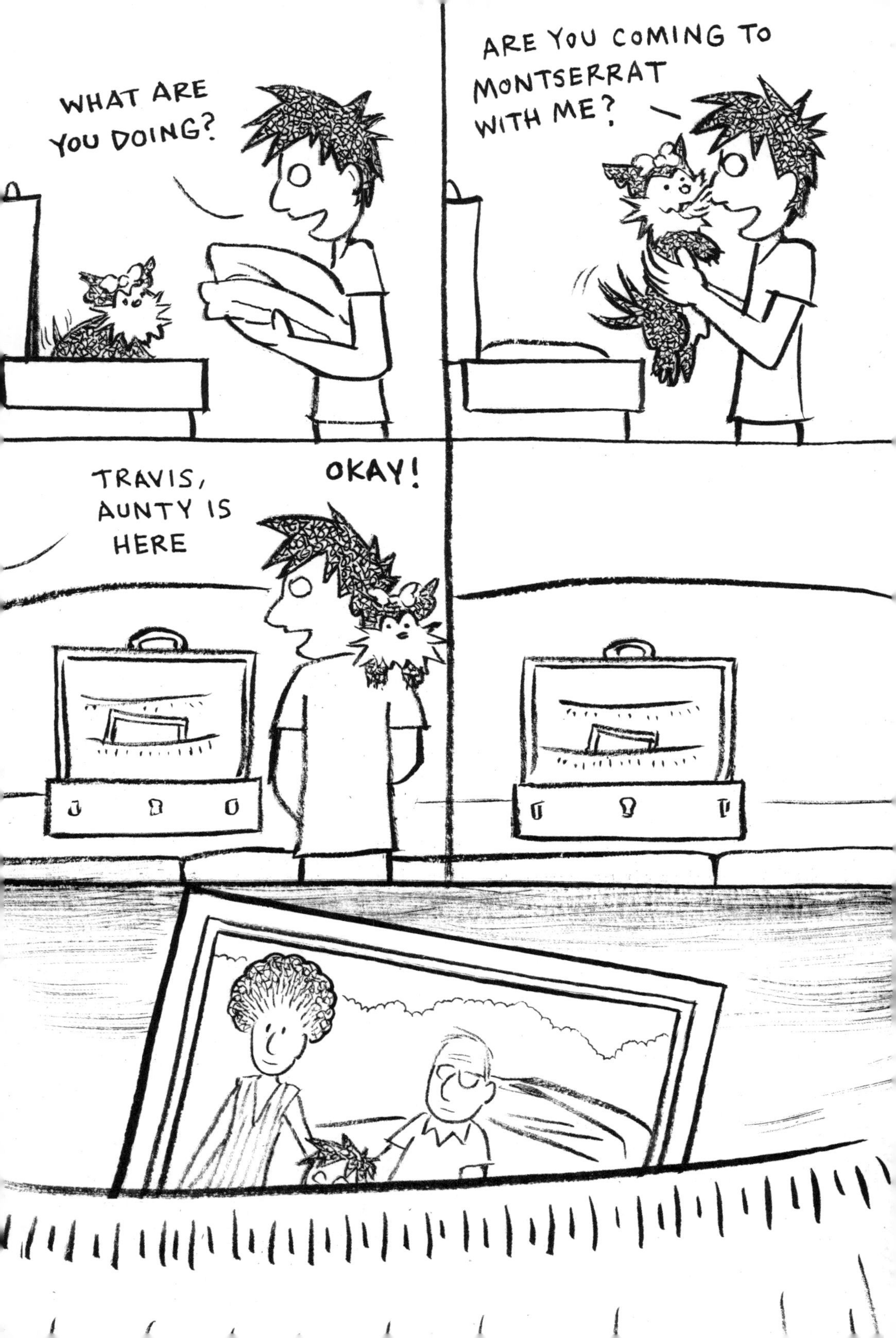
WHAT ARE YOU DOING?
ARE YOU COMING TO MONTSERRAT WITH ME?
TRAVIS, AUNTY IS HERE
OKAY!

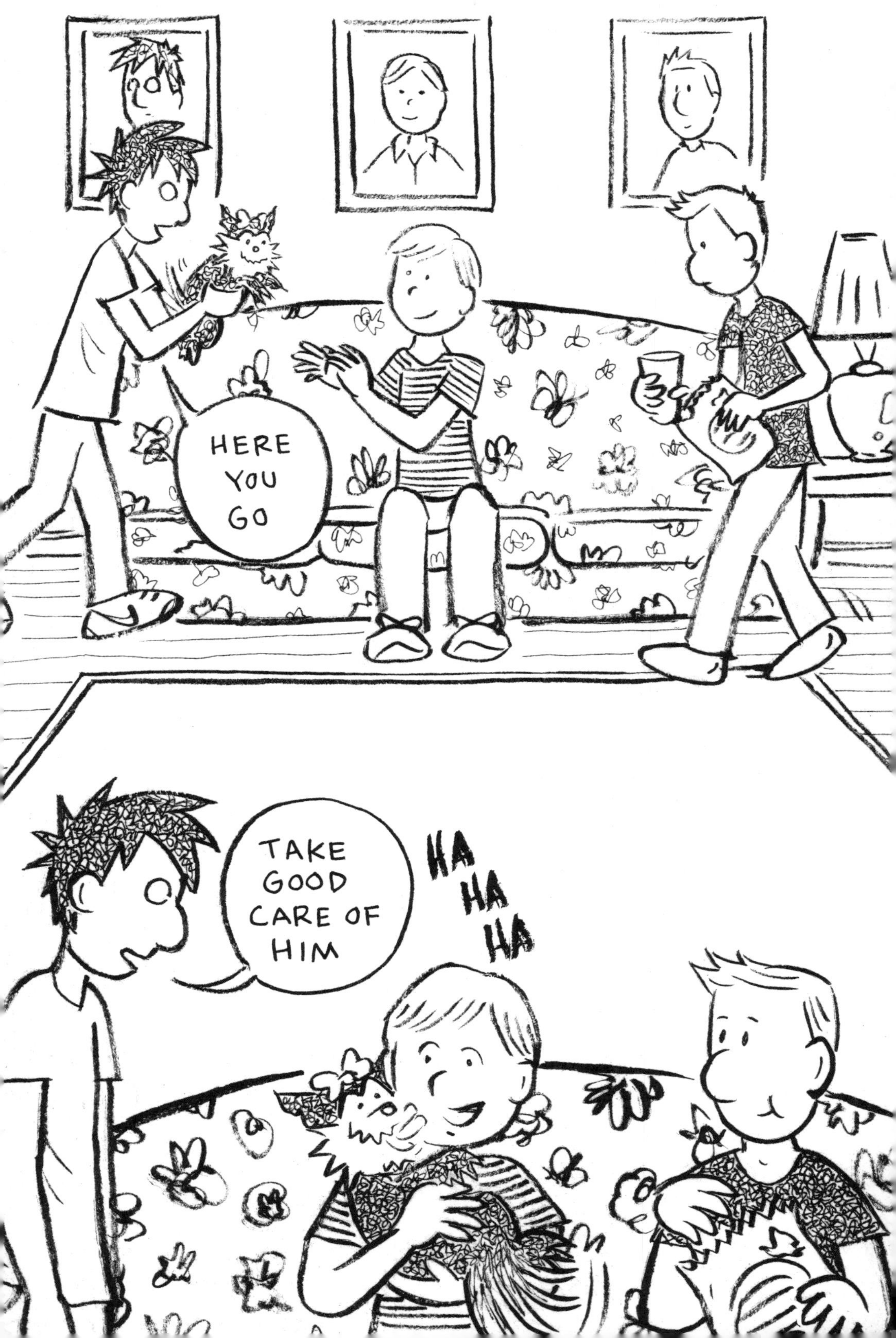
HERE YOU GO
TAKE GOOD CARE OF HIM
HA HA HA

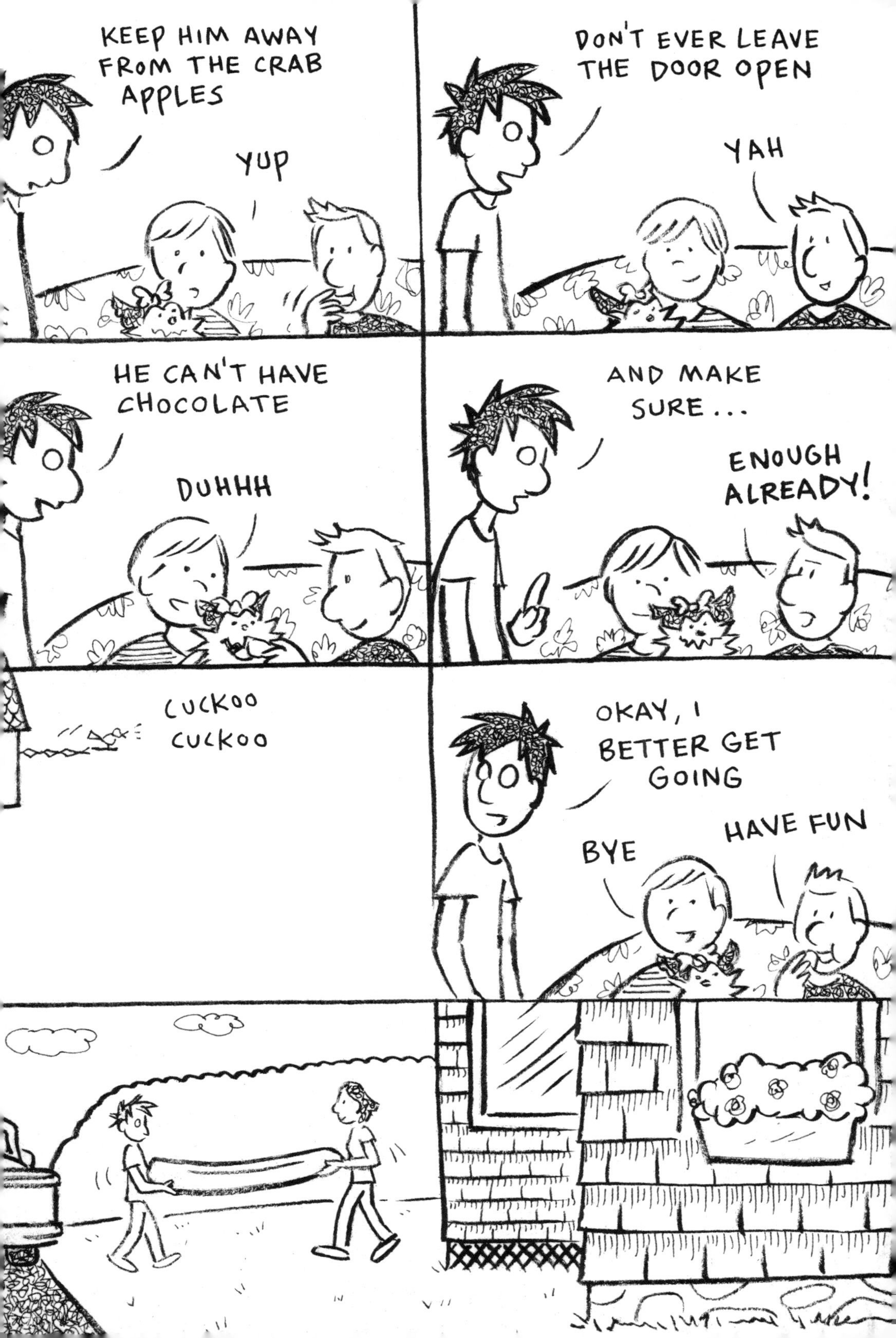
KEEP HIM AWAY FROM THE CRAB APPLES
YUP
DON'T EVER LEAVE THE DOOR OPEN
YAH
HE CAN'T HAVE CHOCOLATE
DUHHH
AND MAKE SURE...
ENOUGH ALREADY!
CUCKOO CUCKOO
OKAY, I BETTER GET GOING
BYE
HAVE FUN

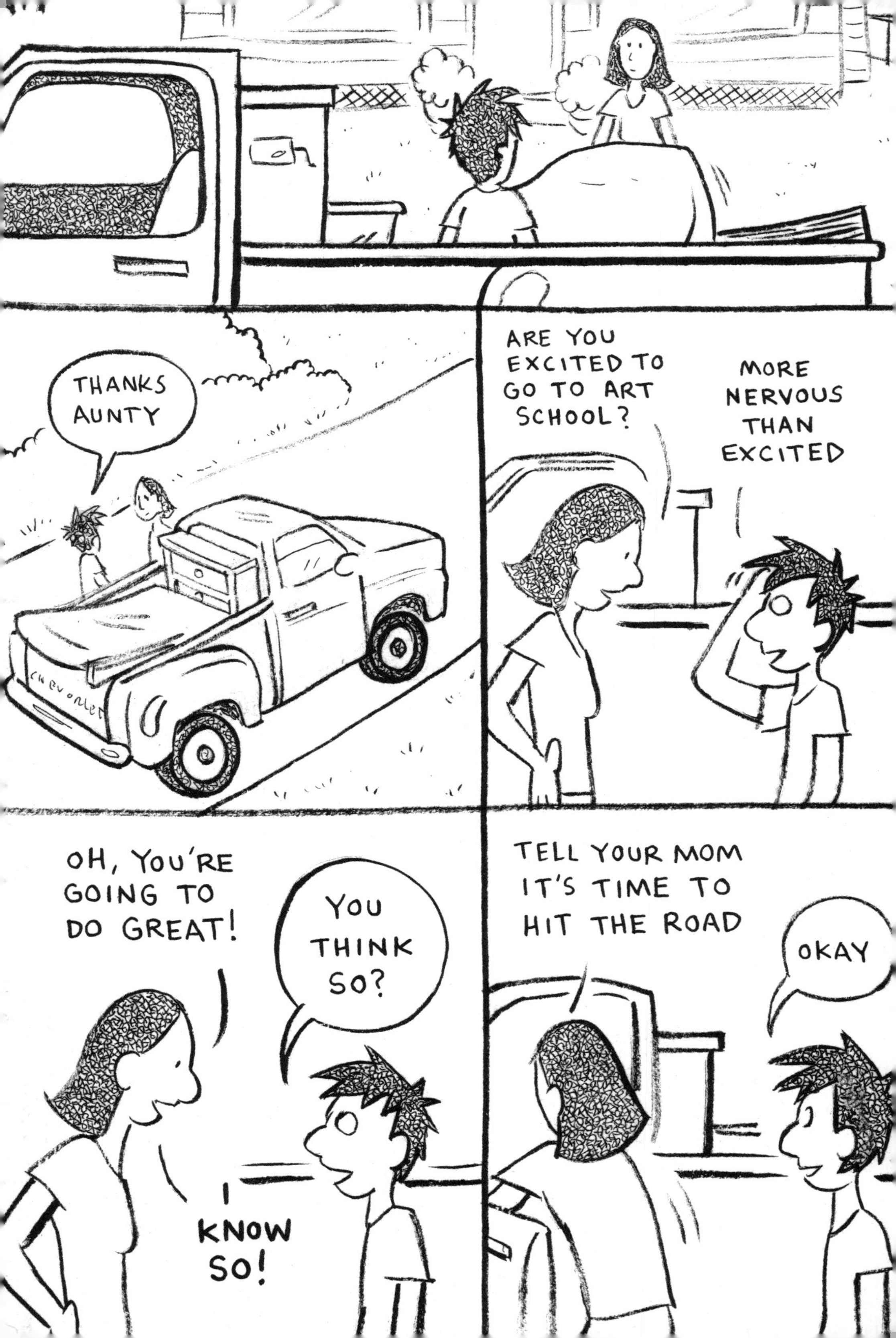
THANKS AUNTY
CHEVROLET
ARE YOU EXCITED TO GO TO ART SCHOOL?
MORE NERVOUS THAN EXCITED
OH, YOU'RE GOING TO DO GREAT!
YOU THINK SO?
I KNOW SO!
TELL YOUR MOM IT'S TIME TO HIT THE ROAD
OKAY

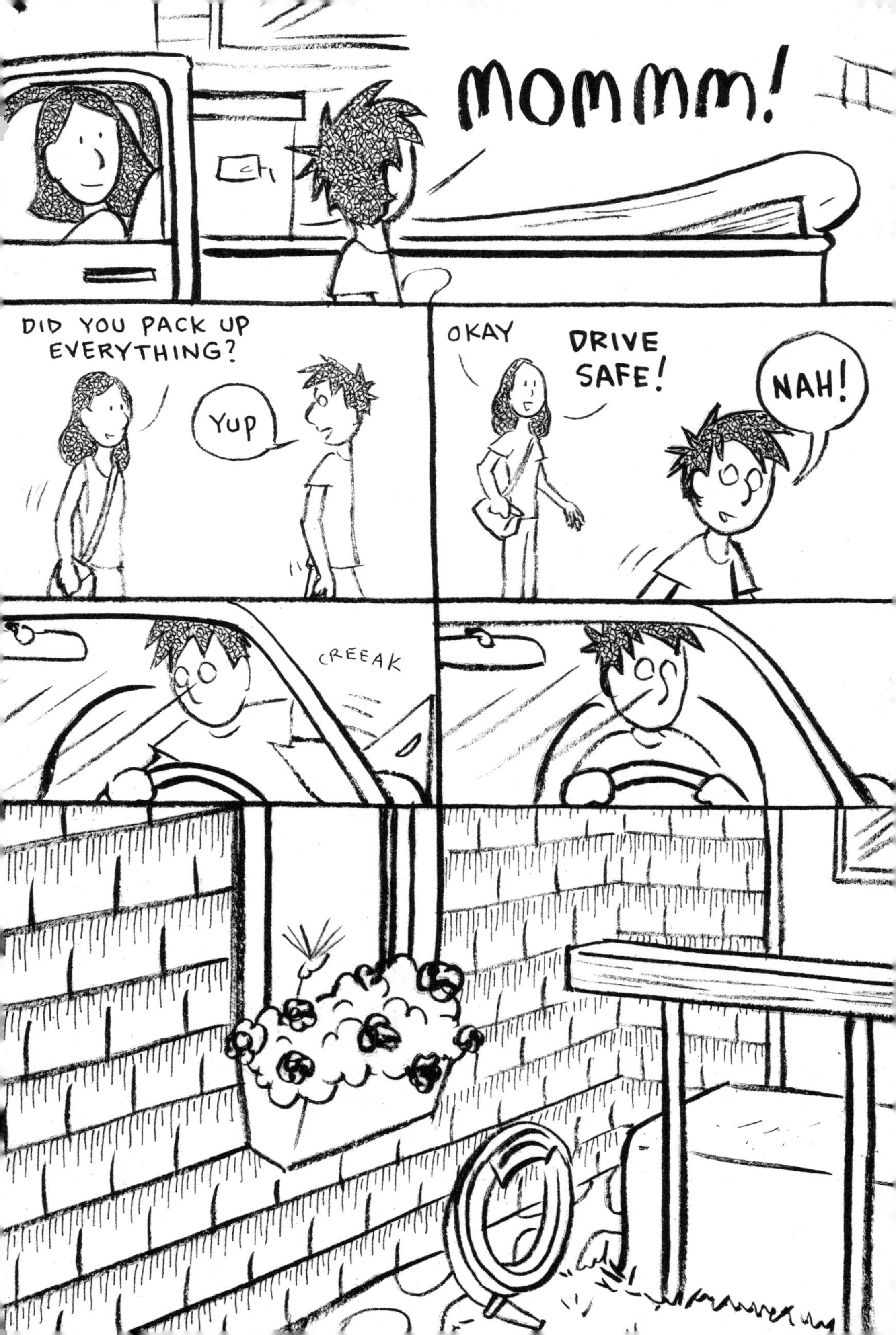
MOMMM!
DID YOU PACK UP EVERYTHING?
YUP
OKAY
DRIVE SAFE!
NAH!
CREEAK

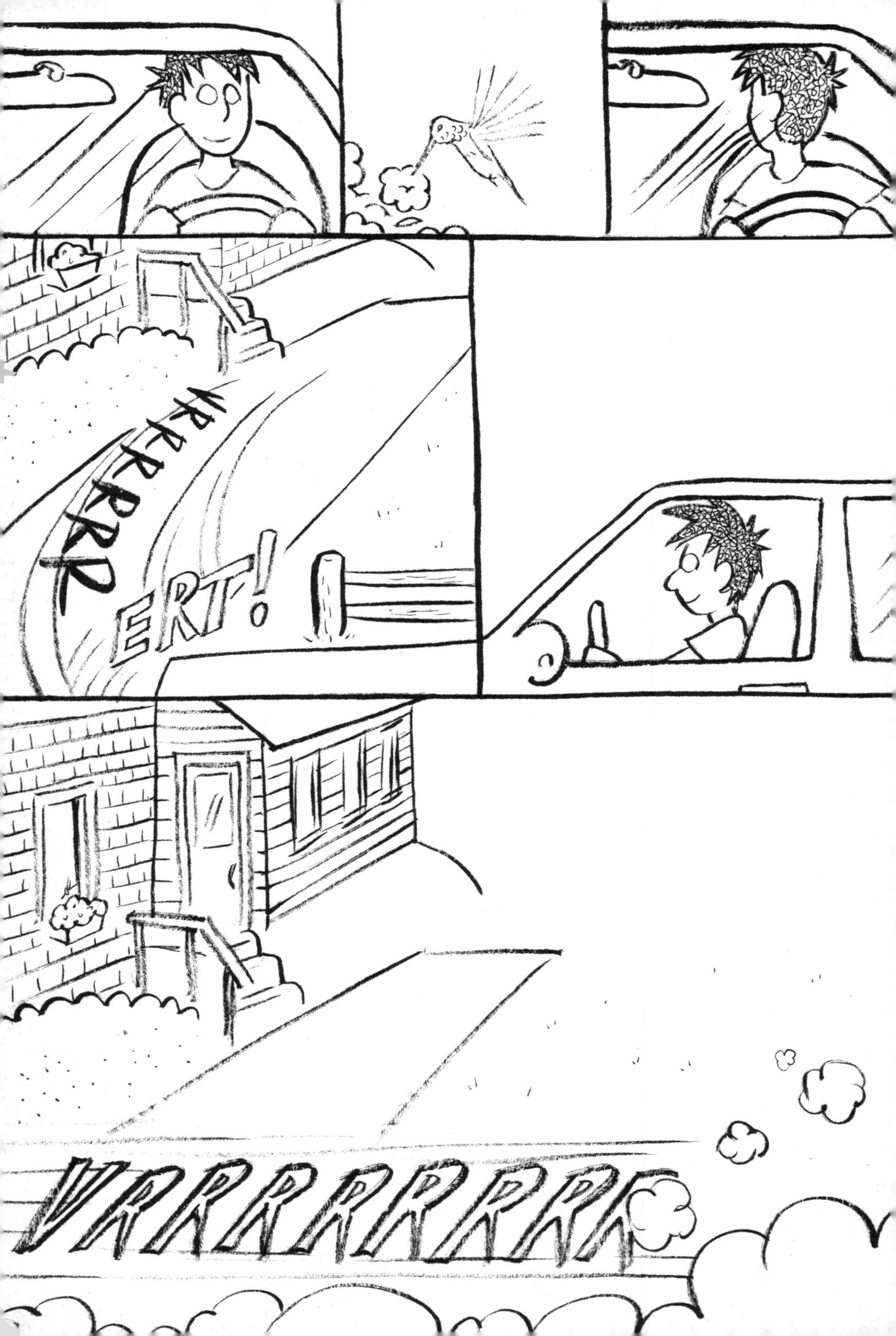
ERT!
VRRRRRRRR

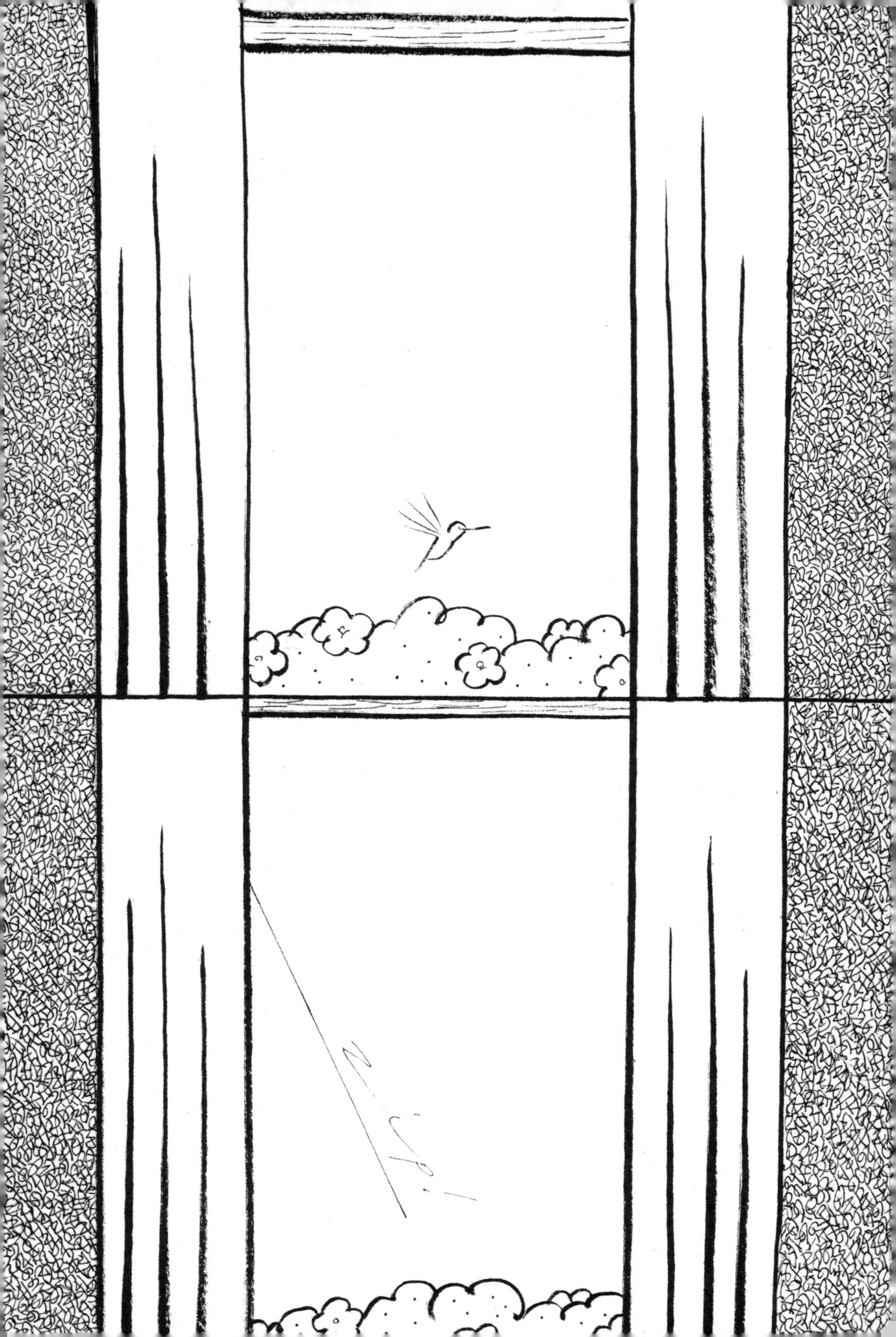
Zip!

Zip!

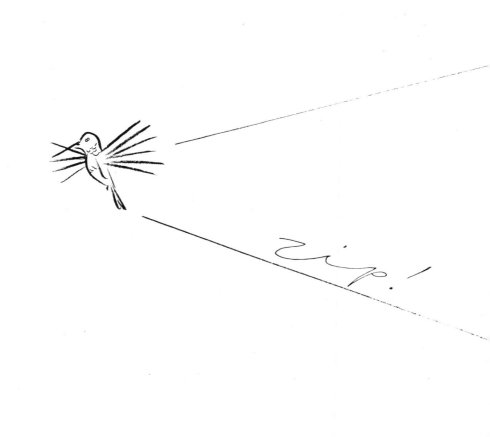

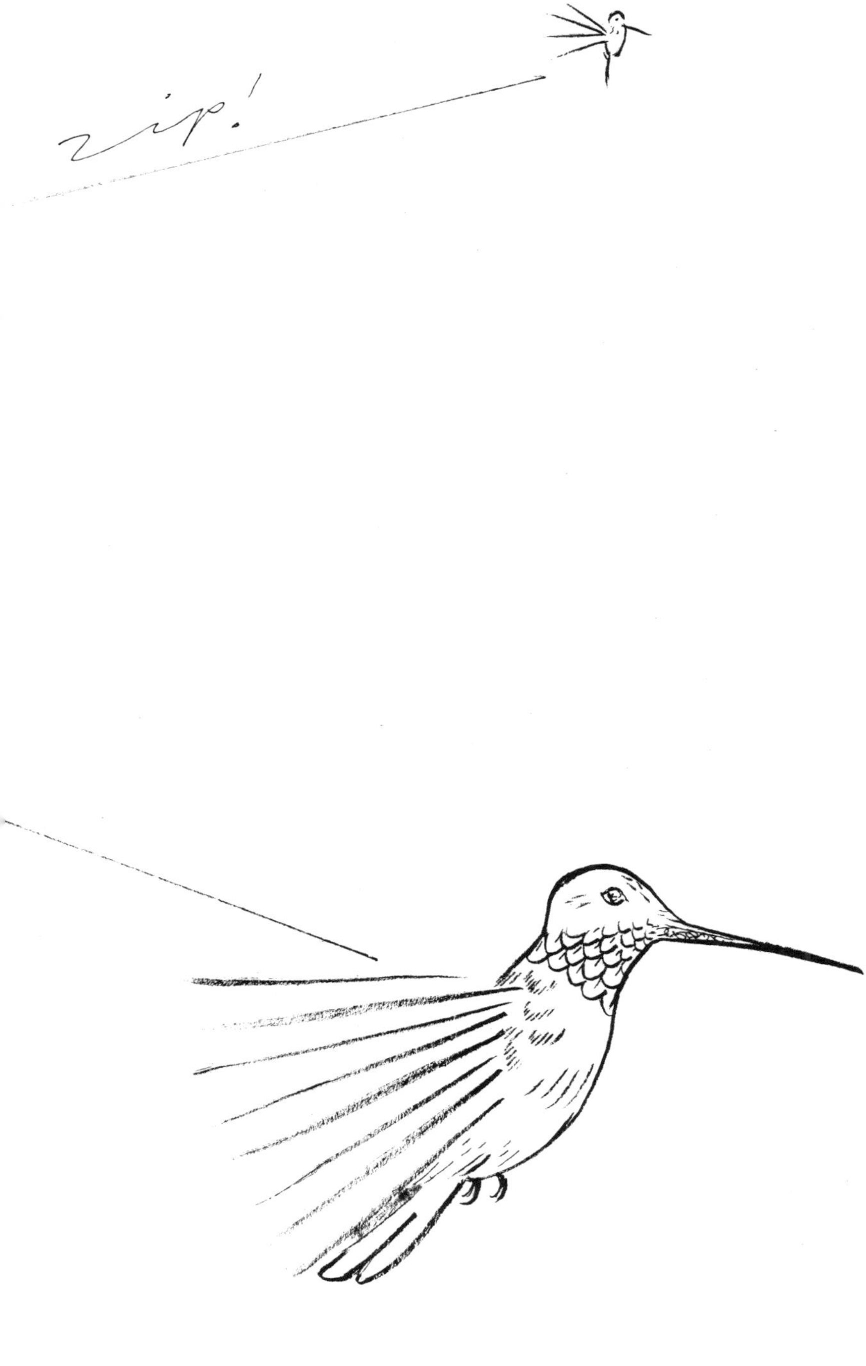
zip!

zip!

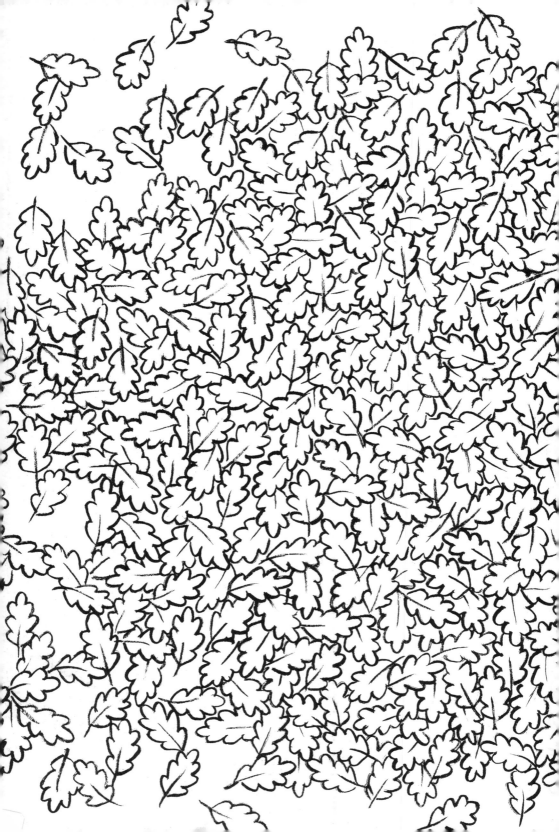